THE PAPERS OF

WOODROW WILSON

VOLUME 49

JULY 18–SEPTEMBER 13, 1918

SPONSORED BY THE WOODROW WILSON
FOUNDATION
AND PRINCETON UNIVERSITY

THE PAPERS OF

WOODROW WILSON

ARTHUR S. LINK, *EDITOR*

DAVID W. HIRST, *SENIOR ASSOCIATE EDITOR*

JOHN E. LITTLE, *ASSOCIATE EDITOR*

FREDRICK AANDAHL, *ASSOCIATE EDITOR*

MANFRED F. BOEMEKE, *ASSISTANT EDITOR*

DENISE THOMPSON, *ASSISTANT EDITOR*

PHYLLIS MARCHAND AND MARGARET D. LINK,
EDITORIAL ASSISTANTS

Volume 49
July 18–September 13, 1918

PRINCETON, NEW JERSEY
PRINCETON UNIVERSITY PRESS
1985

Note to scholars: Princeton University Press sub-
scribes to the Resolution on Permissions of the Association of American University Presses, defining what
we regard as "fair use" of copyrighted works. This
Resolution, intended to encourage scholarly use of
university press publications and to avoid unnecessary
applications for permission, is obtainable from the Press
or from the A.A.U.P. central office. Note, however, that
the scholarly apparatus, transcripts of shorthand, and
the texts of Wilson documents as they appear in this
volume are copyrighted, and the usual rules about the
use of copyrighted materials apply.

Publication of this book has been aided by a grant
from the National Historical Publications and Records
Commission.

Printed in the United States of America
by Princeton University Press
Princeton, New Jersey

INTRODUCTION

THE eight weeks covered by this volume see growing turmoil in Russia and a marked improvement in the Allied military fortunes on the western front. Ludendorff's great offensive fails, and Wilson, banking on eighty new American divisions to provide the decisive edge over Germany in 1919, persists in his twofold policy toward the East. He will refrain from taking sides in Russia's internal affairs, and, in a limited way, will aid the Czech Legion to leave Russia through Vladivostok. Wilson had set forth this policy in an aide-mémoire of July 17, 1918, to the European allies, but they continue to press him to send substantial American forces into Siberia and northern Russia. They argue that, without strong reinforcements, the Czechoslovaks might be crushed. The Allies also warn that Wilson's hands-off policy will permit the Germans to transfer forces from the eastern to the western front, thereby counterbalancing the American contribution and leaving the outcome of the war in doubt.

Wilson, however, continues to reject intervention in Russia as wrong in principle and unrealistic in strategy and, on August 3, issues a public statement of his objections to any military intervention in Russia. He again insists that the western front is the decisive theater and that forces should not be dissipated elsewhere. Soon afterward, he recognizes the Czechoslovaks as belligerents and authorizes money and supplies for them, but he still refuses to send additional troops to Siberia. Instead, he contemplates dispatching to that area an American commission consisting of merchants, agricultural experts, labor advisers, and Red Cross and Y.M.C.A. representatives to promote economic relief through educational and organizational assistance. A complicating factor in these relations is Wilson's irritation with the governments of Japan, Great Britain, and France. He believes that Japan has broken its promises to the United States by sending a larger force into Siberia than the two governments had agreed upon. He is also so angered by the actions of the British commander at Murmansk and Archangel that he threatens to withdraw the small American force in that area from the British general's command. As this volume ends, the thorny problems of extricating the Czechoslovak forces from Siberia and of reaching some kind of workable arrangements in Russia remain unresolved.

Meanwhile, as Allied military prospects brighten on the western front, it becomes more feasible to think constructively of a postwar world. Wilson protests that he has "a single-track mind" and has to concentrate on the war rather than on preparations for a league of nations and the peace settlement. However, he and House study the British Phillimore Report and write their own drafts of a covenant, or constitution, for a league.

Along with his crucial international concerns, Wilson continues to be deeply engaged by responsibilities at home. Reacting to various recent outrages, he denounces mob spirit and lynching in a moving appeal to the American people. He also requests the Attorney General to investigate "slacker" raids and Upton Sinclair's complaint about censorship of domestic publications. On the economic front, Wilson is still engrossed in problems of war production, shipping, food and agriculture, stabilization of prices and wages, the plight of transit companies under inflationary conditions, leasing of coal and oil fields, water power, a war-profits tax, and labor disputes. Also, looking toward the approaching congressional elections, he is cautious about endorsing candidates but still active in working to elect senators who will vote for woman suffrage.

"VERBATIM ET LITERATIM"

In earlier volumes of this series, we have said something like the following: "All documents are reproduced *verbatim et literatim*, with typographical and spelling errors corrected in square brackets only when necessary for clarity and ease of reading." The following essay explains our textual methods and review procedures.

We have never printed and do not intend to print critical, or corrected, versions of documents. We print them exactly as they are, with a few exceptions which we always note. We never use the word *sic* except to denote the repetition of words in a document; in fact, we think that a succession of *sics* defaces a page.

We usually repair words in square brackets when letters are missing. As we have said, we also repair words in square brackets for clarity and ease of reading. Our general rule is to do this when we, ourselves, cannot read the word without having to stop to puzzle out its meaning. Jumbled words and names misspelled beyond recognition of course have to be repaired. We correct the misspelling of a name in a document in the footnote identifying the person.

However, when an old man writes to Wilson saying that he is glad to hear that Wilson is "comming" to Newark, or a semiliterate farmer from Texas writes phonetically, we see no reason to correct spellings in square brackets when the words are perfectly understandable. We do not correct Wilson's misspellings unless they are unreadable, except to supply in square brackets letters missing in words. For example, he consistently spelled "belligerent" as "belligerant." Nothing would be gained by correcting "belligerant" in square brackets.

We think that it is very important for several reasons to follow the rule of *verbatim et literatim*. Most important, a document has its own integrity and power, particularly when it is not written in perfect literary form. There is something very moving in seeing a Texas dirt farmer struggling to express his feelings in words, or a semiliterate former slave doing the same thing. Second, in Wilson's case it is crucially important to reproduce his errors in letters which he typed himself, since he usually typed badly when he was in an agitated state. Third, since style is the essence of the person, we would never correct grammar or make tenses consistent, as one correspondent has urged us to do. Fourth, we think that it is very important that we print exact transcripts of Charles L. Swem's copies of Wilson's letters. Swem made many mistakes (we correct them in footnotes from a reading of his shorthand books), and Wilson let them pass. We thus have to assume that Wilson did not read his letters before signing them, and this, we think, is a significant fact. Finally, printing typed letters and documents *verbatim et literatim* tells us a great deal about the educational level of the stenographic profession in the United States during Wilson's time.

We think that our series would be worthless if we produced unreliable texts, and we go to considerable effort to make certain that the texts are authentic.

Our typists are highly skilled and proofread their transcripts carefully as soon as they have typed them. The Editor sight proofreads documents once he has assembled a volume and is setting its annotation. The Editors who write the notes read through documents several times and are careful to check any anomalies. Then, once the manuscript volume has been completed and all notes checked, the Editor and Senior Associate Editor orally proofread the documents against the copy. They read every comma, dash, and character. They note every absence of punctuation. They study every nearly illegible word in written documents.

Once this process of "establishing the text" is completed, the manuscript volume goes to our editor at Princeton University Press, who checks the volume carefully and sends it to the printing plant. The galley proofs are read against copy in the proofroom at the Press. And we must say that the proofreaders there are extraordinarily skilled. Some years ago, before we found a way to ease their burden, they queried every misspelled word, absence of punctuation, or other such anomalies. Now we write "O.K." above such words or spaces on the copy.

We read the galley proofs at least three times. Our copyeditor gives them a sight reading against the manuscript copy to look for remaining typographical errors and to make sure that no line has been dropped. The Editor and Senior Associate Editor sight read them against documents and copy. We then get the page proofs, which have been corrected at the Press. We check all the changes three times. In addition, we get *revised* pages and check them twice.

This is not the end. The Editor, Senior Associate Editor, and Assistant Editor give a final reading to headings, description-location lines, and notes. Finally, our indexer of course reads the pages word by word. Before we return the pages to the Press, she comes in with a list of queries, all of which are answered by reference to the documents.

Our rule in the Wilson Papers is that our tolerance of error is zero. No system and no person can be perfect. There may be errors in our volumes. However, we believe that we have done everything humanly possible to avoid error; the chance is remote that what looks at first glance like a typographical error is indeed an error.

We thank our editor at Princeton University Press, Alice Calaprice, for her help in the preparation of this volume. We are grateful to Professors John Milton Cooper, Jr., William H. Harbaugh, Richard W. Leopold, and Betty Miller Unterberger—all members of our Editorial Advisory Committee—for reading the manuscript of this volume and for being, as before, constructively critical.

We take this opportunity to welcome Denise Thompson back to our staff after an interval for study. She has served this project in past years in various capacities with intelligence and cheerfulness and now joins us as Assistant Editor. We look forward to a long and productive association.

THE EDITORS

Princeton, New Jersey
October 23, 1984

CONTENTS

Collateral Materials

Diplomatic correspondence, reports, memoranda, and aide-mémoire

ILLUSTRATIONS

Following page 298

ABBREVIATIONS

ALI	autograph letter initialed
ALS	autograph letter signed
CC	carbon copy
CCL	carbon copy of letter
CCLI	carbon copy of letter initialed
CLS	Charles Lee Swem
CLSsh	Charles Lee Swem shorthand
DFH	David Franklin Houston
EMH	Edward Mandell House
FKL	Franklin Knight Lane
FLP	Frank Lyon Polk
FR-WWS 1918	*Papers Relating to the Foreign Relations of the United States, 1918, Supplement, The World War*
FR 1918, Russia	*Papers Relating to the Foreign Relations of the United States, 1918, Russia*
HCH	Herbert Clark Hoover
Hw, hw	Handwriting, handwritten
JD	Josephus Daniels
JPT	Joseph Patrick Tumulty
JRT	Jack Romagna typed
LS	letter signed
MS, MSS	manuscript, manuscripts
NDB	Newton Diehl Baker
OCL	offset copy of letter
RG	record group
RL	Robert Lansing
T	typed
TC	typed copy
TCL	typed copy of letter
TI	typed initialed
TL	typed letter
TLI	typed letter initialed
TLS	typed letter signed
TS	typed signed
TWG	Thomas Watt Gregory
WBW	William Bauchop Wilson
WGM	William Gibbs McAdoo
WJB	William Jennings Bryan
WW	Woodrow Wilson
WWhw	Woodrow Wilson handwriting, handwritten
WWsh	Woodrow Wilson shorthand
WWT	Woodrow Wilson typed
WWTL	Woodrow Wilson typed letter
WWTLI	Woodrow Wilson typed letter initialed
WWTLS	Woodrow Wilson typed letter signed

ABBREVIATIONS FOR COLLECTIONS
AND REPOSITORIES

Following the National Union Catalog of the Library of Congress

AFL-CIO-Ar	American Federation of Labor-Congress of Industrial Organizations Archives
ATT	Tuskegee Institute
CSt-H	Hoover Institution on War, Revolution and Peace
CtY	Yale University
CtY-D	Yale University Divinity School
DeU	University of Delaware
DHU	Howard University
DLC	Library of Congress
DNA	National Archives
FFM-Ar	French Foreign Ministry Archives
FMD-Ar	French Ministry of Defense Archives
FO	British Foreign Office
KHi	Kansas State Historical Society
KyU	University of Kentucky
LDR	Labor Department Records
MH	Harvard University
Nc-Ar	North Carolina State Department of Archives and History
NDR	Navy Department Records
NjP	Princeton University
PRO	Public Record Office
RSB Coll., DLC	Ray Stannard Baker Collection of Wilsoniana, Library of Congress
ScCleU	Clemson University
SDR	State Department Records
TDR	Treasury Department Records
UMWA-Ar	United Mine Workers of America Archives
WC, NjP	Woodrow Wilson Collection, Princeton University
WDR	War Department Records
WP, DLC	Woodrow Wilson Papers, Library of Congress

SYMBOLS

[July 26, 1918]	publication date of published writing; also date of document when date is not part of text
[*August 15, 1918*]	composition date when publication date differs
[[July 9, 1918]]	delivery date of speech if publication date differs
**** ***	text deleted by author of document

THE PAPERS OF

WOODROW WILSON

VOLUME 49

JULY 18–SEPTEMBER 13, 1918

To William Jennings Bryan

[The White House] 18 July, 1918

I earnestly beg that you will not consent to represent the Government of Costa Rica.[1] We have not recognized and cannot recognize that government and it would be very distressing to me to have you put in the position of urging us to do what we cannot do.

Woodrow Wilson.

T telegram (Letterpress Books, WP, DLC).
[1] See WJB to WW, July 17, 1918, Vol. 48.

To Harry Augustus Garfield

My dear Garfield:　　　　The White House 18 July, 1918

I brought up the matter of an industrial army at the meeting of the Cabinet last Tuesday and found that Secretary Wilson and the Labor Department were considering plans of this sort with a hope of producing some general recommendation. I am, therefore, taking the liberty of sending him today your letter of yesterday[1] in order to get his immediate advice, my effort being not to cross wires.

Cordially and sincerely yours,　Woodrow Wilson

TLS (H. A. Garfield Papers, DLC).
[1] H. A. Garfield to WW, July 17, 1918, Vol. 48.

To William Bauchop Wilson

My dear Mr. Secretary:　　　[The White House] 18 July, 1918

The enclosed letter will explain itself and is, as you see, supplemental to the letter I handed you the other day at Cabinet.[1] I hope that it will be possible for us to agree upon some general conclusion as to matters of this sort at an early date, because I fully share Doctor Garfield's apprehension about the coal supply and don't like to act contrary to his judgment that some such action as he suggests will be very helpful.

Cordially and faithfully yours,　Woodrow Wilson

TLS (Letterpress Books, WP, DLC).
    [1] See H. A. Garfield to WW, July 17, 1918, n. 1, Vol. 48.

To Frank Lyon Polk

My dear Mr. Counselor: The White House 18 July, 1918

This[1] certainly affords a very interesting illustration of the eagerness of the Allies to get into the Siberian business. Before we go any further with this Italian suggestion, do you not think it would be well to know somewhat particularly from what part of the Austrian Empire these ex-Austrian soldiers came? Inasmuch as our idea is to cooperate with the Czecho-Slovaks, some sparks might be struck if they were not sympathetic.

Cordially and sincerely yours,   Woodrow Wilson

TLS (SDR, RG 59, 861.00/2838, DNA).
    [1] See FLP to WW, July 16, 1918, Vol. 48.

To William Procter Gould Harding

My dear Governor Harding: [The White House] 18 July, 1918

Thank you for your letter of yesterday.[1] I don't like to trouble you to send me a written memorandum about the cotton situation, but in all matters of that sort it is very valuable for me to have the matter in writing because amidst the multitude of things that are brought to my attention every day an oral conversation does not remain with me. Would you not, therefore, be generous enough to send me such a memorandum with regard to the cotton matter, in which I am very much interested indeed?

Cordially and sincerely yours,   Woodrow Wilson

TLS (Letterpress Books, WP, DLC).
    [1] W. P. G. Harding to WW, July 17, 1918, Vol. 48.

To Gilbert Fairchild Close

My dear Close: [The White House] 18 July, 1918

You need not be sorry for any trouble you have given me, because you have given me none.[1] I want you to follow the course that you think is the course of duty always.

Just between ourselves, I have thought within the last few days that it might be necessary for me to ask Mr. Daniels to give you up to me.[2]

In haste

Cordially and faithfully yours,   [Woodrow Wilson]

CCL (WP, DLC).

[1] Wilson was responding to G. F. Close to WW, July 17, 1918, TLS (WP, DLC). Close had served as a clerk in the office of Josephus Daniels since May 1917. He had recently been transferred to a similar position at the War Trade Board. However, as he explained to Wilson in his letter, he was returning to Daniels' office because he felt more useful there, and Daniels had offered him an increase in salary.

[2] The *New York Times*, July 17, 1918, reported that Wilson had agreed to the enlistment of Charles Lee Swem in the army aviation service. Swem's enlistment took effect on August 1, and Close replaced him at the White House on that date.

Two Letters from Frank Lyon Polk

My dear Mr. President: Washington July 18, 1918.

The Associated Press and the United Press both have telegrams from Tokio discussing the so-called United States proposal and the latest despatch states that the Japanese have accepted the plan proposed by us.[1] The Department has heard nothing. Some statement will probably come from the Japanese tomorrow, I should think. If they accept, it will be necessary to make some statement at once to the Press in view of the very free way the Japanese Government has dealt with their press on this subject. I would be very much obliged if you would indicate to me whether it is your intention to make any general statement at this time, or merely to announce the details of the plan agreed on by the Japanese and this Government, assuming, of course, that the Japanese Government will accept.   Yours faithfully,   Frank L Polk

[1] Many newspapers of July 19, 1918, carried an Associated Press news report, datelined Tokyo, July 16, which outlined an American proposal for joint Japanese-American military intervention in Siberia and stated that the Japanese government had just decided to accept the proposal. The dispatch was based upon reports published in Japanese newspapers on July 16. See, for example, the *New York Times*, the New York *World*, the *New York Herald*, the *New York Tribune*, and the *Washington Post*, all of July 19, 1918. The Japanese government's Advisory Council on Foreign Relations, at its meeting on July 16, had in fact agreed in principle to accept the American proposal, although the council still had to revise and approve the details of the proposed Japanese reply. See James William Morley, *The Japanese Thrust into Siberia, 1918* (New York, 1957), pp. 274-90.

My dear Mr. President: Washington July 18, 1918.

Mr. Bryan came to see me yesterday in regard to the recognition of Tinoco. I told him that you and Mr. Lansing had both been over the case time and time again, and I thought you were not only entirely familiar with the arguments on both sides, but had quite made up your minds as to what course you would pursue. He seemed to be set on taking up the matter with you personally and could not be discouraged.

In this connection, it has just come to my notice that a man named Field has been making most serious charges against Mr. Stabler, Chief of the Latin-American Division,[1] both to you and to the Foreign Relations Committee of the Senate, claiming that he attempted to support Tinoco's backers, and questioning his integrity and loyalty to the Administration. These charges do Mr. Stabler a gross injustice and are absolutely without foundation. I have had a good deal to do with Field in one way or another, and the Secretary and I both have felt that he was thoroughly unreliable. He is the representative of the coffee firm of Montelegre and Bonilla, of New York, the members of which firm are Costa Rican citizens and have a bitter personal feud with the Tinoco family. Field has become the self appointed representative of the Gonzales[2] faction and wishes the Government to use force to remove Tinoco. He continually criticizes the Department for its inactivity along these lines, as well as charging the Department of Justice with negligence. My opinion is, and I believe it to be accurate, that Field, who was a close friend of Ferrara[3] and the Cuban Revolutionists, is very anxious to get Stabler out of the Latin-American Division in order to have him replaced by some one friendly to Ferrara and the Cuban Revolutionary movement.

This may not have come to your attention, and if not, I apologize for bothering you, but on the chance that you may have heard of it, I thought I had better mention it, and if you are interested, I would be very glad to give you further details.

Yours faithfully,   Frank L. Polk

TLS (WP, DLC).
[1] About Woolsey Hopkins Field, see the Enclosure printed with RL to WW, Feb. 7, 1917, Vol. 41. The only reference which the Editors have found concerning his attack on Jordan H. Stabler is a White House memorandum dated August 5, 1918, in Case File No. 1565, WP, DLC, which indicates that Field wrote either to Wilson or to someone on the White House staff on that date, accusing Stabler of "giving away State secrets through his brother who is in Costa Rica." Field's communication was referred to the State Department.
[2] That is, Alfredo González Flores, about whom see the index references in Vol. 41.
[3] That is, Orestes Ferrara, *ibid.*

From Robert Latham Owen

My dear Mr. President: [Washington] July 18, 1918.

On July 6, 1918, Governor Harding, acting for the Federal Reserve Board, addressed a circular letter to the banks of the United States suggesting:

"A judicious curtailment of credits for non-essential purposes."

This was emphasized in the circular in various ways.

Congress authorized the Capital Issues Committee to control the employment of *new capital*, but the constriction of credits to established industries on the theory of a local banker that he does not regard it as essential, merely gives an opportunity to the local banker to raise his rate on industries which he may class as non-essential, or to deny them credit, and by denying them credit bankrupt such institutions.

Mr. President, I cannot but believe it is a serious error in national policy to break down existing established industries whether they are designated essential or non-essential, because when this war closes every present industry, whether called essential or not, will be required as a means of employing the eight million men who will be thrown out of employment in this country, now employed in war industries, including those who will be returning from abroad.

The Government will be obliged to make a gigantic effort to employ such men at living wages on public work,—concrete roads, canals, irrigation, reclamation, etc., etc., in order to avoid domestic disturbances. To close up thousands of industries now operated by men and women beyond the draft age means to close up thousands of avenues for the employment of the unemployed when the war ceases.

We have *priority* regulations giving preference against all industries not engaged in war industries; we have absorbed all skilled labor for war industries, and have already in this war seriously afflicted many industries not essential to war but which have been found essential to the happiness of mankind in times of peace by the actual establishment and maintenance of such concerns. Now to have the twenty-five thousand banks of the United States invited to deny credit to industries not essential to the war will lead to unhappy consequences. Such establishments have been weakened by war conditions as far as it is safe to do it unless the Government is willing to put them out of business, and I cannot conceive that this can be the policy of your Administration. I think it of the highest consequence that the powers of the Government should actively support the welfare of our business men wherever it is possible, as England does, as Germany does. We should improve on their performances, as we did do in framing our banking system, where we put the powers of the Government behind the meritorious credit of every individual business man in America. This is the virtue of the Reserve Act, which enables a business man to obtain good currency on his note when the note is a good note endorsed by a member bank against commodities. This principle of the Reserve Act has not been sufficiently recognized by the Reserve Board in using commodities as a basis of credit.

I remind you that the shipment of what might be called non-essentials for war to the neutral nations can thereby be converted directly into essential materials for war, and moreover, such shipments serve directly to correct the balance of trade which now is causing a discount of the American dollar from twenty to fifty per cent.

Mr. President, I beg you to permit me to suggest that you should immediately appoint a very high class board to expressly study the question of preparedness for the problems of the peace which must follow the gigantic dislocation of war. It will not do to delay. France, Great Britain and Germany are already prepared. We have made no adequate preparation. We should be ready to absorb, if necessary, millions of men in building concrete highways, building canals, reclaiming lands, irrigating lands, etc., etc., in order that we shall leave no soldier returning from war unable to find the means of subsistance with his own labor. This is a duty we owe, both to the soldier in the field and to the people at home who are sacrificing for war.

If the so-called non-essential industries are to be denied credit, it should not be done except upon the advice of some competent authority directly representing the Government of the United States and especially appointed by the Executive for that purpose.

What is to become of the people engaged in making all sorts of things which have already been contracted for and which have been partly manufactured if a campaign is put on to prevent the giving of Christmas gifts? What is to become of the little people engaged in all sorts of manufacture if credit is denied them, and the people able to buy are invited and urged not to buy?

Mr. President, let us not preach pessimism but optimism. We have a right to be optimistic. The increase of the actual values in lands and the products of the land of the United States since 1910 will far more than meet the present cost of the war, including 1919.

The actual output of the fields, mines, forests, etc., fisheries and factories last year amounted to approximately sixty-seven billions of dollars.

The energies of the American people are now tremendously stimulated. Every body is at work; the output of materials, the construction of buildings and the making of machinery has progressed in such a way that our output after the war, if our people are properly employed, will keep this country in a condition of the highest prosperity.

I pray you, do not let your subordinates try to discourage the American people or put any of them out of business.

Most respectfully and faithfully yours,   Robt L. Owen

TLS (WP, DLC).

David Lloyd George to Lord Reading

[London] 18 July 1918.

Private & Personal

Many thanks for your private wire.[1] You will already have heard of the decision in regard to Knox. There is no man in the British Army who knows Russia as Knox does. He knows Russian perfectly. He is not a politician, his whole interests lie in soldiering. In so far as he has politics they are indicated by the fact that his brother[2] was a Home Rule member of Parliament and his family of Irish Protestant Home Rule complexion. It is an absolute mistake to think he was identified with the old regime. He was the one man who consistently pointed out the corruption and inefficiency of the old military system. He alone, in the Czar's days, among the military attachés of the Allies refused to be bamboozled with the optimistic information which was issued to them from official quarters. In consequence of his pessimistic reports he was so unpopular with the old Russian General Staff that Kitchener sent out to Russia a court soldier, Hanbury Williams,[3] who was more acceptable to Russian Headquarters. Orders for Knox's recall were actually issued and they were only cancelled owing to the intervention of Edward Grey and myself. After considering your representations most carefully we decided to confirm the decision to send him to Siberia because he is much the best man for dealing with the military aspects of the Russian problem. From first to last he has been absolutely right in his forecasts of the military situation in Russia. In going out he will not be concerned with politics, but solely with the conduct of efficient military operations. I am certain that he will be of the greatest use in these respects.

As to what you say about the Administration's fears in regard to the sympathy in this country with Russian reactionaries, the last thing that I would stand for would be the encouragement of any kind of repressive regime under whatever guise. I consider that we shall have failed in our war purpose unless by the end of the war Russia is settled on liberal, progressive and democratic lines. Not only do I want it from the point of view of the Russian people, I want it from the point of view of the peace of the world and of the peace and security of the Indian frontier. Reactionary Russia is certain to be aggressive and to be in close alliance with Germany. I should have thought that the relations which we have maintained with the Bolsheviks since the beginning of this year ought to be sufficient proof that we have no desire to encourage reaction in that country and that it is the basis of our policy to leave the Russian people perfectly free to determine for themselves the form of Government under which they are to live.

As to the future the real security against what the President fears lies in the President himself. Intervention in Siberia is necessarily a matter in which the United States must play the predominant part. The other Allies are fully pre-occupied by their commitments elsewhere. If we are to do anything effective in Siberia it must be done in the main by America and Japan. So far as I am concerned I am prepared to back the policy of the President through thick and thin, always provided that it is an effective policy and not a policy of drift. You can tell the President that provided he will really act in Siberia and make it the primary object of his policy to establish effective Russian and Allied control over the whole of the Siberian railway to the Urals before winter sets in, I will give him all the support of which I am capable, whether it be with the Japanese or with the other Allies. What I am frightened of, however, is that we shall drift along until it is too late to save Russia from falling under German domination. I don't believe that the Russian people, suffering as they are from the effects both of autocracy and Bolshevism, can liberate themselves from Germanic penetration and domination unless the Allies can bring effective assistance to bear at once. That effective assistance to my mind means the firm establishment of the Allies in the Northern ports of Russia and throughout the whole of Siberia before the end of this summer. If we once do that we create a rallying point close at hand for all the liberal and democratic forces in Russia, and we shall be able to bring economic assistance and propaganda effectively to bear in Russia itself. If we don't act decisively now I greatly fear that the Germans will find ways and means through pro-German elements in Russia to beat down the truly liberal elements, to round out the Czecho-Slovaks or drive them out of Siberia, and so reduce Russia to such impotence that she will be a negligible quantity for the rest of the war. I am an interventionist just as much because I am a democrat as because I want to win the war. But we can do nothing without America. I hope the President realises the tremendous consequences which hang upon his decision and still more upon the promptitude and vigour with which he gives effect to it.

As to methods of intervention. The Czecho-Slovaks are the key to the position. If we come to their assistance in time we have there a large Slav force, which with American and Allied assistance ought to more than counter-balance even a considerable Japanese force. If they will accept Allied direction it ought to be possible to create a joint Allied political control in Siberia, in which America had the predominant voice, and which would obviate the chief difficulties connected with the use of Japanese in effective numbers. The Czechs are a highly educated democratic people. They would not readily support a reactionary cabal. Their whole record goes to show that their only desire is to avoid taking sides in Russian politics and to fight Germany for the freedom of their country. ⟨We are now at the crisis of the war so far as the Eastern situation is concerned. The Allies are agreed.⟩

I am much attracted by your suggestion about sending a Labour representative. There are two difficulties; one, that we have practically no Labour leaders who have had experience in this kind of work. They are competent Trades Union leaders but as the Henderson mission to Russia[4] shows they are not likely to make a success of this kind of job. Secondly, I am not quite clear about what they are to do. They presumably could not make speeches to a population which understood no English and it would be difficult to give them any position of real influence or authority. If, however, the President proposes to send a powerful political delegation representative of the Allies but in which the United States should take the leading part we would certainly send Liberal or Labour representatives to accompany it.[5]

TC telegram (A. J. Balfour Papers, Add. MSS 49692, British Library).
    [1] Lord Reading to D. Lloyd George, July 12, 1918, Vol. 48.
    [2] Edmund Francis Vesey Knox.
    [3] Lt. Gen. Sir John Hanbury-Williams, chief of the British Military Mission in Russia, 1914-1917; at this time in charge of the British Prisoners-of-War Department in Bern.
    [4] Arthur Henderson, then a member of the War Cabinet, had spent six weeks in Petrograd and Moscow in June and July 1917. His public mission was to persuade Russian socialist factions to support a renewed Russian war effort. He was also authorized to succeed Sir George W. Buchanan as British Ambassador to Russia if, in his opinion, Buchanan was unpopular with the Provisional Government. Henderson soon decided that his mission to the socialists was doomed to failure and that Buchanan was perfectly acceptable to the government. He recommended that Buchanan be retained in his post. See Mary Agnes Hamilton, *Arthur Henderson: A Biography* (London and Toronto, 1938), pp. 123-34, and Robert D. Warth, *The Allies and the Russian Revolution* (Durham, N. C., 1954), pp. 69-72.
    [5] This telegram was based in part upon D. Lloyd George, "Points to be raised in reply to Aide-Memoire," T MS (A. J. Balfour Papers, Add. MSS 49692, British Library).

Sir William Wiseman to Lord Robert Cecil, with Enclosures

My dear Lord Robert,   New York July 18th, 1918.

I must begin with an apology for not answering your letter of May 19th,[1] but this does not mean that I have neglected the matter you wrote to me about.

On the contrary, as you will see by the cable I sent you yesterday,[2] I have been following it up to the best of my ability. I have put off writing to you from week to week because I have been expecting

Col. House's Bureau to complete their preliminary report on the League of Nations which I wanted to send you as a counterpart to the Phillimore Report.[3] Col. House has decided, however, not to issue any report for the present for various reasons which I will describe.

There is really a great amount of interest in America in the League of Nations. Many promiment [prominent] men are studying and conferring on the question. To mention only a few—there is Ex-President Taft; Dr. Lowell, the President of Harvard University; Elihu Root; and Nicholas Murray Butler, of Columbia.

It cannot be said, however, that they agree by any means either as to the scope of a League, or the methods by which it should be put into practice. The President has not appointed any Committee to deal with the subject, and I do not think he is likely to. He told me quite frankly that he was not able to give much thought to the matter now. He himself claims to have a "single-track" mind, by which he means that he can only deal with one problem at a time. At present, as you will readily understand, every moment is taken up with the actual problems of the war. The executive authority of the government is so narrowed down into his own hands that hardly any queston of first-class importance can be settled without his intervening. With regard to the League of Nations, therefore, he has turned the matter over to House for study, and House, in his turn, is making use of the organization which he has created to prepare the American case for the Peace Conference. It is, as you know, my chief duty here to keep in the closest touch with House and this organization of his.

We find that opinion in America regarding a League of Nations may be divided roughly into three sections:

First, there are those who believe that a League should be started now, while the war is in progress, among the Allies, leaving open the question as to whether Germany should be admitted after the war or not. These people would have us enter into a treaty by which the full naval, military, and economic force of all the members of the League would be used against any power which might attempt to disturb the peace of the world.

There is a second group who think that the League cannot be formed until after peace is signed, and that Germany and all other nations should be invited to join, and that each power should contribute something towards the creation of an international police-force to enforce the decisions of the League.

Then there is a third group who do not believe in attempting to create anything of the kind while the war is still in progress, and who doubt the practicability of an international police force. In this connection I would like to make this observation: The war has created, or rather increased the national spirit in America to an extent that one would hardly have believed possible. There is far less international sentiment here than formerly, and I think it would be extremely difficult to persuade the American people in their present temper to hand over to any League of Nations any part of the authority over their armed forces. I am sure that the President has no very definite views as to what form the League should take; and I am also satisfied that since he made his first pronouncement a closer investigation has revealed practical difficulties which will tend to make him very cautious in committing himself to any definite proposal. It is interesting to observe that the United States and the British Empire are the two powers who would be most exposed to a mis-use of the League. Let me attempt to give you an example. Supposing Germany, with the intention of stirring up trouble, persuaded, say, the Persian Government to raise some question affecting Afghanistan, or India, and brought it before the League of Nations: It is conceivable that a cunning preparation of the case might involve a discussion among the League of the whole policy of British rule in India and place the British Government in a position where, in order to make good their case, they would have to disclose much confidential information.

Supposing Germany in the same way persuaded Mexico to raise some question with the States, the American Government might easily find themselves in an equally embarrassing situation, while public opinion here would be very impatient of any interference in their Mexican policy.

I am sending you a copy of a memorandum I wrote for House after talks with him on the Phillimore report, and a subsequent note which I also made at his request. You may take these as representing not so much his considered opinion as thoughts on the subject which are passing through his mind.

In conclusion, I think the encouraging part is the earnest intention of the Government and people of the United States to endeavour to find a means of preventing wars, and not less encouraging is the shrewd commonsense with which they face the obvious practical difficulties.

There is last but by no means least the growing feeling that the English-speaking peoples of the world must in some way form the basis of the League of Nations. This is a view held very strongly by House. He has told me again and again that he wants to work out this problem in close and frank cooperation with the British.

Reading sent you a cable regarding Phillimore's report[4] which I suggested to him might be rather misleading. What happened was this: I gave a copy of the report to House, who decided not to send it to the President because he knew he was too busy to deal with it. I also gave a copy to Lord Reading. Later another copy of the report was sent officially to Lord Reading, asking him to send it to the President. The President acknowledged it; was too busy to deal with it and sent it on to House, as explained in my cable. House did not think it was necessary to mention to the President that he had already received a copy of the report from me.

As you know, Lord Reading contemplates going over very shortly to London to confer with the Government, and I would venture to suggest that you should take that opportunity for discussing the American attitude towards the League of Nations with him. He is, of course, fully aware of the President's and Col. House's views, and has also, I believe, had some discussion of the matter with other prominent Americans.

Yours very sincerely,   W. Wiseman

TLS (FO 371/4365, pp. 145-48, PRO).
  [1] It is missing in the Wiseman Papers, CtY.
  [2] W. Wiseman to R. Cecil, July 17, 1918, T telegram (W. Wiseman Papers, CtY). Wiseman included this comment: "I have discussed the subject generally with the President. He recognises the practical difficulties far better than most people suppose."
  [3] About which see Lord Reading to WW, July 3, 1918 (second letter of that date), n. 1, Vol. 48.
  [4] "Col. House's letter of June 24th is a reply to the Phillimore report. The print was sent to Wiseman some time before it reached me for the President. I received copy on June 29th and sent it to the President who acknowledged it stating that he would write his comments after more careful consideration." Lord Reading to R. Cecil, July 17, 1918, No. 3239, T telegram (FO 115/2427, p. 166, PRO).

E N C L O S U R E   I

MEMORANDUM.

THE LEAGUE OF NATIONS.

This memorandum is intended to serve as a contribution to the study and advancement of the idea for the establishment of a League of Nations to maintain peace. The world-wide acceptance of this idea has been manifested by the production of a number of proposals having the same purpose, all of which have been subjected to criticism. The idea set forth below is largely the result of a study of such criticism and of an effort to find the means to overcome the main objections it has advanced. One objection alone has been disregarded and that is that which passively dismisses the whole subject by qualifying it as impracticable and Utopian.

The nations of the world shall be invited to send plenipotentiaries to a Conference or Parliament for the purpose of establishing a League of Nations to Maintain Peace, along the following lines:

The Conference will first assign to each nation that accepts the invitation and attends the Conference the voting power it will have in the League which the Conference will constitute. The voting power will be fixed with due regard to the population and economic and military importance of each State. The Conference will, by a majority vote, decide to what extent each of these factors will weigh in order that the tabulation of the States may be made with the highest possible degree of fairness.

Once that these general lines are established, the Conference will proceed to definitely assign the voting power of each State by means of a secret ballot of all the nations represented at the Conference. For this vote, each participating nation will be allowed an equal vote. The nation whose voting power is being voted on will abstain from voting.

After each nation has been assigned its voting power, the Conference will proceed to the election of a given number of individuals, nationals of any one of the States participating, to form a Permanent Tribunal of Judges in the High Court of the Nations. The Conference will fix the means of putting forward the candidature of said individuals, who will then be voted for. In this ballot, as in all subsequent ballots, each nation shall use the voting power assigned to it by the Conference.

The individuals will be appointed members of the Permanent Tribunal for life, and the Tribunal will remain in existence for all time as its name implies.

The members of the Permanent Tribunal will elect a President of the Tribunal from amongst their own number.

The Conference will further select and appoint a Permanent Commission of the Conference either from amongst its own members or from amongst those individuals which these members designate.

This Permanent Commission will sit as a body to receive the appeal of any nation participating in the League, for the settlement of any dispute arising between it and any other member-nation.

The Permanent Commission will consider the dispute and endeavour to bring about its settlement by conciliation. Should it fail in bringing about such a settlement and should it consider the matter of sufficient importance it will put the dispute before the Permanent Tribunal.

The Permanent Tribunal will deliberate upon the matter and will pronounce its finding.

The Member-Nations will be held bound to accept this finding.

Should either of the Member-Nations parties to the dispute refuse to abide by the finding of the Permanent Tribunal, this body will summon the Conference of Member-Nations for the purpose of debating on the means to be used to enforce respect of the Permanent Tribunal's finding upon the recalcitrant nation.

The Conference will recommend, by a majority vote in which every nation will vote with the voting-power originally assigned to it, the action which all Member-Nations shall take to enforce the finding of the Permanent Tribunal.

All Member-Nations will be bound to adopt the recommendations thus made by the Conference.

ENCLOSURE II

MEMORANDUM. 22nd June, 1918.

THE LEAGUE OF NATIONS.

The interim Report of the Committee on the League of Nations[1] well fulfils its avowed intention "to serve as a basis for an interchange of views." By the recognition it contains of the existence and importance of the difficulties which stand in the way of arriving at a practical scheme, it encourages criticism on the part of those who do not wish to exaggerate those difficulties but seek rather to suggest methods by which they can be overcome.

Before attempting to make any direct criticism of the detail of the suggestions made in the report it will not be out of place, therefore, to set down some of the general considerations to which the proposal for the establishment of a League of Nations gives rise.

The aim of the League shall be to provide the means of avoiding war. Not only must it seek to prevent that international disputes shall lead to the outbreak of hostilities between two nations. It must also seek to deter any nation, or any group of nations, from embarking upon an aggressive war intended either to despoil some smaller and weaker nation or to force to combat any nation, however strong, for the purpose of self-aggrandizement. It must, in short, be the keeper of the world's peace.

It follows that as a body the League must have functions in the Society of Nations analagous to those of the machinery of the Law in human society. Civilisation has long ago substituted litigation for knives and clubs for the settlement of individual quarrels.

---

[1] That is, the Phillimore Report.

Even before the present war enlightened public opinion sought to substitute arbitration for war as a means of deciding international disputes. The world-conflict now raging has convinced all whose opinion is worth considering that, if civilisation is to endure, no effort must be spared to prevent the recurrence of deliberate wars of aggression.

The main difficulty in the way of constituting the inter- or supernational body which shall act as the tribunal for, and have authority over all nations, becomes readily obvious by pursuing the analogy cited above. In any society the peaceable settlement of disputes can only be secured provided there is some physical force ready, if need be, to carry out the decrees of the court appealed to. In other words, the judge is useless without the policeman. Unless it has the means of enforcing its decisions and can deal with the law-breaking nation as a police force can deal with the law-breaking individual, a League of Nations cannot really guarantee peace to the peoples of the world.

Whilst the citizens of the majority of the nations of the world today desire without doubt to see the creation of the body which shall guarantee them against the miseries and cruelties of war, it cannot be said that they are, as yet, prepared to pay the price of such a guarantee. We say "as yet" because we believe that the world is moving towards the point where all international disputes will be settled by a Court of Nations and its authority upheld by an international police. But that time has clearly not yet arrived. A mechanic in Belgium, a farmer in France, would not stand ready today to fight in a "police" force destined to chastise the Argentine Republic for unjustly warring on Chile.

It therefore becomes necessary to see whether there is any other way in which the proposed League of Nations could bring pressure to bear upon an offending member so that it would desist from war. A return to the analogy of the human society will give two examples which are most worthy of note.

The first is the practice known as "boycotting." Whilst none of the peoples of the earth would be prepared to embark on war for the purpose of enforcing a decision against any one country, the manifest desire that a League of Nations to prevent war shall be constituted and the pathetic faith which exists in the ability of the world's honest statesmen to solve the problems its constitution presents, encourage the belief that it would be less difficult to enlist the co-operation of the peoples towards the enforcement of a decision if the burden that that cooperation would signify were considerably reduced. If the members of the League should bind themselves to suspend all financial and economic relations with the offending member, it is almost certain that such a partial interruption of their own financial and economic activities would be readily assented to by their peoples. The menace of such a step would weigh heavily in the councils of the offending country and those parties or groups within it who opposed the projected war would find themselves notably strengthened thereby.

The second example furnished by human society is not so concrete though none the less important. Not all the offenses that the individual can commit are punishable by law, and, of those that are, not always is the punishment which the judge is authorised to inflict either commensurate with the offence or is it the only punishment which the offender is called upon to bear. Ostracism, public condemnation and scorn are often punishments far more effective than prison sentences, and it cannot be gainsaid, unfortunately, that in certain strata of modern society they are undoubtedly far more effective deterrents from crime than the actual fear of incarceration in a modern jail. Surely by analogy we find here a force which can be of great use in the society of nations. "It doesn't pay" has kept many a man from the risk of prison. If it can be shown to nations that "it doesn't pay" to break the peace of the world, it is legitimate to hope that they also will abstain from offense.

So that whilst at first sight it would seem that to reject the idea of an international police force is to admit that the functions of a League of Nations must be limited to making recommendations and acting in an advisory capacity, it will be found that its authority will not be entirely ineffective if it does not rest on force of arms. The forces outlined above may well prove powerful to the end desired.

Let us now attempt to draw the lines a concrete proposal should follow:

a). A treaty should be drafted creating the League of Nations and all the nations of the world should be invited to sign it. The League will fall short of its ideal and its utility will be seriously impaired so long as it does not include all nations, or, at least, all civilised nations. If it does not include them it will be little more than a defensive alliance between those nations who belong to it.

b). The League should set up a moral standard for nations in their dealings one with the other. Relations between them should conform to the same code that any honourable society imposes on its members. Actions which perpetrated by individuals for personal motives would lead to ostracism and universal condemnation must no longer be condoned, as they are today, under the plea of patriotism. The same stigma must attach to the reprehensible acts of nations as now attaches to the acts of individuals.

c). The League must be universal in its scope and should lay down the principle that any war, however remote and insignificant, is the concern of all the nations of the world.

d). The League shall bind its members to use all means of conciliation between States who are in dispute and shall also bind all members to submit their disputes to arbitration.

e). The League shall bind its members to enforce its decrees by suspending all financial and economic relations with the nation which shall have refused to abide by said decrees.

f). The League shall ever strive to bring about a reduction of armaments, the abolition of national service and state control of the manufacture of all war material.

To turn from the above general considerations to a more detailed study of the Interim Report which has prompted them, the following observations suggest themselves.

There appears to be a contradiction between paragraph 8. of the Report and Article 2. of the "Draft Convention." Paragraph 8. states that no provision has been made for action against a State refusing to abide by the awards of the proposed Conference of Allied States. Article 2. appears to specifically provide for such action.

Paragraph 9. of the Report, section (b), would seem to take a one-sided view of the case it sets forth. Surely the consent to "warlike preparations" during a moratorium would also be of advantage to the State who had already initiated such preparations. An unprepared State would be an added handicap.

Paragraph 19. of the Report refers to Article 17. of the Draft Convention. This article authorises the imposition of conditions on a State seeking to join the Conference. Article 13 gives such a State facilities for joining the Conference at a given moment and for a specific case without the imposition of any conditions.

The Committee's suggestion that some country such as Switzerland, Holland, or Belgium, should be the seat of the League is excellent, and we also agree with the suggestions with regard to the President of the League and to the status of the diplomatic representatives of the countries forming part of the League in the country where its seat is located as ipso facto representatives of their respective governments on the League. Also with the right of member-nations to add other representatives to the Conference.

It does not seem proper that the League of Nations itself should act as a Court of Arbitration. The great disadvantage of this course would be that members of the League would tend to range themselves into two camps; racial and national passions would be aroused and a fair judicial settlement would be difficult to arrive at. A better course would be the selection of three arbitrators, one by each of the belligerents, and the third selected by these two arbitrators. Should they fail to agree on a third, he should then be nominated by the majority vote of the League of Nations.

It would be advantageous if the League of Nations were to be provided with the means of automatically convening its members when conditions between any two States justified the assumption that there existed a danger of their going to war in order that they might insist that they should submit their difference to arbitration, if they were member-States, and procure that they should if they were not.

T MSS (FO 371/4365, pp. 149-55, PRO).

To Joseph Patrick Tumulty

Dear Tumulty: The White House [c. July 19, 1918].

I would be very much obliged if you would answer this and say to the writer that Mr. Svasley[1] quoted the true spirit of what I said to him[2] but that he has here stated more confidently than I had any right to state the expectation that the hopes of the Armenians "will be crowned." I also had no right to say and do not remember saying that I was "resolved that no question should be left unsettled in the general reckoning after the war." I do not remember exactly what I said to Mr. Svasley but I have no doubt that I did express my own resolution to do all that I could to see that the hopes of the Armenians were satisfied and that no question of essential justice involved in the present European situation should be left unsettled in the general reckoning after the war.

The President.

TL (WP, DLC).
    [1] Miran Sevasly, lawyer of Boston and chairman of the Armenian National Union of America.
    [2] "(From *Azk*, July 13, 1918) Mr. Svasley approached the President on the Mayflower [on July 4, 1918], and congratulated him for his speech, calling it a new Magna Charta devoted to the rights of nationalities, and he then expressed the hope to see the principles enunciated in that speech executed in behalf of small nationalities. President Wilson, in reply, said: 'You are justified in your expectations.' Then President Wilson explained to Mr. Svasley why America had not declared war upon Turkey, and, continuing his conversation, the President declared solemnly that the Armenians have nothing to fear, because their question will be solved according to justice, and their hopes will be crowned, and that he had resolved that no question would be left unsettled in the general reckoning after the war." T MS enclosed in Arshag Mahdesian to WW, July 18, 1918, TLS (WP, DLC). Mahdesian, editor of the periodical, *The New Armenia*, published in New York, wished to know if Sevasly had summarized the conversation accurately. *Azk* (*The Nation*) was an Armenian periodical published in Boston.

From Frank Lyon Polk

Dear Mr. President: Washington July 19, 1918.

Replying to your inquiry of yesterday, concerning the Italian ex-Austrian soldiers, I find that almost all of them are "irredenti" and are regarded by the Italian Government as absolutely loyal and trustworthy. The Italian authorities have weeded out all those whom they did not consider suitable and about 300 of the unsuitable men have just arrived in this country en route to Italy. I am of the opinion that these soldiers will cooperate sympathetically with the Czecho-Slovaks, more especially as the Czecho-Slovaks are now fighting with the Italian Army on the Italian Front.

Sometime ago when these ex-Austrians had reached the Far East from European Russia, the Italian Government made inquiries of us regarding their transportation to Italy. This transportation seemed very difficult to arrange at the time and we intimated to the Italian Embassy that possibly the Italian Government might find it wise to leave them there for the present, pending developments in the Russian-Siberian situation.

Faithfully yours,   Frank L. Polk

TLS (WP, DLC).

From William Jennings Bryan

My dear Mr. President: Asheville, N. C. July 19, 1918.

Your telegram received. I appreciate your consideration in desiring to save me from the embarassment of being put in the position of having an appeal for recognition refused, and assume that the information upon which your judgment is based is of such a character that it can be communicated to me. I am anxious to hear what you have learned.

If I am correctly informed—if not, I shall be pleased to have you set me right—Tinoco, who was educated in Belgium and whose wife is daughter of an English woman, after taking the Presidency, as the result of a bloodless revolution (differing entirely from the Huerta one in purpose and method) called an election, was supported by the five living ex-Presidents and the public generally, was elected and was by the Constitutional Convention declared the duly elected President for a term ending in 1923. He offered the United States the use of Costa Rica railroads and harbors for military purposes, secured from Congress a declaration of war against Germany and is now keeping the Government in harmony with the Allies, with the support of all the country except the anti-United

States-pro-Ally element, and that element has little strength except the encouragement given it by our refusal to recognize Tinoco.

I am, as you know, fully in sympathy with your Latin America policy and as unwilling to represent an unjust couse [cause] as you are to have me, but the facts as I understand them explain the recognition already given by Guatamala, Honduras and Salvador and the leading countries of South America and several European countries. The deposed President was unfriendly to us, while Tinoco has not only shown himself a friend, in spite of our refusal to recognize him, but is anxious that Costa Rica shall make a treaty with us similar to the one with Nicaraugua, covering its share in the canal route and including an important island halfway between Panama and Fonseca Bay. I fear a failure to recognize this Government, which has enjoyed popular support for nearly fifteen months, may so encourage the pro-German element as to involve Costa Rica in civil war. As I understand the facts, our failure to recognize the existing and accepted government is not only unjust to Costa Rica and disappointing to friendly republics in South America, but a possible source of danger to us.

Knowing the conscientiousness with which you act, I am glad to aid you if I can, or to be myself corrected if I am in error. If the facts are such as to make the recognition of Tinoco impossible, I would like to learn from you what is necessary to secure for Costa Rica the right to cooperate with us as a sister republic. At present the situation is deplorable and Germany, recognizing the strategic importance of Costa Rica, is using her influence to overthrow Tinoca.

When you honored me with a position in the cabinet, I told you of my deep interest in Latin America; while Secretary, I found my interest deepening and it has not abated. I am willing to go to Costa Rica this fall, if necessary, with a view to rendering any assistance I can. I shall be pleased to suspend for the present the question of representing Costa Rica and confer with you, as a friend of Latin America, with a view of helping a republic in distress.

Please wire me whether you can see me next Monday, the 22nd. If not convenient then—unless you feel that you cannot see me at all—I shall try to find a later date that will suit your convenience. Most of the time until September is taken up with meetings, at each one of which I spend about thirty minutes appealing for support of the Government on each one of its several lines of activity, and I would prefer not to cancel these, unless necessary; but I regard the Costa Rica situation as so serious that I shall be pleased to cancel any of them to secure a conference with you.

With assurances of respect, I am, my dear Mr. President,
                    Very truly yours,   W. J. Bryan

TLS (WP, DLC).

From George Creel

My dear Mr. President: Washington, D. C. July 19, 1918.

I have just seen the men behind the Mooney mass meeting arranged for Sunday afternoon at the Belasco Theatre. Headed by Bourke Cochran,[1] a delegation will be there to call upon you Monday. While ostensibly for the purpose of thanking you for your past interest, this delegation wants to urge you to exercise your powers as Commander-in-Chief to take the entire Mooney matter out of the California Courts, bringing it under Federal jurisdiction.

I know that you will appreciate the importance of this case, but I do not know whether you quite realize the extreme bitterness of labor as the result of it. Between now and the date of Mooney's execution in August, mass meetings are planned from coast to coast.

I do not know what to advise, because I am not lawyer enough to know whether there is anything else that you can do that you have not done already.

If you wish to see this delegation, I can make them stop after thanking you, permitting you to make such answer as you see fit without being compelled to any decision by their suggestions.
                    Respectfully,   George Creel

TLS (WP, DLC).
[1] That is, William Bourke Cockran.

From Samuel Gompers, with Enclosures

Sir: Washington, D. C. July 19, 1918

Of course it was my fault that I did not in advance ask you whether you could spare some time yesterday for the presentation to you of other important matters than the question of prohibiting child labor,[1] and I readily realize that your engagements forbade my even suggesting that you would give me more time than you had at your disposal yesterday.

And yet the matters which I desired to submit to you for consideration were of prime importance and I feel that it is my imperative duty to bring them to your attention in this form.

From many sections of the country there come to me resolutions, telegrams, in the form of petitions and protests regarding the Mooney case, one cablegram from the Secretary of the Parliamentary Committee of the British Trade Union Congress, the Right Honorable Charles Bowerman, all of them urging, even protesting. I know of no one particular thing that is calculated to do the cause of America and the cause of our allies greater injury than the execution of Tom Mooney. I am exceedingly apprehensive of its consequences if it should be permitted to take place. The Mooney case is now and for months has been an international and a political issue, rather than a local or judicial state issue in California, and as the days go on I am sure that feeling and that issue will become intensified. If Mooney should be executed with the general knowledge or belief that his conviction was had upon manufactured or perjured evidence, and of that there is little or no doubt, I repeat that I am apprehensive of the consequences.

Enclosed you will please find copies of a few of the telegrams and a copy of the cablegram which I have received within the recent past, and to which your attention is respectfully called.[2]

Enclosed you will please find a copy of the confidential report made by the American Labor Mission which by direction of the American Federation of Labor I sent to Mexico. It throws a great light upon the situation in Mexico.

You will observe that the American Labor Mission made some recommendations.

1. The plan for the education of the Mexican people as to the cause for which the United States entered into the world war against Germany and Austria.

2. That the best agency to help stabilize relations between the Mexican and the United States governments is the organized labor movement of the two countries.

3. The American Federation of Labor has not the means to conduct such a campaign. Because the Congress has cut the appropriation made for the Committee on Public Information it is practically impossible for that committee to bear the expense.

It has been suggested that it might be borne by the fund which the Congress has placed at your disposal for the purpose of helping to win the war. This fact, as I had the opportunity of saying to you yesterday, was concurred in by Honorable William B. Wilson, Secretary of Labor, Mr. Buyor[3] and Mr. Sisson of the Committee on Public Information, (Mr. Creel at the last moment being unable to attend the conference.) Secretary Wilson will beyond doubt place the matter before you for consideration and action in more concrete form. I have absolute confidence in the official whose name you suggested that I should present this matter to, but I am convinced that these things should receive your careful consideration.

Another phase of the Mexican situation and the relations between it and the United States has come to me in another form and which, as I took occasion to say yesterday, must be presented to you if presented at all. I am under word of honor to convey it to no one but you. I hope that I may have an opportunity of conveying this information to you some time in the late afternoon Monday July 29th, or any hour which may be convenient to you Tuesday July 30th. The Executive Council of the American Federation of Labor will hold a week's session outside of Washington, hence it will be necessary for me to be in attendance with my associates; therefore the suggested dates.

I am very anxious to aid in all things that will benefit our country and our cause, so anxious that I am impelled to present these matters to you for your consideration and action.

I have the honor to be

Yours very respectfully,   Saml. Gompers.

TLS (WP, DLC).
  [1] The United States Supreme Court, on June 3, 1918, had declared, by a five-to-four vote, that the Keating-Owen Child Labor Act of 1916 (about which see the index references in Vols. 37 and 38) was unconstitutional. The majority held that, in attempting to prohibit the interstate transportation of the products of child labor, Congress had exceeded its constitutional authority to regulate interstate commerce. Hammer *v.* Dagenhart, 247 U.S. 251. In the wake of this decision, Wilson and Gompers, like many other progressive reformers, were urgently seeking some alternative means to prohibit child labor. For a discussion of the decision and its impact, see Stephen B. Wood, *Constitutional Politics in the Progressive Era: Child Labor and the Law* (Chicago and London, 1968), pp. 139-202.
  [2] Two TCL and twenty-one TC telegrams (WP, DLC) from various union locals concerning the Mooney case.
  [3] Carl Byoir, one of the three associate chairmen of the Committee on Public Information.

E N C L O S U R E   I

From Samuel Gompers

Sir: Washington, D. C. July 18, 1918

The confidential report of the A. F. of L. Commission to Mexico— a copy of which I have the honor to present to you—was read in my office last Wednesday before Secretary of Labor Wilson, Mr. Felix Frankfurter, two representatives from the Committee on Public Information, Mr. Sisson and Mr. Brayer,[1] Secretary Frank Morrison and me.

Afterwards the recommendations proposed by the commissioners was discussed, all agreed that it was practical and worthy of adoption as to its main features. The Secretary of Labor promised to present the whole matter to you with his suggestions as to its feasibility. It was agreed by us all that the first thing to do was to lay the matter before you with the suggestion that Ambassador Fletcher be consulted as to the practicability of the plan.

Mr. Frankfurter, Mr. Sisson and Mr. Brayer were in accord with the Secretary of Labor and so expressed themselves.

I feel that this is an opportunity for the American Federation of Labor, in collaboration with the Mexican Labor movement, to do a service to the peoples of all Latin America and so present the matter to you whose friendship for Latin America has deepened our hope that something practical can be done to put relations between the United States and Mexico and ultimately Latin America upon a higher plan[e].   Respectfully yours,   Saml. Gompers.

TLS (WP, DLC).
¹ That is, Carl Byoir.

E N C L O S U R E   I I

CONFIDENTIAL REPORT

The Commission of the American Federation of Labor consisting of James Lord, President of the Mining Department of the A. F. of L., Santiago Iglesias, President of the Free Federation of Workingmen of Porto Rico, and John Murray, Secretary of the Pan-American Federation of Labor Conference Committee, arrived in Mexico City on May 22, 1918. Lord and Iglesias returned to the United States on June 3, and Murray returned on June 14.

THE MEXICAN PRESS

Practically every day of this period the German owned press of Mexico City headed by EL DEMOCRATA, kept up a front page attack of scurrilous falsehood against the commissioners from the United States declaring in one instance that the commissioners were "strikebreakers," and in another that they were "betrayers of the labor movement and agents sent to destroy Mexico."

EL PUEBLO, the official organ of the Mexican Government, in an article on its front page of June 7, openly exhorted the unions of Mexico to refuse to have anything to do with the labor commission of the American Federation of Labor.

The same paper in an article of June 3 upon its front page, after a headline which declared the commission was merely an agency of the White House, commenced as follows:

"Samuel Gompers!

"What insulting ignominy and abjection is represented in this name!"

BOLETIN DE LA GUERRA on May 24 had the following headlines

on its front page: "The Strike Breakers Have Arrived—Be Careful Of Their Words—Nothing Good Will Be Accomplished For The Mexican Working Men By Inaugurating Relations With The Political Delegation From The United States."

EL DEMOCRATA on May 23 declared "The yankee commissioners have already arrived in the City of Saltillo to start intervention propaganda among the Mexican workers. * * * The organized working men of Mexico are waiting these agents with fear. * * * The Mexican workers and the syndicalists are not willing to hear the insinuations of this interested Commission and we are ready to maintain our absolute neutrality in regard to the international policy."

Not satisfied with the attacks of EL DEMOCRATA in the morning and EL NACIONALISTA and EL BOLETIN DE LA GUERRA in the afternoon, the Germans covered the billboards of the city proclaiming that "The Yankee Labor Commission Proceeds Without Honor," and that "It is hypocritical in its attempts to bind the ties of international relations."

Two daily papers in Mexico City, EL UNIVERSAL and EXCELSIOR, gave full and fair reports of the A. F. of L. Commission's work.

Felix F. Palavacini,[1] late editor of EL UNIVERSAL, an advocate of Mexico's siding with the Allies, was forced to leave the Capitol after being informed by President Carranza that the writings and policies of EL UNIVERSAL were not in accord with the government.

Palavancini sold his paper to the man who brought him the notice to depart, Rafael Nieto, Sub-Secretary of the Treasury.

On a recent trip to Pachuca, President Carranza noticed that EL DEMOCRATA was not being sold on the train, and asking why, was told that the company having the concession of sales did not care to sell such a badly conducted paper. The President ordered the sale of the paper immediately reestablished. Later the concession of this company was revoked.

President Carranza's defense of his complacence in the face of the conduct of the German owned dailies is that he cannot abridge the freedom of the press, but in the case of Palavancini, who stood for the cause of the Allies, the freedom of the press was denied.

Publicity fair to the United States in Mexico and the cause of the Allies is suppressed by German influence working through Mexican government sources.

MEXICAN UNION MEETING

The theater first hired by the Mexican unions in which it was proposed to hold a public meeting for the A. F. of L. commission

---

[1] Félix Fulgencio Palavicini, an intellectual leader of the Mexican Revolution since the days of Francisco I. Madero.

was closed to the unions at the last moment and the assembly had to be held in another theater. On the day of this meeting EL PUEBLO, the government organ, advertised a lottery of $2000.00 in another theater at which free tickets would be given to the public. But in spite of all these Germanic attempts to keep the workers away from the union meeting the theater finally obtained by the unions was crowded until there was only standing room. The various attempts of German agents in the audience to interrupt the speakers from the United States were promptly suppressed by Mexican union men. Marked applause followed a reference by one of the commissioners to the "bought and paid for" press. This meeting was the proof that organized labor of Mexico stands for friendly, international relations and is not swayed by Germans. Common talk on the street before the meeting was to the effect that the Germans would organize a mob to attack the commission.

GERMAN PAID MOB

That the Germans actually organize mobs in Mexico is proved by the attack upon Ambassador Fletcher when he attended a meeting of the Mexican Chamber of Deputies, was hissed in the Chamber and met a mob at the entrance on leaving which howled, threatened, but failed to frighten the Ambassador who marched through the German-paid gathering without noticing the menace, though inwardly expecting to be man-handled.

The day following this mob attack President Carranza sent an apology to the Ambassador.

A. F. OF L. COMMISSION SEES CARRANZA

The A. F. of L. commission did everything in its power to harmonize its actions and speech in Mexico with all duly constituted authority. Letters of introduction to President Carranza from General Obregon and from Governor Hunt of Arizona were duly presented in an interview arranged and attended by Ambassador Fletcher. President Carranza gave the commission nearly an hour in which to state its case, listening most attentively to Iglesias, whose Spanish is of Spain, but making little comment. Afterwards the Ambassador congratulated Iglesias on his presentation of the aims of the commission and conditions of labor in the United States. Iglesias spoke much of the War Labor Board and its workings for fair play. He gave deserved credit for the establishment of this Board to President Wilson and the American Federation of Labor. Carranza commented that Mexico had government machinery for the settlement of strikes in accordance with the constitution.

MEXICAN LABOR COMMISSION TO U. S.

Ambassador Fletcher went over the situation in Mexico in a series of conferences with the commissioners. He desired particularly that the commissioners should keep him informed as to the sentiment and opinions of the leaders of the organized labor movement in Mexico. He pointed to the condition in Chile where the army is officered by Germans. He drew attention to the results in Turkey where German control and propaganda brought results that might be repeated in some form in Mexico. He offered to help in the sending of the Mexican labor commission to the United States by urging the U. S. Department of Public Information, through its resident Mexican representative, Robert H. Murray, to pay the traveling expenses of the Mexicans. This later plan became unnecessary when the Mexican commission was at last furnished with funds by President Carranza and after the Mexicans had been secretly threatened as "traitors" if they accepted funds from any source other than Mexican. The fear that the Mexican commission might go to the United States uncontrolled by the Mexican government was plainly the reason for the finding of the funds by Carranza at the last moment.

Ambassador Fletcher, with his fluent Spanish and sense of the Mexican viewpoint, is a fitting representative of President Wilson's Latin American policy. Mexico City's comment on him is that he should have come to Mexico sooner—that, possibly, his good work is all too late.

Interview was had with General Pablo Gonzalez. He declared his belief that the government should have control in all labor disputes.

A. F. OF L. COMMISSION WINS MEXICAN UNIONS

Proof that the A. F. of L. commission finally won the confidence of the organized labor movement of Mexico is shown in the resolutions adopted by the MEXICAN FEDERATION OF LABOR (Confedercion Regional Obrera Mexicana) and the FEDERATION OF WORKERS SYNDICATES OF THE FEDERAL DISTRICT OF MEXICO (Federacion de Sindicatos Obreros del Distrito Federal de Mexico). In these resolutions the Mexican unions set forth their desire for an international labor conference and working relations with the American Federation of Labor. They especially desire these relations for the benefit of their brother Mexicans now in the United States (over a million and a half of them) and also for those Mexicans now flocking by thousands over the border into the United States.

MEXICAN UNION MEN FOR ALLIES

Under the cover of confidence statements were made to the commission by Mexican labor leaders expressing their conviction that the best thing for Mexico was to unite with the Allies in the present war. Mexican organized labor is the one and only trustworthy source for spreading the truth throughout Mexico. Its sympathies are with the Allies.

The facts herein presented were gathered by the commission from organized Mexican labor sources, the Ambassador, Associated Press representatives and reliable American and Mexican news writers.

GERMANS TERRORIZE U. S. PUBLICITY

Robert H. Murray, who was himself threatened with jail a few days before the commission's arrival related how many of his publicity plans had been fought by the Germans. German terrorism frightened a Mexican moving picture lecturer, that Murray had hired, out of his job. The Germans held up the pictures of the sinking of the Lusitania for a considerable time in Mexico. Murray gave the commission every assistance in its work. He pointed out how the commission could aid him in circulating some of his publicity, explaining that his only present source of individual distribution was through the hands of American residents in Mexico and they, naturally, could not reach the masses of the people. Mexico today is practically divided into German and Anti-German camps.

FREE PULQUE

German propaganda does not stop at publicity. Two pulque shops, "U 39" and "Hindenburg," see to it that the lowest elements of Mexico City are freely supplied with liquor. This condition of affairs is the more extraordinary because the entire nation of Mexico is turning toward prohibition and the production of pulque has been heavily taxed in order to prevent drunkenness among the people. The German influence which obtained the right to practically distribute it free in the City of Mexico must have been very great.

MEXICAN LABOR FOR U. S.

Mexican delegations of skilled mechanics came almost every day to the commission's rooms at the Hotel Cosmos asking for information as to work in the United States. The commission was forced to reply that this was not a part of its mission and therefore it could give no assistance. Reference was, however, made to Secretary of Labor Wilson in whose office such information might be obtained.

It was at this time that the Mexican government printed a notice in the papers to the effect that Mexican mechanics would not be allowed to cross the border into the United States.

While the Commission was in the Capitol the Mexican government discharged some five thousand government employes. It was stated by Mexican residents that in the course of a few weeks these employes would be at the end of their resources for food.

TEACHERS STRIKE

The school teachers at this same time threatened to strike because the government had turned over to the States the school system and the States had no money to pay teachers. The organized railroad workers also threatened to strike because of a practical 25 per cent reduction in their pay. They were finally induced to accept the cut. The great textile mills of Puebla were idle for over two months in the course of a strike for living wages. This strike was settled just as the commission left Mexico.

ARMY OFFICERS SHOOT WORKERS

The railroad workers have still another grievance, namely terrorism by army officers. One engineer was shot and killed, while the commission was in Mexico, by an army officer who put a bullet through the man as he sat in his engine cab at a station. The excuse was that the engineer had not obeyed orders.

During this same period the dailies of the Capitol contained various accounts of policemen being shot in the streets by army officers. These military men, apparently, refuse to acknowledge any police or civil authority.

ZAPATA

Zapata is not now able to control his followers. Zapatistas are in force within eight miles of the City of Mexico. Zapata is not spoken of as a political factor, but merely as the last refuge of desperate men fleeing for their lives from various government authorities. In almost every state there are factions in revolt against the government.

THE SAFEST RAILROAD IN MEXICO

Attacks were made on five railroad trains while the A. F. of L. commission was in the City of Mexico. One train was looted of many thousands in gold going to pay troops in the North. But one line is considered reasonably safe from the border to Mexico City, the Constitutionalist Railway running from Nuevo Laredo through Monterey, Saltillo, San Luis Potosi, Queretaro, and to the Capitol. The train on which the commission traveled was proceeded by a pilot engine to feel out the way and find possible burnt bridges. The engine of this train was followed by a carload of soldiers, and the last car of the train was a practical fort surmounted with an iron-clad tower.

STARVATION

It needs no report from this commission to tell of the starvation that every traveler witnesses in Mexico. Early morning in Mexico City with its 8000 feet of altitude is chilly, and it is a daily sight to the early riser to see huddled piles of homeless children, some mere babies of five and six years, massed together like pigs on the stone side walks, with scraps of torn sacking covering portions of their naked bodies. One must be careful here in throwing a discarded and sucked fruit skin in the street for upon such fragments the little children pounce and try to extract sustenance. Disease, which follows such conditions, stares one in the face in every direction.

MACHINERY LACKING

Without machinery this country is in desperate straights [straits]. The big ranches, producers of the bulk of Mexico's food, work with the aid of machinery, machinery which is today lacking. The railroads, the mills, the factories, all are being slowly strangled to death for the lack of machinery that cannot be obtained by Mexico, the neutral nation.

General Pablo Gonzalez is reported to have three Japanese officers on his personal staff. He has made certain pro-Ally statements which are considered something of a joke as no official within the reach of Carranza does anything opposed to the President's policies.

MEN WHO MEXICAN LABOR DISTRUST

Gonzalez is thoroughly distrusted by the Mexican labor movement because of his jailing and suppression of the leaders of Mexico's unions in November, 1916. That was the time when Carranza issued his decree of death to strikers which reads as follows:

"Article 1st. The DEATH PENALTY shall be applied, not only to disturbers of the peace mentioned in the Law of January 25th, 1862, but also to: First: Those who may incite workmen to strike in factories and concerns devoted to public service, or who may engage in propaganda to that end; to those who may preside at meetings where such strikes are proposed, discussed or approved; to those who may defend or uphold the same; to those who may approve or subscribe thereto; to those who may attend said meetings, or may not withdraw from the same as soon as they learn their purpose; and to those who strive to render the strike effective after it once has been declared."

GOVERNMENT SIGNS PACT WITH UNION

It was Gonzalez who gave to the Mexican unions the use of the building formerly occupied in the Capitol by the Mexican Jockey Club. They occupied it but a short time until a strike was declared and the general sent his soldiers to put their leaders in jail and close the headquarters. These same unions had volunteered as unions and fought for the cause of Carranza when the First Chief was at his lowest ebb of power with his official residence on the pier of Vera Cruz convenient to flight from Mexico by water. History shows that the uniting of the organized labor movement of Mexico with its provisional government under Carranza turned the scale in favor of the First Chief. The Constitutionalist Government under Carranza and Mexico's only national labor organization in 1915 signed a printed contract which was placarded all over Mexico. This contract between the government and the union—the Casa del Obrero Mundial with a membership of between 50,000 and 60,000—was signed by the Executive Committee of the union and by Rafael Zubaron Capmany representing the government. It was declared that the workers would take up arms for the Constitutionalist Government, that the female workers would attend the wounded, that the union committees should make its propaganda and organization in collaboration with the Constitutionalist cause and that the government would provide such workers with the means of subsistence. With the revolution won for Carranza the Casa del Obrero Mundial was considered a menace by the First Chief. Result was that its leaders were jailed, threatened with death, its assemblies suppressed and the organization wiped from the face of Mexico. This last act was performed principally, by General Pablo Gonzalez. Thus history explains the present sentiment of the workers of Mexico towards President Carranza and General Gonzalez.

DEAD LABOR LAWS

The labor laws of Mexico's constitution adopted at Queretaro in 1917, are practically all dead letters with the exception of the eight hour law which prevails throughout the Southern Republic. One government official recently stated in the Chamber of Deputies that the labor laws of the constitution were impractical and could not be put in force. This statement is credited to the Secretary of Industry, Commerce and Labor, Alberto J. Pani. Great hostility is shown in Mexico by the big capitalists and their political followers to the labor and agrarian provisions of Mexico's constitution.

THE OPEN DOOR TO MEXICO'S MIND

In accepting the A. F. of L. commission's proposals to the holding of an international conference the Mexican labor movement proved that it was the only powerful group in Mexico openly willing to cooperate with the people of the United States. This acceptance was made in spite of the combined German and government influence which desired that there should be no organized labor intercourse between Mexico and the United States during the war.

Publicity and education can only filter into Mexico through the labor movement of Mexico.

ARIZONA

In its reply to the A. F. of L. commission's proposals Mexican organized labor laid great stress upon the aid and protection that the American Federation of Labor could give to the tens of thousands of Mexican workers now in the United States and the added thousands that will soon cross the border. This aid the American

Federation of Labor will undoubtedly see its way clear to give as much for its own protection as that of its Mexican brothers. Arizona, alone, has some fourteen thousand Mexican miners nearly half of whom are now members of unions affiliated with the American Federation of Labor. The labor movement of Mexico has the best and most material of reasons for establishing fraternal ties with the people of the United States.

WHY PRESIDENTS ARE INVITED

It is clear that the proposed international conference on the border line cannot be safely attended by Mexican labor leaders without the consent of the Mexican government. Proof of this has been given during Carranza's rule by the practical suppression of several National Labor Congresses called without government consent. The recent National Labor Congress held in Saltillo in May, 1918, was called by one of the most friendly governors to labor in all Mexico, Governor Mireles[2] of Coahuila. Here Mexico made its first Mexican Federation of Labor, delegates attending from nineteen Mexican States. These things being so it is plain why invitations have been issued asking the attendance of President Wilson, President Carranza and the governors of all States, on both sides of the border to the international conference.

Still another and larger meaning than that of the mere fraternalization of the labor movements will naturally attach itself to this international conference. It will be the binding of the first ties between the two Republics untouched by mining claims, oil claims, commercial claims or questions of private property, claims which have taught hate of all things coming from the "Colossus of the North" to generations of Mexicans.

LATIN-AMERICA WATCHES

Such a conference will affect the entire Latin-American relationship with the United States because of the fact that all Latin-American countries watch the acts of the people and government of the United States in relation to Mexico as typical of what may happen to them individually and collectively.

MEXICAN COMMISSION IN WASHINGTON

The two Mexican labor commissioners, Luis N. Morones, representing the Mexican Federation of Labor, and Salvador Alvarez, representing the Syndicates of Mexico City, had a three days' conference in Washington with the Pan-American Federation of Labor Conference Committee, President Gompers and representatives of international unions. The result was that the following resolutions

---

[2] Gustavo Espinosa Mireles.

were drafted, discussed and adopted. President Gompers handed these resolutions to the Mexican commissioners for their immediate presentation to the Mexican labor movement for adoption, time, place for the conference and conditions being proposed by the American Federation of Labor through its President as authorized by a convention of the American Federation of Labor.

PLAN FOR INTERNATIONAL CONFERENCE

First—That an international conference be held at the earliest possible date, at the most convenient place on the frontier, at which shall be represented the American Federation of Labor and representatives of the organized labor movement of Mexico.

Second—That President Carranza and President Wilson of the two Republics be earnestly requested to be present at this conference for such periods as they may deem proper.

Third—That the governors of the border states be invited to attend this international conference.

Fourth—That the subjects for consideration at the international conference shall be

(a) The establishment of the Pan-American Federation of Labor,

(b) The establishment of better conditions for workingmen who emigrate from one country to another,

(c) The establishment of a better understanding and relationship between the peoples of the United States and Mexico,

(d) To utilize every lawful and honorable means for the protection and promotion of the rights, the interests and the welfare of the peoples of the United States and of Mexico,

(e) To utilize every lawful and honorable means for the purpose of cultivating the most favorable and friendly relations between the labor movements, the peoples and the Republics of Mexico and of the United States.

It is tentatively proposed that the conference shall begin in Laredo, Texas, Wednesday, November 13, 1918, to continue until the business before the conference shall have been completed.

In view of the national importance and the results upon the public mind of all Latin-America that such a conference would have, nothing should be left undone to make it a success. To this end the following practical plan is proposed:

The issuance in the labor press of a series of articles in Spanish and English explaining the good results to the people of both countries of the proposed international conference. To cover the organized labor groups in Mexico and the United States with copies of such a publication will necessitate a weekly edition of at least 50,000.

This confidential report makes no attempt to cover the detailed report of the commission as made to the convention of the American Federation of Labor in St. Paul, Minnesota, wherein it is shown that Mexico has in the neighborhood of half a million organized workers, a body of men and women representing the highest aspirations and organized mentality of the Southern Republic. In this group is the soul of the Mexican revolution as expressed in its constitution. This group holds the door open to international good understanding.

(Signed)   James Lord
      "   Santiago Iglesias
      "   John Murray

T MS (WP, DLC).

Lord Reading to Arthur James Balfour

Washington. July 19, 1918.

Very Urgent, Personal and Secret.

My telegrams 3265 and 3276.[1]

I would suggest that you should send me message relating to the Aide Memoire to transmit to President whom I shall see within next few days, probably Monday or Tuesday.

Confidential. I understand that the French Ambassador before receiving the Note of yesterday expressed to State Department satisfaction of his Government with U. S. proposal to Japan. Please do not mention to French Government that I have reported this to you but I learned it today from my colleague.

You will probably find it difficult to express satisfaction although I think it carries out, allowing for the greater solemnity of a document, what I have anticipated in my message to you.

I am convinced that President thoroughly dislikes the idea of sending American soldiers to Russia and has only consented because he realizes that the U. S. could not fail to support the Czecho-Slovaks. He also fears that once American troops are in Russia action may be taken by French or British which would in his view be interference with Russian domestic affairs—or that otherwise he may be drawn into a much more extensive operation than he intends.

You will realize how important it is therefore that he should express readiness to send U. S. troops with Japanese and as it will assuredly develop under Japanese command.

He is quite convinced that the issue will be fought out on the Western front.

About Thursday next I shall visit House for discussion.

Please inform me immediately of any matters you may wish me to take up before my departure for England.

T telegram (FO 115/2448, pp. 267-68, PRO).
    [1] Lord Reading to D. Lloyd George and A. J. Balfour, July 10, 1918, and Lord Reading to D. Lloyd George, July 12, 1918, Vol. 48.

To the Citizens of Lyon

The White House. 20 July, 1918.

Please request to State Department to send the following message in reply to the enclos[ed] cablegram from citizens of Lyons:[1]

I am deeply gratified and honoured by the message from the population of Lyon assembled on the occasion of the solemn celebration of the fourteenth of July and beg to assure them that it is a matter of the profoundest pride to me that their great city should on that day have given my name to the splendid bridge just completed. I take the liberty of sending them the warm fraternal greetings of the American people who rejoice to be associated with them in the defence of Right and Liberty.   W.W.

WWT MS (WP, DLC).
    [1] [Édouard] Herriot to WW, c. July 15, 1918, translation of telegram, T MS (WP, DLC). Herriot was at this time Senator from the Department of Rhône and Mayor of Lyon.

To Theodore Roosevelt

[The White House] July 20, 1918

Am greatly distressed that the news of your son's death is confirmed.[1] I had hoped for other news. He died serving his country and died with fine gallantry. I am deeply grieved that his service should have come to this tragic end.   Woodrow Wilson.

T telegram (Letterpress Books, WP, DLC).
    [1] Lt. Quentin Roosevelt, an army aviator, had been shot down over German-held territory near Château-Thierry on July 14. Theodore Roosevelt had received word of the crash and presumed death of his youngest son, age twenty, on July 17, but later reports had said that he might still be alive. *New York Times*, July 18-21, 1918.

From Frank Lyon Polk, with Enclosure

My dear Mr. President: Washington July 20, 1918.

I took the liberty of showing your proposed statement to the press *in re* American-Japanese action in Siberia to the Secretary of War as he was discussing this subject with me this morning and the following thoughts occurred to both of us:

(1) The statement on the first page beginning with the words "and that it" and ending "the war against Germany" might prove of considerable value to Germany for propaganda purposes as indicating that we formally had abandoned all hope of reconstituting an Eastern front even out of Russian forces.

(2) This statement further would prove embarrassing in the event that the Allies attempted to reconstitute the Eastern front as an argument for Germany to use to persuade the Russians against assisting the Allies in such action.

Mr. Baker thought that the best line to take would be to lay stress on the fact that we are bending all our energies on the Western front and that we intend to force a decisive issue there rather than to dissipate our energies in trying to reestablish the Eastern front. This, I think, you made perfectly clear in your memorandum to the Allies.

There are some indications that the Japanese are attempting to drive a wedge between the United States and the European Allies. Accordingly, would it not be wise, following the language of your communication to the Allies, to add to this memorandum a paragraph to the effect that the views of the Government of the United States have been communicated to the Governments of Great Britain, France and Italy with the statement that the United States does not wish, by its frank and definite statement of the policy it feels obliged to adopt for itself, to be understood that, in so restricting its own activities it is seeking even by implication to set limits to the action or define the policies of its Associates, and that the Governments of Great Britain, France and Italy have advised the United States that they agree *in principle* with the views of the United States.

France has agreed already and I have no doubt that I can secure the agreement of Great Britain and Italy if you authorize me so to proceed.

The European Allies are somewhat concerned respecting plans for economic reconstruction in Russia, and for this reason, and also if the Japanese are trying to leave them out, they would undoubtedly appreciate being given an opportunity to cooperate in this respect under the leadership of the United States. It therefore might help to add a sentence to the effect that it is the earnest hope of the Government of the United States that its Associates in the war will actively lend their cooperation to the economic and military measures outlined. This would, I am sure, obviate certain embarrassments.

I thought it best to put these suggestions before you at once. Of course I am at your disposal if you wish me to explain them further.

I have heard nothing from the Japanese Ambassador, although he told me late yesterday afternoon that he expected to receive a message from his Government today.

I return herewith your memorandum.

I am, my dear Mr. President,

Faithfully yours,   Frank L. Polk

TLS (WP, DLC).

E N C L O S U R E

[c. July 19, 1918]

STATEMENT for the press *in re* American-Japanese action in Siberia.

In the judgment of the Government of the United States,—a judgment arrived at after repeated and very searching considerations of the whole situation in Russia,—military intervention in Russia would be more likely to add to the present sad confusion there than to cure it; would injure Russia rather than help her out of her distresses, and that it could not be carried out upon a scale and with an efficiency that would be likely to make it of any real advantage in the prosecution of our main object, namely, to win the war against Germany. It cannot, therefore, take part in such intervention or sanction it in principle. Such military intervention as has been most frequently proposed, even supposing it to be efficacious in its immediate object of delivering an attack upon Germany from the east, would, in its judgment, be more likely to turn out to be merely a method of making use of Russia than a method of serving her. Her people, if they profitted by it at all, could not profit by it in time to deliver them from their present desperate difficulties and their substance would meantime be used to maintain foreign armies, not to reconstitute their own or to feed and sustain their men, women, and children.

As the Government of the United States sees the present circumstances, military action is admissible in Russia now only to help the Czecho-Slovaks to consolidate their forces and get into successful cooperation with their Slavic kinsmen and to steady any efforts at self-government or self-defence in which the Russians themselves may be willing to accept assi[s]tance. Whether from Vladivostock or from Murmansk and Archangel, the only present object for which American or allied troops can be employed, it believes, is to guard military stores which may subsequently be needed by Russian forces and to render such aid as may be acceptable to the Russians in the organization of their own self-defence.

The United States and Japan are the only powers which are just now in a position to act in Siberia in sufficient force to accomplish even these modest objects. The Government of the United States has, therefore, proposed to the Government of Japan that each of the two Governments send a force of a few thousand to Vladivostock, the two forces to be equal in number, with the purpose of cooperating as a single force in the occupation of Vladivostock and in safeguarding, so far as it may, the country to the rear of the westward-moving[1] Czecho-Slovaks; and the Japanese Government has consented.

In taking this action the Government of the United States wishes to announce to the People of Russia in the most public and solemn manner that it contemplates no interference of any kind with the political sovereignty of Russia, any intervention in her internal affairs,—not even in the local affairs of the limited areas which her military force may be obliged to occupy,—and no impairment of her territorial integrity either now or hereafter; but that what we are about to do has as its single and only object the rendering of such aid as may be acceptable to the Russian people in their endeavour to regain control of their own affairs, their own territory, and their own destiny. The Japanese Government, it is understood, will issue a similar explicit assurance.

It is also the hope and purpose of the Government of the United States to take advantage of the earliest opportunity to send to Siberia a commission of merchants, agricultural experts, labour advisers, Red Cross representatives, and agents of the Young Men's Christian Association accustomed to organizing the best methods of spreading useful information and rendering educational help of a modest sort, in order in some systematic way to relieve the immediate economic necessities of the people there in every way for which an opportunity may be opened. The execution of this plan will follow and will not be permitted to embarrass the military assistance rendered to the Czecho-Slovaks.

WWT MS (WP, DLC).
[1] By this time, open warfare had broken out between the Czechs and Bolsheviks. The Czechs took control of Vladivostok on June 30 and then began to move westward along the Trans-Siberian Railroad, presumably to rescue their comrades in central Siberia.

From Frank Lyon Polk, with Enclosure

My dear Mr. President: Washington July 20, 1918.

I beg to enclose herewith a copy of a telegram sent by Captain Voska,[1] through the Military Attaché at Paris[2] to the Military Intelligence Branch of the Executive Division of the War Department, which I venture to believe you will find of interest in connection with the present situation in Siberia.

Captain Voska is a close friend of Professor Masaryk, a naturalized American citizen, and was recently given a commission in the National Army to enable the Military Intelligence and ourselves to keep in touch with Czecho-Slovak organizations in Europe, where he now is. Captain Voska has been well and favorably known to the Department for some time and furnished us with valuable information regarding the political situation within the Central Empires and in Russia, which he obtained during his recent visit to the latter country, where he was closely associated with Professor Masaryk and intimately connected with Czecho-Slovak activities. Consequently, his views on the situation in Russia are believed to be of considerable value.

Faithfully yours,   Frank L. Polk

TLS (WP, DLC).
[1] Emanuel Victor Voska.
[2] Maj. Barclay Harding Warburton.

E N C L O S U R E[1]

Paris, July 17, 1918.

No. 229. Capt. Voska, G.S.C., N.A.,[2] after careful investigation suggests that immediate steps should be taken to prevent Japanese intervention in Russia, to which French Government would agree. Instead of Japanese intervention the Czecho-Slovak army should be used together with other military units of Poles and Russians grouped under command of American officers together with an American force of 5,000 men composed of material suitable for instruction and the whole should be known as an American command.

He believes Japanese intervention would throw into arms of Germany the whole Russian element which is now anti-German because Japanese as a nation are more hated by Russians than any other race and that the Czecho-Slovaks under an American command would be heartily welcomed by the Russian people who believe in and have confidence in the Czecho-Slovaks and Americans.

Russian people would rally around such a movement. Prestige of the Czecho-Slovaks would be increased when it became known that they are American units and not French.

Russians dislike French on account of financial support they gave to Ukraine. At present French Government is endeavoring to have Czecho-Slovak army transferred to fighting in France. Voska believes this would be a great blunder and is sure they can do better work in Russia than here. In case of intervention Japanese should only play secondary part. Voska suggests, "It would be advisable for the United States to issue a proclamation showing clearly purpose of the intervention, announcing to the Russian people that it was solely for the purpose of policing their country until such a time as Russian people could establish some form of government."

Warburton.

TC telegram (WP, DLC).
    [1] Baker also sent a copy of the following telegram to Wilson, with the comment: "Captain Voska, who is mentioned in this cablegram from our military attaché at Paris, has doubtless been mentioned to you by Mr. Charles R. Crane. Voska is believed by Mr. Crane to be the most knowing person in the world on Bohemian and Czecho-Slovak affairs, and the opinions expressed to Major Warburton are therefore interesting." NDB to WW, July 20, 1918, TLS (WP, DLC).
    [2] That is, General Staff Corps, National Army.

From Frank Lyon Polk, with Enclosure

My dear Mr. President: Washington July 20, 1918.

For your information I am enclosing a copy of a telegram from the American Consul at Vladivostok dated July 18th, in regard to the Provisional Government of Autonomous Siberia. You will recall that a memorandum[1] which was submitted to you not long ago referred to this Government as the so-called "Tomsk" movement, one of the several movements for the restoration of order in Siberia.

Faithfully yours,   Frank L Polk

TLS (WP, DLC).
    [1] The Enclosure printed with RL to WW, April 22, 1918, Vol. 47.

ENCLOSURE

TELEGRAM FROM VLADIVOSTOK, DATED JULY 18, 1918
No. 52, 5 p.m.

Local representatives of Provisional Government of Autonomous Siberia have presented notes to local Allied Consuls asking them to transmit to their respective Governments request for Allied military intervention in Siberia and Russia, with the object of interning

Austrian and German prisoners and establishing new Russian front against Germany. They express entire willingness to furnish Russian force to cooperate with Allied army provided intervention does not violate territorial sovereignty of Russia which Siberian Government considers its duty to restrain.

Allied Consuls mutually agreed to forward above to their Governments. Tokyo and Peking informed.

Signed,　Caldwell.

T MS (WP, DLC).

From Newton Diehl Baker

My dear Mr. President:　　　　　　Washington. July 20, 1918.

Mr. Polk tells me that you have handed to the several Ally ambassadors the memorandum. I have, therefore, felt that I ought at once to communicate with General Pershing with regard to our forces for the Murmansk expedition.

In General Bliss' cablegram of July 14th[1] you will recall that he says in the discussion of the matter before the Supreme War Council: "I and my colleagues, therefore, agreed upon a small force of at most six, and possibly four battalions, distributed among the four Allies. * * * This plan was strongly supported by General Foch and the Naval authorities."

Under this plan General Bliss points out that the United States would send only one, or at most two battalions, and he proceeds to show that after the military advisers had reached this determination which was in accordance with the recommendation of General Poole, the British commander at Murmansk, the Supreme War Council met, and without asking any further opinion of the military representatives, Mr. Lloyd George, Mr. Clemenceau and Mr. Orlando agreed upon the resolution asking the United States to contribute three battalions, two batteries of artillery and three companies of Engineers.

This is the resolution which General Bliss recommended you to approve; but upon which you have as yet taken no action. Nevertheless, when we asked General Bliss to state for our personal guidance his view of the matter he discussed the whole problem, and ended with the expression of a belief on his part that we ought to be represented in the expedition by only "our fair part."

I am, therefore, writing this to inquire whether your desire is that we should direct General Pershing to carry out the resolution of the Supreme War Council making it three battalions and three companies of Engineers (artillery being out of the question for us

at present), or should I cable General Pershing to send a less number of men for the present in accordance with General Bliss' personal suggestion. My own judgment in the matter is that having
in effect agreed to the Murmansk project as the result of the representations of the Supreme War Council it would be wiser to
instruct General Pershing to prepare three battalions of Infantry
and three companies of Engineers, and notify the British that they
will be ready for transportation to be furnished by them as soon as
he is notified of the port of embarkation and the time. It has been
understood from the beginning that the transportation of these
troops would have to be by the British, and I think we ought to say
positively and at once that the supply of artillery is not possible
unless the British themselves undertake to supply the guns and
rely on us only for artillery personnel.

Respectfully yours,   Newton D. Baker

TLS (WP, DLC).
[1] Actually, T. H. Bliss to NDB and P. C. March, July 12, 1918, Vol. 48.

From Thomas Garrigue Masaryk, with Enclosure

Mr. President,   [Washington] July 20, 1918.

Allow me to call your attention to the enclosed report of our army
in Siberia: it is a very clear statement and an objective representation of the given situation. I am sorry to see that even the leaders
of the Bolsheviki, not only the local Soviets, as I supposed, are not
loyal.

Under given circumstances I am obliged to ask for the help of
the United States and the other Allies for our army in Russia. I had
a conference with Secretary Polk yesterday, and I am submitting
him a short memorandum on the question.

Believe me, Mr. President,

Yours respectfully,   Professor T. G. Masaryk

TLS (WP, DLC).

E N C L O S U R E

TELEGRAM FROM THE BRITISH CONSUL AT VLADIVOSTOK[1] DATED JULY
14, 1918.

Spacek (?) and Girsa[2] send the following for Professor Mazaryk:
Message Begins:

We have received your message of June 28th and sent the following.

We were permitted by the Central Bolshevist Government to leave Russia on the terms prescribed in the agreement on March 26th between the Government of the Peoples Commission and our Army.

We have carried out faithfully and loyally all conditions which this Treaty laid upon us and we have never been involved in Russian domestic politics. The best proof of this is the fact that 13,000 of our men have, notwithstanding the difficulties placed in their way by the Bolshevist local authorities, made a journey throughout the whole of Russia without disputes and that for the last two months they have been in Vladivostok and maintained correct and loyal relations with the local authorities in this city. As long as the Bolshevist Government remained in Russian control this state of things was maintained, but a complete change occurred as soon as the control of the Central Siberian Government was obtained by Magyars and Germans, who were accepted by the Bolshevist authorities, under the guise of Communists and Internationalists, in the Red Army and also even in the Administration of which they now form the nucleus.

Trotsky, in obedience to the German ultimatum, gave orders that our Officers should be outlawed, our troops disarmed, and our men sent to Internment Camps as prisoners under strict control. In consequence of these orders simultaneous attacks were made by Germans and Magyars on our troops along the Line between Penza and Irkutsk. Our Treaty with the Bolshevists, by which we were promised free departure from the country, was treacherously violated by Trotsky's orders and the Germans secured control of the Central Siberian Government.

Being ambushed by the Magyars and Germans our forces were compelled to accept combat in self defence, the result being that we now have in our hands the whole Siberian Railway from Irkutsk to Penza. The Bolshevist Government has everywhere on this line been expelled, without any cooperation on the part of our troops, by the Russian Menshevists and Revolutionary Socialists of the Right. The Bolshevist Central Government of Siberia is hurriedly organizing German and Hungarian prisoners against us. Our troops are welcomed and supported heartily by the Russian people.

In Vladivostok our forces remained for two months completely loyal to the local Bolshevist authorities. When, however, it was learnt that treacherous attacks had been made on our men west of Irkutsk, when we heard of the arrests in Moscow of Maxa Marcovitch and Janic[3] by the Boshevists and when it was clear that preparation had been made in Vladivostok against us it appeared to us that we were in duty bound to go to the help of our fellow countrymen and to join them. With this object Vladivostok was occupied by us on June 29th. A Government opposed to the Bolshevists was immediately formed, and we are now endeavoring to arrange for an advance on Irkutsk by the Chinese Eastern Railway.

In our fighting here most of our opponents have been Magyars and Germans, proof of this being furnished by prisoners and by dead bodies. The Bolshevists have completely lost their popularity with the majority of the Russian people and, in places where they still retain power, this is only with the help of enemy prisoners who hold control of everything by force. We do not mix in any way in Russian domestic affairs, and we find that this secures us the sympathy of the people. Everywhere. We have also kept in close touch with the representatives of the Allies and all our measures are taken with their knowledge and concurrence. All the Allied representatives are in sympathy with us and afford us all the assistance they can, supplying us with medical assistance, arms and ammunition, and guarding our rear. In our opinion it is most desirable and also possible to reconstitute a Russian-German front in the East, but we feel certain that a combined and single minded military effort by the Allied Powers is essential to effect this. We also feel certain that an Army capable of fighting the Germans cannot be raised by Russia herself in the immediate future. The Army must come from outside to begin with.

If a new German-Russian front is established by the Allies we ask for instructions as to whether we should leave for France or whether we should stay here to fight in Russia by the side of the Allies and of Russia.

The health and spirit of our troops are excellent. General Diterichs is in command of the detachment of (?) 14,000 and Captain Gaida of the (?) other portion of 35,000.

Message ends.

T MS (WP, DLC).

[1] That is, Robert M. Hodgson.

[2] V. Spacek and Dr. Vaclav Girsa, formerly a physician in Kiev. All those identified in this and the following note were associated at this time with the Russian branch of the Czechoslovak National Council.

[3] Prokop Maxa, Ivan Markovic, and Frantisek Janik. Maxa was a member of the presidium of the Russian branch of the Czechoslovak National Council. They and numerous other Czechs in Moscow were arrested on Trotsky's orders on the night of May 20-21. The objective of this action was to force Maxa and Bohumir Cermak, the two members of the Czech presidium then in Moscow, to sign an order to the Czech Legion to surrender all weapons to representatives of the Soviet government. About this affair, see Victor M. Fic, *The Bolsheviks and the Czechoslovak Legion: The Origin of Their Armed Conflict, March-May 1918* (New Delhi, 1978), pp. 238-42.

From William Procter Gould Harding, with Enclosure

Dear Mr. President: Washington July 20, 1918.

I take pleasure in handing you, as suggested in your letter of the 18th instant, a memorandum about the cotton situation which contains what I believe to be the essential facts of the case, together with a few suggestions as to how the problem may be met.

Respectfully yours,   W P G Harding

TLS (WP, DLC).

E N C L O S U R E

MEMORANDUM REGARDING COTTON.

The new cotton season begins August 1st. During the month of August new cotton will come into the market to an appreciable extent, although the movement in large volume will not begin until September.

The carry-over, or surplus, from the crop of 1917 amounts to something over 3,000,000 bales, which includes a larger proportion than usual of low grades. The present price of cotton is about 30¢ per pound, basis middling, with differentials for better or lower grades. This excess supply of cotton is about 2,000,000 bales greater than is usual at this season of the year, and because of this fact and for the additional reason that other commodities are being stored in larger amounts than usual, most of the Southern warehouses report that they have but little available space.

The New England manufacturers have been discussing for some time a plan to provide additional warehouse facilities at Boston, Fall River, and other points convenient to the mills, partly with the view of facilitating the financing of cotton by the use of warehouse receipts as collateral, and partly with the object of having an adequate supply available in order to forestall any interruption of transportation next winter on account of climatic conditions.

A committee of New England manufacturers who were in Washington on the 17th instant, stated that mill purchases just now are light, being made to provide for actual requirements only, because of a feeling that the present price of 30¢ per pound will not be sustained, and partly because the price of manufactured cotton goods which has been fixed by the Government at 60¢ per pound for 36 inch sheetings—based on cotton at 30¢ a pound—expires by limitation on October 1st.

Until a price shall have been fixed, effective after that date, mill purchases will probably continue to be light. The recent estimate of the Department of Agriculture indicates a yield this year of something over 15,000,000 bales, exclusive of linters, which would amount to perhaps 1,500,000 bales additional. Assuming that the linters will be readily absorbed by the Government for war purposes, we are confronted with the problem of disposing of the new crop of 15,000,000 bales, plus a carry-over from last year of 3,000,000 bales, or, say, 18,000,000 bales.

The consumption of cotton during the next season in the United States and Canada will probably not exceed 8,000,000 bales. This would leave 10,000,000 bales available for export. Owing to the demands upon ocean transportation for the movement of troops, munitions and supplies, the space available for cotton is limited and it is the opinion of many that it will not be safe to count upon an export movement up to May 1st of more than 3,000,000 bales. This would leave a surplus of 7,000,000 bales to be taken care of. Assuming that unfavorable weather conditions during July and August may curtail production, we are still likely to have a crop of not less than 13,000,000 bales, with a carry-over of at least 5,000,000 bales.

The high cost of labor is reflected in the cost of producing cotton. In 1911 it was thought that 8½¢ per pound was a fair estimate of the average cost of producing cotton. It may be assumed, however, that costs since that time have at least doubled. There is a scarcity of labor on the farms, and the amount of cotton which will actually be picked will depend

(1) upon the labor available, and

(2) upon the price at which cotton can be sold.

Any cotton left in the fields unpicked represents of course, an economic waste, but this memorandum is written upon the assumption that the price will be sufficient to bring out of the fields all the cotton that is grown. It seems probable that labor employed in picking cotton will be paid at the rate of $1.50 to $2.00 per 100 pounds of seed cotton. At $1.50 per 100 this would be equivalent to $22.50 a bale, or 4½¢ a pound. Various estimates have been made as to the probable cost of the production of the present crop, but Southern producers and bankers are unwilling to concede that the cost can be less than 22½¢ per pound.

The sentiment among Southern farmers at this time appears to be averse to price fixing by the Government, although some of the more far-seeing are in favor of such a policy. The Southern bankers as a rule are in favor of price fixing, provided the price be fixed at a figure high enough to cover at least the cost of production. The cotton manufacturers seem reluctant to express themselves, but it appears that they would prefer to have an open market.

With the present outlook which has been foreseen by the trade for the past 60 days, a price of 30¢ per pound seems high. That it has been sustained is due to the tenacious holding of the South and to the feeling that in the event of peace a much higher price would obtain. Without effective support, it seems inevitable that the pressure upon the market of the new crop, or the anticipation of that pressure, will force the market to much lower levels. I am of the opinion, therefore, that it is actually in the interest of the producer of cotton that a price should be fixed before a break in the market occurs.

I understand that legislation will be necessary, and I believe that the power to name the price should be vested in the President. The bill should not state what the price is to be, for whatever figure might be named one element would regard it as too high, and another would think it was too low. But all would be willing to leave it to the judgment of the President, who would not deal with the problem from a local or sectional viewpoint, but solely from the broad and patriotic standpoint of the national interest.

I assume that the price fixed would not be below the cost of production, for it seems clearly in the national interest that all sections of the country remain solvent.

In the case of wheat, a fixed price was made. This was necessary in order to enable the Government to get the wheat. Had any margin for fluctuation been allowed, wheat would have been held back at the farms for higher prices. The situation with respect to cotton is different. I do not understand that there is any immediate need on the part of the Government for cotton. I would respectfully suggest, therefore, that a minimum price for cotton be fixed, representing the cost of production, say 22½¢ per pound, (middling basis) if that be the cost, and that a maximum price of not exceeding 27½¢ per pound (middling basis) be permitted, with the understanding that there would be no obligation on the part of the Government to buy cotton at more than the minimum price, and that it would have the right to commandeer it at the maximum price. This suggestion is made because of the necessity for avoiding congestion of cotton at the ports and at the important cotton towns in the interior.

The warehouses, whose receipts would be available as security for loans of cotton, have a maximum capacity of not more than 6,000,000 bales. It seems desirable, where a large amount of cotton must be held over, to distribute the burden as widely as possible. Should a fixed price be made as in the case of wheat, there would be no incentive on the part of the individual to hold cotton. On the other hand, there would be every reason why he should sell at once. The result would be a terrific strain upon transportation facilities, the congestion of cotton in the towns, and a call upon the Treasury to provide for a very large amount of money to be used in paying for cotton.

With a maximum price fixed as well as a minimum price, the result would be that the banks in the smaller towns would lend freely on cotton and they would have no difficulty in securing rediscounts from the larger banks and from the Federal Reserve banks, because the value of the security would be definitely known. The producer of cotton would sell as little as possible at the minimum price, and as the mills in the United States and Canada will be constantly in the market, there is no reason to believe that the price of cotton would fall to the minimum, so that the probability is the Government would not be called upon to fulfill its obligation to buy cotton at the minimum price. The maximum price, on the other hand, would prevent profiteering and the range between the minimum and maximum would provide for reasonable fluctuations and would offer an incentive to the farmer to hold back his cotton.

I would suggest also, in case it should be decided to ask for legislation authorizing the fixing of a price for cotton, that authority be secured to fix the price of the 1919 crop. A figure could be made sufficiently low (and this might be raised later on, should conditions change) which would avoid any danger of over-production next year, thereby adding further to the value of the present crop.

I deem it unnecessary to discuss the importance of cotton as a national asset and its utility as an auxiliary to our gold reserve upon the return of peace, and will bring this memorandum to a close by stating my firm personal conviction that, as a war measure, price fixing should be applied to raw cotton, as well as to manufactured goods, and that it will be far easier to fix a price downward from the present level of 30¢, than it would be to secure legislation to fix a price upward from a 15¢ level.

I would strongly urge two prices, a maximum price,—fair to the producer and consumer alike—and a minimum price, to be used as a stabilizer.   Respectfully submitted,   W P G Harding.

TS MS (WP, DLC).

From Theodore Roosevelt

Oyster Bay, N. Y., [July] 20, 1918.

I thank you for your courtesy and kindness in telegraphing me, and I deeply appreciate your expressions of sympathy and of approval of my son's conduct.   Theodore Roosevelt.

T telegram (WP, DLC).

From Joseph Patrick Tumulty

Dear Governor: [The White House] July 20, 1918

I only send this[1] to you because I promised Mooney I would do
so.   J. P. Tumulty

TL (WP, DLC).
[1] T. J. Mooney to JPT, July 13, 1918, TLS, enclosing T. J. Mooney to Franklin Griffin,
June 21, 1918, TCL, both in WP, DLC. Mooney, who argued that the crucial evidence
upon which he had been convicted had been discredited, had requested that Judge
Griffin schedule an immediate trial on one of the two indictments still pending against
him on the calendar in Griffin's department of the Superior Court of California.

From the Diary of William Phillips

Saturday, July 20 [1918].

The President sent over a draft announcement on the Siberian
situation, which he had written on his own typewriter. Polk asked
me to read it and comment. Before I had got half through I gasped
"impossible." He said that Baker had first made the same comment.
In it the President set out to show how inopportune intervention
was and why therefore the United States could not approve. In so
doing he was going directly back on his Aide Mémoire in which
he especially pointed out that the Allied governments were free to
take their own course if they so desired. Polk returned the draft
with various suggestions.

Bound T diary (W. Phillips Papers, MH).

To George Creel

My dear Creel,   The White House. 21 July, 1918.

Will you not prepare the way for this little address of mine to my
fellow countrymen[1] in some way that will lead the public to expect
it for (say) twenty-four hours before it appears. I am no expert in
publicity, as you know; but my notion is that a "story" a day or so
in advance to the effect that the President, like all thoughtful people
in the country, had become deeply concerned about the apparent
growth of the mob spirit in the country and that it was understood
he had in view a very earnest and solemn statement on the subject
should come first. Does that suggest something that you can work
out effectively? My only object is to fix the attention of the people
on this protest of mine in the way that will give it the greatest
possible emphasis.   Faithfully Yours,   Woodrow Wilson

WWTLS (G. Creel Papers, DLC).
[1] The statement printed at July 26, 1918.

From Newton Diehl Baker

Dear Mr President: Washington. July 21, 1918

In directing Gen Pershing to select the troops for Murmansk I took the liberty of adding that they should not be allowed to go until Gen Foch had been notified and approved.[1] In the midst of the present great battle it would seem unwise to give a peremptory order detaching troops from his command particularly since the troops sent must be trained troops. Foch may need every man just now while he may spare them easily when things become stabilized again. At any rate leaving the time of their going to him would seem wise   Respectfully,   Newton D. Baker

ALS (WP, DLC).
   [1] See P. C. March to T. H. Bliss, July 22, 1918.

Lord Reading to David Lloyd George and
Arthur James Balfour

                                        Washington. July 21, 1918.
Very Urgent. Personal and Secret.

In any communication you may send for representation by me to the President please bear in mind that his mental attitude is that he is willing to move troops because of necessity of protecting Czecho-Slovaks but that otherwise he is as opposed as hitherto to intervention. I cannot but think that best course is to accept his proposal and let situation develop. If there is no substantial opposition by the Russians to the presence of Japanese or other troops he will be more favourably disposed to your views. I believe the French and Italians will accept his proposals simplicites.

Above all he is opposed to any step approaching the taking of political control by the Allies.

Please do not think I am not giving sufficient weight to your views and especially regarding need for promptest action before winter sets in but I know the situation here too well and the fear the President has that this action of sending small number of troops may commit him heavily against his will.

T telegram (Reading Papers, FO 800/223, PRO).

To Thomas Garrigue Masaryk

[The White House,
My dear Professor Masaryk: c. July 22, 1918]

Thank you for your letter of July 20 with its enclosure. Nothing is giving me more concern at present than the position of the Czecho-Slovak forces in Siberia.

The Secretary of State, the Secretary of War, and I are trying to work out a policy which would be of real service.

Cordially and sincerely yours,   [Woodrow Wilson]

JRT transcript (WC, NjP) of CLSsh notes (C. L. Swem Coll., NjP).

To Frank Lyon Polk

My dear Mr. Counselor,   The White House. 22 July, 1918.

Thank you for your comments and suggestions about this statement. I have cheerfully altered it.[1]

When the right time has come for its release please let Creel handle it. I had a conference with him to-day (about another matter) at the end of which I mentioned this and found that he had the right idea about the publicity desirable.

Faithfully Yours,   W.W.

WWTLI (F. L. Polk Papers, CtY).
[1] Wilson's revised version is printed at Aug. 3, 1918.

From William Bauchop Wilson

My dear Mr. President: Washington July 22, 1918.

I realize the gravity of the coal situation, and share Dr. Garfield's belief in the fruitful possibilities of his program for stimulating production. On the other hand, the problem of devising right incentives is one that concerns all the production departments of the Government, although it may be of more immediate urgency to the Fuel Administration. I am anxious, therefore, that any step taken by the Fuel Administration should have proper regard for the administration of a similar policy for the whole Government.

In seeking cooperative action in this matter, the War Labor Policies Board[1] has evolved a program which has received by [my] approval and which is in process of administration. I have, therefore, asked Mr. Frankfurter, my assistant and Chairman of the War Labor Policies Board, and Mr. Clayton,[2] whom I have made Chief of the Bureau of Civilian Insignia, to confer at once with Dr. Garfield and Mr. Neale, so that there may be no delay in carrying out the action which the Fuel Administration thinks necessary, while at the same time relating such action in a comprehensive way to like action by other departments of the Government.

Faithfully yours,   W B Wilson

TLS (WP, DLC).

[1] The War Labor Policies Board had been established in the Department of Labor in early May. It included representatives from the departments of War, Navy, and Agriculture, the Emergency Fleet Corporation, the Railroad Administration, the War Industries Board, and the National War Labor Board. Its purpose was to secure uniform policies in regard to the distribution of labor, wages, hours, and working conditions in the nation's industries during the war emergency. It was intended to be an administrative agency, in contrast to the quasijudicial and legislative National War Labor Board. However, the W.L.P.B.'s decisions could be carried out only by the governmental departments and agencies represented on the board. Despite the strenuous efforts of Frankfurter as chairman, the board accomplished very little before the Armistice. See Michael E. Parrish, *Felix Frankfurter and His Times: The Reform Years* (New York and London, 1982), pp. 107-14; and Valerie Jean Conner, *The National War Labor Board: Stability, Social Justice, and the Voluntary State in World War I* (Chapel Hill, N. C., 1983), pp. 32-33.

[2] Charles T. Clayton, formerly Assistant Director General of the United States Employment Service.

From Samuel Reading Bertron

My dear Mr. President: New York July 22, 1918.

The situation as regards the public service companies of the Country has now reached a stage where it is exceedingly critical. In many cases they are already in extremis. I feel sure that this problem must be giving you great concern. It is a subject that I have been following for twenty years and with which I have therefore considerable familiarity. There are several solutions, some one of which must be arrived at immediately if this great industry is to be saved, representing as it does an investment of more than ten billion dollars.

If you think that I can be of the slightest use to you I will greatly appreciate the opportunity of discussing the matter with you.

With very kind regards, please believe me,

Very faithfully yours,   S R Bertron

TLS (WP, DLC).

From William Kent

My dear Mr. President: Washington July 22, 1918.

I was greatly impressed by hearing the statement of Mr. Raymond Robbins, of the Red Cross expedition to Russia, and sincerely hope that you will get the information which he is prepared to offer. Mr. Robbins, whom I believe to be accurate and truthful and who certainly had an intimate inside experience, believes, first, that the Soviet Government up to the time of his leaving, was representative of the Russian people and was recognized throughout the length and breadth of Russia, with certain exceptions affected by counter-revolution. In the six thousand mile journey from Petrograd to Vladivostock he found the fullest recognition of credentials furnished him by Lenine.

A matter of great surprise to me was his statement that Lenine was embarking on constructive and productive work. This I should have doubted greatly except that he gave as a specific illustration the protection under the Soviet Government of the plant of the International Harvester Company, employing more than three thousand men, and the abatement in this case of proclamations turning the financial management and the industrial organization over to the workmen.

It is in specific matters like these that we must look for a knowledge of the situation. Somehow, it seems to me as if the whole world of big business had consciously turned loose to yell "pro-German" at all progress or radicalism, whether sane or insane.

I am convinced that Robbins has the documents to prove that much of the information reaching this country through our diplomatic channels is colored by fear and hysteria to a certain extent begotten by social prejudice.

I have followed your course of discouraging Japanese intervention with interest and approval. In my opinion, racial dislike would throw Russia directly into the arms of Germans, if molested by Japanese. We must remember the many centuries when Russia was the barrier to Oriental invasion. If you or I were Russians and saw the Japanese coming, we would embrace the first armed German we met as a possible saviour against the bugaboos of our cradle days.

If you do not find time to see Mr. Robbins, his information seems to me to be worthy of consideration and analysis by someone in whom you have condfidence.

Robbins is naturally a radical, Thacher[1] a conservative. Both men are too strong to be biased by the other. Both report the same things and both agree as to our policy.

Yours truly,   William Kent

TLS (WP, DLC).
[1] That is, Thomas D. Thacher.

From Gilbert Fairchild Close

My dear President Wilson: Washington. July 22, 1918.

Thank you ever so much for your note of July 18th, which came to the War Trade Board after I had left there and which has been forwarded to me here.

I am glad to be back with Mr. Daniels, but I need not tell you that if it should turn out as you suggest in your letter, nothing in the world would please me more.

                    Always faithfully yours,   Gilbert F. Close

TLS (WP, DLC).

From Newton Diehl Baker

Dear Mr. President: Washington. July 22, 1918

Thank you for sending me Upton Sinclair's interesting communication.[1] I think, however, he should be informed that we are now doing absolutely all that public opinion will stand in the interest of conscientious objectors and others whose views do not happen to coincide with those of the vast majority of their fellow countrymen.

I have given directions that all the court martial cases having to do with these people shall be carefully and sympathetically reviewed in the light of the experience gained by the special Board of Inquiry consisting of Judge Mack, Dean Stone and Major Stoddard.[2] The terms of imprisonment which conscientious objectors may, in the last analysis, be compelled to serve, will be served in the Disciplinary Barracks at Fort Leavenworth, where the men have a wholesome, outdoor life and are kept busy upon things that are worth doing. Most of the conscientious objectors who declined to accept military service in any form, however, are now engaged in farm work at a private's pay, through cooperation between the Department of Agriculture and the War Department.

I do not know how many of what Mr. Sinclair calls political prisoners are now under the control of the Department of Justice, but if you care to have me do so, I could find out from the Attorney General whether there are any prisoners under his direction whom he thinks it would be wise to have transferred to Fort Leavenworth.

                    Respectfully,   Newton D. Baker

TLS (WP, DLC).
[1] The Enclosure printed with WW to NDB, July 15, 1918, Vol. 48.
[2] Julian William Mack, Harlan Fiske Stone, and Richard C. Stoddard, chairman. The text of the statement issued by the War Department on May 31, 1918, is printed in the *New York Times*, June 1, 1918, and in the *Official Bulletin*, II (June 1, 1918), 1-2.

Peyton Conway March to Tasker Howard Bliss

Washington, July 22, 1918.

Number 72, Confidential

Reference your 148, the President has decided that he will permit three battalions of infantry to be contributed by the United States to the Murmansk expedition provided General Foch can spare them. These battalions to come from General Pershing's forces. He also has authorized three companies of engineers provided General Pershing can spare them. He has disapproved the furnishing of any artillery. March.   McCain

TC telegram (WDR, RG 407, World War I Cablegrams, DNA).

Two Telegrams from Arthur James Balfour to Lord Reading

[London, July 22, 1918]

VERY URGENT. Personal.

Your telegram personal and secret of July 19th.

For obvious reasons it is not very easy to devise a satisfactory message to President.

On the other hand we view with great satisfaction his resolution to send an American and Japanese force to Siberia. This will we hope be a great encouragement to Czechs and will give them much needed reinforcements. Moreover it admits principle of giving external aid to Russia and we gladly welcome his acceptance of a policy which we know he regards with much misgiving.

On the other hand we cannot pretend for ourselves, nor ought we to convey to him, that we regard size of American-Japanese force as in any way adequate to necessities of the case. To us it seems almost certain that either Allied expedition will fail or that it will have to be largely reinforced; we hope the latter. But these are hopes which you can hardly convey to President. In any case we trust that what President is prepared to do will be done quickly.

As regards President's fears that through French or British action Americans will be dragged into a policy of interfering with Russian domestic affairs you may express to him in most emphatic terms that such interference would be quite contrary to our wishes and to our firm intention. It is of course perfectly true that with best will in the world military intervention is certain to have an effect on Russian parties. Intervening force must necessarily work with those who are prepared to work with it. Indirectly it will strengthen any party which is prepared to fight Germans and injure any party which turns to Germany for assistance. We can only do our best to keep aloof from internal controversies.

[London, July 22, 1918]

No. 4543. Following Memorandum has been approved by Imperial War Cabinet. Begins.

H.M.G. recognize to the full spirit in which Aide Memoire of July 17th is conceived and they sincerely welcome decision of U. S. to assist towards safeguarding Czecho-Slovak army though they entertain serious misgivings that proposed force may prove inadequate for its purpose.

They are also in complete accord with President's proposal to send economic mission through Vladivostock in order to supply material assistance to a people sorely tried by miseries of war and revolution.

These are in themselves most admirable schemes which deserve and will assuredly receive gratitude of America's allies. H.M.G. have however never concealed their view that they are insufficient by themselves to cope with Russian situation, regarded as an element in a great military and political problem with which the Allies are confronted. The arguments indeed which have led us to this conclusion have been so often stated by European Allies that it seems neither necessary nor desirable to repeat them on present occasion. But there are two points, the one military and the other political, on which aide memoire seems so seriously to misconceive attitude of Entente Powers as to require further comment and explanation.

Military misconception bears on relations between Western and Eastern theatres of operations. H.M.G. are entirely in accord with aide memoire in thinking that of these two theatres, Western is the more important. They admit to the full that it is on the West that great effort must be made and they believe that to endanger successes in the West in hope of securing advantages in East would be not only foolish but suicidal. But for this very reason they desire Allied intervention in Russia. Their scheme is not designed to diminish relative strength of Allied armies in the West by sending to Russia American troops who might be fighting in France or Italy, but to increase our relative strength in France by retaining in the East important bodies of Germans and Austrians, achieving this purpose by utilizing forces that are not available for Western front. In our view this can only be done on a considerable scale by enabling Japan should she be willing to employ her unused military strength against the common enemy. If this were possible the gain would be incontestable and nowhere would it be more appreciated than in Western theatre of war. It may be too sanguine an expectation that Russia can with Allied aid recover the military strength she possessed before the Revolution but it is not unreasonable to look forward to a recovery which would constitute a real menace to German occupation of conquered territories, thus absorbing considerable German forces which would otherwise have been employed in France. If this could be accomplished the task of French British and American forces in France next year would be materially lightened.

The second misconception which (as it seems to us) pervades aide memoire, is that Allies in advocating intervention in Russia are not thinking of Russia, but solely of themselves. "Military intervention," says the aide memoire, "even supposing it to be efficacious in its repeatedly avowed object of delivering an attack upon Germany from the East, would be merely a method of making use of Russia, not a method of serving her."

H.M.G. are unable to admit the assumption on which this statement appears to rest. In our view Germany has used and misused the struggle for liberty of the Russian people to serve her own selfish end. Herself the great example of efficient autocracy, she has sedulously fostered in Russia every influence, from extremes of Socialism to extremes of reaction, to paralyze the national will and destroy the national integrity. She has forced the country into a degrading and disastrous peace. Even that peace she has refused to keep. Russian territories which she has forcibly taken under protection she is treating with characteristic brutality. Russia is to her no more than a conquered area from which she can squeeze supplies and Russian people are no more than a subject rabble, to be stripped and plundered in exact proportion to Germany's strength and Russia's weakness.

To H.M.G. therefore it seems that so far from an attack on German forces in Russia being as aide Memoire suggests "merely a method of making use of Russia not a method of serving her," it would confer upon Russian people the most signal service that can be imagined. If Russia is ever to develop along her own lines, if she is ever to regain her self-respect, she must first be free from an alien domination, whole object of which is to shatter her political fabric and exploit her material resources.

Aide Memoire goes even further than making suggestion that Allied intervention is a method of "making use of Russia not of serving her." It suggests that intervention has a political as well as a military object; that it is in some almost sinister fashion designed to foster reaction. We had certainly hoped that our reiterated declarations upon this subject made doubts about our policy impossible. Above all things we desire to keep free from party disputes by which Russia is torn. There is no principle on which we have laid greater stress than that she should manage her own affairs. We wish her to choose her own form of Government and to pursue in her own way her own line of self-development. But unless all the information which reaches us is worthless the best hope (perhaps the only hope) of allowing the voice of Russian people to be heard, lies in the cleansing of the country from German influences supported by German soldiers. This it seems to us can only be accomplished by foreign aid. We regret President cannot see his way to join the Allies in granting such aid. Were it accompanied by a proclamation of the kind approved by the President, and repeatedly suggested by H.M.G., there should be no error or misconception as to motives of the Allies; and there seems no reason to doubt that all the best elements in the country whatever be their political opinions would rally to the Allied standard and make use of Allies support.

We desire to add that in making admittance of the great difficulty of the Russian problem we know how deeply it has engaged the attention of the President, we rejoice to recognise the spirit of disinterested co-operation which animates all his policy whether in the West or in the East, and we firmly count upon its continuance. But there are some questions about which no doubts should be allowed to linger; and among these are points with which we have endeavoured briefly to deal in this Memorandum.

CC telegrams (W. Wiseman Papers, CtY).

To William Jennings Bryan

My dear Mr. Bryan: [The White House] 23 July, 1918

I value your long letter about the Costa Rican situation but beg to assure you in reply that no item of foreign policy has received more frequent or careful consideration by me or has been looked at from more angles, and I feel obliged to retain immovably my position that I will not and cannot recognize a government which originated in individual unconstitutional action. This is a test case and I am sure that my yielding in it would break down the whole morale of our relations, particularly with Central America.

I cannot tell you how many persons have been to me and laid the various aspects of this matter before me. The latest was Mr. Samuel Untermyer, who very earnestly urged the same course upon me that you are urging. But behind it all, my dear Mr. Bryan, there are contending business interests in the United States which we ought to be very careful to disappoint in what is nothing less than an attempt on their part to use the Government of Costa Rica for their own benefit.

I am always sorry to differ from you in any matter of importance, but this is a matter in which I feel bound both by principle and expediency.

Cordially and sincerely yours,   Woodrow Wilson

TLS (Letterpress Books, WP, DLC).

To Robert Latham Owen

My dear Senator: [The White House] 23 July, 1918

I share the anxieties expressed in your letter of July eighteenth and you may be sure have before this repeatedly turned my attention to the industrial and labor problems which we are to face after the war, though I must frankly say that it does not seem to me that just now very much can be done by way of preparation because of our concentration upon other things.

But with regard to "non-essential" industries, I believe I can assure you that the various agencies of the Government have been going very slowly and cautiously. Some industries it has been necessary to curtail because the raw materials which they used were absolutely needed for war purposes, and there were not enough of them to permit their free use in industries which could be dispensed with for the time being, but even in such cases the action of such agencies as the War Industries Board has been very conservative, I believe, and has been a constant subject of discussion amongst us, so that I think the best brains there are in the employment of the Government are being devoted to that subject, and the best consciences also.

Cordially and sincerely yours,   Woodrow Wilson

TLS (Letterpress Books, WP, DLC).

From Leonidas Carstarphen Dyer

Dear Mr. President: Washington, D. C. July 23, 1918.

I note in the St. Louis Republic of this date a statement to the effect that you are deeply concerned as regards mob spirit prevailing in certain sections of the United States. The clipping referred to is attached.[1]

I trust you will permit me to also ask your consideration of the lynchings still prevailing in certain sections of the United States,

and in which the victims are in most cases colored men and sometimes colored women. I hope you will call the attention of the people
of the United States to this outrage going on also, and urge that
they put an end to it and that the orderly procedure of the courts
prevail in this respect also. In connection therewith permit me to
call to your attention a Bill that I have introduced in the House of
Representatives. It is H.R. 11279, a copy of which I attach to this
letter.² I also enclose a copy of some remarks on the subject, and
also a copy of some hearings recently had upon the Bill in the
Committee on the Judiciary of the House of Representatives.³ I
know full well the many important details and responsibilities de-
volving upon you, and in every instance I have done my best as a
Member of Congress to aid you. I feel that you can do a great service
if you would in a vigorous statement urge upon all the people to
respect the rights of citizens and of aliens in the United States,
and that mob law and lynchings cease as an aid to the successful
carrying on of the War as well as the erasing in the life of our great
Nation the serious blot that now is upon it.

Yours very truly,   L. C. Dyer

TLS (WP, DLC).
¹ "Mob Treatment of Disloyalists Worries Wilson: President Will Issue Statement
Demanding Respect Be Shown to Law," St. Louis *Republic*, July 23, 1918. The article
reported that Wilson had been especially disturbed by the lynching of Robert P. Prager (about
which see W. B. Hale to WW, April 6, 1918, n. 2, Vol. 47) and the propaganda which the
German government had made out of that incident.
² Dyer had introduced H.R. 11279 on April 8. This bill made lynching a federal crime on
the ground that it was a denial by a state of the equal protection of the law. Any person
participating in a lynching was to be "deemed guilty of murder" and subject to trial in the
circuit court of the United States having jurisdiction in the place where the lynching occurred.
Any state or municipal officer who failed to make "all reasonable efforts" to prevent a lynching
or to prosecute those who participated in a lynching was made subject to criminal trial in a
United States circuit court, with a fine and/or imprisonment upon conviction. Moreover, any
county in which lynching occurred was made subject to a forfeiture of not less than $5,000
nor more than $10,000 for the use of the family of a victim of lynching, or, if there was no
family, of the United States. 65th Cong., 2d sess., H.R. 11279, printed bill (WP, DLC). The
bill is also printed in full in *Cong. Record*, 65th Cong., 2d sess., p. 6177. Although the House
Committee on the Judiciary held at least one hearing on the bill, it was never reported out of
committee.
³ *Federal Law Against Lynchings: Speech of Hon. L. C. Dyer of Missouri in the House of
Representatives, Monday, May 7, 1918* (Washington, 1918), also printed in *Cong. Record*,
65th Cong., 2d sess., pp. 6176-78; and *To Protect Citizens Against Lynching: Hearing Before
the Committee on the Judiciary . . . on H.R. 11279 . . . Statements of Maj. J. E. Spingarn and
Capt. George S. Hornblower, June 6, 1918* (Washington, 1918).

From Charles Richard Crane

Dear Mr President   Wood's Hole, Mass. July 23 1918

I am glad you are taking your own time and preserving your
usual valuable practice of thinking things through before acting on
Russia. With the best of intentions the chances of doing the wrong

thing by *any* action is infinitely greater than of doing a useful thing. And dont be so much disturbed by the German Bogie there. The Germans *are* industrious but they are *not* omniscient. So far they have made an awful mess of everything since the Brest-Litovsk treaty. Throwing Siberia into the hands of the Checko-Slovaks, instead of letting them quietly proceed out of Russia with their arms, is entirely characteristic. The killing of Mirbach[1]—the most efficient of the Kaiser's aides—is only a symptom perhaps but, as far as it goes, and [an] excellent symptom that the patient is still taking some notice and that the German doctor cannot carry his malpractice too far.

If Mott could arrange to head the Commission for say three months, as a most important symbol, the carrying out of any program would then proceed in good order. With Mott we could get word to the Patriarch of the Orthodox church[2] and to the Metropolitan of the Old Believers[3] and they would soon get their message to every corner of the state that the Commission was entirely a helpful one and to protect it.

And their word should be got to the old Union of Unions, which included the Zemstovos, the Municipalities and the great Co-operatives societies. There are millions in these societies and they worked together most effectively in all of the war and relief processes.

Probably Stevens would know how to take over the railroad and keep it going without making much fuss or any declaration. Affectionate messages to you from Mrs Crane and me,

Always   Charles R. Crane

ALS (WP, DLC).

[1] Count von Mirbach had been assassinated in the German embassy in Moscow on July 6 by two members of the Left Social Revolutionary party. His killing was the centerpiece of a drive by the Left Social Revolutionaries to destroy the peace settlement of Brest-Litovsk and to renew the war with Germany. See William Henry Chamberlin, *The Russian Revolution, 1917-1921* (2 vols., New York, 1935), II, 53-56.

[2] Patriarch Tikhon (Vasilii Ivanovich Belavin). The Sobor, or Council, of the Russian Orthodox Church had chosen Tikhon on November 5/18, 1917, to be the first Patriarch since the time of Peter the Great.

[3] Meletii, Metropolitan of Moscow for the Church of Old Believers of the Belo-Krinista Concord, primate of those with priests among the Old Believers.

From Thomas Nelson Page

Confidential

My dear Mr. President: Rome July 23rd, 1918.

The dozen members of Congress from the middle and extreme west, headed by Judge Tillman, of Arkansas,[1] were received here with great cordiality, and their visit has undoubtedly made an ex-

cellent impression. They were entertained at the Montecitorio by
the hundred or so members of the Chamber of Deputies now in
Rome, and were offered entertainment by the Under Secretary of
Foreign Affairs, the Marquis Borsarelli,[2] and by Under Secretary
of the Interior, Gallenga-Stuart.[3] Their stay here, however, was so
brief that they were only able to accept an official lunch which I
gave them at the Embassy, and at which were present the representatives of the Government, including the representatives of the
Senate and Chamber.

At the reception short addresses were made in which America
and yourself were acclaimed as the paladins of liberty, not only of
Italy, but of the world.

The Representatives left last night for the front where they will
be the guests of the Headquarters General, and will dine to-night
with the King.

I learn also that the Italian Government is providing a special car
to take them back to Paris.

It has been a great pleasure to me to have these gentlemen here,
and the fact that they are the first who even as an informal representation have come directly to Italy has had a great effect and
will continue to bear fruit.

I was pleased to hear from a number of them that, although
Republicans, they were solidly behind you in the great work which
you are carrying out with such wonderful results.

This is the flood tide here for America. From one end of Italy to
the other this is America's day. Our health officer from Naples was
in here this morning and was eloquent over the extraordinary manifestation of enthusiasm shown there on the Fourth of July. He
says women held their babies up in their arms toward the Consulate
crying "vivas" for America. It was the same way throughout Italy.
They are looking now for the coming of the American flag, and the
newspapers are reproducing much more than ever the accounts of
what our gallant men are doing in France. And with what pride
we here are following their deeds, worthy of the glorious deeds of
the fathers. It is felt from one end of Italy to the other that America
has saved the day, and I am shining in the reflected light far beyond
my desserts. They know, however, who has done the trick, and no
orator now would fail to mention your name which always brings
vociferous rounds of applause.

Even The Avanti, the rank Socialist organ, in its attacks on the
war modifies its former virulence and puts its criticisms in the form
of questions.

I was glad to hear from Secretary Baker, in a letter which I
received yesterday, that you are well and fit notwithstanding labors

which I would think must exceed the labors of Hercules. I congratulate myself and our country that your gifts include physical endurance, but I trust that you will be able to get at least some change, if not rest. I am regarded here, even by men younger than myself, as being tough, but there are times when I feel the need for rest and unless something turns up meanwhile, I am going off the first of August for a change and rest. Most of the other Ambassadors, if not all, are away at this time and the members of the Government run off also from time to time. I am going to visit Aix les Bains partly because it is good for the gout, from which my wife is beginning to suffer, but more because so many of our men go there on their leave and I want to see them.

What glorious news is that coming from France. It does begin to look as though the weight of America thrown with its force as has been done this last year is beginning to tell decisively.

I hear that in Germany they are trying to make the people believe that our armies are composed of only the foreign element in America, and that those of the old American stock are not coming.

They will soon be undecieved [undeceived] and then the reckoning will come later on.

There is persistent talk here about an effort to get Baron Sonnino out of the Government. The principal lever now being used is said to be his firm attitude in regard to the Jugo-Slavs and the dismemberment of Austria. This is at present the popular side to espouse. I question, however, if they can turn [him] out unless something unexpected occurs. He is the man who has stood always for fighting the war through to a finish. He says to them, "These are my honest views. I believe this is for the best interests of Italy and of the Allies. I will not dissemble them or vote against my convictions. If you wish other views carried through you must get someone else to do so."

This, at least, I understand to be his attitude and it is an attitude which the Italians understand and appreciate. So I hardly think that it will result in turning out the man who has always represented the idea of beating Austria.

Believe me, my dear Mr. President, always with increasing appreciation of what you stand for in this crisis of our history, and of the history of the world,

Most sincerely yours,   Thos. Nelson Page

TLS (WP, DLC).
[1] John Newton Tillman.
[2] Marquis Luigi Borsarelli di Rifreddo.
[3] Probably Count Romeo Adriano Gallenga-Stuart.

From Newton Diehl Baker

My dear Mr. President: Washington. July 23, 1918.

Sargent, the painter, is reported to me to be at British Head-quarters in France with a commission from the British Government to paint a war picture for preservation in the National Gallery. It has been suggested that while he is there he would have ample opportunity to paint a series of war pictures for the United States, and I am requested to present the matter to you.

I confess my own mind is so full of practical things at the present moment that I hardly feel sure in trying to pass upon the value of art; nor do I know enough about Sargent's work to feel free to suggest that you offer him commissions of the kind suggested. This war is, of course, a very great national event, and the preservation of some of its phases in a permanent form would be a rich national possession.

Should you desire more information I can, of course, get General Bliss to see Sargent, or it might be done through our Embassy in Paris, and full particulars laid before you before any decision in the matter is reached.   Respectfully yours,   Newton D. Baker

TLS (WP, DLC).

Peyton Conway March to Tasker Howard Bliss

[Washington] July 23, 1918.

Number 74 Secret.

RUSH. After a complete study of all American resources, the recommendation of the War Department has been approved by the President that we attempt a program involving the delivery in France by June 30, 1919, of 80 divisions provided the following can be obtained:

First. A change in the ages now prescribed by law for the limits of the draft so as to produce in such a short time the required number of men, the program in its entirety being 80 divisions in France and 18 at home.

Second. That the consent of France and Great Britain is assured for the continued supply of field guns and ammunition and of the heavier calibers until the American artillery program comes through.

Third. That Congress will appropriate the billions of dollars necessary for the 80 division program.

Fourth. That Great Britain will furnish us troop and cargo ships to supply our deficiency in that respect until our shipping program comes through.

The first and third of these requirements while needing legislation can be assumed to be a certainty. The promise already made by Great Britain to continue the use of the present troop ships which are aiding in the transportation of American units will it is assumed practically take care of that deficiency. The deficiency in cargo tonnage is estimated as follows by months.

For August, 1918 1,217,755 DWT. September 1,185,384, October 1,117,734, November 859,949, December 731,274, January 497,016, February 209,641. Our expected production of shipping will take care of the cargo program for 80 divisions from that point on until June 30, 1919. In this connection it may be pointed out that the United States has been continuing the shipment of troops during July on the basis of this program and a little more, the cargo tonnage available in July has not been sufficient for the proper supply of our troops now in France.

Referring to the second requirement, it is understood that the French can continue to furnish guns and carriages and ammunition at least as rapidly as they have been furnishing them up to the present time. It is desired that this be confirmed. March.

McCain.

TC telegram (WDR, RG 407, World War I Cablegrams, DNA).

Lord Reading to Arthur James Balfour

Washington. 23rd July 1918.

[No. 3352.] Very Urgent & Secret.

Your telegram No. 4543.

1. I saw the President today and reproduced to him orally the substance of the memorandum and told him that in due course I should send the memorandum to the State Department. If you wish me to present it textually as sent to me please cable immediately otherwise I would suggest that I be allowed to make some slight changes without altering any important sentences or modifying in any way the sense of the document. I understand that the French Ambassador is making no substantial comment and is accepting the proposals.

2. The President agreed that these proposals were insufficient to cope with the Russian situation viewed as a military problem but repeated his opinion that it was not feasible to send an adequate force there for the reasons which he had given at various times and were stated in the aide memoire.

3. As to the military misconception he was anxious that H.M.G. should understand that it was really not possible for the U.S.G. to

embark on an enterprise of magnitude in Russia, for even though it should be carried out mainly by Japanese troops the equipment and supply would in the main have to come from the U. S. He assured me that after the most careful investigation he was advised and agreed with the opinion that it would be impossible for the U.S.G. to continue to supply and equip troops for the western front and also to undertake to provide for Japanese troops in Russia. He again referred to the difficulty encountered in the U. S. in the production of coal and to the enormous demands for steel which were quite unprecedented. He further said that the result of investigation was to establish that the U.S.G. could not provide and supply and equip 100 divisions by July 1919 and that careful consideration was now being given to ascertaining what reduction from this number would be necessary. He explained in some detail that the reduction of man power in the industrial area by the calling up of increased numbers of troops would have serious effect in the U. S. productive capacity unless indeed Congress was prepared to extend the age for compulsory military service. Of course I pointed out how much greater was the proportion of males serving in France and Great Britain. He answered that was possible because we derived supplies so largely from both America and elsewhere. He concluded this part of the discussion by the observation that it would be idle for the U.S.G. to undertake a task which was obviously an impossible one. He added that the requirements for steel for non-essential industries were being ruthlessly cut down.

4 As to the political misconception: I repeated almost verbatim the words of the memorandum and emphasized the repeated declarations which had been made to him on behalf of H.M.G. of their desire and determination to keep free from party disputes in Russia and from interference in internal political affairs of Russia. The President explained that the words "making use of Russia and not serving her" were not intended by him to convey any suggestion that H.M.G. would foster reaction or would use intervention for political purposes. He hoped H.M.G. would understand that this was not in his mind at all. What he meant was that the introduction of large forces of Japanese into Russia would appear to the people of Russia as if the Allies were using Russia for their own purpose against Germany instead of coming to the assistance of Russia.

I pressed the necessity for immediate action [and the] urgency of the matter. He informed me that no official answer had yet been received from Japan although it had been expected for days past but that no time was being lost and every preparation was being made; that 1000 men were ready at the Phillipines with transport and that the remaining numbers were ready for embarkation on the Pacific coast also with transports available.   R.

T telegram (W. Wiseman Papers, CtY).

From the Diary of Josephus Daniels

July Tuesday 23 1918

Cabinet

Gregory had been to Detroit & reported progress in building liberty motors. Also about submarine detectors.

WW told of a Scotch woman house keeper at White House. She was very suspicious of an unoffending German who made the fires in the White House and came in ominous tones and said "There is a German in the cellar."

WW: In order to disgust child who used slang very precise mother began to use it. Hearing an auto going by & making a noise, the daughter asked what it was & the mother said: "I think it is a tin lizzie panting for juice"

Making Liberty engines for $3,600 & England wanting them

Hw bound diary (J. Daniels Papers, DLC).

From Lord Reading

My dear Mr. President,   Washington July 24th, 1918.

I have the honour to inform you that I have received a telegram from London requesting me to convey to you the following personal message from His Majesty the King.

"It has given me great pleasure to have visited this afternoon the United States ship 'New York' and to have made the acquaintance of Rear-Admiral Rodman[1] and the captains of the remarkable battleship force now operating with my Grand Fleet and I also had an opportunity of seeing representatives from other ships of the squadron. I should like to express my admiration of the high efficiency and general smartness of the force; and the happy relations which exist between the United States squadron and their British comrades, and the unity of purpose which characterizes their work are sure guarantees of the continued success of the Allied arms at sea."

I have the honour to be, My dear Mr. President,

With the highest respect,   Reading

TLS (WP, DLC).
[1] Hugh Rodman, commander of Division Nine, Battleship Force, U.S.N.

To Lord Reading

My dear Mr. Ambassador: [The White House] 24 July, 1918

Thank you for your letter of this morning conveying to me the very kind and interesting message of His Majesty, the King, sent after his visit to our battleship NEW YORK. When you reach London, will you not be kind enough to express to the King in person my appreciation of the message and my pleasure that he found our men so fit? He may be sure that our cooperation with the British Navy is rendered with the heartiest spirit, and I am sure that it will net greater and greater advantages to the cause of the nations associated against Germany.

With the best wishes,

Cordially and sincerely yours,   Woodrow Wilson

TLS (Letterpress Books, WP, DLC).

To Josephus Daniels

My dear Mr. Secretary: The White House 24 July, 1918

I am disturbed to find that the present industrial demands of the country for the supplying of war needs, either directly or indirectly, are in some instances far in excess of the productive capacity of the country and in other instances almost as great as the full capacity of our present organized industries.

The apparent direct and indirect requirements for steel for the last six months of the present year are estimated at about twenty million tons, whereas the greatest productive capacity of the steel industry for an equal period has not exceeded 16,500,000 tons. From the data now in hand, it appears that the Army will need all of the available wool in this country and as much as can be supplied from without by the shipping now available, and so it is with many other materials.

I, therefore suggest it is highly necessary that the various departments of the Government which are placing large contracts of any sort should have a careful re-survey made which would check every considerable item for the purpose of seeing to it that material is not ordered to be in hand until it can actually be used. The war demands must, of course, be met, but it has become necessary that they should not be anticipated. What I fear is an unnecessary curtailment and destruction of the less essential industries, and this may be brought about by the accumulation of material which it is not possible to use as fast as it is received.

I am solicitous that our war programme should be carried out with as little disturbance of our usual industries and our normal economic fabric as possible, and with this in mind suggest that it is of paramount importance that existing plants which have been rendered idle or are likely to be rendered idle by the curtailment of non-essential production should be converted to war uses as far as pos[s]ible. The present tendency in many cases is to create new plants or enlarge old ones without a sufficient survey of such possibilities of conversion.

I would be very much obliged if you would again call the attention of the bureau chiefs of your Department to the fact that I have specially charged the War Industries Board with the conversion of existing plants to war uses and have asked that no new facilities should be provided without consultation with the War Industries Board. If these suggestions are acted upon, many of the hardships that would fall upon business may be lessened or avoided altogether. The War Industries Board is in a position to know the businesses that will have to be curtailed, because of the withdrawal of materials and their adaptation to other uses.

The financial advantage of maintaining industrial efficiency at its best and most economical point is, of course, manifest, and I am writing this letter not because the argument is not plain but because I think it will be advantageous just at this point to have a re-survey all around to see whether the active and energetic directors of production in the departments are keeping these questions in mind.

Cordially and sincerely yours,   Woodrow Wilson[1]

TLS (J. Daniels Papers, DLC).
[1] Wilson wrote the same letter, *mutatis mutandis*, on the same date, to Newton D. Baker, William B. Wilson, William C. Redfield, and Edward N. Hurley.

To Newton Diehl Baker

My dear Mr. Secretary: The White House 24 July, 1918

Thank you for your letter of July sixteenth[1] about the charges presented through Mr. Gompers against the Governor of Porto Rico. It seems to me that you have handled the matter in just the right way, and I am sincerely obliged to you.

Cordially and faithfully yours,   Woodrow Wilson

TLS (N. D. Baker Papers, DLC).
[1] NDB to WW, July 16, 1918, Vol. 48.

To William Bauchop Wilson

My dear Mr. Secretary: The White House 24 July, 1918

I have your letter of the eleventh[1] about the formation of a corporation to carry out the housing programme and write to say that I accept your judgment in the matter. I have found it a sound judgment to follow.

Cordially and sincerely yours,   Woodrow Wilson

TLS (received from Mary A. Strohecker).
[1] WBW to WW, July 11, 1918, Vol. 48.

To Samuel Reading Bertron

My dear Mr. Bertron: [The White House] 24 July, 1918

I have your letter of the twenty-second. I do indeed fully appreciate, I believe, the difficulties that the public service companies are in, but I am sorry to say that no solution has been suggested to me which I thought it feasible to employ, at any rate so far as the federal government is concerned.

In haste   Sincerely yours,   Woodrow Wilson

TLS (Letterpress Books, WP, DLC).

To John Skelton Williams

My dear Mr. Comptroller: [The White House] 24 July, 1918

I have been very much concerned, as others have, about the straitened condition of many of our public utilities corporations,[1] but I have looked into the matter very carefully and in my judgment there is no federal agency which can assume the authority of fixing rates. Moreover, it is my clear judgment that there is a distinct effort just now to unload this function on the Federal Government because the local utility commissions are unwilling to take the responsibility, or it may be the odium, of increasing these rates.

I happen to know something of the situation in one state, namely, New Jersey. If the chief public utility corporation there is in straitened circumstances, it is chiefly due, I am sure, to its own "high finance," and you will notice that the Public Utility Commission of New Jersey has just refused to grant them an advance of rates.

This is a thorny matter and we ought to be very careful how we touch it.

Cordially and sincerely yours,   Woodrow Wilson

TLS (Letterpress Books, WP, DLC).
[1] Wilson was replying to J. S. Williams to WW, July 22, 1918, TLS (WP, DLC).

To Harrison Leroy Beach[1]

[The White House] July 24, 1918

Your letter received.[2] The Administration as between candidates equally loyal never takes part, but in the light of Mr. Slayden's[3] record, no one can claim he has given support to the Administration.

Woodrow Wilson

T telegram (Letterpress Books, WP, DLC).

[1] Co-publisher of the San Antonio *Light*.

[2] It is missing.

[3] That is, James Luther Slayden, Democratic congressman from San Antonio, Texas. When Wilson's telegram was made public on July 25, Slayden, then campaigning in Texas, immediately announced his withdrawal from the primary contest, thus ending a congressional career of twenty-two years. See Ellen Maury Slayden, *Washington Wife: Journal of Ellen Maury Slayden from 1897-1919*, with an Introduction by Walter Prescott Webb (New York, 1963), pp. xi-xiii, 333-34.

To Samuel Gompers

My dear Mr. Gompers:　　　　The White House 24 July, 1918

With regard to the suggestion that I attend the Mexican-American Labor Conference which is being planned for November, I feel bound to say to you now, as I said to you when you mentioned the matter orally, that it is quite clear to me that I cannot attend and that my attendance would involve some political embarrassments because of the peculiarities of Mr. Carranza which I think ought to be avoided.

I am very much interested in the plan for such a conference and hope sincerely that it will succeed, but I do not think that it would be wise for me to be present.

In haste

Cordially and sincerely yours,　　Woodrow Wilson

TLS (photostat in RSB Coll., DLC).

To William Procter Gould Harding

My dear Governor Harding:　　[The White House] 24 July, 1918

Thank you for your memorandum about the cotton situation. Frankly, my mind shies off from price fixing, but Mr. Lever of South Carolina, who came to see me the other day about this same situation, had a series of suggestions to make which seemed to me wise and which seemed likely to meet the situation. If he is no longer in Washington, as I fear he is not, I suggest that you get his secretary to obtain for me a memorandum from him following in substance his conversation with me.

In haste   Sincerely yours,   Woodrow Wilson

TLS (Letterpress Books, WP, DLC).

To James Hamilton Lewis

My dear Senator: [The White House] 24 July, 1918

Thank you for your letter of yesterday.[1] I don't think you need fear any consequences of our dealings with the Bolsheviki, because we do not intend to deal with them.

I am very much interested to hear of your contemplated visit to the other side of the water, but you certainly do not need any caution as to what you are to say. I hope that you will have a very rich experience.

In great haste   Sincerely yours,   [Woodrow Wilson]

CCL (WP, DLC).
    [1] J. H. Lewis to WW, July 23, 1918, TLS (WP, DLC). Lewis suggested that, if Wilson found it necessary to enter into an "arrangement" with the Bolsheviks, he should also make to the American people "some reference to the *big and good things they are doing*, as the country at large knows only of the worst things they did." Such an explanation would, Lewis said, counter Republican charges that the Wilson administration was seeking to bolshevize the United States by such actions as taking over the railroads and telegraph lines. He also suggested making General Leonard Wood the head of the American military forces in Siberia: if Wood was a success in that post, it would redound to Wilson's credit; if he was a failure, it would damage the General's reputation forever. Finally, Lewis announced that he was going to Europe soon to investigate conditions among the American forces there, and he asked Wilson's advice as to what he should say, or avoid saying, in his speeches abroad.

To John Joseph Pershing

My dear General Pershing: The White House 24 July, 1918

It was thoughtful of you to send me the photographs which have come to me this morning of the American troops in action in the attack at Cantigny. It gives me an opportunity that I had not had before of visualising the circumstances of an action like that.

But I am not writing merely to thank you for the photographs. I want also to say how very proud we are of the record our men have been making under you in the recent fighting at the front. It has given a deep sort of pride and joy to the whole country, and my sincere congratulations go out to you and to the immediate commanders of the men who have been rendering so fine an account of themselves.

With the best wishes,

Cordially and sincerely yours,   Woodrow Wilson

TLS (J. J. Pershing Papers, DLC).

From Frank Lyon Polk, with Enclosure

My dear Mr. President: Washington July 24, 1918.

The Japanese Ambassador came in this afternoon and gave me orally the answer of the Japanese Government to the proposals in regard to sending troops to Vladivostok. He said that his Government for political reasons could not bind itself to limit the force to 7,000 as it would be said by the people of Japan, and particularly the opposition, that the limitation was being imposed because of lack of confidence in Japan and its motives. He said of course his Government knew the limitation was not suggested for any such reason, but the political situation in Japan was such that the acceptance of this limitation would be used against the Government, and therefore, much to their regret, they could not accept it.

He assured me it was not his Government's intention to send a large number of troops, but he said that the Japanese Government was convinced that the forces proposed would be too small adequately to protect the rear of the Czecho-Slovacs. He said he had learned from his Military Attache that his Government would send a division which, on a peace footing, would be about 12,000 men, with the understanding that the number of troops that they would send would depend on the amount of resistence that they met from the Bolsheviks, Austrian and German prisoners.

I tried to argue with him as to limiting the number to 7,000 but without success. He reiterated that there was no misunderstanding on the part of the Government of our motives in making the limitation, but they were afraid of public opinion.

He read me a copy of the declaration which they proposed to make, stating that his Government felt that separate declarations would be better than a joint declaration. I enclose a copy of the declaration. I told the Ambassador that I would communicate with you and he would hear from me very shortly.

I suppose the number of troops they intend to send now is not as important as their reserving the right to send more later. He said at the end of the interview that when we were in agreement we could then arrange with the Entente Governments for their participation.   Yours faithfully,   Frank L Polk

TLS (WP, DLC).

E N C L O S U R E

The Japanese Government, actuated by the sentiment of sincere friendship towards the Russian people, have always entertained the most sanguine hopes of the speedy reestablishment of order in

Russia and a healthy and untrammelled development of her national life. Abundant proof, however, is now afforded to show that the Central European Empires, taking advantage of the chaotic and defenceless condition in which Russia has momentarily been placed, are consolidating their hold on that country and are steadily extending their activities to the Russian Far Eastern possessions. They have persistently interfered with the passage of the Czecho-Slovac troops through Siberia. In the forces now opposing these valiant troops, the German and Austro-Hungarian prisoners are freely enlisted and they practically assume the position of command. The Czecho-Slovac troops, aspiring to secure a free and independent existence for their race and loyally espousing the common cause of the Allies, justly command every sympathy and consideration from the co-belligerents to whom their destiny is a matter of deep and abiding concerns. In the presence of danger to which the Czecho-Slovac troops are actually exposed in Siberia at the hand of the Germans and Austro-Hungarians, the Allies have naturally felt themselves unable to view with indifference the untoward course of events and a certain number of their troops have already been ordered to proceed to Vladiostock. The Government of the United States, equally sensible to the gravity of the situation, recently approached the Japanese Government with proposals for an early despatch of troops to relieve pressure now weighing upon the Czecho-Slovac forces.

The Japanese Government, being anxious to fall in with the desires of the American Government and also to act in harmony with the Allies and having regards at the same time to the special position of Japan, have decided to proceed at once to despatch suitable forces for the proposed mission. A certain number of these troops will be sent forthwith to Vladivostock and, if called for by the further exigencies of the situation, another detachment will eventually be ordered to operate and to maintain order along the Siberian Railway. In adopting this course, the Japanese Government remain unshaken in their constant desire to promote relation of enduring friendship with Russia and the Russian people and reaffirm their avowed policy of respecting the territorial integrity of Russia and of abstaining from all interference in her internal politics. They further declare that upon the realization of the objects above indicated they will immediately withdraw all Japanese troops from Russian territory and will leave wholly unimpaired the sovereignty of Russia in all its phases whether political or military.

T MS (WP, DLC).

From Frank Lyon Polk

Dear Mr. President: Washington July 24, 1918

We tried to keep secret the conferences relating to the formation of an American Group, but, have not been entirely successful in doing so. Several articles have appeared in the New York papers, some, apparently, coming from persons in New York and one bearing a Washington date line. The articles do not properly present the situation and it is feared that a misapprehension is likely to grow in the minds of the public.

It seems advisable to me to clarify the situation by making an official announcement. If it is done in this way the point of view of the Government can be presented and the publicity given a proper direction.

I am enclosing a draft of a proposed announcement to be given to the press.[1] It is submitted for your consideration and I will be glad to receive and to follow any directions you may have to give in regard to it.

I am, my dear Mr. President,
Faithfully yours,   Frank L. Polk

TLS (WP, DLC).
[1] It is printed as an Enclosure with WW to FLP, July 26, 1918.

From John R. Mott

My dear Mr. President: New York July 24, 1918

I have continued to think on the personnel of the Commission which you contemplate sending to Russia and in accordance with my promise now write you.

My mind keeps turning to Mr. Lane as the best equipped man to serve as Chairman. I believe it will be wise to send men who will go prepared to remain, if need be, a year or longer, but in the case of Mr. Lane it would be better to have the benefit of his unique abilities but a few months, if necessary, then let another member of the Commission take his place than to have the Commission go forth under any other leadership of which I have so far been able to think.

Naturally one thinks of Mr. Stevens as the one who could best deal with transportation questions. There may be some reason with which I am not familiar why he would be *persona non grata* with important elements in Russia, but unless this be the case, it would seem that his experience, spanning nearly the entire period of the Revolution and especially related to Eastern Russia, should qualify him to make a unique contribution to the entire work of the Commission. If, for any reason, you deem it inexpedient to relate him to the Commission, Mr. Willard impresses me as able to deal with all that pertains to transportation.

If the Commission is called upon to handle diplomatic matters, Mr. Lloyd Griscom[1] is well worth considering. He was, as you know, one of the best ambassadors we have had in Tokyo as well as in Rio and in Rome. In the course of my foreign journeys I had occasion to observe his work and influence at all of these centers and was favorably impressed by his judgment, tact and sympathy. The fact that he has recently entered military service may eliminate him. On the other hand this might not be without its advantage.

Mr. Julius Rosenwald might be a valuable member of such a Commission. He has given attention to all sides of a great commercial and business undertaking which reaches out over a vast agricultural area. He has constructive ability and a winning manner. He has shown the gift of sympathy with other races. I am not unmindful of what might be said of the fact that he is a Hebrew. I recognize the somewhat serious risk which might be incurred. I have so much confidence in the man, however, that personally I would feel like taking chances.

I recognize the necessity of having on the Commission a satisfactory representative of labor. Mr. Duncan, if he were less talkative, less rigid and more tactful, would be ideal. He may still be the best available man, but I would be disposed to raise the question with Mr. Gompers whether he cannot suggest another man who is officially related to the American Federation of Labor and who would in his judgment do even better than Duncan.

I am inclined to think that Professor Ross has already made his chief contribution—one of real value—as a trained sociologist and effective writer as contrasted with one who will be called upon to deal in a practical and constructive way with difficult conditions. I have been trying to think of some one from the Northwest who is an authority on agricultural conditions and who could enter with insight and sympathy into the problems of the peasants of Siberia. Mr. Houston would know whether Mr. Henry Wallace[2] of *Wallace's Farmer* of Des Moines would do. Or he may think of a man related to the demonstration or extension work of one of our Agricultural Colleges who would still better serve this very important purpose.

You asked me to suggest for consideration a suitable representative of the Y.M.C.A. an organization which is in a position to have such a useful part in the rebuilding of Russia. My first choice would be Mr. E. T. Colton[3] who for twenty years has been the colleague of Mr. Brockman[4] and myself and who has had charge of our work in Russia during this trying year. He is now on his way home but I hope would be willing to return soon should it be desired that he do so.

It was particularly gratifying to me to learn from you of your plan to ensure a wise coordination of all that is being done and all that will be done on behalf of Russia by the various departments of the Government and by other agencies (commercial, humanitarian, etc.) here at home. To my mind this is essential to the strengthening of the hands of the proposed Commission and to giving effect to their efforts and recommendations.

Let me reiterate my conviction that you have been Providentially guided from the beginning in your attitude and policy with reference to Russia and the Russian peoples. In the midst of such confused counsels and conflicting national ambitions and in the face of much publicity propaganda, your own course has been all the more remarkable. It is an impressive illustration of the value of having clear guiding principles and also sympathy with the aspirations of what have been aptly called "dark people" groping after larger light and liberty.

I shall be in Washington July 29th or 30th and will report my whereabouts to Mr. Tumulty in case you should wish to see me.

With highest regard   Faithfully yours,   John R. Mott

TLS (WP, DLC).
[1] Lloyd Carpenter Griscom, lawyer and Republican political leader of New York; United States Minister to Persia (1901-1902) and Japan (1902-1906) and Ambassador to Brazil (1906-1907) and Italy (1907-1909).
[2] That is, Henry Cantwell Wallace.
[3] That is, Ethan Theodore Colton.
[4] That is, Fletcher Sims Brockman.

From Thomas Watt Gregory

Dear Mr. President: Washington, D. C. July 24, 1918.

Under date of June 12th you wrote me[1] asking me to make an investigation and advise you with reference to statements made in a telegram sent you June 10th by the Executive Committee of the Washington State Grange, complaining of the treatment given the officers and members of the State Grange of Washington at Walla Walla by local authorities, who summarily broke up the annual meeting of the Grange. The telegram requested you to make a Federal investigation to determine whether the officers and members of the State Grange were disloyal.

I have caused a careful investigation to be made of the whole matter and find that the situation was a very complicated one. It seems that William Bouck, Master of the State Grange and a conspicuous member of the Non-Partisan League, wrote a letter urging higher taxation of war profits, in the course of which he said:

"We have no moral right to saddle upon the next generation a huge debt that profiteers may gloat over their gains in this.

"Buy Liberty Bonds when possible and when needed, but larger war profit taxes should be paid so a smaller amount of Liberty Bonds will be needed.

"Do your part by writing to your Congressman at once, demanding that larger war taxes be required."

This letter was published in the local newspapers at the time of the meeting referred to, and in his annual address Bouck advanced substantially the same argument, namely, that by issuing bonds the burden is shifted from our shoulders to those of our children, and again urging larger war taxes. These remarks of his were seized upon by opponents of the Non-Partisan League, and publicly interpreted by them as an argument against buying Liberty Bonds. As a result of the agitation thus brought about, the local authorities withdrew from the Grange permission to use the School Building in which meetings were being held, and other local officials warned the officers of the Grange not to continue their meetings in Walla Walla. The remarks attributed to the Master of the Grange constitute no violation of law, and I shall so advise officers of the Grange; but I have already advised them that it is impossible for this Department to give a blanket certificate of loyalty to the officers and members of the Grange. I have further advised them that while wrong has been done them, it is beyond the power of the Federal law authorities to take any action in this particular situation.

In my opinion, the issue of loyalty is not raised in any clean-cut manner by the occur[r]ences at Walla Walla, and it is my personal view that they do not merit a further special investigation by Federal authorities.   Respectfully,   T. W. Gregory

TLS (WP, DLC).
  [1] See WW to TWG, June 12, 1918, Vol. 48.

From Clark Howell

Personal

My dear Mr. President: Atlanta. July 24, 1918.

I am calling your attention to the senatorial situation in Georgia, for I cannot believe that you are acquainted with conditions here brought about by two candidates[1] appealing to the loyal sentiment of the people against one[2] who is practically defying your administration in justifying his antagonistic course both before and since this country entered the war.

Hardwick has been back in Georgia now for about two weeks. He is covering as many counties in the state as possible, and he has already been in every part of the state.

I am in very close touch with the situation and hear constantly from every part of the state of Georgia. My frank opinion is that Hardwick has gained so rapidly of late that the prospect of his success, *against a divided vote* of those who are defending the attitude of the administration and of their country in this war, has become an actual menace.

I am not an alarmist but this report comes to me with such force from all parts of Georgia that I feel that it is my duty to present the situation to you as it comes to me; for nothing could be more deplorable than to have this state placed in the attitude of refusing to uphold your course when the sentiment of the people overwhelmingly indorses every step that has been taken to put the whole force of our country back of our men now at the front.

I have been so much impressed with the gravity of the situation that I wanted to go to Washington to talk with you in person about it, but conditions are such that it is impossible for me to leave here at the present time.

So, I am taking this method of communicating with you to give expression to my opinion that the sure, the certain, and the only solution of the problem here, is for you to make the statement that has been pending for so many months, and concerning which assurance has been extended time and again that you were simply "waiting for the right time" to send such a message. If there ever was or will be a right time, it is now.

Unless you see your way clear to take this view of the matter at an early date, I very much fear the outcome of the primary; for, as matters stand now, Hardwick can be nominated by receiving only one-third of the vote of the state. Under existing conditions he is likely to get that, for he is appealing to every discontented element in the state. And he is undoubtedly making marked headway.

I do not presume to suggest to whom, or how you should write, or what you should say. I prefer especially that if you do write, you do make it as an answer to this letter.

If you care to write to me personally, either as editor of the Constitution, or as a member of the Democratic National Committee from Georgia, presenting your view of the danger involved in the situation, and urging the people of Georgia not to permit a minority vote to place them in the attitude of refusing to support the country while at war, such a letter would undoubtedly be handled with powerful effect. And I would, of course, put the full force of the Constitution back of it.

Or, perhaps, it may be better for you to write direct to one of the other candidates making a plain statement of the situation and appealing to their loyalty at this critical time to take such a step as will remove all doubt as to the outcome, and make it no longer possible for the state to be misrepresented as to the result of the primary.

If this fight can be centered to straight out contest between the loyalists on one side and the out spoken or half-hearted tories on the other, there will be no possible doubt of the result.

But it is going to take a bold stroke to bring about such a concentration and nothing could so admirably serve this purpose as a direct expression from you. And this conclusion is emphasized by the fact that this expression has been promised time and again—so many times that the Hardwick element has made all possible use of the argument of "outside interference," and nothing that you could say or do now could give them ground for any additional argument along that line. Whatever there is in that argument has been worked to its final analysis, and yet the force of your attitude has not been felt in full, because it has not been openly expressed.

There is, therefore, every advantage, and no possible disadvantage to accrue from such an expression from you.

The truth is it seems to me that this is the only possible way to absolutely save the situation.

Pardon the length of this letter which goes to you solely as a personal and a confidential expression from me. Anything you may write in reply will, of course, be received in the same way if you should not authorize its publication.

With cordial personal regards, and with best wishes, I am

Sincerely yours,   Clark Howell.

TLS (WP, DLC).
[1] That is, William J. Harris and William S. Howard.
[2] That is, Thomas W. Hardwick.

Lord Reading to Arthur James Balfour and Lord Milner

Very Urgent and Secret.   Washington. July 24th, 1918[1]
No. 3353 Following for Mr. Balfour and Lord Milner.

My telegram No. 3352 of today.

The President's observation that 100 U. S. divisions could not be sent to France by July 1919 was the first definite information I have received of this fact although the doubt has been raised for some weeks as to the feasibility of this extended programme. In addition to the already reported observations of the President at my interview with him today he said that much would depend upon the number of cargo ships which Great Britain could furnish for the purpose of carrying supplies for the American army increased as it would be month by month. I have already indicated this view to you. Even allowing for the increased production of ships in the latter quarter of the year and early part of next year assistance will be required by U.S.G. I expect that other demands may be made upon us for assistance in supply and equipment of U. S. Army as I have already told you.

CC telegram (W. Wiseman Papers, CtY).
  [1] This telegram was written on July 23: Lord Reading to A. J. Balfour, July 23, 1918, T telegram (FO 115/2461, p. 419, PRO).

Lord Reading to Arthur James Balfour

Washington. July 24th, 1918.[1]
No. 3354, Very Urgent and Secret.

At my interview with the President today reference was made to the League of Nations. I informed him that it was being much discussed in England and had been debated in the House of Lords and was the subject of considerable Press comment and correspondence. I informed him that H.M.G. might possibly be asked to discuss the matter in the House of Commons. The President hoped nothing would be done which would even informally bind H.M.G. before there had been full opportunity for interchange of views. He himself has been at work on a paper regarding the Phillimore committee report which he had hoped to have finished before but his time had been so occupied that it was still uncompleted. He was in substantial agreement with Colonel House's letter of June 24th on this subject[2] but this letter was not exhaustive of the President's views. I hope it will not be necessary to take any step in this matter until after my arrival in London.

T telegram (FO 115/2427, p. 167, PRO).
  [1] This telegram was also written on July 23.
  [2] The Enclosure printed with EMH to WW, June 25, 1918, Vol. 48.

From the Diary of Josephus Daniels

1918 Wednesday 24 July
War Council at White House discussed necessity of economizing in steel & making other things go as far as possible

Wrote Henry F not to make any statement until after Michigan primary[1]

[1] About Ford's entrance into the Michigan senatorial primary race, see JPT to WW, June 18, 1918, n. 1, Vol. 48. The primary was to be held on August 27.

Two Telegrams from William Gibbs McAdoo

Glacier Park, Mont., July 25, 1918.

Acting upon a report of the board of railroad wages and working conditions of the wage scale and problems presented by the mechanical crafts of the railroad employees and after thorough consideration I have felt it to be my duty in the public interest as well as the interest of the employees to render a decision fixing a scale of wages for the mechanical crafts which represents a great increase but which nevertheless is below the scale now being paid in the ship yards in the navy yards and perhaps in some munitions plants. I am convinced that the scale now adopted for the railroads is fair and just and that it will be accepted by the great mass of the employees and that they will be contented provided the ship yards and the navy yards do not make a further increase in the wages of their employees as I understand they now contemplate doing. I am informed that the existing scale in the shipyards is highly remunerative and sufficient and that further agitation for increases would cease if it were made clear that the Government will stand upon such wages and refuse to make further concessions. It is impossible for the railroads to run a race with the ship yards and other Government agencies in increasing wages. This competition does not add to the number of skilled employees but merely results in transferring them from one arm of the service to another. More than four hundred thousand men are employed in the mechanical crafts of the railroads and increases in their pay must be general throughout the country and impose a great additional charge upon the people which in turn must be financed by the already overburdened treasury. The shipbuilders having contracts from the government on a cost plus basis are really benefitted by every increase of wages and the Treasury has to take the load to say nothing of the general demoralization in the labor situation resulting from constant changes in rates. I feel that I have gone as far for railroad employees as I conscientiously can and as far as we can justify to the country. Some prominent labor men tell me that they believe confidently that if you should see fit to tell Daniels and Hurley and the other Governmental agencies either employing direct or controlling the wages of labor through the cost plus contracts that existing wages

scales must not be increased and that if you would make an appeal
to labor throughout the country to stand upon the fair and equitable
basis of wages now established labor throughout the country with
practical unanimity would accept your decision and the continuous
agitation now in progress would end with general benefit to the
public to labor and to all industries involved. This is my conviction
also. The decision I have just made increasing the wages of the
mechanical crafts of the railroads which although less than the
ship yards and in some respects navy yard scale means an increased
cost of approximately one hundred seventy five million dollars per
annum. It was unavoidable in view of the wages paid by the ship
yards and other Governmental agencies. Unless we make a stand
now on the existing fair basis there will be no stop to these increases
all of which come back ultimately to the Treasury aggravating us
difficulties and continuing a general unrest throughout the country.
Again I am distressed to burden you with additional problems but
I am sure that you are the only one who can settle this issue
promptly and satisfactorily. I hope you may think it wise to confer
with Daniels and Hurley and Secretary Wilson immediately calling
in Carter[1] director of the division of labor of the railroad administration with a view to action along these lines. The matter will soon
be exigent because ship yard labor in the Pacific northwest is already demanding as I understand it increases in wages beginning
August first. I have advised Hurley that I have telegraphed you
about this situation.   McAdoo.

T telegram (WP, DLC).
    [1] That is, William Samuel Carter.

Glacier Park, Montana, July 25, 1918.
Newspapers indicate that effort will be made to give waterpower
bill precedence over revenue bill when House reconvenes August
nineteenth and that Revenue bill may not be acted upon by House
until early in September. The imperative demands on the Treasury
compelled me to plan sometime ago for beginning, at the latest, a
fourth Liberty loan campaign September twenty eighth and ending
October nineteenth. This would leave free for political campaign
little more than two weeks before election. I should fear to offer
the four and one quarter per cent Liberty bonds authorized by the
fourth Liberty bond bill for subscription before enactment of the
revenue bill. Perhaps you may recall that an important ground for
our insistence upon prompt revenue legislation was the conviction
that new taxes should be determined upon before next Liberty loan
campaign, both in order to give the bonds the benefit of exemption
from definitely increased normal income and other taxes and to

give the people definite knowledge of their tax liabilities before they are asked to subscribe for bonds. Another and most important reason for earliest possible tax legislation was to enable me to sell short time Treasury certificates of indebtedness in anticipation of and receivable for income and excess profit taxes. Protracted delay even in writing the new law is interferring with my plans and prolonged delay in its enactment would, in my judgment, seriously jeopardize the ability of the Treasury to sell sufficient Treasury certificates to finance the Treasury in the intervals between Liberty loans. The financial operations of the Treasury are so colossal now that it will impose an undue strain upon the resources of the banks if we throw upon them alone the burden of taking short time certificates of indebtedness. We must supplement the resources of the banks by selling Treasury certificates of indebtedness available for the payment of income and excess profits taxes in order to reach the great number of taxpayers and to transfer to them through anticipation by them of their tax payments a large part of the load of temporary Treasury financing instead of imposing it wholly upon the banks. To postpone the Liberty loan campaign beyond September twenty eight would, on account of the impending elections, necessitate delaying it until the middle of November, which would make it conclude about the seventh or tenth of December. This would mean that proceeds of fourth Liberty loan would not be available before middle of December and would necessitate a large increase in the amount of the offering, forcing it probably to eight billion dollars. It would also compel the Treasury to refund about three billion dollars of short time Treasury certificates which have already been or shortly will be issued pursuant to program announced by me on June twelfth to banks and trust companies throughout country, all of which mature prior to the middle of December, as they were issued in conformity with the plan to offer the fourth Liberty loan about September twenty eighth. I doubt if this refunding could be done, coming as it will, in the middle of the crop-moving season and at a time when the resources of the banks will be taxed to the utmost. Therefore a material change in the date for the fourth Liberty loan seems to be impossible.

In these circumstances I hope that you may deem it wise to ask Mr. Kitchin to present the revenue bill to the House immediately upon its reconvening and to expedite its passage over all other measures, and that you may ask Senator Simmons to arrange for its expedi[ti]ous passage in the Senate. Knowing as I do the imperative necessities of the Treasury which are becoming more pronounced each day with the constantly increasing appropriations and other demands upon it, I consider it vital that the new revenue bill shall become a law before the end of September. Of course I know that you can use only your great influence to secure this result and the purpose of this telegram is to beg you to exert your influence in this direction immediately.

May I also add that in the hope of accommodating the action of the Treasury to the wishes of Mr. Kitchin, Treasury officials have, by my direction, refrained from making any official suggestion concerning the revenue measure excepting when invited by Mr. Kitchin and, even then, we have supplied data for his consideration in an informal way only. Personally I consider it most unfortunate that Mr. Kitchin and the committee have not invited the Treasury to present its views formally and in detail about the new revenue measure. Such cooperation would have been of the greatest value, but apparently there has been some feeling against the Treasury because of its insistence upon prompt action in this vital matter and I have not felt justified in obtruding my views unless invited by the committee. My profound conviction is that the tax program substantially as outlined in my letter to you on May of June last[1] and in my letter of June fifth to Mr. Kitchin[2] is of vital importance and should be followed as nearly as practicable if the Treasury is to meet the demands imposed upon it by the Congress and if the general financial situation in the country is to be kept sound and strong. It seems to me most important that when the new revenue bill is introduced in the House it shall be of a character which you and the Treasury can wholeheartedly endorse and support. If you think it wise and practicable to indicate to Mr. Kitchin that you would be glad if he and the committee could find it possible in the revenue bill to follow the lines indicated and if he and the committee could avail themselves to the fullest extent possible of the views of the Treasury officials who are familiar with the subject from the standpoint of the Treasury's needs and the general financial situation of the country, I should be very glad.

I am distressed to burden you with this matter and would not if I were not keenly alive to the difficulties confronting the Treasury and of the imperative necessities of the situation. I would be very grateful if you would send for Leffingwell and discuss the situation with him.   W. G. McAdoo.

TC telegram (TDR, RG 56, Office of the Secretary, General Corr., 1917-1932, DNA).
    [1] *Sic.* See WGM to WW, May 23, 1918 (first letter of that date), Vol. 48.
    [2] WGM to C. Kitchin, June 5, 1918, OCL (WP, DLC). This was a revised version of the letter cited in n. 1.

From John R. Shillady[1]

Sir: New York July 25, 1918

The press of July 23 carries special dispatches to the effect that you have under consideration the issuance of a statement concerning mob violence. We trust that you will feel disposed to make this statement and that it will include an unequivocal condemnation of the lynching of Negroes. We are not in the slightest doubt as to your attitude toward lynching, but there are in our judgment special reasons why the President of the United States at this time should speak in the name of the nation in condemnation of the lynching of Negroes.

We respectfully submit the following reasons as justification for our earnest appeal to you to include the lynching of Negroes in a prominent place in any statement you feel disposed to make. In a separate memorandum[2] we are outlining more at length the reasons summarized below:

1. The extraordinary number of lynchings which have occurred since the entry of the United States into the war. (259 Negro victims of mob violence.)

2. The large number of states in which mob outrages against Negroes have occurred since April 6, 1917. (3 Northern and 14 Southern States.)

3. The particularly vicious character of some of these lynchings. In one state three men have been burned and tortured before death and the bodies of two others burned after death. In another state six members of a family were killed at one time; in another, thirteen were lynched from May 17 to May 24, 1918.

We are enclosing for your examination a copy of the report of a special investigator who, on July 10, presented to Governor Hugh M. Dorsey of Georgia the results of his investigation,[3] showing that ten and probably eleven persons (one person had disappeared who is believed to have been lynched) have been lynched as the result of a single episode, instead of six persons as was reported by the press. One of these was a woman eight months pregnant who was said by the investigator to have been lynched hanging by the heels, disemboweled, and in the process giving birth to an eight months old child who was crushed under the heel of one of the lynchers.

4. The failure to punish lynchers in any one of the total number of cases in which Negroes were concerned. In only one case known to us have any indictments been found. Though the alleged lynchers were indicted five months ago, none has been brought to trial.

5. Failure of governors of many states to take seriously protests or inquiries made by responsible organizations and leading news-

papers against lynchings in their states and against the failure of the authorities to punish lynchers.

6. Confessed lack of power by certain governors to act to prevent lynching even when it is a matter of common knowledge that lynchings are likely to occur.

7. The danger to national morale due to wide-spread resentment at this crime by Negroes of the nation and particularly at the failure of responsible authorities of the law to take steps to punish lynchers or to prevent lynchings.

8. The loyal response of the Negroes of the nation to every opportunity to serve as contrasted with the failure of local authorities to act when Negroes are lynched by mobs.

9. The opinion of the Attorney General that the federal courts have no jurisdiction to deal with ordinary cases of lynching, and the opinion generally accepted by competent legal authorities that federal anti-lynching legislation under the Fourteenth Amendment is or is likely to be regarded by the Supreme Court as unconstitutional.

10. The ardent desire of great masses of Americans, white and colored, that the stigma of lynching be removed from America.

11. The heightened prestige at home and abroad which American institutions would receive if energetic efforts were made really to stop the lynching of Negroes.

Respectfully yours,   John R. Shillady

TLS (WP, DLC).
[1] Secretary of the National Association for the Advancement of Colored People.
[2] J. R. Shillady, "Memorandum to Hon. Woodrow Wilson . . . ," c. July 25, 1918, TS MS (WP, DLC).
[3] Walter Francis White to Hugh Manson Dorsey, July 10, 1918, TC MS (WP, DLC). Shillady also enclosed tearsheets of Walter F. White, "The Burning of Jim McIlherron: An N.A.A.C.P. Investigation," *The Crisis*, XVI (May 1918), 16-20.

From William Bauchop Wilson

My dear Mr. President: Washington July 25, 1918.

I have discussed with Mr. Gompers his suggestion of the establishment of a labor paper to aid in counteracting German intrigue in Mexico and in fostering a friendly attitude of mind towards us amongst the common people, particularly the wage workers, of that country.

It seems to me to be a practicable plan to help in creating a better understanding between the peoples and the Governments of Mexico and the United States. It could be financed through the Committee on Public Information. I have asked Mr. Gompers to submit an estimate of the cost, which he has done. It is as follows:

COST ESTIMATE. (weekly)

50,000 copies at $17 per thousand	$850.00
Mailing	40.00
Postage	40.00
English editor	50.00
Spanish editor	50.00
Stenographers (2) Spanish and English	60.00
Office rent, phone, stationery, etc.	25.00
Circulation agents (2) for Mexico and U. S.	60.00
Railroad expenses for agents (2)	80.00
	$ 1255.00
Total until end of 1918	$22590.00

If you are in doubt about the wisdom of authorizing this work, may I suggest that you bring it to the attention of the Cabinet for discussion.   Faithfully yours,   W B Wilson

TLS (WP, DLC).

From Edward Mandell House

Dear Governor: Magnolia, Massachusetts. July 25, 1918.

We are terribly disappointed that you had to give up coming to Magnolia at the last minute. I sincerely hope it is only deferred and that you will be able to come later.

As a matter of fact, the weather is too hot to make travelling pleasant and if I were you I would choose a cooler period. It is pleasant here but the coming and going would have been very trying.

Labor leaders are very anxious for you to see a small group of them on Monday in regard to the Mooney case. I promised to speak to you about it, although they have already taken it up through Tumulty.   Affectionately yours,   E. M. House

I believe a few days here would be of great benefit to you.

TLS (WP, DLC).

From Thomas James Walsh

My dear Mr. President: Washington July 25, 1918.

I venture to express the hope that you will resolve as speedily as possible the question submitted to you by Secretary Houston of making provision from the war fund at your disposal for aiding the farmers in the drouth affected areas of our State to secure seed and feed for fall planting.

We were obliged to appeal to you in this matter because the case does not admit of delay, even until the reassembling of Congress. The planting of fall wheat should begin not later than the fifteenth of August, and you will readily appreciate that if the fund were made available at once, the time is all too brief within which to make the necessary examinations and reports and to put in operation the machinery for distributing. Moreover, I am assured from many sources that settlers who have now met with a second failure are growing despondent and are already leaving, or are preparing to leave the country. Many of them have mortgaged their horses, machinery and whatever cows they may have to the local banks, which, naturally, are proceeding to reduce the security. Mr. Lobdell[1] told me of some Kansas people he met out there on his late trip, who were selling off everything they had preparatory to going to Los Angeles, where they expect to find employment in a shipyard.

If these people could be assured at once that the Government is coming to their aid, at least to the extent of advancing them the money with which to put in another crop, many of them would be induced to stay.

I appreciate how many important matters there are imperatively demanding your attention and I would not think of crowding you in this matter were it not that I feel that any further delay would be disastrous.

With assurances of my very keen appreciation of your interest and sympathy with those in behalf of whom I appeal, I am,

Very truly yours,   T. J. Walsh

TLS (WP, DLC).
[1] That is, Charles Elmer Lobdel.

A Translation of a Telegram from Jean Jules Jusserand to the Foreign Ministry

Washington, no date, no time,
received July 25, 1918.

Nos. 966-970. URGENT. VERY CONFIDENTIAL.

966. In the course of a long interview which I have just had with the President, I explained to him that, if the action in Siberia must have only a limited character, it was nonetheless important that it should be immediate.

He agreed, saying that orders had already been given for the embarkment from San Francisco and the Philippines of 7,000 men and their equipment. But we continue still to lack a Japanese agreement. Viscount Ishii comes each day to bring me soothing words but without any definitive reply, in spite of the concession made concerning the command.

The President confirmed to me the assurance which Mr. Polk had given me that the Allied forces there could move according to necessity and would not have to remain at Vladivostok, being always constituted if so desired as a rear guard.

He foresees, for the rest, a smaller total number raised than that envisaged as possible by the

967. Counselor of the State Department and does not think that it should exceed 20,000 men. He has not, however, arrived at a truly exact idea of this number.

The President has repeated for me a general review of his views which can be summarized as follows:

"The question of the western front dominates everything. Because massive intervention, a reconstitution of the eastern front, and the million and more Japanese thrown into Russia, of whom the English ministers speak with so little prudence, would pose a great threat to our effort in France and are, besides, impossibilities.

"Our resources are considerable but not inexhaustible. You know the figures for coal; as for steel, it is recognized as necessary that we should furnish during the year 20,000,000 tons,

968. up to three and a half millions of which is for us probably impossible.

"Can you imagine what it would be necessary to add to this to carry out so large an expedition? All the calculations that we make with the most ardent desire to satisfy your requests permit us to foresee only a total of eighty divisions in July next instead of the 100 which you asked for and which we at first thought we would be able to furnish you. One could, in fact, have the men, but not without the danger of disorganizing the war industries; the problem of matériel is of the greatest difficulty.

"Studies are going forward.

"I remain persuaded, in spite of the contradictions, that the reconstitution of an eastern front, desirable though that might be (and the East itself is in my thoughts), is an impossibility and out of the question and that the dispatch of troops (among which the yellow element would dominate) would have the gravest drawbacks.

969. "We are trying at this moment and for this reason politely to persuade the Chinese not to insist also upon sending 7,000 men and to content themselves with 1,000.

"We wish to watch, to assist, to serve, not to disturb and irritate.

"The commission will assist in reconstructing the railroads, agriculture, etc. ⁕ ⁕ ⁕ We will organize this aid in such a manner that no one can suspect us of trying to seek commercial advantages after the war. What we bring (clothing, agricultural machinery) will not be a gift, however. It will be bartered for local cereals, hides, and so forth, which we will thus shelter from the Germans."

The President confirmed to me that he would not publish his aide-mémoire but that he wished, it being necessary to inform his country, to issue to the press, when the time was ripe, a brief communique indicating the weight of the question and the motive behind his action.

970. In the course of the interview covered by the preceding telegrams, the President spoke with a marked bitterness caused by the efforts to make him go where he did not want to go, and which have certainly had a reverse effect upon him. He attributes to an outside source the articles (which I have called to your attention several times) appearing in the American press in favor of intervention in Siberia with imposing force, notably those in the *New York Times*.[1] When I tried to shed doubt on these suppositions, he replied to me rather sharply: "They are inspired by London. I know it." There is no need for me to call your attention again to the conclusions which are to be drawn from such marked reactions.

When he manifests to me his ideas, as fixed as ever on the bad effect of depending on the predominance of Oriental troops, I take the lead and mention some Annamese who, by necessity, had to be included in our first contingent but who will soon be replaced.

The commander of the American contingent has not yet been named. He looks, Mr. Wilson tells me, for a young brigadier general.

Jusserand.

T telegram (État-Major, L'Armée de Terre, Service Historique, 4 N 46, FMD-Ar).

[1] The *New York Times* published news reports and articles on the advisability of intervention in Russia in general or Siberia in particular almost every day during June and July 1918. Many of them said that the last chance for the Allies and the United States to "save" Russia from German and Bolshevik domination was being jeopardized by the reluctance of the Wilson administration to commit itself to a definite policy in regard to intervention. The following list is a sampling of such articles printed in the *New York Times* in July: Harold Williams, "Allied Action in Russia Urgent," July 3, 1918; Eugene de Schelking, "The Chief Russian Danger," July 4, 1918; A Military Expert, "Military Critic on Allied Attacks Along West Front . . . Imperative Need of Rebuilding Russian Front by Some Form of Intervention," July 7, 1918, Sect. 4; "Allies Reported Eager to Send Aid to Russia . . . Fear that We May Act Too Late Oppresses Allies," July 14, 1918; Joseph I. C. Clarke, "The War in Siberia," July 20, 1918; and "Says Immediate Aid Will Save Russia," July 21, 1918, Sect. 2.

A Translation of an Extract from the Notebooks of Henri Bergson

[July 25, 1918]

July 25. This conversation [with Wilson on intervention in Siberia], which takes place in the afternoon, is long. The President speaks to me with extreme kindness, almost with emotion, and with a soothing tone which I have never heard from him before. Evidently, he is sorry to have to refuse what I ask him. Jusserand told me before the audience that Wilson had decided to make this declaration[1] because the Allies had seemed to him to wish to force his hand. At the time that they had decided that the expedition would be a Japanese-American one, they had landed English and French troops at Vladivostok. (It is striking, in my opinion, that troops called for by the Czechoslovaks in danger of being killed had to be sent by the Allied governments *before* the American decision.) Furthermore, there have appeared some extraordinary articles in the *New York Times* strongly in favor of intervention, and the President is *convinced* that these articles emanate from the English government. When I raised the possibility that they might have come from the English Ambassador himself, he replied, "I know it." Such, according to Jusserand, must be the reason. But my conversation shows me that the reasons are much deeper than that, and that it is something other than vexation, as Jusserand sees it. (The latter always catalogues disagreeable diplomatic mistakes— of other ambassadors or of our government.)

Returning to the basic question, I begin by telling the President that the Germans still have thirty-six divisions in Russia and that they have already begun to transfer them to our front, that thirty-six divisions represent almost the entire American effort during this year. I point out besides, something even graver, that the Germans have established at Bergzabern and Friedrichshafen two schools for Ukrainian and Finnish officers; that they have announced their intention to constitute Russian armies which Germany will surely use for her own benefit; that here is a counterbalance to the American effort which can prolong the war indefinitely. One can figure out, I say to him, what the Germans, now that they have been checked in their offensive, will do. According to their customary practice, they are going to burrow themselves in on the western front and are going to do what they can to exploit the East, this time to recruit armies there. They are always going to shift from one front to the other. They *have* to proceed thus, or else they are lost.

The President replied that he had no fear of the Slavs whom the Germans could recruit. They will fight badly for Germany. Besides, what is to be done? We are going to come to the aid of the Czechoslovaks in a very limited expedition. But if we wish to do more, it will be necessary to have recourse to the Japanese, and they have already made it known that they will need "supplies," particularly steel, in considerable quantity. Moreover, we will have to equip their men. But at the present time our production does not suffice for the enormous effort that we are devoting to the western front. If it is a great campaign that we must prepare for in the West, then we must renounce making such an effort in the East. What does one wish? The President came back time and again to this idea, declaring that we have here a "material impossibility."

I said to him that this impossibility could be relieved little by little and, for that very reason, out of prudence, we ought by degrees to provide in Siberia and Russia what American production will make possible in the course of time. But no, replies the President, for at least a year longer we will scarcely be able to provide for the needs of the western front.

But why, I asked him, announce publicly that one is going to do the minimum? You will thereby reassure the Germans. The Allies, replied the President, well know the limit of our means and how we cannot make a double effort. "I gave up a long time ago trying to hide anything from the Germans."

But, I told him, you are going to depress the Allies. It is better, he replied, that they should understand what hopes are not realizable.

In sum, this is what I have untangled: the President is always loath to set the Japanese in motion, and he has always hoped to avoid intervention, even the appearance of intervening in Russian affairs. Moreover, recent and current events have combined to give him arguments to support his repugnance and his hope. As far as the Japanese are concerned, for three weeks they have replied neither yes nor no on the subject of that very small expedition decided upon for Vladivostok. Every day, Count Ishii comes to make ambiguous declarations on this subject, from which it results that Japan *will* accept or *may*, however, accept. This confirms the idea of the unreliability of Japan. She asks for enormous supplies, especially of steel, if the expedition is to become important. Evidently Japan asks for more than is necessary. Why? Probably in order to prepare for the other war, the one which will follow this one. War against whom? Japan does not know that herself, but it could be against the Americans. It is impossible that the President does not have these thoughts. The President told me that Japan asks for much money and steel and other things. In an emergency, one could give her money, but, as for the rest, it is impossible.

But on the other hand, the success of our soldiers and of the American soldiers on our front now makes him hope for the coming victory. In these circumstances, to be distracted from our front appears to him to be out of the question. On the contrary, it is necessary to press ahead with all force on the western front.

"Notes réunies ainsi par H.B. lui-même," Hw MS (Papiers d'Agents, Bergson, Vol. 3, FFM-Ar).
[1] The press release printed at Aug. 3, 1918.

From the Diary of Colonel House

July 25, 1918.

The President telephoned Frank Polk this morning at 10.30 that he was leaving tonight for Magnolia. Polk evidently asked whether he had received a memorandum which he had written for him last night. When the President read this he concluded that it would be impossible for him to leave Washington at the moment because of the crisis in the Japanese-Siberian intervention situation. Personally, I think the very hot weather now prevailing had something to do with his decision. Mrs. Wilson is not a lover of heat like the President and she really suffers under it. The temperature in Washington today I am told is insufferable, and I think that had as much to do with the postponement as the Japanese Note.

The President is fretted with the Japanese attitude. They do not wish to limit the size of their forces to be sent in. As a matter of fact, they have never wanted to intervene on an altruistic basis such as the President has insisted upon. They have used all sorts of excuses of which this is one. The President sent rather a peremptory note to our Ambassador at Tokyo, telling him that unless they would agree to intervene upon our terms, there would be no intervention at all with our consent.[1]

The difficulty I think is that there are two parties in Japan. The Civil Government wishes to cooperate with us and sees the necessity for it. The military clique see nothing in such intervention for Japan. They have not the vision to know that in the end it would be better for the Japanese to do the altruistic thing. It is the old story one meets everywhere and the one met since the beginning of the world; "what is there in it for me?" I hope before the war is over we can drive it into the consciousness of individuals as well as nations that from a purely selfish viewpoint, it is better to take the big, broad outlook that what is best for all is best for one.

T MS (E. M. House Papers, CtY).
¹ House had advance knowledge of the telegram, which Polk, after a conversation with Wilson on July 25, had written or wrote soon afterward to Ambassador Morris. About the telegram, see Enclosure II with FLP to WW, July 26, 1918, n. 1.

From the Diary of William Phillips

Thursday, July 25 [1918]

Returned to Washington last night. The Siberian situation remains a tangle. Japan has presented a draft announcement which it proposes to make: talks about cooperation with the Allies; gives the impression that large military units may be sent "in view of Japan's special position in Siberia." I said at once that this was impossible and that if we allowed Japan to proceed without protest we should be approving Japan's procedure in Siberia and thus become a party to what may be most serious developments. The President came over and spent some time in Polk's office. He read the Japanese declaration and was very much upset by it. Polk sent for the Japanese Ambassador this afternoon and told him that it would be wiser to leave out all mention of Japan's special position, etc. Conversations continue and nothing actually seems to be done. Fortunately the Czecho-Slovaks seem to be holding their own and have just taken Irkutsk.

A Statement to the American People

[July 26, 1918]

My Fellow Countrymen: I take the liberty of addressing you upon a subject which so vitally affects the honor of the Nation and the very character and integrity of our institutions that I trust you will think me justified in speaking very plainly about it.

I allude to the mob spirit which has recently here and there very frequently shown its head amongst us, not in any single region, but in many and widely separated parts of the country. There have been many lynchings, and every one of them has been a blow at the heart of ordered law and humane justice. No man who loves America, no man who really cares for her fame and honor and character, or who is truly loyal to her institutions, can justify mob action while the courts of justice are open and the governments of the States and the Nation are ready and able to do their duty. We are at this very moment fighting lawless passion. Germany has outlawed herself among the nations because she has disregarded the sacred obligations of law and has made lynchers of her armies.

Lynchers emulate her disgraceful example. I, for my part, am anxious to see every community in America rise above that level with pride and a fixed resolution which no man or set of men can afford to despise.

We proudly claim to be the champions of democracy. If we really are, in deed and in truth, let us see to it that we do not discredit our own. I say plainly that every American who takes part in the action of a mob or gives it any sort of countenance is no true son of this great Democracy, but its betrayer, and does more to discredit her by that single disloyalty to her standards of law and of right than the words of her statesmen or the sacrifices of her heroic boys in the trenches can do to make suffering peoples believe her to be their savior. How shall we commend democracy to the acceptance of other peoples, if we disgrace our own by proving that it is, after all, no protection to the weak? Every mob contributes to German lies about the United States what her most gifted liars cannot improve upon by the way of calumny. They can at least say that such things cannot happen in Germany except in times of revolution, when law is swept away!

I therefore very earnestly and solemnly beg that the governors of all the States, the law officers of every community, and, above all, the men and women of every community in the United States, all who revere America and wish to keep her name without stain or reproach, will cooperate—not passively merely, but actively and watchfully—to make an end of this disgraceful evil. It cannot live where the community does not countenance it.

I have called upon the Nation to put its great energy into this war and it has responded—responded with a spirit and a genius for action that has thrilled the world. I now call upon it, upon its men and women everywhere, to see to it that its laws are kept inviolate, its fame untarnished. Let us show our utter contempt for the things that have made this war hideous among the wars of history by showing how those who love liberty and right and justice and are willing to lay down their lives for them upon foreign fields stand ready also to illustrate to all mankind their loyalty to the things at home which they wish to see established everywhere as a blessing and protection to the peoples who have never known the privileges of liberty and self-government. I can never accept any man as a champion of liberty either for ourselves or for the world who does not reverence and obey the laws of our own beloved land, whose laws we ourselves have made. He has adopted the standards of the enemies of his country, whom he affects to despise.

Woodrow Wilson.

Printed in the *Official Bulletin*, II (July 26, 1918), 1-2.

A Statement[1]

The White House [July 26, 1918].

Again the Government comes to the people of the country with the request that they lend their money, and lend it upon a more liberal scale than ever before, in order that the great war for the rights of America [and the] liberation of the world may be carried on with ever increasing vigor to a victorious conclusion. And it makes the appeal with the greatest confidence, because it knows that every day it is becoming clearer to thinking men everywhere that the winning of the war is an essential investment. The money that is held back will be of very little use or value if the war is not won and the selfish masters of Germany dictate what America may and may not do. Men in America, besides, have from the first until now dedicated both their lives and their fortunes to the maintenance and vindication of the great principles and objects for which our government was set up. They will not fail now to show the world for what their wealth was intended.   Woodrow Wilson

WWT MS (WP, DLC).
  [1] Written in response to Labert St. Clair to WW, July 20, 1918, TLS (WP, DLC). St. Clair, Assistant Director of Publicity for the War Loan Organization in the Treasury Department, had asked Wilson to write a statement to be used in newspaper advertisements to promote the Fourth Liberty Loan.

From David Franklin Houston

Dear Mr. President: Washington July 26, 1918.

The matter of aid to farmers in drouth stricken regions has occupied much of my thought during the last week or ten days. When I spoke to you Tuesday, I indicated that, looking at the matter strictly on its merits, having in view the National need for wheat and the areas in which we could get the requisite acreage, it seemed that we should concern ourselves primarily with Montana. There wheat growing is a somewhat hazardous but still a legitimate enterprise. In the distressed areas of western Nebraska, Kansas, Oklahoma, and Texas wheat growing is still more hazardous and less legitimate. In these sections it will unquestionably be wise, in the long run, for more of the farmers to place emphasis on live stock, with adequate silos to furnish feed over the months when ordinary feed supplies are insufficient.

Still, in view of the representations I am getting from Senators, Congressmen and others, it seems to me that it would create embarrassment if you were to set aside a fund solely for use in Montana. I think the situation is such as to compel the direction of attention to certain areas and to the condition of a number of farmers outside of Montana. In such other areas the conditions under which loans should be made necessarily would have to be carefully defined. Loans to stimulate indiscriminate planting of wheat would result in sending good money after bad.

My impression is that, if you decide to make any funds available, it would be well for you to determine the maximum amount and to leave it to the Treasury Department and to this Department to work out the details as to the sums to be assigned to the different areas and to be lent to individuals. I imagine, with all the calls on your special fund, you could scarcely make available more than $5,000,000. Bearing in mind that we are now concerned only with fall wheat, apparently from $1,500,000 to $2,000,000 would provide for the legitimate fall wheat planting operations in Montana. This would leave from $3,000,000 to $3,500,000 for use in other sections if it seemed desirable to consider them.

If it is known that any funds are available, of course there will be demands for assistance for all sorts of purposes. People in the sections concerned would have in mind not only the fall but also the spring operations and many other things than wheat. In most areas they would also assume that the object was to stimulate the planting of an increased acreage. If funds are made available, it ought to be indicated that the desire is not to stimulate an increased acreage, or even necessarily to secure the planting of the normal acreage, in the counties that have suffered severely from the drouth, but rather to tide the farmers over this period of distress, to keep them on their farms, and to prevent great, very real sacrifices.

If Congress had acted on our emergency food production bill, we would have had available the sum of $6,500,000 to assist farmers in securing wheat seed, $2,500,000 of which could have been used for loans to farmers on crop liens.

Taking everything into consideration, and bearing in mind the psychology of the farmers in the areas concerned, I am inclined to believe it would be wise for you to make available immediately the five million dollars, if possible, and to assign it to the Secretary of the Treasury, to be expended by the Treasury Department and this Department cooperatively. The Treasury Department could handle the fiscal side of the matter and this Department could furnish the facts bearing on the agricultural needs.

Faithfully yours,   D. F. Houston.

TLS (WP, DLC).

To David Franklin Houston

My dear Mr. Secretary: [The White House] 26 July, 1918

I have your letter of today about the matter of aid to the farmers in the drought-stricken regions and am happy to comply with your suggestion. I hereby put at the disposal of the Treasury Department and the Department of Agriculture, acting in common counsel, the sum of $5,000,000 from the fund for national security and defense, put at my disposal by appropriation of Congress, and beg that you will be kind enough to advise with the Treasury Department, which I suppose will act through the Farm Loan Board in determining the character and extent of the aid to be given.

Cordially and sincerely yours,   [Woodrow Wilson]

CCL (WP, DLC).

To Newton Diehl Baker

My dear Mr. Secretary: [The White House] 26 July, 1918

I have your letter of the twenty-third telling me that Mr. Sargent is reported to be at British Headquarters in France with a commission to paint a war picture for preservation in the National Gallery. I appreciate the interest of such a picture, but for my own part I take very little stock in such things and, while of course any picture by Mr. Sargent would be of the highest value, I don't think it is worth our while to make any similar arrangement with him, and I think I read between the lines of your letter that that is your own judgment.

Cordially and faithfully yours,   Woodrow Wilson

TLS (Letterpress Books, WP, DLC).

To Frank Lyon Polk, with Enclosure

My dear Mr. Counselor: The White House 26 July, 1918

I think it very wise to issue the enclosed statement and am glad you are going to do it.

Cordially and sincerely yours,   Woodrow Wilson

TLS (SDR, RG 59, 893.51/1945, DNA).

ENCLOSURE

China declared war against Germany very largely because of the action of the United States. Therefore this Government has felt a special interest in the desire of China so to equip herself as to be of more specific assistance in the war against the Central Powers. Until the present time the engagements of the United States in preparing to exert effectively its strength in the European theatre of war has operated to prevent specific constructive steps to help China realize her desires. Recently, however, this Government felt that, because of the approach to Chinese territory of the scenes of disorder, a special effort should be made to place proper means at the disposal of China. Consequently, a number of American bankers, who had been interested in the past in making loans to China and who had had experience in the Orient, were called to Washington and asked to become interested in the matter. The bankers responded very promptly and an agreement has been reached between them and the Department of State which has the following salient features:

First: The formation of a group of American bankers to make a loan or loans and to consist of representatives from different parts of the country;

Second: An assurance on the part of the bankers that they will cooperate with the Government and follow the policies outlined by the Department of State;

Third: Submission of the names of the banks who will compose the group for the approval of the Department of State;

Fourth: Submission of the terms and conditions of any loan or loans for approval by the Department of State;

Fifth: Assurances that if the terms and conditions of the loan are accepted by this Government and by the Government to which the loan is made, in order to encourage and facilitate the free intercourse between American citizens and foreign states which is mutually advantageous the Government will be willing to aid in every way possible and to make prompt and vigorous representations, and to take every possible step to insure the execution of equitable contracts made in good faith by its citizens in foreign lands.

It is hoped that the American group will be associated with bankers of Great Britain, Japan and France. Negotiations are now in progress between the Government of the United States and those Governments which it is hoped will result in their cooperation and in the participation by the bankers of those countries in equal parts in any loan which may be made.

Beside the war-like conditions which confront China on her

northern and western borders, there is a further incentive to co-operate with all these Governments, because the war has created a community of interest between them and their citizens and those of other Governments and has broken down barriers which once have existed and has made easier the intercourse between them. It is hoped that if the project succeeds it will serve as an agency through which this community of interest and the consequent expansion of our mutual interests abroad may be adequately and properly expressed.

T MS (SDR, RG 59, 893.51/1945, DNA).

To Thomas Francis Egan[1]

My dear Mr. Egan: [The White House] 26 July, 1918

I am sincerely complimented by the suggestion you make in your letter of July nineteenth[2] in which you ask if I would be willing that the amalgamated Central Democratic Club and the Melrose Democratic Club should assume my name and be called the Wilson Democratic Club. Of course, I should be very much complimented, but may I not make this suggestion: They are working Democratic clubs I have no doubt, and might the impression not be created that they were preparing to work for my reelection? I should not like that impression to be made, and I respectfully suggest that some other name be considered.

Cordially and sincerely yours, Woodrow Wilson

TLS (Letterpress Books, WP, DLC).
[1] His letterhead describes him as a "Lecturer and Publicist" of New York.
[2] T. F. Egan to WW, July 19, 1918, TLS (WP, DLC).

To William Gibbs McAdoo

[The White House] 26 July, 1918

There is no danger of any other bill taking precedence of the Revenue Bill and you may be sure I shall plead for its passage at the earliest possible moment. I will also confer with the ship builders about the matter of your other telegram. I am delighted to hear that your rib[1] is all right and that you are really getting in shape. Don't come back until you have done so. With love from us all,

Woodrow Wilson

T telegram (Letterpress Books, WP, DLC).
[1] "My rib is well. Doctor here confident he can repair my vocal chords. . . ." WGM to WW, July 25, 1918, T telegram (WP, DLC).

From Edgar Rickard

Dear Mr. President: Washington July Twenty-Sixth *1918*

Secretary Houston has requested an expression of opinion as to the desirability of consulting the National Farmers' Advisory Council before submitting to you the joint suggestion of the Department of Agriculture and the Food Administration in regard to announcing a guaranteed wheat price for 1919. We discussed the matter with Secretary Houston this morning, and it seems wise to us to call the National Farmers' Advisory Council together at the earliest date possible, and secure their views; and I believe that this is also the conclusion of Secretary Houston who, I am informed, will personally present to you his views as well as ours, more in detail.

Faithfully yours,   Edgar Rickard

TLS (WP, DLC).

To Edgar Rickard

My dear Mr. Rickard: The White House 26 July, 1918

I quite agree with the Secretary of Agriculture that it would not be wise to fix the price of wheat for the next year without first having a conference with the National Farmers Advisory Council. No matter what the result, they would wish to be consulted, I am sure, and would feel aggrieved if they are not, besides which their counsel may be of capital importance to us. I hope that this will commend itself to your judgment and that you will see your way to arranging an early meeting with them.

Cordially and sincerely yours,   Woodrow Wilson

TLS (Hoover Archives, CSt-H).

To William Bauchop Wilson

My dear Mr. Secretary: The White House 26 July, 1918

Senator Thomas of Colorado came in to me yesterday very deeply concerned about labor matters and brought me, among other things, these enclosures[1] which of course represent a most unwarranted action and position on the part of H. W. Brown, who is trying by quotation from me to dragoon men into joining his organization.[2] I would be very much obliged if you would tell me if anything occurs to you that it would be wise to do.

The Senator was under the impression that the labor situation

in the country was growing worse and the number of strikes multiplying. Is that your own impression?

Cordially and sincerely yours,   Woodrow Wilson

TLS (received from Mary A. Strohecker).
    [1] They are missing.
    [2] Harvey Winfield Brown was business agent for the Newark, N. J., local of the
International Association of Machinists. For an explanation of what he was doing, see
WBW to WW, July 30, 1918.

To Josephus Daniels

My dear Daniels: [The White House] 26 July, 1918

I would like very soon to have a conference with you about shipbuilding wages, and write to suggest that if any changes in the
wage scale in the shipbuilding yards is under contemplation or
asked for, you would be kind enough to postpone the determination
of them until early next week, when I will have an opportunity to
see you and Mr. Hurley and the Secretary of Labor about the matter.

Cordially and faithfully yours,   Woodrow Wilson[1]

TLS (Letterpress Books, WP, DLC).
    [1] Wilson wrote the same letter, *mutatis mutandis*: WW to E. N. Hurley, July 26, 1918,
TLS (Letterpress Books, WP, DLC).

To Claude Kitchin

My dear Mr. Kitchin: [The White House] 26 July, 1918

I hope you will not think I am taking an undue liberty in sending
you the enclosed copy of a telegram[1] I have just received from the
Secretary of the Treasury and adding that every word of it seems
to me weighty with good counsel. I have no doubt, however, that
that will be your own judgment. I only want to keep all our wires
united in one system in order that we may pull together for the
earliest and best possible action.

Cordially and sincerely yours,   Woodrow Wilson[2]

TLS (Letterpress Books, WP, DLC).
    [1] That is, WGM to WW, July 25, 1918 (second telegram of that date).
    [2] Wilson sent the same letter, *mutatis mutandis*: WW to F. M. Simmons, July 26, 1918,
TLS (Letterpress Books, WP, DLC).

From Joseph Patrick Tumulty

Dear Governor: The White House 26 July 1918.

You smiled when I spoke to you about Al Smith,[1] candidate on
the Democratic ticket for election as Governor of New York. I think

you will be very much cheered as the days go on by the turn of the tide in favor of our Party in New York State. It will strengthen and influence opinion in our favor throughout the country. Mr. Roosevelt's secretary[2] handed to me today a letter from Edgar T. Brackett[3] who was the Republican leader in the New York State Senate, from which I have taken the following excerpts:

"I think, as I have always, that from the beginning Uncle Josephus has made good. Whether by your help, Frank Roosevelt's or the help of any one else, his department has come up to the scratch and done its work as it ought to be done. And I always resented the outrageous criticism on the part of certain interests that I believe were not without a sinister motive.

"The convention is in session today. I have not been down this morning, but the latest that came to me last night was that Al Smith was likely to be designated for Governor. If so, and this thing of a Whitman should be again nominated—which may the gods forfend—Smith ought to beat him and I believe will, if the Administration backs him up. He was long in the Assembly when I was in the Senate and he was in the last constitutional convention with me. I appreciate that he is a product of Tammany Hall, but he is a high-minded man, honest to the core, with an experience among the common people that has given him a wide and sympathizing view of affairs generally and in knowledge of the state affairs, I believe he is one of the best equipped men in either party today. He has a winning personality, something of 'a broth of a boy' style, can make a splendid speech, and if he should be elected, I believe would make a good governor. I am not trying to determine democratic policy, but I believe that the Administration can well afford to get behind him with every power of influence and money and elect him, and that, if it is done, it would result in a better feeling than has ever existed between the Administration and Tammany, and would result in Smith being one of the staunchest supporters of the Administration through thick and thin, Tammany or no Tammany. This is the way it strikes a decaying politician, up a very small tree in this edge of the woods."

I had the pleasure of hearing Smith make a speech over two or three years ago in New York. His references to you convinced me that back of them there was a deep-seated, affectionate admiration for you.   Sincerely yours,   J P Tumulty

TLS (WP, DLC).
   [1] The Democratic State Conference, meeting at Saratoga Springs on July 24, had named Alfred Emanuel Smith, at this time President of the New York City Board of Aldermen, as its candidate for Governor of New York. This action made Smith the leading candidate in the Democratic primary contest.
   [2] Renah F. Camalier, private secretary to Franklin D. Roosevelt.
   [3] Edgar Truman Brackett, lawyer of New York and Saratoga Springs; state senator of New York, 1895-1907, 1909-1912.

From Frank Lyon Polk, with Enclosures

My dear Mr. President: Washington July 26, 1918.

On the chance that you may not have seen this telegram from the Military Attache at Tokio,[1] I thought I had better send it over to you, as it is rather interesting, bearing on the Siberian situation. As you will notice they plan not only to send a division to Vladivostok, but also a division to Manchuria.

I also enclose a memorandum of my conversation with the Ambassador.[2] If there is any point you think I have not covered, it would be very easy to send for him and add it, as I feel reasonably certain we will not hear for several days.

Yours faithfully,   Frank L Polk

TLS (WP, DLC).
[1] Capt. Karl F. Baldwin.
[2] Wilson had talked with Polk for an hour, from 11:30 a.m. to 12:30 p.m. on July 25, and Polk of course reflected Wilson's opinions and thoughts in his subsequent conversation with Viscount Ishii.

E N C L O S U R E   I

Tokyo. July 23, 1918.

No. 74. In regard to proposition sending American and Japanese troops to Siberia, counter-proposal from Japan that she send troops to Vladivostok but reserve the right to send other troops elsewhere appears to represent the minimum offer of the present Ministry. If we insist upon original proposal present premier[1] will most likely resign and be followed by a man more radical and difficult for us to deal with. Foreign Minister[2] insists necessary to guard railroads in Manchuria.

Plans indicate 12th division would be used about Vladivostok and 8th division sent to Manchuria. Reserves have been notified to be ready for call but no troops have been moved to my knowledge. Ships have been requisitioned for use in case of necessity but further action depends upon pending negotiations.   Baldwin

T telegram (WP, DLC).
[1] That is, Count Masatake Terauchi.
[2] That is, Baron Shimpei Gotō.

E N C L O S U R E   I I

INTERVIEW WITH THE JAPANESE AMBASSADOR, July 25, 1918.[1]

I said that this Government quite understood the position of the Japanese Government and its motives, and this Government had no desire naturally to criticise or in any way interfere in their independence of action, but the acceptance of the Japanese Government was not an acceptance of our proposal but a new proposal. I enlarged on this and made it quite clear to him that we had suggested a small force and they had come back with a suggestion indefinite as to numbers, not only now, but as to future reinforcements. I said our proposal had primarily at heart the impression which would be made on the Russian mind, as it was believed they would receive a wrong impression unless we were very specific not only as to the number of troops that were being sent by all the Governments, but also that the Japanese forces would not be substantially more than all the Allies. This Government would have no objection to the Japanese sending a division, assuming by that they meant a division on peace footing, that is to say 10,000 to 12,000 men. I pointed out to him that his Government would have the high command and also more troops than all the other Governments. We felt that by sending troops in not only without any limitation as to number, but even indicating that more troops would be sent if the occasion demanded, the natural impression would be created in the Russian mind that this was an expedition which had more in view than merely assisting the Czechs. We felt very strongly that the number should be limited, and if later it appeared that this force was not adequate the question could be discussed and this Government would then be in a position to decide whether they would continue or whether they would withdraw, leaving the Japanese and the other Governments to proceed if they saw fit.

I laid particular stress on the question of supplies and financial aid, as I said that that had also influenced you in limiting the character of the expedition, as this Government could not possibly supply materials or money for an expedition of any size. We were committed to concentrating all our energies on the Western front and therefore it was absolutely out of the question for this country to supply material or money for anything but a very small expeditionary force. I said that as the Government had regarded this very modest program which it had proposed as the only wise and practicable program, the judgment of the Japanese Government that this program would not serve the purpose makes the Government reluctant to act at all.

I then asked him whether I had made myself perfectly clear. The Ambassador said he quite understood our point of view to be that we wanted the expedition limited and felt it was necessary to specify the numbers that were to go in, but he then argued the question as to whether this force could be of any real assistance. He said his General Staff did not think it would, and therefore had as a practical question said that more troops were necessary as a starter and more would have to follow.

He wanted to know whether it was our idea that the forces should not leave Vladivostok. I said that was a military question; that it was our understanding that they should go to that city for the purpose of releasing the Czechs for military movements in the West, but of course, I assumed that did not mean they were actually to stay in the city limits.

He spoke of the necessity of guarding all bridges and controlling the railroad to the north. I said of course I realized the Japanese were closer to the situation and possibly knew more about it, but the fact remained that the President and the Secretary of State, and the Secretary of War had decided on a plan, and if his Government did not think it worth while we would probably be unable to take part in a larger expedition.

He asked whether, assuming his Government was satisfied to send 12,000 men and the other Governments sent their contingents, it would be possible, if later on the question arose, to discuss reinforcements. I told him I had already tried to make that point clear, that of course if later on it should be reported that this force was not adequate to accomplish any results, the Government would discuss the question of sending reinforcements, and that we might agree and send reinforcements or disagree and withdraw.

I then called his attention to the proposed declaration and pointed out that the suggestion that the Japanese Government was anxious to "act in harmony with the Allies" might be inconsistent with our plan, as the Allies had very frequently expressed themselves as being in favor of a large expedition. I told him that if it were made clear that his Government meant by this to act in harmony with the Allies *as far as this particular proposal or expedition was concerned* that would be satisfactory. He said that was his understanding, but he would have this cleared up.

I also called his attention to the words "having regard at the same time to the special position of Japan," and said that it hardly seemed necessary to put that in, as the Lansing-Ishii agreement very clearly indicated our attitude toward Japan, and none of the European powers would question their interest, but putting it in might create difficulties in Russia in spite of their declaration of disinterestedness.

I said I also thought that in view of the fact that they would have the high command and a larger number of troops than any other power, such a declaration was unnecessary. He said he would communicate with his Government and let me know at once.

T MS (WP, DLC).

[1] FLP to R. S. Morris, July 27, 1918, T telegram (SDR, RG 59, 861.00/2424a, DNA), is a summary of this memorandum.

Lord Reading to David Lloyd George and Arthur James Balfour

Washington. July 26th, 1918.

Very Urgent. Personal and Secret.

For the Prime Minister and Mr Balfour.

The Japanese answer to the U.S.G. is regarded by the latter as a counter proposal. It is (a) that the Japanese should send more troops than the 7000 proposed—they talk of 15,000 at least—and (b) that they should not be restricted to the purpose mentioned in the President's proposal, which is that contained in the Aide Memoire sent to you, briefly, of assisting the Czecho-Slovaks.

As regards (a) I do not think there will be very serious opposition on the part of the United States Government, who will rely upon us and the French and the Italians to make with them a sufficient force to prevent the Japanese preponderating in numbers over Allies or at least to any substantial extent. Probably the full demand of the Japanese as to numbers will be somewhat limited as a result of the discussions now taking place, although they will send a larger number than the 7,000 proposed by the U.S.G.

As to (b) the proposal of the Japanese is more seriously viewed by the United States Government. I do not believe that latter will give way upon this point, and in the end the Japanese will probably accept the American formula. It is clear that the formula, which might be described as prescribing for the Allies the holding of the territory behind the Czecho-Slovaks whilst the latter make advances into the West of Siberia, is one which cannot literally be observed, and in truth, I gathered from a conversation of M. Jusserand with the President, reported to me by the former, that the President agrees that the formula cannot be interpreted literally. Nevertheless it must be remembered that the President dislikes having to take part in this military expedition, and that his military advisers support him in this view for other reasons than the President's. Consequently, if the Japanese insist on a formula giving them greater freedom of action, there is some danger of the President withdrawing from his proposals.

I studiously avoid expressing such views to Viscount Ishii as I am now presenting to you, and for reasons which will be apparent to you.

I have no doubt that in the end the Japanese will give way as regards (b) but there may be some delay caused by negotiation to and fro, which I am told here is not unusual in U. S. negotiations with the Japanese. I have again urged the necessity for immediate action but no step will be taken by the U.S.G. until an agreement has been reached with the Japanese.

The Japanese will in the end agree with the U. S. because they so seriously need material assistance from the U. S.

I am now proceeding to New York, as indicated to you yesterday, and shall be there till Monday night when I sail.

Please cable through Wiseman.

T telegram (Reading Papers, FO 800/225, PRO).

A Translation of a Telegram from Jean Jules Jusserand to Stéphen Jean Marie Pichon

Washington, no date,
received July 26, 1918.

No. 972. URGENT. (VERY CONFIDENTIAL)

I spoke to the President of the sentiments of affection and admiration which go out to his compatriots throughout France on account of their wonderful conduct and which is aroused by their heroism and their natural goodness. The two armies rival each other in spirit and valor, and each day we watch with pride the results of their common efforts. Mr. Wilson felicitates himself on this fraternity of arms, a proved case of suffering together, these victories gained in common which will in the future have the most pregnant consequences. He expressed the hope that, in spite of our advance being necessarily slowed, a catastrophe was not impossible for the Germans. Then

973. speaking again in the same terms about a subject which the Secretary of State had already discussed with me (my telegram No. 838), he said to me that:

"This is a point about which I would like to have your opinion. The moment is going to come when the Germans, being driven back or only stopped, will conclude that they have nothing to hope for on the western front. They will then make the most tempting offers of peace—Belgium entirely free, Alsace-Lorraine restored in its entirety, concessions to Italy, etc. Without making precise terms in one sense or another, they will pass by the East in silence. The temptation will be enormous. If we succumb to it, we are lost. Keeping their hands free, the Germans will recover in the East much more than they will have given up in Alsace-Lorraine.

"The temptation will be great above all and perfectly understandable for a country which has suffered as much as yours.

974. "The [group missing] surely understands the extreme gravity of the danger, but what will public opinion say and will it permit, in the presence of such proposals and in spite of growing American aid, the continuation of such hard efforts?"

I have no reason to doubt it, I reply, but I will convey your observations to my government which will view them with satisfaction as, I am sure, new proof of your intention to continue the war to complete victory and which has, I believe, no worry about the state of public opinion.

I spoke again in this connection of the utility in this order of ideas of the reconstitution of the eastern front. "Utility incontestable, in my eyes," Mr. Wilson replied, "but an absolute impossibility." He then repeated the same arguments which are familiar to you. "I remain convinced that it is on the western front that we must concentrate our efforts and that all questions will be settled there by a single blow provided we persevere to the necessary extent."   Jusserand.

T telegram (État-Major, L'Armée de Terre, Service Historique, 6 N 53, FMD-Ar).

A Translation of a Telegram from Henri Bergson to Stéphen Jean Marie Pichon

Washington, no date [July 26]
received July 27, 1918.

979. URGENT. For the Minister on behalf of Mr. Bergson.

The intention announced by President Wilson to declare publicly that he would do only the minimum in order to succor the Czechs seemed to me so unfortunate that I believed that I had to undertake, independent of our Ambassador, a special démarche with him. In a long interview yesterday, I insisted on the danger that he would create in tying his hands for the future. Returning to the heart of the matter, I explained again how all the American effort was in danger of being neutralized by the resources which the Germans could derive from Russia, how the thirty-six divisions which they still have there and which they begin to transfer to our front would counterbalance a whole year of American efforts, how schools for Ukrainian and Finnish officers recently established in Germany indicate a general project to reorganize the Russian military forces to the benefit of the Germans, how one could not understand [980] why we should not do everything possible in order to prevent that which, once accomplished, would lead to such a prolongation of the war. I added that, in announcing publicly a fixed intention of not going beyond a certain point, Mr. Wilson has relieved the Germans of all worry about the East, and that we must, on the contrary, create for them the largest number of preoccupations as possible in order to cause them to disperse their efforts as far as possible. Finally, I spoke of the depressing effect that this declaration could have in France and England. But I ran into most vigorous resistance and a resolution [group passed] reiterated and pressing incidents have not been able to shake him. I asked myself if the attitude of the Japanese could not be the principal cause. From the beginning the President has seemed loath to make, seriously, an appeal to the yellow people who inspire here mistrust and fear. But here, after waiting three weeks for their response, we have the Japanese asking for a considerable quantity of coal, steel, etc. and important financial help. In a pinch, says Mr. Wilson, one could give them money but it is impossible to [981] furnish the rest to them (the provisions of the United States do not suffice for the needs of the western front), and it will be so at least for another year. Besides, the success achieved these days by French soldiers with the assistance of the Americans seems to have confirmed Mr. Wilson in the hope of obtaining a rapid and radical solution on the western front and in the conviction also that it is necessary to concentrate all his effort there. Thus present circumstances seem to him to support his arguments in the sense of his reluctance [répugnances] and of his hope. He wishes to seize the moment in order to bind himself by a public declaration. But events will probably be too powerful. If the Japanese really need what they ask for, there are perhaps insurmountable difficulties in acting in a grand way at once. But our action could develop, and no doubt circumstances could render such development necessary.

Jusserand.

T telegram (État-Major, L'Armée de Terre, Service Historique, 4 N 46, FMD-Ar).

From Robert Russa Moton

Tuskegee Institute,
Dear Mr. President: Alabama July 27, 1918

I am writing to thank you for the wise, strong, frank, patriotic statement on mob violence which appeared in the daily papers yesterday.

You can hardly realize how much this will mean to the colored people. To those who have sought in an unselfish way to guide the race along channels of rational thought and patriotic action, your remarkable statement will be a source of much encouragement and hope.   Yours very truly,   [R. R. Moton]

No rational person white or black in North or South could take exception to a single sentence

CCL (R. R. Moton Papers, ATT).

From William Julius Harris

My dear Mr. President: Atlanta, Georgia, July 27, 1918.

I have been speaking daily for several weeks and feel confident that I will receive sixty per cent. of the total vote of the State, but, under our Primary Law, it is possible, with several candidates in the race, for Senator Hardwick to be nominated, although he receives only twenty per cent. of the total vote.[1] If I could have the race between only Senator Hardwick and myself, I would not lose over fifteen counties of the one hundred and fifty-two counties in the State. I feel absolutely confident of this.

There are certain difficulties in my way, which I feel you should know. Major Cohen has made a political machine of the Atlanta Journal and its employees, and Clark Howell has done almost as bad with the Constitution. The Constitution and the Journal have ceased entirely any fight on Hardwick. These two papers are practically the only daily papers read in all of North Georgia and while, editorially, they have taken no stand, in their news columns they are doing everything within their power to confuse the peoples' mind in regard to the Senatorial race and keep them from centering on me, by making it appear that Howard is speaking to large crowds in South Georgia when, as a matter of fact, he rarely has as many as one hundred to hear him. There are thousands of people in the State who are friendly to my candidacy and are loyal to the administration, but they wish to vote for the strongest man to defeat Hardwick and the Atlanta papers try to make it appear that Howard is conducting a wonderful campaign, and that Howard is as much the Administration's candidate as I am. In South Georgia, and there are sufficient votes to nominate in what we call South of Macon— the papers are friendly to me and the conditions are all that we could ask, except in less than a dozen counties. Mr. Howard is devoting most of his speeches to making false statements about me and my work on the Trade Commission. He has resorted to every artifice of the trained demagogue and the ward politician. He has a number of times brought Mr. Hurley's name into the campaign because of my relations with him and in his speeches, where there are Watson[2] followers, he has stated that Hurley was one of the high priests in the Catholic Church; that he was contributing $25,000.00 to my campaign, and trying to create the impression that I am running in the interest of the Catholics. Mr. Howard charges, among other things, that I worried you to death all last year with trying to get your endorsement for the Senate and interfered with your duties and has, time and again, charged that I sent five men to Washington to get you to endorse me, and that you declined. Although I deny them, he continues to make the charges. I have not indulged in mudslinging and have conducted my campaign on a high plane when he was daily resorting to his low methods. The Atlanta Journal daily gives from one to three columns to his speeches making false statements about me, which the paper knows are false.

Major Cohen will never forgive you for not allowing him to dictate who shall be United States Senator, so as to help re-elect Senator Hoke Smith to the Senate. Clark Howell is equally as disappointed in not being able to select the Senator from his faction. They both resent the fact that my election will mean that the National Administration will have the full cooperation of the party in Georgia without the assistance of the Journal or the Constitution.

Clark Howell sent me a copy of a letter he had written you[3] and it displeased me very much, as he has done everything he could to confuse the situation instead of to help. He is on record in a public statement as saying that he will unreservedly support for the Senate any one you endorse. He realizes that the chances are ten to one that I will be elected and that this condition was brought about not by his assistance, but over his opposition. At the same time he does not wish Howard elected because of his close relations to Hoke Smith. I sincerely hope that you may not commit yourself to Clark Howell either way. If you should not endorse me, the letter would be used by him to injure me. He would stop short of nothing in order to bring about my defeat if he could, except that it might elect Howard.

On account of the Primary Law, which would enable Hardwick, as a minority candidate, to be elected and receive not more than twenty per cent. of the votes of the State, and as the issue is loyalty to the Government and to our Commander-in-Chief, it seems to me absolutely necessary that you let the people of Georgia know the importance of the election of a Senator and that you hope the loyal vote will not be divided; that you endorse my candidacy as the one who has developed the most strength to defeat Hardwick, and express the hope that Mr. Howard and the other candidates may withdraw.

It had not been my purpose to annoy you in reference to the Senatorial situation and I would not have done so had it not been for the letter written you by Mr. Clark Howell. Any message you may wish to deliver to the people of Georgia, I sincerely hope may not be addressed through Mr. Clark Howell or Major Cohen. We need the friendship of the Journal and the Constitution, but the editors have acted so badly that I hope they will not be allowed to gain any prestige in this matter. We need their cooperation and, when you express your choice, they will support me, as they will be afraid of public sentiment if they do not.

I suppose you have seen the impartial poll of the Editors, Chairmen of the Democratic County Committees, and the one thousand Fish and Game Wardens from every Militia District in the State. This impartial poll shows that I am stronger than Mr. Howard in nine-tenths of the counties. Members of the Legislature in three-fourths of the counties of the State inform me that I shall carry their counties.

In Mr. Howard's letter to you,[4] when he informs you that he will make the race for the Senate, he states that if at any time his candidacy might make possible Hardwick's election, he will withdraw. If you would be willing to write him that there is danger of this at this time and request him to withdraw and express the hope that the others might do so and leave the race to Senator Hardwick and myself, Mr. Howard would withdraw at once. In fact, I believe he would be more than pleased to receive such a letter, so as to give him an excuse for retiring.

On account of the attitude of the Atlanta papers, unless you do express your choice, they are going to do everything within their power to confuse the issue, which might result in Hardwick's election.

I know it is your policy not to take part as between two loyal candidates, but Mr. Howard and his friends can no longer be considered loyal, as they are cooperating with Hardwick to bring about my defeat. There is absolutely no doubt of this.

With assurances of high regard, I am,

Most sincerely yours,   Wm J. Harris

TLS (WP, DLC).
    [1] Under Georgia's long-standing county-unit system, enacted into law by the Neill Primary Act of 1917, a candidate for United States senator, governor, or other elected state office who received the largest popular vote in a county in a party primary was to be considered to have carried the county and be entitled to its unit votes (that is, two votes for every representative which the county had in the lower house of the General Assembly) in the party's state convention. See Albert Berry Saye, *A Constitutional History of Georgia, 1732-1968* (Athens, Ga., 1970), pp. 356-59, 412-14.
    [2] That is, Thomas E. Watson.
    [3] That is, C. Howell to WW, July 24, 1918.
    [4] The letter is missing, but see WW to W. S. Howard, April 12, 1918, n. 2, and WW to W. S. Howard, April 20, 1918, n. 1, both in Vol. 47.

From Newton Diehl Baker

My dear Mr. President: Washington. July 28, 1918.

I enclose a letter from Senator Chamberlain,[1] to which I have not as yet replied beyond a formal acknowledgment.

When the plan for our 80-division program is taken up there will undoubtedly be a discussion of some phase of universal service, and I would like to have the benefit of your judgment and wishes before formulating a policy on the subject. I think the General Staff of the Army, including General March, are disposed to feel that it would be a helpful thing to bring out the young men of the country within the limits of two years below the minimum draft age for annual encampments and training for a period of four or five weeks. This would mean that in the Summer-time boys of 17 and 18 (if the minimum draft age is fixed at 19) would be gathered into encampments scattered around over the country and given the elements of military drill and some experience in camp life. Each young man would thus have two periods of, say, five weeks in two years. It would add something to their availability to military service, make it easier to gather them into actual training camps later, if necessary, and would have the very great social value of a substantially universal medical inspection of the youth of the country, with consequent advice and correction of minor faults of health. Such a plan would not be costly and ought not, I believe, to agitate the opponents of universal service. It would not, of course, satisfy the advocates of universal service, but would be accepted by them as a beginning upon which they could later build.

I have stated the General Staff position without indicating my own belief, which, so far as I have thought it out, is about as follows: That the General Staff plan would be a good plan during the period of the present war, if it could certainly be controlled and not made a permanent military policy. After this war is over, assuming its favorable termination with the principles of an unmilitarized world, I believe we ought to encourage and enlarge military training in colleges, technical schools and high schools, with the view to having at all times in the country a body of men from whom officers can be rapidly made, and a sprinkling of men throughout the country to whom the discipline of military life is familiar, so that the sanitary necessities of army life will be known should another mobilization of the military strength of the nation be necessary. I am afraid, however, that if we were to undertake the General Staff plan at this time, without very definite statements that it was a policy adopted for this war only, it would have a serious effect both at home and abroad, first as an evidence of our uncertainty as to the issue of the present war and, second, as to the reality of our belief in the possibility of such international arrangements as would make permanent militarization unnecessary.

Respectfully yours,   Newton D. Baker

TLS (WP, DLC).
¹ G. E. Chamberlain to NDB, July 17, 1918, TLS (WP, DLC).

To Frank Lyon Polk

My dear Mr. Counselor: The White House 29 July, 1918

I do not feel that I can adequately reply to this very gratifying and interesting communication from the President of Salvador,¹ but I would be very much obliged if you would have our representatives in Salvador convey to President Melendez the following message:

"Your Excellency's very generous letter of the fourth of July has just been placed in my hands and I am availing myself of the earliest opportunity of expressing to you the very deep appreciation with which it was received and read. It is delightful to feel that a mutual understanding is being established among the nations of the Americas which promises to constitute a genuine and permanent foundation of friendship, and I beg Your Excellency to believe that the speech to the Mexican editors,² to which you so kindly refer, came without premeditation from my very heart. I wish you also to know that it expressed something very much more than my own personal feeling and policy, for I believe that it expressed the real attitude of the people of the United States and the policy which they would always wish to see their Government adopt and pursue. I join with you in looking forward with the highest hope and confidence to such a union of minds and purpose in America as will lead to abiding peace and friendly cooperation."³

Cordially and sincerely yours,   Woodrow Wilson

TLS (SDR, RG 59, 710.11/375, DNA).
¹ C. Meléndez to WW, July 4, 1918, TLS (SDR, RG 59, 710.11/375, DNA).
² It is printed at June 7, 1918, Vol. 48.
³ This was sent as FLP to F. D. Arnold, July 31, 1918, T telegram (SDR, RG 59, 710.11/375, DNA).

To Charles Sumner Hamlin¹

My dear Mr. Hamlin,   The White House. 29 July, 1918.

I know Mayor Ole Hanson so well and know him to have so unusual a spirit and point of view in public matters and so unusual a knowledge of the public interest, that I am taking the liberty of writing this line to say that I sincerely hope that it will prove possible for the Capital Issues Committee to meet his wishes with regard to the work he wishes to see the city of Seattle undertake.[2] I believe in what he proposes in principle and feel sure that it can be done without unjust prejudice to private interests.

Faithfully Yours,   Woodrow Wilson

WWTLS (C. S. Hamlin Papers, DLC).
  [1] He was at this time chairman of the Capital Issues Committee of the War Finance Corporation, as well as a member of the Federal Reserve Board.
  [2] The City of Seattle had petitioned the Capital Issues Committee to approve the issue of $5,500,000 of municipal bonds to construct a new hydroelectric plant. The plant was to be situated on the Skagit River about 110 miles from Seattle. The project is described in detail in C. S. Hamlin, "In the matter of the petition of the Mayor of Seattle . . . ," CC MS, enclosed in C. S. Hamlin to WW, July 31, 1918, TLS (WP, DLC).

From Charles Sumner Hamlin

Confidential.

Dear Mr. President: Washington July 29, 1918.

I have just received your note of July 29th and hasten to reply that I concur fully in what you say. I spent yesterday almost continuously from 8 A.M. to 7 P.M. going over the record and, in my opinion, there is today in Seattle a very serious, critical condition as regards the supply of power.

Speaking personally, I feel that that [*sic*] the application of the Mayor should be granted on a showing that the proposed project is practical as to time, foundations, etc. Personally, also, I realize the vital importance, and am sure I shall be joined in this feeling by my associates, of doing everything to preserve a municipal plant, such as this, and permitting it to develop along proper lines.

In this case there is some embarrassment from the fact that Mr. Taylor,[1] the engineer appointed by the San Francisco district committee of the Capital Issues Committee, and Major Sever,[2] representing the Power Administration of the War Industries Board, have both reported against the advisability of permitting the Seattle company to enter into this new development during the course of the war. After a careful study of their reports, without considering the evidence offered by the City of Seattle, I am perfectly satisfied personally that, notwithstanding their conclusions, the facts stated in their records show, as I have stated, a serious, critical situation, demanding immediate attention and fully warranting approval of the application of the city.

I have called a conference of engineers for Wednesday morning, representing the War Industries Board, the City of Seattle and the

Stone & Webster Company, the principal competitors of the Seattle company in that district, and I hope that out of this we shall be able to reach an adjustment of the matter which will give the City of Seattle an opportunity to do what it desires. I am at work writing a memorandum, stating my views in full, for submission to the Capital Issues Committee, and I will send a copy of this to you as soon as it can be written out, I hope by tomorrow.

In this connection, may I suggest to you that you request Mr. Baruch, of the War Industries Board, when Major Sever's report is considered by that board, or by Mr. Darlington,[3] the head of its Power Administration, to invite the Capital Issues Committee to attend the meeting of the War Industries Board, in order that there may be a free interchange of views on this question. You will understand that the War Industries Board, through its Power Administration, has, I think, power to forbid this development, no matter what the opinion of the Capital Issues Committee may be; but I feel quite confident that a discussion of the whole question with men of the standing of the War Industries Board, will result in a decision that the Mayor should be permitted to proceed with his project.

Before Secretary McAdoo left I wrote him a letter expressing the hope that some member of the Capital Issues Committee might be appointed on the War Industries Board, because of the fact that we frequently have questions where the mutual jurisdiction apparently overlaps, and that such an appointment would prevent our being at cross purposes. Mr. Baruch replied that this was not practicable, but that possibly, at some future date, some representative from the Treasury might be appointed to this board. I think, however, that a suggestion from you that, in this particular case, no action should be taken on the report of Major Sever without a full conference with our committee, would accomplish the desired result.

There is another matter in this connection on which I want to write you briefly. You may remember, sometime ago, Mayor Hanson charged that the manager at Seattle of the branch bank of the Federal Reserve Bank of San Francisco[4] had accused him of being disloyal. I think he wrote you and that you forwarded the letter to Governor Harding,[5] who sent the letter to the Federal Reserve Bank of San Francisco. Later, Mr. Elliott,[6] the assistant Federal Reserve agent,—I believe on June 22d—replied to Governor Harding that deputy Governor Calkins[7] of the San Francisco Bank was convinced that this manager had said nothing reflecting on the patriotism of Mayor Hanson. I find, however, in the record, that there was a statement sent to Governor Lynch[8] of the San Francisco Bank to the effect that the three men coming to San Francisco, of whom one was Mayor Hanson, "possess the minimum amount of patriotism and I think they should be curbed." Mr. Elliott in his letter to Governor Harding, stating that nothing had been said reflecting on the patriotism of the Mayor, did refer to a letter sent by the manager, but said that it expressed a confidential opinion and that Mayor Hanson had learned its contents, and that there was some leak at the bank which the Secret Service should investigate. Governor Harding, however, to my mind, was fully justified in writing, as I believe he did to you,⁹ that, in view of Mr. Elliott's letter, no statement had been made reflecting on the patriotism of Mayor Hanson. As a fact, however, as I have stated, there was such a letter.

The entire record of this case, including the above letters, were sent to the Senate last week, in response to a resolution. My recollection is that, based upon Governor Harding's letter, you wrote or telegraphed the Mayor that his patriotism had not been questioned.¹⁰ I thought I would let you know these facts as, undoubtedly, Mayor Hanson will call the manager of the branch bank to account for what he wrote.   Very sincerely yours,   C S Hamlin

TLS (WP, DLC).
  ¹ He cannot be further identified.
  ² Maj. George Francis Sever.
  ³ Frederick Darlington.
  ⁴ Clifford John Shepherd.
  ⁵ O. Hanson to WW, June 17, 1918, T telegram (WP, DLC); WW to W. P. G. Harding, June 18, 1918, TLS (Letterpress Books, WP, DLC).
  ⁶ That is, Edward Graham Elliott.
  ⁷ John Uberto Calkins.
  ⁸ James Kennedy Lynch.
  ⁹ W. P. G. Harding to WW, June 22, 1918, TLS (WP, DLC). Harding quotes the text of Elliott's telegram of the same date.
  ¹⁰ WW to O. Hanson, June 24, 1918, TLS (Letterpress Books, WP, DLC).

To Bernard Mannes Baruch

My dear Baruch: [The White House] 29 July, 1918

I have become greatly interested in the question now before the Capital Issues Committee of the War Finance Corporation as to whether the City of Seattle is to be permitted to secure the capital necessary to undertake very essential municipal work. There are a great many influences working against the city administration, with which I for one have have [sic] no sympathy whatever. Your engineer, Major Sever, has, I am told, reported adversely to the project. I write now to beg that you will not accept his adverse judgment before going into the matter very fully. When Major Sever's report is considered by the War Industries Board, or by Mr. Darlington, the head of the Power Administration, I would be very much obliged if you would invite the Capital Issues Committee to attend the meeting and would yourself be present, in order that there might be a complete interchange of views on this question. My own very definite judgment is that the city should be allowed to do what that peculiarly fine fellow, Ole Hanson, is so eager to have it undertake, and I have gone into the matter sufficiently to believe not only that it can be done with equity to all concerned, but that it is of the highest importance. We must do nothing unfair to Stone and Webster, but we must see to it that they don't tighten the grip of their monopoly.

Always
Cordially and faithfully yours,   [Woodrow Wilson]

CCL (WP, DLC).

To Charles Richard Crane

My dear Friend: [The White House] 29 July, 1918

Your letter of July twenty-third has comforted me greatly. I have to do some very lonely thinking about the Russian business, and to have any assurance from you that, on the whole, I am handling the thing as promptly and as wisely as the circumstances permit gives me the deepest comfort.

Cordially and sincerely yours,   Woodrow Wilson

TLS (Letterpress Books, WP, DLC).

To James Gray McAllister[1]

My dear Doctor McAllister: [The White House] 29 July, 1918

Your letter of July twenty-fifth[2] gave me a great deal of pleasure, and it was certainly very thoughtful of you to repeat to me the interesting conversation you heard between your youngsters. We are looking forward with a great deal of interest to hearing you when you come to the Central Presbyterian Church here. We are sticking it out through the summer because there does not seem to be any public business which I can transact from a distance. One of the compensations will be that we shall have the pleasure of seeing you again.

Cordially and sincerely yours,   Woodrow Wilson

TLS (Letterpress Books, WP, DLC).
[1] At this time Professor of Bible Introduction, English Bible, and Biblical Theology at the Louisville Presbyterian Theological Seminary.
[2] It is missing.

To John R. Mott

My dear Mott: The White House 29 July, 1918

Thank you warmly for your carefully considered letter about the personnel of the Russian Mission. You may be sure it will be very useful to me.

Pardon unavoidable haste.

Cordially and faithfully yours,   Woodrow Wilson

TLS (J. R. Mott Coll., CtY-D).

To Ethel Morgan Lyle Wyatt[1]

My dear Madam: [The White House] 29 July, 1918

I am very much touched that you should have had the generous thought of naming your son, who was born on the Fourth of July, after me, and I beg that you will accept my warm assurances of gratification which such an act of friendship causes me.[2]

I am also very much complimented that you should ask me to be one of the lad's godfathers. I feel constrained to say that I cannot do that, because I feel that if one undertakes that very sacred relationship, he ought to place himself in a position to fulfill the responsibilities of it, and that is manifestly in this case impossible. I know that you will appreciate my scruple in this matter and will believe that my declining to be the lad's godfather does not in the least subtract from my deep appreciation of your generosity.

Sincerely yours,   Woodrow Wilson

TLS (Letterpress Books, WP, DLC).
    [1] Mrs. Harvey Lyle Wyatt, who lived at Milbourne Lodge in Esher, England.
    [2] Wilson was responding to Ethel M. L. Wyatt to WW, July 7, 1918, ALS (WP, DLC). The son was named Woodrow Lyle Wyatt. He was later a Labour M.P.

From Jean Jules Jusserand

Dear Mr. President   Washington July 29. 1918

I had not failed to cable to my Governt. a summary of our conversation of Wednesday last, and especially of what you said concerning the tempting offers of a free Belgium, Alsace restituted, etc., which the Germans are sure to make, the moment they find their hopes of a solution on the Western front shattered. They will propose all sort of advantages there, and be silent on Eastern Europe, counting on its possibilities to more than recoup themselves. If we were so imprudent as to listen to offers which years of sufferings might cause to appear tempting, we should be lost.

I answered, if you remember, that I felt no doubts; that, in spite of all trials, neither the French Governt. nor the French people would yield to any such temptation, for the reason that we do not fight for a gain but for a cause.

My Government's, answer, just received, is a confirmation, pure and simple, of what I said. Mr. Pichon's cable reads: "I have been most favorably impressed by the passage of your telegram in which you say that, according to the settled views of the President, a peace leaving to Germany a free hand in Russia, would be for us all a real defeat. I have shown your telegr. to Mr. Clemenceau, who joins me in asking you to inform the President that we are in complete accord with him on this point. Tell him, please, that he may entirely depend on our resolution. We, and with us all the French statesmen, would consider that to abandon Russia to Germany would be tantamount to losing the war. Whatever happens, we shall not change. No doubt is possible concerning the state of mind of the French people as to this. We believe moreover that the British Governt. entertains similar dispositions."

In the rest of the same telegram due praise is given to the fine conduct of the American troops, resulting in a fraternity of arms, the consequences of which will be both happy and lasting.

I had taken the liberty of stating to you, Mr. President, on the same occasion that though the contemplated action in Siberia must needs be of limited scope, it would, it seems, be advantageous not to state this too clearly, but keep the Germans guessing. They might feel anxious, and anxiety is not a force. I read in to-day's papers an extract from the "Volkszeitung" of Cologne, showing that they begin to be seriously anxious indeed as to Siberia and that, with their congenital incapacity to understand in others a feeling they are unable to experience, namely disinterestedness, they wonder what advantages America may have reserved for herself in the East. It could only do them good, as I think, that they should continue guessing.

Believe me, dear Mr. President

Very respectfully and sincerely yours   Jusserand

ALS (WP, DLC).

From Claude Kitchin

My dear Mr. President: Washington, D. C. July 29, 1918.

I wish to acknowledge receipt of your letter of July 26th, enclosing copy of a telegram from Mr. McAdoo to you, under date of July 25th.

I entirely agree with Mr. McAdoo in what he says.

The Committee hopes to be able to report the bill by the time the recess agreement terminates, that is, by August 19th, and at once to begin its consideration in the House. I wish to assure you that the Committee will make every effort to do this. In my opinion, the bill will be ready to be reported to the House by August 19th.

Cordially yours,   Claude Kitchin

TLS (WP, DLC).

From Lord Reading

My dear Mr President,   New York July 29/18

As I leave the United States for my visit to England I am filled with admiration for the splendid part your forces are taking in the war and I think of the gratification their conduct must afford you. I am permitting myself the luxury of expressing this thought to you who have given us this most valuable help when we stood so much in need of it.

I am, my dear Mr President

Yours very sincerely   Reading.

ALS (WP, DLC).

From George Foster Peabody

Dear Mr President,   Saratoga Springs New York July 29th 1918

One need never doubt your capacity to do effectively the thing you decide upon. I must thank you for the noble and heart-searching address to your fellow countrymen which is bound to prove of very great service in furthering the tremendous advance of real democracy which the world has begun under your inspiring and heartening leadership. It thrills one to hear continuingly the echoes of the response made by the simple people—so many "still in economic serfdom"—in Russia China Italy Austria France and England "to the words of President Wilson." Again throughout your own country there will more widely and deeply resound words of hope because of this clear statement of the conditions governing "the reign of law, based upon the consent of the governed and sustained by the organized opinion of mankind"

I am with every grateful regard

Very respectfully yours   George Foster Peabody

ALS (WP, DLC).

Joseph Patrick Tumulty to Frank Lyon Polk

My dear Mr. Polk: The White House July 29, 1918.

The President asks if you will not have the following reply sent to the accompanying message:[1]

"Your telegram sent on July twenty-eighth has met with a very hearty response in my own heart and I am sure will meet with an equally warm response in the hearts of everybody in the United States. We know the deep waters of suffering through which Serbia has passed and our sympathies not only, but our profound friendship and an eager desire to help, follows your courageous people throughout every stage of the present tragical course of the war. I am sure that justice to Serbia stands at the very top of any programme of justice in the thoughts of every thinking and patriotic man in the United States. Please accept my warm personal greetings. Woodrow Wilson."   Sincerely yours,   J P Tumulty

TLS (SDR, RG 59, 763.72/10860, DNA).
   [1] N. P. Pašić to WW, July 28, 1918, T telegram (SDR, RG 59, 763.72/10860, DNA). This was a plea on behalf of the Serbians, Croatians, and Slovenes in Austria-Hungary on the fourth anniversary of the outbreak of the war.

Tasker Howard Bliss to Peyton Conway March

Versailles. July 29th [1918]

Number 162 Secret.

For the Chief of Staff.

In third paragraph of your 73[1] occurs the following two sentences "It regards the Italian front as closely coordinated with the western front, however, and is willing to divert a portion of its military forces from France to Italy if it is the judgment and wishes of the Supreme Command that it should do so. It wishes to defer to the decision of the Commander in Chief in this matter, as it would wish to defer to all others." The words "Supreme Command" are of importance in connection with the following. The convention of Doullens on March 26th gave General Foch certain consulting and coordinating powers but without specific power to issue orders to enforce coordination. This led to friction and resulted in the convention of Beauvais on April 3rd in which specific powers were given to General Foch to issue orders necessary to carry out his plans. Neither the convention of Doullens nor that of Beauvais gave any powers in respect to the Italian Front. The Supreme War Council in session at Abbeville May 2 and 3 vested in General Foch over the Italian front the powers of the Doullens convention namely consulting and coordinating powers. But the Italian Government refused to allow him any power of command on the Italian front until there should be Allied armies operating in Italy in the same sense as in France. There are now Allied troops in Italy but they are amalgamated with the Italian army and do not form separate Allied Armies as in France. The words "Supreme Command" are the words habitually used by the Italians designated for their Commander in Chief. But I assume that those words as used in your number 73 mean General Foch the Allied Commander in Chief in France where he has full powers as such. The Italian section here has submitted a proposition coming from General Diaz for a possible reenforcement of the Italian Army by the transfer of at least 20 divisions from France to Italy including several American divisions but exact number not stated. On the above assumption I have objected to its consideration until it should be approved and urged by General Foch after necessary consultation with General Pershing. I have stated that Government of the United States would not even then consider a proposition for diverting American troops now in France to Italy under any other conditions. If I am right I recommend that Italian Ambassador be informed that the words "Supreme Command" in your number 73 do not mean "Commando Supreme" but mean General Foch the Inter-Allied Commander-in-Chief in France. This is important though it may not appear so.   Bliss

TC telegram (WDR, RG 407, World War I Cablegrams, DNA).
    ¹ P. C. March to T. H. Bliss, No. 73, July 22, 1918, "Strictly Confidential. Rush," TC telegram (WDR, RG 407, World War I Cablegrams, DNA). This telegram embodied the text of Wilson's aide-mémoire printed as an Enclosure with WW to FLP, July 17, 1918, Vol. 48. The telegram to Bliss ended as follows: "The foregoing is furnished you for your guidance in dealing with such military international questions as involve the United States."

A Translation of a Telegram from Jean Jules Jusserand to the Foreign Ministry

Washington, 29 July [1918].

No. 1004. URGENT. In the course of the conversation which I have just had with the President I talked with him particularly about the Siberian question.

He told me that the Japanese response to the urgent American counterproposition had not yet arrived. He has expressed himself on the first offers of Japan as had the Acting Secretary of State to me, showing the same aversion to accept the transformation of his limited project into a virtually unlimited enterprise. "We naturally would not know how," he said, "to pronounce an interdiction of action vis-à-vis Japan, any more than for other countries; but that does not take into account the aid for which we have greater need elsewhere."

He believes that the response will be inspired by domestic political considerations, which will enable the [Japanese] general staff to accept his views.

I asked him if he had thought in terms of publishing a proclamation of disinterestedness. He replied, "Yes, but only in general terms," and that he would think more about it. He energetically blames the Japanese draft for its allusions to interests in the neighborhood of Japan. Nothing could cause a more unfavorable impression among the Russian people, and this is what Mr. Wilson wishes above all to avoid. I spoke also about the dispatch of doctors, medicines, and supplies being expedited by the American Red Cross in order to succor the wounded Czechs and Russian refugees who must arrive in the near future at Vladivostok and to extend his action where the need will exist.

Mr. Wilson told me that it would be like an advance guard of the projected economic commission. All preliminary steps are now being taken so that, when agreement is reached, this commission, in which the Red Cross will also have an important role to play, can start right in.   Jusserand

T telegram (État-Major, L'Armée de Terre, Service Historique, 4 N 46, FMD-Ar).

From the Diary of Josephus Daniels

July Monday 29 1918

P. A. Davison[1] wanted to send a mission to Siberia to help the Russians, but wanted to cross no wires with the plans of the President.

(WW: "It would be a Republican mission and I am preparing large plans which will include YMCA work[."])

[1] That is, Henry Pomeroy Davison.

To John Palmer Gavit

My dear Gavit: [The White House] 30 July, 1918

I am ashamed to have taken so long to reread the essays contained in my little volume, "An Old Master,"[1] but I don't know anything harder than reading my own stuff when it is cold. At last I have read these essays, however, and I have the distinct judgment that it would not be wise at this time to republish either the essay entitled, "The Character of Democracy in the United States,"[2] or the one entitled, "Government Under the Constitution."[3] Circumstances have thrown many new lights upon the subjects of these essays since they were written, and while I still think they were true and valid judgments at the time I wrote them, I would alter the perspective very materially if I were to write them now. If they were republished at this time, people would not realize even if the dates were given just when they were written and might accept some opinions in them as indicating my present attitude, when they do not. I hope, therefore, that the house will postpone the republication of this particular volume.

I am very much interested to see that you are with Harper & Brothers.

Cordially and sincerely yours,   Woodrow Wilson

TLS (Letterpress Books, WP, DLC).
 [1] Wilson was replying to J. P. Gavit to WW, July 9, 1918, TLS (WP, DLC).
 [2] Printed at May 10, 1889, Vol. 6.
 [3] Printed at June 26, 1893, Vol. 8.

To Newton Diehl Baker

My dear Mr. Secretary: The White House 30 July, 1918

I have read with a great deal of interest your letter about Senator Chamberlain's desire to take early action about a plan for universal military training, and hasten to say that I agree with your own judgment in the matter, only I go a little further. I think we are doing now just as much as we ought to do and that *any* plan of this sort, even the modest plan now proposed by the General Staff, must be declined in the interest of economy of effort and efficiency.

Cordially and faithfully yours,   Woodrow Wilson

TLS (N. D. Baker Papers, DLC).

From John Franklin Fort, with Enclosure

My dear Mr. President: Washington July 30, 1918.

Since I saw you the other day I have taken up with Mr. Glasgow, of the Food Administration,[1] the report which our Commission sent you[2] as to the 2½ percent turnover up to the limit of 9 percent on the packers' capital and borrowed money (called by Mr. Hoover "borrowed capital," which is an entire misnomer).

Mr. Glasgow and I have reached a conclusion as to the parts of the report which the Food Administration wished us to change, which they thought reflected upon them. We also went over Mr. Hoover's letter to you,[3] which he wished published, if you published the report as originally made.

I see no reason why either our report or Mr. Hoover's letter should be published. Mr. Hoover's letter to you, if you will pardon me for saying so, I think is unfair. Our report, as to the reasonableness of the percentages allowed, was not of our own initiative, but was made because your committee requested us to do so, as appears on its face.

It would appear from Mr. Hoover's letter that he seems to think he is required to explain and that he must defend himself against statements in our report. This is, of course, erroneous, as when he made his percentages they were made without knowledge of their probable effect, and ours are made after a knowledge of what has resulted under them. He should not, therefore, be criticized in any way.

Mr. Glasgow and I have arranged a correction in the original report, omitting certain things to which Mr. Hoover objected, and which I submitted to you personally last Monday, and I think that matter is now all straightened out.

Mr. Hoover's letter reads as if there were matters at issue between this Commission and the Food Administration. Of course, there are none. Our report is not and was not intended to be controversial. It was only intended to be a finding of facts; that, and that alone.

But, now that we know that the profits are excessive, some action can be taken if deemed necessary in the public interests.

I am returning with this letter the original report as corrected by Mr. Glasgow and myself (with certain of the exhibits in the original omitted and retained here in our files) for your consideration, and for such use as the Food Administration may find it can make of it.

With great respect, I remain
                    Your obedient servant,   John Franklin Fort

TLS (WP, DLC).
    [1] That is, William Anderson Glasgow, Jr., counsel for the Food Administration.
    [2] See HCH to WW, July 8, 1918, n. 2, Vol. 48.
    [3] See *ibid.*, n. 1.

E N C L O S U R E

From William Byron Colver and Others

Sir: Washington June 28, 1918.

On May 27, 1918, the President's Committee on Meat Policy in its report to you suggested that the Federal Trade Commission report to you before July 1 on the reasonableness of the present profit regulation of meat packing companies as imposed by the Food Administration.

Immediately upon your direction that this be done, the Commission undertook the task, and finds:

I. That the maximum profits for the five largest packers under the Food Administration regulations are unreasonably high. These rates of profit are estimated to be from two and one quarter to three times as great as those earned in the pre-war years of 1912, 1913 and 1914.

II. That the plan of regulation makes impossible adequate certification; so that, to safeguard the public interest, the plan should be changed.

Supplementing these conclusions, the Commission makes the following specific recommendations:

(1) That the present segregation of the business of the packers into classes be discontinued, and, for the current year at least, the regulation apply a single rate to the licensee's entire business, including foreign business and domestic subsidiaries and affiliations, without segregation or exemption of any kind.

(2) That Net Worth (actual invested capital represented by stock issued and surplus) as of November 1, 1917, be the basis upon which the allowed rate of profit be computed for all packers large and small, and that gross sales as a basis, as well as "net investment" which now applies only to the five chief packers, be discontinued. "Net investment" including as it does borrowed money, may be subject to abuse by reason of excessive borrowing, and is a very difficult figure to certify to; while "net worth" is simpler, fairer as between different packers, and more just to the public.

(3) That the rate be a sliding scale, based on volume, in weight, of animals slaughtered; thereby stimulating production of meats, without directly encouraging expansion into other lines.

(4) That the normal rate for the five chief packers be seven percent on net worth, with one-half percent increased allowance for every ten percent increase in weight slaughtered, and one-half percent decrease in rate for every ten percent decrease in weight slaughtered; the maximum profit allowed not to go above nine percent. It is probable that this rule would result in about eight percent, which is one percent more than their actual pre-war earnings.

(5) That the maximum allowed the smaller packers be nine percent, increasing on a sliding scale to eleven percent, but without a decreasing scale.

(6) That profits in excess of the prescribed rates be either turned over to the Treasurer of the Unted States, or applied against future government purchases.

(7) That all meat packers, as well as slaughterers, be included within the regulation except that no licensee doing an annual business of less than $500,000.00 be subject to federal limitation of profits. (The minimum limit for Canadian packers is $750,000.00).

In reaching these conclusions and recommendations, the Commission has been assisted by a committee of three of its staff, to which committee was assigned the task of collecting the pertinent facts bearing on the situation. A more detailed report of a committee is enclosed herewith,[1] in which will be found a further development of the various points already raised:

The report is in the form of a final report of the committee to the Commission and is signed by Messrs. Walter Y. Durand, Stuart Chase and Perley Morse & Company, Certified Public Accountants.

In connection with its own report and that of its committee, the Commission has on file supporting data and exhibits (notably a full transcript of hearings in which Mr. Morse examined the officers of the five chief packing companies in regard to the present regulation), and will be glad to submit on request such additional material as may be necessary to a more complete understanding of the situation.

Very respectfully,   William B. Colver. Chairman.
                      John Franklin Fort Commissioner.
                      Victor Murdock Commissioner.

TLS (WP, DLC).
    [1] Walter Y. Durand *et al.* to the Federal Trade Commission, June 24, 1918, TCL (WP, DLC).

From William Bauchop Wilson

My dear Mr. President: Washington July 30, 1918.

I am in receipt of your letter of July 26th relative to a visit to you by Senator Thomas of Colorado who expressed deep concern about labor matters and brought you clippings of advertisements by H. W. Brown of the Machinists' Union quoting excerpts from your Buffalo speech,[1] detached from the qualifying sentences surrounding it and putting a construction upon it to accomplish his own partisan purposes.

Several instances of this character, on one side or the other, have been brought to our attention, and the only way we have been able to meet them has been by quoting the full text, or at least the qualifying sentences of the speech or document which partisans have sought to distort to their own advantage.

Several weeks ago, the threatened general strike of machinists of Hudson, Essex and Bergen Counties, New Jersey, was brought to our attentiion. It was being handled by Mr. Brown on behalf of the machinists, who at times seemed determined to precipitate a strike, using the excerpt from your Buffalo speech and also certain clauses from the plan of labor adjustment adopted by the War Labor Board,[2] as justification for his position. We endeavored to offset his strike propaganda by another quotation from your Buffalo speech— viz., "Nobody has the right to stop the processes of labor until all the methods of conciliation and settlement have been exhausted," and by quotations from the War Labor Board's plan for labor adjustment. We finally learned that he was endeavoring to precipitate a strike for the selfish purpose of compelling the War Labor Board to give immediate consideration to their grievances in preference to other cases pending before it. A few shops did strike, but the bulk of them continued to work, and the whole question was finally adjusted through the War Department.

I think Senator Thomas is unduly alarmed about the labor situation. It is true that New England is somewhat of a storm center at the present time. The most important strike there is that of the General Electric Company at Lynn, Massachusetts, affecting approximately 14,000 workers. The workmen are willing to submit their case to the War Labor Board and return to work immediately, but the company has thus far refused to do so and is insisting upon the matter being handled by the Massachusetts State Board of Arbitration and Conciliation. The same company having agreed to submit disputes with its employees at Schenectady, N. Y., and Pittsfield, Mass., to the War Labor Board, the workmen are insistent that the dispute in Lynn should take the same course.

The next most important controversy is that of the shoe cutters at Brockton, Mass. It is the result of a jurisdictional dispute between two labor organizations, and has no justification from the stand point of wages or conditions of employment. The employees of the United States Rubber Company, to the number of 1,400, are on strike for increased wages. The Massachusetts State Board of Arbitration is handling the case and is hopeful of a speedy adjustment. Eight hundred and seventy-five employees of the Smith and Wesson Company, Springfield, Mass., are on strike for higher wages. We are advised that the company is six weeks ahead of its orders and consequently prefers to fight it out rather than enter into any kind of negotiations, particularly in view of the fact that since the organization of the company, more than sixty years ago, it has never dealt with organized labor directly or indirectly.

While we always have a considerable number of disputes in the process of adjustment that have not reached the strike stage, these are the only important strikes in the East. At Cleveland, Ohio, 4,000 garment workers are on strike. Here the workers are willing to submit the case to the War Labor Board or the conciliation services of the Department of Labor. The manufacturers have thus far declined to do either. We have asked the War Labor Board to take jurisdiction, and they will begin hearings on the 31st.

The only other serious condition in the country is at Butte, Montana, where a strike is threatened in the copper mining and smelting industry because of a jurisdictional quarrel between the members of the metal trades unions and the metal miners and smeltermen's union. The companies have trade agreements with all of their workmen with union shop conditions. We are trying to keep the men at work while we endeavor to work out their jurisdictional troubles, but will not know until Wednesday or Thursday whether or not we have succeeded.

While the labor situation is not as good as it was in April, May and June, and a number of under-currents are moving in various sections of the country, I can see no cause for alarm so far as strikes are concerned. I am very much more worried about the labor "turn-over" than I am about strikes. I look upon "labor turnover" as an individualistic strike; the protest of the individual who is either unwilling or unable to induce his associates to engage in collective protests. I am satisfied that it is resulting in very much more loss than grows out of all our strikes and lockouts. We are putting forth all of the energy of the Department in an effort to reduce it to a minimum.   Faithfully yours,   W B Wilson

TLS (WP, DLC).
    [1] It is printed at Nov. 12, 1917, Vol. 45.
    [2] About this, see N. Carlton to WW, June 17, 1918, n. 1, Vol. 48.

From Furnifold McLendel Simmons

My dear Mr. President: New Bern, N. C., July 30, 1918.

Your letter of the 26th instant has been forwarded to me from Washington; also telegram from the Secretary of the Treasury, dated July 25, urging prompt passage of the new revenue bill.

I am in entire accord with the reasons of the Secretary and, so far as I am able, I shall be glad to lend myself to carrying out his suggestions.

With high esteem, I am,

Cordially yours,   F. M. Simmons.

TLS (WP, DLC).

From Samuel Gompers

Sir: Washington, D. C., July 30, 1918.

Under your advice, as you know, I took up the matter of Porto Rico in conference with Secretary of War Baker, General McIntyre, and Mr. Iglesias, and I believe we have arrived at a just course of action. As a result of our conferences, Secretary of War Baker wrote you his conclusions enclosing my letter addressed to him dated July 11th, and recommending the appointment of a Commission to make an investigation in Porto Rico. In my opinion the investigation should include that which goes to make up the work and life of the Porto Rican workers.

In my letter to Secretary of War Baker, I have respectfully suggested for your consideration the following:

1. That the suggested investigation be conducted under the director of the National War Labor Board.

2. That the commission to make the investigation be appointed by the President of the United States.

3. That the commission be made up of four or six persons representing (a) employers, (b) employes,—both to be appointed by the President, and (c) that each group select a man to act in the capacity of adviser and to preside alternately at meetings; and that each group consist of two or three persons.

4. That the commission act upon the same principles and methods as formulated by the National War Labor Conference Board and which were by Presidential Proclamation put into practice and operation.

5. That the commission have power and authority to summon witnesses, to scrutinize books and documents, to undertake mediation and conciliation and to make complete investigation and report its findings and recommendations to the President of the United States and to the National War Labor Board.

The commission as above suggested could make an investigation and recommendations that would be most influential in establishing the basis for better industrial relations, remove much, if not all, the cause of industrial unrest, and bring about a sound and equitable basis in all relations of the lives of the people of Porto Rico.

On behalf of the American Federation of Labor, I have the honor to submit to you the following names of American citizens, with the earnest request that two of them be appointed by you as members of the Commission to go to Porto Rico:

John J. Fitzpatrick,[1] President Chicago Federation of Labor.

H. B. Perham,[2] President, Order of Railway Telegraphers.

James Lord, President Mining Department, A. F. of L.

Domingo Collazo, New York, as trustworthy interpreter for the commission.

I respectfully submit that a practical effort ought to be made to give these people of Porto Rico the real opportunity which democracy implies, and with which I know you have the most sincere and practical sympathy.

Respectfully yours,   Saml. Gompers.

TLS (WP, DLC).
  [1] That is, John Fitzpatrick. He had no middle name.
  [2] That is, Henry B. Perham.

Peyton Conway March to Tasker Howard Bliss

Washington, July 30, 1918

Number 76. Confidential

With reference to your 162, the State Department has been directed to communicate to the Italian Ambassador here the following statement of policy. "It is the firm hope and set purpose of the United States to have its expeditionary force assembled as an American army just as the Italian army is now assembled and as the armies of Great Britain and France on the Western Front. The President is not adverse to having a gradual and relatively small increase made in the American combatant forces now associated with the Italian army on the Italian front but he believes that this should be done with the consent of the Commander in Chief, General Foch, to whom the President feels obliged to defer in the matter of detaching American forces from the French front where they are now engaged. The President's idea therefore would be that the main body of the American army will ultimately be assembled as one army occupying its own position on the French or Western front with such relatively small bodies of American troops associated with the Italian Army on the Italian front as may from time to time seem advisable and not inconsistent with the general purpose above expressed. The President is, however, particularly anxious to have the Italian Government know that this view is dictated by the President's feeling that the course suggested will lend the greatest assistance to the Allies generally and that it is entertained in harmony with the most sincere and earnest wish to render every possible aid to the Italian Government and its great army on the Italian front." March.   McCain.

TC telegram (WDR, RG 407, World War I Cablegrams, DNA).

From the Diary of Josephus Daniels

1918 Tuesday 30 July

Cabinet. Gompers wanted to buy certain Mexican papers to help make favorable sentiment to Americans. WW No. Labor had helped Carranza and then C had turned on union labor. Instead of helping a subsidized paper, making propaganda, reacted. Witness German use of money to buy papers & writers.

I brought up action of King of England in decorating Rodman and Strauss[1] & advocated their non-acceptance. Sentiment was they could not be returned but that Secy. of State should inform European governments this Gov. did not desire such decorations to be given. I telegraphed Sims and approved his declination to accept tender from Italy

President discussed his letter to Slayden[2] saying he had not supported the administration & said Burleson had gotten him into that trouble.

"You wrote the telegram" said WW

B explained at request of Texas editor he had drafted telegram & sent to Tumulty for WW to sign if he thought fit, but said he did not think WW would sign. B's brother-in-law nominated.[3]

Hardwick and Vardeman due such letter

How far should it go.

[1] Rodman had been made a Knight Commander of the Order of the Bath. Rear Adm. Joseph Strauss, commander of the naval force mining the North Sea, had been made a Knight Commander of the Order of St. Michael and St. George.
[2] He meant WW to H. L. Beach, July 24, 1918.
[3] Carlos Bee, lawyer of San Antonio and a former member of the Texas Senate, had defeated Alva Pearl Barrett, another lawyer of San Antonio, in the contest for Slayden's congressional seat in the Democratic primary election held on July 27.

To George Creel

My dear Creel: The White House 31 July, 1918

The Secretary of War has just shown me a letter from a friend of his,[1] who has had the opportunity to see things from the inside

in Mexico, and there is one passage in it which I am going to take
the liberty of quoting in order that you may do anything that it is
possible for you, incidentally, to do to let our newspapers know how
dangerous it is to take news from Mexico that is unverified. The
passage is as follows:

"When one is on the ground, they become conscious of the fact
that the whole drive of German propaganda is to the end of so
exaggerating small incidents as to create ill feeling between Americans and Mexicans. As an illustration in point, an oil man with
whom I came in chance contact told me of a drunken brawl in
which some of his men became involved in Tampico, or near Tampico, one of them being killed in resisting arrest. This same incident
appeared in northern papers as an anti-American riot. There is no
need to bore you with a recitation of such cases though there are
a plenty of them. The point of it all is, that many of our newspapers
have unconsciously fallen into the habit of taking such stories without question and thereby simply playing the German game."

Always   Faithfully yours,   Woodrow Wilson

TLS (G. Creel Papers, DLC).
¹ Samuel Wilson, manager of the Kansas City, Kansas, Chamber of Commerce, to
NDB, July 27, 1918, TLS (N. D. Baker Papers, DLC).

To Franklin Potts Glass

My dear Glass: [The White House] 31 July, 1918

Just because you desire it I wish I could fall in with your judgment
about my writing a letter about Mr. Huddleston,¹ but I have can-
vassed this policy in my mind very carefully again and again, and
it seems to me that it would be a very great mistake, and result in
a very serious reaction, if I were to do in many cases what I did in
peculiar circumstances in the case of Mr. Slayden. From what you
tell me it would look as if Huddleston were pretty sure to get what
is coming to him at the primaries.

In haste   Faithfully yours,   Woodrow Wilson

TLS (Letterpress Books, WP, DLC).
¹ Glass' letter, to which Wilson was replying, is missing. Huddleston was George
Huddleston, Democratic congressman from the Birmingham, Alabama, district. For
Wilson's later intervention in the primary contest, see WW to F. P. Glass, Aug. 9, 1918.

To Emmett Jay Scott

Dear Mr. Scott: [The White House] July 31, 1918.

Your letter of June 26th[1] has been called to my attention, and I am both interested and pleased with the report it gives of the meeting held in Washington by leaders of thought and opinion among the negro citizens of the country. The problems considered by the conference, of special importance to the people whom they represent, are grave and weighty, and the whole state of feeling throughout the country will be helped by the frank and calm consideration given to these matters. In the meantime, it is cheering to see that the fine philosophy of democracy, which is at this time the inspiration of the great effort of our country, was felt and expressed by these conferees as the dominating thought which ought to control all Americans in the present crisis.

Cordially yours,   [Woodrow Wilson]

TL (Letterpress Books, WP, DLC).
[1] The Enclosure printed with G. Creel to WW, July 5, 1918, Vol. 48.

To Josephus Daniels

My dear Daniels: The White House 31 July, 1918

I have your letter with the enclosures,[1] which I am returning, but just between you and me, I am not keen to do anything for Senator Shields. There is very little reciprocity in the business, and, therefore, I feel justified in standing upon my general principle that I will not make exceptions to the rules which have hitherto governed the appointments at large. If I am wrong, forgive me.

In haste   Faithfully yours,   Woodrow Wilson

TLS (J. Daniels Papers, DLC).
[1] JD to WW, July 31, 1918, TLS, enclosing J. K. Shields to JD, July 25, 1918, T telegram; J. K. Shields to L. C. Palmer, July 25, 1918, T telegram; and L. C. Palmer to Navy Department, July 26, 1918, TLS, all in J. Daniels Papers, DLC. Shields had nominated Jesse Carmack as a midshipman at the United States Naval Academy. Young Carmack had passed all his examinations for entrance, but it then came to light that he was a duplicate nominee and, hence, that no vacancy existed for him under the regular appointment procedure. Shields was now urging that Carmack be appointed to an at-large vacancy in place of an officer's son who had previously been nominated but failed to qualify.

To David Baird[1]

My dear Senator Baird: [The White House] 31 July, 1918

The whole subject of woman suffrage has been very much in my mind of late and has come to seem to me part of the international situation as well as a question of capital importance to the United States. I believe that our present position as champions of democracy throughout the world would be greatly strengthened if the Senate would follow the example of the House of Representatives in passing the pending amendment. I, therefore, take the liberty of writing to call the matter to your serious attention in this light and to express the hope that you will deem it wise to throw your vote and influence on the side of this great and now critical reform.

Sincerely yours,   Woodrow Wilson

TLS (Letterpress Books, WP, DLC).
[1] Republican senator from New Jersey, who had been appointed to fill the vacancy caused by the death of William Hughes.

Two Letters from Frank Lyon Polk

Dear Mr. President: Washington July 31, 1918.

I return herewith the communications from Mr. Lewis Warfield[1] which you sent me under date of the twenty-fourth and twenty-ninth instant.

With reference to Mr. Warfield's letter, dated July twenty-third,[2] I find that Mr. House knows nothing whatever about Mr. Warfield, and that Mr. Auchincloss has conferred with him several times with reference to a plan of Mr. Warfield to put into operation a timber property in which he has an interest in Mexico.

The only suggestion made by Mr. Warfield that I believe may be productive of good, is the one with reference to Pastor Rouaix,[3] who, I believe, is now in California. Such reports as we have received concerning this man indicate that he is above the average Mexican governmental officials in intelligence and general ability. It may possibly be wise for you to see him if he comes to Washington. I shall take the liberty of communicating further with you about this matter.

I do not think that any useful purpose would be served by adopting the suggestion made in Mr. Warfield's confidential memorandum, dated July twenty-seventh.[4]

Following the lead indicated in your speech to the Mexican editors on June seventh, the Department has made an earnest effort so to modify the embargo policy of this Government as to permit the resumption of commercial dealings between this country and Mexico. With the cooperation of the Food Administration and the War Trade Board, we have made available for Mexico many products heretofore denied. From time to time the list of these products will be augmented by other commodities, which, on account of our increased production thereof in this country, we can now spare.

One of the most difficult problems still presented in connection with Mexico is the determination of the Mexican Government to nationalize the oil producing lands of the country. The effect of such nationalization would be to confiscate vested interests owned by citizens of the United States. We are working hard for a settlement of this controversy, and on the practical question of the continued production and shipment of oil, I am in close touch with Secretary Daniels, Doctor Garfield and Mr. Baruch.

The financial situation in Mexico is very bad. This Department has stated, over and over again, to those who have approached it with reference to making a loan to Mexico, that the United States Government is entirely sympathetic to the making of such a loan by American interests, provided (1) the terms are liberal to the Mexican Government and do not involve the granting of large concessions by the Mexican Government to the bankers. (2) Some machinery is set on foot by the Mexican Government to provide for a fair and impartial adjudication of claims of citizens of the United States against the Mexican authorities. (3) Some assurance is given by the Mexican Government that the proceeds of a loan will be applied for productive enterprises and not simply to military expenditures.

No headway has been made in straightening out the Mexican finances. One reason for this is that President Carranza seems to be very confident that he will secure all the financial backing necessary from Germany after the war.

It seems to me that Ambassador Fletcher is doing a difficult job well, and that no particular advantage can be gained by adopting the suggestions made by Mr. Warfield.

I am, my dear Mr. President,

Very sincerely yours, Frank L Polk

[1] Transportation engineer of New York and consultant on railroad and street-railway construction projects; also involved in various shipping ventures. See "Record of Lewis Warfield as a Transportation Engineer . . . ," T MS, enclosed in L. Warfield to JPT, Dec. 8, 1917, TLS (WP, DLC).

[2] L. Warfield to WW, July 23, 1918, TLS (WP, DLC). Like most of the numerous letters in WP, DLC, from Warfield to Wilson, Tumulty, and other persons, this one was both wordy and vague as to just what its author wanted. As he had done on earlier occasions, Warfield volunteered to assist Wilson in the improvement of Mexican-American relations. He was eager to participate in what he called the "Pan-American movement." He also believed that he could be of particular assistance in arranging much-needed financial aid for Mexico.

[3] Minister of Agriculture and Public Works in the cabinet of Venustiano Carranza. Warfield stated in his letter that Rouaix, an old acquaintance of his, was coming to Washington in about two weeks and suggested that Wilson appoint a committee of economic experts to confer with him.

[4] "Memorandum re Mexico's necessities," June (not July) 27, 1918, T MS (WP, DLC). The "suggestion" was that the United States Government lend money to Mexico for industrial and other development.

My dear Mr. President: Washington July 31, 1918.

The attached copy of a letter from the Italian Ambassador[1] presents the question of whether this Government will agree, in principle, to share with the Governments of France, Great Britain and Italy in the maintenance of the Russian Legation in Roumania, where Russian funds are now exhausted.

I believe our answer should be in the affirmative and am referring this question to you as it would seem necessary that any advances by this Government would have to come from the National Security and Defense Fund. I do not feel that the decision to contribute to the support of the Russian Legation at Jassy need necessarily commit us to a general policy to maintain other Russian diplomatic missions abroad. The situation at Jassy is peculiar. Furthermore, as far as I am informed, the only other Russian mission at present in need of funds is that in Spain. I would be glad to know if you can see your way clear to my answering the Italian Ambassador in the affirmative.

At the same time perhaps you will care to consider what answer should be made if the same question arises in regard to any other Russian missions abroad, notably that in Spain. I have had some anxiety regarding the latter mission because of the very strong hold which German propaganda has in Spain and the critical situation which has been produced by the Russian mission in that country being in danger of collapse through lack of so small an allowance as $5,000 a year. I may add that Russian diplomats, with the single exception of the Chargé d'Affaires in Portugal, have repudiated any allegiance to the Bolshevik authorities and have remained steadily at their posts until they can receive orders from some stable and representative Russian Government. They have maintained their loyalty to the cause and, as far as I can ascertain, their conduct generally has been praiseworthy under very trying conditions.

                        Faithfully yours,   Frank L Polk

TLS (WP, DLC).
    [1] V. Macchi di Cellere to FLP, July 23, 1918, TCL (WP, DLC).

From Josephus Daniels

Dear Mr. President: Washington. July 31. 1918.

The enclosed telegram from Admiral Knight[1] would seem to need an answer as early as one can be made. Will you please indicate what answer shall be sent?

                        Sincerely yours,   Josephus Daniels

ALS (WP, DLC).
    [1] It is printed as Enclosure II with FLP to WW, Aug. 1, 1918 (first letter of that date).

From William Charles Adamson

Dear Mr. President: Carrollton, Ga. July 31st, 1918

I have been in Georgia three days. I heard Mr. Harris speak to-day. I dont find the situation as favorable as I could wish.

Hardwick will not campaign in but one-half the counties. He claims that he will secure a plurality in them and secure the nomination. I dont believe that, but with so many candidates in the field there is confusion in the minds of patriotic voters and there is danger that that [sic] Hardwick will secure the delegations in many counties.

Howard ought to quit, then Harris would be easily nominated. Can you not devise some safe and easy way to induce Howard to get out of the race. With your fertile mind, tempered and regulated by prudence and propriety I believe that you can suggest some way to eliminate Howard.

I am desperately in earnest about the matter.

Yours truly, W. C. Adamson

TLS (WP, DLC).

From John Skelton Williams

My dear Mr. President: Washington July 31, 1918.

I have the honor to report to you that at a meeting of the Capital Issues Committee, held this morning at eleven o'clock, the matter of the application of the City of Seattle for authority to proceed with its plans for financing a certain hydro-electric development, at an estimated expenditure of approximately $5,500,000, was thoroughly discussed for several hours and the views of various parties in interest presented and considered.

After the hearing the Committee went into executive session, and voted unanimously to approve the application, subject to certain conditions relative to the interchange of electric power between the City and the Stone & Webster Electric Companies, which both parties to the controversy informed the Committee would be acceptable.

Respectfully and faithfully yours, Jno Skelton Williams

Other than Mr Hamlin & the writer I do not believe that the members of the Committee are aware that this subject has been brought to your attention. J.S.W.

TLS (WP, DLC).

James Brown Neale to Harry Augustus Garfield[1]

Dear Mr. Garfield: [Washington] July 31, 1918

I would not venture to suggest the wording of the President's Proclamation urging increased coal production in case he decides to make one, but perhaps you may think it wise to outline for his approval the thoughts to be expressed. I therefore offer the following:

To All Those Engaged in Coal Mining:

The existing scarcity of coal is creating a grave ⟨menace⟩ *danger*—in fact the most serious which confronts us—and calls for prompt and vigorous action on the part of both operators and miners. Without an adequate supply our war program will be retarded; the effectiveness of our fighting forces in France will be lessened; the lives of our soldiers will be unnecessarily endangered and their hardships increased, and there will be much suffering in many homes throughout the country during the coming winter.

I am well aware that your ranks have been seriously depleted by the draft, by voluntary enlistment, and by the ⟨needs⟩ *demands* of other essential industries. This handicap can be overcome, *however,* and sufficient coal can be mined in spite of it, ⟨in only one way, namely, by⟩ *if* every one connected with the industry, from the highest official to the youngest boy, ⟨giving⟩ *will give his best work* each day for the ⟨prescribed hours, his very best efforts.⟩ *full number of work hours.* The operators must be zealous ⟨as to⟩ *as never before to bring about the highest* efficiency of management, ⟨as to good⟩ *to establish the best possible* working conditions, and ⟨as⟩ to accord⟨ing⟩ fair treatment ⟨as never before,⟩ *to everybody,* so that ⟨the best opportunities⟩ *the opportunity to work at his best* may be ⟨afforded to the⟩ *accorded every* ⟨workmen.⟩ *workman.* The miners ⟨must⟩ *should* report for work ⟨each⟩ *every* day, unless prevented by unavoidable causes, and ⟨must⟩ *should* not only stay in the mines the full ⟨prescribed⟩ time, but ⟨must⟩ also see to it that they ⟨produce⟩ *get out* more coal than ever before. The other workers in and about the mines ⟨must⟩ *should* work *as* regularly and faithfully so that the work of the miner *not* be retarded in ⟨no wise.⟩ *any way.* This will be especially necessary from this time forward for your numbers ⟨will⟩ *may* be further lessened by the draft, which will ⟨induce⟩ *induct* into the Army your fair share of those not essential to industry. Those who are drafted ⟨and⟩ *but* who are essential will be given deferred classification and it is their patriotic duty to accept it ⟨,and⟩. *And* it is the patriotic duty of their friends and neighbors to hold them in high regard for doing so. The *only* worker ⟨deserving of⟩ *who deserves* the condemnation of his community is the one who fails to give his best in this crisis; not the one who accepts deferred classification and works regularly and diligently to increase the coal output. A great task is to be performed. The operators and their staffs alone can not do it, nor can the mine workers alone do it; but both parties ⟨in interest,⟩ working hand in hand with a grim determination to rid the country of its greatest ⟨draw-back toward⟩ *obstacle to* winning the war, can do it. It is with full confidence that I call upon you to assume the burden of producing an ample supply of coal. You will, *I am sure*, accept this burden and will successfully carry it through and in so doing you will be performing a service just as worthy as service in the trenches and ⟨you⟩ will win the applause and gratitude of ⟨all.⟩ *the whole nation.*

TL (WP, DLC).
[1] Words in the following document in angle brackets deleted by Wilson; words in italics added by him.

From the Diary of Josephus Daniels

July Wednesday 31 1918

War Council. Discussed big profits steel men had made and Baruch talked of the meeting of Union Labor to try to compel steel men to admit unions into that industry. WW said grave problems after the war were such that he almost hoped the war would continue until his term of office expired. He said democratization of labor would not come through war between capital & union labor and collective bargaining but through partnership. If big industry does not invite labor to place on directorate and share in profits & responsibility, it will invite worse. Labor is entitled to this & when steel companies make big money labor should have better pay

I advocated Gov. fixing prices & if necessary commandeering coal & ore & preventing excess profits. Baker thought best way was to lay heavy excess profit tax—very difficult to fix varying prices and some concerns had to pay out more to produce coal &c

From Fred Thomas Dubois[1]

Dear Mr. President: Washington, D. C., August 1, 1918.

An unusual political situation has arisen in Idaho which you can patriotically and effectively solve. Senators Borah and Nugent[2] are, have been, and will continue to be your loyal supporters. I know that you desire the return of both of them to the Senate. It cannot be otherwise. Senator Borah will have no opposition in his own Party and is very strong with the Democrats, so that his election is absolutely assured. Senator Nugent cannot be elected without the open support of Senator Borah. Senator Borah will give this open support to Senator Nugent, provided you will make it plain that you desire the return of these Senators.

Congress will probably be in continuous session and you need Senator Nugent here as he is a member of the Finance Committee, and you need Senator Borah here because he is one of your most effective and reliable supporters at all times. The Power Trust and other sinister influences in Idaho are anxious to have a representative in the Senate. If there is a partisan fight, the Republicans will elect both Senators, and the one who succeeds Senator Nugent will be a thorn in the side of Senator Borah as well as of your Administration. The peculiar intimate relations which these two Senators occupy towards you, and your aims and objects, not only make it advisable, but in my judgment make it your duty, to indicate your wish that they be returned without opposition. Prompt action is required on account of the primary laws. Senator Borah and I are very close and confidential friends and I can assure you that he will be pleased to emphasize what I am taking the liberty of writing to you if you will ask him. We can secure a Democratic Senator in Idaho who will be loyal to you in this way, and in my judgment only in this way.

Sincerely yours,   Fred T Dubois

P. S. I tell you truthfully that people of all parties in Idaho desire to aid you, and will accept and follow your suggestions. D.

TLS (WP, DLC).
  [1] United States senator from Idaho, 1891-1897, and 1901-1907. Elected as a Silver Republican in 1900, he had switched to the Democratic party shortly thereafter and had since been active in Democratic party politics. He had managed Champ Clark's presidential nomination campaign in 1912. At this time, he lived in Washington and was vice-president of the First National Fire Insurance Co.
  [2] That is, William Edgar Borah and John Frost Nugent. Nugent, a Democrat, had been appointed by Governor Moses Alexander, also a Democrat, to fill the vacancy created by the death of Senator James Henry Brady, a Republican.

To Albert Sidney Burleson, with Enclosure

Confidential.

My dear Burleson: The White House 1 August, 1918

Here is the note to Senator DuBois about which we agreed this afternoon.

In haste,   Faithfully yours,   Woodrow Wilson

TLS (A. S. Burleson Papers, DLC).

ENCLOSURE

To Fred Thomas Dubois

Personal and Confidential.

My dear Senator: The White House

The Postmaster General has discussed with me the situation in regard to the senatorial contest in Idaho. I had already had some of the main aspects in the situation brought to my attention.

I am free to say that the return of Senator Borah and Senator Nugent together would be entirely satisfactory to me, for I have appreciated very much Senator Borah's friendly and helpful attitude and know that his support can be counted on, but I think you and he will both appreciate my scruple about saying anything for publication. The truth is I hesitate upon the grounds of principle to seem to be selecting United States Senators, either directly or indirectly, or to seem to be exercising a direct guidance over the electors, who, I am sure will make their own proper assessment of men and measures. It is for that reason that I feel constrained to express these views to you only in this private way. After all, the interests of the country are paramount just now, and I feel confident that this Idaho situation can be worked out in the real interests of the country as a whole.

Cordially and sincerely yours, Woodrow Wilson.[1]

TCL (A. S. Burleson Papers, DLC).
[1] This letter was sent: WW to F. T. Dubois, Aug. 1, 1918, CCL (WP, DLC).

Two Letters to William Bauchop Wilson

My dear Mr. Secretary: The White House 1 August, 1918.

At my Wednesday conference yesterday with the heads of the new departments lying for the most part outside the Cabinet, we discussed the very difficult and important question of cooperating with regard to increases of wages in the various industries in whose full efficiency the Government is now so much interested. We agree, as I am sure you will agree, that there should be a very careful coordination of action among the several agencies of the government with regard to increases and equalizations of wages, and I know that you have been devoting a great deal of time and thought to this whole question.

McAdoo, for example, has just fixed the wages of machinists and shop men in general for the railroads, and in that connection sent me the enclosed telegram,[1] which was the occasion of our discussion yesterday. Baruch and Hurley and Daniels and Garfield are all very anxious to have your advice and cooperation in this important matter, and I am writing now to suggest that it will be very serviceable if you would get into personal consultation with these gentlemen and help them to draw any skeins which at present may be tangled into a consistent pattern.

Cordially and faithfully yours,   Woodrow Wilson

TLS (LDR, RG 174, DNA).
  ¹ See WGM to WW, July 25, 1918 (first telegram of that date).

My dear Mr. Secretary: The White House 1 August, 1918.

Dr. Garfield told me yesterday that you had approved, in principle at any rate, of such a recommendation as the enclosed, proposed by Mr. Neale.¹ I would be very much obliged to you if you would indicate whether you think I ought to say substantially what Mr. Neale has outlined for me in the enclosed.

Cordially and sincerely yours,   Woodrow Wilson

TLS (received from Mary A. Strohecker).
  ¹ Actually, the message, "To All Those Engaged in Coal Mining," embodied in J. B. Neale to H. A. Garfield, July 31, 1918.

To Charles Sumner Hamlin

My dear Mr. Hamlin: The White House 1 August, 1918.

Thank you very much for your note of yesterday and the memorandum enclosed² about the hydro-electric development proposed by the authorities of the city of Seattle. I am heartily glad to learn that the action of the Capital Issues Committee was favorable and am very glad indeed to have this detailed memorandum before me.

Cordially and sincerely yours,   Woodrow Wilson

TLS (C. S. Hamlin Papers, DLC).
  ¹ That is, the letter and memorandum cited in WW to C. S. Hamlin, July 29, 1918, n. 2.

To John Skelton Williams

My dear Mr. Comptroller: [The White House] 1 August, 1918

Thank you very much for your letter of yesterday about the Seattle development. I am heartily glad to learn that the Capital Issues Committee unanimously approved of it.

Cordially and sincerely yours,   Woodrow Wilson

TLS (Letterpress Books, WP, DLC).

To Josephus Daniels

Personal and Confidential

My dear Daniels: The White House 1 August, 1918.

I wish I could give Knight the information he desires about the troops to be sent to Vladivostock, but unhappily the Japanese Government is trying to alter the whole plan in a way to which we cannot consent, and for the time being at any rate the whole matter is in suspense.

Cordially and faithfully yours,   Woodrow Wilson

TLS (J. Daniels Papers, DLC).

To Jean Jules Jusserand

My dear Mr. Ambassador: [The White House] 1 August, 1918.

I acknowledged orally the other day your kind note of July 29th about the reassurances you had received from your Government on the matters which had given me some concern and about which I had spoken to you, but I want to make this more formal acknowledgement and say how much obliged I am to you for your careful report of the opinion of M. Clemenceau and M. Pichon with regard to the attitude of the French people at this time. It has given me a great deal of encouragement.

Cordially and sincerely yours,   [Woodrow Wilson]

CCL (WP, DLC).

To Alvey Augustus Adee

My dear Mr. Adee: [The White House] 1 August, 1918.

Saturday, I know, will be the thirty-second anniversary of your service as Second Assistant Secretary of State, and I want to convey to you my sincere congratulations not only, but my thanks for the services you have rendered this administration, and an expression of my admiration for the valuable services you have rendered from the first.

It has distressed me very much indeed to learn of your sorrow in the loss of your sister-in-law,[1] who I know was your only companion, and I hope that the sympathy of your friends will be a source of real comfort to you.

Cordially and sincerely yours,   Woodrow Wilson

TLS (Letterpress Books, WP, DLC).
[1] Ellen Skeel (Mrs. David Graham) Adee had died on July 16.

From Frank Lyon Polk, with Enclosures

My dear Mr. President: Washington August 1, 1918.

I am enclosing three telegrams from Admiral Knight which have been received by the Navy Department within the last twenty-four hours, which give a very full statement of the situation of the Czecho-Slovacs based upon authoritative information.

Yours faithfully,   Frank L. Polk

TLS (WP, DLC).

E N C L O S U R E   I

PARAPHRASE OF A TELEGRAM FROM ADMIRAL KNIGHT
RECEIVED JULY 31, 1918.

By sufficient majority giving also control of mayor and duma, Bolsheviki have city election.

Result due to division opposition factors and wide abstination from voting. Difficult situation created especially as several members elected Duma now being held by Czechs for recent efforts to create disorder. Among those former Soviet president[1] who will be probably chosen directly.

800 British troops expected Aug. 2d when same number Czechs will be withdrawn for service at front leaving total military force here 2,000 to which added 1,000 from ships. USS BROOKLYN has 250 guarding munitions, consulate and patroling. Russian manager cable station recently shot wounded by discharged employee. Proposal made that Allies declare martial law for prevention repeat. I refused assent considering it unjustifiable although other disorder probably will occur. Nothing alarming present local situation.

At request Czech General,[2] Japanese government sending cruisers, gunboats, four destroyers, to estuary Amur River to prevent rumor[ed] active Russian gunboats commanded by German officers and protect Japanese and Allies' subjects in Nikolevsk.[3]

Japanese flagship ASAHI now here, will be relieved by HIZEN. Acknowledge. 18030.

[1] Unidentified.
[2] Mikhail Konstantinovich Dietrichs.
[3] Nikolayevsk or Nikolayevsk-on-Amur.

ENCLOSURE   II

PARAPHRASE OF TELEGRAM RECEIVED FROM ADMIRAL KNIGHT
JULY 31, 1918

Have just received information of unfavorable development in
Lake Baikal front where small body from the Western area are in
danger of being overwhelmed by concentration of enemy forces of
combined war prisoners and Red Guards which are now moving
away from Semyonoff front, where they have been, to combine with
already liberated force at Chita and vicinity.

Czech General at Vladivostok feels it necessary to move almost
immediately via China Eastwards towards Chita; leaves only 1500
men in Eastern Siberia. This is great reduction of force which has
hitherto been proposed to hold enemy from Habarovsk direction
(north) and makes situation much more serious than it has been
considered. Force which may move on Vladivostok after withdrawing this force may reach ten thousand.

If it is true that Allied forces other than 800 British are to be sent
here soon, it is urgent that they arrive earliest possible date.

Recent triumph of the local Bolsheviki in the election is likely to
cause internal unrest, especially when it becomes known that Czechs
are moving west.

Request information whether Allied troops are to be sent here
and when.

ENCLOSURE   III

PARAPHRASE OF TELEGRAM RECEIVED AUGUST 1,
FROM ADMIRAL KNIGHT AT VLADIVOSTOK.

General Dietrichs (apparently the Czech commander NB.) at
conference of Allied Naval and Military representatives today, reported important information received from Lake Baikal front; he
developed fully situation Ussuri front between Nikolsk and Habarovsk and outlined his plan for immediate movement westwards
and explained the necessity for it: also gave much information about
attitude of Cossacks and peasants. The whole situation was discussed by the conference.

Line from south end of Lake Baikal, south to mountain range,
is being held by 4000 Czechs. Communication with Irkutsk is over
difficult mountain trails, tunnels having been destroyed. Including
those withdrawn from Irkutsk and several thousand who have been
opposing Semyonoff and have recently defeated him, all enemy

forces in region Baikal to Blagovestchensk is concentrating against them. Czechs who have penetrated this region in disguise, report force of about 25,000 well organized, including 9,000 mounted. Horses are plentiful in this region. Forces commanded by Major General von Taube.¹ It is believed that critical period of campaign is approaching. Czechs feel urgent necessity to hasten to assistance even though realizing that their force is inadequate and that they leave Vladivostok imperfectly defended. Propose to send temporarily one batallion 750 men to Ussuri front, one batallion Nikolsk, one batallion Vladivostok and withdraw one of these batallions when British (800) arrive on the 2nd August.

Czechs 6,500 effectives, on their way from Manchurian border to Lake Baikal. About the 6th of August one French batallion is due here and will proceed to Nikolsk or Ussuri, giving total force covering Vladivostok approximately 3,000. Opposing forces between Nikolsk-Habarovsk, known to be about 15,000 of whom 6,000 are war prisoners. All military representatives at conference believe that proposed movement by Czechs is hazardous and that local situation at Vladivostok will be far from favorable but agree that the Czechs have no choice.

Evidence indicates that sentiment of population is against Bolsheviks and against Germany but peasants will not use force and have no arms even if willing to fight. The Cossacks are wavering and very unreliable. Many of them are actually in the ranks of the enemy. Result of parley with Cossacks and peasants convinces that no help is to be expected from either class; that the country will welcome release from Bolshevik rule, but will not help to secure it. In conclusion, all evidence indicates that coming six weeks will probably decide the issue and that help designated in insuring safety of Czechs should come immediately. If not all can be sent now, few thousand despatched immediately by transports now at Manila may avert disaster, as Czech movement westwards must occur 10 days before contact with enemy; or regiment from Tientsin could be transported to Harbin by railroad in three days, marines from Peking taking their place. Urge this be accomplished.

It is stated by General Dietrichs that it would be much easier to form his plans if he knew what help to expect and at what time. His opinion is that 10,000 men needed to clear Amur line, and 25,000 for safe advance to Irkutsk; in this opinion all naval and military representatives in conference agreed after carefully studying situation. Am confident it is minimum not maximum.

It is confirmed by many civilians from the interior that the population can be expected to show friendliness but not active help until Bolsheviki and war prisoners are eliminated, after which reinforcements may be expected, especially from former soldiers, presenting possibility of new Russian army.

T MSS (WP, DLC).
  [1] Aleksandr Aleksandrovich Taube, former czarist general, at this time chief of staff of the Red Army command in Siberia.

From Frank Lyon Polk

My dear Mr. President: Washington August 1, 1918.

As you know one of the most pressing problems confronting Mexico at the present time is that of financial reconstruction. President Carranza has frequently been urged by those interested in the continuance of good relations between the United States and Mexico to apply to the United States Government for a loan. This he has always refused to do, partly by reason of pride and partly because Germany has consistently held out before him tempting offers of extensive financial assistance after the war. He has stated, however, that he would accept a loan from private bankers in the United States. American bankers, on account of present conditions in Mexico, will not move in this matter unless requested so to act by the United States Government.

I suggest that you authorize me to confer with representative American bankers with the object of inducing them to initiate negotiations with the Mexican Government for a substantial loan. The immediate effects of such negotiations, I believe, would be,

(1) To show to the Mexican Government and people that we earnestly desire to assist them in the friendly spirit of your speech of June seventh to the Mexican editors.

(2) To render ineffective much of the German influence in the Mexican Government which influence, in part at least, is obtained by German promises of financial support after the war.

(3) Possibly to relieve the present oil situation by diverting the attention of the Government from that source of revenue to the [c]offers of our bankers.

The ultimate success of the negotiations, is, of course, more than doubtful, on account of the many considerations involved. It would seem wise to me, however, to make a beginning, but I shall await your instructions before acting.

I am, my dear Mr. President,
                    Very sincerely yours,   Frank L Polk

TLS (WP, DLC).

From Charles Richard Crane

Dear Mr President   Woods Hole Mass August 1 1918

I am sure Russia gives you much anxiety. Her fearful present as well as her undefined future—the present and the future—of all the gifted slavic peoples—is perhaps a greater problem for the welfare of the world than the war. Fortunately the war is now going well—men, ships and equipment are now moving well and the soldiers, as well as the rest of our people, are transported at finding something really worth while to which they can dedicate their all. Life is found to be worth living and worth giving. Democracy is justifying herself and setting an inspiring example to the ages.

With Russia you will have to be as steady and as patient as you have been with Mexico. Roughly speaking it is the Mexican situation multiplied about ten times both in area and in population, and for the Russian problem as for the Mexican one there is no such thing as "expert" advice. Old Russia, like old Mexico has passed away forever and any understanding of the previous states gives little help in interpreting what is passing at present. In both states the political and social cement has run out leaving a vast human desert and no one is clairvoyant enough to be able to devine how the new cement will be constituted.

In navigating your ship by the stars you are pursuing the wisest possible course. Every other state—especially Germany—which has pretended to know and has tried to act, has blundered. Your prestige is higher than ever there—certainly higher than it was a year ago and any program you propose will be accepted as the expression of a wisely sympathetic friend. Russia is fundamentally Slavic and also Christian and you have near you the best and wisest of Slavs, Masaryk, and the best and wisest of Christians, Mott, to consult about moves that are more or less technical. You three are trusted by the whole world—and especially by the slavic world—and will do what is possible as opportunity offers. There is an old tradition that Russia will someday be saved by Siberia and I hope to have some word with Reinsch about it when we go to see the first launching at Hog Island next week.

Affectionate messages to you both from Mrs. Crane and me. We would take good care of you if you would come up to visit us and also you might avoid a very persistent letter writer.

                         Always sincerely   Charles R. Crane

ALS (WP, DLC).

From Walter Hines Page

My dear Mr. President: London. Augt. 1. 1918.

I have been struggling for a number of months against the necessity to write you this note; for my doctors now advise me to give up all work for a period—my London doctor says for six months. I have a progressive digestive trouble which does not yield to the usual treatment.[1] It's the war, five London winters, the monotony of English food and the unceasing labor wh. is now the common lot. I am ashamed to say that these have now brought me to something near a breakdown. I have had Sir Wm. Osler as well as two distinguished London physicians for several months. The digestive trouble has brought other ills in its train (I'm glad to say no organic disease); and I am assured that they will yield to freedom from responsibility and complete rest for a time in a dry, warm climate and that they are not likely to yield to anything else.

I see nothing else to do, then, but to bow to the inevitable and to ask you to be kind enough to relieve me and to accept my resignation to take effect as soon as I can go to Washington and make a somewhat extended report on the work here which, I hope, will be of some use to the Department; and I ought to go as soon as possible—say, in September. I cannot tell you how great my disappointment is that this request has become necessary.

If the world and its work were so organized that we cd. do what we should like to do, I shd. like a leave of absence till the winter be broken and then to take up my duties here again till the war end. But that, of course, is impracticable. And it is now a better time to change Ambassadors than has before come since the war began. My five years' service has had two main phases—the difficult period of our neutrality and the far easier period since we came into the war. But, when the war ends, I fear that there will be again more or less troublesome tasks arising out of commercial difficulties.

But for any reasonable period the Embassy's work fortunately can now go on perfectly well with Mr. Laughlin as chargé—until my successor can get here. The Foreign Office like him, he is *persona grata* to all other Departments of the Government, and he has had a long experience; and he is most conscientious and capable. And the organization is in excellent condition.

I venture to ask you to have a cable message sent to me (to be deciphered by me alone).[2] It will require quite a little time to pack up and to get away.

I send this, Mr. President, with more regret than I can express and only after a struggle of more than six months to avoid it.

                              Yours sincerely,   Walter H. Page

ALS (WP, DLC).
    ¹ Actually, Page was suffering from congestive heart failure and many complications.
See John Milton Cooper, Jr., *Walter Hines Page: The Southerner as American, 1855-1918*
(Chapel Hill, N. C., 1977), pp. 390-96.
    ² Wilson's reply is printed at August 24, 1918.

From Newton Diehl Baker

My dear Mr. President: Washington. August 1, 1918.
    Raymond Fosdick told me a story which is so significant that I
take the liberty of writing it to you.
    A Y.M.C.A. Chaplain in France was having a meeting attended
by a large number of soldiers. For his own information he asked
each person present to write on a piece of paper and pass up to
him what he regarded as the three cardinal sins. The vote was
unanimous as to No. 1; nearly unanimous as to No. 2, and a large
majority for No. 3. In their order they were:
    No. 1—Cowardice,
    No. 2—Selfishness,
    No. 3—Big-Head.
This seems to me to show a very extraordinary change on the
part of the men in their attitude toward life and its problems.
                Respectfully yours,   Newton D. Baker

TLS (WP, DLC).

A Translation of a Letter from Jean Jules Jusserand to Stéphen Jean Marie Pichon

                        [Washington] August 1, 1918
    Protocol. No. 37. As authorized by Your Excellency's telegram
No. 1398,¹ I had sent from New York the two Gobelin tapestries,
"The Nuptials of Psyche" and "The History of Other Times," and
I begged Mrs. Wilson kindly to choose between the two.
    Mr. Guiffrey² accompanied us to the White House and, with his
great competence in questions of art, furnished to the Chief of State,
who was present with Mrs. Wilson, useful and interesting infor-
mation.³
    The first of these tapestries is so much the more beautiful that,
in spite of its enormous dimensions (it touched the ceiling of the
East Room, where it was presented, and formed a fold on the par-
quet floor) the choice was made quickly and, in accord with her
husband, Mrs. Wilson pronounced in favor of "The Nuptials of
Psyche," expressing the most vivid admiration for a work which

only France knows how to produce and only the French would know how to appreciate. She wished to express her gratitude in writing, and she has written the enclosed letter by hand in which she says:

"The gift is itself so rare and beautiful that it will always command my admiration. But since, besides, it represents the friendship between our two countries and the gracious thought of your government, I will never look at it without an enchanted feeling.

"My admiration for France and the French people is so profound that I am particularly happy to possess so marvelous a specimen of an art for which France is celebrated in the world."

To those who conceived the idea of this gift must go the sincerest compliments, for it has certainly produced happy and long-standing effects.

TL (Papiers Jusserand, Vol. 17, pp. 235-36, FFM-Ar).
    [1] It is missing.
    [2] Jean Guiffrey, for many years Adjunct Curator of Paintings at the Louvre; he was about to be appointed Curator of Paintings and Drawings at that institution. He had been Visiting Curator of Paintings at the Museum of Fine Arts in Boston from 1911 to 1914.
    [3] The meeting described in this telegram took place on July 30. For a somewhat different account of what transpired, see Edith Bolling Wilson, *My Memoir* (Indianapolis and New York, 1938), pp. 164-65.

From the Diary of Josephus Daniels

1918 Thursday 1 August

Vance McCormick. New York politics. WW agreed that Osborne should come out and give Al Smith a free & open field[1]

    [1] William Church Osborn had announced his candidacy for the Democratic nomination for Governor of New York on July 14. He had declared himself to be the candidate opposed to Tammany Hall and to the rumored candidacy of William Randolph Hearst for the governorship. Although Tammany Hall itself soon put an end to the discussion of Hearst as a candidate, Osborn repeatedly declared that he would remain a participant in the primary contest, despite pleas that he withdraw to insure party unity. The endorsement of Alfred E. Smith for the governorship by the Democratic State Conference at Saratoga Springs on July 24 did not alter Osborn's determination to remain in the race. He conducted a rather low-key campaign in August, making frequent attacks on Charles F. Murphy and his Tammany organization but avoiding adverse comment on Smith. Smith defeated Osborn in the primary election on September 3 by a vote of 199,752 to 32,761. *New York Times*, July 15, 17, 18, 24, and 25, Aug. 7, 14, 18, 22, 25, 27, and 28, Sept. 4 and 5, 1918; James Malcolm, ed., *The New York Red Book, 1919* (Albany, 1919), p. 455.

To William Sowden Sims

Confidential

My dear Admiral: [The White House] 2 August, 1918.

I am sincerely obliged to you for your letter of July 13th acknowledging mine introducing Mr. Blythe.[1] It was very gratifying to me to hear thus directly from you the impressions you are gathering on the other side of the water, and I am glad to avail myself of this opportunity to say how well it seems to us all that you and the officers associated with you have been managing what must at times be the rather difficult task of keeping in close cooperation with the British naval forces.

I am sure that you all must have been heartened by recent events on the Western front. Both at sea and on land our men are splendidly justifying our confidence in them and are winning more and more golden opinions at home and abroad.

Please feel free at any time to write to me, for your letters will always be welcome.

Cordially and sincerely yours,   [Woodrow Wilson]

CCL (WP, DLC).
[1] See W. S. Sims to WW, July 13, 1918, Vol. 48.

To Samuel Gompers

Dear Mr. Gompers: [The White House] 2 August, 1918.

Thank you for your letter of July 30 about the investigation of labor conditions in Porto Rico. I shall take the matter up promptly with the Secretary of War and have no doubt that I shall have his very earnest cooperation.

Cordially and sincerely yours,   Woodrow Wilson

TLS (Letterpress Books, WP, DLC).

To Newton Diehl Baker

My dear Mr. Secretary: [The White House] 2 August, 1918.

Enclosed is Mr. Gompers' plan for conducting the investigation into labor conditions in Porto Rico.[1] I know you approve of it in principle. Do you approve of it in detail as he has outlined it?

Cordially and faithfully yours,   Woodrow Wilson

TLS (Letterpress Books, WP, DLC).
[1] That is, S. Gompers to WW, July 30, 1918.

To George Creel

My dear Creel: The White House 2 August, 1918.

Please read the enclosed letter from Mr. Gompers[1] and tell me what you think of his plan of disbursement through the Federation of Labor. My idea would of course be to have the funds pass through your hands primarily. Do you think it would be feasible to use the instrumentalities that he refers to just as we have been using the Y.M.C.A.?

Cordially and faithfully yours,   Woodrow Wilson

TLS (G. Creel Papers, DLC).
[1] That is, S. Gompers to WW, July 19, 1918.

To Winthrop More Daniels, with Enclosure

My dear Daniels: The White House 2 August, 1918

Will you not be kind enough to read the enclosed memorandum and give me an expression of any opinion that you may be willing to express about the wisdom of attempting what is suggested in it? Certainly something ought to be done in the premises, but my judgment is not at all clear what it ought to be.

Cordially and faithfully yours,   Woodrow Wilson

TLS (Wilson-Daniels Corr., Cty).

E N C L O S U R E

MEMORANDUM SUGGESTING THE APPOINTMENT OF A
FEDERAL ADVISORY COMMISSION ON PUBLIC UTILITIES.

Increases in the cost of materials entering into public utility construction, maintenance and operation; difficulty and delay in securing these materials; scarcity of labor and great advances in labor costs; loss of engineers and trained operatives who have gone into the military service; and scarcity and high cost of capital during the war period, have combined to increase the difficulties of public utility operation to an unprecedented extent.

That the services of the public utilities are vital to the welfare of urban communities and also vital to the efficiency and success of the military branches of the Government in the conduct of the war is now universally recognized.

On account of the increase in the demand for service, the gross revenues of some utilities have increased so much as to make unnecessary any increase in rates; in other cases increases in rates have already been granted. But it is asserted by public utility men that the costs of service have in most cases increased out of proportion to the increase of revenues, and that in a great many cases financial relief must be promptly secured if the service is to be properly maintained and extended and the bankruptcy of the utility companies avoided.

The problem is one of immense and immediate importance. However, if public utility rate increases be allowed wholesale, without proper investigation of each particular case, it may not only work an additional hardship to the people generally, already burdened with high prices and war contributions, but may also arouse their resentment and do more harm than good. It may appear that under the cover of war necessity these corporations are freeing themselves from the salutary regulation which has been gradually developed and are abrogating their franchise contracts under the protection of the national administration.

The public is prepared loyally to bear the necessary burdens of the war, but it has a right to expect that public service corporations should show a willingness to bear some part of this burden, and not ask for rate increases sufficient to put them back into the financial status of their most prosperous years, with their war taxes shifted upon the consumers. The public should pay the necessary cost of public utility service, but it wants guaranties that the cost is not greater than necessary.

Another factor of tremendous importance in connection with rate increases as applied to street railways, telephone systems and lighting plants is the probable curtailment of use. Experience shows that rate increases often result in a great diminution of the service, which largely neutralizes the desired effect of higher rates in increasing the revenues and injures the community which depends so largely upon good public utility service for its development. This involves a reversal of the Country's established social policy with respect to urban utilities.

Public utilities occupy an unusual position because they are subject, even in normal times, to regulation by public authority, as to service, as to rates and as to capitalization and investment. In many cases their rates are limited by the terms of their local franchises, and in most cases they have no authority to increase rates without the approval of established commissions.

The power of regulation is vested in state and local commissions or boards, many of which, however, are poorly equipped for making speedy investigations and rendering prompt decisions in matters of such vast importance as the increase of rates. In the absence of complete investigation and full understanding of the problem, both in its local and its national aspects, the commissions often hesitate to grant relief even where it is realized that it is needed.

Under these circumstances it has been suggested by the utilities that the Federal government assume jurisdiction to grant rate increases or to authorize the disregard of service standards, thus going over the heads of the state and local authorities if a way can be found to do it; or, at least, that the President issue a statement to the effect that the national emergency requires general acquiescence in the demands of the utilities for financial relief.

It would be unfortunate to ignore or break down the existing regulatory machinery established by the states and cities, even if it were possible to do so. It is better to cooperate with existing agencies; to put existing machinery into more effective operation.

It is suggested that the President consider the appointment of an advisory Federal Commission on Public Utilities, to be composed of able and experienced men who are thoroughly familiar with public utility problems from the point of view both of the public and of the utilities, men who are thoroughly competent to understand the financial and other needs of the utility corporations and to cooperate with local authorities in devising methods of meeting those needs.

The Commission would not be a judicial body to hear cases formally and render decisions, but rather an investigational body to gather information and formulate recommendations. In many cases, the Commission's action would be informal, the local authorities and the utilities being assisted in coming to an agreement as to the relief to be granted. In other cases, the Commission would make a formal recommendation as to increase of rates or change of standard, and thereby give the local authority the support of its influence and prestige. In many cases, the public is opposed to increasing rates because of lack of confidence in the claims of the company as to its needs. The recommendation of a responsible Federal Commission, which has investigated a given case and which can certify to the facts and needs of the utility, would, in most cases, remove the objection of the public and take away the political aspect of the question.

The Commission could also recommend economies in operation, restrictions of free service, relief from the burdens of taxation or other measures supplementary to or in place of straight increases in rates.

The Federal Commission would have no legal power to enforce its recommendations, but it would have great influence everywhere by virtue of the high standing of its personnel, its ability to gather full information, the fact that it is an unbiased federal agency and has the support of the federal administration. It would gather information from all available sources, receive written statements from representatives of the public as well as from the utilities, and do everything possible to secure fair and just treatment for the utilities and as uniform and consistent practice as possible among the various states and cities. It is believed that it would aid very greatly in making public utility regulation effective, and might be found desirable to continue as a permanent arrangement after the war.

The Bureau of Standards would cooperate with such a commission by reporting upon standards of service and safety and the efficiency and economy of operation, and doing the scientific and engineering investigation needed in the work of the commission.

Prepared for the President by the Bureau of Standards.

William C. Redfield

TC MS (Wilson-Daniels Corr., CtY).

From Joseph Patrick Tumulty

Dear Governor: [The White House] August 2, 1918

I am sending you a letter from Mr. Leffingwell,[1] Acting Secretary of the Treasury. I think you ought to supplement Mr. McAdoo's letter to Kitchin by a letter from you to Kitchin, urging the views expressed by Mr. McAdoo in favor of war profits taxes. Now is the time for us to make our record for the country will look upon war legislation that does not include a provision for a tax on war profits as a capitalistic tax bill. This letter to Kitchin should be written with the idea that it can be given out and used in connection with any campaign we may have to carry on in urging this legislation.

I beg to call your attention to two editorials from the New York WORLD[2] which clearly set forth the issue involved in this vital matter.

As Mr. McAdoo well said in his telegram of May 23rd, "The laboring men of the country, the great mass of the people of the country, will not rest content while corporations engaged in war industries pay huge dividends from Government war contracts or Government price fixing."   Tumulty

TLS (WP, DLC).
[1] R. C. Leffingwell to WW, Aug. 2, 1918, TLS (WP, DLC). Leffingwell, at McAdoo's request, enclosed R. C. Leffingwell to WGM, July 31, 1918, and WGM to R. C. Leffingwell, Aug. 1, 1918, TC telegrams (WP, DLC). Leffingwell reminded Wilson that, in his special message to Congress of May 27, 1918 (printed at that date in Vol. 48), he had indicated his expectation that taxes upon war profits would be a major source of additional revenue. He also recalled to Wilson's attention the letter from McAdoo to Wilson of May 23, 1918 (printed in *ibid.*) which had initiated the discussion of a war-profits tax, as well as the slightly revised version of that letter which McAdoo had sent to Claude Kitchin on June 5 (see WGM to WW, July 25, 1918, second letter of that date, n. 2).

In his telegram to McAdoo of July 31, Leffingwell reported that Claude Kitchin had told Daniel C. Roper, Commissioner of Internal Revenue, that he was opposed to a war-profits tax. The congressman preferred to increase the rates of the existing excess-profits tax. However, Kitchin said, if McAdoo and Wilson insisted, and would accept the responsibility, he would insert such a tax in the pending revenue bill. However, Kitchin proposed to wait until McAdoo had returned to Washington and then to seek a conference on the subject with him and Wilson. Leffingwell suggested the text of a telegram which McAdoo might send to Kitchin in order to spur him to immediate action.

McAdoo's telegram of August 1 to Leffingwell included the text of a revised version of the proposed telegram to Kitchin which McAdoo intended to send immediately, if Wilson approved. The revised text reads as follows: "Roper has advised me of his talk with you Wednesday STOP I greatly appreciate assurance you give him of your desire to meet as far as you possibly can views of the Treasury STOP I should be very sorry to have progress on the revenue bill delayed for conference concerning war profits tax as I understand you suggest STOP This is a matter which has engaged my earnest thought and in order that you may know my view without delay I take the liberty of telegraphing to confirm and reinforce the program outlined in my letter to you of June fifth and to express the conviction that that program is sound and reasonable STOP I earnestly hope that it may commend itself to you and the committee STOP I regard the war profits tax as an integral and indispensable part of that program STOP As a result of the further consideration of the subject which has been given since I wrote you I am confirmed in my opinion that a flat war profits tax of eighty percent should be imposed STOP Of course ample safeguard should be provided against hardship in extraordinary cases in the application of such a rate STOP The adoption of an eighty percent war profits tax should render unnecessary and I believe undesirable any increase in the existing excess profits tax rate STOP It is my strong conviction that the taxation of genuine war profits is the only way to reach the real war profiteering and that it is at the same time a thoroughly justifiable measure upon economic grounds as well as a certain and indispensable producer of a large part of the required revenue STOP The patriotic producers of America should be content if one fifth of their war profits are secured to them especially when we reflect that these men who are fighting and dying in France to save the liberties of those who stay at home and to make it possible for them to continue in business are limited by Act of Congress to three hundred ninety six dollars per year and give their blood in the bargain STOP Should we be more partial and tender to those who are protected in safety at home than we are to those who make the supreme sacrifices for us on the field of battle STOP I sincerely trust also that amendments which express as [experience has] shown to be desirable if not essential to the provision affecting the determination of the excess profits taxes may be adopted."

² "Dodging the War-Profits Issue," New York *World*, July 30, 1918, and "An Example of War Profits," *ibid.*, Aug. 1, 1918.

To Russell Cornell Leffingwell

My dear Mr. Secretary: The White House 2 August, 1918.

Thank you for referring to me the telegram which Mr. McAdoo purposes sending to Mr. Kitchin about the war profits tax. I agree with the position of the Secretary and entirely approve of his sending the telegram as he has formulated it.

Cordially and sincerely yours,   Woodrow Wilson

TLS (TDR, RG 56, Office of the Secretary, General Corr., 1917-1932, DNA).

To Claude Kitchin

My dear Mr. Kitchin: [The White House] 2 August, 1918.

I hope that you will not think that I am offering too many suggestions about the revenue measure, but there is one thing to which

I referred in my special message to Congress which I feel that I ought to return to, in order to let you know how important it is, in my judgment. I refer to a war profits tax as distinguished from a mere excess profits tax.

I most earnestly hope that the Committee on Ways and Means will embody a distinctive war profits tax in the measure which they are now engaged in formulating. I think that such a tax is not only defensible in principle, but that the public opinion of the country would rightly hold us responsible if we did not impose such a tax. It is manifestly equitable. I do not believe that the manufacturers of the country who are now making profits directly from war work would object. On the contrary, I think that they would feel a certain pride in sharing the burdens of the war directly with the men who are giving their lives for the safety of America and the freedom of the world.

I think the Secretary of the Treasury has apprised you of his own very deep interest in this particular form of taxation, and I am very glad to emphasize my concordance with his view.

If you will be kind enough to present this view to the committee as coming from my most earnest conviction in the matter, I will be sincerely and warmly obliged to you.

Cordially and sincerely yours,   Woodrow Wilson

TLS (Letterpress Books, WP, DLC).

Three Letters to Joseph Patrick Tumulty

Dear Tumulty: [The White House] 2 August, 1918

I would be very much obliged if you would send word to the Commissioners that I am perfectly willing that they should release the pamphlet they refer to, for publication.[1]

The President

[1] Wilson was responding to J. F. Fort to WW, Aug. 1, 1918, TLS (WP, DLC). Fort requested, on behalf of the Federal Trade Commission, Wilson's permission to publish the report on the meat-packing industry cited in W. B. Colver et al. to WW, July 3, 1918, n. 2, Vol. 48.

Dear Tumulty: [The White House, c. Aug. 2, 1918]

Yes, Mrs. Wilson and I are going to attend,[1] but I am a good deal disturbed by the references in this memorandum to the speakers' stand. Hurley gave me explicit assurances that I would not have to make a speech and I understood that there were to be no speeches.

I am merely going to attend. I would be very much obliged if you would make sure that this is the general understanding.

The President.

[1] The launching of the freighter *Quistconck*, the first one completed at the Hog Island Shipyard near Philadelphia, on August 5. Wilson's reference to a "speaker's stand" is puzzling: the attached White House memorandum and itinerary make no mention, even indirectly, of a speaker's stand.

Dear Tumulty: [The White House] 2 August, 1918

I have just read the article here referred to, and while there is no objection to its republication so far as any of its contents is concerned, I hope you will say to Mr. Wildman that I see no timeliness in it and I am sorry to say that I cannot approve of its republication.[1]   The President.

TL (WP, DLC).
[1] Wilson was responding to Edwin Wildman to JPT, July 27, 1918, TLS (WP, DLC). Wildman, president and editor of the New York *Forum*, requested Wilson's permission to reprint in a current issue Wilson's article "The Proper Perspective of American History," New York *Forum*, XIX (July 1895), 544-59. This article appears in somewhat expanded form in this series as "The Course of American History," printed at May 16, 1895, Vol. 9. Wildman declared in his letter that the article was "of great interest and significance at this time."

To Joseph Patrick Tumulty, with Enclosure

Dear Tumulty: [The White House] 2 August, 1918

I do not like this. It is a mere means of advertisement, but I suppose the only thing to do is to send a formal line of appreciation.

The President

TL (WP, DLC).

ENCLOSURE

From Joseph Schick

Hon. Sir!   Philadelphia, Pa. July 29 1918

Perhaps it may give you a moment of pleasure in this your hour of stress to know that the above concern in esteem for your illustrious self has named its principal street in a large tract of land composed of 62 acres named "Eagleville Heights" as follows "Wilson Boulevard"

"Pershing Avenue" altho not bordered with trees as is the above named B'vard, adjoins it.

All we hope for is that "Wilson Bvard" may be to Norristown and

Philadelphia Pa what President Wilson means to the whole world just now.

May long life and happiness be in store for you is the fervent wish of   Respectfully yours,   Workmans Co-operative
Realty Co
per Joseph Schick

ALS (WP, DLC).

To William Bauchop Wilson

My dear Mr. Secretary: The White House 2 August, 1918.

I am warmly obliged to you for your kind letter of July 20th [30th], reviewing very fully the matters to which Senator Thomas, of Colorado, recently called my attention. I am glad to find your own view of the labor situation on the whole reassuring, because I am sure that the whole field is very much more visible from your office than it is from Senator Thomas's.

Cordially and sincerely yours,   Woodrow Wilson

TLS (received from Mary A. Strohecker).

To Robert Russa Moton

My dear Mr. Principal: [The White House] 2 August, 1918.

Thank you sincerely for your letter of July 27th. I am happy to know that my statement against mob violence appears to you to have struck the right note. I hope with all my heart that it will be effective in checking this terrible evil.

Cordially and sincerely yours,   Woodrow Wilson

TLS (Letterpress Books, WP, DLC).

To Frank Lyon Polk

My dear Mr. Counselor: [The White House] 2 August, 1918.

I answered orally this morning your note of yesterday about getting the bankers interested in a loan to Mexico. I am merely writing this line to confirm our conversation, and to say that I hope you will make the effort.

Cordially and faithfully yours,   Woodrow Wilson

TLS (Letterpress Books, WP, DLC).

To Jessie Woodrow Wilson Sayre

My precious little Girl,   The White House. 2 August, 1918.

My heart has been specially full of you ever since Frank left. If you can in any way feel conscious of the loving thoughts I am constantly sending your way, you can, I am sure, never be very lonely. You are so brave and fine that I know you never allow yourself to admit that you are lonely, but I know that the absence of dear Frank must every day make a deep difference, even when you do not allow it to go the length of unhappiness, and I want you to feel all the time how my thoughts keep you company, how full my heart is of you and the dear little ones. I am so glad that Frankie is proving such good company for you. That makes an immense difference. But if at any time you need *any* of us do not hesitate to say so and we will come! Edith joins me in sending a heartful of love.

No, indeed, I do not share the idea that there is any real danger to Nantucket or to those who come and go to and from the island from the submarines.[1] Those are dangerous waters for the submarine, both because they are comparatively shallow and because they are so constantly under observation and so hard to get away from if you are once observed. If the stupid submarine commanders should seek to create terror anywhere, it would be on some crowded coast like that of New Jersey, not on remote Nantucket. I should not feel in the least uneasy there myself, although at present the naval people think it might be taking unnecessary risks for me to cross the open waters opening from Long Island Sound, if I did so in the slow and easily recognizable Mayflower. I do not share their uneasiness about such a trip, but everybody here threatens to raise a row if I insist upon it at present.

It is delightful, dear Girlie, to read your cheerful letter,[2] God bless you! Please give our dearest love to Frank whenever you write; and tell us what you learn of his work and movements when you can. We are always hungry for letters from you. My warm regards to Mrs. Sayre and my thanks and best wishes to the young friend who is staying with you till Nevin comes. Margaret sends heeps of loving messages. Helen is away, at York Harbor.

Your loving Father

WWTLS (RSB Coll., DLC).

[1] Six German submarines are known to have operated in North American waters between May and October 1918. The earliest of these, *U-151*, created the so-called submarine scare of 1918 by its extensive destruction of coastwise merchant ships and other small vessels off the shores of New Jersey and Delaware in May and June. At least three German submarines were operating off the North Atlantic coast of the United States and Canada as of August 2. Of these, the most conspicuous was *U-156*, which on July 21 attacked and severely damaged the American tug boat, *Perth Amboy*, and sank the four barges she

was towing within plain sight of many people on the beaches near Orleans on Cape Cod. The same submarine sank an American fishing schooner off Cape Porpoise, Maine, on July 22 and a British motor schooner at the entrance to the Bay of Fundy on August 2. See United States Office of Naval Records and Library, Historical Section, *German Submarine Activities on the Atlantic Coast of the United States and Canada* (Washington, 1920), and James M. Merrill, "Submarine Scare, 1918," *Military Affairs*, XVII (Winter 1953), 181-90.

² Jessie W. W. Sayre to WW, July 25, 1918, ALS (WP, DLC).

From Frank Lyon Polk

Dear Mr. President: Washington August 2, 1918.

The British Embassy have received a message from Mr. Balfour to the effect that the final report of the committee sitting in London under the Chairmanship of Lord Phillimore is now on its way to Washington. Mr. Balfour states that the recommendations of the interim report,¹ handed you by Lord Reading a short time ago, have not been altered, but that the final report explains and enlarges the considerations upon which the interim report was based. Mr. Balfour goes on to say that he hopes that you will not express any final conclusion on the scheme of the Committee until you have had an opportunity of seeing the final report.

I am, my dear Mr. President,
                    Very sincerely yours,   Frank L Polk

TLS (WP, DLC).
¹ About which, see Lord Reading to WW, July 3, 1918 (second letter of that date), n. 1, Vol. 48.

From George Creel

My dear Mr. President,   Washington, D. C. August 2, 1918

Sunday, August 4, is Remembrance Day in Great Britain, marking England's entrance into the war. Our representative there cables urgently in the matter of a short statement from you to the English people. May I also take the liberty of suggesting some word to the American people asking them that they bear in mind the significance of the day.

All Chicago is insistent that you come there to speak on Labor Day. Shall I tell them that it is impossible—or is there any hope? Our great war exposition opens in Chicago on Labor Day, and it is the biggest thing since the World's Fair.

May I have a copy of your remarks to the Lithuanians¹ for my own personal information?

I am attending to the matter of unverified news from Mexico.

Victor Morawetz² wants to go to Europe as a volunteer worker of the Committee. The State Department has no objection, but I would like your view.

Is their [there] any reason, from your standpoint, why Kerney[3] in Paris should not accept the services of James Hazen Hyde?[4]

Respectfully,   George Creel

TLS (WP, DLC).

[1] Remarks to a Committee of Lithuanians, May 3, 1918, JRT transcript (WC, NjP) of CLSsh (C. L. Swem Coll., NjP).

[2] Corporation lawyer of New York, best known as co-counsel, with Francis Lynde Stetson, for J. Pierpont Morgan in the organization of the United States Steel Corporation; author of *A Treatise on the Law of Private Corporations Other Than Charitable* (Boston, 1882) and *The Banking & Currency Problem in the United States* (New York, 1909).

[3] That is, James Kerney, who was at this time the representative of the Committee on Public Information in Paris.

[4] About Hyde, see the index references in Vols. 14 and 16 of this series. He had been living in Paris in recent years.

From Ben Johnson

Washington, D. C.

Dear Mr. President: August Second Nineteen eighteen.

Herewith I am sending to you a copy of "The Menace,"[1] which came to me through the mail.

I have marked an editorial paragraph therein for the purpose of bringing it to your attention, since it maligns about forty per cent of the American army.

I say "forty per cent" because I am told that about that per cent of the Army and Navy is composed of Catholic young men.

The charge made by The Menace is bound to be false; and, in my opinion, the author of the statement has subjected himself to arrest and prosecution for disloyalty for thus branding our army.

Then, too, it seems to me to be an awful thing that the Catholic boys in the army, as well as their families here, must realize that the Nation itself for which they are offering their lives is disseminating, through the mails, the horrible charge that they are disloyal and dishonest.   Sincerely yours,   Ben Johnson

TLS (WP, DLC).

[1] It is missing. However, as B. Johnson to WW, Sept. 30, 1918, TLS (WP, DLC) reveals, it was the issue of August 3, 1918. In this letter, Johnson quoted the "editorial paragraph" which he found objectionable: "If all the Roman Catholic grafters connected with army and navy work were suddenly retired to civilian life at least half of the secret service men and inspectors would have to resign for lack of employment." *The Menace*, a virulently anti-Catholic weekly magazine, was published in Aurora, Mo., by Wilbur Franklin Phelps.

From Bernard Mannes Baruch

My dear Mr. President: Washington August 2, 1918.

The Seattle municipal matter, I think, has been settled satisfactorily.

What a delightful breath of human interest Mayor Hanson brings with him!   Sincerely yours,   B M Baruch

TLS (WP, DLC).

From Alvey Augustus Adee

Dear Mr President: [Washington] August 2. 1918

Your letter has touched me very deeply. In all my years of service my single aim has been to show each day the same aspiration to be worthy of my trust that I could have shown on the first day, and I am indeed proud to know that I have deserved your confidence.

I am very grateful for your sympathy in my bereavement. It is indeed hard to face life absolutely alone.
                            Very sincerely   Alvey A. Adee

ALS (WP, DLC).

A Press Release[1]

                                    [c. Aug. 3, 1918]
STATEMENT to the press in re American-Japanese action in Siberia.

In the judgment of the Government of the United States,—a judgment arrived at after repeated and very searching considerations of the whole situation,—military intervention in Russia would be more likely to add to the present sad confusion there than to cure it, and would injure Russia rather than help her out of her distresses. Such military intervention as has been most frequently proposed, even supposing it to be efficacious in its immediate object of delivering an attack upon Germany from the east, would, in its judgment, be more likely to turn out to be merely a method of making use of Russia than to be a method of serving her. Her people, if they profitted by it at all, could not profit by it in time to deliver them from their present desperate difficulties, and their substance would meantime be used to maintain foreign armies, not to reconstitute their own or to feed their own men, women, and children. We are bending all our energies now to the purpose, the resolute and confident purpose, of winning on the western front, and it would in the judgment of the Government of the United States be most unwise to divide or dissipate our forces.

As the Government of the United States sees the present circumstances, therefore, military action is admissible in Russia now only to render such protection and help as is possible to the Czecho-Slovaks against the armed Austrian and German prisoners who are attacking them and to steady any efforts at self-government or self-defence in which the Russians themselves may be willing to accept assistance. Whether from Vladivostock or from Murmansk and Archangel, the only present object for which American troops will be employed will be to guard military stores which may subsequently be needed by Russian forces and to render such aid as may be acceptable to the Russians in the organization of their own self-defence.

With such objects in view the Government of the United States is now cooperating with the governments of France and Great Britain in the neighbourhood of Murmansk and Archangel. The United States and Japan are the only powers which are just now in a position to act in Siberia in sufficient force to accomplish even such modest objects as those that have been outlined. The Government of the United States has, therefore, proposed to the Government of Japan that each of the two governments send a force of a few thousand men to Vladivostock, with the purpose of cooperating as a single force in the occupation of Vladivostock and in safeguarding, so far as it may, to [the] country to the rear of the westward-moving Czecho-Slovaks; and the Japanese Government has consented.

In taking this action the Government of the United States wishes to announce to the people of Russia in the most public and solemn manner that it contemplates no interference with the political sovereignty of Russia, no intervention in her internal affairs,—not even in the local affairs of the limited areas which her military force may be obliged to occupy,—and no impairment of her territorial integrity either now or hereafter; but that what we are about to do has as its single and only object the rendering of such aid as shall be acceptable to the Russian people themselves in their endeavours to regain control of their own affairs, their own territory, and their own destiny. The Japanese Government, it is understood, will issue a similar assurance.

These plans and purposes of the Government of the United States have been communicated to the governments of Great Britain, France, and Italy, and those governments have advised the Department of State that they assent to them in principle. No conclusion that the Government of the United States has arrived at in this important matter is intended, however, as an effort to restrict the actions or interfere with the independent judgment of the governments with which we are now associated in the war.

It is also the hope and purpose of the Government of the United States to take advantage of the earliest opportunity to send to Siberia a commission of merchants, agricultural experts, labour advisers, Red Cross representatives, and agents of the Young Men's Christian Association accustomed to organizing the best methods of spreading useful information and rendering educational help of a modest kind, in order in some systematic way to relieve the immediate economic necessities of the people there in every way for which an opportunity may open. The execution of this plan will follow and will not be permitted to embarrass the military assistance rendered to the Czecho-Slovaks.

It is the hope and expectation of the Government of the United States that the governments with which it is associated will, wherever necessary or possible, lend their active aid in the execution of these military and economic plans.[2]

WWT MS (WP, DLC).
    [1] This statement was published in the *Official Bulletin*, II (Aug. 5, 1918), 1-2.
    [2] This statement was sent to the American diplomatic representatives in Great Britain, Russia, France, Italy, Japan, and China, and to the American Consul at Harbin. See *FR 1918, Russia*, II, 328-29.

To Joseph Patrick Tumulty

Dear Tumulty: [The White House] 3 August, 1918

In no circumstances should any message sent to our office be given out in response to letters like this.[1] There is a very savage partisan fight on in the Northwest against the Non-Partisan League, and repeated attempts have been made to draw us into it. I think the best plan is simply to ignore letters of this sort altogether.

                                        The President

TL (WP, DLC).
    [1] Wilson was reacting to Thomas E. Cashman to JPT, July 30, 1918, TLS (WP, DLC). Cashman, proprietor of the Clinton Falls Nursery Co. of Owatonna, Minn., asked Tumulty for the original or a copy of a telegram from Arthur Charles Townley to Wilson in which Townley had said that the farmers of the Northwest would be satisfied to get the same price for the wheat crop of 1918 that they had received for the one of 1917. He gave no reason for his request. The telegram he referred to was A. C. Townley to WW, March 20, 1918, Vol. 47.

To George Creel

My dear Creel: The White House 3 August, 1918.

Answering the several matters referred to in your letter of yesterday:

My embarrassment about taking special notice of August 4th, the day of Great Britain's entrance into the war, is that I have not done so in other similar cases, and discriminations are very dangerous. As a matter of fact, I did send a message to England to be used tomorrow.[1]

As for the Chicago invitation for Labor Day, I do not want to say No, and yet I dare not say Yes. Suppose you just leave it in abeyance, as I have done in writing to Chicago myself.

You are quite welcome to the enclosed copy of my remarks to the Lithuanians for your personal information.

I do not know Victor Morawetz, but something vaguely sticks in my mind which makes an interrogation point stand up about him. Am I not right in thinking that he has been a writer on banking subjects and that his connections are almost altogether banking connections?

There is a very definite reason, from my standpoint, why Kerney should not accept the services of James Hazen Hyde. Mr. Hyde may have reformed in a handsome manner, but when I knew him he was a capital ass, and I cannot imagine that he can be of real service. Moreover, I do not like to have him associated with us. This may be prejudice, but it is very strong.

In haste,   Always faithfully yours,   Woodrow Wilson

TLS (G. Creel Papers, DLC).
  [1] WW to George V, c. Aug. 4, 1918, printed in the *Official Bulletin*, II (Aug. 5, 1918), 1. It reads as follows: "America cordially extends her hand to Great Britain upon this anniversary of Great Britain's entrance into the present war in which the forces of civilization are engaged against the forces of reaction, and rejoices with her that the two nations stand side by side in so great a cause. Woodrow Wilson."

To Harry Augustus Garfield

My dear Garfield: [The White House] 3 August, 1918.

I am very glad to send you with my signature the proclamation which Mr. Neale suggested, and I hope with all my heart that it may be effective along the lines that you and he hope for.

No doubt Creel, of the Committee on Public Information, can tell you the best channels of wide publicity, if you think it necessary or care to consult him.[1]

Cordially and faithfully yours,   Woodrow Wilson

TLS (Letterpress Books, WP, DLC).
  [1] It was published over Wilson's signature as "To All Those Engaged in Coal Mining" in the *Official Bulletin*, II (Aug. 12, 1918), 2, and was widely distributed in coal-mining areas.

To Ben Johnson

My dear Mr. Johnson: [The White House] 3 August, 1918

What you call my attention to in "The Menace" is quite in line with many other things of the same sort of which that extraordinary publication has been guilty. I shall take pleasure in calling the attention of the Postmaster General to what you have marked, and you may be sure anything that the law permits will be done.
Cordially and faithfully yours,   Woodrow Wilson

TLS (Letterpress Books, WP, DLC).

To Albert Sidney Burleson

My dear Burleson: [The White House] 3 August, 1918.

Will you not look at this extraordinary thing that Representative Ben Johnson has sent me? I have written him as follows:

"What you call my attention to in "The Menace" is quite in line with many other things of the same sort of which that extraordinary publication has been guilty. I shall take pleasure in calling the attention of the Postmaster General to what you have marked, and you may be sure anything that the law permits will be done."[1]
Cordially and faithfully yours,   [Woodrow Wilson]

CCL (WP, DLC).

[1] B. Johnson to WW, Sept. 30, 1918, TLS (WP, DLC), continued the discussion. Johnson reported that William Harmong Lamar, the Solicitor for the Post Office Department, in a letter to him of August 31, had stated that there was "no law authorizing the exclusion from the mails of this publication, so long as it does not contain matter the circulation in the mails of which is prohibited by the espionage or some other law." Johnson insisted that, by defaming soldiers and sailors who adhered to the Roman Catholic faith, the editorial paragraph in question did in fact violate the Espionage Act, and he again requested that action be taken against *The Menace*. WW to B. Johnson, Oct. 2, 1918, TLS (Letterpress Books, WP, DLC), stated that he was again calling the matter to the attention of the Post Office Department "in the hope that Mr. Lamar may review his decision in the light of the arguments and citations you supply." There is nothing further on this subject in WP, DLC.

Two Letters to Frank Lyon Polk

My dear Mr. Counselor: The White House 3 August, 1918.

Thank you for your letter about Lewis Warfield. He is evidently just one of those extraordinary persons who want to take the Mexican matter out of our hands for various reasons.

You may be interested in the enclosed[1] which Tumulty sent me the other day, and which I send you for whatever it may be worth.
Cordially and faithfully yours,   Woodrow Wilson

TLS (F. L. Polk Papers, CtY).
¹ L. Warfield to JPT, July 12, 1918, TLS (WP, DLC).

My dear Mr. Counselor: The White House 3 August, 1918

I do not know much about Tereschenko,¹ but I have an instinctive feeling that it would not be wise to let him pass through the United States and "take counsel with the Government of the United States concerning Russian affairs." Perhaps, however, you know more about him than I do and will correct this judgment.

Cordially and sincerely yours,   Woodrow Wilson

Aug 6, 1918 Spoke to Pres. at Cabinet & agreed not to let T. come at present FLP

TLS (SDR, RG 59, 861.00/2471, DNA).
¹ That is, Mikhail Ivanovich Tereshchenko, Russian Minister of Finance from March to May 1917, and, afterwards, Foreign Minister of the Provisional Government. Jailed and then exiled by the Bolsheviks, he was living in Norway at this time and had undoubtedly asked for the State Department's aid in returning to Russia.

Two Letters from Frank Lyon Polk

My dear Mr. President: Washington August 3, 1918.

I am sending you the following report merely as a matter of record.

The Japanese Ambassador called this morning and told me that his Government cordially appreciated the frank expression of the views of the United States Government; Japan was glad there were no fundamental differences between us; and they had no intention of sending more men than was necessary to assist the Czechs, and the only difference between the two Governments was as to the number that was necessary.

He said his Government still felt a larger force than proposed was essential, but in view of the necessity for immediate action, and in view of the attitude of this Government, his Government authorized him to say that they accepted our proposals, reserving the question as to the sending of additional troops to Vladivostok or elsewhere until circumstances should arise which might make it necessary.

He said that his Government has explained this last point by saying it might be necessary for the troops to move out of Vladivostok in order to prevent the slaughter of the Czechs, or it might be necessary to send reinforcements for this same purpose. He said his Government felt that such a slaughter would be a misfortune on humanitarian grounds and on political grounds, as it would hopelessly injure the prestige of all the Governments concerned if a slaughter took place which could have been prevented by prompt action of the Allied forces. He said that in such an emergency it was his Government's intention to consult this Government and the other Governments, but it was conceivable that there might be no time for consultation, in which case the Japanese Government wished to say frankly that they would be compelled for the reasons already stated to move without consultation. He said it meant a great deal to his Government to be in accord with the United States, and they felt that they had met our views on all the disputed points.

I asked him two or three times whether it was his understanding that the Japanese forces would be limited to ten or twelve thousand men, and he said that in view of the fact that such a number had been mentioned by me in our previous conversation, and in view of the fact that his Government stated they accepted our proposal, he felt there was no question on that point.

I asked him whether it was their intention to send troops anywhere else. He said no, not as far as he knew, and he thought that he had been fully informed on this point.

He showed me a copy of their proposed statement, and they had made the amendments we had suggested, that is, that his Government was in accord with the Allies as to *this* expedition. They had stricken out the reference to Japan's particular interest. He said that now that we were in agreement his Government had given out their statement in Tokio on August second,[1] and they were getting ready to move the troops.   Yours faithfully,   Frank L Polk

[1] K. Ishii to F. L. Polk, Aug. 2, 1918, *FR 1918, Russia*, II, 324-25. This memorandum began with a lengthy preamble setting forth the situation in Siberia and the necessity for intervention. The remaining portion reads as follows: "The Japanese Government, being anxious to fall in with the desires of the American Government and also to act in harmony with the Allies in this expedition, have decided to proceed at once to dispatch suitable forces for the proposed mission. A certain number of these troops will be sent forthwith to Vladivostok. In adopting this course, the Japanese Government remain unshaken in their constant desire to promote relations of enduring friendship with Russia and the Russian people and reaffirm their avowed policy of respecting the territorial integrity of Russia and of abstaining from all interference in her internal politics. They further declare that upon the realization of the objects above indicated they will immediately withdraw all Japanese troops from Russian territory and will leave wholly unimpaired the sovereignty of Russia in all its phases whether political or military."

My dear Mr. President: Washington August 3, 1918.

I am calling to your attention a telegram which the American Consul at Vladivostok has transmitted to be brought to the attention of the Red Cross. It describes the condition of the Czecho-Slovak troops; most of them are reported to be without under-clothing and their uniforms much worn. I have brought this matter to the attention of the Secretary of War but it seems to me that you will also want to consider whether we should not make some special effort to provide for the safety of these men. It is raw and cold in Siberia even in September, and in October cold weather sets in with temperatures ranging below zero. The transit time to Vladivostok is so long that I believe you will agree that if we are able to do anything at all, a decision should be made in a very short time.

I may add that the telegrams we have received from Admiral Knight and from the Consul, confirm the fact that the Czecho-Slavs are not provided with clothing to survive a Siberian winter.

Faithfully yours,   Frank L Polk

TLS (WP, DLC).

From Gordon Auchincloss

My dear Mr. President: [Washington] August 3, 1918.

I enclose a paraphrase of a telegram from Mr. Balfour to Lord Reading[1] which expresses warm approval of your general scheme of an Economic Mission to assist Russia and states that the British Government will be glad to cooperate in any way that may be required.

In the Aide Memoire handed the Allied Ambassadors on July 17th speaking for the United States you stated that it was our purpose and hope at the earliest opportunity to send to Siberia a commission to relieve the immediate economic necessities of the people of Russia. Your proposed statement to the press respecting Siberia (which has not yet been given out) states that the United States hopes and expects that the Governments with which it is associated will "whenever necessary or possible" lend their active aid in the execution of our military and economic plans.

The enclosed telegram which deals with important features of such a mission may be said fairly to indicate the desire of not only the English but also the Japanese, and to a less extent the French and Italians, to participate with us in our plan.

I have been very guarded in what I have said to the Allied representatives concerning our plans for an Economic Mission. I suggest that you authorize me to advise these representatives, in the sense of your proposed press statement, pointing out to them that until you have nominated the chief of the Mission you would prefer not to discuss the details.

I am, my dear Mr. President,
Very sincerely yours,   [Gordon Auchincloss]

CCL (G. Auchincloss Papers, CtY).
[1] A. J. Balfour to Lord Reading, July 25, 1918, T telegram (FO 115/2448, pp. 280-82, PRO).

Colville Adrian de Rune Barclay to Robert Lansing

My dear Mr. Secretary,   [Washington] August 3rd, 1918.

I have been requested by Mr. Balfour to transmit to you the enclosed sealed packet addressed to the President of the United States.

This packet is understood to contain a communication addressed to the President by the Lord Mayor of Dublin, with reference to the question of compulsory military service in Ireland.[1] I understand that it was arranged with the United States Embassy in London that this packet should be transmitted to me for delivery unopened to its high destination, and an assurance was given by the American Embassy that in deference to the wish of His Majesty's Government no publicity would be given to its contents in the United States.

I shall be much obliged if you will be good enough to forward the packet to the President in conformance with Mr. Balfour's suggestion, should there be no objection.

Believe me, my dear Mr. Secretary,

Yours very truly,   CB

CCLI (FO 115/2397, pp. 362-63, PRO).
[1] L. O'Neill to WW, June 11, 1918, printed LS (WP, DLC).

From the Diary of William Phillips

Saturday, August 3 [1918].

Great news continues coming in regarding the French-American offensive. Soissons has fallen and immense supplies have been captured. The Germans appear to be in full retreat towards the Vesle.

At last the Japanese reply has come. Ishii brought a copy of the announcement this morning; but just previous Japanese troops were sent to Siberia. We do not know how many—probably about 12,000. The Japanese have moved in circles all around us. They have beaten us out everywhere. Not only have they secured our consent to a Japanese command, but their troops have entered Siberia before ours even began to move. This is not the way it should have been—in fact it is just the opposite of the way the President intended it. The result of indecision and playing the lone hand! I don't like the picture that the situation presents.

The President came over this afternoon and was closeted with Polk for half an hour. He was indignant with the Japanese and thought that they had got the better of him. Polk, however, prevailed upon him to let the matter stand as it is and to issue our announcement[1] this afternoon so that it will appear together with the Japanese announcement which has just reached the United States through press channels. Baker joined the conference and by four o'clock instructions were issued by the War Department to begin moving our few thousand troops from the Philippines and Hawaii to Vladivostok. I sent for representatives of the British, French and Italian embassies—the Ambassadors had all gone out of town— (Lord Reading is on his way to England), and Polk handed them copies of our announcement before giving it to the press. We also cabled the announcement in full to London for Francis at Murmansk; Paris and Rome; Peking for Harbin; Tokyo, and also to Vladivostok via the Navy.

A telegram from Vladivostok this morning[2] states that the Czechs have suffered a severe reverse and are in full retreat. As soon as the British and French units arrive they will be dispatched westward at once.

[1] That is, the press release printed at Aug. 3, 1918.
[2] A. M. Knight to JD, received Aug. 3, 1918, T telegram (SDR, RG 59, 861.00/2494, DNA).

From George Foster Peabody

Dear Mr President   New York Aug 4th 1918

May I express my deep satisfaction with the conclusion reached by you respecting the method of extending aid to the Russian people and heartening the Czecho Slovak Allies. I have felt a serene confidence in your wisdom in dealing with this complex situation but am none the less greatly rejoiced to read the illuminating statement of your acting Secretary of State and realize how truly it discloses the heart back of your true sympathy with the struggling peoples of the earth.

May I also say that to my mind the part that the U. S. of A has had in rightly assisting the statement from the Japanese Government is one of the most signal instances of true and successful statesmanship in diplomacy.

I beg also to enclose to you a letter just received from our Negro Secretary of the Institute Y.M.C.A. Doctor Moorland[1] is a fine man and at some suitable time I believe it would greatly help your work for spreading of true democracy if you could permit him to report to you of the important work under his direction. The Secretary of War was as always fine in his courteous audience with Dr. Moorland and as you will see promptly acted in the matter of the unfortunate action that had been taken at Camp Grant.[2]

You will appreciate that nothing can be more helpful to the country than to build up with the help of your administration the race pride of the Negroes. It is being done sir I am glad to realize. I am
    With high respect
                    Faithfully Yours   George Foster Peabody

ALS (WP, DLC).
    [1] The Rev. Dr. Jesse Edward Moorland, senior secretary of the Colored Men's Department of the Young Men's Christian Association. His letter is missing in WP, DLC, and there is no copy in the J. E. Moorland Papers, DHU.
    [2] Maj. Gen. Charles Clarendon Ballou, commander of the all-black 92nd Division, had issued an order to his men, then at Camp Grant near Rockford, Illinois, to stay away from places of entertainment where managers and owners objected to their presence on grounds of race. The colored officers of the division sent a strong protest to the Secretary of War. They said that colored men who were willing to die for their country should be able to enjoy its amusements and pleasures. Undated clipping, datelined Washington, April 18, 1918, in J. E. Moorland Papers, DHU.

To Myron S. McNeil[1]

My dear Mr. McNeil: The White House. Aug. 5, 1918
    Replying to your letter of the 23rd of July,[2] let me say that it is always with the utmost hesitation that I venture to express an opinion about candidates for election, either to the Senate or to the House, because I feel that it is not from any point of view my privilege to suggest to the voters of a state what their action shall be. But upon questions of fact I am at liberty to speak. You call my attention to certain statements made on behalf of Senator Vardaman, in which an effort is made to create the impression that I would not regard the return of Senator Vardaman to the Senate as a verdict against the present administration. Such statements are calculated to put a very false face upon Senator Vardaman's candidacy. Senator Vardaman has been conspicuous among the Democrats in the Senate for his opposition to the administration. If the voters of Mississippi should again choose him to represent them, I not only have no right to object; I would have no right in any way to criticise them. But I should be obliged to accept their action as a condemnation of my administration, and it is only right that they should know this before they act.
                    Very truly yours,   Woodrow Wilson

Printed in the Jackson, Miss., *Daily Clarion-Ledger*, Aug. 11, 1918.
    [1] Lawyer of Hazelhurst, Miss. He was described by the *Clarion-Ledger* as "formerly a strong supporter of Senator Vardaman."
    [2] It is missing.

Two Letters from William Bauchop Wilson

My dear Mr. President: Washington August 5, 1918.

I am in receipt of your letter of August 1st inclosing telegram from Secretary McAdoo relative to stabilizing wage rates, and in accordance with your suggestion I will endeavor to have a conference with Secretaries McAdoo, Baker and Daniels and Messrs. Hurley and Garfield sometime during the coming week when I can get them all together.

I do not believe the question of standardizing and stabilizing wages has reached the stage of development where it would be advisable for you to issue any statement or proclamation concerning it. It is one of those situations where the evil is easily seen, while the remedy is difficult of application. The whole question is complicated by the attitude of large numbers of employers and employees towards each other, by variable costs of living in different localities, the lack of proper classification of trades and crafts, the absence of any uniform differential in the wage rates paid to different degrees of skilled labor, the need of stabilizing of living costs concurrently with stabilizing the wage rates, and a number of other equally important phases.

The War Labor Policies Board has had numerous conferences with representative employers and employees, and we believe we are making progress, although there are a great many conflicting interests that have to be harmonized in order to achieve success.

Faithfully yours,   W B Wilson

My dear Mr. President: Washington August 5, 1918.

I have received your letter of the 22d ultimo, inclosing letter addressed to you by Mr. Samuel Gompers[1] in which he quotes a resolution adopted by the American Federation of Labor Convention requesting that the controversy between the Street and Electric Railway Employes of St. Paul and Minneapolis and the Twin City Street Railway Company be brought to the attention of the National War Labor Board. Acting upon the suggestion contained in the resolution, I have submitted the entire subject matter to the War Labor Board.   Faithfully yours,   W B Wilson

TLS (WP, DLC).
[1] WW to WBW, July 22, 1918, TLS (Letterpress Books, WP, DLC). The letter from Gompers to Wilson of July 18, 1918, is missing.

From David Baird

My dear Mr. President: Camden, N. J., August 5, 1918.

I beg leave to acknowledge the receipt of your esteemed favor of July 31st, regarding my attitude on the question of Woman Suffrage, which came to hand today.

While I have the greatest respect for your opinion on any question and deep admiration for your patriotism and am pledged to support you throughout my short term as a United States Senator in your program for the conduct of the war, as has been proven by my vote on several occasions, still I cannot agree with your present view that the adoption of the Woman Suffrage Amendment at this time is vital to the winning of the great struggle for the supremacy of democracy throughout the world.

Would it not be better to leave the settlement of this extraneous question to calm and clear minds when the war is over? May it not be disposed of with better judgment then than now when we are engrossed in the tremendous task of raising armies of millions of men and borrowing billions of dollars to finance the greatest conflict of all times? The disputed question as to whether women should be enfranchised by Federal amendment or by State legislation may properly be deferred, it seems to me, until after we have freed the world of the terror of the Hun.

My State and your State rejected woman suffrage by 50,000 majority. I do not know that the people of New Jersey have since changed their minds on this subject. As many have petitioned me against Woman Suffrage as have favored it and I can frankly say my mind is still open, although from principle I should be against it according to the vote in my State—I being a believer in the good Republican principle of the rule of the majority.

I still insist that your letter to me does not clearly state that the enactment of the Woman Suffrage Amendment is necessary to winning the war. However, it is not my purpose to attempt to get into any controversy with you on this question, which may not be decided during my brief term. In my judgment, further consideration of this subject and others likely to destroy the unity of the Nation should be postponed until after the war. In a short time my term in the Senate will be ended and as my successor in all probability will be Governor Walter E. Edge,[1] who favors the adoption of the Federal amendment for Woman Suffrage, surely the Suffragettes can await his advent in the Senate, and may urge his election on the ground that he endorses your present views on this subject, as well as supports you in all your policies to win the war and to make no peace without victory for the principles of democracy throughout the world.

I am, with the greatest respect,

Sincerely yours,   David Baird

TLS (WP, DLC).
  ¹ The leading Republican candidate for the senatorship to succeed Baird. Edge was elected in November 1918.

From Winthrop More Daniels

My dear Mr. President: Washington August 5, 1918.

Your letter of August 2, with the enclosed memorandum, reached me by messenger this afternoon.

I have no doubt that some of our Public Utilities are in a sorry plight owing to increased costs and unchanged rates. I incline to think, however, that the Advisory Federal Commission on Public Utilities with power to investigate but not to fix rates is not the remedy that is required. State Commissions, if they do their duty, are the proper instruments to meet the difficulty.

In New Jersey, under Donges'¹ leadership, the Public Service Gas and Public Service Electric were allowed on their bills to consumers to add a "war surcharge" printed in red ink, and specifically so designated—*"war surcharge."* Donges left the Commission for the War Appraisal Board. The Public Service Trolley Lines had also asked for an increase, but Walter Edge, fearful that he should be held in part responsible for the action of a board containing a majority of his own appointees and of the same political party as himself, butted in to prevent a rate increase which he felt would react unfavorably upon his own political aspirations. I am fairly confident of this and Donges will tell you the same thing. How far these and similar influences have prevented a needed temporary concession of increased rates generally, I do not know. The memorandum from Secretary Redfield, however, greatly exaggerates the inability of State Commissions to gather information or make investigations. I incline to think that the attempt of a Federal Commission to exercise these functions and to recommend rates would seem like an attempt to supersede state and local bodies; and so long as the proposed Federal Commission has no power to increase rates, I doubt whether it could in large measure impose its counsels of perfection upon the state and local authorities.

My mind rather works in the direction of forcefully urging the state and local Commissions to do their duty in the premises and to accord prompt relief where such investigation as is possible shows it to be necessary, with the reservation, to which I think most Public Utilities would agree, that an excess of net revenues should be impounded as a public trust after it reaches a certain stipulated figure, and that a temporary war surcharge, indicated as such on the face of the bills rendered and self-expiring 60 days after the termination of the war, would be a longer step in the right direction.

Donges is living with me at present, and I shall take the liberty of showing him Secretary Redfield's memorandum and of advising you further in the premises.

I return the enclosed memorandum.

Believe me, with all good wishes,

Very sincerely,   W. M. Daniels

TLS (WP, DLC).
[1] Ralph Waldo Emerson Donges, president of the Board of Public Utility Commissioners of New Jersey, 1913-18.

From John Palmer Gavit

Dear Mr. President: Wolfeboro, N. H., August 5, 1918.

Your letter of July 30th has been forwarded to me up here on the shores of the beautiful Lake Winnepesaukee, whither I have fled for a breathing-spell. I wish you might be here for a space and sit down with me under the pines and get a respite from the wearying business that must weigh very heavily these fearful days.

I take it for granted that your wish must be law in the matter of postponing publication of "An Old Master." Certainly we shall not republish without your full consent the two essays that you mention. In any event, nothing will be done until I return to New York at the end of this month. I suspect that the omission of those two essays will make the bulk of the book so small as to discourage its publication. Later on, perhaps we can look about and find one or two of your other essays that can be included to replace the ones you wish to have left out. But we shall do nothing at all without your full knowledge and consent. I forward your letter to the office for their information. With cordial regards, I am always,

Sincerely yours,   John P. Gavit

TLS (WP, DLC).

From Thomas Garrigue Masaryk

Mr. President: [Washington] August 5, 1918.

With the deepest satisfaction I thank you for your decision to help our Czechoslovak Army in Russia.

Mr. President, you heve [have] repeatedly announced the principles in which American citizens have been bred, the principles of liberated mankind, of the actual equality of nations, and the principles according to which governments derive all their just power from the consent of the governed. The decision of the third of August to us constitutes a guarantee that these American principles will be realized. It is for these principles that our nation has been contending not only in this war, but already long ago; it is for these principles that our boys are shedding their blood on the endless plains of Russia and Siberia.

Your name, Mr. President, as you have no doubt read, is openly cheered in the streets of Prague,—our nation will forever be grateful to you and to the people of the United States. And we know how to be grateful.

Believe me, Mr. President,
                    Yours very sincerely,   Th. G. Masaryk.

TLS (WP, DLC).

To Samuel Gompers

My dear Mr. Gompers: [The White House] 6 August, 1918.

I know you will be glad to read the enclosed copy of a letter I have just received from the Secretary of Labor.[1]
                    Cordially and sincerely yours,   Woodrow Wilson

TLS (Letterpress Books, WP, DLC).
[1] That is, WBW to WW, Aug. 5, 1918 (second letter of that date).

To Newton Diehl Baker

My dear Mr. Secretary: The White House 6 August, 1918.

I must admit I do not know what is the right of the law in this matter to which Mr. Russell Harrison calls my attention.[1] I would like very much to have your own judgment.
                    Cordially and sincerely yours,   Woodrow Wilson

TLS (N. D. Baker Papers, DLC).
[1] Russell Benjamin Harrison to WW, Aug. 3, 1918, TLS (WP, DLC). Harrison, a lawyer of Indianapolis and the son of President Benjamin Harrison, called Wilson's

attention to what he considered an "error of judgment" on the part of Provost Marshal General Enoch H. Crowder. Crowder, acting under new provisions concerning the registration and drafting of aliens contained in the Army Appropriations Act of July 9, 1918 (40 *Statutes at Large* 845), had, on July 10, 1918, issued an order instructing all local boards to exempt from the draft all citizens or subjects of nations neutral in the war who had declared their intention of becoming citizens of the United States. However, he had also included in the order a list of belligerent nations whose citizens or subjects were not to be exempt from the draft. One of those nations was Russia. Harrison believed that, subsequent to the signing of the Treaty of Brest-Litovsk, Russia could only be considered to be a neutral. For the United States now to draft Russian citizens could only create friction between the two nations.

To Walker Downer Hines[1]

My dear Mr. Hines: [The White House] 6 August, 1918.

Thank you for your letter of August 5th.[2] I appreciate the embarrassment which is sure to arise out of the decision of the War Labor Board with regard to the unclassified laborers of the Chicago Elevated Railroad, and am going to take the liberty (because I am afraid it is too late to reverse this partricular action) of calling the attention of the War Labor Board to difficulties of this sort, which I am afraid may arise more and more frequently.

Cordially and faithfully yours,   Woodrow Wilson

TLS (Letterpress Books, WP, DLC).
[1] Assistant Director General of Railroads.
[2] W. D. Hines to WW, Aug. 5, 1918, TLS (WP, DLC). Hines informed Wilson that William H. Taft and Francis P. Walsh, acting as arbitrators on behalf of the War Labor Board, had just rendered a decision which granted a minimum wage of forty-two cents an hour to all unclassified laborers of the Chicago Elevated Railroad. Since this company had a Chicago-to-Milwaukee line which closely paralleled lines of several steam railroads between the two cities, the decision would result in employees of the Chicago Elevated working almost side by side with employees of the steam lines having minimum wages, set by the Director General of Railroads, ranging from 19.4 to 33 cents per hour. Hines also pointed out that the forty-two-cent minimum wage was considerably above the average for other workers in the Chicago area.

To William Bauchop Wilson

My dear Mr. Secretary: The White House 6 August, 1918.

The enclosed concerns a matter which we are all puzzled how to handle, and I send it to you in the hope that you will have an opportunity to call the attention of Mr. Taft and Mr. Walsh to this particular case, not with a view, of course, of interfering with this individual decision or suggesting a re-consideration, but merely in order that we may effect the cooperation which it is so difficult to effect and yet so necessary in equalizing, so far as it is possible, the wages paid in given localities to given classes of employees. I am sure that Mr. Taft and Mr. Walsh will see the importance of this and will be glad to cooperate when it is possible.

Cordially and sincerely yours,   Woodrow Wilson

TLS (LDR, RG 174, DNA).

From Frank Lyon Polk, with Enclosure

My dear Mr. President: Washington August 6, 1918.

I enclose an important despatch from Berne, giving the substance of an interview between Doctor Herron and two prominent Catholics. I first thought of sending you a digest in order to save your time, but I thought you would probably prefer to read Doctor Herron's report without any editing by me.

Yours faithfully,   Frank L Polk

TLS (WP, DLC).

E N C L O S U R E

George Davis Herron to Hugh Robert Wilson

Dear Mr. Wilson: Geneva, July 1, 1918.

This memorandum has to do with a conversation which was not only unexpected, but, so far as I am concerned, profoundly undesirable.

I have hesitated, and still hesitate, to put before you, for such transmission as you deem proper, the question to which the conversation leads. As you will see, the question is: "If the Pope asks the President to establish the Society of Nations, will the President respond (a) favorably, (b) unfavorably, or (c) find the acceptable way of telling the Pope to keep out?" And have Catholic leaders or emissaries any right to ask for advance knowledge or intimation as to what the President would do, in the event of such Papal procedure?

But perhaps I should tell how the question came—giving, as nearly as I can recall, its evolution.

Of course my personal opinions, as expressed to the two gentlemen who sought the interview, can have no interest to the State Department. Yet I must report all that took place, in order to present the final and crucial question in its true setting.

On Thursday, June the 27th, I received a telegram from Professor Stephen Bauer, of the University of Bâle, and also Secretary of the International Bureau of Labor Legislation, requesting me to meet him at Lausanne the next morning on "a matter of great importance." I could not even guess what was wanted; but I knew Professor Bauer to be a careful as well as much-occupied man, so decided that there must be good reason for so imperative a summons.

If I had known beforehand what the nature of the meeting was to be, I should not have gone; and even now I would wish not to put the question that concludes this memorandum. The chief value accruing from the interview,—if my account of it has a value,—is in the fact that it is an incident of the present dangerous activity of the Catholic Hierarchy in the direction of peace.

When I arrived at the appointed place, I found Professor Bauer accompanied by Dr. Feigenwinter,[1] Nationalrat, and political leader of the Catholic Church in Switzerland. The conversation began in so general a way,—Dr. Feigenwinter seeming to assume that it was I who desired the interview,—that I was puzzled, for a time, to know why I had been sent for. It came out, however, that he had lately come from the new Papal Nuncio to Switzerland,[2] with whom he is in intimate contact, and for whom he appeared to be preparing the way for a future conversation with myself.

Dr. Feigenwinter began by producing a copy of "La Liberté," the daily journal of Fribourg, where immense Catholic and Jesuit activities are now centered, and whence they are now reaching out through all Europe. He called my attention to a long article in criticism of my alleged hostility to the Pope,—or rather to the Pope's attitude toward the war,—in my little book of a year ago, "The Menace of Peace."[3] He said that the view expressed in that book had produced a painful impression upon Catholics in general, and was a cause of sorrow at Rome. He wished to know if I had to any extent modified my views since then, and would I write a reply to the article in "La Liberté," using some conciliatory expressions toward the Holy See.

Not knowing whither the conversation was leading, and becoming uneasy as to its antecedent motive, I felt that I must make clear beyond any question or doubt my purely personal capacity. I did not know, I stated, in what capacity Dr. Feigenwinter had come to me; but he must clearly understand that this conversation, so far as I was concerned, was merely an incidental exchange of individual views between two private gentlemen. I could neither speak nor listen to him with any thought in his mind that I represented anybody but myself, or that I was acting in any capacity that could be considered even *officieux*, much less official. There must be no misunderstanding, on his part, that any response I might make would be in the nature of sheer personal opinion, without any shadow of exterior authority behind it. I did not know the opinion of the American Government, nor of a single member of that gov-

[1] Ernst Feigenwinter, lawyer of Basel, member of the Swiss National Council (the lower house of the national legislature).
[2] Msgr. Luigi Maglione, provisory papal representative in Bern since February 1918. The position of nuncio to Switzerland had been suppressed in 1873 and was only reestablished in 1920, at which time Maglione assumed the post.
[3] George Davis Herron, *The Menace of Peace* (London and New York, 1917).

ernment, nor of a single member of the American Legation in Bern, concerning the participation of the Pope or the Catholic Church in the problems of this war and the ensuing problems of peace.

Dr. Feigenwinter having agreed to this understanding, I proceeded to say that, so far as my observation of the course of the Pope's political actions went, I personally saw no reason for holding any other view of them than the one he deplored. As clearly and courteously as I was able to do so, I explained to him how it came that every Papal participation in the war—as well as every non-participation—had appeared, in the eyes of the peoples of the Allied countries, to place the Vatican on the side of the Central Powers. Whether it were deservedly so or not, it was no less a fact that the influence of the Catholic Hierarchy had thereby steadily diminished in the Allied countries, since the beginning of the war, and had steadily increased in the Central Empires. The Vatican had not only lost, it was still loosing [losing], the spiritual respect of the nations at war with the autocratic governments and the autocratic principle.

I gave him different instances of this decreasing influence. I quoted to him a very serious and able editorial in a recent number of the "London Times."[4] I told him of one of the best French bishops, and of many French priests, now favoring the establishment of a French National Church at the end of the war. I explained to him what a shock it was to the moral sense of mankind that, when the Allies had graciously acceded to the Pope's request to suspend attack upon Cologne on the day of Corpus Christi, and when the German armies then proceeded to fire upon Paris upon the very day and hour of the unhindered Cologne procession, this unimaginable moral treachery and barbarity brought forth not one word of Papal rebuke to Germany.

I assured him that this decay of Papal influence was not due to any hostility to the Catholic Church in itself, but due to the political conduct of the Papacy since the war began. In the first place, the mere profession of neutrality on the part of the Holy Father had been an offense to French and Anglo-Saxon mankind, to say nothing of Belgium. The peoples could not regard the Pope as an international politician, balancing the interests of one nation against

---

[4] "The Allies and the Holy See," London *Times*, June 1, 1918. The editorial noted the incident on May 30, the day of the Feast of Corpus Christi, which Herron mentions in this paragraph, and then continued with a discussion of what it meant concerning the attitude of the British people toward the Pope. "The British people . . . ," it said, "are uncertain whether the Vatican is not neutral towards the high moral and religious issues underlying the war, issues in regard to which they regard neutrality as inadmissible. They feel that the war is essentially a contest between right and wrong, between organized devilry and the principles of Christian civilization. Hitherto, they have seen no unmistakable sign that the Holy See is unreservedly with the right and against the wrong. They have seen, to their regret, many signs in many countries that the Roman Catholic hierarchy has been with the wrong against the right."

another: they looked to him as a spiritual authority—as a power joining issue with world-wrong in its assault upon world-right. When a great conflict like the present was upon the world; when it began with the most shameless and cynical violation of a sacred treaty, with the invasion of a small and unoffending nation by a great military empire; then for him who calls himself the Shepherd of the Peoples, who is officially named the Viceroy of God, to refuse to take sides, to be absolutely silent about incredible and universal wrong, and all for the sake of his political interest,—this seemed to the Allied peoples to be an abdication, on the part of the Pope, of his spiritual office, indeed of the Holy See's reason for being. And, in the next place, even the profession of neutrality had not been real. Every exercise of the Papal power, since the beginning of the war, had been, as I had already declared, on behalf of the Central Empires nor once on behalf of the Allies.

I stated that I personally deplored the situation in which the Pope found himself. Not in the whole history of the Papacy had there been set before a Pope such an opportunity for a real shepherdship of the world. If, at the moment that the war began, the Pope had proclaimed the sacredness of treaties, and the wickedness of the destruction of weak nations by the powerful, the whole world would have rejoiced in such a shepherdship; the church would have wielded a power which no conceivable political advantage could place in its hands. I, and thousands like me, who find no satisfactory churchly home and yet who above all else are believers in the final and literal establishment of the Kingdom of Christ, might have run as if upon wings into the fold of the Church if the Pope had taken this stand.

To all this I received only the most sophistical and indeed juggling of answers. One was the statement that the German Catholics had always been true internationalists, and had been always ready to obey the Holy Father, while the French had always been nationalists, had always been disobedient, even in ancient times but especially since the time of Lammenais.[5] And the excuse for Cologne and Paris was, that the procession of Corpus Christi took place in Cologne on Friday—the Friday on which the Allies abstained from attack—but that it was other religious processions than Corpus Christi which took place in Paris, Corpus Christi coming later, on Sunday. Besides, the French had not asked the Pope to intervene on their behalf and the Germans had.

After advancing, for a considerable time, this quality of defence of the Pope as an internationalist, Dr. Feigenwinter came at last to

---

[5] That is, Hugues Félicité Robert de Lamennais (1782-1854), French priest and religious philosopher, whose advocacy of democratic principles and separation of church and state ultimately caused his writings to be condemned by Pope Gregory XVI.

the real point of the interview: Could I personally ascertain if the American Government either desired or would be willing to enter into diplomatic conversations with the Vatican concerning questions of peace? It would not do for the Pope to suffer the humiliation of making such advances, unless he had some assurance beforehand that they would be favorably met. I naturally stated that I possessed absolutely no information upon this subject, nor could even inform him if information could be obtained. It seemed to me that the way to such information would be for the Vatican to proceed through the American Embassy in Rome. But Dr. Feigenwinter replied that before any official inquiry could be made, the Vatican must have some personal assurance upon the subject—but assurance that would be certain and authoritative. He then argued, for awhile, that the American Legation in Bern, or the American Embassy in Bern, should take steps to inquire if the Vatican was ready to enter into conversation with the American Government on the subject of peace. It was the American Government, not the Vatican, that should make the initial inquiry.

I then raised the question as to why the Pope, if he wished to set himself and the Church in a better light before the Allied peoples, did not declare to the world his indorsement of the Society of Nations according to the program of President Wilson. He could do this by addressing the President directly. As the Shepherd of the Peoples, he could ask the President to call for the immediate establishment of this Society. And here, I think, I came upon the core of the whole interview—not the Society of Nations per se, but the recognition, in a political manner, of Papal spiritual supremacy.

Dr. Feigenwinter wishes to know,—and I suppose he is making this inquiry on behalf of Rome,—indeed he stated distinctly that he would make further inquiry of Rome,—if there is any way of ascertaining what the President would do in case the Pope should appeal to him to call for the immediate or early establishment of the Society of Nations—the Pope also calling upon the nations to lay down their arms and unreservedly submit all questions regarding the war to the tribunal of that Society.

It is possible, indeed, that the question of how the Pope should intervene might have taken some other form if I had not anticipated the conclusion with my own question. But it would have been only as to form: the question of the attitude of the American President to Papal intervention for peace would have risen as the reason for an conclusion of the interview. But since the question has been raised, I do not feel like taking upon myself the responsibility of refusing to transmit it to you. If you think best to transmit it to the State Department, and if it should be that this question comes before the President, I should certainly accompany it with a prayer that his answer be negative, or that he make no answer at all.

On reflection, I think I should regard it as one of the greatest calamities of history if it should turn out that the Society of Nations were to receive its realising impulse from the Pope—that is, if the result of this were the presence of the Vatican at the Peace Table, and the restoration of a measure of Papal political power. If one could conceive of anything so miraculous as a disinterested appeal of the Pope to the President,—to the Pope acting purely in his capacity as "Pastor of the World,"—without official calculations or political demands,—then one might welcome his appeal as an impulse creative of the Society of Nations. But history warrants no expectation of such a miracle—especially the history of the last four years.

I would like to make three or four observations in closing.

I. It may be that both Dr. Feigenwinter and myself were being used for an end that [n]either of us were quite aware of; and this notwithstanding the fact that he is the political leader of the Swiss Clericals, and that he is a stalwart and brainy man, apparently well able to take care of himself and to know what he is about. On the other hand, a far cleverer man than either the Catholic leader or myself is Professor Stephen Bauer—the one who brought about the interview. Ever since it took place, I have been puzzling myself over three or four phases of it which I could not then understand. And one of these is the apparent assumption of Dr. Feigenwinter that the appointment was at least partly due to some expressed desire of mine. I think, on reflection, that it is quite possible, even probable, that Professor Bauer made us each think the interview was of the other's seeking. Professor Bauer is very much a man of the world: He has travelled the world over, has lectured in the principal American universities, and is a finished cosmopolitan gentleman, with a wide circle of acquaintance. But he is no less a Viennese, even after twenty-five years at the University of Bâle; and no less a persistent Catholic, with Jesuit antecedents and training, even though his father was a Jew. He is in close relations with leading Catholic personalities, and showed me a somewhat lengthy letter from the present Pope to himself, written before his election to the Papacy, in the Pope's own handwriting, concerning questions of labor legislation. And I am convinced that Professor Bauer is an active (though honorable from the Papal point of view) principal of a veiled propaganda to procure the presence of the Pope or his representative at the Table of Peace. I think this is probably the motive behind his recent persistent and persuasive cultivation of my company.

II. The Catholic efforts to procure a peace that shall be favorable to Germany are now pervading Switzerland, and are marching through France and England as well. A large number of German priests have visited, and continue to visit, the French-Swiss priests of both the City and the Canton of Geneva, seeking to persuade French-Swiss Catholics to pacifist opinions and measures. Fribourg and Einsiedeln are each becoming a small Rome. Prince von Bülow visits Einsiedeln regularly, sometimes twice a week, and German Catholic activities go out from there in every direction. Fribourg has become the popular center of German and Jesuit activities which are designed for the Latin and Anglo-Saxon nations. The pacifist propaganda of Switzerland is passing largely into the hands of these Fribourg leaders, who are continuously in telegraphic communication with Chancellor Hertling.

III. The initiative of the Pope in the direction of the Society of Nations, if such initiative should be taken by him, would have only what would be an essentially false motive. It would not be the Society of Nations in itself the Pope would be caring about; it would not be for the creation of a democratic and righteous peace he would be laboring; it would not be the realisation of an actual kingdom of heaven among men that would concern him; his motive would be the rehabilitation of the influence and authority of the Catholic Papacy among the nations at war with the Central Powers.

IV. *Finally, what to me is the most menacing and outstanding fact of the increasing international Catholic activity in Switzerland is this: The Vatican is watching and preparing for the psychological moment wherein to snatch the initiative of the Society of Nations from President Wilson, and to use this initiative for the glory of the Church, for Papal rehabilitation, and for the salvation of the Central Empires. I am persuaded, too, from remarks which passed between Dr. Feigenwinter and Professor Bauer, as well as from activities now proceeding from Fribourg, that there is some secret understanding about this initiative between Germany and the Vatican. If the Vatican can take the initiative in this great matter, Germany and Austria will instantly give an affirmative response, thereby placing the Allied governments in a position of extreme embar[r]assement, and at the same time tending to create an uprising among the Allied peoples against their governments— against the continuation of the war. This is a subject that I intend to investigate further; but even as far as I have gone, I am convinced it is a possibility that ought to have the instant and urgent consideration of the President and our government.*

Respectfully submitting the above, I remain,

Faithfully Yours,   George D. Herron

TLS (WP, DLC).

From Thomas Garrigue Masaryk, with Enclosure

Mr. President: [Washington] August 6th, 1918.

Permit me to call your attention to the enclosed statement of Captain Hurban,[1] of our army in Russia, who arrived in Washington a few days ago. It is a fairly good report of the development of the situation which led to the conflict with the Russian authorities. In it you will find full justification of the decision to assist our army taken by you a few days ago.

Believe me, Mr. President,

Yours very sincerely,   Prof T. G. Masaryk.

TLS (WP, DLC).

[1] Vladimir S. Hurban, formerly with the Czechoslovak Legion in Siberia, at this time a military adviser to Masaryk.

E N C L O S U R E

I came to Washington to give a detailed report of our army now in Russia, to the commander-in-chief, the president of the Czechoslovak National Council, Professor T. G. Masaryk.

We in Siberia were almost completely cut off from the rest of the world, and already on our way, in Honolulu, we were very glad to see in the papers, how the United States,—not only the government, but also the public,—sympathetically follow our progress through Russia and Siberia, to which there is hardly any equal in history.

The history of the origin of our army, of its operations on the Russian front, and its march around the world to the French front will some day read like a phantastic romance, before which the imaginations of Wells fade into prosaic, matter of fact stories. It will be, of course, a romance with documents written with blood.

Much of it is already known to the American public. It may, however, prove interesting to outline a general picture of the events as they presented themselves to my eyes. It is not customary for a soldier to give interviews; but under exceptional circumstances I was permitted to give an authentic report to the American public.

Our Army in Russia was organized from Czech and Slovak prisoners of war under almost insurmountable difficulties. We were cooperating with the Russian Army, and since summer 1917 practically the only army on the Russian front, capable of any military action in the proper sense of the word. In July, 1917, during the first revolutionary offensive under Kerensky it was only our army that really attacked and advanced.

When the Bolshevik Soviet Government signed the peace treaty at the beginning of March, our army, of about 50,000 men, was in

Ukrainia, near Kiev. The former Ukrainian Government, to escape the Bolsheviks, threw themselves into the arms of the Germans and called for German help. When the German and Austrian armies began their advance into Ukrainia, the position of our army was almost desperate. We were in a state which has concluded peace, into which, however the Germans were advancing and occupying larger territories without resistance; the Red Guards of the Soviets did not represent any real military power.

The Germans advanced against us in overwhelming numbers and there was danger that we would be surrounded on all sides, on the right and left flank; our rear was not covered and the Germans were liable to attack us from the rear. We had no lines of communication behind us, no stores of materials and no reserves; everywhere there was disorganization, and anarchy, and the Bolshevik Red Guards seized the locomotives and were fleeing East in panic.

Under these circumstances Emperor Charles sent us a special envoy with the promise, that if we disarm, we will be "amnestied" and our lands will receive "autonomy." We answered that we will not negotiate with the Austrian Emperor.

As we could not hold a front, we began a retreat to the East. Already then in agreement with the Allies, (our army had been proclaimed a part of the Czechoslovak army on the Western Front, and thus allied with the French army) it was decided to transport our army over Siberia and America to France. We began the difficult retreat from Kiev. The Germans in an overwhelming force were trying to prevent our escape; about a hundred miles behind us they seized the important railroad junction at Bachmač, which we were obliged to pass in our trains on our retreat to the East.

When we arrived at Bachmač the Germans were already waiting for us. There began a battle lasting four days, in which the Germans were badly defeated, and which enabled us to get our trains through. The commander of the German detachment which was defeated by us at Bachmač, offered us a 48 hours' truce, which we accepted, for our duty was to leave Ukrainia; but the truce was canceled by the German chief commander, Linsingen,[1] yet too late; our trains had already gotten away. We lost altogether about 600 men in dead, wounded and unaccountable, while we buried 2000 Germans in only one day.

In this manner we escaped from Ukrainia. Our relations with the Bolsheviki were still good. We refrained from meddling with Russian internal affairs and we did not react to the appeals of the

---

[1] Gen. Alexander von Linsingen, formerly commander of the German forces in the Ukraine, at this time commander in chief in Brandenburg.

different anti-Bolshevist circles. Therefore when we found ourselves on the soil of the Soviet Russia, we tried to come to an
agreement with the Bolshevik Government with respect to our departure, or respectively, passage through Russia. But already then
signs were visible that the Bolsheviks—either under German influence or because we then represented the only real power in Russia—will try to put obstacles in our way. We made it clear to the
Bolsheviki, that if we were not absolutely loyal, it would suffice to
order one of our regiments (our army was then, in March, near
Moscow) to take Moscow, and in half a day there would be no
Bolshevik Government; for then we were well armed, having taken
from the front everything we could carry, so as to prevent it from
falling into the hands of the Germans (each of our regiments had
200 to 300 machine guns) and nobody in Russia, to say nothing of
Moscow, could have at all contemplated an attempt at opposition;
Moscow, moreover, would have received us with open arms. But
we were determined to leave as the army of a friendly, brother
nation, an army which in spite of all bad experiences, wished Russia
the strengthening of real democracy. Knowing Russia as we did,
we understood that the misfortune of the nation was the Tsarist
regime, which had held the nation in darkness. Although we could
not sympathize with the Bolshevik Government, we as guests refrained from all action against it, and remained absolutely loyal to
it.

To prove indisputably our loyalty we turned over everything, all
our arms, with the exception of a few rifles which we kept for our,
so to say, personal, safety (10 rifles for each 100 men) to the Bolsheviks. The equipment we turned over to the Bolsheviks including
arms, horses, automobiles, aeroplanes, etc. was worth more than
1,000,000,000 rubles, and it was legally our possession, for we took
it away from the Germans, to whom it was abandoned by the fleeing
Bolsheviks. This transfer of the equipment was of course preceded
by an agreement made between us and the Moscow government,
by which we were guaranteed unmolested passage through Siberia,
to which the government pledged to give its unconditional support.

Already then there were signs that the Germans were beginning
to be uneasy about our movement. Today we have documentary
evidence of the fact that in March the Germans considered our
progress as a naive adventure, which will soon end in failure. When
they saw, however, that the "impossibility" as they called it, was
becoming a reality, then they began to do their best to frustrate
our efforts, and organized an army of agents against us. As I had
said above, the Bolsheviks though not exceptionally friendly to us,
restrained so far from all direct action against us. Their only desire

in this respect, to which they devoted much money, was to persuade our volunteers to join their Red Guard. After getting our support and the support of the Letts, Lenine and Trotzky felt, they would be safe. This agitation was carried on vigorously and not by very honest methods; we did practically nothing to oppose it, but we knew our men; our people are too well educated politically and in every other way, to be carried away by the methods of Lenine and Trotzky.

More dangerous was the work of German agents who, under the mask of internationalism found their way into the Soviets. In every Soviet there was a German who exercised a great influence over all its members because of his superior intelligence. Soon there came the news that the German and Magyar prisoners of war were organizing in Siberia and were being armed by the Bolshevicks under the pretense that they were going to fight against "World Imperialism." We have proofs now that the Germans were planning to provoke our conflict with the Bolsheviks and to destroy us piecemeal with the aid of the armed prisoners of war.

Under such circumstances we began our pilgrimage East. I was in the first train (there were then eighty trains of us) which was to prepare the way. It is no exaggeration when I say that if our men were to choose between two routes, one of which would lead through five lines of German fortifications, and the other through friendly Soviet Russia, they would have chosen the first route. There can be no greater torture for a soldier hardened by many battles than the constant abuse and difficulties which were thrown in our way by people to whom we were loyal, of whom we knew that they were doing wrong without knowing it and whom we could destroy by a single move of our fingers. Our men were patiently suffering it all, although sometimes it was mighty hard to keep them from losing their patience; but we were determined to leave Russia without a conflict. Notwithstanding the fact that we kept our word, that we surrendered all arms with the exception of the few necessary, our progress was hindered and unending negotiations were to be repeated in every seat of a local Soviet. We were threatened by machine guns, by cannons, but we patiently stood it all, although the Bolshevik Red Guard could have been disbanded by a few of our volunteers. After 57 days of such tiresome travel our first train arrived in Vladivostok where we were enthusiastically received by the Allied units stationed there.

When the Germans saw that we, notwithstanding all their intrigue, were nearing Vladivostok, they have exercised a direct pressure on Lenine and Trotzky; for the things that were later committed by the Soviets, cannot any further be explained away by ignorance. The trains were stopped at different stations so that they finally were separated by a distance of over 50 miles from one another. Provoking incidents of all kinds were the order of the day. The arming of the German and Magyar prisoners was begun on a large scale. One of the orders of Čičerin, the Bolshevik foreign Minister reads: "Dispatch all German and Magyar prisoners out of Siberia, stop the Czechoslovaks." Three members of our National Council who were sent to Moscow for an explanation of the stopping of our trains, were arrested. At the same time our trains were attacked in different stations by the Soviet troops, formed mostly of German and Magyar prisoners.

I will recall the Irkutsk incident. Our train—about 400 men, armed with ten rifles and 20 hand grenades, was surrounded by a few thousand Red Guards armed with machine guns and cannons. Their commander gave our men ten minutes to surrender their arms, or be shot. According to their habit, ours began negotiations. Suddenly there was heard the German command, "Schiessen!" and the Red Guards began firing at the train. Our men jumped off the train, and in five minutes all the machine guns were in their possession, the Russian Bolsheviks disarmed and all the Germans and Magyars done away with.

The Siberian Government which resides in Irkutsk and which, as it appeared later, ordered this attack, can thank only the intervention of the American and French consuls that it was not destroyed by our rightly embittered volunteers.

To what extremes our loyalty was carried, is shown by the fact, that although perfidiously attacked, and although we disarmed the Red Guard in Irkutsk, we still began new negotiations, with the result that we surrendered *all* our arms, on the condition that all German and Magyar prisoners will be disarmed and disbanded, and that we will be allowed to proceed unmolested. The Siberian Government guaranteed us unmolested passage, and taught by bitter experience that it is dangerous to attack even unarmed Czechoslovaks, let us proceed to Vladivostok. True, this concerned only the trains in the vicinity of Irkutsk; the trains west of Irkutsk were—under the orders of Moscow—attacked in the same manner, but always with the same result: everywhere the Bolsheviks were disarmed.

The arrest of the members of our National Council, which took place immediately before these treacherous attacks, then thousands of armed Germans and Magyars in the vicinity of Omsk, Krasnoyarsk and Chita, forced our army between [the] Volga and Irkutsk to take the Siberian administration into their hands (toward the end of June). But even at this stage we were trying to enter into negotiations with Moscow. But Moscow, i.e: Lenine and Trotzky, proclaimed us murderers and began mobilization against us. Under these circumstances our troops were forced to take possession of the bridges over the Volga.

I must mention the fact, that our defense, which, as said, was necessitated by treacherous attacks and everywhere resulted in the disarmament of the Bolsheviki, was joyfully greeted by the majority of the Russian population. Anti-bolshevists took advantage of the situation and overthrew the Soviets. We did not interfere with their internal affairs even after the open conflict. We only disarmed those who attacked us, to make repetition of attacks impossible.

The Germans were trying to spread rumors that our volunteers committed brutalities during these battles. That is not true. The fact is this: Russian-Bolshevists taken by our troops were disarmed and sent home, but the Magyars and German prisoners, taken with arms in hand, were killed. That was made known to them beforehand. The Austrians hanged all our wounded whom they captured on the Italian front, and they attacked one of our trains of wounded in Siberia. The four years of a struggle for life taught us to be on guard. We did no harm to German or Magyar prisoners who did not oppose us although they were our enemies; we could have killed thousands and thousands of them, but we allowed them to leave Siberia in peace, if they desired to go home. When, however, they treacherously attacked us, they must be made harmless. We made an official announcement that every German and Magyar caught by us with arm in hand, will be given no quarter.

On the contrary we could cite many instances of unprecedented brutalities committed on our wounded by the German and especially Magyar prisoners.

In Siberia there are today some hundred thousand German and Magyar prisoners, a great number of whom are armed. It is these men who offer considerable resistance to our army—the Russian-Bolsheviks surrender after the first shot.

The Bolsheviks gave a sufficient proof of the fact that they are not capable to rule. The number of their fighting supporters is very indefinite. They consist chiefly of hungry masses, loth to work, who are getting 30-40 rubles a day in the Red Guard. They have no workers among them. A great number of the Bolshevik officials steal just like the officials of the Tsar's regime. Industry, commerce, transportation, everything is at a standstill, and there is nothing to eat. That spells failure of the Bolshevist government; the Bolsheviks are now doing everything to maintain their power. They obey the Germans and Austrians to keep themselves in power. The Germans, however, do not want a consolidation of Russia.

What will happen in the future, I am unable to tell. The fact is, Russia is ill, today powerless. If left to her fate, the Germans will obtain full control of her. But the consolidation of Russia is possible. That depends entirely on the good will of the Allies. Russia needs effective, firm, friendly help, for today she is herself completely helpless. Russia needs order, which today the Russians are incapable of upbuilding. The Russians are exhausted, they lost faith in themselves, and they need rest to recover. The majority of them are excited people who therefore cannot organize. The Allies knowing the psychology of Russia of today, and knowing the real strength of Russia, will extend their help in the proper manner. I think that our army can be of great assistance in this task; all of our boys have learned Russian in the four years of war, and know how to treat the people; they know the Russian people and Russian situation, and they desire only the good of Russia. It was the Czechoslovaks, who were always accused of exaggerated Russophilism by the Germans and Magyars; it is the irony of fate that we had to suffer so just in Russia. We hope and desire that our sacrifices be not offered in vain.   Vladimir S. Hurban.

T MS (WP, DLC).

From George Creel

My dear Mr. President,   Washington, D. C. August 6, 1918
    The question of the use of foreign languages in the United States, written or spoken, is one that keeps calling for consideration and decision. The Administration has not yet spoken, nor has Congress legislated save with reference to the filing of translations with postmasters, but, nevertheless, local agitations are many in number and very definite in results.
    One State, for instance, has proclaimed the following rules:
    "First—English should and must be the only medium of instruction in public, private, denominational or other similar schools.
    Second—Conversation in public places, on trains or over the telephone should be in the English language.
    Third—All public addresses should be in the English language.
    Fourth—Let those who cannot speak or understand the English language conduct their religious worship in their homes."
    In other States similar prohibitions have been put into effect, and sudden and fundamental changes are being worked not only in the school, the church, and the press, but in the whole social structure.
    There does not seem to be any effort at distinction, the language of allied and neutral countries being put under the ban as well as enemy languages.

There can be no denial of the evil attempted to be cured. In our schools, our churches, our press, and in our social life, English should be the one accepted language, and this must, of necessity, be our goal. But the ideal of tomorrow cannot alter the facts of today. We must face and accept the condition that there are hundreds of thousands of foreigners in this country who cannot speak any language but their own. If we are to institute an instant drive against the use of foreign languages, either written or spoken, we shut off these thousands from contact with American life, driving them further into ignorance and aloofness, and utterly robbing us of opportunity to win their understanding and cooperation.

As you know, we have organized all of the foreign language groups along lines of patriotic endeavor, and to each in its own language are carrying the meaning and needs of America. A first response was the great Fourth of July celebration that pledged our millions of foreign born to the ideals and purposes of democracy.

This work, so vitally necessary and so rich in results already, will be sharply limited if prejudice continues to be substituted for orderly and intelligent procedure. In my opinion, the whole matter is one for deliberation and decision by Congress. If, however, communities feel compelled to initiate their own action, is it not fair and wise to ask that such action be confined to enemy languages, exempting the tongue of neutrals and friendly belligerents?

Respectfully,   George Creel

TLS (WP, DLC).

From Theodore Marburg, with Enclosure

Dear Mr. President: Upper Saranac, N. Y. Aug. 6-18

May I suggest the following as a possible method of furthering a cause you have so much at heart and which you have already done so much to advance?

Immediate, direct action by the chancelleries, through the Versailles Council instead of through a conference, to secure at once certain institutions of a league intended to be permanent. These would naturally be a court, a council of conciliation and a quasi-legislature.

In respect of the court, the line of least resistance would be to set up the Court of Arbitral Justice already agreed upon by all the States assembled at the Second Hague Conference. It remains only to decide on a method of selecting the judges for it. If its nature and functions require modification, as some think, in order to fit it to meet the needs of the League, consideration of such modifications had best be postponed, had they not, to a future time?

As to the Council, the present Versailles Council could easily be developed into a true Council of Conciliation by adding members to constitute special sections.

The quasi-Legislature is needed in order to devise positive measures for the common good.

I am aware that any league set up now cannot be the kind of league we hope to have ultimately. It cannot proclaim intention to discipline the recalcitrant member so long as the Central Powers remain outside the League for that member to fall back upon for assistance; and it must include a feature we would naturally lay aside later, namely, defensive and offensive action which it is now called upon to take against an outside group. But to set up a rudimentary league now would have many advantages. Next in importance to your bringing the league project so prominently to the attention of the world was your action, through Col. House, in getting the Versailles Council established. Can it not be developed forthwith, in some such manner as the above, to function more fully as a real league?

In order to avoid burdening you with further comment on a subject to which you yourself have given so much thought, I am relegating to a separate sheet the reasons which seem to me to call for immediate action.

I am, with great respect,

Yours sincerely   Theodore Marburg

TLS (WP, DLC).

E N C L O S U R E

Reasons for developing the Versaillrs [Versailles] Council now into a rudimentary internationational organization intended to be permanent. (From an article written recently for the London Daily Chronicle by Theodore Marburg.)

The successful conduct of the war would be promoted by more complete cooperation of the Allies.

Organization, affected now, may prove to be the nucleus of a permanent league.

Broad community of interest is more patent in the face of common danger and opposing interests are more readily reconciled at such a time.

It is of the utmost importance that the Allies should present a common front at the peace table and, in order to effect this, they must reach an understanding, so far as possible, on specific questions in advance of the peace conference.

The settlement of questions arising among the Allies during the war will be facilitated.

The creation now of an organization involving habits of common action and fixed relations with one another will tend to hold the Allies together after the war.

The proclamation of just aims by such an organization will disabuse the mind of the German people of the idea that the Allies seek their permanent injury and will thus tend both to shorten the war and to draw a liberalized Germany to the group.

T MS (WP, DLC).

To Thomas Garrigue Masaryk

My dear Mr. Masaryk: [The White House] 7 August, 1918.

Your letter of August 5th is greatly appreciated. I have felt no confidence in my personal judgment about the complicated situation in Russia, and am reassured that you should approve of what I have done.

Cordially and sincerely yours,   Woodrow Wilson

TLS (Letterpress Books, WP, DLC).

To Victor Fremont Lawson[1]

My dear Mr. Lawson: [The White House] 7 August, 1918.

I am warmly obliged to you for your interesting and enlightening letter of August 5th.[2]

My apprehension about immediate legislation would be this: that it would create a false impression on the other side of the water, particularly among the more active socialists and labor elements (though I do not couple these together in my thought). They would think that it was a counsel of despair with regard to having any other basis for peace after the war except force and, what they have been so uneasy about, namely, universal military service.

Moreover, you know that what I have at heart is something which I have to admit that I have not been able to find time to work out in detail, namely a combination of military with industrial training. I should wish such a system, if worked out, to be national in character and adapted in large part to conditions, which we cannot yet clearly forecast, which will follow the war.

These are just hastily dictated lines, in which I am throwing my thought at you in unchiseled chunks, but I know that you will read more than I have written.

I am greatly reassured by your generous approval of my action with regard to Russia. It is a matter of the most complex and difficult sort, and I have at no time felt confidence in my own judgment about it.   Cordially and sincerely yours,   Woodrow Wilson

TLS (Letterpress Books, WP, DLC).
    ¹ Publisher and editor of the *Chicago Daily News*.
    ² V. F. Lawson to WW, Aug. 5, 1918, TLS (WP, DLC). This was the continuation of a correspondence, the earlier portion of which is missing. Lawson, on behalf of the Universal Military Training League, was promoting a scheme for such training in the United States, the nature of which is not clear from this letter. He argued that this or a similar scheme should be enacted into law immediately, while public opinion was favorably disposed toward it. He stressed that, under the league's proposal, the President would decide when the program should be put into operation and that, therefore, it could be inaugurated after the conclusion of the war.
    In a postscript, Lawson praised Wilson for his "constructive, and, there is every reason to hope, adequate plan of relief and national reconstruction in Russia."

To George Foster Peabody

My dear Mr. Peabody: The White House 7 August, 1918.

Thank you for your recent letters. They have cheered me very much. And thank you also for having let me see the enclosed letter to you. I am heartily glad to be able to serve my colored fellow-citizens in any way that I can, as I think you know and as I hope they are beginning to believe.
    In haste,
                    Cordially and sincerely yours,   Woodrow Wilson

TLS (G. F. Peabody Papers, DLC).

To Winthrop More Daniels

Personal.

My dear Daniels: The White House 7 August, 1918.

Thank you for your letter of the 5th about the proposal with regard to public utilities. Perhaps I like it all the better because it agrees with the judgment that I had formed about the matter. I am re-assured to have your confirmation.
    In haste,
                    Cordially and sincerely yours,   Woodrow Wilson

TLS (Wilson-Daniels Corr., CtY).

To William Cox Redfield

My dear Mr. Secretary: [The White House] 7 August, 1918.

After you have read the enclosed letter from Commissioner Daniels, will you not be kind enough to return it to me? I must say that my own judgment corresponds with his in this difficult matter.

Cordially and sincerely yours,   Woodrow Wilson

TLS (Letterpress Books, WP, DLC).

Two Letters to Clark Howell

Personal and Private.

My dear Mr. Howell: [The White House] 7 August, 1918.

I received your letter with more surprise than I have expressed in the accompanying letter, because you will remember that you sent me word through Mr. Woolley of the Interstate Commerce Commission that you regarded the situation as unsatisfactory, but that you would do anything that I suggested. I sent my suggestion very promptly, not only through Mr. Woolley but through others, and you did not accept it. The present anxieties among loyal men in Georgia are partly due to that fact, and I hope that you will do everything in your power to correct a mistake which seems to me to have been very serious indeed.

Very truly yours,   [Woodrow Wilson]

My dear Mr. Howell: [The White House] 7 August, 1918.

Allow me to acknowledge the receipt of your letter of July 24th, which has been supplemented by a number of others from prominent citizens of Georgia bearing the same inquiry as to the attitude of the national administration with regard to the pending contest for the United States senatorship in Georgia. Your own letter, I observe, is addressed to me by you in your capacity as a member of the National Democratic Committee, and I assume that it is your feeling that it is proper for me to answer the question in the interest of the party as a national unit.

I must say, however, that I have been surprised by the question, because I had supposed that the people of Georgia fully understood my attitude. The recent correspondence between Mr. William Schley Howard and myself,[1] which I understand has been published, is surely self-explanatory. I have never undertaken, and I never would presume to undertake, to dictate to the voters of any State the choices they should make, but when my views have been sought by those who seemed to have a right to seek them, I have not hesitated to give them. I gave them most frankly to Mr. Howard when he asked for them.

Senator Hardwick has been a constant and active opponent of my administration. Mr. William J. Harris has consistently and actively supported it. In my opinion the obvious thing for all those to do who are jealous for the reputation of the party and the success of the government in the present crisis is to combine in the support of Mr. Harris.   Very sincerely yours,   [Woodrow Wilson]

CCL (WP, DLC).
  ¹ See WW to W. S. Howard, April 12, 1918, and April 20, 1918, both printed in Vol. 47.

From William Bauchop Wilson

My dear Mr. President: Washington August 7, 1918.

I have your letter of the 6th instant, inclosing a communication from Walker D. Hines, Assistant Director General of the United States Railroad Administration, relative to the difference between the wage rates for certain classes of labor established by the Railroad Wage Board for railroad employees and those established by the National War Labor Board for the Chicago Elevated Railroad employees. I have already brought this matter to the attention of the National War Labor Board but have not yet been advised what steps would be taken to arrange the difficulty.

This is one of the minor phases of a very big problem. The most acute part of it lies in the fact that the flagmen employed at crossings are paid jointly by the railroad company and the street car company. I do not imagine that more than one hundred men are involved in this phase of the situation, yet anyone can readily understand the complication that will arise through one board awarding 19.4 cents per hour and another board awarding 42 cents per hour applicable to the same individuals.

Every portion of the Government intrusted with the responsibility of production or transportation for war purposes has felt keenly the necessity for getting results, no matter what the effect might be on others. They have felt it incumbent upon them to deal with their own labor problems in their own way. Of course there will be lack of uniformity under such circumstances. Fortunately we have been able to work harmoniously with all of them and have endeavored to keep things running as smoothly as possible.

I do not make these statements in any form of adverse criticism.

We did not have the machinery in existence at the beginning of the war to deal with these problems through a unified administration, and the machinery established by the different departments, boards and administrations have been very helpful in many ways, even though leading to complications in others. I firmly believe, however, that we will continue to have the kind of difficulties mentioned in Mr. Hines' letter until these matters are all handled by some central organization.

In addition to that I am of the opinion that the following things are needed in order to standardize and stabilize wages and working conditions in the United States:

A basic eight-hour workday, with a uniform system of paying for overtime.

A proper definition of each craft or kind of labor, skilled and unskilled, with the same terminology applied to the same kind of labor in all parts of the country.

A uniform wage rate for each craft or kind of labor notwithstanding differences in cost of living in different localities.

Piece-work prices made to conform to the day wage rates as nearly as possible.

Properly weighted family budgets prepared by the Bureau of Labor Statistics and a record made monthly of the changes in the cost of living, the wage rate to rise or fall during the ensuing month one cent per hour for each change of eight cents per day in the cost of living shown by the investigations made by the Bureau.

All questions of dispute arising out of this arrangement to be decided by the National War Labor Board.

I do not know whether or not a program of this kind can be "put over," but we are strenuously working to that end.

Faithfully yours,   W B Wilson

TLS (WP, DLC).

From Upton Beall Sinclair

My dear President Wilson: Pasadena, California August 7, 1918

I thank you for sending me the letter from Secretary Baker dealing with my suggestions concerning "political prisoners."[1] Mr. Baker discusses principally the matter of conscientious objectors, and it may not be clear as to just what persons I have reference to. I do not refer to men of draft age who have refused military service. The arrangements you have made concerning them are as fair as I could ask. The people I have reference to are those who are in jail for violation of the Espionage Laws, by carrying on propaganda against the draft or against our participation in the war. I exclude all those who may have been plotting with the enemy, or who may have used violence of any sort. My reference is to persons whose opposition has been openly and honestly expressed, and is based upon religious or humanitarian grounds; and my purpose is to suggest that you should display toward them the same kind of enlightened humanity which you have displayed in the case of those who have refused military service. I am not asking that they should be in any way petted or pampered. On the contrary, one of my objections is that many of them are kept in idleness, whereas they would be glad to work if given the opportunity; also that able-bodied men are required to guard them, whereas they might, if properly approached, be guarded by their own word of honor.

For there is a fundamental difference in character between such prisoners, and the criminals with whom they are at present confined. Men who have given a life-time's devotion to the highest ideals of humanity, and whose only fault is that they have not been able to adjust their minds to the present sudden and desperate emergency, are people who deserve all possible consideration. Granting that for the present it is necessary to restrain them, it is certainly possible to do it in some way other than that of brute force. To such men and women the most precious thing in life is self-respect, integrity of character. It [If] they were presented with an opportunity to give a pledge that they would m[a]ke no effort to escape, that they would not mail uncensored letters, nor see unauthorized visitors, nor make any effort to carry on propaganda during the period of their restraint, it might be that some of them would refuse this pledge, but certainly those who gave it might be relied upon to keep it. Consider, for example, the case of Mrs. Rose Pastor Stokes. I do not know what would be her attitude toward the proposition I am here making, but having known her intimately for many years, I can say that I would be willing to stake my life upon her word, once given. The same is true of Eugene Debs, Adolph Germer, Scott Nearing, Art Young, Max Eastman, Floyd Dell, Prince Hopkins, Frederick Krafft,[2] and many other men in jail or under indictment whom I personally know.

It is my proposition that people of this character, having given their pledge, should be treated with the same liberality which such prison-reformers as Thomas Mott Osborne and Ben Lindsey have proven can be granted to the most dangerous of common criminals. I ask that they should be confined, not in "disciplinary barracks" under the ordinary regimen of convicts, but should be taken apart and given an opportunity to operate a farm and to construct a farm-colony which, after the war, may be used for the care of partly incapacitated soldiers. I am sure that public opinion would assent to this step, if it were presented by you with your customary clearness.

Many of these political prisoners are, of course, not prisoners of the Federal government, but of state and county authorities. Perhaps you have not the right to take over the control of such prisoners, but I am sure that upon invitation from you, the various state and county officials would cheerfully turn them over to Federal control. I urge this, because the clergyman whose case caused me to write you my first letter,[3] is a prisoner here in Los Angeles County, and is held under conditions which are truly atrocious; and I am sure that this must be the case with many others who are lodged in city and county jails.

I remember reading something in the life story of August Bebel which made a great impression upon me. He was sentenced to two years confinement for violation of the anti-Socialist laws, and he states that at the beginning of his confinement he was a victim of tuberculosis, but at the end of his confinement he was cured. As I write, word comes to me that Secretary Baker is on his way to Leavenworth to inspect the place where political prisoners are confined. I will ask him to answer frankly the question whether he considers this place one in which a man would be likely to be cured of tuberculosis. I have been confined in two American prisons, once for playing tennis on Sunday, and once for walking up and down in front of 26 Broadway; I have visited a score of other prisons, and inspected them, and I feel sure that in none of these places was a man ever cured of tuberculosis—on the contrary thousands were dying of tuberculosis contracted while in the prisons.

The reason for my appeal to you is that I am defending the liberality of the American government as against the German government, among radicals and social revolutionists, not merely of America, but of Europe as well; and I can not carry on this propaganda with success, so long as there is any circumstance in which I have to admit that German practice may be more liberal than American. I am sure you will understand this point without further elaboration. I know that you wish to be as liberal as possible, consistent with the winning of the war. I present to you here a way to accomplish everything possible toward winning of the war, with less expenditure of government money and time, and less embitterment and political opposition.

Very sincerely,   Upton Sinclair

TLS (WP, DLC).
[1] NDB to WW, July 22, 1918.
[2] Persons not heretofore identified in this series were Adolph Germer, national sec-

retary of the Socialist party and an organizer for the United Mine Workers of America; Art Young, political cartoonist, a frequent contributor to *The Metropolitan*, *The Masses*, and *The Liberator*; Floyd Dell, an associate editor of *The Masses*; Prince (he later spelled it as "Prynce" or Pryns") Charles Hopkins, a wealthy Socialist from Santa Barbara, Calif.; and Frederick Krafft, Socialist candidate for Governor of New Jersey in 1916.

[3] Printed as an Enclosure with WW to NDB, July 15, 1918, Vol. 48.

From Joseph Patrick Tumulty

Dear Governor: The White House August 7, 1918

Our friends in New Jersey, without consulting us in any way, selected Senator Johnson[1] of Bergen County to make the fight for Senator. In my opinion Johnson has none of the qualities of a winning candidate and his selection will be practically a confession of judgment in favor of Edge.

Judge Hudspeth wrote me this morning and told me what has been done, and I have written him, without in any way attempting to convey your opinion, telling him how I personally feel about it. There are so many reports coming to me from day to day, especially from Republican sources, that we have a great opportunity to beat Edge, that it would be a neglect of our duty to the State to allow this election to go by default.

I believe that if you will authorize me to say to Tom Haight[2] that it is his duty to make the fight, he will do so. I hate to burden you in these days, but I am sure that we can win a Senator in New Jersey if Haight will consent to run. I would not have you write Haight, but suggest that you write a letter to me—which I will not let get out of my possession—telling me that you think it is Haight's duty to run. If he should be defeated, there are many places where the services of such a fine man could be utilized. Only yesterday, Mr. Hurley was telling me that the Shipping Board is very much in need of good lawyers.   J P Tumulty

TLS (WP, DLC).
   [1] James A. Courvoisier Johnson, lawyer of Englewood, N. J., and New York, Democratic state senator from Bergen County, 1911-1913.
   [2] Thomas Griffith Haight, judge of the United States District Court in Newark.

From Joseph Wingate Folk

                              St. Louis, Mo., August 7, 1918.

I have been nominated for Senator by about forty thousand majority. Permit me to assure you again that I shall stand by you and in the Senate your policies will be my policies. With sincere regards.
                                        Jos. W. Folk.

T telegram (WP, DLC).

A Translation of a Telegram from Jean Jules Jusserand to the Foreign Ministry

Washington, received August 7, 1918.

No. 1050   Following my telegram 1045.[1]

I asked the President, whom I saw today, if he intended to publish, in connection with the sending of troops to Siberia, a more formal declaration of disinterestedness than the one contained in his communique to the press of the day before yesterday.

He replied: "I was caught short because of the publicity given unexpectedly by Japan to the result of our pourparlers. On my part, I had to publish something immediately. I intend to be held to this declaration of disinterestedness, which I would try if I could to address directly to the Russian people, who have no government; but we will do whatever is necessary so that they, meanwhile, should know it." . . .[2]   Jusserand.

T telegram (État-Major, L'Armée de Terre, Service Historique, 4 N 46, FMD-Ar).
   [1] J. J. Jusserand to the Foreign Ministry, received Aug. 6, 1918, T telegram, *ibid.* Jusserand reported on the answer which he had received from the State Department when he had asked why the statement to the press printed at August 3, 1918, had been published so suddenly. The reply was essentially the same as that of Wilson quoted in the above telegram.
   [2] Here follows a brief commentary by Jusserand.

To William Bauchop Wilson

My dear Mr. Secretary: The White House 8 August, 1918.

Just today the enclosed letter[1] turns up, which shows that the decision of the National War Labor Board in regard to the wages on the Chicago Elevated Railroad system has a wider range of possible meaning and effect than I had at first realized. I would appreciate it very much if you might bring these considerations, which are profoundly important, to the attention of Mr. Taft and Mr. Walsh, together with an expression of my concern about them.
          Cordially and faithfully yours,   Woodrow Wilson

TLS (LDR, RG 174, DNA).
   [1] Britton Ihrie Budd to JPT, Aug. 6, 1918, TLS (WP, DLC). Budd, president of the four elevated railway companies of Chicago as well as of the Chicago, North Shore, & Milwaukee Railroad, pointed out several other inequities in wages created by the recent decisions of the War Labor Board in regard to employees of electric railways.

To Joseph Patrick Tumulty

My dear Tumulty: The White House 8 August, 1918.

I am very much concerned about the Senator situation in New Jersey, and it seems clearer to me every day that it is really the duty of Judge Haight to allow himself to become a candidate for the Democratic nomination. I know what sacrifice this will involve on his part, but I also know of his unusually strong sense of public duty, and I hope with all my heart that you will present this aspect of the matter to him, along with my strong hope that he may see it in the light that we do.[1]

Always faithfully yours,   Woodrow Wilson

TLS (J. P. Tumulty Papers, DLC).
[1] For whatever reason, Haight did not run for the nomination. As it turned out, Wilson's old friend, George Mason LaMonte, was the Democratic candidate for senator.

To Samuel Gompers

My dear Mr. Gompers: The White House 8 August, 1918.

Your letter of August 5th[1] gives me real pleasure. I knew the errand upon which you had gone to Chicago and am mightily pleased by your report of the results.

I have been thinking a great deal about the Labor Day celebration in Chicago, and thinking with a genuine desire to be present if it should be possible, but I dare not, as you know, create expectations because I never know from one day to another what I am free to do away from Washington. All I can say, therefore, at present is that I shall keep this matter in mind with a great deal of interest and sympathy.

Cordially and sincerely yours,   Woodrow Wilson

TLS (S. Gompers Corr., AFL-CIO-Ar).
[1] It is missing.

To Frank Lyon Polk, with Enclosure

My dear Mr. Counselor: The White House 8 August, 1918.

I think that with regard to the matter you discussed in the letter which I return with this, that this is one about which we ought to go very slowly and with a very careful preliminary determination of large questions of policy. I do not like what Mr. MacMurray reports with regard to the British and Japanese ministers, and I think they are going too fast. They are trying to scoop everything while the war is in course and are thereby making the difficulties of settlement when the war is over every day greater. My advice is that for the present we instruct MacMurray to protest against any present effort to settle questions of this kind.

Cordially and faithfully yours,   Woodrow Wilson

TLS (SDR, RG 59, 893.102 Han/18, DNA).

E N C L O S U R E

From Frank Lyon Polk

My dear Mr. President: Washington August 2, 1918.

In a telegram dated July 30, 1918, copy of which is herewith enclosed,[1] the American Chargé d'Affaires at Peking reports that the British and Japanese Ministers[2] have suggested for early discussion by the Allied colleagues a proposal to request the Chinese Government to internationalize the former German and Austrian concessions in Tientsin and Hankow, and asks whether he shall concur in such a proposal.

A prompt decision is thus called for which brings up for immediate consideration the question of whether it would not be better for us to endeavor to obtain from the Chinese Government these splendid locations for American settlements.

The actual situation is briefly as follows:

There are four classes of foreign settlements at the open ports of China. 1. International in which the foreign residents, of certain property qualifications, without regard to nationality, elect their municipal government and control the area set aside by China for the residence of foreigners. Examples are the international settlements at Shanghai and Amoy. 2. Concessions made to single nations, each nation having a district of its own controlled by its own people, though in most cases admitting other Europeans to residence under certain restrictions. There are five such concessions at Hankow: British, French, German, Russian and Japanese. There are eight such settlements at Tientsin: British, French, German, Japanese, Austrian, Italian, Russian and Belgium. There are two at Canton: British and French. At none of these ports is there an international settlement. 3. The settlements established by China, under Chinese municipal control, but separate from the adjacent Chinese city. Such are found at Changsha, Tsinan and elsewhere. 4. Settlements at open ports outside the Chinese city but without any definite area set aside for them as at Chefoo and Newchwang.

The leased territories of Kuantung, Manchuria, (including Dairen and Port Arthur), Weihaiwei, Kiaochow, Kowloon, and Kuangchouwan are in an entirely different category.

Aside from the leased territory of Kiaochow, which includes the port of Tsingtau and is now in Japan's possession, Germany had at the outbreak of the war but two concessions in China, one at Tientsin and one at Hankow.

After China declared war on Germany and Austria the Chinese Government took over control of those concessions and they are now being administered by Chinese Officials.

The United States has no concessions of its own nor any settlement under its sole control. It once owned a concession at Tientsin but abandoned it ma[n]y years ago when American trade at that port was insignificant. In 1901, after the "Boxer" troubles the American Government attempted to recover control of the site, but China objected because two important Chinese companies, The China Merchants Steamship Company, and the Chinese Engineering and Mining Company, held the wharfage and were unwilling to give it up since no good location on the river would be left to them. China offered instead the location afterward set aside for Austria, but it was considered unsuitable for our purposes.

If the former German and Austrian concessions are made international it appears inevitable that in the long run the nation having the largest representation there will place the others at a disadvantage as is the case in the purely national settlements.

On the other hand if we own these concessions it will be in this way, and this way only that we can be sure of controlling adequate wharfage and docking facilities for our greatly increased merchant marine.

The public expenses involved in the organization and maintenance of these establishments would be met easily by the revenues now being collected on wharfage dues, real estate, licenses, etc.

Finally as regards the effect on the Chinese of our joining the ranks of the concession owning powers, it seems probable that instead of its producing an unfavorable impression it will be looked upon as a manifestation of our desire and intention to build up and put on a permanent and effective basis our friendly interest in the country and its future development.

I shall be glad to know whether the enclosed telegram to Peking on this subject meets with your approval.[3]

Faithfully yours,   Frank L Polk

TLS (SDR, RG 59, 893.102 Han/18, DNA).

[1] J. V. A. MacMurray to RL, July 30, 1918, T telegram (SDR, RG 59, 893.102 Han/18), which Polk follows closely in his first paragraph.

[2] That is, Sir John Newell Jordan and Baron Gonsuke Hayashi.

[3] Polk's proposed telegram is missing in the State Department's files. The following telegram was sent instead: "The American Government considers it inadvisable to discuss at present the internationalization of the settlements mentioned. You are instructed to protest against any effort to settle such questions now." RL to P. S. Reinsch, Aug. 28, 1918, T telegram (SDR, RG 59, 893.102 Han/17, DNA).

To Theodore Marburg

My dear Mr. Marburg: The White House 8 August, 1918.

I have read your letter of August 6th with a great deal of interest, but, alas, you do not know of course as intimately as I do how difficult the conferences at Versailles are. I would despair of getting such action as you suggest discussed there in the midst of the other matters bristling with practical difficulties which the Council has to handle; and moreover we are not at present represented at that Council, and in a matter of the sort to which you refer it is of capital importance that we should be.

It is unnecessary to add how much I appreciate your interest in these matters and how welcome your suggestions always are.

Cordially and sincerely yours,   Woodrow Wilson

TLS (WP, DLC).

To John George David Knight[1]

My dear General Knight: [The White House] 8 August, 1918.

I have your letter of August 6th[2] about suspending the eight-hour provisions of the law with regard to laborers engaged in construction, maintenance and repair of municipal buildings, bridges, street and roadway pavements; street and alley cleaning; disposal of city refuse, and the construction, operation, maintenance and repair of water and sewerage systems of the District, but before acting upon the recommendation which your letter contains I would like to be sure that you and your fellow-Commissioners are clear that such an order is absolutely necessary. I have become very uneasy of late at the number of exceptions which have been made with regard to the eight-hour provision of the law and have come to the conclusion that I am not justified in extending the exemptions further unless there is a clear case of public necessity.

Cordially and sincerely yours,   Woodrow Wilson

TLS (Letterpress Books, WP, DLC).
    [1] Brigadier General, U.S.A., Ret.; at this time a member of the Board of Commissioners of the District of Columbia.
    [2] J. G. D. Knight to WW, Aug. 6, 1918, TLS (WP, DLC).

To Francis Joseph Heney

My dear Mr. Heney: [The White House] 8 August, 1918.

I am writing to say how sorry I am that I did not have an opportunity to see you before you left and to thank you for the devoted and painstaking labor you gave to your work as Special Counsel of the Federal Trade Commission. It is hard, amidst my rushing days, to keep aware of how my friends come and go in Washington, or I should have asked the pleasure of seeing you before you left.

Cordially and sincerely yours,   Woodrow Wilson

TLS (Letterpress Books, WP, DLC).

To Frank J. Hayes

My dear Mr. Hayes: The White House 8 August, 1918.

May I not tell you what profound gratification I have derived from the following item in the United Mine Workers' Journal of July 25th:

"On July 5, the wives and sweethearts gathered about a thousand mine shafts from the Pacific to the Atlantic and checked off the men as they reported for work. Over every mine flew an American flag, emblematic of the second line of defense, of which the miners are a chief factor. And at each pit mouth hung a quotation from President Wilson."

It is very delightful to feel that I am thus brought into comradeship with the workers who are doing such essential labor for the support of the government and of the liberties of free men everywhere.   Cordially and sincerely yours,   Woodrow Wilson

TLS (UMWA-Ar).

To George Creel

My dear Creel: The White House 8 August, 1918.

I am sorry to disappoint the National War Savings Committee, but I know that Mrs. Wilson would not be willing to make any statement such as they suggest. Her chief anxiety is to keep out of the papers, and she has confined herself, and I am sure will confine herself, to those things with which she has been obliged to form a sort of official connection.

In haste,   Faithfully yours,   Woodrow Wilson

TLS (G. Creel Papers, DLC).

To Joseph Wingate Folk

My dear Governor Folk: [The White House] 8 August, 1918.

I appreciate very much your telegram of August 7th and the generous assurance which it brings of your support of the administration and its policies in the Senate. I feel, as I have no doubt you do, that a peculiar responsibility rests upon us all just now, not only to think straight but to act with unity and vigor in a cause which is perhaps greater than the public men of any time have ever been called upon to deal with. Every assurance such as you give me adds to my confidence in the eventual outcome.

Cordially and sincerely yours,   Woodrow Wilson

TLS (Letterpress Books, WP, DLC).

From Newton Diehl Baker, with Enclosure

My dear Mr. President: Washington. August 8, 1918.

I enclose a telegram which came to-day from General Pershing. The statements of Mr. Lloyd George are of course at variance with all we have been led to expect, but they may not be final statements of conclusion on his part but rather preliminary to some sort of negotiation he has on foot with Mr. Clemenceau. In any case, I do not think we should allow our program to hesitate at this juncture.

Respectfully yours,   Newton D. Baker

TLS (N. D. Baker Papers, DLC).

E N C L O S U R E

From HAEF *To* The Adjutant General, Washington, D. C.
Number 1,567 August 7th Confidential
For the Chief of Staff

Paragraph 1. Following telegram from Mr. Lloyd George to Mr. Clemenceau dated August 2d repeated for information of the Secretary of War:

Subparagraph A. "Recent dispatches from Washington give reason to believe that the United States Government has abandoned its program for putting 100 divisions on the Western front by July 1919 and that the greatest possible number would only comprise 80 divisions. We have also been advised that this program reduced to 80 divisions can only be realized if Great Britain should continue to furnish its help for naval transportation. Because of the serious character of this information I immediately made a preliminary study of the question with the minister of naval transportation Sir Joseph Maclay. I regret to declare that we shall not be able to continue our help as far as cargoes of merchandise are concerned and that we shall probably have to cut down the tonnage assigned for troop transportation. In the last few months we have lost several troop transports of large tonnage, notably the Justicia, which could carry 5,000 men and 10,000 tons of materiel per trip. As far as merchandise shipping is concerned we are already grappling with serious difficulties. Every day Austrialia and New Zealand ask for a help we are unable to give them. In Lancashire 40,000 cotton workers at least are idle because of lack of raw material and to increase the cotton supply we have been forced to cut short our program for cereal supply. Another very serious difficulty results from the lack of coal by reason of our need of man-power to keep the armies going in the recent military crisis. The coal question is giving us the greatest anxiety because the situation in France and

Italy as well as our own munition production depends upon a suitable coal supply. By reason of the lack of coal a large number of ships have been subjected to delay in our ports and our whole program of naval transportation has been shaken up by these facts. This increases our difficulty to help the Americans in executing their program with regard to merchant shipping. While continuing naturally to do our best for the allies in the future, as we have in the past, I think it best to let you know without delay what difficulties we may meet in attempting to realize the American program in its entirety."

Subparagraph B. The foregoing telegram was handed to me confidentially. The views of the British Prime Minister as shown therein seem to be an indication of his attitude on the question of aiding us with shipping to carrying out even the 80 division program. It suggests the desirability of an early and complete understanding with the British Government on this subject.   Pershing.

T telegram (N. D. Baker Papers, DLC).

From William Cox Redfield

My dear Mr. President: Washington August 8, 1918.
Respectfully returning herewith letter to you of the 5th instant from Mr. W. M. Daniels, Chairman of the Interstate Commerce Commission, permit me to say that I concur in thinking well of the suggestion embodied in the latter part of his letter.
                    Yours very truly,   William C. Redfield

TLS (WP, DLC).

From William Gibbs McAdoo

Dear Governor: En route, Aug. 8, 1918.
I have just received the enclosed telegram from Leffingwell about Warburg.[1] As I am not familiar with the situation, not knowing what, if any, action you have taken, I shall be greatly obliged if you will telegraph me at White Sulphur Springs Friday, August 9 (and as early in the day as possible) your suggestions as to what, if anything, I should do in the matter. I am quite willing to ask him to remain, as Leffingwell suggests, until I get there Monday and we can discuss the situation, but if we do that, it will make it extremely awkward not to reappoint him. I would push right on to Washington tonight and talk to you in person about this matter Friday if the doctor had not commanded me very sternly to rest

two or three days after this long hot trip and the strain I have put on my voice while having to use it on the train across the country. It is for this reason that I cannot reach Washington until Monday, the 12th.

Nell is in fine form and I am all right again. We look forward with great pleasure to seeing you and Edith very soon. With best love for each of you, I am

Affectionately yours,   W G McAdoo

TLS (WP, DLC).
    [1] R. C. Leffingwell to WGM, Aug. 8, 1918, T telegram (WP, DLC). Leffingwell reminded McAdoo that Paul M. Warburg's term as a member of the Federal Reserve Board expired at midnight on August 9. He informed McAdoo that Warburg's letter discussing the question of his reappointment (P. M. Warburg to WW, May 27, 1918, Vol. 48) had never been even acknowledged by the White House. Leffingwell had consulted with McAdoo's "other advisers" about the matter and they had reached the following conclusions: "We here, fear that to allow him [Warburg] to go out of office and leave town in present state of record, will give appearance of cruelty and ingratitude to one who has until now been treated as loyal and trusted servant of Administration and if it becomes known, will antagonize and embitter large and loyal element in community of which he is one, and at same time unnecessarily flout strong sentiment in his favor which has developed in press[,] banking community and reserve banks. It is clearly desirable to keep matter open until your return and if he is not to be reappointed until name of his successor has been determined, therefore, I venture to suggest you send him a kindly telegram expressing your sympathy with and understanding of his feeling and your own consciousness of difficulty of problem involved and asking him to remain here and give board benefit of his advice and assistance until after your return when matter can be definitely determined. If this course commends itself to you, I suggest that you also telegraph President and advise him immediately to write a short and kindly letter to this member on similar lines."

Frank Lyon Polk to Joseph Patrick Tumulty, with Enclosures

My dear Mr. Tumulty: Washington August 8, 1918.

I have the honor to enclose herewith, for communication to the President, a message from Messrs. Girsa, Spacek and Houska[1] of Vladivostok, members of the Czechoslovak National Council, to Professor T. G. Masaryk, dated July 31st.

I am, my dear Mr. Tumulty,

Very sincerely yours,   Frank L Polk

TLS (WP, DLC).
    [1] Vaclav Houska.

E N C L O S U R E   I

Message from Dr. Girsa, Spacek and Houska, Vladivostok, (members of the Czechoslovak National Council) to Professor T. G. Masaryk, dated July 31.

Begins: Our advance guard has now reached the river Ussuri,

the Vladivostok detachment having lost 170 wounded and 80 killed, while the enemy have had considerably heavier losses. The enemy have good and plentiful equipment, and we are still in need of much to complete our equipment, more especially artillery, aircraft, and cavalry, and we need considerable assistance from the Allies in this respect. The Bolshevists have proclaimed a forced mobilization in the district between Tchita and Habarovsk, but this is no less unpopular with the inhabitants than the previous voluntary mobilization. The enemy have now a total of some 50,000 men operating against our two forces. The advance guard of our Western group has reached the South shore of Lake Baikal at Kultuk. They are in a critical position and require help from us immediately, but we cannot supply this unless the Allies, by immediately landing troops to protect our rear, free us from Vladivostok, and also support us by sending one division with our force. When they do this we can immediately advance towards Tchita on the Manchurian Railway, and we could thus connect in five weeks with our force advancing from Irkutsk. We could then proceed either to Dairen or Vladivostok, if the winter is to be spent here. Our men are in excellent spirits and health. Rest will be required after operations are finished, and military technical reorganization could be undertaken during this period of rest. The task immediately before us is to set free our force and to concentrate it either in Vladivostok or at some other point. In undertaking this, we maintain the principle of keeping ourselves free from Russian domestic affairs, unless our interference is absolutely essential for the protection of our force and for carrying on military operations. This attitude is recognized by the population, who are therefore friendly disposed to us. We ask you to place at once before the Allies:

(a) The question of the completion of our armament and equipment, and

(b) The need for expediting military support, which Japan would have already given if they had obtained the official concurrence of the United States. This point is an essential one for us.

Bolshevism now seems to be disappearing, and continues to exist only owing to the forcible support of the Germans and Magyars of the "International Army." The movement against the Bolshivista has been strengthened thruout Russia by our action, and reports have been received indicating the deposition of Soviets in Russia, and it is also stated that a coalition central government has been created in European Russia, including Milyukov and Rodzianko. A temporary Government of autonomous Siberia has been set up in Western Siberia and it is stated that the Russian Central Government will be recognized by this Government. Conditions are not so

favorable in Eastern Siberia owing to the disputed [dispute] between the Bolshevists and General Horvat. We request your opinion, in view of the new situation thus presented, as to whether we
should stay in Russia, supposing this to be possible, and if so, under
what conditions. Please communicate to us for our information the
results of our formations in America and further, whether it will
be possible to make use of our surplus officers with these detach-
ments, and also whether, supposing that we remain in Russia, we
can depend upon completing our army with volunteers from the
United States. We should also like details as to our forces in Italy
and France.   Message ends.

E N C L O S U R E   I I

Note to the Report from Vladivostok, dated July 21, 1918.

The part of the Czechoslovak Army, situated between the River
Volga and Lake Baikal is armed only by such weapons as they had
taken from local Red Guards. They have no stores of ammunition,
for in May 1918, the Bolsheviks have removed all arms and ammunition to Chita, where they maintained a base against Semenoff.
For this reason the Germans and Magyar Prisoners, operating between Lake Baikal and Vladivostok, are well armed, and for this
reason is the position of our army critical.

Capt. Vlad. Hurban.

T MSS (WP, DLC).

From the Diary of Josephus Daniels

August Thursday 8 1918

WW called at my office with Baker & we decided not to allow
any volunteer enlistments until Congress completed the present
Army draft law.[1]

President thought too many men, who wished to volunteer instead of being drafted, were rushing into the service who ought to
remain at home, & a plan should be worked out by which such
men should not have to ask exemption

[1] That is, an amendment to the Selective Service Act, approved by Wilson on August
31, 1918, which extended the draft ages from twenty-one to thirty to from eighteen to
forty-five.

To Paul Moritz Warburg

My dear Mr. Warburg: [The White House] 9 August, 1918.

I hope that my delay in replying to your letter concerning your retirement from the Federal Reserve Board has not given you an impression of indifference on my part or any lack of appreciation of the fine personal and patriotic feeling which made that letter one of the most delightful and gratifying I have received during these troubled times. I have delayed only because I was hoping that the Secretary of the Treasury would be here to join me in expressing the confidence we both feel, alike in your great ability and in your unselfish devotion to the public interest.

Your retirement from the Board is a serious loss to the public service. I consent to it only because I read between the lines of your generous letter that you will yourself feel more at ease if you are left free to serve in other ways.

I know that your colleagues on the Board have not only enjoyed their association with you, but have also felt that your counsel has been indispensable in these first formative years of the new system which has served at the most critical period of the nation's financial history to steady and assure every financial process, and that their regret is as great as my own that it is in your judgment best now for you to turn to other methods of service. You carry with you in your retirement from this work to which you have added distinction, my dear Mr. Warburg, my sincere friendship, admiration, and confidence, and I need not add, my cordial good wishes.

Cordially and sincerely yours,   [Woodrow Wilson][1]

CCL (WP, DLC).
[1] There is a WWsh draft of this letter in WP, DLC.

To Joseph Patrick Tumulty

Dear Tumulty: [The White House] 9 August, 1918.

What do you think of the suggestion that Commissioner Daniels makes on the marked paragraph on page 2 of the enclosed letter?[1] If it strikes you favorably, what do you think is the best way to act upon the suggestion?   The President

TL (WP, DLC).
[1] The paragraph beginning "My mind rather works in the direction" in W. M. Daniels to WW, Aug. 5, 1918.

From Joseph Patrick Tumulty

Dear Governor: [The White House] 9 August, 1918.

The reports that come to the White House every day with reference to the situation of the street railways make is [it] necessary that some action be taken by you.

The recent action of the War Labor Board in recommending that action be taken by you and their wage increase awards pending before the Board, making the increased wage scale apply to all utility corporations without regard to their financial condition seems to me to make action on our part imperative.[1] The War Labor Board take the position that the question of the financial condition of the companies disputing these awards is not a point in issue. For instance, in New Orleans the War Labor Board has just announced an award which will increase the wages payable to the men from approximately $2,600,000 to over $4,700,000. The aggregate earnings of this company applicable to fixed charges and dividends for the last twelve months are two millions and a half, whereof two millions represented fixed interest charges. The company cannot therefore meet the Labor Board's award. See letter to Mr. Tumulty from Mr. Francis T. Homer, dated August 7.[2]

It now looks as if in the months to come we will have to appoint a railway administrator.

This matter is so fraught with danger that we cannot proceed too slowly. I do not know whether Mr. Daniels' way to handle it is the proper way. I would suggest that you write to Mr. Daniels, saying that your mind is "to let" on the subject, and asking him to prepare for you, so that you can consider it, such a statement as he indicated in page 2 of his letter. To issue a statement right now embodying Mr. Daniels' idea would be equivalent to announcing a policy, which we might have to recede from in the months to come.

                                                            J.P.T.

TL (WP, DLC).
[1] About the recommendation by the War Labor Board that Wilson take action to raise street railway fares and his response thereto, see n. 1 to the Enclosure printed with JPT to WW, July 5, 1918, and WW to W. H. Taft and F. P. Walsh, July 9, 1918, both in Vol. 48. In the wake of that correspondence, Taft and Walsh had decided to proceed with the specific cases pending before the board and, on July 31, made awards in twenty-two cases. In all cases, they recommended substantial increases in the minimum wage to be paid to the several classes of workers and in each case they also recommended that the state or local agency having the power to set rates for the particular utility concerned grant an increase in fares sufficient to cover the cost of the wage increases. For a detailed discussion of the background, as well as the effect, of these awards, see Valerie Jean Conner, *The National War Labor Board*, pp. 68-88.
[2] It is missing.

To Alexander Monroe Dockery

My dear Governor Dockery: [The White House] 9 August, 1918.

Thank you very warmly for your list of the Democratic nominees for Congress in Missouri.[1] I am particularly glad to see that Shackleford[2] did not obtain a renomination.

May I ask what your interpretation is of the attitude of Mr. W. T. Bland,[3] of Kansas City, who defeated Mr. Borland[4] at the primaries? I had a good opinion of Borland, and had heard that Mr. Bland was allied with the forces that approve and support Senator Reed. Is that your own analysis of the situation?

Cordially and faithfully yours,   Woodrow Wilson

TLS (Letterpress Books, WP, DLC).
  [1] [A. M. Dockery], "NAMES AND POST OFFICE ADDRESSES OF DEMOCRATIC NOMINEES FOR CONGRESS SELECTED AT THE MISSOURI STATE PRIMARY ELECTION HELD TUESDAY, AUGUST 6, 1918," T MS (WP, DLC).
  [2] That is, Dorsey William Shackleford.
  [3] William Thomas Bland, former lawyer; recently retired as president of a wholesale drug company in Kansas City, Mo.
  [4] William Patterson Borland, congressman from Kansas City, Mo.

To Franklin Potts Glass

[The White House] 9 August, 1918.

Your message received.[1] I do not feel at liberty to make any discrimination between candidates equally loyal, but I think I am justified in saying that Mr. Huddleston's record proved him in every way an opponent of the Administration.

Woodrow Wilson[2]

T telegram (Letterpress Books, WP, DLC).
  [1] It is missing.
  [2] This telegram was printed in the *Birmingham News*, Aug. 9 and 10, 1918.

To Newton Diehl Baker

Dear Baker,   The White House 9 Aug., 1918

This is serious,[1] and—how characteristic after urging the 100 division programme! We must now insist that the decision be definite and final as to what they can do. Would that we were dealing with responsible persons!   W.W.

WWTLI (N. D. Baker Papers, DLC).
  [1] The Enclosure printed with NDB to WW, Aug. 8, 1918.

From the White House Staff

The White House.

Memorandum for the President: August 9, 1918.

Secretary Daniels telephones to ask if he, Mr. Baruch, Mr. Polk, and Mr. Garfield may see the President today on the Mexican Oil situation.[1]

T MS (WP, DLC).
[1] See the extract from the Daniels Diary printed at Aug. 9, 1918.

From Edward Mandell House, with Enclosure

Dear Governor: Magnolia, Mass. August 9, 1918.

Here is a copy of a letter from Lord Robert Cecil in reply to the one I wrote him about the League of Nations.

I do not agree with his conclusions. He would make the League an innocuous affair and leave the work where it is now.

I enclose a clipping[1] from an English paper giving Arthur Henderson's view of the subject, which I think more nearly represents the body of opinion everywhere.

Affectionately yours,   E. M. House

TLS (WP, DLC).
[1] " 'Parliament of Man': Mr. Henderson on the Task of a League of Nations," unidentified newspaper clipping (WP, DLC). Henderson declared that the organized working-class movement wanted a "peace of reconciliation" and a league of nations which would be an "international legislature" in which the peoples of the world would be truly represented and a body which would have "overriding political authority" in world affairs.

ENCLOSURE

Lord Robert Cecil to Edward Mandell House

Confidential.

My dear Colonel House: London. July 22, 1918

I am extremely grateful to you for your letter of June 24th.[1]

There are indeed a large number of opinions about a league of nations, but I am struck with the fact that certain broad principles seem pretty generally accepted. One is that international disputes may be divided into two classes, though it is obvious that the definition of classes must be rather nebulous. Still, broadly, almost everyone thinks that only the less important disputes can really be disposed of by a tribunal of arbitration, and that I am sure is true.

In any dispute between two nations involving vital national interests neither of them would be ready to accept the decision of any external tribunal. Nor do I understand that you disagree with that view, though you believe that it might be useful to have a preliminary discussion before a tribunal, and then a reference to a council of the nations.

You may be right, but I have a kind of feeling that it would be impossible to construct, even for this purpose, a tribunal that would command sufficient confidence to do useful work in vital international disputes.

The Phillimore scheme, as you will remember, proceeds on a different plan. It relies on making the two disputing nations, or groups of nations, bring their quarrel for open discussion before an international conference. This very much carries out your idea that we must rely on international public opinion as our chief guarantee of peace. The real trouble is, how are we to secure that the disputants *shall* bring their dispute before the council of nations? For that purpose, according to the Phillimore scheme, coercion is to be employed.

Since I sent you our scheme I have seen the French proposals.[2] Generally speaking, I am not very much impressed with them, but there is one suggestion which seems to me very important, and that is that we should utilize the international organizations which we are now constructing for the control of raw materials and other things as a lever to compel the nations of the world to accept a league of peace. The suggestion is that we might make participation in those organizations dependent on adhesion to the league of peace, which seems a very fruitful suggestion and well worth investigation.

I notice that you propose that the components of the league should make a profession of faith to the effect that they will abide by a code of honour. I think it would be all to the good to have such a profession included in the instrument by which the league of peace was constructed, but I am afraid I do not think that by itself it could be relied upon. The example of Germany in this war shows that under pressure of false teaching and national danger there is no crime which a civilized nation will not commit, and the same has been found true over and over again in history.

I am convinced that unless some form of coercion can be devised which will work more or less automatically no league of peace will endure. You refer to the history of the civilization of individuals; but surely the great instrument of law and order has been the establishment of the doctrine of the supremacy of the law. So long as codes of laws were only, or mainly codes of honour or good conduct they were always disobeyed by anyone who was sufficiently powerful to do so, with the result that we in this country had to endure periods of anarchy culminating in the Wars of the Roses.

On the Continent things were even worse, and it was very largely the luck of having here so vigorous a ruler as Henry VII, combined with his skill in devising a means of coercing the barons and feudal chiefs that really laid the foundations of our present civilization. The Star Chamber by its subsequent history achieved an evil reputation, but at the time of its institution by Henry VII it was a most valuable instrument for coercing the forces of disorder.

I admit that I do not see my way to the institution of an international Star Chamber, but I do believe that the means of control conferred by the complications of modern finance and modern commerce should be very powerful, and if they should be strengthened by such a scheme as the French propose I do believe that we might devise an efficient sanction for the commands of a league of peace. One great danger, however, I see in the way:

The French suggest that it should be confined to democratically governed nations—at least so I understand them.

I cannot help feeling that this is a most dangerous path for us to travel. After the Napoleonic wars public opinion in Europe believed that Jacobinism was the great danger to peace, just as we believe, with more justification, that Prussian Militarism is what we have mainly to fear. Accordingly, the principal nations entered into the Holy Alliance, with a view to suppressing Jacobinism whenever they saw it raising its head. Very soon Great Britain withdrew from the League, but it persisted with the most disastrous results for many years in Europe.

I am dreadfully afraid that we may make the same mistake now. Prussian Militarism is indeed a portentous evil, but if, misled by our fear of it, we try to impose on all the nations of the world a form of government which has been indeed admirably successful in America and in this country, but is not necessarily suited for all others, I am convinced we shall plant the seeds of very serious international trouble.

It is for the same reason that I am reluctant even to accept your principle that we ought to guarantee each other's territorial integrity. I am sure we ought to guarantee, as far as it can be done, the observance of all treaties, and as a corollary we ought to provide means for their periodical review, but I do not know that territorial integrity should be specially singled out from other treaty obligations and as it were crystallized for all time.

I hope these observations will not seem to you very desultory and unintelligible, but the subject is a difficult and complicated one.

Again thanking you very warmly for sending me your letter.

Believe me,   Yours very sincerely,   Robert Cecil.

I am in hopes that this Government will adopt the Phillimore Report as a basis of discussion with their allies.

TCL (WP, DLC).
    [1] Printed as an Enclosure with EMH to WW, June 25, 1918, Vol. 48.
    [2] A French commission on postwar international organization, headed by Léon-Victor-Auguste Bourgeois, had presented its report to the French government in June 1918. That government in turn had forwarded it to the British government for its information. The Bourgeois commission had recommended a "Société des Nations" consisting of an international council, a tribunal, and a secretariat. It also had proposed a scheme for an international army, organized under an international general staff, to carry out the decrees of the tribunal and defend members of the league from outside aggression. George W. Egerton, *Great Britain and the Creation of the League of Nations: Strategy, Politics, and International Organization, 1914-1919* (Chapel Hill, N. C., 1978), p. 74. For an English translation of the Bourgeois commission's report, see David Hunter Miller, *The Drafting of the Covenant* (2 vols., New York, 1928), II, 238-46.

From Frank Lyon Polk, with Enclosure

Dear Mr. President: Washington August 9, 1918.

Dr. Herron has been having further conversations with di Fiori,[1] who maintains that he is the representative of the Bavarian Government and King. Di Fiori says that Bavaria will undertake to bring it about that Germany shall propose peace upon the basis of his memorandum if he (Herron) expresses his personal conviction that such action would be favorably considered by you. Di Fiori's plan is to induce the other German states to join with Bavaria to bring pressure to bear upon Prussia.

I enclose the despatch from Berne[2] transmitting the full report of the conversations between Herron and di Fiori,[3] together with Mr. Phillips' brief summary of the conversation.[4]

Through our own and French sources of information we hear that di Fiori is regarded as a dangerour [dangerous] Ludendorf agent. Dr. Herron, however, appears to trust him, and refers to him as a special friend of Colonel Sondenburg.[5]

Do you not think that Dr. Herron is perhaps a little out of his depth and that unless we caution him against continuing conversations of this nature, the impression will be strengthened in Germany that he is an agent of this Government?

                    Faithfully yours,   Frank L. Polk

TLS (R. Lansing Papers, NjP).
    [1] About the beginning of these conversations and the principals involved, including Robert de, not di, Fiori, see WW to RL, July 8, 1918, and its Enclosure, Vol. 48.
    [2] P. A. Stovall to RL, No. 3788, July 11, 1918, TLS (SDR, RG 59, 763.72119/1834, DNA), the covering letter.
    [3] [G. D. Herron] "OPENING CONVERSATION," T MS dated July 6, 1918, *ibid.*, a forty-one-page memorandum describing the second series of conversations between Herron and De Fiori, which began on July 1. The Enclosure cited in n. 1 is a telegraphic summary of these conversations, based on Herron's preliminary oral report to Stovall. This memorandum of July 6 should not be confused with an undated earlier one of

forty-seven pages, which described the first series of conversations, June 7-10. This earlier memorandum is summarized in n. 1 to the Enclosure cited in n. 1 above.

4 It is printed as the Enclosure. It refers to the same conversations in early July as those reported in the Enclosure cited in n. 1, but Phillips' text is based on Herron's full report rather than on Stovall's preliminary summary.

5 Alphons Falkner von Sonnenburg, actually head of the censorship office in the Bavarian Ministry of War.

E N C L O S U R E

Substance of further conversations between Dr. Herron
and Mr. di Fiori, representing the
Bavarian Government

On July first di Fiori returned to Geneva after submitting to the Bavarian Government a memorandum of his previous conversation with Herron, in which the latter outlined the purposes of America in the war. He conferred principally with Professor Foerster, who occupies "the Royal Chair in the University of Munich," the occupant of which can only be chosen by the King, and Colonel Sondenburg, the Bavarian Minister of War. Di Fiori's memorandum was submitted also to the King, Crown Prince and later to the whole Government. Sondenburg said "the words of Mr. Herron are true. Either we must force Prussia to make peace or Germany is ruined."

Di Fiori brought back to Herron "peace proposals," official in the sense that they are "the proposition which the Bavarian Government will proceed to act upon if it receives the necessary encouragement or assurance." If it receives encouragement, the plan is for Bavaria to communicate with the other German states and so bring pressure to bear upon the German Government. Di Fiori's memorandum is given on page 7, and comprises:

1. Restoration of Belgium;
2. Self-Administration for all the Austrian peoples, including the Germans;
3. Complete restoration of Serbia, with free access to the Adriatic;
4. Restoration of Poland;
5. All Balkan questions to be referred to the Peace Conference for a final settlement;
6. America to mediate between England and Germany in all questions relating to colonial possessions; also in all German-English questions of the Balkans;
7. Disarmament; and
8. Society of Nations.

Conversations regarding Alsace-Lorraine followed at length. Di Fiori's idea seems to be that Germany will consent to give Alsace-Lorraine as many rights as England will give Ireland. He mentions that separation of Alsace-Lorraine from Germany would be against the wills of the "present peoples of Alsace-Lorraine."

Discussions followed regarding the Society of Nations. Di Fiori says the principal questions are:

1. The total future relations with England; and

2. The German position in the Society of Nations. "If Germany knows that she is in no danger of destruction and no danger of economic ostracism if she sues for peace, she will reach out her hand." Herron replies that the most important thing to the non-German world is some sure sign of repentance or change of purpose on the part of Germany, that Germany would never reach peace by bargain, intrigue and negotiation.

Di Fiori says that Bavaria will undertake to bring it about "that Germany shall propose peace upon the basis of his memorandum" if Herron expresses his personal conviction that such action would be favorably considered by the President. Herron replies he is not convinced that the door, if opened, would lead to any result, and is not convinced that the actual destruction of Germany is not essential to true progress.

Herron's concluding remarks: He believes that Bavaria's proposed action is against Prussia and not in cooperation with the general peace offensive; that there is great tension now between Bavaria and Prussia. He thinks that Bavaria, in making its proposal to us has given a hostage or a weapon into our hands and that a rejection of these proposals "even though it be purely personal and unofficial" or even the "refusal to make any answer whatever," may have an immense effect upon a part of Germany. Indeed, it may be that these Bavarians have put us in a position to strike a blow that would be equal to a victory on our part on the field of battle.

T MS (SDR, RG 59, 763.72119/1834, DNA).

From the Diary of Josephus Daniels

1918 Friday 9 August

Jas. A. Garfield, Judge Proctor[1] representing oil companies had conference with Polk, Baruch, & Garfield in Navy Department. They had been ordered to file their holdings by Mexican government. They said their lawyer advised them if they did so they would acknowledge the right of that Gov. to confiscate their property & would do it. We suggested it might be wise to file a protest. Lansing had already protested. Garfield & Requa seemed to lean toward the oil men, Baruch & [I] not.[2] We went to see the President and he decided the oil men could not stampede us. I told oil men what they wanted amounted to a declaration of war

[1] James Rudolph Garfield, at this time counsel for the Oil Producers Association, an organization of American companies with interests in Mexican oil fields, and Frederick Cocke Proctor, lawyer of Houston and general counsel for the Gulf Oil Refining Co.
[2] For the background and results of this conference, see Mark T. Gilderhus, *Diplomacy and Revolution: U.S.-Mexican Relations Under Wilson and Carranza* (Tucson, Ariz., 1977), pp. 80-86.

To Frank Lyon Polk

My dear Mr. Counselor: The White House 10 August, 1918.

I hope with you that Herron will not go any further with these conversations with di Fiori.

In the first place, though the basis of discussion proposed by di Fiori is in some respects a very fair and promising one, you will notice that the usual thing has happened. There is absolutely no mention of the situation in the East. These suggested terms ignore the existence of Russia, and it is plain to me that Bavaria would have no difficulty in inducing the Prussian government to propose negotiations on this basis, because I am convinced that it is ready to agree to concede practically anything that it is necessary to concede in the West and in the Balkans, if only it is left with a free hand in the East and Southeast.

At the same time I am puzzled to know just how to check Herron in this matter without seeming to have less trust in him than I actually and genuinely have. The course that occurs to me as best in the circumstances is to have Stovall communicate to Herron the suggestion that he say substantially this to di Fiori: that he has so dintinctly [distinctly] gained the impression that the government at Washington objects to indirect approaches of this kind and is definitely determined to entertain only official suggestions coming from accredited representatives of a government, that he has come to the conclusion that it would prejudice matters rather than promote them to seek to ascertain the attitude of our government in the way that di Fiori has hoped that he (Herron) might be willing to attempt to ascertain it.[1]

I do not think that it would be wise to state any of our reasons to Herron, as for example the reason I have just given, of the absolute omission of the Eastern question, because although I have entire confidence in Herron's integrity, such information would inevitably constitute a part of what was in his mind and would inevitably, I should think, come out in any future conversations of this sort he might have, and make the impression that he had means of knowing what sort of proposals would be acceptable to us.

Cordially and sincerely yours,   Woodrow Wilson

TLS (R. Lansing Papers, NjP).
¹ This message was embodied in RL to Amlegation, Bern, Aug. 13, 1918, T telegram (SDR, RG 59, 763.72119/1834, DNA).

To Winthrop More Daniels

The White House Washington
My dear Daniels: 10 August, 1918.

The situation about the public utility corporations is certainly becoming increasingly serious. My inclination is to adopt the policy suggested in the closing paragraph of your recent letter to me about the subject, and yet I am not a little in doubt as to what it may become *necessary* to do. Would it be imposing too much upon your kindness and good nature to ask you to draw up such a statement as you would suggest that I make by way of announcing the policy suggested in your letter? I would be very much indebted to you if you could and would do that.

Cordially and faithfully yours,   Woodrow Wilson

TLS (Wilson-Daniels Corr., CtY).

From Arthur Capper¹

Dear Mr. President: Washington D. C. August 10, 1918

Permit me to call to your attention and careful consideration the crisis with reference to our method of financing the war. As you are aware, a certain class in the United States desires to have the major portion, if possible three-fourths or four-fifths, of the cost of the war met by bond issues. The enclosed resolutions² adopted by the National Grange and the State Granges of Washington and Pennsylvania and by the American Federation of Labor, similar to those adopted by many organizations of farmers show the conviction of the producers and toilers of America that at least half of the cost of the war should be met by current taxation.

This Farmers' National Committee on War Finance has secured data and submitted the same to the Ways and Means Committee of the House showing that at least twelve billion dollars can be raised during the present fiscal year by current taxation, without in any way interfering with the health and efficiency of the people of the country, or preventing the necessary expansion of industries vital to the energetic prosecution of the war. The patriotic record of the farmers of the country in subscribing to Liberty Loans needs no comment. We feel very strongly, however, that in line with your address on the revenue bill to Congress on May 27th,[3] the time has arrived for a Liberty Tax Bill. The press of the country in announcing the new loan will be affected by the amount of revenue to be secured in the revenue bill now being framed. It is certainly a question whether it will be wise to attempt to raise over six billion dollars by a loan. It is beyond question that it will be much easier to raise a six billion dollar loan after a revenue bill has been adopted which will enforce the principle of equality of financial sacrifice.

Chairman Sherley of the Committee on Appropriations reported recently that the estimated appropriations for the current fiscal year ending June 30, 1919 amount to approximately thirty billions of dollars. We feel that it is most deplorable that the demand of the American people for a revenue bill which will [re]cover into the Public Treasury excess and war profits, surplus incomes, and the unearned increment of land speculators, should be set aside, and its importance belittled by the assertion that essential Liberty Loans are a substitute for a just tax bill. We know that an enormous amount of energy can be saved by the prompt enactment of a revenue bill before the new loan drive is started. We also wish to call to your attention the fact that the people of the country will not brook the repudiation of their mandate, which you so eloquently and logically expressed to Congress in your address on the revenue bill.

May we call to your attention the rapid growth of the concentration of credit, the evils of which you portray in "The New Freedom"? The Pujo Investigating Committee reported:

"The resources of Morgan & Co. are unknown. Its deposits are one hundred and sixty-three million."

That report showed that the resources of the banks directly connected with Morgan & Co. are one billion, six hundred million dollars, "aside from the vast individual resources of Messrs. Morgan, Baker, and Stillman"; to which should be added the resources of the Equitable Life Assurance Society, controlled through stock ownership of J. P. Morgan, amounting to five hundred and four million dollars, a grand total of two billion, one hundred and four million. There has been marked concentration of banking deposits since the war began, and at present the deposits of the National City Bank are, in round figures, six hundred and eighty-one million; of the Guaranty Trust Co. five hundred and sixty million.

Even more marked concentration of credit has been developed within the last few years in England and in Germany. A revenue bill which secures twelve billion dollars through taxes such as we have urged upon the Ways and Means Committee will tend to retard this dangerous concentration of credit. It will be a marked democratic achievement in the direction of the new freedom.

The remarkable machinery developed for securing loans in small amounts for the war shows that this money can be obtained from those of small means. Our Government might with propriety emulate the example of New Zealand and compel people to loan a certain proportion of their income to the government for the war, if such compulsion were necessary. The socialization of credit has made large progress during the war, and it can be fully established as the democratic method of financing public undertakings. The big financial interests of the country would naturally prefer to loan to the government, and to have the wages of the workers taken in taxation direct and indirect. We are grateful that you have expressed your opinion of those of large wealth or moderate wealth who, in these days, attempt to carry the selfish higgling of the market into their relations with the Government.

We therefore ask that as the privileged interests of the country are endeavoring to reduce the amount to be raised by taxation, and to place the major portion of the cost of the war upon future generations, that you make it clear that the Liberty Loans are not designed to interfere in any way with the enactment of a Liberty Tax Law, to which task you summoned Congress. The American people are not in a mood to temporize with our kaisers of finance. The fathers and mothers and wives of the men now in the service, and who are to go into the service in vastly larger numbers, will not forget it if there be any dual standard for wealth and men during the war. They will back you in your sincere effort to put men and property upon a par and will demand of Congress that they give you loyal support in this your effort. Of course we shall work our best for the Liberty Loan and make every effort to see that whatever amount is needed by the Government is not only secured, but that the over-subscription is large.

Yours very truly,   Arthur Capper

TLS (WP, DLC).
[1] Governor of Kansas. He wrote as chairman of the Farmers' National Committee on War Finance, whose headquarters were in Washington.
[2] Resolutions on financing the war adopted by the National Grange in 1917, the Pennsylvania State Grange in 1917, the Washington State Grange in 1918, and the American Federation of Labor in June 1918, CC MSS (WP, DLC).
[3] It is printed at that date in Vol. 48.

From The White House Staff

                                           The White House.
Memorandum for the President: August 10, 1918.

Dr. John M. T. Finney, of Baltimore, a trustee of Princeton University, who is now a Colonel in the Medical Corps, United States Army, has just reached the United States from France. He says he has a personal message to the President from General Pershing and asks if he may see the President for not to exceed two or three minutes on Monday or Tuesday.

Colonel Finney can be reached at the Office of the Surgeon General, Room 264, War Department.[1]

T MS (WP, DLC).
[1] Wilson saw him at the White House at 5:45 p.m. on August 13. Pershing had sent Finney to the United States to ask Wilson to appoint Brig. Gen. Merritte Weber Ireland as Surgeon General of the Army. Wilson told Finney to see Newton D. Baker about the matter but also promised to speak to the Secretary of War himself. Ireland was appointed Assistant Surgeon General with rank of major general on August 23; he was named Surgeon General on October 4. See John M. T. Finney, *A Surgeon's Life: The Autobiography of J. M. T. Finney* (New York, 1940), pp. 193-98.

From Alexander Monroe Dockery

My dear Mr. President: Washington August 10, 1918.

I am just in receipt of your favor of the 9th instant and hasten a reply.

The nominee in the Tenth District of Missouri is Harlan Eugene Read, instead of William Reid, as it was given to me over the phone the day before yesterday. The Tenth and Twelfth Districts are the Districts represented by Representatives Dyer and Meeker[1] and usually give decisive Republican majorities.

I note your inquiry as to the nominee in the Kansas City District. I have understood that he has always been a consistent supporter of the war policies of the Administration, but I will put this question at rest by some inquiries I am sending out today to Missouri on my own account. As soon as I receive replies, will be able to advise you definitely.

By the way, I transmit herewith a statement showing the total amount of deposits in the Treasury up to and including yesterday, on account of the sales of war-savings and thrift stamps.[2]

                              Sincerely, your friend,   A M Dockery

TLS (WP, DLC).
[1] That is, Leonidas Carstarphen Dyer and Jacob Edwin Meeker.
[2] T MS (WP, DLC). The amount was $575,370,750.26.

From Paul Moritz Warburg

Chevy Chase, Md.

Dear Mr. President,   Saturday, Aug. 10th, 18

Permit me to thank you for your gracious letter of August ninth.

It is a genuine satisfaction for me to be assured by you that I have been able to gain your confidence and—as you so generously put it—your friendship and admiration. I thank you sincerely for those words and for having given me the great opportunity of serving the country—and of serving it at this time.

I leave my post in the confident hope and with the heartfelt wish that the Federal Reserve System under your wise leadership may continue to develop as a tower of strength in war and in peace.

faithfully and respectfully yours   Paul M. Warburg

ALS (WP, DLC).

To George Huddleston

[The White House] 12 August, 1918.

I certainly have no wish to do any injustice.[1] Let the record speak for itself.   Woodrow Wilson

T telegram (Letterpress Books, WP, DLC).
    [1] Huddleston had sent the following telegram to Wilson, probably on August 10: "Newspapers publish telegram from you stating that my record proves me in every way an opponent of the administration. My friends and myself doubt the genuineness of this telegram. If genuine we believe that it has been procured by misrepresentations as to my real attitude. We ask as an act of justice to my constituents and to me, that you disclose the representations which induced you to send the telegram. I have supported every measure supposed to have been favored by the administration, except possibly four. No word of criticism of the administration has ever passed my lips. I have supported your policies in Committee on Foreign Affairs with unquestionable loyalty. Your telegram coming at the last moment before the election does a cruel injustice." Printed in the *Birmingham News*, Aug. 10, 1918.

To Newton Diehl Baker

My dear Baker: [The White House] 12 August, 1918.

Poor Yager apparently has been a good deal distressed by the unjustified attacks of the labor people on him in Porto Rico and sends me the enclosed letter,[1] which ought really to go to you.

Can I not correctly assure him that we are entirely satisfied that he has done his duty in these matters, and even more than his duty, and that if any commission is appointed it will be merely to clear matters up and make it evident to everybody that the charges were unfounded?

Cordially and sincerely yours,   Woodrow Wilson

TLS (Letterpress Books, WP, DLC).
¹ The Editors have not found this enclosure. A White House memorandum says that it was a letter from Yager to Wilson dated July 30, 1918, "Regarding labor conditions in Porto Rico, and charges made against Governor Yager by the labor leaders."

From Clark Howell

My dear Mr. President: Atlanta. August 12, 1918.

I am attaching herewith two pages from this morning's Constitution containing features that explain themselves.¹ To say that they created a sensation in the state puts it mildly.

In regard to your "personal and private" letter, sent with the one for publication, I have only to call your attention to the file of my correspondence with Mr. Woolley, of the Interstate Commerce Commission, to convince you that if any "mistake" was made when I first called your attention to the senatorial situation in Georgia through him, it was through no fault of mine.

I went into the matter fully with Mr. Woolley asking him to present the situation to you, and to urge that you send a letter expressing your view at that time, as you have done now.

Mr. Woolley wrote me of his conference with you stating that "at the proper time" you would send such a letter. I replied to him that whenever you did so I would follow you, and I have done so—just as I am always ready to do.

If the letter had been written at the time that I so strongly urged it through Mr. Woolley, I believe that Howard would have been kept out of the race.

Our mutual friend, Col. Edw. T. Brown, came to me a few weeks ago with your message concerning the situation. I told him I was ready to follow your lead at any time.

I took this position simply because I knew that *you* and *you only* could save the situation.

However, all this is "water that has gone over the wheel," and I am making this statement simply that I may not be placed in the attitude of having brought about a condition which both of us are now trying to correct.

I am sure that your letter will have a good effect, and that it will go far toward clarifying the situation.

With cordial personal regards, I am
                    Sincerely yours,   Clark Howell

TLS (WP, DLC).
¹ The first was the front page. In the center, under the headline "President Woodrow Wilson Urges Voters of State to Support Harris Against Hardwick for the Senate," appeared a toned-down version of C. Howell to WW, July 24, 1918, and WW to C. Howell, Aug. 7, 1918 (the Enclosure printed with the "Personal and Private" letter of the same date). The second clipping was an editorial, "The President Supports Harris

for the Senate." It declared that the *Atlanta Constitution* had no choice but to follow Wilson's lead in supporting Harris over "Herr Hardwick." The "peculiarities" of the Georgia primary law (about which see W. J. Harris to WW, July 27, 1918, n. 1) made it quite possible that Hardwick could be renominated with only a minority of the votes unless everyone united behind Harris.

Two Letters from Newton Diehl Baker

My dear Mr President,   Washington August 12, 1918

Please think no more of my vain proposal—it must seem very inconsiderate to you. Of course I must not set an example of disintegration when we are all more troubled about that than anything else. But I do believe I am young enough to be a soldier; at least I am not old enough to control a very impulsive desire which must spring from some reminiscent youthfulness! I am really very sorry I troubled you with it

Faithfully yours,   Newton D. Baker

ALS (WP, DLC).

My dear Mr. President: Washington. August 12, 1918.

I return herewith the letter of Mr. Russell Harrison.

The question presented is by no means easy. The quotation which Mr. Harrison makes from the order of General Crowder of July 10 is accurate; but where shall we classify Russia if not in the list of belligerents? When Russia had a stable Government she declared war against the Central Empires and became one of the principal and one of the earliest belligerents. After the revolution, Mr. Kerensky's Government was recognized by the United States and their ambassador received here, representing that Government. We have never recognized any other government in Russia, and if the present classification of Russia as a neutral is made to rest upon the Brest-Litovsk Treaty that would, it seems to me, constitute a recognition by the United States of the Lenine-Trotsky Government which made that Treaty. My personal belief in the matter is that the classification made by General Crowder is wise and that Russia ought to be retained in the class of belligerent countries, so far as the administration of the draft law is concerned, until such time as you determine to accord formal recognition to some other Government in Russia and recognize the withdrawal of Russia from the belligerent class by the action of such authorized and recognized Government.

I am disposed to think that the presence of American troops at Murman and Vladivostok implies that we regard Russia as a belligerent; otherwise it would be the duty of Russia to use force to disarm and intern our forces for the period of the war.

Respectfully yours,   Newton D. Baker

TLS (WP, DLC).

From William Thomas Bland

My Dear Mr. President: Kansas City, Mo., August 12, 1918

At the recent Democratic primary election in the Fifth Congressional District of Missouri, I received a very large majority over Mr. Borland, the present incumbent.

I am a Virginian by birth, a son of an ex-Confederate soldier, traditionally a Democrat, and have been an enthusiastic supporter of your policies not only during, but prior to the war. My only son (in fact only child),[1] and my only nephew (who is also an only child), are in the fighting service of our country.

The normal Democratic majority in this District is approximately ten thousand, and the nomination should be equivalent to election, and particularly at this time, when the people are so enthusiastic in the support of your policies to the end that we may win an early victory.

As I am not personally known to you, or you probably do not remember me although I have met you personally three times, I am writing to assure you that in event of my election, you will have an earnest, unswerving, and enthusiastic supporter of your policies in the lower house of the Congress. I realize the vital importance of unity of thought and action at a time like the present, and during the trials and responsibilities which the future must bring to yourself and to the nation.

Sincerely and respectfully yours,   Wm. T. Bland

TLS (WP, DLC).
[1] William Thomas Bland, Jr.

A Translation of a Telegram from Jean Jules Jusserand to Stéphen Jean Marie Pichon

[Washington] August 12, 1918

No. 374. As I have just informed Your Excellency, the President has once more spoken to me of the difficulty that the United States would have in furnishing the minimum of coal and steel which is expected from it during the present fiscal year in view of the normal war effort. It was one of the arguments which Mr. Wilson made in advance for a limited effort in Siberia. The figures which I furnished on this occasion to Your Excellency were only too eloquent. The needs exceed all that the United States has ever produced, and the means of production, on account of the growing demands of conscription, are diminishing.[1] . . . .

During the last interview which I had with the President, he told me that he would not leave Washington this summer (we have had this week forty degrees[2] of heat in the shade, with much humidity). I expressed the thought that the voyages which he could readily make on the Potomac, from Saturday to Monday aboard the *Mayflower*, might afford at least a rest very conducive to his health. He replied no, that he had given them up. "Coal is too scarce to use it in excursions. One must practice what one preaches."

This detail can serve to show not only the President's personal disposition but also that the danger is serious and that nothing must be neglected to remedy it.

T telegram (Papiers Jusserand, Vol. 17, pp. 264-66, FFM-Ar).
    [1] Here follows a summary of Wilson's appeal to coal miners enclosed in J. B. Neale to H. A. Garfield, July 31, 1918.
    [2] Centigrade.

To Joseph Patrick Tumulty

Dear Tumulty: [The White House] 13 August, 1918.

Will you be kind enough to send a telegraphic message to the Mayor[1] as follows:

"The President asks me to acknowledge your important telegram of yesterday and to express his opinion that as the existing law is interpreted, the Federal Government has no power to take over electric railways and lighting companies. The condition under which such companies operate in different parts of the country vary by so wide a variation that no common rule, it would appear, or method of relief could be applied to them; and it is the President's judgment that it is imperatively necessary that local and State authorities should take the action necessary for immediate relief."

The President

TL (WP, DLC).
    [1] Martin Behrman of New Orleans. Wilson was replying to M. Behrman to WW, Aug. 12, 1918, T telegram (WP, DLC). Behrman called Wilson's attention to the "acutely critical condition" of the New Orleans Railway and Light Co., a condition which he attributed to the wage increases recently awarded by the War Labor Board and to the continued increase in the cost of fuel and other materials. The company was totally unable to meet its operating costs, and the city could do nothing further to help. "I realize," Behrman concluded, "the condition to which I refer is common to these instrumentalities throughout the country and therefore may I not suggest that the only solution as I see it in this crisis which threatens our financial and industrial welfare is

for the Federal Government to intervene and take over or in some manner operate these properties as has been done with respect to other necessary war activities. I cannot too strongly impress upon you the emergency which we face."

To Charles Richard Van Hise

My dear Dr. Van Hise: [The White House] 13 August, 1918.

I have your letter of August 8th.[1] The important convention which you are expecting to hold in Madison in November will, you tell me, be under the auspices of the League to Enforce Peace. I am a very warm advocate of a league to enforce peace, but my embarrassment is that the association calling itself by that name has a particular programme which I have not thought it wise to endorse, warmly as I approve the underlying principle, and any official representation of the administration at a convention under the auspices of the League would be apt to carry with it and imply endorsement of the particular constitution of a league of nations which the association advocates.

I have explained to officers of the League on more than one occasion that my judgment is that questions of the particular constitution to be proposed for the league should for the present be postponed, but the League of course cannot postpone its suggestions, because they have already been made.

I need hardly add that I write this in the most cordial spirit toward the League itself.   Sincerely yours,   Woodrow Wilson

TLS (Letterpress Books, WP, DLC).
  [1] C. R. Van Hise to WW, Aug. 8, 1918, TLS (WP, DLC). Van Hise requested that a representative of the Wilson administration, preferably either John W. Davis or Franklin K. Lane, attend the convention and give an address on "The Purposes of the War."

To Arthur Capper

My dear Governor Capper: The White House 13 August, 1918.

I have your letter of August 10th and realize the very grave importance of the question of taxation which it presses upon my consideration, and I beg to say that my whole influence has been exerted and will continue to be exerted in the direction of the raising of as large a proportion as possible of the funds now needed by the government by means of taxation, and of taxation along such lines as your own letter suggests.

Cordially and sincerely yours,   Woodrow Wilson

TLS (A. Capper Coll., KHi).

To Newton Diehl Baker, with Enclosure

My dear Baker: The White House 13 August, 1918.

Here is a memorandum (on thin paper) which was prepared by Dr. McLaurin[1] and handed to me by Dean Fine, and I also enclose Fine's subsequent letter to me.

They both concern the college matter we discussed yesterday, and I should have handed them to you at that time.

Cordially and sincerely yours,   Woodrow Wilson

TLS (N. D. Baker Papers, DLC).

[1] Richard Cockburn Maclaurin, CC MS (N. D. Baker Papers, DLC). Maclaurin, President of the Massachusetts Institute of Technology, outlined a plan for a Students' Army Training Corps intended to keep college students in school until their draft numbers were reached and, at the same time, to provide a pool of men suitable for officers' training or specialized technical training. Maclaurin proposed that all physically fit students over eighteen years of age be given the opportunity to enlist in the S.A.T.C. They would remain at their studies, with part of their time devoted to military training, until their draft numbers came up. They would then be assigned either to active duty at an officers' training camp, to an enlisted men's training cantonment or detachment, or to continue the special technical training in which they were engaged.

This plan was almost immediately superseded by a much more elaborate scheme already being evolved by the War Department. In this program, the Students' Army Training Corps enrolled almost all college-age students and, in effect, took over most of the college and university campuses during the autumn of 1918 for military or technical training. The students enlisted voluntarily, became subject to military discipline, and were entitled to an army private's pay during their stay at college. Participation by colleges and universities was voluntary, but almost all of them did participate. The program came to an end soon after the Armistice, before its full impact could be felt or assessed. For a brief description, see "The Government Takes Over the Nation's Colleges," *Current History*, IX (Nov. 1918), 265-68.

E N C L O S U R E

From Henry Burchard Fine

My dear Tommy,   Princeton New Jersey Aug. 10th. 1918

In our conversation yesterday we considered the case only of men pursuing a course in liberal studies at the colleges. I didnt say all there is to be said in favor of granting exemptions to certain students of this class on terms like those proposed in Maclaurin's memorandum. It certainly would be an unhappy thing were liberal studies to be wholly interrupted in this country for the period of the war. Their footing is none too secure at present and were they to be altogether discontinued as the proposed draft law, if without exemptions, would probably cause them to be, their fate in the years to come would be very problematical.

But it is not for the purpose of continuing our discussion of yesterday that I am writing this letter. I wish to offer a suggestion regarding another class of students in our colleges and engineering schools—those who are preparing themselves for the study of medicine or for work in applied science, especially chemistry or engineering. Men trained to do the work for which such students are preparing will be as much needed as soldiers in the war itself if this be prolonged, and there will be an immense need for them in the years immediately following the war. It is of vital importance therefore that the new draft law should not be such as to decrease this body of students. But that is not enough. Their number should be greatly increased.

The engineering schools cannot fully meet this need even in their own field. Why therefore should not the Government make it possible for the colleges which have the requisite teaching force and equipment to lend their aid? Such colleges could provide excellent instruction of the kind needed by the institution of intensive courses to be continued throughout the year in applied chemistry and engineering and premedical subjects. The Government—through one of its existing committees or a new one—could control these courses by announcing a list of subjects in which it would hold examinations at the end of one, two, and if thought wise three years—the papers to be prepared and read by Government examiners.

If such a system were instituted the only concession under the proposed draft law that need be made to the student pursuing one of these intensive courses and in his first year would be this: In case he were drafted in the course of the year and the college authorities reported that he was at the time well up in his studies, to permit him to remain until the end of the year in order to take the Government examination—with the understanding that if he failed in these examinations he would be sent at once to one of the camps, but that if he passed them he would be ordered to continue his studies—as a member of the U. S. Army on furlough for purposes of study.

These first year examinations should of course not be restricted to men enrolled in a college or engineering school. They should be open to any boy of the proper age who chose to apply for them, and if he passed them he should be ordered to some college for the continuance of his studies during the ensuing year.

If such a plan were adopted the committee in charge could readily determine how to deal with the men now about to begin the second or a higher year of their college or engineering studies.

In particular—though this may seem a little to one side of the main subject of this letter—the system of Government examinations applied to the engineering schools would be a much more satisfactory means of determining what engineering students who come under the draft should be permitted to continue their studies than the present rule which exempts those whom the school authorities report as being of the quality of the men who in their institutions have in past years ranked in the first third of their classes. The Government's committee and not the individual schools would determine who should be exempted.

I am sorry to be troubling you with so long a letter. But I can but feel my suggestion is of real importance. It has for its purpose the meeting of a vital need and one which thoughtful people throughout the country regard as vital. And its terms seem to me such as to provide a way for making the colleges and engineering schools of immediate use in meeting the needs of the country for the period of the war and the years immediately following it without in any way treating college students as a privileged class—even granting as I am not ready to do that to treat students pursuing liberal studies in the manner proposed by Maclaurin would be treating *those* students as a privileged class.

I cannot tell you what a pleasure it was to me to have such a fine visit with you yesterday, and to find you looking so well notwithstanding your carrying the burdens of the whole civilized world on your shoulders.

I am here only for the day. I return to Skaneateles[1] tonight.

As ever   Affectionately Yours,   Henry B. Fine

ALS (N. D. Baker Papers, DLC).
[1] In the Finger Lakes region of New York.

From a Committee of the American Federation of Labor

Sir: Washington, D. C., August 13, 1918.

On the 29th of July a delegation of six hundred representatives of organized labor appointed a committee consisting of members whose names are furnished on the attached list to go before the President on July 30th upon the Mooney case. When the committee visited the executive offices it was communicated to them that the President requested that the matter be presented in the form of a memorial, and in compliance therewith the enclosed memorial is furnished.[1]   BY DIRECTION OF THE COMMITTEE.

TL (WP, DLC).
[1] W. Bourke Cockran *et al.* to WW, Aug. 8, 1918, TLS (WP, DLC).

From Franklin Potts Glass

My dear Friend: Washington, D. C., Aug. 13, 1918

Please excuse my delay in thanking you most warmly for your telegram of last Friday to me at Birmingham. I left Birmingham a few hours after it came, spending Saturday and Sunday at Tate Spring, Tenn., in counsel with my partner[1] on some important business matters. I reached here yesterday, and have been on the jump ever since my arrival.

Your telegram created a great sensation in Birmingham. I immediately printed it in a special edition of the News, within an hour after its receipt, and many thousands of copies were circulated during the evening. It brought Huddleston and his leaders up with a jerk, and for about 24 hours some of them acted like they were crazy men. He fired off to you a very impudent telegram of protest, and a lot of his leaders called upon me with a written demand that I should give out all of the correspondence and telegrams, from myself and any others, that had been sent to you. This I flatly refused to do, and ignored their whole attempt to muddy the waters.

The assumption of Huddleston and his leaders, as I construed it, had a two-fold base; first, that you were a weakling and an ignoramus, and that you did not know what you were talking about in your telegram. Second, that you had been overwhelmed with misrepresentations by me. My judgment was that his course last Saturday was the climax of his own demonstration of his antagonistic attitude to you.

The News and your other friends in Birmingham immediately defined the issue as a square one between you and Huddleston as your persistent and bitter opponent, and called upon the voters of the district to decide where they stood—with you or against you. My information has been that a large percentage of his vote left him in droves, because you had so forcefully torn the lion's skin from the ass's back.

Your friends went to work with redoubled energy Friday night and Saturday. They sent out scores of speakers and about 25,000 photographic reproductions of your telegram to me. The primary is going on today, and I confidently expect Huddleston's distinct defeat. Many of your friends were sorry that they did not have your verdict a week earlier. I am confident that the three days' time in which they have had to work will result in Huddleston's defeat.[2]

Again I most heartily and cordially thank you for your final decision in the matter. I also congratulate you upon your admirable letters condemning Vardaman and Hardwick.

Sincerely yours,   Frank P. Glass

TLS (WP, DLC).
[1] Victor Henry Hanson, publisher and president of the *Birmingham News*.
[2] Huddleston won the primary on August 13 by 7,650 votes to 3,134 votes for Frederick Mitchell Jackson, a businessman of Birmingham, and 2,063 votes for the Rev. Dr. Alfred James Dickinson, pastor of the First Baptist Church of Birmingham.

Samuel Gompers to Joseph Patrick Tumulty

Dear Sir: Washington, D. C., August 13, 1918.

In a letter received from President Wilson, August 2d, he advised me that he had taken up with Secretary of War Baker my letter of July 30th regarding the investigation of labor conditions in Porto Rico.

I am greatly desirous, for reasons I am sure you understand, that some definite action should be taken on this at the earliest moment and I would greatly appreciate that you give to the Bearer, Mr. Santiago Iglesias any information you may have upon the matter.
                    Very truly yours,   Saml. Gompers.

TLS (WP, DLC).

From the Diary of Josephus Daniels

                                1918 Tuesday 13 August

Cabinet. Shall men in military services run for office? Baker said they should be disenrolled when they accepted nomination. McAdoo agreed. Suppose Pershing should be candidate for President? asked McAdoo. I would bring him home at once said Baker.

I: In Civil War Garfield[,] Hayes & others were elected to Congress. There are two sides to question President thought nothing should be done until after election & then they should vacate military positions.

Discussed Labor questions & steadily mounting pay.

Should men at work have medals? Yes, if some arrangement free from abuse could be devised Could it be?

To Thomas H. Daniel[1]

My dear Mr. Daniel: [The White House] 14 August, 1918.

Replying to your letter of August 12th,[2] let me say that I have perfect confidence that the people of South Carolina will judge rightly in the senatorial contest,[3] and I have not the least fear that they will believe that Mr. Blease is or can be a friend of the administration. The record of his opinions is already written, and it is a little late to expunge it.[4]

Sincerely yours,   Woodrow Wilson

TLS (Letterpress Books, WP, DLC).
    [1] Washington correspondent of the *Spartanburg*, S. C., *Herald*.
    [2] It is printed, along with Wilson's letter, in, e.g., the Charleston *News and Courier*, Aug. 16, 1918.
    [3] See WW to A. F. Lever, June 7, 1918, n. 2, Vol. 48.
    [4] Nathaniel B. Dial defeated Blease in the Democratic senatorial primary on August 27, 1918, by a vote of 65,064 to 40,456.

To Thomas Watt Gregory

[The White House]

My dear Mr. Attorney General: 14 August, 1918.

The enclosed letter from Upton Sinclair[1] has made considerable impression on me. I wish you would read it and make any comments upon it that you would like to make, before I answer it. I would like your "lead."

Cordially and sincerely yours,   Woodrow Wilson

TLS (Letterpress Books, WP, DLC).
    [1] U. B. Sinclair to WW, Aug. 7, 1918.

To Russell Benjamin Harrison

My dear Mr. Harrison: [The White House] 14 August, 1918.

Realizing the importance of the many collateral considerations surrounding the question that you raised in your letter of August 3rd,[1] I took it up for serious discussion with the Secretary of War.

The Secretary of War and I agree that we are under something more than a logical necessity in the matter of the classification of Russia as a belligerent. Where shall we classify her if not in the list of belligerents? When she had a stable government she declared war against the Central Empires and became one of the principal and one of the earliest participants in the war. After the revolution, the Government of the United States recognized the revolutionary government and received its Ambassador here. We have recognized no subsequent government in Russia, and if we were now to classify her as a neutral, we would necessarily base that classification upon the Brest-Litovsk Treaty, which we have never recognized as binding and which we cannot recognize as binding without accepting the Lenine-Trotsky Government.

General Crowder, therefore, was shut in to the classification which he adopted, and it does not seem to me possible to alter it without involving international misunderstandings and difficulties which would be of the widest influence and of the most serious consequence. I am sure this reasoning will appeal to you as conclusive, however unacceptable the practical results.

I beg that you will be kind enough to consider this letter as confidential.

Cordially and sincerely yours,   Woodrow Wilson

TLS (Letterpress Books, WP, DLC).
  ¹ See WW to NDB, Aug. 6, 1918, n. 1.

To Robert Lansing, with Enclosures

My dear Mr. Secretary,   The White House. 14 August, 1918.

I hope that you will reply to this to this effect:

The Government of the United States is bound in candour to say that it would be gravely embarrassed if the British Government should take the action suggested. The plan of action recently proposed by the Government of the United States, accepted by Japan and acquiesced in in principle by the Government of Great Britain is now in course of execution. Only a small part of the troops have reached Vladivostock. When all [are] assembled there they will number, approximately twenty-five thousand. It should, in the judgment of the Government of the United States be left to a later time and other circumstances, not yet developed, to consider radical alterations of the whole scale and character of action in Siberia. The President has several times stated to Lord Reading the unalterable facts which must of necessity limit military action and the supplying of armies in Siberia and hopes that he will be kind enough to set those facts before the Government in London more fully than is possible in a cable message.¹   W.W.

WWTLI (SDR, RG 59, 861.00/2501, DNA).
  ¹ Lansing repeated this paragraph, with only a few minor changes in wording, in RL to C. A. de R. Barclay, Aug. 14, 1918, TLS (FO 115/2449, pp. 65-66, PRO).

E N C L O S U R E   I

Handed to FLP by
British Chargé Aug 12, 18.

MEMORANDUM.

No. 894 In view of recent reports, the British Government feel the greatest concern over the critical position in which the Czech forces in Siberia now find themselves, and it is felt that all the Allies are under an obligation of honour to provide for the safety of these troops.

If it were in their power the British Government would be glad to give further help, but they have unfortunately no means of doing more than has already been done in this direction.

The only possibility of saving the situation by immediate action seems to lie with the Japanese.

In these circumstances the British Government earnestly hope that the United States authorities will feel it possible formally to request the Japanese Government to despatch at the earliest possible moment such military assistance as the military experts of the Czech and Japanese forces may consider desirable and necessary. Such a procedure would be in accordance with the public declaration of the United States Government, as the present state of affairs is clearly one of emergency, demanding the application of extraordinary measures.

The Japanese authorities have pointed out to the British Government that no formal request has been received from them by Japan with a view to sending the increased help now evidently necessary for the Czechs. In view of what the Japanese Minister of Foreign Affairs has said on this point, and considering the deep resentment which would be felt in Great Britain at any disaster to the Czech forces, the British Government feel that it will be incumbent on them to make a request of this nature, unless the United States Government have grave objections to such a course.

A recent report on the position of the Czech forces is attached to this memorandum.

BRITISH EMBASSY, WASHINGTON, August 12, 1918.

T MS (SDR, RG 59, 861.00/2501, DNA).

ENCLOSURE II

PARAPHRASE OF A TELEGRAM FROM THE BRITISH CONSUL
AT VLADIVOSTOCK TO THE FOREIGN OFFICE.
August 9, 1918.

Representations have been made by Dr. Girsa of the Czech National Council to the effect that the Czechs in Siberia are daily being placed in a more and more critical position. They have insufficient supplies of clothing, boots, military material, arms and ammunition, and their numbers are being reduced. The position of the troops between Samara and Irkutsk is even worse. The forces at the disposal of the enemy are constantly increasing; they are fully supplied with aeroplanes, automobiles, and artillery, and their organization is being perfected. There are now only two months before the beginning of winter and the Czech troops in Central Siberia will be lost unless help can reach them by then. Dr. Girsa urged that the Allies should extend their plan of operations and send a stronger force and also supplies, more especially aeroplanes and artillery; the forces so far proposed to be sent by the Allies are certainly inadequate.

The positive statement is made by the General in command of the Czechs that not less than three Allied divisions are imperatively necessary to deal with the situation on the Manchuria-Irkutsk front. The prisoners of war have now obtained control of the trans-Baikal Province, where they are terrorizing the inhabitants and forcing them to enlist in the Red Forces.

BRITISH EMBASSY WASHINGTON.

August 12, 1918.

CC MS (FO 115/2449, p. 49, PRO).

Two Letters to Robert Lansing

My dear Mr. Secretary: The White House 14 August, 1918.

This is a very moving address from the Polish Colony of Moscow.[1] I dare say it is not possible at present to find any channel through which to acknowledge or reply to it. We can only file it and remember it.   Cordially and faithfully yours,   Woodrow Wilson

TLS (SDR, RG 59, 860C.01/124, DNA).
[1] "AD[D]RESS TO THE PRESIDENT AND TO THE PEOPLE OF THE UNITED STATES OF AMERICA," T MS (SDR, RG 59, 860C.01/124, DNA).

My dear Mr. Secretary,   The White House. 14 August, 1918.

I think that it will suffice, for the present, to reply to this,[1] that of course there will be cordial cooperation in this matter when our people charged with it get over there, but that until they do this Government will not have the information [necessary] to the determination of the means by which the liaison is to be effected.[2]

W.W.

WWTLI (SDR, RG 59, 861.00/2548, DNA).
[1] British embassy, Washington, Aug. 11, 1918, T MS (SDR, RG 59, 861.00/2548, DNA). This memorandum stated that the British government had appointed Sir Charles Norton Edgecumbe Eliot as High Commissioner in Siberia. Eliot would represent His Majesty's Government in all political questions which came before the Allies and would

be in control of all British agents in Siberia, other than military or naval commands. "An important part of his duties," the memorandum continued, "will be to promote the closest possible co-operation amongst the Allied forces and their leaders." The memorandum concluded by stating that the British government attached "the very greatest importance to the question of facilitating combined action by the Allies in Siberia" and hoped that the United States Government would "co-operate to this end, either by themselves appointing a High Commissioner in Siberia or in whatever other way they may consider most advisable in the circumstances."

[2] Lansing replied to this effect in RL to the British embassy, Aug. 20, 1918, T MS (FO 115/2449, pp. 151-52, PRO).

From William Bauchop Wilson

My dear Mr. President: Washington August 14, 1918.

In accordance with the suggestion contained in your letter of the 8th instant, I submitted the accompanying communication from Mr. Britton I. Budd, of the American Electric Railway Association, relative to the decision of the National War Labor Board in the case of the Chicago Elevated Railroad System, to Messrs. Taft and Walsh, Joint Chairmen of the Board, asking them to give it their very serious consideration in view of the fact that complications might follow a discrepancy in the wages paid under this award where it pertained to joint employees one-half of whose compensation is paid under the wage schedules adopted by the Railroad Administration.

I am transmitting herewith a communication from Mr. Walsh,[1] in which he states that this case was submitted to Mr. Taft and himself as sole arbitrators and that the award provided for the appointment of an examiner to act for the Board in the interpretation and enforcement of the same, with the right of summary appeal to the arbitrators from any disputed point of application or interpretation. Mr. Walsh says the machinery provided seems to be working as designed, as the alleged inequalities and inconsistencies of the award have been referred to the examiner in accordance with the plan and are now receiving consideration.

It would appear, therefore, from the statements of Mr. Walsh that the matters complained of in Mr. Budd's letter are in process of adjustment, although the joint arbitrators, Mr. Taft and Mr. Walsh, have not yet had an opportunity of considering the whole matter as Mr. Taft is at present in Canada.

I am returning herewith the communication which you inclosed.

             Faithfully yours,   W B Wilson

TLS (WP, DLC).
[1] F. P. Walsh to WBW, Aug. 13, 1918, TLS (WP, DLC).

From Newton Diehl Baker

My dear Mr. President: Washington. August 14, 1918.

Replying to your note of August 12th, I think that Governor Yager is now satisfied with the letters that we have sent him with reference to the labor controversy reviewed in his letter to you.

The long letter to you is the result of a request made by the Chief of the Bureau of Insular Affairs to the Governor that he send a full statement of the case so that the Bureau would have the facts available, if necessary.

The matter, however, has now been disposed of and I understand, quite to the satisfaction of the Governor.

I am inclosing a draft of a suggested reply to the Governor.[1]

Sincerely yours,   Newton D. Baker

TLS (WP, DLC).
[1] WW to A. Yager, c. Aug. 15, 1918, TLS (Letterpress Books, WP, DLC).

From Winthrop More Daniels, with Enclosure

My dear Mr. President: Washington August 14, 1918.

Your letter of August 10th was received by messenger yesterday. I have tried to sketch such a statement as you suggest. I do not of course know the particular representations that have been made to you with reference to the predicament of the public service companies. My own knowledge comes from interurban electric lines not under Federal Control to which the Commission has generally accorded increased rates and fares, and partly from my knowledge of conditions in New Jersey. If I can be of further service in this matter please command me.

With all good wishes,   Sincerely yours,   W. M. Daniels

TLS (WP, DLC).

E N C L O S U R E

August 14, 1918.
TO REGULATORY COMMISSIONS AND CONSUMERS:

Of late my attention has been repeatedly called to the financial predicament or the threatened predicament in which many of our public utility corporations find themselves. Sharing, as these concerns do, with industries generally the burden of increased costs, occasioned by greater wages of labor, higher cost of coal and the enchanced prices of supplies generally, they have labored and are laboring under the disadvantage of not being able to raise their fares and charges except with the consent of various administrative bodies. The attention of State Commissions was directed to this situation some months ago by the Honorable Max Thelen,[1] who on October 16, 1917, at the 29th annual meeting of the National Associaton of Railway Commissioners, in his presidential address said:

"While the position of the steam railroads of the country, taken as a whole, is thus gratifying, the same statement cannot be made with reference to certain of the street railroads, gas and electric companies, warehousemen and other utilities. These classes of public utilities, as a whole, have not enjoyed the increase in business which has come to most of our steam railroads. To the applications of these utilities for authority to charge higher rates based on large increases in operating expenses frequently without commensurate increases in the volume of business, the various state commissions must give prompt and sympathetic consideration. In a number of instances, higher rates have already been authorized and in other cases increases must hereafter be allowed. In passing on these applications, however, careful consideration must be given by all parties to the question whether it is fair and just that the entire abnormal burden which has been caused by the war should be shifted from the public utility to its consumers who largely must pay increased prices for everything they buy without in many cases themselves receiving a compensating increased salary or wage."

Since the outbreak of the war there have been effected by the Interstate Commerce Commission and by the United States Railroad Administration very considerable increases in interstate railroad fares and freight rates. Increased costs of all kinds constitute the controlling reason for permitting these increases. The Interstate Commerce Commission has also in many instances upon the application of interstate electric roads including interurban roads not under Federal control, permitted these carriers to increase their fares and rates, in many instances not wholly up to the level of the rates and fares carried by interstate steam railroads, but to a higher level than prevailed before the war. All of these increased rates which the Commission has permitted to be filed, charged, and collected are not definitively approved but are permitted on a *prima facie* showing of need, and left subject to attack or complaint. In some jurisdictions state and local Commissions have also very commendably granted increased rates and charges to be collected by public utilities such as gas, water, and electric companies and also trolley roads. Consumers everywhere are fully aware of the fact that compared with increased prices generally the increase in the rates charged by public utilities has been essentially moderate.

There has been proposed for my consideration the institution of a special federal commission with power to investigate and to recommend increased rates for local utilities during the war. This proposal has not as yet commended itself to me for several reasons. Such a commission would seem to supplant the state and local regulative bodies which are now specifically charged with this task. Moreover the proposed federal body would have no power other than to recommend higher rates which it might think justified. It could not have the intimate knowledge of the financial history of such local utilities as is possessed by the state Commissions; nor could it more readily investigate where investigation either before or after an increase in rates is necessary.

It is not impossible that unless adequate relief to public utilities can be afforded by the authorities primarily charged with this duty the Federal government may have to consider as a war measure the taking over of public utilities generally and the fixing of their rates. But for the present this pressing burden devolves upon state and local Commissions having power to fix rates and I prefer not to assume that these bodies will fail promptly and generously to consider the financial necessities of public utilites subject to their control.

I am advised that in some instances disputes have arisen over rates and charges where there exist municipal contracts or ordinances naming the rates which may be charged by public utilities for their services. In some instances the municipalities have insisted upon their rights under these ordinances or contracts. These disputes in my judgment may properly be postponed until the exigencies of the war are over, and I make bold to suggest that the public utility companies themselves would be willing to agree that such increased rates, fares or charges as they are permitted to make during the war, shall be considered as in no wise affecting or prejudicing the essential character of the contracts or ordinances to which I have alluded, but that the legal rights of the parties involved shall be considered at the expiry of the present emergency without being prejudiced by the *ad interim* waiver of the claimed contractual rights and obligations. The granting of appropriate additional rates and charges may also in my judgment be limited by a special agreement with the public utility companies that all net revenues in excess of what is needed to continue paying present rentals, interest on obligations, and dividends at stated moderate rates shall be impounded as a quasi-public trust and not disbursed in current dividends but remain available for the payment of future dividends or interest charges or for providing extensions and betterments in the future as required by regulatory commissions. I also suggest that such increased rates as may be conceded could be made to expire within a reasonable time after the close of the war or sooner, if exigencies permit.

The need of public utilities for higher rates seems warranted in the first instance to enable them to make headway against rising costs of all kinds. Many public service corporations require higher rates to insure their continued financial solvency and operating efficiency. It is now profoundly necessary to stabilize the investment market in order to contribute to the success of the Government's policy of floating its war loans. These considerations conclusively warrant and require prompt and generous action on the part of commissions and even more widely on the part of the consuming public. I therefore urgently call upon all state and local Commissions to make prompt response to the demonstrated needs of public utilities and, under appropriate restrictions, to accord them the necessary increases in rates, fares and charges. I also appeal confidently to the great body of my fellow citizens who constitute the customers of these public utility companies to recognize the immediate necessities of these public service agencies, and to pay cheerfully such increased rates and charges as may be necessary to effect our one main and dominating purpose, the winning of the war.

T MS (WP, DLC).
    [1] President of the California State Railroad Commission, January 1915-June 1918; at this time Surveyor of Contracts for the General Staff in the War Department.

From Samuel Gompers

Sir: Washington, D. C., August 14, 1918.

The Senate Committee on Military Affairs has incorporated a provision in the new draft act stipulating that those registrants who are placed in exempt or deferred classes shall become subject to military draft if they do not remain steadily at work when physically able. The amendment in this respect reads as follows:

"Persons engaged in occupations or employments found to be necessary to the maintenance of the military establishment, or the effective operation of the military forces, or the maintenance of national interest during the emergency, provided, that, when any person shall have been placed in a deferred or exempted class for any of the reasons in this paragraph set forth, he shall not be entitled to remain therein unless he shall in good faith continue, while physically able to do so, to work at and follow such occupation, employment, or business, and if he fails so to do shall again become subject to the draft; the President shall make regulations for enforcing this provision."

This provision clearly means that the Act will provide not military draft alone, but draft for all labor in occupations at home.

The membership of the American Federation of Labor has but one purpose in this war—to win the war. Its purpose is to so conduct itself as to give the greatest possible strength to our country.

The American Federation of Labor has given every service at its command to make the military draft a success thus far, and it will continue to do so. It has voluntarily rendered full and unselfish service in industry. It has taken great pride in giving freely its best service to the Republic.

The American Federation of Labor must, however, protest most emphatically against any measure which aims to place the working people of the country under draft compulsion in industry. American labor would at once regard such a measure as a direct attack upon its integrity, and affront to its pride in past achievement and a suspicion concerning its motives for the future.

It will be unnecessary for me to recall to you the record of conduct and achievement made by American Labor since our country entered the war, but May I call to your attention the fact that in England where there exists legislation affecting Labor in a much more compulsory manner than in the United States, there has been a record of more wide-spread disaffection and stoppage of work.

American Workers ask but one thing and that is that they may have the opportunity to work under conditions that will permit them to give their best service to the country. They are ardent in their desire to serve fully and continuously. They recognize fully what is at stake in this great struggle. They need no compulsion, and I am sure I voice their views when I say that they will feel the keenest resentment at any attempt to compel them to give that which they are already giving gladly in a cause which they hold more sacred than life.

It seems to me improbable that this proposed compulsory legislation meets your conception of what needs to be or ought to be done and I express to you the protest of Organized Labor against the contemplated compulsory provision in the belief that it will find agreement in your own view of what is just and right.

Respectfully yours,   Saml. Gompers.

TLS (WP, DLC).

From Eleanor Orbison Beach[1]

Dear Mr. Wilson, Princeton N. J. Aug. 14. 1918

Have you heard the latest Princeton joke? Priest,[2] the druggist, said to Mr. Osgood[3] one day "This is a funny world!" "Yes it is," said Mr. Osgood, "But to what particular thing do you refer, Mr. Priest?" "Well," said Priest, "here's Woodrow Wilson president of the United States and boss of creation, and here's Andy West keeping a boarding house!" The Graduate College is now full of people who live and board there, as perhaps you may not know, and the fact creates a great deal of amusement.

But I am not writing to tell you this. I want to ask very respectfully and earnestly whether there is any position in France to which you could appoint my husband. Dr. Nason,[4] a Presbyterian minister, was recently for many years consul in Grenoble—and yet he didn't know French. Sylvester does and has lived in France and has had a good deal of practical experience there. He is a capital business man and enjoys practical affairs. Our three daughters[5] are going to be in Paris indefinitely. They are doing very good war work at present. After the war they can get good positions there as secretaries as they know French, German and some Italian and Spanish. They don't care for Princeton any more, for the same reason that it has become distasteful to us. Since the close of the Wilson régime the old atmosphere is gone. Not only that but, as we have never been able to conceal very successfully our feelings of partisanship and of devotion to yourself and your ideals, the situation here is not an entirely happy one for us. Can't you send us to Grenoble or Nice? Or Florence? I know Italy pretty well. An uncle and aunt of mine were consuls in Venice for years and after my uncle's death my aunt lived in Florence until her death. I have known many of our consuls abroad and know something about their duties. May I add that I have often wished we could be more fitly represented in foreign cities as far as social qualities education and cu[l]tivation are concerned?

Dear Mr. Wilson, as you *are* "boss of creation" couldn't you think up some useful post for us abroad where we could be near our children! It is so lonely here without them and we can't afford journeys back and forth either for them or for us.

Begging forgiveness for troubling you, believe me as ever, yours faithfully, Eleanor Beach (Sr.)

P.S. Sylvester is away on his vacation and has no inkling of my sudden determination. I don't want him to know, either, unless my request is looked upon favorably by you.

ALS (WP, DLC).
   ¹ Mrs. Sylvester Woodbridge Beach.
   ² Joseph Priest, pharmacist and confectioner, 4 Mercer St., Princeton.
   ³ That is, Charles Grosvenor Osgood, Jr.
   ⁴ The Rev. Dr. Charles Pinckney Holbrook Nason, Consul at Grenoble, 1901-1913. Before 1901, he had spent some thirty years in various Presbyterian pastorates.
   ⁵ Mary Hollingsworth Beach, Sylvia Woodbridge Beach, and Cyprian Woodbridge Beach.

From the Diary of Josephus Daniels

August Wednesday 14 1918

War Cabinet. Discussed how to obtain water & power at Hampton Roads and elsewhere without giving too much money to private owners. Decided for Baruch to make study in conjunction with War & Navy

RR wished to use 180 engines belonging to Russia. They were paid for with money G. B. loaned Russia. Decided to use them & to replace them later & to assure Russia they would be ready when R. had transportation and could use them.

WW. Referred to C. Kitchin as that distinguished stubborn North Carolinian who when he made up his mind would never open it. Loves to argue. Reminded him of a certain Englishman who (Jeffers)¹ loved to argue. One night he was ill. Some one out doors called out All is well & the sky clear with stars shining. He rose from his bed, saying "I doubt it" & pointed out a small cloud in the sky.

   ¹ He probably referred to George Jeffreys, 1st Baron Jeffreys of Wem, notorious for his hectoring and bullying of witnesses.

Tasker Howard Bliss to Newton Diehl Baker and Peyton Conway March

Versailles. August 14th [1918].

Number 180 Secret

For the Secretary of War and the Chief of Staff.

Paragraph 1. The personal letter of the Secretary of War number 5 dated July 28 just received says that your studies into possibilities of 80 division program were being sent to me with a view to my taking up with my British colleagues question of assistance in cargo tonnage. These studies not yet received without which I can do nothing definite. Can a full abstract of requirements be cabled to me? Meanwhile I suggest careful consideration of the following.

Paragraph 2. Some days ago Mr. Hoover asked me to consider

whether an agency could be created that could coordinate all other allied and inter-allied agencies controlling such questions as food supply, allocation of shipping for different lines of trade, etc. He believes that if this could be done demand for food and other things could be greatly reduced, thus releasing much tonnage for military programs. In subsequent interviews I told him I did not believe such a coordinate agency could work successfully; that individual nations refuse to surrender certain interests to inter-allied control; that existing inter-allied agencies can be controlled only by another allied agency or by a dictator; and that I believed the former useless and the latter impossible.

Paragraph 3. There is only one solution to Mr. Hoover's problem and I believe it is in the power of the United States Government alone to attain it. Our allies must agree upon some one question as absolutely paramount and agree to subordinate all other questions to it. In that way alone can we determine the sacrifices that must be made in subordinate matters in order to attain the paramount results and also whether the allies will endure these sacrifices. Everything now points to favorable conditions for launching a conclusive campaign on the western front next year, and if enemy's resistance is crushed on this front it will cease everywhere. Therefore I believe that the United States should aim at the successful termination of the war in 1919 and make that the paramount question. Our Allies agree that it can be ended only by American troops, supplies and money. But when the end comes they want certain favorable military situations to have been created in different parts of the world that will warrant demands to be made of the United States as perhaps the principal arbitrater of peace terms. To secure these favorable situations they are constantly considering schemes that would result in diversions of military efforts from this front. If sufficiently favorable military situations are not created on certain secondary theaters by beginning of Autumn next year the Governments of our Allies may be willing to continue through 1920 and at the cost of United States troops and money a war which may possibly be ended with complete success for us by operations on the western front in 1919. But if the mass of the peoples here knew that the United States was demanding a policy that successfully ends the war in one year they would support it and would endure any possible sacrifices to carry it through. As it is now no one proposes to them a definite object for sacrifices demanded of them. We merely ask for as many soldiers and guns and airplanes etc., as possible but the nation[s] will not make their maximum sacrifices blindly. They will make them only for a definite object which they know justifies them. They have a definite object in getting all the food supplies that they can and in keeping open all the lines of trade that they can. They will make further sacrifices in these directions only when the military men tell them that these temporary sacrifices will bring the end of the war into definite sight. The military men asked of the United States the 100 division program. This would give a certain numerical superiority next summer but no one knows whether it is on a definite plan for what the inter-allied Commander-in-Chief expects to be the final campaign or whether it only leads to another one for which a like demand will be made. The time has come to plan a campaign with reasonable hope that it will be the last one. The United States was obliged to cut that program to one of 80 divisions because it knows that the world will not surrender the necessary tonnage unless it has reasonable hopes that this is the final supreme sacrifice. If the allied Commander in Chief can now inform the United States that a certain definite military effort on their part will give him reasonable belief that the next campaign will be conclusive the United States will be in a position to demand of all the Allies including itself the sacrifices without which the necessary tonnage cannot be made available.

Paragraph 4. Preparatory to an interview which Marshal Foch asked with them the military representatives have submitted to him their individual views on the situation. We are on substantial agreement on the essential points. My expressed opinion is that with a superiority of approximately one million rifles by next July maintained for a few months we can accomplish our objects next year. Marshal Foch has this under consideration but when I saw him today he was not prepared to express an opinion. This year the Germans with a superiority of 250,000 rifles failed to reach a vital objective, but it is generally believed that with double that superiority they would have been successful. The allies must go further than the Germans to reach a vital objective but there is good reason for believing that we will be successful with double the superiority that would probably have made them successful. By next July French rifle strength will diminish to 650,000, British rifle strength will diminish to 420,000, and Belgian rifle strength will be 42,000. If the 80 division program can be carried out American rifle strength fit for the front lines July next will be 1,184,000. That excludes ten divisions which will not have been here two months and which include 169,000 rifles. Total allied rifle strength in France fit for line on July 1st next 2,302,000. Total German rifle strength will be 1,378,000. This will give an approximate allied rifle superiority next July of 924,000. But if obliged to do so the Germans might withdraw divisions from Russia to the number of 32 which might reduce allied superiority to 637,000 rifles. If the 100 division program could be carried out the allied rifle superiority July next would in the first case be 1,127,000 and in the second case 850,000. The foregoing calls for the execution of a minimum program of 80 divisions by July 1st next. It would be much safer if the 100 division program could be carried out.

Paragraph 5. If Marshal Foch will state that the 80 division program gives reasonable assurance of a final campaign next year I feel sure that United States can demand and secure the necessary tonnage. If he should demand the 100 division program in order to have the same assurance my hope is that the Allies will make the necessary sacrifices to carry out a plan which has for its definite object the conclusion of the war on this front next year. If we cannot do this we must deliberately contemplate a campaign of 1920 with its untold losses in life and money most of which will be American. I had a long interview with Marshal Foch today on this subject. He left me with the distinct understanding he would promptly inform our President of the definite efforts which we must make by next summer to give good hope of ending the war by winter. If he does this I suggest that our government immediately put the proposition before its allies with the demand that all contribute in the necessary efforts. If the United States give its money and blood the others can diminish their secondary demands and give the necessary ships. The peoples will not sacrifice much without a definite object; with a definite object they can sacrifice a good deal more. It is not improbable that this supreme effort of the United States to be made here at a definite time and with a definite object in view may be the only thing that will hold the allies together for another year. If it becomes evident that the war is to drift into 1920 some nations here may accept terms that will make all our sacrifices a sheer waste. If Marshal Foch should not submit a definite proposition my present opinion is that it would be wise for our government to force this issue at the next meeting of the Supreme War Council.   [Bliss]

TC telegram (WDR, RG 407, World War I Cablegrams, DNA).

From the Diary of William Phillips

Wednesday, August 14th [1918].

The President is indignant with the British memo of a day or two ago regarding additional Japanese military forces in Siberia. He has drafted a stiff reply, which may get us into trouble because it is not in entire accord with the public announcement that nothing in our

program regarding Siberia should be taken to mean a limitation of
action on the part of the Allied governments.

This morning, while we were seated around the Secretary's desk
in our weekly Cabinet meeting, the President stalked in. He apol-
ogized humbly when he saw what he had done.

Peyton Conway March to Tasker Howard Bliss

[Washington] August 15th 1918.

Number 80 Confidential Extra Rush

Paragraph 1. With reference to your number 180 paragraph 1.
Have you not received our number 74 dated July 23.[1] This cablegram sets forth the decision about the 80 division program and
gives specifically what assistance will be necessary from the powers
in order for us to carry it through. We have been expecting daily
a report from you as to whether that assistance can be granted. If
you have received our number 74 your paragraph 1 number 180
is not understood.

Paragraph 2. On the assumption that our number 74 has been
withheld from you it is repeated here entire to save time. . . .[2]

Acknowledge.   March   McCain

TC telegram (WDR, RG 407, World War I Cablegrams, DNA).
  [1] It is printed at that date.
  [2] Here follows the text of No. 74.

Austin Melvin Knight to Josephus Daniels

8-15-18

From: Flag Brooklyn Vladivostok
To: Secnav Washington.

Refer to communication from General Dieterichs and Czechs-
Slovak forwarded by Consul to State Department[1] this date urgently
requesting that the assistance to Czechs by American and other
forces be extended to Manchuria front and Baikhar [Baikal] region
instead of being confined to Ussuri front. Unable to learn where
impression originated that assistance proposed is to be limited to
any one area but in some way this impression has become wide-
spread and appears to be generally accepted. It is even believed
American Forces are to remain Vladivostok. Possible Japan officials
know something not known to myself and have communicated it
confidentially to others Paragraph. Have been asked for information
by Czech General who stated that all his plans depended upon
knowledge of cooperation to be expected. Replied that had not

information beyond that given in proclamation by U S Government.
Acknowledge 15015   Flag Brooklyn

TC telegram (NDR, RG 45, Naval Records Coll. of the Office of Naval Records and
Library, Subject File, 1911-1927, WA-6 Russia: Siberia, Conditions in Vladivostok, 1917-
1919, DNA).
    ¹ It reads as follows: "98. Following is a summary of a report by General Dietrichs,
commanding Czech forces, and of the transmitting letter of Doctor Girsa, member Czech
National Council, showing the necessity of more extensive Allied military assistance to
save their troops in western Siberia. The fact is that war prisoners are being armed
faster than allied assistance can arrive under present plans, and force considered sufficient when asked for six weeks ago is now inadequate. This is clearly shown by telegram
from Consul Ray forwarded by my 95, August 13, 5 p.m. which also shows that large
number war prisoners will have to be fought on other fronts if not fought in Russia. I
therefore earnestly recommend immediate extension of plans to provide sufficient force
to reach Irkutsk before winter.
    "Following is summary of letter of Doctor Girsa:
    "In sending you statement addressed by General Dietrichs to Czecho-Slovak National
Council regarding military hostility our troops, we have the honor to request you to
communicate to your Government our following appeal. It is clear that the position of
our troops becomes daily more severe whereas enemy forces are growing. Therefore the
task of our eastern detachment becomes, if not impossible, at least very difficult without
any guarantee of success. Our troops will of course cheerfully fulfil their duty, but we
feel obliged to point out to the Allied powers that this may mean the loss of the troops
participating. If our troops do not reach their destination by winter (within six weeks)
our troops will be lost, which would be a great gain for Germany and a loss to the Allies.
Russia would be entirely at the mercy of Germany.
    "Having received so many proofs of the sincere sympathy and active help of all the
Allied powers we venture to point out that our object—the liberation of our troops in
Siberia from Germans and Hungarians—can be achieved only in case the Allies do not
confine themselves to operations on the Khabarovsk front, but grant our troops sufficient
military assistance in our advance on Irkutsk. Doctor Girsa, Member Czecho-Slovak
National Council.
    "Following is summary of report of General Dietrichs:
    "The limiting of Allied assistance to Khabarovsk front makes question of re[dis]tribution
Czecho-Slovaks between Lake Baikal and Volga River assume critical form as enemy
forces will be withdrawn from Khabarovsk front to strengthen Irkutsk front, forcing
Czechs to remain in western Siberia over winter, insufficiently provided with munitions,
money and clothing. Enemy can concentrate 30,000 organized Germans and Hungarians, 70 guns, and 200 machine guns in Chita-Baikal area, where Czecho-Slovaks will
have 5,000 men with 6 to 12 guns and limited ammunition. Czech force of 8,000 cannot
be now concentrated on Manchurian border before September with 900 miles to cover
by fighting to reach other body our troops, during which it is possible enemy may attack
in overwhelming force and drive our western body of troops still further west placing
between me and them permanent obstruction in the form of strong military force or
destruction of railway.
    "I do not wish to deal with the position of Czecho-Slovak western group in case
pressure from Baikal region is accompanied by pressure by Germans in Volga River
area. It is evident that eastern group of armed German war prisoners will endeavor to
break through to west, join Germans advancing from Volga, and that strength of eastern
enemy group will increase as Czechs retreat westward, enemy forces being augmented
by recruits from war prisoners now disarmed by Czechs.
    "In this attempt the eastern German-Hungarian group takes very small risk because
they can rely upon food being supplied by Bolshevik authorities restored by their advance
and in the event of reverse they would be no worse off than on Khabarovsk front, where
a large proportion of them at critical moment appeared to be in prison camps or at work.
    "It should be pointed out that regardless of high fighting qualities of the 13,000
Czecho-Slovaks their chances of success against 30,000 German-Hungarian war prisoners cannot be regarded with complete confidence considering Czechs' great lack of
artillery, machine guns and cavalry, and fact that with Bolshevik assistance enemy
forces can be increased to 35,000 or 40,000 men.
    "No time should be lost as only six weeks remain for military operations in which
time every effort should be made to carry out these operations as swiftly and successfully
as possible. This can be done only by the Allies' extending their operations to the
Manchurian-Transbaikal front with large forces. General Commandant Czecho-Slovak
forces in Siberia." J. K. Caldwell to RL, Aug. 15, 1918. *FR 1918, Russia*, II, 346-48.

Helen Hamilton Gardener to Joseph Patrick Tumulty

My dear Mr. Tumulty: Washington, D. C. August 15, 1918.

This morning I received from Mrs. Catt a letter which asked me to telephone you, if I were able, in regard to getting certain information which she feels she must have if it is possible to get it, as she is having a conference on Saturday with Mrs. Park, and they are planning the moves to make next week in the matter of the suffrage amendment when the Congress reconvenes.

She wants me to ask you if you know, or can learn, *definitely* whether we can rely upon Senator Shields to vote for the amendment. Of course, if you know, and do not wish to write the fact, you could tell Miss Husbands,[1] who will bring this to you, simply to say to me that the vote will be all right, and I shall understand; or you could telephone it to me at my home if that would please you better. We are hoping that he has made a definite statement one way or the other to the President.

I am going to give Mrs. Catt's letter to Miss Husbands for you to read if you care to do so. The matter of the half pairs of which it speaks is, of course, confidential, as all of it is between us. The Woman's Party has tried to disturb that matter, as it has everything else, in its intense determination not to allow the vote to go through under Mr. Wilson's Administration, or at least during this session of Congress.

Mrs. Catt wants to know also whether Senator Key Pittman would be an acceptable "whip" for us at the White House. Senator Hollis has for sometime acted in that capacity, but got pretty tired of it toward the last, and as he says frankly, he is not personally interested in woman suffrage. Senator Pittman is, and would be, perhaps, more active in pushing and in getting the many things done that are necessary aside from what Senator Jones[2] does, but of course, we would not want to ask any one to do this special kind of work unless he were wholly acceptable to the Administration.

Senator Lewis, the official "whip," has never acted for us in this matter and is now, I believe, in France. Who will act as general "whip" in his place? Probably he may be a person who could act for us also. Senator Curtis has always acted for us on the Republican side.

If you feel that you can give me this information, Miss Husbands could take your dic[ta]tion and bring it to me if you cared to give it to her, and if not, will you kindly let me know at your earliest convenience in order that I may give the facts to Mrs. Catt.

I am writing this to you, but am telling Miss Husbands to give it to Mr. Forster and ask him to reply in case you are not there, and I shall be grateful to either of you as always for your helpfulness and courtesy. I am still unable to leave my room or I would come myself. Miss Husbands is entirely to be trusted.

Sincerely yours,   Helen H. Gardener

TLS (WP, DLC).
[1] Julia M. Husbands, an assistant to Mrs. Gardener.
[2] Andrieus A. Jones of New Mexico, chairman of the Woman Suffrage Committee of the Senate.

Sir William Wiseman to Lord Reading

[Magnolia, Mass.] August 15, 1918.

CXP 700. With reference to your CXP. 724 of August 14th:[1]

The President asks me to tell you that he has no intention of making any public statement regarding LEAGUE OF NATIONS and hopes that H.M.G. will not publish Phillimore report.

I had long conversation with him today which I will report fully tomorrow.

T telegram (W. Wiseman Papers, CtY).
[1] Lord Reading to W. Wiseman, Aug. 14, 1918, T telegram (W. Wiseman Papers, CtY).

From the Diary of Colonel House

August 15, 1918.

The President and his party arrived this morning on schedule time around nine o'clock. We had four or five motors, including our own, at their disposal, some open and some closed, so all kinds of weather might be met. The President was at breakfast when we arrived. I sat with him until he had finished. Gordon, Janet, and Loulie were also at the station to meet them. The President and I led the way in our limousine and the balance followed to the Coolidge home.[1]

Instead of going to his room to refresh himself, the President went with me to the beautiful loggia overlooking the sea and we at once plunged into a discussion of the League of Nations. I knew intuitively that this was the purpose of his visit, although I had no intimation from him. He started off by saying that he had written the Platform for the Indiana Democratic Convention of the other day;[2] that he had given it to Secretary Baker to take out and put through. Baker returned and reported "we put it through just as you wrote it except we cut your six pages down to three."[3] "This," the President said, "is what I have done with your constitution of a league of nations.["] He then proceeded to read it as he had re-written it.[4] As a matter of fact, he has cut but little except he has tried to reduce the number of articles to thirteen, his lucky number. To bring this about he has been compelled to have an addenda.

He takes two or three of the first clauses and incorporates them into the "Preamble." He has cut out the Court. We were in absolute disagreement about this and I finally contented myself by the feel-ing of assurance that the Peace Conference would maintain my position. The balance of the document is about as I wrote it. The only change of note is that I provided only for two belligerent nations and he makes the machinery include two or more, which is as it should be.

We discussed the advisability of making a statement in regard to it, and we agreed that it would be best not to do so. He has delayed it so long that the British are pressing to put out the Phille-more Report, and it would not do to anticipate them since I have asked the British Government not to make the report public. The President gave even a better reason. He thought if it were published in advance of the Peace Conference it would cause so much crit-icism in this country, particularly by Senators of the Lodge type, that it would make it difficult to do what we both have in mind at the Peace Conference. He also thought that some of the American group favorable to a league would feel that we had not gone far enough and other[s] would feel that we had gone too far. We con-cluded that if a governmental report was made by any of the Allied Nations at this time it would inevitably cause more or less friction and would increase the difficulties of getting a proper measure through at the Peace Conference. I am sure this is true just now. However, if the President had taken the lead earlier and had pushed the matter vigorously, he might have given out his own conception of what a league of nations should be, and have rallied the world around it.

The President thinks, and I agree with him, that a league of nations might be incorporated in the Peace Treaty. In our discussion I stated that, in my opinion, it seemed impracticable to think of the smaller nations as members of the league on equal terms with the larger ones. He dissented quite warmly and said to exclude them would be to go contrary to all our protestations concerning them. I agreed to this and said when I sat down to write the Covenant I had in mind the participation of every nation both great and small. However, the difficulties were so apparent that I was afraid it was an idealistic dream that could not be made practical. There are fifty odd nations, and of these there are not more than twelve at the outside that would do any serious fighting in the event of a great war, or be of service in financing it, and yet the forty, under the plan we have drawn up and to which we both agree, could overrule and direct the twelve.

The President was deeply concerned at the attitude I took and yet he was compelled to recognize my argument. He wondered if we could not include all the nations that would be at the Peace Conference with a tentative understanding that other nations might be taken in later. I did not push the discussion further, but rather acquiesced in the suggestion, having in mind that at the Peace Conference all of the great nations would probably take my view, and that we could then form a league of nations which will give to those actually carrying the responsibility the main direction of it.

He has promised to give me a copy of the draft he has made. He says he will have to make it himself but will do so when he returns to Washington.

He asked if I had thought of the person[n]el of the American representation at the Peace Conference. He recalled, he said, that I thought there should be at least five. I told him the number was immaterial; that if he went, he would practically be the commission. I thought he should place a republican upon it, and the republicans of the country would expect him to choose either Roosevelt, Taft or Root. He at once dismissed Taft and Roosevelt as impossible and argued against Root. He said he had a lawyer's mind and since he was getting old his mind was narrowing rather than broadening. Nevertheless, I thought Root, at the moment, was the best in sight.

He wanted to know if I thought he could take Newton Baker. I thought not because he would then have to take Daniels and perhaps Redfield. Lansing from the Cabinet was all I thought should be taken. I am not certain that I would like to be a delegate. Unless I change my mind I think I should prefer not being one unless, indeed, the President should not go himself. In that event, I would want to be a delegate. From what the President has said I am sure he will leave this to me. It is a matter of indifference to him whether I go as a delegate or merely in an advisory capacity to him. He always speaks of us as one. There are many reasons why it would be better for me to be on the outside and, unless I change my mind, I shall go in that way. It would be consistent with my entire career.

After we had finished our conversation we strolled to the beach, the Secret Service men following. I introduced several of our neighbors to him and we then sat alone with Grayson on the veranda of the Billy Coolidge bungalow[5] and watched the bathers, talking fitfully of national and international affairs.

The President and Mrs. Wilson took lunch with us. The only other guests were Gordon and Janet, Grayson and Wiseman. After lunch we took a long motor ride, and in the evening we dined with them at the Coolidge home, which is within a stone's throw of ours. We left early.

[1] The Wilsons were staying at the summer home of Clara Amory Coolidge, widow of Thomas Jefferson Coolidge, Jr., located on Coolidge Point in Manchester, Mass.
[2] It is printed at June 15, 1918, Vol. 48. It could not have been written much later than this date, since the Indiana State Democratic Convention met on June 18, 1918.
[3] Actually, the Indiana Democratic platform incorporated Wilson's platform verbatim.
[4] It is printed as an Enclosure with WW to EMH, Sept. 7, 1918. Wilson's WWT draft, which he edited and revised as what is known as his first Paris draft, is printed at January 8, 1919.
[5] The summer home of William Henry Coolidge, a lawyer of Boston.

From Helen Hamilton Gardener

Washington, D. C.

My dear Mr. President: AUGUST SIXTEENTH 1918.

Although I have been in a hospital for several weeks past I have watched with keen interest and gratitude your efforts in our behalf.

Since I shall not be able to take a very active personal part in the coming effort to put the suffrage amendment "over the top," I am taking the liberty to write to you now to say that I hope that you will give us the benefit of any suggestions that may come to you as to the best moves for us to make—*or avoid.*

We work, of course, in harmony with the Republican leaders as well as with the Democratic, but we really have no *one* keen, well-informed "master-mind" in the Senate to guide and help us to make only wise and firm moves—which is so vital at the present moment.

I have wondered if you would feel it possible—or will[ing]—to come out with anything like an appeal to the Senate to not permit this measure to fail, and to handle it as a vital war measure—a question that must be settled *now* and settled right.

Your vision in this, as in other great questions, is so clear and so comprehensive—so inclusive of its future bearings on world, as well as on national politics—that if you once made the people see what it means for America's Senate to go wrong on this great principle at this time, it seems to me the reaction from "back home" could hardly fail to be great enough to push some of the men, like Overman and Trammell, over the fence. I believe that you will pardon me for the suggestion, even if you do not approve of it.

With the ownership of the Courier-Journal of Kentucky[1] now in the hands of a man who is a suffragist that state can be made to know that its senators are not "standing by the Administration," and Kentucky has a strong suffrage sentiment. The country generally does not realize yet the bearings of the present suffrage situation upon national and international politics—nor that the Administration feels strongly that the time has come to take this step.

If you could feel that the time has come for you to say to the Senate and the country some of the splendid things you have said to individuals—with the clarity of diction that is yours—it seems to me that even if we fall one or two votes short, the reaction will surely put those voting against it in an indefensible position "back home," and place you and the whole question before the world in the clear light where none can misunderstand.

If I did not believe that this is one of the vital questions for us *all* at this time, I would not venture to send this to you now, but I am very sure that you will understand me fairly. To be ill and obliged to fall out of the fighting and useful line at this critical time is a great grief to me, and so this is a "cry from Macedonia."

Very gratefully and sincerely yours,   Helen H. Gardener

TLS (WP, DLC).
[1] Robert Worth Bingham, a wealthy lawyer and former Mayor of Louisville, had, on August 6, 1918, purchased a two-thirds interest in the Louisville *Courier-Journal* and the *Louisville Times* from Henry Watterson and William Birch Haldeman. Watterson continued to write occasional editorials for the *Courier-Journal* as "Editor Emeritus."

Elihu Root to Edward Mandell House

My dear Colonel House,   Clinton, N. Y. August 16' 1918.

I promised to give you in writing the substance of some things I said during the luncheon at your apartment some time ago.[1]

The first requisite for any durable concert of peaceable nations to prevent future war is a fundamental change in the principle to be applied to international breaches of the peace.

The view now assumed and generally applied is that the use of force by one nation towards another is a matter in which only the two nations concerned are primarily interested, and if any other nation claims a right to be heard on the subject it must show some specific interest of its own in the controversy. That burden of proof rests upon any other nation which seeks to take part if it will relieve itself of the charge of impertinent interference and avoid the resentment which always meets impertinent interference in the affairs of an independent sovereign state. This view was illustrated by Germany in July 1914, when she insisted that the invasion of Serbia by Austria-Hungary was a matter which solely concerned those two States, and upon substantially that ground refused to agree to the conference proposed by Sir Edward Grey. The requisite change is an abandonment of this view, and a universal formal and irrevocable acceptance and declaration of the view that an international breach of the peace is a matter which concerns every member of the Community of Nations,—a matter in which every nation has a direct interest, and to which every nation has a right to object.

These two views correspond to the two kinds of responsibility in municipal law which we call civil responsibility and criminal responsibility. If I make a contract with you and break it, it is no business of our neighbor. You can sue me or submit, and he has nothing to say about it. On the other hand, if I assault and batter you, every neighbor has an interest in having me arrested and punished, because his own safety requires that violence shall be restrained. *At the basis of every community lies the idea of organization to preserve the peace. Without that idea really active and controlling there can be no community of individuals or of nations.*[2] It is the gradual growth and substitution of this idea of community interest in preventing and punishing breaches of the peace which has done away with private war among civilized peoples.

The Monroe Doctrine asserted a specific interest on the part of the United States in preventing certain gross breaches of the peace on the American Continent; and when President Wilson suggested an enlargement of the Monroe Doctrine to take in the whole world, his proposal carried by necessary implication the change of doctrine which I am discussing. The change may seem so natural as to be unimportant, but it is really crucial, for the old doctrine is asserted and the broader doctrine is denied by approximately half the military power of the world, and the question between the two is one of the things about which this war is being fought. The change involves a limitation of sovereignty, making every sovereign state subject to the superior right of a community of sovereign states to have the peace preserved, just as individual liberty is limited by being made subject to the superior right of the civil community to have the peace preserved. The acceptance of any such principle would be fatal to the whole Prussian theory of the state and of government. When you have got this principle accepted openly, expressly, distinctly, unequivocally by the whole civilized world, you will for the first time have a Community of Nations, and the practical results which will naturally develop will be as different from those which have come from the old view of national irresponsibility as are the results which flow from the American Declaration of Independence compared with the results which flow from the Divine Right of Kings.

The second proposition which I made was that the public opinion of the free peoples of the world in favor of having peace preserved must have institutions through which it may receive effect. No lesson from history is clearer than this. Very strong public feeling may produce a mob which is simply destructive, or a multitude of expressions of opinion which get nowhere by themselves; but to accomplish anything affirmative some particular person must have delegated to him authority to do some particular thing in behalf of the multitude. The original forms of the institutions created to give effect to popular opinion is not so important. Our elaborate institutions of government have grown from very simple beginnings developing to meet requirements from generation to generation. The important thing is that there are officers who have the right to act and the duty to act in doing things which are necessary to preserve the peace.

Some rudimentary institutions have already been developed by agreement among the nations. Provision has been made by the Hague Convention for machinery making it very easy to submit questions of international rights to a tribunal for decision. It has also been made easy to determine the truth when there is a dispute about facts through a Commission of Enquiry, as in the Dogger Bank case.[3]

International usage arising under the concert of European powers has also made it a natural and customary thing for the powers to meet in conference when any serious exigency arises for the purpose of discussing the way to avoid general injury. All of these inchoate institutions, however,—the Arbitral Tribunal, the Commission of Enquiry, the Conference of Nations,—depend entirely upon individual national initiative. No-one has any authority to invoke them in the name or interest of the Community of Nations which is interested in the preservation of peace. The first and natural stop [step] in the development of these institutions after the adoption of the new principle of community interest in the preservation of peace will be an agreement upon someone or some group whose duty it will be to speak for the whole community in calling upon any two nations who appear to be about to fight to submit their claims to the consideration (I do not now say 'decision,' but consideration) of the Tribunal as it is now or may hereafter be organized, or the Commission of Enquiry, or the Conference, as the case may require. It will be exceedingly difficult for any nation which has explicitly acknowledged the community interest and right, to refuse such a demand in the name of the community, and it could not do so without clearly putting itself in the wrong in the eyes of the entire world. I do not say that it would be impossible for a nation to reject such a demand, but it would be much more difficult than it is now, and much more improbable; for example, the whole contention upon which Germany sought to save her face while she was using the Austrian ultimatum to Serbia as the occasion for going into a general war would be completely destroyed. *Behind such a demand of course should stand also an agreement by the powers to act together in support of the demand made in their name and in dealing with the consequences of it.*

The question how far that agreement should go brings me to the third proposition which I made, and that is that no agreement in the way of a league of peace or under whatever name should be contemplated which will probably not be kept when the time comes for acting under it. Nothing can be worse in international affairs than to make agreements and break them. It would be folly, therefore, for the United States in order to preserve or enforce peace after this War is over to enter into an agreement which the people of the United States would not regard as binding upon them. I think that observation applies to making a hard and fast agreement to go to war upon the happening of some future international event beyond the control of the United States. I think that the question whether the people of the Country would stand by such an agreement made by the President and Senate would depend upon the way they looked at the event calling for their action at that future time when the event occurs,—that they would fight if at that time they were convinced they ought to, and they would not fight if at that time they were convinced that they ought not to. It may be that an international community system may be developed hereafter which will make it possible to say "We bind ourselves to fight upon the happening of some particular event," but I do not think that system has so far developed that it is now practicable to make such an agreement. Of course, it may become so before this War is over. No-one can tell. We are certainly rather nearer to that point than we were two or three years ago.

I think this covers what I said. I have not undertaken to add to it anything about disarmament, which I consider essential, nor about the necessity of wiping out the military autocracies who have brought on this War. I think that must be done in order to have secured peace. So long as Hohenzollerns and Hapsburgs remain on the throne, we shall have to be perpetually on the alert against unrepentant professional criminals. Their agreements will always be worthless; their purposes will always be sinister; and, while we can make it much more difficult, we can never make it impossible for them to start again to shoot up the world.

Faithfully yours,   Elihu Root

TLS (E. M. House Papers, CtY).

[1] See the extract from the House Diary printed at April 11, 1918, Vol. 47.

Sir William Wiseman to Lord Reading

[Magnolia, Mass.] August 16, 1918.

No. CXP 701. PERSONAL & VERY SECRET.

Yesterday I showed COLLIER [WILSON] a paraphrase of your No. 724 of 14th. BEACH [HOUSE] was present during most of interview. COLLIER remarked that he was glad of the opportunity of further discussion because when he last saw you he had not read the PHILLIMORE report, and moreover he had been obliged to discuss with you a variety of subjects in a short interview. He asked me to cable you and say that he has no intention of making any public statement regarding the constitution of a LEAGUE OF NATIONS. In the first place, such a statement on his part would be a target for criticism here. One section of the Senate, led by Lodge, would say that he had gone to[o] far in committing the United States to a Utopian scheme, and, on the other hand, the League enthusiasts would criticize him for not going far enough. Great harm might be done the scheme by arousing such controversy at this time. In the second place, he has not yet determined in his own mind the best method of constituting the League. He has ideas on the subject but not worked out in detail. I asked what his ideas were. He replied—"Two main principles; there must be a League of Nations, and this must be virile, a reality, not a paper League." I asked what he thought of the PHILLIMORE report. "It has no teeth," he replied; "I read it to the last page hoping to find something definite, but I could not." I asked whether he would appoint a Committee similar to Phillimore's to report on the subject, so that H.M.G. could ascertain the American view. He said he would not be in favour of appointing such a committee. "How then," I asked, "are we ever to exchange views and urge a common basis, because no one nation can make a league all by itself." He agreed it would be necessary to find common ground, and said he would like nothing better than to discuss the whole matter perfectly frankly with MR. LLOYD GEORGE, who he felt would substantially share his views. As this is impossible at present he would be glad to discuss the question with anyone H.M.G. care to send to him. In further conversation COLLIER said he thought the LEAGUE OF NATIONS ought to be constituted at the Peace Conference and not before. If we formed the league while we were still fighting, it would inevitably be regarded as a sort of

Holy Alliance aimed at Germany. This would not be the purpose of the American people. Germany should be invited to join the family of nations, providing she will behave according to the rules of the Society. COLLIER sees grave danger in public discussions of the scheme now. Each nation, he fears, would become committed to its own plan and find fundamental objections in the methods proposed by others. It would, he thinks, even endanger the solidarity of those nations fighting Germany. He feels very strongly on this point and asked me to urge you from him to use your influence against the publication of the Phillimore report. He feels sure its publication would create much controversy here and that he would not be able to avoid expressing his opinion, when he would have to say definitely that he did not endorse the report. This would look like an important divergence of view between the two Governments and might have very ill effects. He asked me this morning if I had cabled you, and said he felt much relieved as you would appreciate his position, and be able to prevent the report being published.

I have tried faithfully to repeat the conversation which took place at intervals throughout a whole afternoon. In addition I will give you a few general impressions.

I think COLLIER looks to economic pressure to supply the main force which might be used to support the League. He feels there must be force, but recognises the practical difficulties. He has come up here to discuss the whole war situation with BEACH, but particularly the League of Nations. COLLIER referred to the anti-British feeling still existing here as an additional reason for avoiding any appearance of friction between the two Governments. I reminded him that this might also create an anti-American sentiment in England, which happily did not now exist. He agreed that it was a possibility which too many Americans overlooked.

Regarding GERMAN peace offers, COLLIER said U. S. representatives abroad had been instructed to listen and report anything that was said, without holding out any hope that such unofficial offers would be considered by U.S.G. The right policy, he said, would be for the German Government to state their terms through properly accredited representatives, so that they might be then considered officially by all the associated belligerents.

In conclusion, I would venture to urge you to impress COLLIER's views regarding Phillimore report on H.M.G. He is willing, even anxious, to discuss the League of Nations in all its phases with us, but for[e]sees endless trouble and controversy if immature conclusions are made public and the nations through their press become engaged in public argument in support of various methods. He has given us this clear warning, and it may easily embarrass our whole relations with him if we cannot meet his views.[1]

T telegram (W. Wiseman Papers, CtY).
¹ Reading sent a copy of this dispatch to Lloyd George: T MS enclosed in Lord Reading to D. Lloyd George, Aug. 19, 1918, ALS (D. Lloyd George Papers, F/43/1/14, House of Lords Record Office).

From the Diary of Colonel House

August 16, 1918.

The President played golf this morning with Grayson and Mrs. Wilson. He later came to us for lunch. The other guests were Mona and Randolph,¹ Mrs. T. Jefferson Coolidge Jr. and her son Billy.² After lunch the President and I went into my study for an hour's conference. There were many matters discussed. The vacancy at Copenhagen, the possibility of Walter Page breaking down in London and his successor, and various other subjects. I suggested Frank I. Cobb for London. The President thought well of Cobb but did not think well of having newspaper men head our embassies. He thought Cleveland Dodge was not physically equal to it. As a matter of fact I do not believe he thinks Dodge is the right type of man, and in this I am in partial agreement.

There are two vacancies on the Federal Reserve Board, and two vacancies on the Federal Trades Board about which he is anxious. I had no suggestions to make. I cannot get my mind upon appointments and he is very much in the same condition.

In speaking of the Irish he surprised me by saying that he did not intend to appoint another Irishman to anything; that they were untrustworthy and uncertain. He thought Tumulty was the only one he had come in contact with who was. It is curious that he should pick him as an exception to the rule. Dudley Malone and some others have brought him to this frame of mind and he does the Irish an injustice. However, he never means half he says and so stated to the crowd when we returned to the veranda. He said "House is always afraid that I am about to do something foolish because I unload my mind on him without reserve, and he is afraid I might do some of the things I tell him I want to do."

I sounded him on another term, and I see evidence of his being a candidate. I have had such a long and wide experience in this direction that I am able to detect the trend of a candidate's mind before he, himself, is more than half aware of it. The President thinks he does not want re-election, but I am convinced will acquiesce if urged. I am opposed to a third term in ordinary circumstances but after looking over the different possibilities, I have come to believe that it may be necessary for the President to undertake another four years. The end of the war is drawing too near the end of his term to make it possible for him to properly solve the many problems arising at the Peace Conference, and the after war problems which are certain to need wise solution. There is no one but the President who has the proper background and outlook. The Republican Party is devoid of suitable material, nor is there anyone in the Democratic Party who could fill the President's place in such work.

After our conference we motored into Boston and took supper at my daughter's house in Chestnut Hill. Mona and Randolph had gone to York Harbor, but Mona telephoned arranging with her servants for our coming. Chestnut Hill was practically deserted, the people being in the country since it is a purely residential town of the wealthy.

When we drove up in two automobiles and went into the house a policeman on the beat eyed us with suspicion. After remaining in the house a few minutes the President, Grayson and I walked out the back way, strolling around the grounds and taking a walk in the neighborhood. We did not know until after we returned that the policeman had followed us and had stopped one of the Secret Service men to tell of his suspicions. He said he knew the owners of the house were away, and having seen us drive up to the front door with two machines, one of which he thought was for the "loot," and then come out the back way bare-headed convinced him something was wrong and he was about to put us under arrest. The Secret Service man had some difficulty in making him believe that it was the President of the United States he had under suspicion.

We had an excellent supper and afterward motored back through Revere Beach and along the shore to Magnolia. The air was crisp and the moon beautiful. I think the President and Mrs. Wilson enjoyed the trip thoroughly.

[1] That is, Mona House Tucker and Randolph Foster Tucker.
[2] William Appleton Coolidge.

From Newton Diehl Baker

My dear Mr. President: [Washington] August 17, 1918.

I enclose a cablegram from General Bliss[1] which, I confess, not only disturbs me but surprises me very much, because it seems to imply that General Bliss has not received the cablegram which I sent him of the fifth of August, containing full and detailed statements with regard to the subjects about which he inquires. General March has sent a cablegram repeating that of August 5th, and seeking to learn whether the original was in any way suppressed from delivery to him.

The suggestion made by General Bliss seems to me essentially wise. There must be a show-down on this subject. The tremendous effort which America is making, and the vast force which we will have in 1919 will win the war, if our allies want it won, and are willing to make any correspondingly devoted effort.

It was with this thought in mind that I suggested the wisdom of my going to Europe, and having the whole matter finally agreed on. I still think that the wise course, although I believe it would save time to send General Bliss a cablegram directing him to take the whole matter up with the military advisers in the form of a resolution to be presented to the Supreme War Council, and let him get that far along with it before I go to Europe, when I could take General Bliss with me and go from one place to another until we together got all of the details definitely set out and agreed upon as engagements for concerted action among the Allies.

Respectfully yours,   [Newton D. Baker]

CCL (N. D. Baker Papers, DLC).
[1] That is, T. H. Bliss to NDB and P. C. March, No. 180, Aug. 14, 1918.

From Hamilton Holt

To the President: New York August 17 1918

You may possibly be interested in the leading editorial in this week's Independent entitled "No Divided Counsels at Washington."[1]

As far as I know it is the first time in the existence of The Independent that we have advocated to the American people electing a Democratic House of Representatives.

Very respectfully   Hamilton Holt

TLS (WP, DLC).
[1] The Independent, XCV (Aug. 17, 1918), 210-11.

From William Albert Ashbrook[1]

Dear Mr. President: Washington, D. C. August 17, 1918.

I hesitate to intrude upon your time, but having just returned from Ohio, and learning first hand from many of my farmer friends of the dissatisfaction which exists over the regulation of farm products, and being unable to secure any information from other sources, I am constrained to appeal to you. I might say that I addressed an inquiry to Mr. Pennell,[2] Chief of the Wool Division of the War Industries Board, who was unable to give satisfactory reply. I then wrote to Mr. Baruch, Chairman of the Board but my inquiry was ignored.

I believe the farmers are quite as patriotic as any other class, and will cheerfully carry any burdens that may be placed upon them, providing they do not believe that they have been discriminated against. I was many times asked why the price of wool and wheat was regulated and the price on cotton was permitted to soar. I will frankly confess I was unable to give any satisfactory explanation. I represent what was at one time the largest wool producing district in the state of Ohio, and is still one of the foremost. The wool grower seemed resentful that the price of his product is regulated and no steps taken to regulate the price of cotton. I have no doubt that some satisfactory explanation can be made and it is for the purpose of securing this information, and to promulgate it among the dissatisfied which prompts me to address you.

Permit me also to make the observation that the farmer would not complain of the price fixed on wheat if some action was taken to regulate and control the prices of farm machinery, binder twine, and other costs entering into its production.

Thanking you in advance for an early response, believe me,

Very sincerely,   William A Ashbrook

TLS (WP, DLC).
  [1] Democratic congressman from Ohio.
  [2] Actually, Lewis Penwell, chief of the domestic wool section of the textile division of the War Industries Board.

Josephus Daniels to Austin Melvin Knight

[Washington] August 17, 1918

15015 In accordance with President's statement[1] sent you our forces are not intended for intervention in Russia but solely for the purpose set forth in that statement period This Government has agreed with Japan to send a combatant force of about 7000 men which with hospital and auxiliary units will total about 9000 men period The object of the small allied force is first to hold Vladivostok and second to safeguard as far as possible the country in rear of the westward moving Czecho-Slovak troops period The prime consideration at present is the security of the base at Vladivostok 18017

Secnav

T telegram (NDR, RG 45, Naval Records Coll. of the Office of Naval Records and Library, Telegrams—Outgoing, Feb. 6, 1917-May 31, 1919, DNA).
  [1] That is, the press release printed at Aug. 3. It was conveyed to Knight in JD to A. M. Knight, Aug. 3, 1918, T telegram, ibid.

Tasker Howard Bliss to Peyton Conway March

Versailles August 17 [1918].

Number 183 Confidential. For the Chief of Staff.

Paragraph 1. Receipt today of your Number 80 is acknowledged.

Paragraph 2. I received your Number 74 but in the light of paragraph 1 of your cablegram of today it was apparently entirely misunderstood. It came on day of arrival of Mr. Stettinius and I at once showed it to him. Your cablegram stated deficiency in cargo tonnage that must be supplied from August to February inclusive but with no statement that anything was expected to be done here. I assumed that it was intended that I should impress on my colleagues the difficulty in the execution of the 80 division program and that no one should count on it as an assured fact until definitely informed by the United States that it could be carried out. Accordingly I gave them emphatic caution. Both Mr. Stettinius and I assumed that the question of tonnage would be taken up in the usual way by existing councils of shipping experts. This seemed to be confirmed by cablegram received by Mr. Stettinius from Secretary of War dated August 4th in which it was stated "We count with confidence on the British tonnage assistance." No one at Versailles is informed as to shipping details. Nevertheless on receipt today of your Number 80 I took up with British colleagues your statement of deficiency cargo tonnage. They said all they could do was to *refer* it to British War Cabinet which they did.

Paragraph 3. The last sentence your Number 74 stated your understanding that French could continue their assistance in artillery program and added "It is desired that this be confirmed." When I showed this to Mr. Stettinius he said that he was here with large staff to consider matters relating to armament and munitions and that he would take up our artillery necessities with the French Minister of Munitions and also with the Inter-Allied munitions council at its meeting on August 14th. Independent investigations with the same French officials could not be proposed at the same time by him and myself and we have waited for the result of his. I am informed today by Colonel Dunn and Mr. Gifford,[1] of Mr. Stettinius' staff, that a detailed statement was prepared in collaboration with General Wheeler[2] showing our artillery requirements from the French. This was to be presented by Mr. Stettinius to the French with information that the 80 divisions program was entirely tentative until we knew that among other things these requirements could be met. I understand that he may have already received information on this subject both from British and French. He is absent today at French front and I shall have a conference with him on his return at 9:30 tonight.   Bliss.

TC telegram (WDR, RG 407, World War I Cablegrams, DNA).
    [1] That is, Walter Sherman Gifford. Colonel Dunn was probably Beverly Wyly Dunn, a retired army ordnance expert who had been recalled to active duty in 1917.
    [2] Brig. Gen. Charles Brewster Wheeler, chief ordnance officer for the American Expeditionary Force.

Sir Eric Drummond to Sir William Wiseman

[London] August 17, 1918.

No. 736. URGENT: *Please deliver following message to* COL. HOUSE *from* MR. BALFOUR:

We have observed with interest the concentration of CARRANZA'S opponents under the leadership of ROBLEZ DOMINGUEZ.[1] It is reported that the latter will take action before the end of the month, when his immunity as a member of Congress expires. This may well happen even if he receives no external assistance.

In the meantime DOMINGUEZ has asked H. M. GOVERNMENT to transmit message to his correspondent in NEW YORK in order to establish a Bank credit. We have not yet complied with the request and we think you ought to be informed of it. As you are aware, there seems overwhelming reason to believe that CARRANZA is intriguing with GERMANY, that he has been promised GERMAN cash, and that he is organizing MEXICO as a base for German submarines.[2]

In these circumstances we should certainly regard with satisfaction any genuine MEXICAN movement which would provide a Government whose external policy would be friendly to the associated Powers and whose internal policy would do something to secure honesty and order in the public administration.

(Message ends).

Following PRIVATE *for* W. *from* MR. BALFOUR:

I need hardly add, for your personal information, that what we most wish to have is PRESIDENT WILSON'S own views. But I am well aware that asking for it direct is not always the best way to get it.

T telegram (W. Wiseman Papers, CtY).
    [1] Alfredo Robles Domínguez, architect and engineer, a supporter of the late Francisco I. Madero and former *Carrancista* governor of the Mexican Federal District. For details of Robles Domínguez' unsuccessful plot to overthrow Carranza, see Friedrich Katz, *The Secret War in Mexico: Europe, the United States, and the Mexican Revolution* (Chicago and London, 1981), pp. 479-84.
    [2] For earlier notes and documents relating to this subject, see n. 1 to the Enclosure printed with RL to WW, March 27, 1918; WW to E. W. Pou, May 1, 1918, n. 1; and A. J. Balfour to Lord Reading, May 7, 1918, all in Vol. 47; and Lord Reading to A. J. Balfour, May 23, 1918, and RL to WW, June 4, 1918, n. 1, both in Vol. 48. For a discussion of the evidence concerning the construction of a German submarine base in Mexico, see Katz, pp. 425-27.

From the Diary of Colonel House

August 17, 1918.

The President did not play golf this morning but instead we took a drive around Eastern Point and the Magnolia Shore Road. They came to luncheon as usual and we dined with them. Peter and Hetty Higginson[1] lunched with us. In our luncheon arrangements we have only invited some member of Mrs. Coolidge's family. We have done this in order to avoid offending the sensibilities of our friends. No one could object to our having Mrs. Coolidge's connections because the President and Mrs. Wilson are occupying her house.

After lunch we had our usual conference for an hour or more. We discussed Russia and the Economic Mission. I was surprised to find that he did not have anyone in mind to head this mission and asked for suggestions. He thought there was no haste because he believed the military forces should go in before the economic. My opinion is that he has done the whole thing badly. I would have featured the economic part of it and sent in that section before the military, or at least have cooperated with it.

I spoke to him about Pershing and Goethals and urged that Pershing's wishes be repected since everything was going well in France. I did not think Goethals was a man to work easily in a subordinate position. Goethals would have been all right if my suggestions regarding Stettinius had been carried out,[2] but Goethals under Pershing would be quite different from Goethals under Stettinius. The President assured me that nothing would be done contrary to Pershing's wishes. I shall send Pershing a cable in regard to this when the President leaves, and it will be attached to the diary.

I spoke to him about the Council of National Defence as a reconstruction committee. I found he did not have them in mind for such work, nor indeed, did he seem impressed with the necessity of it. He thought matters could be adjusted as they arose later. I shall take the matter up with him again.

In speaking of the Peace Inquiry, I asked whether we were spending too much money. He thought not. He feels toward the Inquiry very much as I do. He has not the kind of mind that can use such detailed data as they are preparing but he thinks it will be necessary to have it because there will be times when we will have to be given certain facts. I added that the work they were doing would be necessary for the Conferences which must inevitably be held after the Peace Conference was over in order to do the "buttoning up" of the agreements made.

I asked if he had in mind my going abroad this Autumn. My thought was that it would be unnecessary. He agreed to this and said it would be a mistake for the reason it would be generally thought the war was narrowing to a close and that my mission abroad was for that purpose. It would be unfortunate if such a belief became prevalent for it would have a tendancy to a lessening of effort.

We discussed Bulgaria but came to no conclusion as to what should be done.[3] After we were through they went motoring. I remained at home to get at an accumulation of correspondence.

[1] Francis Lee Higginson, Jr., and Hetty Appleton Sargent Higginson. He was a member of the firm of Lee, Higginson & Co.
[2] See EMH to WW, June 3, 1918, and NDB to WW, June 8, 1918, both in Vol. 48.
[3] That is, whether the United States should declare war against Bulgaria.

From Robert Lansing, with Enclosures

My dear Mr. President: Washington August 18, 1918.

On Friday, the 16th, I asked the Japanese Ambassador to come and see me in regard to a report that Japanese troops were being sent to Manchu-li on the Manchurian border not far from Chita, the western junction of the Eastern Manchurian and Amur River Railways. He evidently anticipated the purpose of the visit for he brought with him a telegram from his Government. The substance of the telegram he sent to me last night, and I enclose it to you. He also said that the Japanese Government were sending between 3,000 and 5,000 troops to Manchu-li and that these troops were part of forces stationed in Manchurian garrisons further south.

I am also enclosing a letter from the French Ambassador on the Siberian situation which is in substance a repetition of statements made to me on Saturday morning.

To complete the documents in the case I am appending a telegram from Admiral Knight to the Secretary of the Navy, under date of the 15th,[1] and also a report by General Diterichs in command of the Czechs at Vladivostok, forwarded by Consul Caldwell on the 15th.[2]

A careful consideration of the facts as disclosed by these communications convinces me that the situation is developing in a way which differs considerably from the plan originally determined upon and compels a consideration of the policy which should be adopted in reference to the new conditions presented.

I believe that the evidence points to an intention on the part of the Japanese to send a larger number of troops to Vladivostok than the 13,500 already sent, while I feel sure that they will increase the force operating at Manchu-li in the event that the pro-German troops should be superior. Of course they assert that the Manchurian force will not go beyond Chinese territory, but in view of the importance of the Chita junction I am not sure that that is not their objective.

We are informed that on July 7 Irkutsk was captured by the Czecho-Slovaks, that between that city or between Lake Baikal and the Chinese border there are about 25,000 of the opposing forces largely composed of armed German and Austrian prisoners, and that that section of the railroad is entirely in their hands.

We are also informed that Czech troops, estimated variously at from 2,000 to 6,000, have reached Harbin from Vladivostok, which is apparently an utterly inadequate force to push westward to Irkutsk in the face of the largely superior numbers near Manchu-li.

In addition to this the Germans and Austrians and the Red Guard are in strong force (estimated 80,000) north of Vladivostok along the Amur, so that it will require all the Czechs remaining in the city together with the allied forces landed to resist an attack on that port.

The question seems to be, therefore, what course should be taken to open a way to relieve the Czecho-Slovaks in Western Siberia. Under present conditions a military advance westward seems practically impossible. I do not see how we can permit a deadlock to continue, because to do so would destroy the whole value of the enterprise and seriously imperil the lives of all the Czechs west of Irkutsk, who will if captured be treated as traitors.

Frankly I think that the situation is getting beyond our control and that unless we revise or modify our policy to meet these new conditions we will be placed in a very embarrassing situation, especially so if any disaster should occur to the Czechs in the west.

I think, too, that whatever is to be done to relieve the Czecho-Slovaks must be done speedily since winter will set in within eight or ten weeks and the rigorous climate will cause great suffering unless we can reach them with supplies, of which, we are informed, they are so sorely in need.

I am not prepared to offer advice in the matter but I do feel that we must assume that Japan, with the pressure of the present situation together with the undoubted approval of the Allied Governments, will assert that military conditions require her to send a much larger force both to Vladivostok and to the western border of Manchuria.

If the Japanese Government indicate their purpose to take such action, what ought we to say?

If we reach the conclusion that Japan will follow this course in any event, would we or would we not be in a better position to control the situation in the future by asserting that present con-

ditions require Japan to send sufficient troops to open the railroad
to Irkutsk and to keep it open so that we can send supplies to the
Czechs?

I raise these questions for consideration only and not as an
expression of opinion. My only suggestion is that the situation calls
for prompt consideration.

Faithfully yours,   Robert Lansing

TLS (SDR, RG 59, 861.00/2602½, DNA).
  [1] A. M. Knight to JD, Aug. 15, 1918; see also JD to A. M. Knight, Aug. 17, 1918.
  [2] Printed in n. 1 to A. M. Knight to JD, Aug. 15, 1918.

E N C L O S U R E   I

Kikujiro Ishii to Robert Lansing

Dear Mr Secretary,   Washington August 17 1918.

As I promised you yesterday I beg to send you herewith enclosed
a short sketch of what I explained to you verbally about the situation
in the border town of Manchulie.

Yours sincerely   K. Ishii

ALS (SDR, RG 59, 861.00/2602½, DNA).

E N C L O S U R E   I I

IMPERIAL JAPANESE EMBASSY
WASHINGTON

The forces of the Soviet, virtually under command of the armed
German and Austro-Hungarian prisoners, have recently pressed
back the Semenoff's troops to the borders of China. Part of the town
of Manchuli has been bombarded by them and the Japanese residents numbering some two hundred fifty have been compelled to
take flight to the town of Hailar. The Chinese troops stationed at
Manchuli were powerless to cope with the Soviet forces and only
succeeded by means of a compromise to check their invasion into
the town.

It is further reported that part of the Soviet forces seem to have
penetrated into the Chinese territory, proceeding eastward around
the north of Manchuli.

T MS (SDR, RG 59, 861.00/2602½, DNA).

Tasker Howard Bliss to Newton Diehl Baker and
Peyton Conway March

Versailles. August 18 [1918]

Number 184 Confidential.

For the Secretary of War and the Chief of Staff. The following instructions have been issued by the British War Office to General Poole commanding allied forces at Archangel and Murmansk.

"Paragraph 1. Your main object is to cooperate in restoring Russia with the object of resisting German influence and penetration, and enabling the Russians again to take the field side by side with their Allies for the recovery of Russia.

Paragraph 2. In order to effect the above object your immediate aim should be to establish communications with the Czechs, and assisted by them probably secure control of the Archangel-Vologda-Ekaterinburg railroad and the river and railroad lines of communications between Archangel and Viatka.

Paragraph 3. At the same time you should endeavor to promote resistance to the enemy by all means at your disposal including: A. Organization of armed force to resist the Germans. B. The support of any administration which may be disposed to be friendly to the Allies. C. The affording of relief to the civil population. D. Judicious propaganda.

Paragraph 4. According to our latest information the Czechs and anti-Bolshevik forces are in possession of Ekaterinburg and the whole of the Siberian railroad from the neighborhood of Penza to Lake Baikal. It is however reported that 16,000 Bolshevist troops with 60 guns are in possession of the railroad between Perm and Ekaterinburg. Though it is true that Allied forces have actually landed in Vladivostok and more are en route, they are at present strictly limited in number in accordance with the view of the United States as to the amount which they consider necessary to establish and maintain communications with the Czechs near Lake Baikal and act as an escort to an economic mission. It may or may not be found that these numbers are sufficient to ensure the attainment of the above objects and possibly therefore they may be increased. It is improbable however that in the near future any allied forces other than Czechs will reach western Siberia. Under these circumstances in all probability the Czech troops and their sympathizers now in western Siberia will turn eastwards for safety rather than stretch out to you via Perm and Viatka. They may even not be able to maintain their present positions. You will be constantly informed of modifications in the above situation as they occur.

Paragraph 5. It will not be possible to send you more fighting troops this season than those already notified. Every effort will however be made to provide such arms and supplies as you may consider necessary and which it may be possible with the limited shipping available to place at Archangel before the closure of that port.

Paragraph 6. The events of the next few weeks alone can show whether, should the number of allied forces be inadequate, the Czechs can hold out and Russians in sufficient numbers rally to you to secure your immediate objects as in two above.

Paragraph 7. Should it become apparent that you will be unable to realize the object named in paragraph 2 you should concentrate your efforts on the object named in paragraph 3 and the immediate defense of Archangel during the ensuing winter months."

Paragraph 8. Further reference my number 183.[1] Mr. Stettinius informed me last night that he had submitted to French and English statement of artillery requirements for the 80 division program and hoped for an official reply on Aug. 21. He has reason to hope the reply will be favorable.   Bliss.

TC telegram (WDR, RG 407, World War I Cablegrams, DNA).
[1] That is, T. H. Bliss to P. C. March, Aug. 17, 1918.

From the Diary of Colonel House

August 18, 1918.

The President slept late as it was Sunday and I did not see him until they came to lunch. Our other guests were Mrs. Sargent[1] and Charles Auchincloss.[2] I had a long talk with Dr. Grayson this morning as to the President's health and as to whether he thought he could stand another term. Grayson thought he might go for another ten years if nothing untoward happened. This new development will disconcert McAdoo and I doubt very much whether he continues in the Cabinet. He certainly will not after this term if the President should be re-elected.

I have a long letter from Senator Root about the League of Nations. I gave it to the President to read aloud. He marked some of the passages and we discussed the letter in detail. He thinks Root has the wrong idea, but I felt that I could bring him around to our view. I shall try to do this and if he cannot be brought around, I fear Mr. Root will not be of the Peace Commission. There is no use getting a man on the Commission who will be antagonistic to the President for it will only make for trouble.

I spoke to the President of a letter I had received from McAdoo sometime early in June in which he had asked my advice upon three points: Whether he should resign from both the Railroad Directorship and the Treasury; whether he should resign from one or the other; or whether he should continue with both with the prospect of dying from the strain. I told of my reply to which he agreed. He thought, however, that McAdoo had better give up the railroads rather than the Treasury. The railroads, he thought, was more of an administrative matter, and the Treasury was more the business of a statesman. He put this to me in a way which he evidently wished me to convey to McAdoo so that he would choose the Treasury rather than the railroads. I have an idea what was in the back of his mind, but I did not indicate it. The President thinks, so he says, that McAdoo's throat is too bad for him to go out on another Liberty Loan speaking tour, therefore, he will put a ban upon it and will make a more limited tour of the country himself. Trouble is brewing between the two, for McAdoo is not the sort to take this kindly.

We dined with them[3] at the Coolidge home.

[1] Marion Coolidge Sargent, widow of Lucius Manlius Sargent.
[2] Charles Crooke Auchincloss, lawyer of New York, brother of Gordon Auchincloss.
[3] That is, the Wilsons.

From Robert Lansing

My dear Mr. President: Washington August 19, 1918.

The Governments of France, Italy and Great Britain, as you have seen by the reports, have given recognition to the Czechs as a sovereign nation or at least to the Czech National Council,[1] in terms which are assumed to be a full recognition. Doubtless this was induced by our public expression of sympathy with the national aspirations of the oppressed races.

In view of this action by the Allied Governments I think that we ought to consider whether it is expedient to make a further declaration giving more complete definition to our attitude in order to encourage the Czecho-Slovaks in their struggle against the Central Powers.

Although I feel strongly that Austria-Hungary as an Empire should disappear since it is the keystone of Mittel-Europa, I do not think that it would be wise to give full recognition to the Czecho-Slovaks as a sovereign nation. Without discussing the legal objections a serious embarrassment would be the effect on the Jugo-Slavs, who would undoubtedly clamor for similar recognition and feel offended if it was not granted. In any event I think the declaration would have to contain a reservation as to territorial limits, which would materially weaken it.

Two other courses seem open in case it is deemed to be advisable to make any declaration at this time:

First. We might recognize the belligerency of the Czecho-Slovak revolutionists in view of their military organization operating in Siberia and Eastern Russia against Austrian loyalists and their German allies. I think that it would be proper in such case to recognize the Czecho-Slovak Council with Masaryk at its head as a *de facto* Revolutionary Government and give to it such aid as seems expedient. Basing this action on the state of belligerency the Jugo-Slavs would have no similar ground to claim recognition. As you know the jealousy of Italy and the desire of Serbia to absorb the Jugo-Slavs rather than to become federated with them makes it necessary to be cautious in deciding on a policy.

Second. It may be wise, in order to avoid any future charge of deception or secretiveness, to adopt a more general policy by issuing a frank declaration that the utter subservience of Austria-Hungary to Germany, whether the result of coercion, fear or inclination, forfeits whatever right the Dual Monarchy had to be treated as an independent state; that the nationalities aspiring to be free from Austro-Hungarian rule are still more entitled to be saved from German domination; that such nationalities should receive not only the sympathy but the material aid of all nations who realize the evil ambitions of Germany's rulers; and that this Government is prepared to advance the cause of national freedom by assuming relations with any council or body of men truly representative of revolutionists against the Austro-Hungarian Government, who seek national independence by force of arms.

Such a declaration would avoid the question of defined territory and of naming any particular nationality, though the latter would later have to be done when a military organization was in actual operation.

If this course should be adopted, it would give Austria-Hungary notice that at the peace table we would oppose the continuance of the Empire in its present form and within its present boundaries. To that extent it would limit our freedom of action; but, if you have definitely decided that that should be the policy, its declaration can do little harm since Austria-Hungary is and will continue to be a tool of Germany.

It would cause a profound impression and would deeply affect the nationalities involved; it would put heart into the patriots now attempting to organize revolutions in the Empire; and it would be a notification to the world that this Government intends to support and give substantial aid to all little nations which have been held in subjection against their will by the exercise of superior force.

I submit the foregoing as a proper subject for discussion at this time.   Faithfully yours,   Robert Lansing.

TLS (SDR, RG 59, 763.72/11132A, DNA).
[1] The Italian government and a representative of the Czechoslovak National Council, on April 21, 1918, had signed an agreement providing for the creation of a Czechoslovak army in Italy. France had recognized the Czechoslovak National Council as the supreme authority of the emerging Czechoslovak nation on June 29. Great Britain followed suit on August 9. See Thomas Garrigue Masaryk, *The Making of a State: Memories and Observations, 1914-1918* (London, 1927), pp. 448-51; Eduard Beneš, *My War Memoirs*, trans. Paul Selver (London, 1928), pp. 286-95, 382-84, 397-412; and *FR-WWS 1918*, I, I, 802-803, 816, 824.

From George P. Hampton[1]

Dear Mr. President: Washington. D. C. August 19, 1918

We have been in conference with Congressmen Sims and Ferris and Secretary Baker with reference to the water power bill reported by Mr. Sims, Chairman of the Committee on Water Power, to whom we have made the following suggestion which we respectfully submit for your consideration.

Congresssman Ferris informed us that you told him that if the bill passed with the recapture clause as it now stands,[2] you would veto it. It seems to us, however, that the bill itself is contrary to the democratic principles for which we are contending not only through armed forces but through intellectual discussion and enactment of legislation. Does it not violate the principle for which, as you stated so accurately, we are fighting this war,—to afford all peoples participation upon fair terms in the economic opportunities of the world? We feel so very distinctly, and that it would be a great mistake at this time to alienate even under form of lease any of the water power of the country which is so greatly needed for the prosecution of the war and for the rehabilitation of our industry after the war. We think that the Federal Government should develop the water power itself and ask whether it will not be feasible to have an administration bill introduced to provide for such Government development.

Both Congressmen Sims and Ferris and Secretary Baker agreed to this principle, but raised the question whether Congress would be willing to pass such a bill. It seems to us that they would be,

[1] Manager and director of legislation for the Farmers' National Headquarters, the Washington office of a group of national farmers' organizations.
[2] About which see S. Ferris to WW, June 27, 1918, Vol. 48.

and Congressman Sims thinks that with help from the Administration it could be put through the House.

The railroad situation has developed an additional argument for Government developement of water power, for motor power for the railroads. The Director General of Railroads, in explaining the necessity for increasing freights, pointed out that the railroads were obliged to pay in 1915, $1.13 for a ton of coal, and in 1918, $2.95 per ton. While the consumption of coal is estimated to be only about one-third greater in 1918 than in 1915, the increased cost of coal is $345,840,000—the figures for 1915 being $137,860,000, and for 1918 $489,700,000. We are threatened with a coal shortage and we shall have this condition probably for two or three years. The railroad consumption of coal this year is estimated at 166,000,000 tons.

Mr. E. W. Rice, Jr.,[3] President of the American Institute of Electrical Engineers, recently stated:

"It is terrifying to realize that 25 per cent of the total amount of coal which we are digging from the earth each year is burned to operate our railroads under such inefficient conditions that an average of at least six pounds of coal is required per horse power of work performed. The same amount of coal burned in a modern central power station would produce an equivalent of three times that amount of power in the motors of an electric locomotive, even including all the losses of generation and transmission from the source of power to the locomotive.

"But this is not all. It is estimated that something like 150,000,000 tons of coal were consumed by the railroads in 1917. Now, we know from the results obtained from such electrical operation of railroads as we already have in this country that it would be possible to save at lease [least] two-thirds of this coal if electric locomotives were substituted for the present steam ones. On this basis there would be a saving of over 100,000,000 tons of coal a year. This is an amount as large as the total coal exported from the United States during 1917."

While, of course, water power can not be immediately utilized for electrification of the railroads, a big beginning could be made in a few months. A marked reduction in freight rates on agricultural products will be possible with cheaper costs of transportation, to the advantage of producers and consumers. If the water power of the country now in public hands is developed by private companies they will seek a large return, and will secure the speculative and natural value of these resources for themselves.

You may know that in 1915, the various state granges and the

---

[3] Edwin Wilbur Rice, Jr., president of the General Electric Co.

National Grange in their annual convention adopted resolutions opposing the principal of leasing natural resources which could be developed by the Government, and insisting upon the retention of the fee of lands "containing fuel, and fertilizer minerals, forests, and water power." You may also know that the National Conservation Association approved these resolutions and that the Farmers' Union, American Societies of Equity, the Gleaners, and other farmer organizations throughout the United States passed resolutions showing that the farmers were practically of one mind in their position on conservation legislation. A fifty year lease is altogether too long for public welfare. The British Labour Party conference recently adopted a declaration "that the Labour Party stands for the provision, by the Government itself, of the score of gigantic super-power stations by which the whole kingdom could be supplied, and for the linking up of present municipal and joint stock services for distribution to factories and dwelling houses at the lowest possible rates." It stated: "The conference notifies that the Labour Party will offer the most strenuous opposition to this great national service being entrusted on any terms whatsoever to private capitalism."

It seems to us also that Senate Bill 2812 which passed the Senate January 7, 1918, and is now in conference, is similarly unwise and a backward step. This bill authorizes "exploration for and disposition of coal, phosphate, oil, oil shales, or gas," under terms which indicate that the drafters have no disposition to "make ready for the birth of a new day" as you have so aptly phrased it. The report on this bill of the House Committee on Public Lands, #563, estimates that the tonnage of bituminous, semi-bituminous, and lignite coal in public ownership in accessible areas amounts to fifty billion tons, and that the value of phosphate in its natural state in public lands is ninety billion dollars. This bill, as Secretary Daniels has pointed out, threatens the supply of oil in naval reserves needed for the Navy. How much oil and gas there is in public land is not known. The resolution of the National Grange which we have quoted indicates the opposition of this important body of farmers to such legislation as well as to the alienation of publicly owned iron and copper ores. On this point also the British Labour Party is equally explicit, for the conference referred to, urges that the coal mines now in Government control should not be handed back to their capitalistic proprietors, "but that the measure of nationalization which became imperative during the war, should be completed, at the earliest possible moment by the expropriation on equitable terms of all private interests in the extraction and distribution of a nation's coal (together with iron ore and other minerals)." The conference suggested the practical methods of governmental distribution of these natural resources. Distribution by the Government of natural resources owned by the Government at cost would mean a considerable reduction in the cost of coal and of farm implements and machinery.

You have had, unfortunately, frequent occasions to realize that there are some Americans who are anxious to lose in America the war for democracy which we shall assuredly win in Europe.

Should not the Administration now undertake an offensive against those who are seeking to exploit the natural resources for selfish gain? Can we consistently take a less progressive and fundamental attitude on these questions of industrial democracy than the British Labour Party?   Yours very truly,   Geo. P. Hampton

TLS (WP, DLC).

From Jessie Woodrow Wilson Sayre

Dearest, Dearest Father,   Siaconset Mass. Aug. 19th 1918.

I don't suppose you got my telegram which I sent to Washington,[1] not knowing that you were in Mass. Mother Sayre died very suddenly on Wednesday.[2] She had been very well—for her—for at least fo[u]r weeks and only that afternoon had expressed enthusiasm about a proposed picnic on the Friday. "She really felt well enough for picnics now." She woke from her afternoon nap with a severe headache and feeling very weak, and at one o'clock in the morning she died. I think she must have had three strokes, but she was so peaceful, and for the most part unconscious, that we hardly knew.

I went with her and Nevin to Bethlehem Pennsylvania where she was buried. It was in one sense a hurried trip and might have been tiring, but Nevin took such tender care of me that I came home feeling much better. It was good to have something to *do* because the shock was so very sudden. On my way back I stopped to see Dr. Davis—Philadelphia is only one hour from Bethlehem—and he approved of all I had done. Because, you see, dear Father, I am hoping if all goes well that you will have another grandchild in February. So you needn't worry about me at all.

I miss her very, very, much. She was always adorably sweet to me, and I grieve also for Frank's sake, but for her own sake, no, she had had four such miserably feeble and ailing years.

Dear, dear Father, I love you so, and I *hope* your vacation will do you so much good. *Don't* go back to that awful heat—not till you are thoroughly refreshed! Dearest love to Edith.
          Ever devotedly your little girl   Jessie

P.S. Frank gets home in 3 weeks now! Please tell Edith its all right about Alice's present[3] and thank her warmly for me.   Jessie.

ALS (WP, DLC).
¹ It is missing.
² Martha Finley Nevin (Mrs. Robert Heysham) Sayre had died early in the morning of August 15.
³ Alice Wilson, daughter of Mr. and Mrs. Joseph R. Wilson, Jr., was married to the Rev. Isaac Stuart McElroy, Jr., in the Blue Room of the White House on the evening of August 7. The bridegroom's father, the Rev. Dr. Isaac Stuart McElroy, performed the ceremony. The younger McElroy was at this time stated supply at the Presbyterian church of White Sulphur Springs, W. Va. For accounts of the wedding, see the *New York Times* and the *Washington Post*, Aug. 8, 1918, and Edith Bolling Wilson, *My Memoir*, pp. 166-67.

Peyton Conway March to Tasker Howard Bliss

Washington, August 19, 1918.

Number 81 Confidential

With reference to your 183, in view of paragraph 3 your 140[1] transmitting Resolution Number 2 of the Supreme War Council at the last session reported "First that General T. H. Bliss is requested to ascertain in what measure the American Government can furnish the tonnage necessary to transport to France troops called for in approved program" our Number 74 was sent to you direct instead of "assuming that the question of tonnage would be taken up in the usual way by existing councils of shipping experts." The cablegram in question indicated clearly that the British Government intended to give us the tonnage both for the additional troop transport and cargo transport necessary for the increased program. However on August 7th General Pershing sent us his Number 1567[2] which contained a copy of a very confidential cablegram from Mr. Lloyd-George to Clemenceau dated August 2d in which he completely reverses his former position and states among other things "I regret to declare that we shall not be able to continue our help as far as cargoes of merchandise are concerned and we shall probably have to cut down tonnage assigned for troop transportation." If Pershing has not given you a copy of this cablegram get it from him.   March.

TC telegram (WDR, RG 407, World War I Cablegrams, DNA).
¹ T. H. Bliss to RL *et al.*, July 2, 1918, printed as an Enclosure with P. C. March to WW, July 3, 1918, Vol. 48.
² Printed as an Enclosure with NDB to WW, Aug. 8, 1918.

From the Diary of Colonel House

August 19, 1918.

The President played golf this morning and I did not see him until he came to us for lunch. After lunch we had our usual conference, in fact, the conference continued practically all the afternoon as he did not leave our premises until we all went to the Coolidge house for an early dinner. Part of the time we sat on the lawn in the sun with Mrs. Coolidge and Sir William Wiseman.

The President looks a different man from what he did when he arrived. He feels rested and looks it. When I told him that Dr. Paul Reinsch, our Minister to China, was lunching with us tomorrow, he remarked that he could not remember just what conclusion he and Reinsch had come to at their conference in Washington. This indicated, he said, that his mind was becoming "leaky." He had Reinsch write a memorandum[1] afterward of what they had agreed upon and send it ot [to] him. He does this now in almost every instance in order not to further burden an already over-burdened mind.

I spoke to Mrs. Wilson about this condition and told her how much I disapproved of the President's method of conducting his work. He does too much detail and does not delegate enough of it to others. Mrs. Wilson's answer was that when he delegated it to others he found it was not well done. My reply to this was that it was better to have it not so well done than to overburden himself. My contention was, and is, that he should give himself ample leisure to think clearly upon the big problems that confront him and not have his mind wearied with detail someone else could do.

The President and party left at eight o'clock. Gordon, Janet, Loulie and I went to the station to see them off. The President asked Gordon to go down with them on their special but he concluded to go to New York with his brother. The President made much of baby Louise while he was here. He does not seem over fond of children and I was surprised at the affection he showed her.

[1] It is printed as an Enclosure with WW to RL, Aug. 22, 1918 (first letter of that date).

To Newton Diehl Baker

My dear Baker: The White House 20 August, 1918.

I felt confident that a protest of the sort that is embodied in the enclosed letter from Mr. Gompers would come, and yet I am convinced that it is based upon a misapprehension of the law proposed. As I understand the proponents of the revision referred to, it is merely this: that when a man is once exempted because of his employment in indispensable services, his exemption remains valid only so long as he continues in those services.

It would undoubtedly bear the appearance of enforced labor if we were to make the principle work automatically and administer it in such a way that a man would immediately be called to the colors the moment he ceased to be engaged in a preferred occupation. Cordially and faithfully yours, Woodrow Wilson

TLS (N. D. Baker Papers, DLC).

To William Thomas Bland

My dear Mr. Bland: [The White House] 20 August, 1918.
Your letter of August 12th has given me the greatest pleasure. It certainly conveys most generous assurances and makes me feel that I shall be strengthened by the presence of a new friend in Congress, a feeling, I need not tell you, most reassuring and necessary to me in these times of anxiety and strain.

It was certainly a generous impulse which led you to write, and I shall look forward with pleasure to being associated with you.
Cordially and sincerely yours, Woodrow Wilson

TLS (Letterpress Books, WP, DLC).

To Robert James Drummond[1]

My dear Dr. Drummond: [The White House] 20 August, 1918.
Your letter of the 25th of July,[2] which has just been laid before me, brings me the deepest gratification. Such a message as you sent me from the General Assembly of the United Free Church of Scotland goes straight to my heart. I know the spirit in which it was passed and therefore receive the message as a tonic and a message of heartening friendship. If you have any channel through which you can do so, I hope you will convey to the members of the Assembly an expression of my warm gratitude.

May I not also thank you, sir, personally for your very generous words of approval and friendship? They make me very happy.

With warmest good wishes,
Cordially and sincerely yours, Woodrow Wilson

TLS (Letterpress Books, WP, DLC).
[1] The Rev. Dr. Drummond was pastor of the Lothian Road United Free Church in Edinburgh and Moderator of the Assembly of the United Free Church for 1918.
[2] It is missing.

To Charles Sumner Hamlin

My dear Mr. Hamlin: [The White House] 20 August, 1918.
I do not wonder at your deep indignation[1] at the outrageous editorial from the Business Chronicle of the Pacific Northwest, of

which you sent me a copy.[2] I sincerely hope that some legal proceedings will be justified by the law. I cannot help suspecting that the editorial was inspired by the "Power" interests which wish to monopolize the whole development of electrical power supply in the Northwest.

Cordially and sincerely yours,   Woodrow Wilson

TLS (Letterpress Books, WP, DLC).
    [1] Wilson was responding to C. S. Hamlin to WW, Aug. 15, 1918, TLS (WP, DLC). Hamlin enclosed a typed copy of the editorial cited and quoted in n. 2 below with the comment: "You will notice that the editorial directly charges us with political corruption." He added that he had recommended to McAdoo that he send the editorial to the Attorney General "to ascertain whether we have any recourse against this paper for its unreasonable, and almost treasonable, attack."
    [2] "BY WAY OF INTERPRETATION: What was the Consideration?," *Business Chronicle of the Pacific Northwest*, Aug. 3, 1918, T MS (WP, DLC). It reads as follows: "In a spirit of pardonable curiosity Seattle tax payers would be vastly interested in learning just what were the secret political bargains that oily Ole [Hanson] entered into at the National Capital enabling him to put across the Skagit power project and to return to the city next week as the central figure in a Roman triumph. Did he perchance 'collect his pay' for recent spellbinding services to the Democratic Party when he last turned his political coat of many colors; did he promise to keep out of the way of Wesley Jones' reelection ambitions in the coming Senatorial race in return for that unctuous officeholder's pressure brought to bear on [the] Capital Issues Committee; or—what? Whatever this misfit Mayor did do in the way of political chicanery, it is Seattle tax payers who will have to furnish the cash to liquidate the obligation, and who, without having any voice in the matter, are made the cat's paw for pulling this demagogue's nicely toasted chestnuts out of the fire of Bolshevik politics. There is no use in crying over spilt milk. If Seattle business men and property owners will now highly resolve that no more political adventurers of the type of this man Hanson shall ever again be placed in the mayor's chair, possibly, for the city's future welfare, the lesson may be worth even this exhorbitant price."

From Newton Diehl Baker

My dear Mr. President: Washington. August 20, 1918.

I have carefully considered Mr. Gompers' suggestion regarding an investigation of labor conditions in Porto Rico which you were good enough to send me on the second; and, while you know I approve in principle, I am not sure that the method suggested by Mr. Gompers is the wisest which we might pursue.

In arriving at a satisfactory solution of the problem there are several aspects of the situation which it is important to bear in mind. There is in Porto Rico comparatively little industrial unrest as we are accustomed to use the term in this country; and there is comparatively little union labor trouble. The outstanding cause of the economic conditions which exist there is the fact that in a purely agricultural community there is a population of approximately 350 per square mile. The production per capita is much less than would be required to maintain normal standards of living from an American standpoint. The problem is primarily agricultural rather than industrial.

In sending a commission to Porto Rico we should, of course, recognize the practically autonomous government of the Island; and, while sending an American commission would not be unpopular, the Americans, in their several fields, must be recognized experts, and not men who would be less well known, or less able than any one of a number of Porto Ricans.

We should not recognize any of the political parties of Porto Rico. Parties there, as in other Latin countries, bear a somewhat different relation to the problems of government from the parties here. The Free Federation of Labor in Porto Rico is also the Socialist political party of the Island. It would immediately create antagonism to select a representative of this party, either by appointing a Porto Rican member thereof, or a person allied therewith in the United States. In selecting, therefore, for any commission which you appoint, a representative or representatives of labor, I feel sure that he or they, even though members of the American Federation of Labor, should be selected not as representatives of the Federation, but as representatives of our Government who are deeply interested in improving conditions of labor, and in bettering the living conditions of the workers in Porto Rico.

The experience of the Government in dealing with somewhat similar questions in this country, as I have been able to observe it, leads me to question the expediency of so large a commission as Mr. Gompers suggests. I should personally deem a board of three preferable to one of six. All of the members of such a board might, it seems to me, be wisely selected by you to represent the Government. Their personal prestige, and their ability to attack cooperatively the problem which will be presented to them, would seem to me to be greater under such a method of selection than under the method suggested by Mr. Gompers.

As to Mr. Gompers' suggeston that the principles of the War Labor Board should be applied by the proposed commission, I am not entirely clear. They were, I assume, adopted after a matured consideration of conditions in the territorial United States, and primarily of the industrial conditions here. I had not supposed that the conference board which produced these very admirable principles was made up of men familiar with Porto Rico or its problems. If you find yourself in agreement with me in these doubts, might it not be well to leave to the board which you may appoint the determination of what broad principles should be applied in Porto Rico, after they have familiarized themselves with local conditions and with the specific problems which are pressing for solution?

I do not understand that Mr. Gompers suggests that the Board should be empowered to subpoena witnesses or documents. I assume that unless legislative action is to be sought, which I do not understand to be your intention, we must rely largely upon the investigating and mediating functions of the board.

Respectfully yours,   Newton D. Baker

TLS (WP, DLC).

From Charles Richard Crane

Dear Mr President   Wood's Hole August 20 1918

I plan to spend next Monday and Tuesday—the 27th and the 28th—in Washington. As they will be the last days before leaving for China, I would very much prize one more talk with you. If you can fit me in please remember the kind of people I shall be seeing during the next few months who will be intensely interested to know in which direction you are thinking and in what way they may be helpful. Of course I shall see many of your friends and devoted supporters between Washington and the Pacific coast. In the Far East I shall also see many Americans who will long to have the latest word from home and news of the country and you. I shall have to make the best guess I can as to the way we are drifting and the way you would like to see us head.

Still beyond these two groups are the people of Northern and Eastern Asia—their destinies and their relations with us and one another. I feel that these various subjects could furnish material for a five minutes interview—possibly even longer—and on Monday morning I shall take the liberty of calling up your office to ask if there is any word for me.[1]

We were glad to provide you with real President's weather during your minute visit to Massachusetts and hope that you will be tempted back here again some day.

Affectionate messages to you both from the Houston-Crane families.   Always devotedly   Charles R. Crane

ALS (WP, DLC).
[1] Crane had lunch with Wilson and Dr. Grayson at the White House on August 27.

From Valentine Everit Macy

Washington D. C.
My dear Mr. President: August Twentieth Nineteen Eighteen.

Under the provisions of the agreement establishing the Shipbuilding Labor Adjustment Board, the Board has been holding daily hearings for the past two weeks.

Christening the *Quistconck* at Hog Island, August 5, 1918

The Senate Committee on Military Affairs. Senator Chamberlain is in the front row, second from the left

John F. Stevens

Major General Leonard Wood

Sir Eric Drummond

General William S. Graves in center; to his left, General Rudolf Gajda

General Grigorii Mikhailovich Semenov

Vice Consul L. S. Gray and Consul General Ernest L. Harris

The requests presented by the representatives of the International Unions appearing before the Board are of such character as to vitally effect [affect] the entire war program of the nation. The situation is such that we believe it essential that our Board should present in person our information to you. As our former decision for the Pacific Coast expired on August first last, it is important that a new decision should be promptly rendered if confusion and discontent are to be avoided.

May I therefore ask for an appointment for the Board in the near future?[1]   Respectfully, V. Everit Macy

TLS (WP, DLC).
 [1] Wilson saw the board at the White House at 5 p.m. on August 27. As WW to WBW, Aug. 28, 1918, indicates, the principal topic of discussion was the coordination of labor policy among all governmental labor boards and agencies involved in the war effort. See also Willard E. Hotchkiss and Henry R. Seager, *History of the Shipbuilding Labor Adjustment Board, 1917 to 1919*, Bulletin of the United States Bureau of Labor Statistics, No. 283 (Washington, 1921), pp. 42-43.

Sir William Wiseman to Arthur James Balfour

[Magnolia, Mass.] August 20, 1918.

No. CXP. 704.

Begins: No. 114. Mr. HOUSE asked me to thank you for your cable No. 736 of the 17th., and to reply in the following sense:

In the course of the general conferences which have taken place here during the past week, MR. HOUSE showed the President your cable No. 736. The PRESIDENT immediately expressed himself as much gratified that you should have been good enough to have cabled MR. HOUSE. It was, he said, a very encouraging proof that H.M.G. intend to exchange views quite frankly with the U.S.G. on the MEXICAN situation. For his part, he intends to be equally frank. This he considers most important in the interests of all concerned and of the ideals which we are both trying to achieve.

The PRESIDENT most earnestly hopes that H.M.G. will not contemplate supporting DOMINGUEZ with money or otherwise, either directly or indirectly. You will recollect that the PRESIDENT has adopted a carefully considered and, for his part, unalterable policy regarding MEXICO and the Latin-American States generally. The guiding principle of this policy is non-interference with the internal affairs of the Latin-American States and non-recognition of revolutionary leaders. By refusal to recognize leaders who succeed in capturing the reins of government by violence, the PRESIDENT believes he will discourage such movements: indeed, he thinks this policy has already had its effect in Latin-American countries. While it is practically true that the UNITED STATES are not entirely satisfied with the attitude of CARRANZA, or with the situation in MEXICO, they believe the position is improving, and that as the Allies' success increases on the Western Front the pro-German element in Mexico will lose influence. U. S. hope that economic assistance will help Mexico to recover her stability. Any allied support of a counter-revolutionary movement would, in the PRESIDENT's opinion, be fatal to such a policy. The source of the support must inevitably become known and would destroy the structure of friendly relations with Mexico which U.S.G. have so patiently built up and put them back to the unhappy condition of several years ago. The PRESIDENT will insist that the Mexican Government shall deal with the Oil supply of the country in accordance with the recognized principles of international law and the rights of foreign nations.

I gather there is a feeling in Administration circles that it is a pity H.M.G. have not a representative at Washington specially charged with Mexican affairs, who could be to some extent in sympathy with the policy of the U.S.G.—with whom the State Department could take counsel freely on the various difficult phases of this perplexing problem. LORD READING can tell you exactly what is meant by this observation. (Message ends).

T telegram (W. Wiseman Papers, CtY).

Sir William Wiseman to Lord Reading

[Magnolia, Mass.] August 20, 1918.

No. 703. The PRESIDENT has asked me to cable you regarding the economic policy of the Allies towards Germany. He had understood that the Allied Governments decided that they would not officially resort to punitive trade policy advocated by the Paris Conference. He was disturbed, therefore, on reading the reports of MR. LLOYD GEORGE's speech of July 31st to the National Union of Manufacturers,[1] which seemed to recommend the crushing of Germany's trade after the war. I gather that the PRESIDENT's views on the subject are substantially as follows:

He fully appreciates the value of the economic weapon which the Allies, particularly Great Britain and the United States, possess, and he is in favour of using that weapon to the full in order to bring Germany to her senses and to ensure that a just peace when signed will be scrupulously observed. He is convinced, however, that it is a great mistake to threaten Germany now with any kind of punitive post-war measures against her trade. In his view this threat is one of the strongest levers with which the German militarists suppress the growth of any Liberal movement in Germany. They point out, he thinks, to their people that the Allies, especially Great Britain, are manifestly jealous of Germany's commercial position, and that if the Allies are not forced to accept a German peace they will crush Germany's trade. The PRESIDENT thinks that we ought to adopt the line that we have no desire to deny Germany her fair share of the world's commerce, and that it is her own militarists who are ruining her trade by prolonging the war and obliging us to maintain a blockade. It is true that the Allies will come to the Peace Conference practically controlling the supply of the world's raw material, but there will be no need to advertise that fact or to threaten anyone. Everyone—especially the Germans—will be quite aware of the facts. For your own private information, I may tell you that the PRESIDENT will try to get Congress to give powers to the Executive to control American raw-material exports for a period of years after peace. While this would not be openly aimed at Germany, it would be a formidable weapon for the United States to bring to Peace Conference.

The PRESIDENT hopes you will take this up with the PRIME MINISTER so that Great Britain and the United States can arrive at some common policy on this important and far-reaching question.

COL. HOUSE says he fears that if the Allies persist in making similar statements regarding their economic policy, the PRESIDENT will feel obliged, as he did once before,[2] to make some statement dis-associating this country with that policy.

T telegram (W. Wiseman Papers, CtY).
[1] David Lloyd George, at the request of the National Union of Manufacturers, had spoken in the House of Commons to a deputation of some 200 heads of business firms. His subject was postwar international economic problems of reconstruction. He did not go into specific details of a postwar economic plan, but he did indicate that the British government would support basic industries essential to national security and economic well-being. Then he issued a warning to Germany: "The longer the war lasts the sterner must be the economic terms we impose upon the foe. And I think the sooner he realizes that the better. He is fighting to impose his own economic terms upon the Allies. He will never succeed in doing so. As far as that is concerned we must be in a position to determine the conditions which we regard as fair, without having them imposed on us by the will of the enemy. If he goes on fighting, imposing greater burdens on us, destroying our young manhood, and guilty also of outrages which shock humanity . . . the sterner will be the terms that will be imposed on him." Later portions of his remarks make it clear that he had in mind the control of raw materials and transportation, with preference in both being given to trade with the dominions and the Allies over trade with the former enemy nations. He also made one pointed remark about the United States. He noted that the resolutions of the Paris Economic Conference (about which see RL to WW, June 23, 1916, Vol. 37) had been arrived at in 1916. "Up to the present time," he said, "America has expressed no opinion on the Paris resolutions, and it is vitally important that the policy of America and the policy of this country should be in complete agreement on economic problems as well as on other problems." This summary and the quotations are taken from the "official report" of Lloyd George's remarks in the London Times, Aug. 2, 1918.
[2] About this incident, see RL to WW, Feb. 16, 1918, the Enclosure thereto, and WW to RL, Feb. 16, 1918 (fourth letter of that date), all in Vol. 46.

Lord Reading to Sir William Wiseman

[London] August 20, 1918.

No. CXP. 738. URGENT: Surveying situation, I feel seriously concerned regarding matter of the SIBERIAN expedition, and I am, therefore, explaining matters to you in order that you may discuss them with COL. HOUSE. I promised him to speak quite frankly and now do so in the hope in any event that we may ascertain his views and that between us we may derive some benefit from these cable conversations.

On the one hand, news received by H.M.G. of the CZECHO-SLO-VAKS causes undoubted anxiety lest forces despatched consequent upon the recent arrangement with the PRESIDENT prove inadequate in number to protect the CZECHO-SLOVAKS or to help RUSSIANS resist their oppression. Natural consequence of this view would be attempt to induce the PRESIDENT to agree to further JAPANESE divisions being despatched. But, on the other hand, H.M.G. desires to respect the PRESIDENT's views, and therefore abstains from further request to him directly or indirectly for the addition to the military force. I am bearing in mind facts stated to me by the PRESIDENT, when he explained limitations which must necessarily be placed upon military action in consequence of the necessity of providing requisite supplies and have pressed these views upon H.M.G. Nevertheless I cannot but see that there is danger in allowing matters to remain for any length of time as they now are, and indeed they cannot remain, they must develop from day to day and may possibly cause acute situation at any time. For example, should disaster overtake CZECHO-SLOVAKS, there will be an outcry here of the public, who will attribute disaster to delay in sending the expedition or to inadequacy of the forces composing it. There will be public agitation, and, strive as H.M.G. may and will to prevent it, this may react upon the relations between United States and ourselves.

At the audience which I had last week HIS MAJESTY expressed serious anxiety about these matters, which he discussed fully, and with every regard for the views of U.S.G. The KING's observations, apart from their own value, reflect the opinion of the public. What is most in my mind is that, should any misfortune occur, and should there be any public outcry, it will have tendency to affect the PRES-IDENT's influence, which is now so powerful with our people and in France and elsewhere in world councils. This is a point which is constantly presented to my mind, and every effort should be made to counteract happening of any event which would minimize the PRESIDENT's influence.

Viewing all, is there any course which COL. HOUSE can suggest, or is he of opinion that notwithstanding danger to which I have called attention we should nevertheless do nothing further at the moment and merely await events. It is the serious risk involved in this latter policy which prompts me to send this cable.

T telegram (W. Wiseman Papers, CtY).

From the Diary of Colonel House

August 20, 1918.

Miss Denton[1] and I have been overwhelmed with crank and every other kind of letters. I recognize the handwriting of some that come to me as being the same who also write the President in my care. My habit is to throw these letters in the waste-basket and not give them to the Secret Service men. They indicate, however, how many thoroughly unbalanced minds there are in the country. Some of them accuse me of a pro-Catholic leaning, some of an anti-Catholic, some pro-British and some anti. Every conceivable public question seems to be on the minds of these cranks and it is a wonder the President does not come to harm even though he is as carefully guarded as he is.

Wiseman, who has been taking his vacation at Magnolia, has given me letters and cables from his Government. One of these refers to the Mexican situation and was from Balfour to me. The President read it and was much annoyed and asked me to have Sir William send the despatch which went today, a copy of which is a part of the record. Sir William and I also wrote a cable regarding raw materials. It is a criticism not only of Lloyd George, but of the Allied Governments. This cable, too, is a part of the record. Both of these cables the President requested me to send through Wiseman, asking me to use his name as freely as I thought necessary in order to bring about the desired results.

In talking with the President the other day I called his attention to the necessity of not offending the British Government in a way that would offend the entire British nation. The British people, as a whole, I told him, were with him; the British Government and the reactionary element in England were against him. In his desire to hit the Government and the reactionary forces he might, if he were not careful, hurt the *amour propre* of the British people as a whole. This, I thought, would be unfortunate. The President said he realized the truth of what I said and would use the necessary caution.

Dr. Paul Reinsch took lunch with us. I found him an intelligent, scholarly man. In speaking of Russian intervention he agreed heartily with the proposal I had suggested to the President, i.e. Hoover, etc. I asked him for suggestions as to the head of a mission and, strangely enough, he made the same suggestion Gordon made last night before leaving, and that was, Roland Morris, our Ambassador at Tokyo. I shall look into this further and perhaps suggest his name to the President.

¹ That is, Frances B. Denton, House's confidential secretary.

To George P. Hampton

My dear Mr. Hampton: [The White House] 21 August, 1918.

I have your interesting and impressive letter of August 19th about the water power legislation and shall take pleasure in consulting Members of the House Special Committee about it.

In haste,   Sincerely yours,   Woodrow Wilson

TLS (Letterpress Books, WP, DLC).

To Scott Ferris

My dear Mr. Ferris: [The White House] 21 August, 1918

I must say that the enclosed letter jumps with so many of my own notions that I have been very much impressed by it and am taking the liberty of sending it to you in the hope that you will let me know if you think it would be wise to make the attempt which Mr. Hampton suggests.

In haste,

Cordially and faithfully yours,   Woodrow Wilson

TLS (Letterpress Books, WP, DLC).

To Helen Hamilton Gardener

My dear Mrs. Gardener: [The White House] 21 August, 1918.

I am greatly distressed to know that you have been in the hospital and are not yet getting back your former strength. I can realize how it distresses you to give up the work in which you have been so actively and intelligently engaged.

You may be sure that the suggestion contained in your letter of August 16th will sink in my mind and that I will keep my eye open for suitable occasions when I may either in the way you suggest or in some other way be influential in bringing about the result we both desire.

    With the best wishes and most sincere sympathy,

Cordially yours,   Woodrow Wilson

TLS (Letterpress Books, WP, DLC).

To Robert Lansing

Dear Mr. Secretary: [The White House] 21 August, 1918.

    I have received a letter from a Mrs. J. L. Boggs, of Batesville, Arkansas,[1] in which she calls my attention to an unusual case as follows:

    "Last December a Spanish exchange tutor from Mexico, came to Arkansas College. In less than a week after his arrival the dormitory burned. With it went also his books, clothes, money, and to crown it all, his passports. We have made efforts, many and futile, to duplicate them. So far we have failed. Here he is, a stranger in a strange land, homeless, moneyless, except as he follows the wheat fields. He wrote me that if he 'could not now serve Jesu, he could work hard for Uncle Sam.' His name is Rodolfo Torres. The name of his home town is unfamiliar to me, but I can easily get it if necessary. His State is Tamalipas and the nearest big town is Mexico City. Now you see why we are driven to ask the Great White Father in Washington to help out of a very real tragedy one of 'these little ones?' "

    Is there not some way in which the unfortunate situation of this Mexican could be relieved?

Cordially and faithfully yours,   Woodrow Wilson

TLS (Letterpress Books, WP, DLC).
  [1] Lily G. (Mrs. J. L.) Boggs to WW, c. Aug. 17, 1918, ALS (WP, DLC).

To Kate Drayton Mayrant Simons[1]

My dear friend: [The White House] 21 August, 1918.

    I am distressed that you should be distressed about the stopping of the enlistments. It was a measure which it was absolutely necessary to take if the Government was going to exercise any real selection and prevent enlistments on the part of men who were more needed where they are than in the army, and you may be sure that I would make an exception in the case of your son Mayrant if I dared do so. I really dare not, because it would leave me without excuse in other cases and I should be obliged to do for all others similarly situated what I did for him.

I beg you to believe that he will not in the long run suffer by the new order. He has only to wait until he is called, and I do not know of anything that should prevent his going on for the present with his studies, as you wisely desire him to do.

It was a real pleasure to hear from you again and to be reminded of the old days in Atlanta.[2] I hope that in spite of the distress which the war has brought, you are well and enjoying the useful work that you are doing.

In haste, with warmest good wishes,

Cordially and sincerely yours,   Woodrow Wilson

TLS (Letterpress Books, WP, DLC).
    [1] Mrs. S. Lewis Simons of Summervile, S. C. She had been a close friend of Wilson's during his sojourn in Atlanta in 1882-1883. See the index references under Kate Drayton Mayrant in Vol. 13.
    [2] "Befriend me Friend of my youth, when all the world was coleur de rose, & the halo of those days, more than of the White House, still lingers around you." Kate D. M. Simons to WW, Aug. 11, 1918, ALS (WP, DLC).

From Thomas Watt Gregory

My dear Mr. President: Washington, D. C. August 21, 1918.

In your communication of August 14th, 1918, you sent me the enclosed letter from Upton Sinclair, dated August 7th, 1918, and asked for my comments, which might assist you in deciding upon your answer.

I suspect that, at the present writing, Mr. Sinclair has an exaggerated notion of the number of prominent or leading radicals or pacifists confined in penal institutions for anti-war utterances. He mentions, as illlustrations of the kind of persons he has in mind, Eugene Debs, Adolph Germer, Scott Nearing, Art Young, Max Eastman, Floyd Dell, Prince Hopkins, Frederick Krafft and Mrs. Rose Pastor Stokes. Of these only one, namely Frederick Krafft, is in a penitentiary for violation of the Espionage Act. Mrs. Stokes has been found guilty and sentenced, but is out on bail pending appeal. If Prince Hopkins is confined at all, it must be under a state and not a federal proceeding. The others named are under indictment but not yet tried. The number of persons of the class which Mr. Sinclair has in mind now actually confined in penal institutions is small, much smaller, I feel sure, than Mr. Sinclair realizes.

He suggests a sort of farm colony for these "political" offenders, without guarding other than their own word of honor, instead of the regular penitentiaries and the usual guards. The Espionage Act, under which these cases fall, provides for "imprisonment."

Detention on a penal farm might satisfy the requirements of the word "imprisonment"; and it might be within your power to use your emergency war fund for the purposes of establishing a special institution of that nature for the detention of the class of persons under discussion. Such institution would, however, have to be a penal institution, and certainly guarding and supervision by federal officers would be a practical necessity. So if Mr. Sinclair has in mind a place with none of the characteristics of a penal institution, there is no present statutory authority for carrying out that idea.

He refers to the wretched conditions in some state institutions to which these offenders have been committed. This is a matter, however, over which the federal government has absolutely no control; nor would either the state or federal governments have the power to adopt his suggestion that all such offenders be surrendered into federal custody.

Coming to the larger and less technical considerations raised by his letter, I believe that, on thinking them over thoroughly, we must come to the conclusion that nothing quite of the nature proposed by Mr. Sinclair can be justified or is practicable. I realize perfectly the class of persons he has in mind. They are men and women who have not the slightest sympathy with Germany, whose loyalty, in so far as they have national loyalty, is exclusively for the United States, who are intensely sincere, who have no converse whatever with the enemy or agents of the enemy and are guilty of no secret action against the interests of this country, but who, by reason of intense convictions and propagandist temperaments, give public voice to sentiments which are deemed by the Department of Justice and the trial court and jury to be obstructive of the prosecution of the war, and, consequently, a violation of the express provisions of the Espionage Law.

The utterances or propaganda of these men and women are of two types,—the one type being that which proclaims this war as a war by and for the benefit of capitalistic interests; the other that which proclaims participation in the war as utterly irreconcileable with Christianity. The "Christian pacifists" who have been prosecuted are a mere handful in number, so that substantially all who are involved in Mr. Sinclair's suggestions have been or will have been convicted of publicly advancing the proposition that this is a war for capitalism and not for democracy.

The Espionage Law may fairly be said to embody the public opinion of the country, speaking through its legislators, that propaganda which is obstructive of the war must, in the interests of public safety and of the success of the war, be treated as a crime of a serious nature, carrying with it imprisonment for a considerable period, and that success in the war is a matter so vital to this country and its institutions, that a deliberate impeding of that success, from whatever motive, must be treated as a serious offense. The grant of special privileges to persons found guilty of that offense, would be, if not something in the nature of an apology for the policy embodied in that law, at least a casting of doubt upon the wisdom of that policy. Furthermore, such a course would seriously impair the beneficial effects of that law. The Espionage Act, like any other penal statute, is intended to have a deterrent effect, and this deterrent effect would be greatly reduced by the adoption of a policy to make things extremely comfortable and pleasant and dignified for persons who violate that Act. Mr. Sinclair's plan, if carried out, might even result in holding these people up to public admiration, thus destroying practically all the efficacy of the Espionage Act as a deterrent of anti-war propaganda. It would be far better for you to exercise the pardoning power in the few cases to which Mr. Sinclair's observations justly apply, for that method of meeting the problem would still leave the Espionage Act intact.

The "political" offenders of the class referred to by Mr. Sinclair do present an anxious and many-sided problem. Where, however, the Department of Justice has come to the conclusion that the Espionage Act has been violated and a trial court and jury have concurred in that opinion, I believe, after much reflection, that it is better not to grant any exceptional favors to the persons thus found guilty.   Faithfully yours,   T. W. Gregory

TLS (WP, DLC).

From Jouett Shouse

PERSONAL

Dear Mr. President: Washington, D. C. August 21, 1918.

If the amendments to the Draft Act get through the House this week it is my present purpose to attend the Democratic Party Council[1] at Topeka, Kansas, on Tuesday of next week. My Democratic colleagues feel, as do I, that we should have definite personal representation at that Council in order that we may help as far as possible to formulate a platform that will be strong and effective.

We have gone over the platform recently adopted at the Indiana Democratic Convention[2] and we approve for the most part its utterances. We believe, however, there should be changes made in the platform, in its description of war accomplishments more particularly, to bring it down to date. We also favor a more definite statement as to continued government control and operation of the railroads, telephone and telegraph lines.

We believe the recommendations of the Federal Trade Commission relative to the control of the packers should be carried out by legislation. We feel that emphasis should be laid on the fact that our party has passed through the House a resolution submitting an amendment to the constitution providing for equal suffrage and that attention should be called to the effective efforts which you are exerting to have that resolution passed by the Senate. We think there should be mention also of the prohibition legislation of the Sixty-fourth and Sixty-fifth Congresses. These two last-named propositions will especially appeal to Kansas, where we have equal suffrage and where we have had prohibition for a great many years. We believe, furthermore, there should be mention made of the liberal pension legislation of this and the preceding Congress as Kansas has a very large number of old soldiers.

I am requested by my colleagues to submit to you these suggestions, with a copy of the Indiana platform; to ask that, if in the multiplicity of your duties you can do so, you be good enough to go over that platform, to make any suggestions of change which you think are wise and as far as you can to so revamp it as to make it the most effective possible expression of the principles of Kansas Democracy.

I know this is asking a great deal. But I am sure it is near to your heart, as it is to ours, that we shall continue to hold the present Democratic representation from Kansas. I may say to you, while in my judgment we are certain to lose a Democratic Senator from our state, we have a splendid chance not only to continue the five present Democratic Congressmen but to regain the Second District and perhaps to defeat Representative Campbell[3] in the Third District.

To this end every effort that we are capable of exerting will be put forth. We believe we will have your cooperation and the cooperation of the national administration generally, for there will be no battle ground upon which the Republican party will wage a harder campaign than the five districts in Kansas now represented by Democrats.

I expect to leave Washington Saturday afternoon and I want to urge that you shall give me your suggestions before that time. The copy of the Indiana platform which I enclose was secured from Chairman Ferris of the Congressional Campaign Committee. It is the only copy he has and he requests that it be returned by you.

Assuring you of my deep appreciation of the splendid help which you can give and with great respect, I have the honor to be

Sincerely yours,   Jouett Shouse

TLS (WP, DLC).
    ¹ A meeting of the Democratic leaders of Kansas.
    ² It is printed at June 15, 1918, Vol. 48.
    ³ Philip Pitt Campbell.

A Message

The White House, Aug. 22, 1918.

TO THE SENATE AND HOUSE OF REPRESENTATIVES:

I transmit herewith a report by the Acting Secretary of State submitting a draft of a joint resolution authorizing the admission into the United States of aliens who are refugees from conditions created by the war.[1]

I earnestly recommend this humane project to the favorable consideration of Congress.   [Woodrow Wilson]

CC MS (WP, DLC).
    ¹ F. L. Polk to WW, July 19, 1918, CCL (WP, DLC). Polk called Wilson's attention to the plight of some 1,800 Serbian refugees presently in Russia. Polk believed that, for humanitarian reasons, they should be admitted into the United States. However, he pointed out that the present immigration law would prohibit their admission since they could not meet its requirements of guaranteed employment and ability to support themselves. Hence, he and William B. Wilson had drafted a congressional joint resolution to permit the entrance both of the Serbians and others who might thereafter be in need of similar assistance. The draft joint resolution is missing. However, it was introduced as S.J. Res. 171 by Senator Thomas P. Gore on September 3 and referred to the Senate Committee on Immigration. It was reported favorably by the committee on the same day. Gore, on September 6, asked the Senate for unanimous consent to consider the resolution. Senators Lodge, Smoot, Thomas, and Brandegee were willing to admit the 1,800 Serbians but objected that the resolution was so broad that it would allow almost anyone—even a "Bolshevik"—to enter the United States until six months after the conclusion of the war. Gore thereupon withdrew his request for unanimous consent and Lodge moved to return the resolution to the Committee on Immigration. It never reemerged therefrom. *Cong. Record*, 65th Cong., 2d sess., pp. 9868, 9888, 10059-60. The resolution is printed in *ibid.*, p. 10059.

To Robert Lansing, with Enclosure

PERSONAL AND CONFIDENTIAL

My dear Mr. Secretary: The White House 22 August, 1918.

The enclosed is a memorandum which Mr. Reinsch at my request made of a conversation I had with him recently.[1] I agreed with him at the time in the judgments he here expresses, and have no doubt that he expressed the same judgments to you. I will take the liberty of discussing this with you at an early date.

Cordially and sincerely yours,   Woodrow Wilson

TLS (SDR, RG 59, 893.51/1979, DNA).
    ¹ At the White House on August 13.

E N C L O S U R E

August 14, 1918.

MEMORANDUM ON CHINESE FINANCE.

The primary and immediate need in the Chinese political and financial situation is,

(1) To establish China's public finance on a sound basis by making government loans openly on equitable terms and for purposes which will constructively develop the Chinese Government and country, guarding against the diversion of such loans to alien purposes;

(2) The radical suppression of the present debauching practice of making so-called industrial loans the proceeds of which are diverted to corrupt political and military machinations.

This urgent need can be fully met only if all loans made by foreign nations to the Chinese Provincial and Central Governments are embraced in a joint cooperative agreement conceived in the interest of the Chinese people. It is therefore highly desirable that all loans, inclusive of those for industrial purposes, should be included in the arrangements now being made for placing Chinese finance on a sound basis.

Should it prove impossible to include all industrial loans, the following would be an absolutely irreducible minimum, short of which no relief can be expected in the Chinese situation;

(1) The immediate completion of the International Chinese Public Loan Consortium for the purpose of making administrative and industrial loans to the Chinese Government, and the appointment of capable, accredited representatives of the national groups at Peking with the duty to elaborate the details of financial assistance and of securities, so as to devise a sound system of financial support to the Chinese Government;

(2) The making of an agreement among the governments participating in this arrangement, to the effect that each power will carefully scrutinize any and all loans made by its nationals for industrial purposes and will insist upon their bona fides, and that each government will communicate to its associates in this arrangement, within thirty days after conclusion, the text of any such agreements for industrial loans made to the Chinese Central or Provincial Governments or to corporations representative of the same.

The condition of affairs in China calls for immediate action if disgrace to the Allies, danger to their interests and irredemiable damage to the Chinese people are to be avoided.

Paul S. Reinsch.

TS MS (SDR, RG 59, 893.51/1979, DNA).

Four Letters to Robert Lansing

My dear Mr. Secretary,   The White House. 22 August, 1918.

I must admit that I recollect very little of what I have hea[r]d of Mr. Terestchenko,[1] but I have a very definite instinct that we ought not to be parties to getting into Russia, either by the eastern or the western door, any more "leaders" who represent recent months of blunder and ineptitude.   Faithfully Yours,   W.W.

WWTLI (SDR, RG 59, 861.00/2608, DNA).
   [1] Tereshchenko did eventually reach Archangel "incognito" on October 18, 1918, according to D. R. Francis to RL, T telegram, Oct. 20, 1918 (SDR, RG 59, 861.00/3002, DNA). Francis asked for a visa for Tereshchenko so that he could go on via the United States to Omsk as a courier for the Russian Minister at Stockholm.
   On October 24, Lansing cabled Francis that the "Department will now be pleased to have Tereshchenko visit the United States in the capacity of private individual and to facilitate his departure for Siberia." RL to D. R. Francis, Oct. 24, 1918, T telegram (SDR, RG 59, 861.00/3002, DNA).

My dear Mr. Secretary,   The White House. 22 August, 1918.

I return these papers for your file.[1] It is not necessary for me to comment further on the question with which they are concerned. It is plain to both of us that we are taking the right course in Norway and cannot accept the suggestions of method made by the Navy Department in their very natural eagerness to see the northern barrage effective.   Faithfully Yours,   W.W.

I informed Admiral Benson of the Presidents reply on Aug. 22, PM. WP

WWTLI (SDR, RG 59, 763.72111/7097½, DNA).
   [1] Office of Naval Operations to Chief of Naval Operations, Aug. 22, 1918, T MS (SDR, RG 59, 763.72111/7097½, DNA). This memorandum declared that Norway's existing surface patrol against German submarines was ineffective and hence did not fulfill Norway's obligations as a neutral nation. Her proposed increase of the surface patrol would be no more effective and would render the Allied mine barrage of the North Sea ineffective also. "The only recourse for the Allies," particularly the United States, it concluded, "is to demand of Norway that she take the steps which they, the Allies, after years of war experience, do find to be most efficacious. And if Norway will not do it, the Allies must do it for her." What the "most efficacious" steps were, the memorandum did not specify, but it stated that the Allies should, "as far as lies in their power, guard Norway against unjust reprisals."

My dear Mr. Secretary: [The White House] 22 August, 1918.

Some time ago the Italian Ambassador made very earnest representations to us in favor of permitting the construction in our shipyards of twelve non-sinkable transports of a sort which had been originated in Italy. I was of course very anxious to accommodate the Italian Government in such a matter and took the question up with the Chief of the Bureau of Construction and Repair of the Navy Department[1] as well as with the Ship Production Committee and the Engineering Department of the United States Shipping Board.

I now have the united judgment of these gentlemen[2] to the effect that the construction of these ships would require from eighteen months to two years, and that in view of the length of time which would be required to construct them, it seems very doubtful whether we ought in view of the pressing and immediate necessities of the war to set aside the necessary ship-yard space for their construction.

Will you not be kind enough to convey this judgment to the Italian Ambassador, with an expression of my very genuine regret that this should be the result of the investigation?

Cordially and sincerely yours,   Woodrow Wilson

TLS (Letterpress Books, WP, DLC).
[1] Rear Adm. David Watson Taylor.
[2] Conveyed in E. N. Hurley to WW, Aug. 16, 1918, TLS (WP, DLC).

My dear Mr. Secretary,   The White House. 22 August, 1918.

I agree with you that it is time that we took definitive action in this important matter,[1] and my inclination would be to take the second course you outline; but I am restrained by considerations which I shall take pleasure in explaining to you orally at our next interview. They are rather to[o] complex for a brief memorandum like this.

The first alternative you suggest is, it seems to me, the one we should now accept. It to a certain extent carries with it by implication the principle of the second, but is as far as we need go at this time.

I would be very much obliged if you would prepare and let me see the public announcement you would think it best to issue.

Faithfully Yours,   W.W.

WWTLI (SDR, RG 59, 763.72/11132½, DNA).
[1] See RL to WW, Aug. 19, 1918.

From Louis Brownlow

My dear Mr. President: Washington August 22nd, 1918.

The representatives of several patriotic societies and organizations in Washington which intend to celebrate Lafayette's birthday on the sixth of September have asked the Commissioners to name the hitherto unnamed bridge which carries Connecticut Avenue over Rock Creek in honor of Marshal Joffre, it being the purpose to attach the name-plate to the bridge as the principal event of the Lafayette Day celebration.

I am very much in sympathy with the purpose to do honor to France and also to Marshal Joffre. I believe the French Ambassador already has been told of the petition presented to the Commissioners to name the bridge in honor of Marshal Joffre. The suggestion also has been made that the bridge be called the Bridge of France. I do not think it would be proper, however, for the Commissioners to take any action that might be in questionable taste.

If there is any suggestion you would like to make with respect to the matter I will be very pleased to receive it as will my fellow Commissioners.   Yours very truly,   Louis Brownlow

TLS (WP, DLC).

To Louis Brownlow

PERSONAL AND CONFIDENTIAL

My dear Brownlow: The White House 22 August, 1918.

Personally I should feel very cordial towards the suggestion that the Connecticut Avenue bridge over Rock Creek be named in honor of Marshal Joff[r]e, but perhaps you do not know that our repeated attentions to the Marshal have created some heartburnings and some awkward situations in France, because the intimation seems to them to be that we trust Marshal Joff[r]e more than we trust their present military leaders. I am obliged reluctantly to say, therefore, that I do not think it would be politic at this time to confer that name on the bridge.

Perhaps the best suggestion among those you name is to call it the Bridge of France, because that would not attempt a discrimination among persons who take time to be, even in these critical days, very jealous of one another.

Cordially and sincerely yours,   Woodrow Wilson

TLS (WC, NjP)

To Joseph Patrick Tumulty

Dear Tumulty: [The White House] 22 August, 1918

I would be obliged if you would acknowledge this[1] for me and say that it has been brought to my attention. I do not trust Wheeler in the least and do not want to have anything to do with him, and

I must say I have not had time to read this report. Apparently the Chamber of Commerce of the United States is bent upon giving us as much gratuitous criticism as possible.[2]

The President

TL (WP, DLC).

[1] Elliot Hersey Goodwin to WW, Aug. 17, 1918, TLS (WP, DLC). Goodwin, the secretary of the Chamber of Commerce of the United States, requested an appointment with Wilson for Harry A. Wheeler, president of the chamber, to discuss a report on the Federal Trade Commission. He enclosed a copy of the report: Rush Clark Butler to the board of directors of the Chamber of Commerce of the United States, Aug. 14, 1918, TS MS (WP, DLC). Butler, a lawyer of Chicago, was chairman of the chamber's committee on the Federal Trade Commission. Tumulty accurately characterized the report in a covering note to Wilson on August 20: "This is a bitter attack on the Federal Trade Commission." The eighteen-page report charged that the F.T.C. had repeatedly exceeded its statutory powers, had failed to complete important investigations long in progress, had employed unfair procedures in its work, had abused its powers of publicity, and had been grossly careless in matters of fact. It concluded that the only way that public confidence in the F.T.C. could be restored was for the President to fill the two existing vacancies in the commission with "men whose training, temperament, experience, and reputation for sound judgment qualify them for the positions, and whose interests will be single to the Commission's work."

[2] When the Chamber of Commerce received no more than a formal acknowledgment of its report from the White House, it took its case to the public. An extensive summary of the report appeared in the *New York Times*, Sept. 2, 1918.

To James Francis Byrnes

My dear Mr. Byrnes: The White House 22 August, 1918

I would be very much obliged to you if you would at some early time drop in to see me at the White House in order that I may discuss with you some phases of the new appropriation bills. You have always rendered such generous service to the administration and to the government as a member of the Committee on Appropriations that I am anxious to seek your advice.

Cordially and sincerely yours,   Woodrow Wilson

TLS (J. F. Byrnes Papers, ScCleU).

To Jouett Shouse

My dear Mr. Shouse: The White House 22 August, 1918.

I quite agree with you that the Indiana platform, if used by the Kansas Democrats, ought to be brought down to date, and I think that it is not only legitimate but desirable that the Kansas Democrats should add any declaration of principles to the Indiana platform to which they attach sufficient importance. But beyond that I do not feel like going, because I think it is of the essence of effectiveness in these matters that there should be as little guidance as possible from outside and that the declaration of principles should come with as much spontaneity as possible from the men in counsel with each other.

Cordially and sincerely yours,   Woodrow Wilson

TLS (J. Shouse Papers, KyU).

A Memorandum by Scott Ferris

[c. Aug. 22, 1918]

Memorandum from Postmaster General Burleson in reference to the Water Power Bill—handed him by Mr. Scott Ferris.

If President Wilson is willing and can do so without offending Secretaries Baker, Lane and Houston, it would be extremely helpful if he would write a short note to Mr. Sims, Chairman of the Water Power Committee, saying, inasmuch as the House of Representatives has four times passed a Water Power Bill, each time carrying a recapture clause practically identical with the original Administration Water Power Bill as it was originally agreed upon, I am very much in hopes the judgment of the House will be to reject the Committee Amendment and recur to the original Administration Bill as it was originally agreed to at the White House conference and as it was delivered to Mr. Pou of the Rules Committee for introduction and consideration by the Congress.

Note, I do not think this will in any way embarrass or wound the feelings of Secretaries Baker, Lane or Houston. I think it will enable us to pass the bill through the House promptly. I think this will keep the bill free from criticism and attack. I think this will insure a better bill to come out of conference. The testimony of the bond brokers and water power people in the hearings are to the effect that the bill carrying the net investment insurance provision as distinguished from the "fair value not to exceed cost provision" is better than the Shields bill itself. If this be true the bill that would emerge from conference would be worse than the Shields bill. This would bring down the wrath of the people on the bill—bring about newspaper criticism and valid objections to such an extent that I think the President would be compelled to veto it and we would lose out on water power legislation all around. If the President cares to have the exact four provisions as they passed the House, or to amplify this matter in any way, it can be had by glancing at a copy of my minority report which is attached and printed in the back of the report of the pending water power bill.[1]

T MS (WP, DLC).
[1] This enclosure is missing.

To Thetus Willrette Sims

My dear Mr. Sims: [The White House] 22 August, 1918.

I am going to venture to say to you as Chairman of the Special Water Power Committee, what I hope that you will not think I am taking too great a liberty in saying; namely, that inasmuch as the House of Representatives has four times passed a Water Power Bill, each time with a recapture clause practically identical with the pending Water Power Bill as it was originally proposed by the Administration and agreed upon in informal conference, I am very much in hopes that it will be the judgment of the House to reject the Committee Amendment and recur to the original bill in the form in which it was delivered to Mr. Pou of the Rules Committee for introduction and consideration by the Congress. I am very much concerned about this feature of the bill and have had the privilege of being so intimately associated with those who have from time to time conferred about it that I am venturing to make this earnest suggestion.   Sincerely yours,   Woodrow Wilson

TLS (Letterpress Books, WP, DLC).

To Edwin Barfield Chappell[1]

My dear Doctor Chappell: [The White House] 22 August, 1918

Through the courtesy of the Honorable Joseph W. Byrns,[2] I have received your letter[3] suggesting a call by me to the Sunday Schools of the United States to rally in a special way during the coming winter, in order to preserve the interests of religion and keep alive the cause of religious education in the days to come. I need not tell you that the object you have in mind has my earnest and profound sympathy, but I do not believe that it would be wise for me to do what you suggest. I have this very distinct scruple: I do not believe that I ought to assume to be the leader and guide of organized agencies already under direct stimulation from the bodies of citizens which they represent. The Sunday Schools of the country have a very vital spiritual union through the instrumentality of many conferences and organizations, and I believe that they will respond to the call of their own representatives quite as loyally as they would respond to a call from anyone like myself, who would be coming in from the outside and might be considered unaware of the fine spirit and the fine work which already characterizes the Sunday Schools. I feel bound in conscience to be very chary in assuming that I have a right to speak to and for everybody. I am sure that you will appreciate this scruple.

Very sincerely yours,   Woodrow Wilson

TLS (Letterpress Books, WP, DLC).
¹ Editor and chairman of the Sunday School Board of the Methodist Episcopal Church, South; chairman of the Sunday School Council of Evangelical Denominations, 1917-1918.
² Joseph Wellington Byrns, Democratic congressman from Tennessee.
³ E. B. Chappell to WW, Aug. 17, 1918, TLS (WP, DLC).

To Eleanor Orbison Beach

My dear Mrs. Beach: [The White House] 22 August, 1918.

Your letter has interested me very much and you may be sure that my confidence in your husband is such that I would be willing to confide any duty to him which he was willing to assume, but if I may intrude my own personal judgment I would say that just because Princeton has fallen away from some of her old ideals, it is the very place he should not leave because no leaven that remains in the lump should be taken out. I hope and pray that that will be his own judgment.

The latest Princeton joke which you quote to me is certainly very diverting and I thank you for having given me the pleasure of seeing it.

I also thank you for telling me of your daughters, who I hope are keeping very well as well as very busy.

With warmest regards to you both,

Cordially and sincerely yours,   Woodrow Wilson

TLS (Letterpress Books, WP, DLC).

To Jessie Woodrow Wilson Sayre

My precious little Girl,   The White House. 22 August, 1918.

Your telegram *did* reach us at Magnolia, having been forwarded from Washington, as dear Edith's letter has already told you; but, while my heart longed to get into communication with you, to let you know how deeply and tenderly we were thinking of you, I simply did not know how and felt that I had to wait until I knew you were back at Siasconsett. Edith wrote as soon as we got here, and we have been thinking of you all the time, with the sort of love and sympathy which *ought* to have reached you, of its own sheer strength, if it did not.

It was all very distressing and you came through it finely, my dear little girl! We did not know of the extra physical strain you were bearing, and are profoundly grateful that you took no harm from the shock and the journey and that Davis gave you a clean bill of approval. Above all things, take care of yourself.

And now,—how are you going to manage? Do you not *need* some woman to come up and keep you company? Would you like me to suggest it to Helen when she gets home? She is odd about many things. She has just been up with her friend Mrs. Thomas[1] at York Harbor because Mrs. Thomas was alone and really needed her, and I am sure she would wish to come to you if she felt that *you* really needed her. But she is doing Red Cross work here (in which she is useful but not indispensable) and does not feel that she ought to go away from it just for pleasure or any kind of loafing, but only if she is really needed somewhere else. She will be here in about a week, I believe. How long can Nevin stay, and what plan had you formed for the interval (if there is to be one) between his going away and Frank's return?

I am delighted to hear that you expect Frank so soon. It lightens my anxiety about you not a little, to say nothing of the pleasure of having the dear boy himself on this side of the water again! For my heart is constantly full of you, my sweet Jessie, and I wish with all my heart that my special dear ones were where I could keep them, as it were, always in sight!

Our little stay on "the north shore" refreshed us very much indeed; and it was quite long enough. To have made it longer would have meant that I must return to overwhelming arrears of work here which could not be brought to me there. We were beautifully taken care of and have fallen back into the old routine with a new zest and freshness.

Nell and Mac came back from the West very much toned up and are both looking as fit as can be. They are in New York now on some railway business.

How stupid it was of me not to say anything about Alice's wedding when I last wrote you. I would not like Alice to hear me say that I forgot all about it.

Edith joins me in dearest love to you and the babies and is as deeply interested as I am in the happy coming event, if you will and can take care of yourself. I hope you know how deeply and tenderly I love you and how constantly you are in my thoughts! Give Nevin my warmest regards and my heartfelt thanks for the tender care he is taking of you.   Your devoted Father

WWTLS (photostat in RSB Coll., DLC).
[1] She cannot be further identified.

From Robert Lansing, with Enclosure

My dear Mr. President: Washington August 22, 1918.

I enclose to you a letter which I have just received from Mr. George Kennan which I think you will find of sufficient interest to read. Attached to the letter is a Memorandum on the equipment of an expeditionary force in Siberia[1] which, being from one who understands the climatic conditions, should, in my mind, be sent to the War Department for its information. I believe Mr. Kennan's statements can be implicitly relied upon as to the rigorous winter which our men will have to endure in eastern Asia.

Faithfully yours,   Robert Lansing

TLS (WP, DLC).
[1] Wilson sent this memorandum to Baker on August 24.

E N C L O S U R E

George Kennan to Robert Lansing

Baddeck C. B.
Dear Mr. Secretary: Nova Scotia August 18 1918

You were good enough to ask me, once upon a time, to write you freely about international affairs—more particularly Russian affairs—and if I avail myself again of this permission, it is only because I desire to be helpful as far as I can. There are two or three considerations, connected with the expedition to eastern Siberia which seem to me important.

1. The choice of a Chief Commissioner. The success of negotiations with the Russians will depend largely upon the knowledge, judgment and tact of the man selected to conduct them. I do not know, of course, what policy the President has decided upon; but, in any course of action, much must necessarily be left to the judgment and discretion of the man who heads the Commission. The Root Commission of last year did not influence the course of events in Russia in the slightest degree, partly because the people generally did not get into sympathy with it, and partly because the Commission itself did not understand what was going on around it. This was reported to me from Russia at the time, and it became sufficiently evident from the talk of Mr Root when he returned. He did not seem to me to have grasped the significance of the events that he had witnessed, nor to have foreseen the results that the forces in operation would almost certainly bring about. Consequently, he was unduly hopeful and optimistic. Whether he could have influenced the course of events if he had regarded them rightly and had

appreciated their significance, I do not know; but he seemed to me to have lacked the information or the judgment that he ought to have had. In an automobile, efficiency depends very largely, if not wholly, upon the mixture of air and gas in the carburetor, and in the Root carburetor the American air and the Russian gas did not mix at all—they did not even get into contact.

The head of the Commission to eastern Siberia will be in a position to exert far more power and control over the course of events than Mr Root could exert, for the reason that he will be backed by force, and will bring economic and other assistance of which the Siberian population is in urgent need. It is doubly important, therefore, that he should be a big enough man for the job, and that he should have a cool head, sound judgment, and wide knowledge of men and affairs. He will not attempt, I presume, to exercise any political control over the Russians, nor to decide what form of government they shall have; but he cannot help exerting influence, and it is highly important that such influence should be wisely directed. Of all the men I can think of, Franklin K. Lane would be the best, if he were willing to go and if he could [be] spared for a few months from the Interior Department. He has a sympathetic comprehension, at least, of Socialistic ideals, and that would help him very much in dealing with a population in which there is a very considerable admixture of Social Revolutionists. At the same time, he is practical and level-headed, and knows what Socialism can and cannot do. He is also accustomed to deal with big affairs and to look at things in a broad way.

2. The best equipped and most competent Head Commissioner, however, might fail, in a country unfamiliar to him and among a people whom he does not know, if he were not provided with facilities for getting full and accurate information. He should therefore have a small staff of expert and trustworthy Russians, who know the country and the people, and who can give him, or collect for him, the information necessary to the formation of a sound judgment on current events. These men could also act as intermediaries in his dealings with the local government and the people. He would wish, of course, to select these men himself; but if I were in his place, some of the men whose characters and capabilities I should consider are:

a. Mr Konovaloff,[1] a minister in the cabinets of both Prince Lvoff and Kerensky, who is now living in Washington or New York.

b. Mr Novosseloff,[2] President of the All-Russian Tanners' Union, a concern which has about forty branches in European Russia and Siberia. (I sent you a copy of his brochure on the Bolsheviki).[3]

c. Baron S. A. Korff,[4] of the Helsingfors University, who was Vice

Governor General of Finland under the First Provisional Government.

d. Dr Nicholas Russel,[5] of Nagasaki, Japan.

All of these men except Dr Russel you have probably met, as they went to Washington in the early summer to offer information to our Government with regard to Russian affairs. All speak English well, with the possible exception of Konovaloff whom I have not personally met.

Dr Russel is a Russian by birth and education, but he migrated to the United States as a political refugee many years ago, became a naturalized American citizen and settled in the Sandwich Islands, where he bought an estate. He was for some time a member of the Territorial Assembly of Hawaii and ultimately was elected its Speaker. In 1906 he came to Japan to help me in carrying on a liberal campaign of enlightenment among the Russian prisoners of war. He soon acquired the full confidence of the Japanese Government, and was allowed by General Terauchi[6] (then Minister of War) to distribute liberal literature and organize meetings in all the prison camps. He is a man of high culture, an author of some note, a most persuasive orator in both Russian and English, and has really extraordinary tact in dealing with all sorts of people. Since the Russo-Japanese war he has been practicing medicine in Nagasaki, and I presume he now speaks Japanese as well as Russian and English. I was closely associated with him for many months in Japan, and in my judgment he would be a most useful man, in many ways, to such a Commission as it is proposed to send to Siberia. Before coming to the United States he lived for some time in the Balkans, so that he has some acquaintance with the Czecho-Slovaks and other Slav nationalities in southeastern Europe. He is a man of attractive and sympathetic personality, and as a physician, a persuasive speaker, and a writer who is familiar with Russian psychology and conditions, he could be useful to the Commission in manifold ways. I do not know whether he would be willing to go to Siberia or not, as I have not heard from him directly since last year; but he is a patriotic Russian and a most ardent hater of the Germans. His address is No. 9 Bund, Nagasaki, Japan.

I enclose on a separate sheet some suggestions for the winter equipment of the expeditionary force. This is not in your province, but you are the only Cabinet officer I know except Secretary Lane, and if my ideas seem to you worth consideration, you will know what to do with them. Inasmuch as I have spent four winters out of doors in eastern Siberia, I may fairly claim to know something about climatic conditions there. Perhaps our army quartermasters are equally well informed, but when I remember the deficiencies in the equipment of General Shafter's[7] army in Cuba in 1898, I don't feel sure of it.

With sincere regard and esteem I am

Faithfully yours   George Kennan

TLS (WP, DLC).
[1] That is, Aleksandr Ivanovich Konovalov.
[2] S. S. Novosseloff (or Novoselov).
[3] This was probably S. S. Novosseloff, *The Bolsheviki and the American Aid to Russia* (*An Open Letter to the American-Russian Chamber of Commerce of New York*) (New York, 1918).
[4] Baron Sergei Aleksandrovich Korff.
[5] Kennan identifies him thoroughly below.
[6] That is, Masatake Terauchi.
[7] Maj. Gen. William Rufus Shafter (1835-1906) had commanded the American forces which captured Santiago de Cuba in July 1898. His men were seriously hampered by malaria and yellow fever, and he was severely criticized for alleged deficiencies in provisions and equipment.

From Robert Lansing

My dear Mr. President: Washington August 22, 1918.

I lay before you a communication from the French Embassy in relation to the sending of High Commissioners to Siberia[1] and also a memorandum from Mr. Phillips on the subject.[2]

Personally I feel that in view of our policy it would be unwise to do this and that this is another move to impress our action in Siberia with the character of intervention rather than relief of the Czechs. The suggestion that our High Commissioner be the head of an international commission seems to be a bait to draw us into this policy which has been so insistently urged by Great Britain for the past six months.

It would relieve the situation if you authorized me to say to the Ambassadors that we did not intend to appoint a High Commissioner and to state to the press that at present we had no intention of making such an appointment.

If we decline to cooperate in this I believe that the Commission will have little weight.   Faithfully yours,   Robert Lansing.

TLS (SDR, RG 59, 861.00/2659, DNA).
[1] J. J. Jusserand to RL, Aug. 12, 1918, TLS (SDR, RG 59, 861.00/2507, DNA). Jusserand stated that his government believed that an "inter-Allied civilian board" should be created to coordinate Allied policy within Russia. "That board," he continued, "should have the last say in all questions flowing from the assistance brought to Russia by the Allies, decide the political disputes, give the economic, financial and technical directions, define the relations between the Allied Governments and the local authorities." If the American government agreed to the proposal, the chairmanship of the board would go to the United States. A few Russians might be attached to the board in an "advisory capacity."
[2] It is missing in WP, DLC, and in the files of the Department of State.

Two Letters from Newton Diehl Baker

Dear Mr. President: Washington. August 22, 1918.

The so-called Houston Riot[1] took place on August 23, 1917. From the time of the arrival of these colored troops at Houston until the day of the riot there was more or less continuous trouble over the enforcement of so-called Jim Crow laws, provisions for separate drinking water facilities, and other race differentiations. There were some instances of assaults committed upon colored soldiers by Houston policemen and, generally, verbal disputes and clashes were of frequent occurrence. On August 23 two police officers raided a crap game in the colored section of the city, the game being in process among some colored boys who fled for refuge into the house of a woman. One of the officers undertook to arrest the woman, but a negro soldier nearby interfered and was arrested by the officer, with perhaps unnecessary violence. Some controversy arose later in the day between the officer who made this arrest and Corporal Baltimore,[2] a negro member of the Military Police stationed in the city of Houston, which resulted in Baltimore being shot at, struck over the head with a revolver, and arrested. The news of this incident reached the camp and spread among the colored soldiers, with the result that later in the day a mutinous band of colored soldiers, seeking revenge on the police of Houston, left the camp, armed, approached the town, and committed the various murders, assaults, and acts of terrorization which characterized the riot. In all, fifteen persons were killed and twelve others were feloniously assaulted and wounded.

An investigation was of course at once ordered by the Department Commander,[3] and I sent the Inspector General[4] from Washington to investigate the matter, with the view to assuring prompt, but fair and just, trials of all persons implicated in the mutinies and murders. The persons arrested were tried in three groups, and the records of their trials are in my office and are known, respectively, as the Nesbit Case, the Washington Case, and the Tillman Case. In each instance the Court was properly constituted, was composed of officers of long experience and sobriety of judgment, and in each case the defendants were represented by able counsel. The Nesbit Case was concluded on the 30th of November, 1917, the defendants being charged with sedition, mutiny, murder, assault with the intent to commit murder, and wilful disobedience of orders with re-

---

[1] About which, see NDB to WW, Aug. 24, 1917, and the Enclosure thereto, both in Vol. 44, and index references to the Houston riot in that and subsequent volumes.
[2] Charles Baltimore.
[3] Maj. Gen. James Parker.
[4] That is, Maj. Gen. John Loomis Chamberlain.

gard to ammunition. Five of the defendants were acquitted; four were convicted of wilful disobedience and sentenced to brief terms of confinement in the United States Disciplinary Barracks at Fort Leavenworth, Kansas; fifty-four were convicted of murder, mutiny, assault with intent to commit murder, and disobedience of orders, and of this number forty-one were sentenced to life imprisonment in the United States Penitentiary at Fort Leavenworth and thirteen were sentenced to death. Within a very brief period thereafter the Commanding General of the Southern Department having reviewed the record and confirmed the sentences, the thirteen men sentenced to death were executed by hanging. This order was wholly within the power of the Commanding General of the Southern Department under the Articles of War, which in time of war do not require death sentences to be forwarded for review by the Judge Advocate General and confirmation by the President. The record, however, was filed in the War Department and has been examined by the Judge Advocate General;[5] it is without prejudicial error in matter of law and the evidence overwhelmingly sustains the judgment of guilty as to all the defendants, alike as to those who were capitally executed and those who were sentenced to terms of imprisonment. There can, therefore, be no question but that the law of the land prevailed and that justice was done to the defendants in the Nesbit Case, and in dealing with the matters hereinafter to be stated it is my judgment that in whatever action you take there should be a memorandum setting forth the proceedings in the Nesbit Case, the care with which the trial was surrounded, its freedom from error, and the justice of the conclusion reached.

In view of the speed with which the death sentences in the Nesbit Case were executed, some feeling was aroused in the country, based upon the fear that such expedition was inconsistent with that opportunity for careful review which our laws ordinarily accord in cases where the death penalty is imposed. I therefore directed that in all subsequent cases where the death penalty is imposed in the limits of the continental United States, as distinguished from the area of conflict in France, sentence should be suspended, the record reviewed in Washington, and the sentence submitted for your action. It is for this reason that the records in the Washington Case and the Tillman Case are now presented to you.

The Washington Case involved fifteen persons. The trial was concluded on December 22, 1917. Five of the fifteen were found guilty of all specifications and sentenced to death; three were found guilty of all specifications with minor exceptions and sentenced to

[5] That is, Maj. Gen. Enoch H. Crowder.

ten years imprisonment; and seven were found guilty of the specifications with other modifying considerations and sentenced to seven years imprisonment.

The Tillman Case, concluded March 26, 1918, involved forty persons, of whom eleven were sentenced to death, twelve to life imprisonment, nine to fifteen years imprisonment, five to two years imprisonment, two were acquitted, and as to one the charges were dismissed.

The prison sentences imposed in the foregoing cases are not required to be reviewed by the President; there are, therefore, presented for your action in these cases sixteen death sentences.

Because of the very great gravity both of the offenses and the penalties in these cases I have caused the voluminous records to be examined independently by several experienced members of the Judge Advocate General's Corps and by the Judge Advocate General himself. I have also personally gone over much of the record and I am obliged to concur with the unanimous judgment expressed by all who have examined these records, that they are without serious flaw as to matters of law, that the Court in each instance was properly constituted and composed of men of the highest character, that all rights of the accused were safeguarded, and that in spite of the fact that there were manifest evidences of a concert of agreement among the accused not to testify and to withhold material facts from the Courts, nevertheless the judgments are sustained by the overwhelming weight of the testimony.

While these cases were still pending on review a formidable petition was presented to you,[6] signed by many members of the colored race, urging clemency, and letters came from all parts of the United States, some addressed to you directly and some through the War Department, the purport of which were to urge you to regard the provocation of race discrimination as a ground for the exercise of the commuting power, and urging further both that an adequate penalty had been exacted in the executions of those convicted in the Nesbit Case and that the people of the colored race in the United States are manifesting so loyal an attitude toward the Government in the war and are giving such repeated evidence of patriotic devotion to the national cause both by their service in the Army and their purchases of Liberty Bonds and patronage of other patriotic causes, that the Government ought to recognize their loyalty by a concession against the extreme penalty executed upon so many members of the race. In the meantime, many months have elapsed since the beginning of these trials, months which have for the most

[6] It is printed at Feb. 19, 1918, Vol. 46.

part been consumed by the excess of care with which the trials have been surrounded to ensure against accidental error or injustice. Nevertheless, the time has passed and the execution now of these death penalties, it is said, would come as a shock and re-open an old race wound.

Admittedly, the offense of which these soldiers were guilty is one of the greatest gravity. When the Government places high-powered weapons in the hands of soldiers and gives them thereby the power of life and death over the civilian population of the community, the responsibility of those so entrusted is manifoldly increased, and unless the Government sternly requires respect for the lives of civilians at the hands of its armed soldiers the principles of liberty themselves would be menaced by the forces organized for their preservation. Among those killed by these mutinous and riotous soldiers were innocent bystanders and citizens of Houston who with the utmost good will sought to quell this unhappy riot. In some instances perfectly harmless persons having no relation whatever to any of the wrongs of which the rioters complained were shot in cold blood, simply because they came within the reach of the frenzy of this mob. With this sense of duty and responsibility I have still sought in my examination of these cases to distinguish and discriminate as to degrees of guilt among these maddened men, with the thought that while it will be necessary for you, as Commander-in-Chief of the Army, sternly to uphold the principles of discipline which ought to make this sort of outbreak impossible, nevertheless it might be possible for you to discriminate and, by commuting the sentences of those associated in these acts of violence but not directly shown by the evidence to be individually responsible for murder, to make a merciful concession to the considerations which have been urged upon you in the letters and the petition above referred to.

In the Tillman Case this principle of discrimination would show that Private William D. Boone deliberately shot an already wounded man who was on his hands and knees, killing him under circumstances of great brutality and barbarity; but the remaining men in the Tillman Case, while deeply engaged in the riotous assemblage, are not shown by the record actually and with their own hands to have killed designated individuals.

In the Washington Case, Privates Babe Collier, Thomas Mc-Donald, James Robinson, Joseph Smith, and Albert D. Wright were accused and convicted, in addition to the charges of mutiny, rioting, etc., alleged in the other cases, of the murder of E. M. Jones, and the record shows that while Mr. Jones was driving along the road in an automobile he was halted by Collier, McDonald, and Wright, whereupon the whole five fell upon him, shooting him from both sides of the road and killing him. These are the five as to whom the death penalty was imposed in that Case, and the evidence obviously justifies the conviction.

My recommendation, therefore, is that the five sentences of death in the Washington case be confirmed, and that the death sentence in the case of William D. Boone (Tillman Case) be confirmed, that the remaining ten death sentences in the Tillman Case be commuted to life imprisonment, and that this action be taken by you in a comprehensive memorandum reviewing all the cases, pointing out the gravity of this occurrence, the propriety of the result in all these cases, and the fact that the action taken by you as a matter of clemency in the ten cases in which commutation is granted is not to be regarded as expressive of any doubt on your part that full justice was done in the trials, but is a recognition of the fidelity of the race to which these men belong, a recognition of the valiant military service which colored soldiers are now rendering in France, and an expression of your hope that no such incident will ever again disgrace the military service of the United States.

If these recommendations meet with your general approval, or if you will indicate to me any modification of them which you desire to make, I will be glad to prepare for your signature such memoranda and orders as will carry them into effect.

Respectfully yours,   Newton D. Baker

My dear Mr. President: Washington. August 22, 1918.

I have your letter of the twentieth enclosing a letter from Mr. Gompers.

I said to the House Committee that the Senate provision really did no more than the War Department was now doing, so that it was, in effect, a legislative declaration of a policy already adopted and operating. I do not think we ought to use the draft law to settle bona fide disputes between labor and capital, but I am equally clear that a man who is put in a deferred class by reason of his indispensable relation to war industry, ought not to retain the deferred classification when he ceases to be a laborer in that industry.

With this I think Mr. Gompers and his associates agree. They are rather afraid that the provision in the bill will be misunderstood by labor than that it will be unfairly operated. The House Committee, however, decided to leave the amendment out, and I suppose the question will have to be settled in conference. I shall be equally satisfied to have the provision left in or taken out. In my

judgment we now have full power to do the thing which the amendment covers.   Respectfully yours,   Newton D. Baker

TLS (WP, DLC).

From Thetus Willrette Sims

My dear Mr. President: Washington, D. C. August 22, 1918

General debate on the water power bill has closed. Further consideration has been postponed until the man power bill passes the
House but we will probably have time to take up the water power
bill and finish its consideration before the Ways and Means Committee will have the revenue bill ready for consideration. We are
therefore in the amendment stage of the bill which is the all important stage.

As the bill was finally reported by the Committee there is no
matter of serious difference except the so-called net investment
amendment. As you know, Mr. Ferris is very bitterly opposed to
that amendment, Mr. Doremus[1] agrees with him and so do I, but
as Chairman having charge of the bill and representing a majority
of the Committee rather than my personal views it is rather em-
barassing for me to do what I feel my duty will require me to do
in the present case.

You requested the three Secretaries to prepare a bill for you.[2]
Naturally I must suppose that they gave the preparation of that bill
their most deliberate and serious consideration. You presented the
bill they had prepared and given you and which met with your
approval as a basis upon which you asked that a special committee
be created by special rule in order that all questions of water power
legislation should be included in one bill. You stated to us at the
time we met you in conference that you approved the fundamental
provisions of the bill. You finally gave the bill to Mr. Pou, Chairman
of the Committee on Rules so that it might not appear that you had
any feeling or preference as between the several committees that
had heretofore had jurisdiction of water power legislation.

Mr. Pou immediately had the bill printed and a thousand copies
of same distributed among the members of the House. This was
all done before the Committee on Rules had brought in a rule
providing for the establishment of a special committee in compliance with your request. Being satisfied with the fundamental provisions of the bill I strongly urged the Committee on Interstate and
Foreign Commerce to agree to this special rule. Mr. Doremus helped
me in the matter but it was rather an uphill task to get the Com-

mittee to agree to it but finally it did so. The fundamentals of that bill were given to the House as the deliberately considered necessary provisions of a water power bill carefully prepared by the three Secretaries carefully scrutinized by yourself and approved by all concerned. The House, feeling it to be the last word from both you and the three Secretaries, adopted the rule creating the committee. The committee was appointed and I was honored with the chairmanship of same. But the railroad control bill was then up for consideration by the Committee on Interstate and Foreign Commerce therefore I could not call the water power committee together or take any steps whatever in the consideration of the proposed water power bill.

Several weeks after the committee had been created Mr. O. C. Merrill,[3] Chief Engineer of the Bureau of Forestry in the Department of Agriculture, came to see me and stated to me that the three Secretaries requested that this bill which you had given us be referred back to the three Secretaries, that there were certain amendments which the three Secretaries wanted in the interest of clarity and simplicity. I told Mr. Merrill that the bill which you had given to us and which had been printed at the request of Mr. Pou was not a pending bill before the Committee in the sense that it could be referred by Committee action but that if the three Secretaries desired to look over the bill with a view to changing its phraseology thereby making it more clear and simple they could do so and the committee would take up their suggestions and consider same when organized.

About two weeks afterwards Mr. Merrill came to my committee room late one afternoon and brought what he said was a bill with the suggested amendments proposed by the three Secretaries and also handed me a letter signed by the Secretaries. Assuming of course that the amendments had been submitted to you by the three Secretaries and approved by you I never even read the bill or the letter but went immediately to the floor of the House and had the letter put in the Congressional Record[4] and had a thousand copies of the amended bill printed at once and also a thousand copies of the letter.

It was a number of days after that time when Mr. Ferris asked me if I had read these proposed amendments. I told him I had not. He suggested that I read them immediately as he regarded the changes made in the bill as fundamental. I then read the bill and found that Mr. Ferris was exactly right, that instead of changing the phraseology so that the fundamental provisions of the bill would be more easily understood that the basic provisions of the bill had been completely changed. For instance, the bill you gave us provided for a license period of not exceeding fifty years. This had been changed to a specific, arbitrary fifty year period with no power to provide for a less period without the consent of the licensee. A second license period was provided for the holder of the original license and the tender of this second license was made mandatory upon the part of the Commission. The recapture provision of the bill you gave us provided for recapture upon a basis of fair value not exceeding actual cost. This provision was stricken out almost bodily and the so-called net investment provision substituted for it.

It is evident to me that the Secretaries never considered these amendments as thoroughly as they should have been considered. I could never believe that radically fundamental changes in the bill would have been suggested and pressed by the three Secretaries without first being submitted to you and having your approval.

Now, in all fairness and justice to myself as Chairman of the Water Power Committee and to the members of the three committees and to the House of Representatives who concurred in making a revolutionary change in the procedure of the House in order to consider a bill given to us by you that radical and fundamental changes in that bill should not have been prepared and suggested by the Secretaries and given the stamp of administration approval without you or any member of the committee being consulted as to the effect these proposed changes would have upon the bill.

I of course took it for granted that Mr. Merrill was in all good faith representing the Secretaries in doing what he did and that they were doing what you approved. I feel absolutely sure that neither the committee nor the House of Representatives would have suggested any such amendments or would have consented to them on any other theory than that they had received your consideration and approval. The committee has acted on all the amendments but the net investment amendment is the bone of contention and I ask you, if you are willing to do so, to let me know whether or not these proposed amendments were submitted to you and whether or not they were approved by you, especially the net investment amendment as written in the reported bill.

I would like very much to have your reply before we begin considering the bill for amendment because I feel in all good faith I must oppose this net investment amendment.

I must assume that the three Secretaries gave the whole matter exhaustive consideration before they handed you a bill. If they did so and then afterwards radically changed almost every fundamental provision of the bill it is to me a very strange proceeding. Therefore, I cannot believe that they did so with a thorough knowledge of the effect of the amendments upon the bill.

Very sincerely yours,   T. W. Sims

TLS (WP, DLC).
  ¹ Frank Ellsworth Doremus, Democratic congressman from Detroit.
  ² About which, see DFH to WW, Nov. 30, 1917, n. 1, Vol. 45.
  ³ Oscar Charles Merrill.
  ⁴ NDB, FKL, and DFH to T. W. Sims, Feb. 27, 1918, printed in *Cong. Record*, 65th Cong., 2d sess., p. 2942.

To Robert Lansing

My dear Mr. Secretary,   The White House. 23 August, 1918.

I hope you will do just what you here suggest.¹ The other governments are going much further than we and much faster,—are, indeed, acting upon a plan which is altogether foreign from ours and inconsistent with it.

Please make it plain to the French Ambassador that we do not think cooperation in *political* action necessary or desirable in *eastern* Siberia because we contemplate no political action of any kind *there*, but only the action of friends who stand at hand and wait to see how they can help. The more plain and emphatic this is made the less danger will there be or [of] subsequent misunderstandings and irritations.²   Faithfully Yours,   W.W.

WWTLI (SDR, RG 59, 861.00/2660, DNA).
  ¹ In RL to WW, Aug. 22, 1918 (second letter of that date).
  ² Lansing's reply to Jusserand was RL to J. J. Jusserand, Aug. 31, 1918, TCL (SDR, RG 59, 861.00/2507, DNA). Lansing stated that he assumed that there would be the fullest cooperation in relief activities (as distinct from any political activities) between the representatives of the United States and those of the Allied nations in Siberia. As to cooperation in political and economic matters, Lansing made the following declaration: "Since the beginning of the Revolutionary movement this Government has maintained an attitude of strict impartiality as between contending political parties and, as it contemplates no change in this attitude, it deems cooperation in any political action impossible and believes it would be as unnecessary as it is undesirable. It prefers to occupy a position in Eastern Siberia merely as a friend who stands at hand ready to help in the most practical and wholehearted manner. While, therefore, this Government cannot see its way clear to concur in the suggestion that a representative of the United States should assume the Chairmanship of such an inter-Allied Board, I beg to express my appreciation of Your Excellency's courtesy and consideration. Furthermore, I improve this opportunity to inform Your Excellency that, while the matter of the extension of economic relief to the Siberian people is receiving constant and attentive consideration, this Government has not as yet definitely determined upon the action it will take in that respect."

To Robert Lansing, with Enclosure

My dear Mr. Secretary,   The White House. 23 August, 1918.

No doubt it is only fair that the British and other allied governments should know what we are doing, but I beg that you will add
to this telegram instructions to our representative at Christiania[1]
to intimate to the British minister and the others[2] that we are not
in sympathy with the course they are taking as outlined in Schoenfeld's No. 1040, which I enclose. This should be done, of course,
unofficially, but very plainly, so that they may understand that they
shall not draw us into any unneutral action towards Norway of any
kind. You will have to make it pretty plain because it is evident that
Schoenfeld is inclined to do what his British and French associates
desire.   Faithfully Yours,   W.W.

WWTLI (SDR, RG 59, 763.72111 N83/61, DNA).
  [1] Hans Frederick Arthur Schoenfeld, Second Secretary of the American legation in
Christiania, at this time Chargé d'Affaires.
  [2] Sir Mansfeldt de Cardonnel Findlay, British Minister; Abel Chevalley, French Minister; and Giulio Cesare Montagna, Italian Minister.

E N C L O S U R E

Christiania, August 21, 1918.

Urgent. 1040. Absolutely secret. British Minister informs me that
on the nineteenth instant he delivered to the Minister for Foreign
Affairs[1] an aide memoire which described as unsatisfactory the
reply dated August twelfth of the Norwegian Government to his
representations regarding mining Norwegian territorial waters, reiterated the arguments in support of such a course, cited specific
instances which had been observed by British naval forces at great
risks to themselves of violations by German submarines of Norwegian neutrality, and which contained a statement that would be
construed, and was intended to be construed by the Norwegian
Government, as a warning that if within a short period the measures
demanded by the situation be not carried out, action would be taken
to close Norwegian waters in the area affected by means of mines.

British Minister informed me in strictest confidence that the War
Cabinet in London had decided that within fourteen days, presumably counting from the nineteenth instant, the area in question
would be mined by British or Allied naval forces if the Norwegian
Government shall not, by that time, have taken the necessary measures. He said that the British Embassies at Washington, Paris and
Rome had been directed to recommend the issuance of instructions
to this Legation and to the French and Italian Ministers here to
give warning to the Norwegian Government.

I understand, meanwhile, that the British Minister has not given the Norwegian Government an intimation of an actual time limit within which Norway must take the measures deemed necessary, and that he is deferring doing so until our Allied colleagues and particularly this Legation are instructed to give such warning.

British Minister has also been authorized in his discretion and if it prove opportune to do so, to state to the Norwegian Government that it may count on aeroplanes and anti-aircraft artillery to be supplied by Great Britain in the unlikely event that Germany should attack Norway if her territorial waters are mined. As to this, I do not know whether the British Minister has made such a communication to the Norwegian Government.

My Allied colleagues are of opinion, which I share, that actual hostilities by Germany are unlikely. As to the instructions referred to in my 1037 of yesterday as having been sent to Norwegian Legations in Washington, London, Paris, and Berlin demanding explanation of the violations of Norwegian waters by belligerent submarines, it would seem that if the Germans deny having used Norwegian waters they cannot logically object to the Norwegians mining said waters; if the Germans admit having used them, the Norwegian Government has a better case for mining than ever.

I have been unable to telegraph the London Embassy this and previous telegrams on this subject by reason of the absence of an unquestionably secret code between this Legation and the Embassy.   Schoenfeld.

T telegram (SDR, RG 59, 763.72111 N83/61, DNA).
[1] That is, Nils Claus Ihlen.

To Newton Diehl Baker

My dear Mr. Secretary: [The White House] 23 August, 1918.

I agree with your judgment with regard to Mr. Gompers' suggestion concerning the investigation of labor conditions in Porto Rico.[1]

I assume that you have been giving some thought (though I dare say you have as little time to do so as I have) to the personnel of such a commission as you have in mind for Porto Rico. If you have, I would be very glad indeed to know the names that have occurred to you, in order that we may combine our judgments in the matter.
                    Cordially and sincerely yours,   Woodrow Wilson

TLS (Letterpress Books, WP, DLC).
[1] See NDB to WW, Aug. 20, 1918.

From Newton Diehl Baker, with Enclosure

Dear Mr. President: Washington. August 23, 1918.

I enclose for your information and file a copy of letter No. 16 from General Bliss. I ask your particular attention to the suggestion contained in the last part of the letter as to the method of raising the question of our military effort. Do you think it would be wise to have such a telegram as General Bliss suggests sent in your name to the three Governments for their action, before I start to Europe?[1] As I understand it, General Bliss recommends that you send such a telegram, calling on the three Governments to unite with you in a request to General Foch for a definite statement as to the program necessary to end the war in 1919. Upon a definite statement being given by General Foch, General Bliss feels that we would all then be able to work toward a definite program and count just the sacrifices each country would have to make to carry it out.

Respectfully yours,   Newton D. Baker

TLS (WP, DLC).
[1] This remark reveals that Baker and Wilson by this time had decided that the former should undertake a second mission to Europe. Baker sailed on a troopship on August 31 and arrived in France on September 7. As NDB to WW, August 17, 1918, suggests, his principal objective was to secure from the Allied governments a formal agreement to supply sufficient shipping to implement the eighty-division program. *New York Times*, Sept. 9, 1918, and Daniel R. Beaver, *Newton D. Baker and the American War Effort, 1917-1919* (Lincoln, Neb., 1966), p. 172.

E N C L O S U R E

Tasker Howard Bliss to Newton Diehl Baker

No. 16

My dear Mr. Secretary: Versailles. August 7, 1918.

I have received a rather curious request from General Diaz, Chief of Staff of the Italian Army, through the Italian Military Representative here, for information as to what would be the line of action taken by the United States Government on a proposition to have a lot of Russian officers serve with the different Commands of the Allied Troops who may be sent to Siberia. I do not know what particular concern this is of General Diaz, but I suppose it comes up because of pressure originating wth the innumerable Russian societies in Europe. In fact, he says that it relates to a proposition of what is called "The League for the Regeneration of Russia," to have Russian officers now scattered all about Europe serve with these Allied Commands in Siberia. The countries of the various Allies here are filled with Russian officers "out of a job." They are all anxious to get on the American pay-roll and I fancy that the Governments here, who are supporting a great number of them, would be rather glad to unload as many as possible on us. My own opinion is that it is a very delicate question, and that if we were to tie ourselves up with any of these Russian officers, whether from motives of charity toward them, or any other, we might create a great deal of trouble for ourselves and for the Commander-in-Chief of any American forces that might be in Siberia.

I have had to make a polite response to the letter asking for the information for General Diaz, and I have replied in substance that:

1). My Government has formulated no policy on this subject;

2). It would take no action in such a matter except on the advice of any Commander-in-Chief that it might have with the Allied forces in Siberia;

3). The policy of the United States is to conduct its own military operations with its own forces, officers and men;

4). I would transmit the substance of General Diaz' request for such action, if any, as might be desired to be taken in Washington.

This is the only form in which I propose to communicate it, and if you could intimate to me whether my above reply is correct, nothing further will be needed.

August 9th.

For some reason the courier from France to Washington does not leave this week. I am informed that he will not go until Sunday. As there are a number of enclosures to go with this I shall hold my letter until that date.

Sunday afternoon I shall probably have to leave for the Head-quarters of our 33d Division at Moulliens-aux-Bois. The King of England is staying at General Rawlinson's Headquarters at Flixe-court, not far away, and he has asked General Pershing and myself to be there on Monday morning next to receive the decorations which he has conferred.

General Pershing was here on Monday and I had an interview with him about various questions which may possibly be taken up at the next meeting of the Supreme War Council. The date of this meeting has not yet been determined but there is reason to think that it will be somewhere about the middle of the month. Mr. Lloyd-George has asked to have it in London but I think that this is not likely. At the present juncture it would be, I should think, impossible for Marshal Foch and the other Commanders-in-Chief to go so far away. I feel quite sure that one question will come up that will concern Marshal Foch and he would have to be present. That question is the one of extending his powers over the forces on the

Italian Front so that they shall be the same as those which he exercises over the Allies in France. Therefore, I think it most likely that the Council will meet at some other point in France, probably Versailles.

In my interview with General Pershing I was very glad to hear him say with great cordiality that he was thoroughly pleased with the way in which I had supported him in every question which came up which concerned his command. As I think I told you once before, there has never been any ultimate difference of opinion between him and myself.

I have also had two most interesting interviews with Mr. Hoover. When he arrived in Paris he asked me to come and see him at the Hotel Crillon, where he occupied the same apartment that you had while there. In the course of our conversation he asked me my opinion as to the practicability of establishing some agency which would have supreme control over all of the various Allied and Inter-Allied agencies now existing, such as those which control the food-supply question, the allocation of tonnage for different lines of trade, tonnage for military uses, etc. He believes that if this could be done, demands for food and other things could be greatly reduced, thus releasing much tonnage for carrying out the military program. After giving careful consideration to this, in a subsequent interview, the night before he left for London, I told him that I did not believe such a coordinating agency could work successfully; that individual nations refused to surrender certain interests to Inter-Allied control; that existing Inter-Allied Agencies could be controlled only by an-other Allied Agency or by a Dictator; that I believed the former useless and the latter impossible.

I believe that there is only one solution to Mr. Hoover's problem and that it is in the power of the United States Government alone to give it. The Allies must agree upon one question as absolutely paramount and agree to subordinate all other questions to it to the utmost possible limit. Therefore I suggest the following for your consideration, as a purely military proposition.

I believe that the United States should aim at a successful termination of the war in 1919, and should make that the paramount question and in all of its dealings with its Allies should keep that question to the front. You may think that this is purely an academic question; that our Allies will say that they are as much interested in ending the war in 1919 as we can be. That of course, is what they would say; but in practice they may not be ready to do the things and to make the sacrifices which will be necessary to end the war in that time. They all agree that it can be ended only by American troops, supplies, and money. But I can see it in every discussion at which I am present, and in nearly every paper that is submitted to me, that when the end comes they want certain favorable military situations to have been created in different parts of the world that will warrant demands to be made of the United States which they think will be, perhaps, the principal arbiter of peace terms. If these sufficiently favorable military situations are not created on certain secondary theatres by the beginning of the Autumn of next year our Allies may be willing to continue through 1920, *at the cost of United States troops and money*, a war which may possibly if not probably be ended with complete success, as far as we are concerned, by operations on the Western Front in 1919.

If the mass of the people in Europe knew that the United States was demanding that the Allies should make every effort to end the war in 1919, our Government would be supported by the common people of every nation, and I believe that they would endure any possible sacrifice to carry it through. Now they do not see even a suggested time for the end. The time has come to plan a campaign with reasonable hope that it will be the last one and not merely one that will lead to another. What warrant will our Government have in proposing that its Allies should agree to such a policy?

If the proposed 80-Division Program can be carried through, the United States will have in France before the middle of next year more than the rifle strength of all our Allies on the Western Front combined. If the Allied Commander-in-Chief can now inform the United States that a certain definite military effort on their part will give him reasonable belief that the next campaign will be final, the United States will be in a position to demand of all the Allies the necessary sacrifices without which the tonnage cannot be made available. He has asked of the United States the 100-division Program. When informed that the United States can only contemplate an 80-division Program and that it may be unable even to carry that through, he has apparently accepted that decision without question. Either of these programs, if carried through, would give him a certain numerical superiority in rifles next summer, but no one knows whether either of these programs is asked for on a definite plan for what he expects to be the final campaign or whether it is only to lead to another one for which a like demand will be made.

As you know, the Supreme War Council at its last session directed the Military Representatives, in conference with Marshal Foch and the Allied Commanders-in-Chief in the other theatres to study and report to the Supreme War Council their views as to the military attitude to be taken in the Autumn of this year (after the conclusion of the present active campaign), the following winter, and next year. This at once brings us to the question "Can we expect to be in such a relative position next year as will warrant a serious offensive campaign? And if we believe that we may be in a position to warrant such a campaign, what will be its object? Will its object be merely to push the Germans back a few miles further towards the Rhine, or can we, beginning now, make such preparations as will give us good ground for believing that we can absolutely crush German resistance on this front, end the war here next year, and, therefore, necessarily, end it on all other fronts?" On the answer to these questions I think very possibly depends the fate of the present Allied Governments in Europe a little later than this date next year, with all the consequences that such a change of Government may have on the final issue of the war.

The Military Representatives are to have a conference with Marshal Foch some time next week. Each of us have submitted to him in writing our views, in anticipation of that interview. We are all of us agreed on what I believe to be the essential points, except that, naturally enough, the Representatives of our Allies cast more side glances at the situation in the Balkans, in Palestine, Mesopotamia, and elsewhere than I do. We are agreed that the war will almost certainly have to be ended on the Western Front. I want, and I think that the United States wants, that the war should be ended there as quickly as possible. My colleagues, evidently representing confidential views that they receive from their own Governments, want to have certain things done in the Balkans, Palestine, Mesopotamia and elsewhere, before the war ends, which in my opinion cannot be done without diminishing the chances of ending the war on the Western Front in 1919. What Marshal Foch's views will prove to be, when we meet him, I do not now know; but after our conference I am sure that our views and his will be in harmony.

There are certain things that we are all in substantial agreement about.

First: From 1916 to the beginning of the Campaign of 1918, the rifle strength of the two sides has varied from approximately 250,000 in favor of the Allies through the Campaign of 1917, to approximately 250,000 superiority in rifle strength in favor of the Germans at the beginning of the campaign of this year. I am speaking, of course, of the relative strengths on this Western Front. With this rifle superiority the Allies up to the end of the Campaign of 1917 "blew bubbles" in the German line but without breaking it; with the same superiority in 1918 the Germans "blew bubbles" in the Allied line but without breaking it. But it is generally admitted that the German bubbles were more dangerous to the Allies than the Allied bubbles were to the Germans. This is due to the fact that the Germans have had a comparatively small distance to go from the average positions they have held, in order to reach vital Allied points; while the Allies, to reach corresponding German vital points, must go several times that distance. In other words, it is probable that if in March the Germans had had double their then superiority in rifles (500,000 instead of 250,000) they would have reached vital points and have possibly brought on a decision of the war. Therefore, (assuming the German morale and war supplies hold out for another year), in order that the Allies may push through to vital points, that is to say to points which will cause the whole German line to crumble, the Allies must have at least double the superiority that the Germans would probably have had to have in order to have enabled them to reach vital Allied points this spring and summer. In other words, the Allies must have a superiority of not less than 1,000,000 rifles on the line on the Western Front, which means a more or less approximate superiority in machine guns, artillery, airplanes, tanks, etc.

Second: The French rifle strength will probably diminish to 656,000 by July 1 next. The British rifle strength will diminish to 420,000, and the Belgian rifle strength to 42,000. If our 80-division Program can be carried out, American rifle strength, fit for service on the line on July 1 next, will be 1,184,000. That figure excludes 10 divisions which will not have been here two months and which divisions will include 169,000 rifles. Thus, the total Allied strength in France, fit for service on the line on July 1 next, will be approximately 2,302,000. The total German rifle strength will be approximately 1,378,000. This will give an approximate Allied rifle superiority on July 1 next, of 924,000. But, the Germans have still 32 divisions in Russia. If a situation should be created on the Western Front next summer such that the Germans would feel obliged to transfer these 32 divisions, the Allied rifle superiority would be reduced to 647,000.

In the foregoing I have given no consideration to the British estimate that the Germans will secure by March 1 next, approximately 400,000 recruits from the border Russian states. Nor have I assumed the possibility of a situation developing in Italy which would warrant the withdrawal of Austrian troops from that front to assist the Germans on the Western front.

If the 100-division Program could be carried out, the Allied rifle superiority on July 1 next would, assuming Germany withdraws no divisions from Russia, be approximately 1,127,000 and, if Germany withdraws all of her divisions from Russia, it would be 850,000.

As I have said, we do not know whether Marshal Foch believes that he can crush German resistance on this front with either the 100-division Program or the 80-division Program could either of them be carried out. But every day the conditions appear more and more favorable provided we can secure the proper superiority next year, for launching the final and decisive offensive for the purpose of ending the war by the winter of 1919. If Marshal Foch will say to the President that, as Inter-Allied Commander-in-Chief, he has good grounds for believing that he can push the Campaign of 1919 to a decisive conclusion on the 100-division Program or the 80-division Program or with any other definite and fixed military effort which the United States must make, I think that the United States Government has the solution of Mr. Hoover's problem in its own hands. It can then say to its Allies "Our common Commander-in-Chief believes that with certain assistance from the United States by a fixed date in 1919 he can end the war in that year. Do you want it to end in 1919?" There would be but one answer from all Europe to that question. The United States could then say "We must all sacrifice everything to the limit of endurance in order that we can make the necessary effort." I believe that only by some such procedure can we get the necessary tonnage to carry out any program that would do more than keep the war going through 1919 with the certainty of a campaign in 1920. Our losses are beginning now. Next year, instead of hearing of the losses of many hundreds of thousands of our Allies on the Western Front, it will be hundreds of thousands of Americans and a constantly reducing proportion of our Allies. They have lost frightfully in the past, but that does not require the war to be prolonged until our losses equal theirs. It is safe to say that already our American troops have saved the situation here. No Englishman or Frenchman with whom I talk but admits that were not the Americans already here in considerable force the war would be now over, and settled adversely to the Allies. We have already saved France and Europe. We have a right to demand that the hundreds of thousands of young Americans, the present hope of their country and the future hope of the world, who are now ready to give their lives for the common cause, shall not be sacrificed unless it be an absolute necessity. Is it not worth while to save the blood and treasure that must be spent in 1920 if we can, by any possibility, end the war in 1919?

No one, in my opinion, but the United States can bring this question to a head. The Military Representatives cannot do it. But at the next meeting of the Supreme War Council (and there is no time to be lost) the United States Government can ask its three colleagues to join with it in directing their common Commander-in-Chief on the Western Front to state the exact reinforcements which he must have from the United States by a fixed date in 1919 in order to give him reasonable hope that he can end the war on this front in that year. Then, instead of working on the problem of how to secure the tonnage to bring over 100 divisions or 80 divisions, we will work on the problem of how to secure tonnage *to bring over the men necessary to end the war next year*. With a definite object like that before them, I believe that the people of the Allied nations will make, for the few months necessary, the supreme effort and endure to the last degree the extreme hardship necessary to provide that tonnage. They will not do it so long as they feel we are simply asking for *as many men as we can get*. That latter is the principle which inspires other interests; the Manchester cotton manufacturer asks for as many thousand bales of cotton as he can get and takes whatever he can get, whether it is as much as he asked for or not. And so for the Food Controllers and all other interests that want shipping. They say that when the military men ask for 100 divisions or 80 divisions or 50 divisions they are doing it without a definite plan; that they simply want to get as many as they can so that they will be able to carry one campaign through and be ready for the following one, and for the one thereafter. But if they knew (what we do not yet know) that what the military men ask for is what is believed necessary to accomplish a definite object, namely to end the war in 1919, I believe that the other interests will be ready, for the first time, with some cheerfulness to yield their demands in favor of the military program.

And so, in a nut-shell, it is this: Do we want to end the war in 1919 or not? If we do, the first step is to get a declaration from the responsible military men as to what effort the United States must make in order to so end the war, and then demand of the Allied world that every other secondary interest,—trade, food, clothing, etc.,—be sacrificed to the last limit in order that this effort can be made.

I do not see that any harm can come from our learning from the responsible military men what they *hope* to accomplish next year with our troops and supplies. It is possible, of course, that Marshal Foch, in reply to a question as to what force he must have in order to reasonably hope to have a final campaign in 1919, would make a demand for an effort by the United States which it could not possibly comply with, but I doubt if he will do so. At any rate, there is everything to be gained by knowing what our probable status will be, as to the termination of the war, by the maximum effort which we *can* make, and, as I have said a dozen times, I think the only way to determine what is the maximum effort that can be made is in a statement from the responsible military men that they have good reason to believe that that effort will be a final one. If we had the superiority of 1,000,000 rifles now, it is possible that we might beat the Germans this year. If we do not do it, if they dig in on the former Hindenburg line and can hold it, their position next year will make that superiority necessary and, personally, I believe that it will be enough, provided it can be maintained for a few months.

It is possible that I could bring this result about by submitting a Joint Note which, if adopted by all of the Military Representatives, would be telegraphed to each of the Governments for approval. But I think it quite certain that one of the Military Representatives here will not agree and therefore the whole thing would fall through. Moreover, I should not attempt to introduce the draft of such a Joint Note unless I knew in advance that my Government fully approved it. And, of course, you may not approve it.

The only other way to accomplish it is for one of the four Governments which constitute the Supreme War Council to state that it requests that at the next meeting of the Supreme War Council action should be taken on a line indicated by it. I doubt if any of the three Prime Ministers here will take it up except at the request of the United States.

If the general idea that I have outlined should be approved in Washington, the whole matter would come to a head if the Government of the United States should send a telegram to its three colleagues, expressing its hope that a supreme joint effort may be made in 1919 that will avoid the enormous expense in blood and money that will follow a continuation of the war beyond that year; that it therefore hopes that the other members of the Supreme War Council will join with it in instructing the Inter-Allied Commander-in-Chief to promptly inform the Allied Governments of the force which he must have at an approximate date next year in order to bring the campaign on the Western Front to a final conclusion in that year; all of which is necessary in order that the Allies may determine whether that joint effort may be made, at the cost of no matter what sacrifices provided those sacrifices are endurable.

In that way alone can we know what our maximum effort is probably to be, and exactly what are the sacrifices that must be made in order to accomplish it. And it seems to me reasonable to hope that, with the knowledge that these sacrifices are directed to no vague end *but to the termination of the war in 1919*, all interests that are now reluctant to make further sacrifices will cheerfully agree to do so for the few months that will be necessary.

Cordially yours,   Tasker H. Bliss

TCL (WP, DLC).

From John Humphrey Small

My dear Mr. President: Washington, D. C. August 23, 1918.

Referring to the water power bill pending in the House. The enclosed clipping is from the New York Sun.[1] Upon the general subject of development of water power I have for several years been giving some study to the matter and have lamented the existing conditions which seemed to prevent agreement upon a bill which would protect the public, and at the same time encourage capital and individual enterprise to develop our water power resources. I had reached the conclusion that the last bill presented by Secretaries Lane, Houston and Baker would accomplish this result. Regarding the recapture provision of the bill, I am of the opinion that the Net Investment clause is superior in many respects to any provision heretofore considered. On the other hand I was of the opinion that the recapture provision advocated by Mr. Ferris of Oklahoma, would not encourage water power development, but would result in a continuation of the past condition of inertia. The mere fact that the Net Investment provision had received the approval of the three Secretaries indicated that it would receive the approval of the House, as it has already received the approval of a large majority of the special Water Power Committee. I think Secretaries Lane and Houston are especially well qualified to reach a wise conclusion regarding this provision of the bill.

I hope you will not oppose the Net Investment clause as last recommended by the three Secretaries.

Very respectfully,   Jno. H. Small

TLS (WP, DLC).

[1] "Washington, Aug. 14.—President Wilson to-day let it be known through Representative Ferris, Oklahoma, that he is opposed to the clause in the present water power bill that would force the public to pay an exorbitant price to regain control of water power sites leased to private corporations by the Government. 'The President feels as I do, that the public should be forced to pay only actual value and not the original investment,' Mr. Ferris said." "To End Water Power Graft," New York *Evening Sun*, Aug. 14, 1918.

Sir William Wiseman to Lord Reading

[New York] August 23, 1918.

CXP 708. URGENT: My reply to your No. 738 of 20th. was really dictated by COL. HOUSE. This is the first opportunity I have of adding my own observations.

There is a feeling in the State Department that the Allies and United States are at cross-purposes regarding the objects of the expedition to Siberia.

U.S.G. have consented to lend their aid solely for the purpose of helping the CZECHO-SLOVAKS escape from their dangerous situation and leave the country in safety.

U.S.G. are beginning to think that the Allies want to use the expedition for a different purpose, namely to assist the CZECHS to maintain and increase their position in Russia. There is a feeling that the CZECHS are not making any attempt to retire.

I have pointed out that they are probably surrounded and cannot retire until a strong enough relief force reaches them. The military position, however, does not seem clear to U.S.G. Nor is our task made easier by MAZARYK, who seems quite satisfied, or so I understand, though I have not seen him myself.

I have always thought that time and circumstances would modify the PRESIDENT's original policy regarding RUSSIA, and I see indications even now that this is so. The danger now is—to be quite frank—that he is beginning to feel that the Allies are trying to rush, even trick, him into a policy which he has refused to accept. He is well aware that he is committed to the task of rescuing the CZECHS, but thinks the Allies are already trying to change the character of the expedition into a full-fledged military intervention with the object of reconstituting the Eastern Front.

If I may offer a suggeston it is that the JAPANESE Commander[1] should report that he cannot be responsible for the safety of the CZECHO-SLOVAK forces unless further troops are despatched at once, and that message should be conveyed to the PRESIDENT together with the statement that the Japanese are only awaiting his agreement to rush more troops to the rescue.

You will realize that I personally am not fully acquainted with the position, being away from Washington and only seeing some of the cables.

If I am to do anything further in this matter, I should much appreciate a cable from you giving me confidentially the latest news and your own views for my guidance.

CC telegram (W. Wiseman Papers, CtY).
[1] Gen. Kikuzo Otani.

To Walter Hines Page

[The White House, c. Aug. 24, 1918]

I have received your communication of August 1st. It caused me great regret that the condition of your health makes it necessary for you to resign. Under the circumstances I do not feel I have the right to insist on such a sacrifice as your remaining in London. Your resignation is therefore accepted. As you request it will take effect when you report to Washington. Accept my congratulations that you have no reason to fear a permanent impairment of your health and that you can resign knowing that you have performed your difficult duties with distinguished success.

Woodrow Wilson.[1]

Printed in Burton J. Hendrick, *The Life and Letters of Walter H. Page* (3 vols., Garden City, N. Y., 1924-26), II, 396.
[1] The Editors have not found the original of this telegram in WP, DLC, or in the W. H. Page Papers, MH.

Two Letters to Robert Lansing

My dear Mr. Secretary,   The White House. 24 August, 1918.

The substance of this communication[1] I approve, but I hope that you will yourself go over it and reconsider the forms of expression. It is practically a literal transcript of Admiral Benson's memorandum, many of the sentences of which seem to me unsuitable for textual communication to the Government of Norway,—for example, the sentence beginning "It may be well to inform the Norwegian Government," which sounds like instructions to the Minister, not like the text of a formal memorandum to be handed the Foreign Minister. Will you not go over it with a fine-tooth comb and get the Admiral's language, which was for us, out of it?[2]

I take it for granted that there is no secret, or reason for reticence about the existence of the barrage.

Faithfully Yours,   W.W.

WWTLI (SDR, RG 59, 763.72111 N83/59, DNA).
[1] It is missing in the files of the Department of State.
[2] The message sent is RL to H. F. A. Schoenfeld, Aug. 27, 1918, T telegram (SDR, RG 59, 763.72111 N83/59, DNA); printed in *FR-WWS 1918*, 1, II, 1782-84.

My dear Mr. Secretary: The White House 24 August, 1918.

I am warmly obliged to you for having let me see this interesting and helpful letter from Mr. George Kennan. I have taken the liberty of having a copy made for my own files.

I take it for granted that Mr. Kennan is himself too old to take charge of the civilian work we are planning in Siberia.

Cordially and faithfully yours,   Woodrow Wilson

TLS (RSB Coll., DLC).

To Hamilton Holt

My dear Mr. Holt: [The White House] 24 August, 1918.

I had already noticed and read with very deep and genuine appreciation the editorial in The Independent, "No Divided Counsels at Washington." I thank you for it with all my heart. It rings true to the highest sort of public spirit.

Cordially and sincerely yours,   Woodrow Wilson

TLS (Letterpress Books, WP, DLC).

Two Letters to Newton Diehl Baker

My dear Baker: The White House 24 August, 1918.

I have your letter of the 24th [22d][1] about the "Work or Fight" amendment to the Man Power Bill. I quite appreciate the fact that you urge, namely that the power exists and might almost be said to be automatically exercised without any express authorization, but it is a serious matter to put anything in the bill which will prejudice it in the view of any influential part of the public, and I am going to take the liberty, as I have opportunity, to oppose its incorporation.

Cordially and faithfully yours,   Woodrow Wilson

TLS (N. D. Baker Papers, DLC).
[1] Second letter of that date.

My dear Mr. Secretary: The White House 24 August, 1918.

I have read with great care your letter of August 22nd about the Houston Riot cases of August of last year and find myself agreeing in the judgments you express in that letter. I would be very much obliged to you if you would be generous enough to prepare for my signature such memoranda and orders as would carry your conclusions into effect and at the same time explain the action as frankly as it should be explained to the public.

Cordially and faithfully yours,   Woodrow Wilson

TLS (N. D. Baker Papers, DLC).

From Robert Lansing

My dear Mr. President: Washington August 24, 1918.

I thank you for your letter of August 22 and for the memorandum, which you enclosed, of Mr. Reinsch's recent conversation with you in regard to Chinese finance.

I have carefully read the memorandum and am glad to find Mr. Reinsch's views in complete accord with those of the Department as set forth in the plans already formed and in process of execution for the organization of an international consortium to make loans to China.

I note that it is your desire to discuss the memorandum with me at an early date.   Sincerely yours,   Robert Lansing

TLS (WP, DLC).

From Edward Mandell House

Dear Governor: Magnolia, Massachusetts. August 24, 1918.

Now that the expected has happened and Page has actually resigned[1] I would like to make another suggestion other than Frank Cobb—that is, Solicitor General Davis.

I do not know Davis very well but those that do think very highly of him. He is one of the best friends that Lansing has—perhaps the best—which would insure very cordial working relations with the State Department. He has an income, I am told, of $12,000. or $15,000. This would be nearly sufficient during the war, and Cleve Dodge would doubtless be glad to supplement it as he did in the case of Page.

If Davis is what his friends claim, he is more of the ambassadorial type than Cobb. I do not know either Mrs. Davis or Mrs. Cobb.[2] You probably know them both. Mrs. Cobb has done some translating for the Inquiry in both French and German, therefore, I take it, she is a woman of cultivation.

Affectionately yours,   E. M. House

TLS (WP, DLC).
[1] House had learned of Page's resignation through a telephone call from Gordon Auchincloss. House Diary, Aug. 24, 1918.
[2] Ellen Graham Bassell Davis and Margaret Hubbard Ayer Cobb.

Two Letters from Newton Diehl Baker

Dear Mr. President: Washington. August 24, 1918.

I have communicated with Mr. Stettinius and find him thoroughly sympathetic with the plan for the reorganization of the air service by using the place of the Second Assistant for that purpose. I want to be sure, however, before moving in the matter, that the plan has your approval in its details. The plan is as follows:

1. Mr. Stettinius' resignation will be accepted and he will be regarded as the special agent of the War Department in France with full power, by delegation from the Secretary of War, to do the things he is now doing, which, by the way, he is doing very discreetly and effectively, limiting himself entirely to War Department interests and bringing about very helpful understandings with our Allied Munitions Departments in the matter of joint programs.

2. Send Mr. Ryan's name to you for transmission to the Senate as Second Assistant Secretary of War.

3. Issue a War Department order establishing the Air Service under the direction of the Second Assistant, thus requiring the Bureau of Aeronautics and the Bureau of Aircraft Production both to come under the head of Mr. Ryan, acting for the Secretary of War in their coordination and control.

4. Appoint Mr. Potter[1] chief of the Bureau of Aircraft Production, the place which Mr. Ryan now holds but which in a general way Mr. Potter has filled for some time, his appointment being recommended by Mr. Ryan.

If this program meets with your approval I would like to get it done as quickly as possible, so as to get the situation settled and Mr. Ryan's hand laid to his new job before he goes abroad with me.   Respectfully yours,   Newton D. Baker

[1] That is, William Chapman Potter.

Personal

My dear Mr. President: Washington. August 24, 1918.

General Crowder is getting ready for the registration under the new draft Act, which will have to be preceded by a proclamation from you. I enclose a copy of your proclamation under the original Act, and a suggested draft of the inducement for the new proclamation.[1] The formal parts can, of course, be added as the statute may require.

As the proclamation now stands I feel sure you will want to chasten and modify its language. Confidentially, I do not mind

saying that I am weary of the slaughter from cutting out rhetoric from the draft which he submitted to me before I reduced it to the form in which I submit it to you.

Respectfully yours,   Newton D. Baker

TLS (WP, DLC).
[1] This enclosure is missing.

From Edward Mandell House

Dear Governor: Magnolia, Massachusetts. August 25, 1918.

Have you thought of Vance McCormick as a possibility for London? He made a fine impression over there last Autumn. He is progressive, has sufficient money, and has a good knowledge of war conditions which would be useful. His mother and sister[1] could do the household honors for him.

I had thought of Bainbridge Colby as a suggestion but I am told the Washington crowd who have been working with him do not think much of his ability outside of writing and speaking.

Then, there is Ellery Sedgwick. He is progressive, has sufficient means and a wife[2] who would know how to maintain the position. Sedgwick has stood up for you in this country[3] in a way that excites my admiration. He is not from New York which is an advantage.

Affectionately yours,   E. M. House

TLS (WP, DLC).
[1] Annie Criswell (Mrs. Henry) McCormick and Anne McCormick.
[2] Mabel Cabot Sedgwick.
[3] That is, as editor of the *Atlantic Monthly*.

To Newton Diehl Baker

CONFIDENTIAL

My dear Mr. Secretary: The White House 26 August, 1918.

I have your letter of August 24th asking my formal approval of your plan about the reorganization of the Department for the purpose of putting the Air-Craft administration under a unified control, and I write to say that I do approve each and all of the steps which you set forth in that letter.

May I not suggest that at the time this is done, it should be explained to the representatives of the press that the change is made with the entire approval (I believe at the suggestion?) of Mr. Stettinius himself? This seems to me prudent because, as you know, Mr. Stettinius enjoys so high a reputation in many quarters that I should not like the impression to go forth, even for a day or two, that he had in any way been set aside.

Cordially and faithfully yours,   Woodrow Wilson

TLS (N. D. Baker Papers, DLC).

To Thetus Willrette Sims

My dear Mr. Sims: [The White House] 26 August, 1918.

Pardon me for not having replied sooner to your important letter of August 22nd.

I am free to reply to it that I did not see the draft of amendments to the Water Power Bill which were introduced by Mr. Merrill and his associates after the bill was first put in the hands of your special committee. I do not approve of them, and it is my earnest hope that the Congress will see fit to pass the bill as it was originally drafted and provisionally agreed upon in our informal conference.

Cordially and sincerely yours,   Woodrow Wilson

TLS (Letterpress Books, WP, DLC).

To Jessie Eldridge Southwick[1]

My dear Mrs. Southwick: [The White House] 26 August, 1918.

It was certainly very kind of you to write me your letter of August 22nd, which came to me under cover to Mrs. Wilson, and I am grateful that you should be so much concerned about slanders which are being circulated to my disadvantage.[2]

But I feel confident that you can dismiss the slanders which you were kind enough to tell me about without the least concern as to the harm they may do, because they are so entirely false in every particular that they can do, I believe, no harm. I have found that lies take care of themselves. They are so inconsistent with each other, of necessity, and are so colored with all sorts of impossible allegations that they break down of their own absurdity. These particular lies are almost grotesque in their falseness.

I am quite aware that efforts of this sort are constantly being made to discredit me, with what motive I find it difficult to conjecture, but I have steeled my heart to endure them because, although it is very distressing to be so maligned, my own conscience so entirely acquits me that I cannot bring myself to take the malignancy too seriously.

With genuine appreciation of your kindness and solicitude,

Sincerely yours,   Woodrow Wilson

TLS (Letterpress Books, WP, DLC).
¹ Mrs. Henry Lawrence Southwick of Brookline, Mass. Her husband was President of the Emerson College of Oratory in Boston.
² Jessie E. Southwick to WW, Aug. 22, 1918, ALS (WP, DLC). She related some of the "dangerous slander" circulated about Wilson, especially on "Wall Street." For example, Wilson had bargained with Wall Street to bring on the war and, as a result, had come to be worth sixty million dollars. Another tale had Mrs. Wilson having been at one time "completely under the influence" of Count von Bernstorff. A third story had Wilson appointing a man to the Supreme Court as a form of payment of blackmail. Mrs. Southwick said that she wrote as a strong partisan of Wilson who hoped to assist in the scotching of such rumors.

Two Letters from Herbert Clark Hoover

Dear Mr. President: Washington 26 August 1918

Guaranteed Price for the 1919 Wheat Harvest

You are already aware of the recommendation of our Agriculture Advisory Board to the effect that while they consider the price fixed by you of $2.26 per bushel at Chicago for No. 1 Northern Wheat for the 1918 harvest is a fair price, they now recommend that the increasing costs of production of next year's crop warrant an increase in price by twenty cents a bushel and that a guarantee should be given now upon this basis.

We all desire to secure a stimulative return to the farmer and at the same time to be just to the consumer and the Government. While the farmers have recommended an increase, the consumers of the country are protesting against such an increase.

In considering whether a guaranteed price should be given for the growing of wheat next year (the only industry guaranteed by the Government), we must realize that it involves considerable national risk. It is impossible to conceive that our wheat production, even without a guarantee, will not equal our own demand, and therefore the object of a guarantee must be solely to secure a surplus for feeding the Allies, and in this sense it must be realized that this surplus will not be needed in Europe until 1920. If there be peace or increased shipping available in the meantime, the Allies will supply themselves from the large stores of much cheaper wheat from the Southern Hemisphere, where between 300,000,000 and 400,000,000 bushels are even now available. Our Government might best quite well be plunged into a loss of anything up to $500,000,000 in giving such a guarantee or [of] a high level of price maintained to our own people for a long period.

A guaranteed price stabilizes the price and eliminates speculation from our prime food. As you are aware, there has been a great deal of fluctuation in the prices of secondary small grains, ranging from levels above the comparative price of wheat to levels at present lower than the comparative prices, due largely to irregularity in inland and ocean transport. If wheat were unstabilized also, and subjected to these same fluctuations, together with the threat of large supplies from the Southern Hemisphere, confidence of our farmers might quite well be undermined and cause them to relax their efforts in grain production, and speculating on breadstuffs would bring only harm to both producer and consumer.

In view of all the factors involved, I am of the opinion that we must take the risk of giving a guarantee. But it does seem to me that before increasing this liability above the present level, and thus imposing an additional burden upon our consumers and a greater risk upon the Government, the matter should be subjected to searching inquiry into the true costs of production and therefrom determine such a fair minimum for the farmers as will maintain the present acreage.

It appears to me that such an inquiry by a commission independent of all interests, is not insuperable, despite the complexity of local economic differences, provided this inquiry be directed to determine in a broadminded way the increased cost of labor and material consumed by the farmer over, say, the average three year pre-war period and to determine a stimulative increase in profits over that represented in the average pre-war price of wheat. It would not only be a sound guide to yourself in determining the basis of the guarantee, but also an assurance to the consumers of the country.

Many of the factors cannot be determined until the volume of the next harvest can be well approximated, and pending this time and such inquiry, I would suggest that the guarantee be given upon the present price basis, with the additional assurance from you that if the results of the above inquiry warrant, it will be increased.

If an increase should result from such inquiry, it will be necessary to evolve the Administrative machinery by which the increase would apply only to those farmers who had disposed of their 1918 wheat; otherwise we will be faced with considerable and possibly embarrassing hoarding by some minority.

I have the feeling that with the above assurances of a preliminary guarantee, and the possibility of an entirely fair readjustment of prices upward, our farmers will feel warranted in continuing their fine endeavor to meet the demand.

Yours faithfully,   Herbert Hoover

Dear Mr. President: Washington 26 August 1918

In further ampli[fi]cation of the memorandum which I sent you this morning, of the wheat guarantee, I send herewith a letter addressed to Judge Glasgow in my absence by Mr. Barnes, the head of our Cereal Division, which elaborates other arguments than those I have brought to bear on the situation.[1]

Faithfully yours, Herbert Hoover

TLS (WP, DLC).
[1] J. H. Barnes to W. A. Glasgow, Jr., Aug. 8, 1918, TLS (WP, DLC). Barnes strongly objected to the proposal to raise the guaranteed price of wheat from $2.26 to $2.46 per bushel at Chicago. If anything, he argued, the existing price of $2.26 was too high. Any rise in the price would result in a vast increase in the acreage planted in wheat and hence in a huge surplus which the government would be obliged to buy at the guaranteed price. This in turn would have disastrous effects both on the domestic and overseas markets.

From Newton Diehl Baker

My dear Mr. President: Washington. August 26, 1918.

Mr. Barclay, of the British Mission, was waiting for me after you left this afternoon, to read me a cablegram which he had just received from Lord Reading, and of which he was to send me a paraphrase in the morning. In effect, it said that Lord Reading had been asked by the Prime Minister to take up the question of the shipping necessary to enable us to carry out the 80-division program. He had been handed a copy of my cablegram to General Bliss on the subject, showing the amounts of tonnage needed by us for the various months from now until the Spring of 1919.[1] These amounts are larger than my recollection of this afternoon, but show a rapidly diminishing amount of tonnage needed from January 1. Lord Reading desired confirmation of the figures, and his cablegram was not discouraging. He asked Mr. Barclay to find out whether there was any chance of my being there shortly, as he thought he would be able to work it out more quickly and certainly if I could be there.

From this, it looks as though an effort was going to be made to straighten out the matter, and I will ask Mr. Barclay in the morning to confirm the figures to Lord Reading and to tell him that he can expect to see me very shortly.

Respectfully yours, Newton D. Baker

TLS (WP, DLC).
[1] P. C. March to NDB, July 23, 1918.

From Scott Ferris

My dear Mr. President: Washington, D. C. August 26, 1918.

I am in receipt of your good note of August 21st, transmitting to me a letter from Mr. George P. Hampton, Manager and Director of Legislation of Farmers' National Headquarters. I am returning his letter herewith. I am at a loss to know just where Mr. Hampton got the impression that I had quoted you on what you would do with reference to vetoing the water power bill even tho it passed with the present Recapture Clause.

I do not recall your having said anything of the kind to me, and am sure I didn't say anything like that to Mr. Hampton. The truth of the matter is I have not talked with Mr. Hampton at all. I have had some conversation with Mr. Marsh,[1] Director of Publicity, and in talking with him may have said to him that if we passed the Water Power Bill through the House more favorable to the Water Power interests than the Shields Bill, then what would emerge from conference would be more favorable than the Shields Bill and I was afraid the President would be driven to veto it. I do not recall even making it as strong as that, but I know that was in my mind and I may have said that much.

I have no recollection of your telling me that you would veto the Bill and of course made no such statement to Mr. Marsh.

Now, coming to your statement regarding the advisability of Mr. Hampton's plan of developing the Water Power of the country [by the] Federal Government I sometimes get so disgusted with the bickerings and selfishness of the water power interests who try to get everything for themselves and leave nothing for the Government and public, that I am almost driven to that conclusion myself. I confess during these war times, however, when the Government is carrying such a load and burden with all sorts of obligations, it does not seem proper to me that the Government should take on this added responsibility. I repeat, however, if we did not have the burden of war on us and all the tremendous expenses it entails, I am so heartsick with the selfishness of the water power interests who are determined to gobble up everything and get the water power away from the Government without giving anything for it, that I am almost driven to the same conclusion that both yourself and Mr. Hampton express.

I have delayed answering your letter, trying to see Mr. Hampton and Mr. Marsh, and ascertaining where they got the impression that I had been quoting you regarding any contemplated veto on your part. I shall try to see them yet. I think Mr. Marsh is a good man and it is possible that he either misunderstood me or got the conversation he had with me confused with one he had with some one else. Anyway, I shall be glad to correct his impression about the matter as soon as I see him, for I know your generous and helpful attitude on water power legislation all the way through does not entitle you to be mis-quoted or in fact, to be quoted at all.

Thanking you for your good letter—also the Hampton letter, and expressing appreciation for the thousand other considerations you have given this tedious subject, I am

Gratefully yours,   Scott Ferris

TLS (WP, DLC).
¹ Benjamin Clarke Marsh, Secretary and Director of Publicity for the Farmers' National Headquarters.

To Herbert Clark Hoover

My dear Hoover: The White House 27 August, 1918.

Our conversation of yesterday and your memoranda of the 26th have been entirely convincing to me in the matter of a guaranteed price for wheat, and I would be very much obliged if you would have a public statement prepared, continuing the present guarantee and stating, as you suggested yesterday, the circumstances under which it may be reconsidered. I shall be very glad to make any suggestions concerning it, if you will be kind enough to let me see it when it is prepared.

In haste,   Faithfully yours,   Woodrow Wilson

TLS (Hoover Archives, CSt-H).

To John Humphrey Small

My dear Mr. Small: [The White House] 27 August, 1918.

I am sorry to find myself differing with the opinions expressed in your letter of August 23rd about the Water Power bill, and I think it important that I should correct some of the impressions which you evidently have about certain features of the bill.

I do not understand that the Net Investment provision and the Recapture provision as rewritten in fact emanated from the Secretaries of War, Interior, and Agriculture, but from certain subordinates of theirs who, of course in perfect good faith and with the best intentions, suggested these amendments with the permission of those Secretaries.

You seem to be under the impression too that unless the Net Investment feature is put in and the changed Recapture clause, private capital will not go into water power enterprises. I am sure you are mistaken about that. With the constantly increasing cost of fuel, water power is becoming more and more valuable, not to say invaluable, and I have not the least fear as to the future of water power development. And if private capital does not undertake it, undoubtedly the governments of the State and Nation will undertake it.

I am personally strongly opposed to the Net Investment provision and to the altered Recapture clause and am sorry that the impression should have got about that the Secretaries to whom you refer, and whose judgment I respect as much as you do, are the real authors of those clauses.

Cordially and sincerely yours, Woodrow Wilson

TLS (Letterpress Books, WP, DLC).

To Scott Ferris

My dear Mr. Ferris: [The White House] 27 August, 1918.

I am very sorry you were troubled in your mind about the implication in Mr. George P. Hampton's letter that you had been quoting me with regard to a veto of the Water Power Bill in certain circumstances. That did not give me the least concern because I knew that you did not do anything of the kind, and I am very much obliged to you for your interesting letter about Mr. Hampton's suggestion. I find myself concurring in your judgment.

In haste,

Cordially and sincerely yours, Woodrow Wilson

TLS (Letterpress Books, WP, DLC).

To Thomas Watt Gregory

My dear Gregory: [The White House] 27 August, 1918.

The enclosed letter is from the wife of a man whom I very greatly esteem,[1] and although she says that her husband would not approve of her writing this letter, yet I would be very much obliged if you would be kind enough to have the case to which she refers looked into, in order that we may form our own judgment as to whether the right course was pursued or not.[2]

Cordially and faithfully yours, Woodrow Wilson

TLS (Letterpress Books, WP, DLC).
[1] Katherina Tappe (Mrs. Ambrose White) Vernon to WW, Aug. 20, 1918, ALS (WP,

DLC). She stated that two alien enemy seamen, Anton Slivinski and Carl Klück, from a German ship in Boston harbor at the time of the entrance of the United States into the war, had been paroled for the period of the war under the custody of her husband. Recently, without warning and without any breach of the parole on their part, the two men had been seized and sent to internment at Hot Springs, North Carolina. She believed that this action was a violation of the terms of the parole which the men had signed and requested that Wilson look into the matter.
    [2] Gregory's reply is TWG to WW, Sept. 18, 1918.

To Newton Diehl Baker, with Enclosure

My dear Baker: The White House 27 August, 1918.

I am returning the enclosed[1] with my suggestion for the addendum. I quite agree with you that it is hard work clearing up the under brush of General Crowder's rhetoric, and I hope you will approve of the form that I have given it. I take it for granted that General Crowder is sure of the facts which I repeat in my draft.

Cordially and faithfully yours,   Woodrow Wilson

TLS (N. D. Baker Papers, DLC).
    [1] As has been noted, Baker's revision of Crowder's statement is missing.

E N C L O S U R E

Fifteen months ago the men of the country from twenty-one to thirty years of age were registered. Three months ago, and again last month, those who had just reached the age of twenty-one were added. It now remains to include all men between the ages of eighteen and forty-five.

This is not a new policy. A century and a quarter ago it was deliberately ordained by those who were then responsible for the safety and defence of the nation that the duty of military service should rest upon all able-bodied men between the ages of eighteen and forty-five. We now accept and fulfill the obligation which they established, an obligation expressed in our national statutes from that time until now. We solemnly purpose a decisive victory of arms and deliberately to devote the larger part of the military man power of the nation to the accomplishment of that purpose.

The younger men have from the first been ready to go. They have furnished voluntary enlistments out of all proportion to their numbers. Our military authorities regard them as having the highest combatant qualities. Their youthful enthusiasm, their virile eagerness, their gallant spirit of daring makes them the admiration of all who see them in action. They covet not only the distinction of serving in this great war but also the inspiring memories which hundreds of thousands of them will cherish through the years to come, of a great day and a great service for their country and for mankind.

By the men of the older group now called upon, the opportunity now opened to them will be accepted with the calm resolution of those who realize to the full the deep and solemn significance of what they do. Having made a place for themselves in their respective communities, having assumed at home the graver responsibilities of life in many spheres, looking back upon honorable records in civil and industrial life, they will realize as perhaps no others could, how entirely their own fortunes and the fortunes of all whom they love are put at stake in this war for right, and will know that the very records they have made render this new duty the commanding duty of their lives. They know how surely this is the Nation's war, how imperatively it demands the mobilization and massing of all our resources of every kind. They will regard this call as the supreme call of their day and will answer it accordingly.

Only a portion of those who register will be called upon to bear arms. Those who are not physically fit will be excused; those exempted by alien allegiance; those who should not be relieved of their present responsibilities; above all, those who cannot be spared from the civil and industrial tasks at home upon which the success of our armies depends as much as upon the fighting at the front. But all must be registered in order that the selection for military service may be made intelligently and with full information. This will be our final demonstration of loyalty, democracy and the will to win, our solemn notice to all the world that we stand absolutely together in a common resolution and purpose. It is the call to duty to which every true man in the country will respond with pride and with the consciousness that in doing so he plays his part in vindication of a great cause at whose summons every true heart offers its supreme service.[1]

T MS (N. D. Baker Papers, DLC).
    [1] There is a WWsh draft of this statement in the C. L. Swem Coll., NjP. Wilson's statement was incorporated in his Proclamation of August 31, 1918, which appointed September 12, 1918, as the day for registration of all male citizens between the ages of eighteen and forty-five. The text, which included detailed regulations, was published in the *Official Bulletin*, II (Sept. 3, 1918), 1, 2, and 6.

To Newton Diehl Baker

My dear Baker: The White House 27 August, 1918.

As the enclosed letter[1] recites, the Young Men's Christian Association is short of the men and women it absolutely needs on the other side of the water, not because they have not the men and women ready to go, but because of a duplication of authority in the matter of looking into the antecedents and loyalty and what not of the people they want to send. The Y.M.C.A. authorities themselves look into those matters very carefully and scrupulously, and then it seems the Intelligence Department of the Army, and perhaps the Navy also, look into them. This tangle of threads ought surely to be cut, and the people waiting to go ought to be allowed to go if the Y.M.C.A. authorities confidently vouch for them, and you will note that there is a particular opportunity for a lot of them to go next Monday who might not be able to go for a long time afterwards. Won't you give instructions which will cut the threads and, if necessary, put those to whom you give the instructions in touch with the Navy and with the Department of State?

Cordially and faithfully yours,   Woodrow Wilson

TLS (WDR, RG 407, Adjutant General's Office, Central Decimal File 080-YMCA, DNA).
[1] J. R. Mott to WW, Aug. 24, 1918, TCL (WDR, RG 407, Adjutant General's Office, Central Decimal File 080-YMCA, DNA).

To Joseph Patrick Tumulty

Dear Tumulty: [The White House] 27 August, 1918.

Won't you write a kind letter to Mr. Stokowski,[1] pointing out to him how impossible it is for me to decide a queston of this sort[2] and suggesting this to him: It is not a question which can be decided on its merits, but only by the feelings and present thoughts of the audiences to whom the Philadelphia Orchestra and the other orchestras of the country play. It would be unwise to attempt "a settlement" of the question, because feeling changes and will no doubt become perfectly normal again after the abnormal experiences through which we are passing. Please express my appreciation of his confidence in my judgment.   The President

TL (WP, DLC).
[1] Leopold Anthony Stokowski, conductor of the Philadelphia Orchestra since 1912.
[2] Wilson was responding to L. A. Stokowski to WW, Aug. 20, 1918, ALS (WP, DLC). Stokowski raised once again the question of whether or not music by German and Austrian composers should be played in the United States for the duration of the war. He conceded that German opera, any music by living composers of Germanic origin, and the German language should be banned during the continuance of the conflict. However, he suggested that the instrumental music of the great classical masters such as Bach, Beethoven, Mozart, and Brahms belonged to all mankind and could not, and should not, be considered to be an exclusive possession of the German-speaking nations. He pointed out also that France and England allowed the playing of such music. He asked Wilson to decide the question and promised to abide by his decision.

Two Letters from William Gibbs McAdoo

CONFIDENTIAL.

Dear Mr. President: Washington August 27, 1918.

I am greatly concerned about the state of Crosby's health. He is quite ill in London and I think a month or perhaps two months of rest is imperative. This is a decided misfortune because it is most essential for the Treasury that the work Mr. Crosby is doing in London and Paris shall be carried forward uninterruptedly and efficiently. The recall of Mr. Cravath,[1] owing to his familiarity with our problems—a familiarity gained after seven months of active work and experience—added to Mr. Crosby's illness, seriously cripples me at a time when my need is great. I think it is of the utmost importance to send Mr. Cravath back to London immediately and I shall be deeply grateful if you will review this matter. I am convinced that you have had erroneous information about Mr. Cravath and that a very great injustice will be done to him if he is recalled, to say nothing of the serious harm that will be done to the Treasury's work in Europe at this time.

Will you not give this your kind consideration and help me if it is possible to do so.

Of course, if there are conclusive reasons why you think Mr. Cravath should be recalled, I shall, as you know, cheerfully acquiesce. This matter is really exigent and I shall be glad to discuss it with you as soon as you can give me a moment.

Affectionately yours,   W G McAdoo

[1] That is, Paul Drennan Cravath, corporation lawyer of New York, at this time counsel to and a member of the United States Treasury Mission to the Inter-Allied Council on War Purchases and Finance. McAdoo enclosed with this letter P. D. Cravath to WGM, Aug. 24, 1918 (two letters of this date), TLS (WP, DLC). These letters indicate that Cravath's recall was connected with accusations that one of his law partners, Carl August de Gersdorff, had been involved in pro-German activities before the entrance of the United States into the war. Cravath did not directly mention his own difficulty but strongly defended the American-born De Gersdorff against these charges. The problem was soon straightened out, and Cravath returned to his post in Europe.

Dear "Governor":   Washington August 27, 1918

As you know, the Fourth Liberty Loan Campaign begins September 28th. My voice is in excellent shape again, but I purpose making only a few speeches, principally in the East.

If you could manage to make a trip through the West and speak for the Liberty Loan, you would render service of inestimable value in this connection. At the same time, I think you would do a great service to the country by giving the people of the West an opportunity to see you and to get in close touch with you. Their admiration and affection for you is so deep that it would gratify you to meet them, and it would, in my judgment, enormously stimulate their enthusiasm in every direction. You have not been in the West since you became President, and I think there is a feeling out there that you are inclined to forget your friends in the West. It is a good-natured feeling, and is flattering to you. There is nothing of resentment in it. Their eagerness to have you visit them, as evidenced to me in so many ways during my recent visit to the West, is really beautiful.

If you would do this, I would suggest that you accept the invitation of the American Bankers Association to address their Annual Convention at Chicago on the 26th or 27th of September. This would be a very effective way of initiating the Liberty Loan Campaign as the bankers are such an immensely important element in the success of the Loan. A suitable itinerary from Chicago westward could very easily be arranged.

There is just one personal phase of the matter which I venture to speak of—that is, the belief which is quite current throughout the country, due to irresponsible rumors, that my health has been seriously impaired and that I am not able to make another Loan Campaign. For this reason, I should be glad if you would let me make the announcement that you are going to make the Western trip, if you should decide to do so. I think I could put it in such a way as to dispel the impression about the state of my health which might otherwise be created.

Affectionately yours,   W G McAdoo

TLS (WP, DLC).

From Herbert Clark Hoover

Dear Mr. President: Washington 27 August 1918

In thinking over our discussion yesterday with regard to the coordination of economic effort in Europe among the four nations, with a view to the provision of sufficient tonnage to fill the American Army program, I feel that I perhaps neglected to emphasize one point that dominates my own conclusions on the subject. That is that I believe that whoever is sent to deal with this matter should not only have your complete confidence, and as your personal representative be able to coordinate directly with the Prime Ministers of Europe, and at the same time to head up all of the American economic representatives in Europe, but that above all things, he should be able to remain there constantly during the next twelve months. In my view the problem cannot be solved by a temporary negotiation or declaration of principles. New phases of the matter will arise daily and new adjustments will be required constantly, for such a program will tax the whole economic capacity of the four nations to the utmost limit, and we can only expect to get that maximum output from an industrial point of view, the maximum curtailment of consumption on all sides by a continuous effort and adjustment. I could recite a score of adjustments that are needed at the present moment referring to combined activities of the Food Administration, War Trade Board, Treasury, War Industries Board, Shipping Board, etc.

A typical such question lies in the provision of timber for the American Army from Spain and Switzerland. This would mean a great saving in tonnage and would need to be accomplished by a negotiation in which we undertook to supply and even transport larger amounts of other commodities to these nations than programs hitherto, but it would represent a very much less tonnage than the transportation of timber from this country to our own Army. Such a transaction involves the American Army, War Trade Board, Treasury, Food Administration, etc.

As I stated above, these problems will arise every day and every week, and it appears to me that a solution can best be accomplished by some individual who can formulate and coordinate the views of all three of the European governments, together with ourselves, and present a consolidated front of economic action as we have now on the military side.

I write this in view of the fact that I feel that Mr. Baker's large responsibilities must mean that his visit to Europe could only be temporary in any event, and that if he could be accompanied by such a representative of yours as above mentioned, it would go far to produce the situation that I feel is necessary.

Yours faithfully,   Herbert Hoover

TLS (N. D. Baker Papers, DLC).

From Stephen Samuel Wise, with Enclosure

My dear Mr. President: [Washington] Aug. 27, 1918

In discussing with you this afternoon[1] the Zionist development, I failed to give you a copy of the so-called Basle program[2] which is, and from its inception has been, the whole platform of Zionism,— namely, "The object of Zionism is to establish a publicly recognized, legally secured homeland in Palestine for the Jewish people." You will note that no reference is made in this platform to the character of the suzerainty which might obtain over such homeland, and that the Balfour Declaration, likewise silent on this subject, involves no challenge of the present suzerainty and leaves that for determination at the Peace-table.

May I remind you that the date of the Jewish New Year is Friday, Sept. 6th. It would be deeply moving to the Jewish people in this and every land to have your message in time for announcement on that day.   Faithfully yours,   Stephen S. Wise

TLS (WP, DLC).
    [1] At 4:30 p.m. at the White House. For an account of the interview, see Stephen S. Wise, *Challenging Years: The Autobiography of Stephen Wise* (New York, 1949), pp. 191-94. Wise therein says that he and Wilson discussed the draft which is printed as an Enclosure below.
    [2] This enclosure is missing. The Basel Program was adopted by a congress of Zionist leaders called together by Theodor Herzl, which met in Basel from August 29 to 31, 1897. For a full translation of this brief but very basic document of the Zionist movement, see Melvin I. Urofsky, *American Zionism from Herzl to the Holocaust* (Garden City, N. Y., 1975), p. 24.

E N C L O S U R E

I have watched with deep interest the reconstructive work which the Weitzman Commission has done in Palestine at the instance of the British Government, and I welcome this opportunity, moreover, to express the satisfaction which I have felt in the progress of the Zionist movement in the United States and in the Allied countries since the declaration by Foreign Secretary Balfour on behalf of the British Government that Great Britain favored the establishment in Palestine of a national home for the Jewish people and promised to use its best endeavors to facilitate the achievement of that object, with the understanding that nothing would be done to prejudice the civil and religious rights of non-Jewish people in Palestine or the rights and political status enjoyed by Jews in other countries.

I think that all Americans will be deeply moved by the report that even in this time of stress the Weitzman Commission has laid the foundation of the Hebrew University at Jersualem, with its promise of spiritual rebirth.[1]

T MS (WP, DLC).
    [1] For the letter as sent, see WW to S. S. Wise, Aug. 31, 1918.

Sir William Wiseman to Sir Eric Drummond

[New York] Aug. 27. 1918.

No. CXP. 716. *No. 116.* In reply to your No. 746 of August 24th.[1]: Whilst the President's strong belief that territorial changes and other problems arising out of the war should be dealt with at a general peace settlement justifies the idea that he is opposed in principle to any separate peace, it is not true that he has made any declaration such as the Times Athens correspondent attributes to him.

I have discussed relations of U. S. with Turkey and Bulgaria with both Col. House and the President. The President's views are broadly as follows:

He has no sympathy for Bulgaria, nor does he believe in the so-called "traditional friendship" with the States. He does not regard the Bulgarians as dupes of the Germans with whom he classes them. Whilst he admits that a declaration of war against Bulgaria might achieve a certain political advantage he is reluctant to declare a war which would be unaccompanied by any definite military action on the part of the U. S., considering such a situation empty and undignified. Nevertheless I think he could be persuaded to take the step, but I gather from your No. 710 of July 27th.[2] that this would be undesirable unless a declaration of war on Turkey had been previously made. His views regarding Turkey are somewhat different. He has no sympathy or liking for the Turks, but he believes that the presence of American missionaries and others has up to now prevented massacres and atrocities which would otherwise have occurred. Advisers whom he trusts (mostly connected with various educational and religious organizations in Turkey) have convinced him that a terrible outburst of savagery would follow on a declaration of war. This reason, a curious one I admit, added to the fact that he cannot see any direct military advantage to be gained and only an indirect political one, make him definitely opposed to the idea of a declaration of war on Turkey by the U. S.

[1] "Correspondent of the TIMES at ATHENS telegraphed on August 18th. that he learns from authentic source that the PRESIDENT has declared that he would be unwilling to approve discussion for separate peace with BULGARIA and TURKEY even if such suggestion should come from the Allied Governments. Can you throw any light on this report?

"Have you been able to make any progress regarding question of declaration of war on TURKEY by U.S.G. and threat to declare war on BULGARIA? If there are difficulties, could you indicate their nature, so that LORD READING may be fully informed before he returns?" E. Drummond to W. Wiseman, Aug. 24, 1918, T telegram (W. Wiseman Papers, CtY).

[2] "You will no doubt bear in mind that we attach great importance to an immediate declaration of war on TURKEY by U. S. Government. In our view it would be a mistake to make threat on BULGARIA until war on TURKEY has been actually declared." E. Drummond to W. Wiseman, July 27, 1918, T telegram (W. Wiseman Papers, CtY).

Sir William Wiseman to Lord Reading

[New York] August 27, 1918.

No. CXP. 712. For your confidential information, the PRESIDENT has taken no steps whatever with regard to an Economic Commission for SIBERIA. He has no one in mind to send as chief representative, and does not seem in any hurry to develop the idea. I send you this because I understand that British and French are proceeding with their arrangements for economic commissions.

Lord Reading to Sir William Wiseman

[London] August 27th, 1918.

No. 748. (A). It has been suggested to me (? from FRENCH source) that the PRESIDENT and STATE DEPARTMENT are at the present moment somewhat irritated with H. M. Government because, according to them, articles in the British press cabled out to Washington have conveyed the impression that we intend to push on the campaign in SIBERIA at all costs and to commit ALLIED and AMERICAN forces regardless of AMERICAN opinion. Informant states that the President thinks Press attitude is due to official instigation.

(B). Paragraph (A) is for your personal information, and I should like to have your own views as to whether any recently cabled articles have created the alleged impression, and, if so, whether U. S. Government are of opinion that articles were officially instigated. So far as I have been able to discover there is no ground for this opinion. H. M. Government are very alive to the danger of such a course, and in any event would not act in this way, however strong their views.

(C). In any case I should like you to talk to COL. HOUSE in the following sense:

I have noticed that some articles in the British Press on the subject of Allied assistance to CZECHO-SLOVAKS have displayed some slight note of impatience regarding alleged inadequacy of the force and dilatoriness in despatching it. As explained in my telegram No. 738 of the 20th: I have pressed the President's views upon H.M.G., and the latter's views are set out fully in the same telegram. So far as Press is concerned, I personally, and I am sure H.M.G. also, would very much regret if anything were written which might even have the appearance of urging further committal in SIBERIA regardless of AMERICAN opinion, or which might tend to produce in however small a degree any public difference of opinion on the matter between the two countries. I am keeping careful eye on the situation.

(D). Following for your personal information:

The same informant says the President's irritation is also due to the latter's belief that we have urged in TOKYO that JAPANESE expeditionary force should be sent further West than the President either approved or desired. We have, of course, done nothing of the sort, but I should be glad to have your own view as to whether this belief exists.

T telegrams (W. Wiseman Papers, CtY).

To William Bauchop Wilson

My dear Mr. Secretary: The White House 28 August 1918.

A conference which I had yesterday with the gentlemen who are charged with the responsible duty of trying to adjust wage questions in the shipyards[1] brought afresh to my mind the necessity of coordinating all our efforts in the matter of the allocation of labor, the determination of rates of wages, and the many other questions affecting the welfare of laborers which it has seemed right for us to take part in answering.

I write, therefore, to make this suggestion and request: that you call a conference of representatives of the War Labor Board, the Ship Labor Adjustment Board, the Cantonment Adjustment Commission, the Board of Railroad Wages and Working Conditions, and the Labor Bureau of the Fuel Administration, and urge upon them my hope and desire that they can by common counsel establish a common policy in regard to all these matters, and attemp[t] a fair and equitable control over them which will give the working men of the country and the employers alike assurance of some degree of stability and of definite principles of action.

These several agencies are, I am sure, all working with the highest purpose, and when their conclusions are inconsistent with one another it is only because they are not in conference and have no method by which they can accom[m]odate their actions to a single principle and understanding.

There are pending questions with regard to wages which are pressing and whose decision I do not in fairness to the workmen like to hold off, but I am sure that the workmen of every war industry will be glad to see a fixed policy arrived at, and therefore I count with confidence upon their willingness to await the outcome of the effort which I hope you can now make in accordance with these suggestions.

Cordially and faithfully yours,   Woodrow Wilson

TLS (LDR, RG 174, DNA).
[1] See V. E. Macy to WW, Aug. 20, 1918, n. 1.

To Herbert Clark Hoover

My dear Mr. Hoover: The White House 28 August, 1918.

I appreciate the considerations urged in your letter of yesterday, and you may be sure will have them in mind in the arrangements I shall attempt to make.

In haste,
                    Cordially and sincerely yours,   Woodrow Wilson

TLS (Hoover Archives, CSt-H).

To Newton Diehl Baker

My dear Baker: The White House 28 August, 1918.

I am sure you will read with interest and appreciation of the considerations he urges, the letter which I send you from Mr. Hoover. I hope that either this week or in your later observations you may be able to suggest somebody who can keep the adjustments going which it may be possible for you to arrange.

I am particularly interested in the suggestion about timber which Hoover makes in this letter.
                    Cordially and faithfully yours,   Woodrow Wilson

TLS (N. D. Baker Papers, DLC).

To Ruth Thomas James

My dear Mrs. James: [The White House] 28 August, 1918.

It is with deep and genuine grief that I hear of the death of your distinguished husband.[1] He had won the affection of everybody who really knew his quality, and I was proud to count myself among his closest friends. His loss is a very great one to me personally, to the great party which he served, and to the country which in common with the rest of us he loved and to which he sought to give his best.

With warmest sympathy,
                    Cordially and sincerely yours,   Woodrow Wilson

TLS (Letterpress Books, WP, DLC).
   [1] Her husband, Senator Ollie M. James, had died of an acute infection of the kidneys on August 28.

From Robert Lansing

My dear Mr. President: Washington August 28, 1918.

I enclose to you a letter which was handed to me this afternoon by the Italian Ambassador[1] and which he practically asked me to deliver to you.

I also understand that he is asking to have an interview with you upon the subject.

The only thing that I said to the Ambassador was that, while I appreciated the fact that there was in a measure a diplomatic and political argument in favor of a larger contingent of American troops in Italy, it seemed to me that the military considerations were far superior and that it was my impression the matter was one which would depend upon General Foch's views as to the wisdom of what he proposed.   Faithfully yours,   Robert Lansing

TLS (WP, DLC).
[1] V. Macchi di Cellere to RL, Aug. 28, 1918, TLS (WP, DLC). As Lansing indicates below, this ten-page letter presented an elaborate argument in favor of stationing a sizable contingent of the American army on the Italian front for the duration of the war.

From Joseph Patrick Tumulty

Dear Governor: The White House August 28, 1918

In the matter of the Georgia Senatorship which we discussed yesterday, Congressman Lee[1] of Georgia called this morning and confirmed the impression that I had that unless the support of the Atlanta Journal can be thrown to Harris there is great probability that Howard may win. The psychological importance of the Atlanta Journal's turning away from Howard in the last week of the campaign would be of immeasurable value in helping Harris. You suggested that I should write to John S. Cohen editor of the Atlanta Journal, apprising him of the situation and asking for his support. I tactfully approached Congressman Lee with reference to this suggestion and he was afraid that it would not make the impression that would be necessary.

Could you not drop a line to Mr. Cohen, telling him how sorry you were that you missed him on his last visit and saying to him that in view of the attitude of the rest of the country and particularly of the South on the defeat of Vardaman and Blease,[2] Georgia now has an opportunity to rebuke those who have not been loyal. Intimate to him that it has come to you from several sources that the Journal has given great publicity to Howard's speeches and in fact has belittled Harris's candidacy in every way. Say that the impression has gone forth that the Atlanta Journal is really antagonistic to you and to the Administration, which, of course, you do not believe. Tell him how important it is that Harris should be elected, of the fine effect it will make upon the country. And say to him that in view of the attitude of the Atlanta Constitution, which is now openly supporting Harris, you think it is the duty of the Journal, in order that all false impressions may be removed, to come out and openly advocate Harris's election.   J.P.T.

TL (WP, DLC).
    [1] That is, Gordon Lee.
    [2] In the primary election held in Mississippi on August 20, Pat Harrison was nominated for senator by a vote of 56,715. Vardaman received 44,151 votes; former Governor Edmund Favor Noel, 6,730. About Blease's defeat, see WW to T. H. Daniel, Aug. 14, 1918, n. 4.

From Perl D. Decker[1]

Dear Mr. President: Washington, D. C. August 28, 1918.

I have been thinking very much since yesterday about the interview which you were so kind as to give me. This is the first time that I ever had the pleasure of talking to you by myself. I wish that every Member of Congress could have a similar experience. To be frank, I went to your office with considerable trepidation expecting to meet an austere and stern man who I was afraid would be antagonistic and even harsh. Instead I found a man gentle and magnanimous trying to look at the thing from the other fellows standpoint, but withal forceful and so clear thinking that I was quickly convinced that you were absolutely right in not granting my request, and also somewhat ashamed of myself for not seeing it the same as you did before I came to you. In other words your kindness and consideration made me feel like I was talking to my teacher or even to my father.

I took more of your time yesterday than I intended to take going over my record. But as I told you then, I have supported every proposition which you as our Commander in Chief have recommended for the winning of this war. I have done this not half heartedly, but with zeal and whatever ability I possess. I am sure that you believed me yesterday when I told you that whatever mistakes I may have made could not be attributed to improper motives. I had nothing to gain politically. There was no desire to favor Germans or German sympathizers for there are practically none in my district.

I am in deep distress in my district. The St. Louis Republic which is owned by Mr. Francis whom you appointed Ambassador, has been opposing me, not only for nomination but also for election. It has had much to say about my record before the declaration of war but has had nothing to say about what I have done since the declaration of war. In other words it has given it out that it will support a Republican to take my place. Mr. Francis I am sure knows nothing about this, but the Republicans are saying "that since Mr. Francis owns the Republic the Republic would not oppose me unless the President wanted it done." In other words they are saying I am "persona non grata with the administration."

I am a member of the Interstate and Foreign Commerce Committee of the House. The bill providing for the compensation and the regulation of the railroads after they were taken over by the government, and the bill providing for the taking over of the telegraph and telephone lines were reported from this committee.

I supported in the committee and on the floor every feature of these bills as recommended by the administration, and was told by the men that represented the Departments that I had been "very helpful."

There is now before our committee H.R. 12776, "a bill to provide further for the national security and defense and for the more effective prosecution of the war by furnishing means for the better utilization of the existing sources of electrical and mechanical power and for the development of new sources of such power, and for other purposes."

In the cloak room the other day a bunch of congressmen were talking real politics. One congressman made a statement that met with much agreement. It was that "the President is a good sport." This was said with the utmost respect. I am going to appeal to your "spirit of good sportsmanship." I am going to ask you to write me a letter requesting me to call at your office and see you relative to H.R. 12776 above referred to.

This will be of great help to me and I need your help. I have a sincere desire to serve in Congress during the remainder of this war and do all I can in my humble way to help you and your administration in the great work which you have before you. Ordinarily to be defeated for Congress would have no terror for me, but at my age[2] it would be a serious thing to be defeated under circumstances that might place upon me for life the suspicion of disloyalty. Very respectfully, P. D. Decker[3]

TLS (WP, DLC).
[1] Democratic congressman from Missouri.
[2] He was born September 10, 1875.
[3] Tumulty added a note: "Dear Governor: This is a very human letter from Congressman Decker, and I hope you will read every word of it. J.P.T." JPT to WW, Aug. 29, 1918, TL (WP, DLC).

From William Byron Colver

My dear Mr. President: Washington 28 August 1918

The Commission has prepared in bill form, suggested legislation which follows its recommendations in the matter of the Meat Packing Industry which report was submitted to you under date of July 5th.

We are enclosing a copy of this suggested legislation[1] to you with the idea that you may wish to take the initiative.

By direction of the Commission.

Yours very truly,   William B Colver.

TLS (WP, DLC).
   [1] "*A Bill* TO PROVIDE ADEQUATE TRANSPORTATION AND DISTRIBUTION FACILITIES FOR LIVESTOCK AND FOODS," T MS (WP, DLC). This bill authorized the President, acting through the Director General of Railroads, to acquire and operate stock cars, refrigerator cars, and special equipment cars, as well as stockyards and other distribution facilities on behalf of the United States, and to build new cars and distribution facilities as needed. The bill also appropriated $500,000,000 to be used as a revolving fund for these purposes.

From William Gibbs McAdoo

Dear Governor: Washington August 28, 1918.

In line with the policy of the Government affecting political activity of Government employees, and also because I think it highly essential that the railroad employees of the country should not be used in any way for political purposes, I contemplate issuing an order of which the enclosed is a copy.[1] Before doing so, I should be very glad to know if this meets with your approval.

My own judgment is that we should lay the foundation now for the removal of the railway employees of the United States from pernicious political influences as far as it is possible to do so. To my mind, the possible organization of the railway employees in the future by unscrupulous or designing men for political purposes is the most dangerous feature of Government control of the railroads.

Cordially yours,   W G McAdoo

TLS (WP, DLC).
   [1] WGM, "*Press Notice*: TO ALL OFFICERS AND EMPLOYEES IN THE RAILROAD SERVICE OF THE UNITED STATES," Aug. 31, 1918, T MS (WP, DLC). This order forbade any officer, attorney, or employee of any railroad under federal control to engage in any political activity or political fund raising. It also prohibited any such person from becoming a candidate for political office, other than service on a local school or park board, and from interfering with the free exercise of individual suffrage by any other employee of the federally operated railroad system. It was published in the *Official Bulletin*, II (Sept. 3, 1918), 3.

Colville Adrian de Rune Barclay to the Foreign Office

Washington. August 28th, 1918

No. 3865 Dr. Masaryk's last news is to effect that there are nearly 30,000 German prisoners with 200 machine guns and 70 cannon in Vladivostock region. There are under 5000 Czechs at Irkutsk short of munitions, and if these are defeated prisoners and Bolsheviks could then attack there further West. He considers two divisions of Japanese (say 40,000 men) immediately necessary. These could not be supplied at present from this country. He had interview with Secretary of State at end of last week when latter suggested bringing the Czechs from the West to force passage to Vladivostock where they would obtain supplies and then return to the West. When M. pointed out impossibility of this, Secretary practically admitted he did not know what to do and requested M. to prepare a memo on the situation. This he is now doing making need of Japanese help who alone can supply the man power his chief point.

M. warned me that State Department feel irritated with H.M.G. for having pressed them so hard over the Siberian question, and they are disposed to attribute the constant articles in the press which take same view as H.M.G. to this Embassy. For this belief I need hardly assure you there is no ground whatsoever. It shows however that we shall do well to abstain from any further pressure and to await result of M.'s memorandum.

An informant of mine who saw President yesterday says he expressed resolve to do nothing until he was sure what were the real wishes of the Russian people.

Attitude of Chief of Staff[1] is that he is bending all his energies to Western front and therefore entirely discourages any activity in other quarters.

T telegram (FO 115/2449, pp. 183-84, PRO).
[1] That is, Peyton C. March.

To Robert Lansing

CONFIDENTIAL

My dear Mr. Secretary: The White House 29 August, 1918.

You know how much pains we have taken to make arrangements for the purchase of supplies in this country by the Allies on the same terms with our own government and with our civil population. I am sorry to say that the English government has not been equally generous, or perhaps I should say equally successful, in arranging that supplies that this government purchases in England should be purchased upon the same terms upon which sales are made to the British government and to the civilian population of Great Britain. I would be very much obliged to you if you would convey a very earnest intimation to the British government of our hope and expectation that this reciprocal arrangement should be made as promptly and completely as possible. The discriminations I have heard of have disturbed me a good deal, and while I am sure that the men at the top of the government over there would be willing to make a cordial response to such representations, I am equally sure that the traders with whom they are consulting are not equally willing. You will know how to give emphasis with courtesy.

Cordially and sincerely yours,　Woodrow Wilson

TLS (SDR, RG 59, 811.24/251½, DNA).

To Edward Nash Hurley

CONFIDENTIAL

My dear Hurley:　　　　　　[The White House] 29 August, 1918.

There is a matter which has been giving me some concern and about which I am sure you will let me write you with perfect frankness.

The English, as I need not tell you, are making a great many determined efforts to see to it not only that they are not put at an economic disadvantage after the war, but that they secure now by as tight arrangements as possible every economic advantage that is within their reach. They are stimulated to do this by their consciousness that our shipbuilding programme will give us a very considerable advantage over them in the carrying trade, and therefore in world commerce, after the struggle is over. I therefore write to suggest that it is wise for us not to talk now or publicly plan now the use we shall make of our shipping after the war, because while it is true, contrary to the English impression, that we do not intend to seek any unfair advantage of any kind or to shoulder anybody out, but merely to give the widest possible currency to our own goods, the impression made by past utterances has been that we, like the English, are planning to dominate everything and to oust everybody we can oust.

It is past hoping for that they should believe us to be fair and square, perhaps, and therefore is it not best to say nothing about it? My object is to give them not even the slightest color of provocation or excuse for what they are doing.

Cordially and faithfully yours,　[Woodrow Wilson]

CCL (WP, DLC).

To William Gibbs McAdoo

My dear Mac: The White House 29 August, 1918

I think the enclosed statement is absolutely all right, and I am glad you are going to issue it.

Affectionately yours,   Woodrow Wilson

TLS (W. G. McAdoo Papers, DLC).

From Royal Meeker, with Enclosure

My dear Mr. President: Washington August 29, 1918.

I beg leave to suggest that you appoint immediately a Textile and Clothing Administrator to bring about regulation and control of the prices and qualities of textiles and clothing in the same way as the Food Administrator has regulated and controlled the qualities and prices of foodstuffs. The benefits to the people from the activities of the Food Administration are statistically demonstrable, and the need for a similar policy of regulation and control of textiles and clothing is likewise demonstrable by the statistical method.

The Food Administration began its activities in May, 1917. For your information I enclose a tabular statement showing variations in prices of food and clothing at wholesale and variations in prices of food at retail. The index numbers are calculated on the basis that 1913 equals 100.

Unfortunately, we have no strictly comparable figures showing variations in prices of clothing at retail for the whole country. We do know the changes in prices of clothing in the shipbuilding centers in which we have made cost of living studies. The percentage price changes in these cities were computed on the basis that 1914 equals 100 because it was impossible to get dependable price data as far back as 1913.

You will note that the wholesale food index in May, 1917, was 191, while in July, 1918, it was 185, being a *decrease* of more than 3 per cent since May, 1917. On the other hand, the wholesale cloths and clothing index in May, 1917, was 173, while in July, 1918, it was 249, being an *increase* of more than 44 per cent. Surely there is a reason. No one would have the temerity to say that a scarcity exists any more in textiles than in food. Neither has the demand for clothing increased to a greater extent than the demand for foodstuffs. The difference between the decrease of more than 3 per cent in average prices at wholesale of foodstuffs and the increase of more than 44 per cent in the average prices at wholesale of clothing represents the difference between *public* control of prices in the interests of the people and *private* control of prices for the benefit of the private price controllers.

Quite naturally the Food Administration has been able to control wholesale prices much more effectively than retail prices. You will note that the retail food index for May, 1917, was 151 and that there has been a pretty consistent increase in retail food prices from that date to July, 1918, when the retail food index reaches 167, showing a percentage increase of more than 10 per cent.

The increase in cost of food in the families studied in our cost of living investigation is less than that shown in our retail food price index, although it is not possible to compare family expenditures in May, 1917, with July, 1918. We are now tabulating the retail prices for August, 1918, of the different items consumed by workingmen's families, as found in the shipbuilding centers included in our budget study. The figures thus far obtained are from Southern cities only and show that clothing has increased in price since 1914 by from 91½ per cent to 127 per cent. Furniture and furnishings purchased by workingmen show an increase in these same cities of from 104 to 131 per cent. Expenditures for clothing constituted from 11 to 14 per cent of the total family budgent [budget] in Southern cities and from 15 to 16 per cent of the total family budget in Northern cities. Food is, of course, a much more important item, ranging from 45 to 54 per cent of the total family expenditures in Southern cities and from 40 to 45 per cent in Northern cities. Next in importance to expenditures for food, however, come expenditures for clothing, and prices of clothing have increased already to an alarming extent. Dry goods merchants are frightening people to death and inducing them to purchase much more clothing than they have any earthly need for by telling them that the prices of the new stocks of clothing are to be much higher than they now are.

I sincerely trust that you will seriously consider my suggestion and at once take steps to transfer the regulation and control of clothing consumption and prices from the hands of private individuals intent on acquiring profits to the hands of a competent public Administrator charged with the duty and vested with the authority to see to it that the people obtain standard goods at reasonable prices.   Sincerely yours,   Royal Meeker

TLS (WP, DLC).

ENCLOSURE

Index numbers of wholesale prices of food and cloths and clothing and of retail prices of food in the United States, January, 1917, to July, 1918.

(1913 = 100)

Year and month	Food articles at wholesale	Cloths and clothing at wholesale	Food articles at retail
1917.			
January	150	161	128
February	160	162	133
March	161	163	133
April	182	169	145
May	191	173	151
June	187	179	152
July	180	187	146
August	180	193	149
September	178	193	153
October	183	191	157
November	184	202	155
December	185	206	157
1918.			
January	188	209	160
February	187	213	161
March	178	220	154
April	179	230	154
May	178	234	158
June	180	243	162
July	185	249	167

T MS (WP, DLC).

Two Letters from William Gibbs McAdoo

Dear Mr. President: Washington August 29, 1918.

I, of course, realize that the most important industries in the country regard themselves as of such vital importance to the prosecution of the war that they urge that men employed therein should either be exempted from the draft or given deferred classifications. I also realize that it is a very perplexing problem and that exemptions should not be granted unless an overwhelmingly convincing case is made in their favor.

Whatever may be said of other industries, there can be no difference of opinion about the primary and vital importance of the maintenance of sufficient railroad transportation in this country to meet the demands of war industries, as well as the imperative needs of the civil population. Transportation is absolutely fundamental to the whole problem, and any crippling of the transportation machine brings a train of disasters and difficulties which I think every intelligent man will admit that we should, if possible, avoid.

The railroads are now a Governmental agency. Every officer and man in the railroad service of the United States is an employee of the Government. It is, in effect, a part of the military arm of the Government, and as such it is to my mind clear that no drafts should be made upon its essential employees and no impairment of its effectiveness should for one moment be considered.

The railroads are suffering so much from the shortage of labor and from the drafts already made by the War Department that I am impelled to beg you to intervene and prevent any further drafts upon the railroad employees of the country. Unless this is done and done immediately, I am quite sure that there will be a very serious breakdown in transportation at a very early date.

I have been straining every nerve and every officer of the railroads has been keyed to the highest pitch to overcome the railroad demoralization of last winter and to perfect a machine which will perform the service demanded of it. We have accomplished extraordinary results already, but we cannot hold the ground thus far gained unless we can maintain our organization.

I am sure you will acquit me of any desire to ask for railroad officers and employees any consideration which is not in the interest of the country. Our whole military program is limited by what we can accomplish in railroad transportation in the United States. Therefore, the consideration I ask for the officers and employees of the railroads, who are in the employ of the United States, is in my opinion in the best interest of the country and of vital importance to the military operations of the Government.

I enclose a memorandum which I shall be very glad if you will read,[1] together with suggested orders which I ask that you sign.[2] I know, of course, that you will want to discuss this matter with the Secretary of War. I shall only be too glad to take the subject up with him myself if you care to have me do so. A critical situation faces the railroads and it can be saved only by your prompt action.

Cordially yours,   W G McAdoo.

My dear Mr. President: Washington August 29, 1918.

The situation regarding public health work in this country is serious and is steadily becoming worse. This is due to an acute shortage of sanitary and medical personnel and an impending disintegration of the Federal, State and local health organizations.

The Federal Public Health Service is now charged with grave responsibilities of which the following are the most pressing:

Sanitary supervision of areas adjacent to military cantonments and of other areas to which soldiers and sailors have access; sanitary supervision of Government works and adjacent zones; cooperation with State and local health authorities in sanitary work; sanitary supervision of shipyards and shipyard personnel; cooperation with the Labor Department and Ordnance Department in the hygiene of war industries; medical and surgical care of seamen of a greatly increased merchant marine; patients under the War Risk Insurance Act and injured Federal employees; operation of a National system of maritime quarantine; control of the interstate spread of disease; control of venereal diseases; railroad sanitation.

An added emphasis has been given to all these responsibilities by the Executive Order of July 1, 1918, placing all public health activities incident to the prosecution of the war under the supervision and control of the Secretary of the Treasury.

To meet these responsibilities, conservative estimates show that a minimum of 2,300 medical and sanitary experts must be added immediately to the scientific personnel of the Public Health Service.

Public opinion is holding this Department responsible for the discharge of these grave responsibilities, consequently they must be fully met. To do this, the problem becomes one of adequate personnel and funds.

An analysis of the present availability and distribution of the medical personnel of the country shows that the estimated needs of the military forces and local draft and advisory boards will require over 60,000 of the 120,000 available physicians of the country, besides about 4,000 other sanitary experts, thus leaving but 60,000 physicials [physicians] and an insignificant number of other sanitary experts for all medical and sanitary needs of a population now estimated at 110,000,000. Moreover, disintegration is now threatening the personnel of Federal, State and local health organizations.

Many State organizations have already been seriously depleted by enrollment of their personnel with the military forces. Sixteen commissioned officers of the Public Health Service have already resigned, or expressed a determination to leave the Service for duty in the Army.

Unless some immediate action is taken, it seems inevitable that a large number of the commissioned force of the Public Health Service will apply for duty with the Army, even though these officers (216) have been excluded from the operation of the draft law. The situation is much more serious in the case of noncommissioned scientific personnel of the Service which composes by far its greatest part. Under the proposed extension of the draft age 85 per cent will be subject to call.

It is evident from this stat[e]ment of the situation that, not only will it be difficult to secure the force for larger public health work, but, in the absence of early action, the disintegration of the present force will reach such a stage as to prevent the Service from carrying on its present activities.

Furthermore, it should be recognized, as a matter of public psychology, that the needs of the Army are paramount in the public mind. This has led to the enrollment with the military forces of a large proportion of the available medical and sanitary professions. Many thousand more are now applying for enrollment. Moreover, the proposed extension of the draft age will place the military authorities in control of practically all the active available medical and sanitary personnel of the country. It necessarily follows that provisions for maintaining the present forces and provisions for additional forces for the Public Health Service should take into account both the attitude of the medical and sanitary professions and the proposed extension of the draft age, and furnish comparable opportunities for patriotic service.

Foreseeing this situation, over sixteen months ago the Public Health Service prepared a resolution (Senate Joint Resolution No. 63, still pending in Congress) which provided for a sanitary reserve corps of officers to be commissioned by the President in the Public Health Service. This would place the expert sanitarians needed for public health work in the service of the Government with commissions comparable to those of the medical reserve corps of the Army and Navy.

Since adequate protection of the health of the civil population is essential to winning the war, I have to recommend that the following steps be taken to enable this Department to carry out its responsibilities in the premises:

1. That public health work be recognized by Executive Order as

essential war duty on a parity with that of the medical corps of the Army or Navy.

2. That the scientific personnel of the Public Health Service, who are now, or may hereafter be commissioned, or appointed in that Service, shall be placed by the Provost Marshal General in the same class as medical officers of the Public Health Service commissioned under the act of 1889.

3. That officers of the medical and sanitary corps of the Army and Navy be transferred for duty in the Public Health Service in such numbers and for such periods as may be required and military necessity may permit.

4. That Senate Joint Resolution No. 63, providing for a sanitary reserve corps of the Public Health Service be passed without delay.

5. That an urgent deficiency appropriation of $10,000,000 be obtained from Congress for public health work.

Each of these five recommendations are so related that their approval as a whole is essential to the proper protection of the health of the military and industrial forces and the civil population.

In the event that these recommendations meet with your approval, I am enclosing the text of an executive Order and an urgent deficiency estimate which I hope you will sign and approve.[1] I also enclose a suggestion for a letter to Hon. Thetus W. Sims,[2] Chairman of the Committee on Interstate and Foreign Commerce of the House of Representatives, who has charge of Senate Joint Resolution No. 63 in the House. I trust you will see fit to bring to Mr. Sims' attention in some such manner the necessity for this legislation.

Cordially yours,   W G McAdoo

TLS (WP, DLC).
  [1] T MS and WGM to WW, Aug. 23, 1918, TLS, both in WP, DLC.
  [2] T MS (WP, DLC).

From Joseph Patrick Tumulty

Louisville, Ky., Aug. 29, 1918.

Have talked with Stanley[1] about attitude of Senator James successor on suffrage. Think I have made an impression. It would help very much if you would wire or write Stanley arguing importance of matter in connection with James' successor. Regards.

Tumulty.

T telegram (WP, DLC).
  [1] That is, Governor Augustus O. Stanley of Kentucky.

From Robert Lansing, with Enclosure

My dear Mr. President: Washington August 29, 1918.

I call your attention to the marked passage on page two of the enclosed telegram (4470, Aug. 26, 4 pm) from Berne. If you see no objection to making the informal declaration suggested I will so instruct Mr. Stovall. It strikes me that it would be opportune.

Faithfully yours, Robert Lansing.

TLS (SDR, RG 59, 860C.01/132, DNA).

ENCLOSURE

Pontarlier August 26, 1918.

4470. Jan Perlowski a reliable Pole with whom Department is familiar, informed Wilson[1] that he received message from Warsaw from reliable circles to following effect. Von Hintze[2] is anxious to show immediate settlement with Poland as tangible result his activities as opposed to Kuhlmann's dilatory policy. Hintze therefore pressing Austria hard to obtain acceptance German solution Polish problem. Austria in no shape to resist because of internal condition. Poland's game is to play one against the other and endeavor at all costs to prevent Austrian and German Governments coming to accord over Poland.

They submit therefore following question "If independent United Poland, with access to the sea desired to contract a voluntary union with a neighboring state, Germany excepted, if that union were the price of concessions which that state needs make els[e]where to assure a general peace, would the principles of your government be opposed thereto." Perlowski explained that a favorable answer to this question would enable the Poles in Vienna to stiffen auspicious resistance to German demands and spoil Hintze's endeavors toward a solution. Perlowski stated matter was most urgent.

Wilson felt he had no right to give even an expression of personal opinion in this connection.

If Department desires to give an expression of opinion Perlowski could transmit it as views of the Department or personal views of Wilson according as Department desires.

In addition to and entirely separated from the foregoing, I respectfully suggest that this furnishes a good opportunity to allay uneasiness instigated by Germany's propaganda in Poland as to Poland's (?) reconstituted Russia. Some such informal message as following might be given "Recent events in Russia have caused no change in the principles governing the action of the American Government toward Poland's future, principles which have already been clearly stated by President Wilson." In this connection consult my telegram number 4450, August 23, 5 pm.[3]   Stovall

T telegram (SDR, RG 59, 860C.01/132, DNA).
[1] That is, Hugh R. Wilson.
[2] That is, Paul von Hintze, who had succeeded Kühlmann as German Foreign Secretary on July 9.
[3] P. A. Stovall to RL, Aug. 23, 1918, T telegram (SDR, RG 59, 860.01/129, DNA); printed in *FR-WWS 1918*, 1, I, 874-75.

From Robert Lansing

My dear Mr. President: Washington August 29th, 1918.

I hesitate to trouble you again with the subject of supplies for the Czecho-Slovaks, but I fear there is no other course. The Red Cross is sending underwear, socks, sweaters, shirts, cloth for suiting and gloves, together with some shoes and sole leather furnished by the Russian Embassy. Further than that there seems to be no effort to send supplies of any kind and no effort being made to send supplies of a military character. Unless supplies leave the United States within the next three weeks it will be impossible to reach the Czechs, because the winter sets in very early and most rigorously in that climate.

May I be so bold as to suggest that you designate some one person and clothe him with sufficient authority to get the information which seems to be necessary before any shipment can be commenced and to report to you? This seems to me to be the only solution of a situation which is at present chaotic, in which no one seems to have authority and in which there is no directed energy.

From a casual investigation, I am satisfied that there are supplies of a military character in this country which can not possibly be used by our armed forces and which can be most suitably used by the Czechs. This applies to rifles, ammunition, machine guns and various other necessary equipment of a military character.

Of course the work which the Red Cross is doing I feel should not be confused with or sub-ordinated to the direction of any person whom you may designate, and I think that it should be continued in the same independent manner, but I do feel that any other relief which it is contemplated should be sent to the Czechs should be supervised and directed by one person with sufficient authority to co-ordinate all the efforts which will be necessary to get any relief to them.

I am, my dear Mr. President,

Faithfully,   Robert Lansing.

TLS (SDR, RG 59, 860F.24/9A, DNA).

From William Kent

Dear Mr. President: Washington August 29, 1918.

Senator George Norris, of Nebraska, has won out in the Republican primaries. During my life in Washington, I have found him one of the best, most faithful and intelligent men in either House of Congress, and I have known him both in the Senate and in the House. I have never known a time when he would not take up and champion any good cause brought to his attention. He represents pre-eminently the progressive sentiment of the Senate, along with men like Kenyon, Owen, and our lamented friend, Ollie James. I have done what little I could toward furthering his primary campaign, and if necessary, shall go to Nebraska to help in his election. I sincerely hope that the Administration will not feel under obligations to take sides in the Nebraska contest, and in the event of your being asked, trust that you will carefully investigate Norris' position, which has been of the strongest along the lines of conservation and preventing the looting of the public domain.

Yours truly,   William Kent

TLS (WP, DLC).

Three Letters from Newton Diehl Baker

My dear Mr. President: Washington. August 29, 1918.

Mr. Fosdick has talked with Mr. Cleveland Dodge, Mr. George W. Perkins, Mr. Mortimer Schiff and others in New York about the joint drive for the seven agencies engaged in war work. He has today received word that Mr. Mott returned to New York, conferred with his associates, and says that if the War Department wants the plan he will join in and work heartily for it.

Mr. Dodge, Mr. Perkins, Mr. Schiff and others believe the plan wise, but they recognize that it has some difficulties with their constituencies which Mr. Mott pointed out to you.

The net result of all these conferences and of all the thinking Mr. Fosdick and I have been able to do on the subject, leads us very firmly to the belief that a joint drive alone will prevent an unpleasant religious controversy in the country, with unhappy consequences alike to the Y.M.C.A., and some of the other agencies involved. It is the belief of those whom Mr. Fosdick has seen, and is his belief and mind [mine], that if the joint drive were made pursuant to a request from you their acquiescence in it would be understood by their constituencies in a way impossible if they voluntarily went into such an enterprise. Mr. Mott feels, however, that you should not make a statement on the subject until after Tuesday in order that he may adjust the minds of some of his Chicago co-workers to the new phase of the question.

I have asked Mr. Fosdick to keep in close touch with the matter and to report to you on or after Tuesday, when, unless some change takes place, it seems to me that it would be wise for you to issue a joint request to these seven societies to unite their appeals in order that the spirit of the country may be expressed without distinction of race or religion in favor of what is a common service to the soldiers of the country.

In order to prepare this thing for acceptance among the various societies, we have secured a reduction in the estimated budget of the Catholic War Council from $50,000,000. to $30,000,000., and of some of the other agencies in smaller but proportionally like amounts. This makes the gross amount to be sought smaller, and leaves any surplus which may be proportionally distributed available to supplement what the Y.M.C.A. now feels to be an insufficient estimate in their own budget by reason of the increased rapidity with which troops are being assembled in Europe.

In the meantime, there is some duplication in the work done by these societies, and I am asking Mr. Fosdick and Dr. Keppel in my absence to seek to bring about a committee which will represent these seven societies and work in collaboration with Mr. Fosdick with a view to preventing duplication by agreements upon jurisdictional limits of the work to be done by the several societies. There is some work, for instance, now done by the Y.M.C.A., which may properly go over to the Red Cross, and there are some phases of the work in France done by both the Y.M.C.A., and the Knights of Columbus which may still be done by both, but not duplicated in particular places. Conference would undoubtedly lead to agreement eliminating useless expenditure and thus make the amounts received in the pending appeal more nearly adequate to the expanding needs of the several societies.

These last observations are made because Mr. Cleveland Dodge and Mr. George W. Perkins sent a note to me in which they expressed apprehension lest the total amount asked for by the Y.M.C.A. in its budget should turn out to be insufficient after the large number of societies grouped in the single drive secure their distributable proportions of the surplus.

Respectfully yours,   Newton D. Baker

My dear Mr. President: Washington. August 29, 1918.

In talking with General Crowder about the wish you had expressed that we could find some way to have the Department heads designate classes of persons for deferred classification, we found ourselves constantly facing the old objection, class exemption, which has proved a fruitful source of embarrassment in connection with Emergency Fleet exemptions and Navy exemptions, which were the only two granted in that generalized form. The machinery which has now been drawn up provides for a district advisory committee, composed of one person representing the industrial interests of the country and selected by the Department of Labor, and representing both employer and the employe; one selected by the Department of Agriculture with similar relations respecting agricultural employments; and the third a representative citizen selected by the District Exemption Board, who will have as his function to consider the remaining employments, such as banking, insurance, etc., which have to do with the general industrial and commercial life of the community. If a regulation were added, for instance, which authorized the class exemption of chief clerks by a simple designation of their title, it would be found that there are many chief clerks in minor offices of the various Departments scattered throughout the United States who are young, replaceable, and not specially trained or technically indispensable, while if the several Department heads address letters to their subordinates throughout the country, asking them to bring to the attention of the expert adviser appointed by the District Board the cases of all their assistants and employes who are deemed indispensable, with short recitals of the supporting data upon which the claim ought to be presented, the Advisory Board will of course present the matter to the District Board with its recommendation and thus secure the deferred classification in appropriate cases without imposing upon the Department heads the burden of an enumeration by name of their widely scattered employes throughout the United States.

I feel very sure that the foregoing plan will save us from the embarrassment which would arise if we undertook to start class exemptions at all; it would be followed inevitably by suggestions that we should make class exemptions of mine workers, munitions workers, railroad employes, and other great groups whose personnel undoubtedly ought for the most part to be deferred, but in the lists of employes of each there are a number of men who can be readily replaced and ought to be; and if such class exemptions were entered into it would amount to distributing the exemption power practically away from the District Boards and into the hands of representatives of the great industries scattered all over the country and, therefore, not under the actual supervision and centralized control of those who here in Washington are responsible for their actions.

If this solution of the problem seems satisfactory to you, I will ask General Crowder to write to each member of the Cabinet, to each Board, and to the heads of the Y.M.C.A., Red Cross, etc., apprising them of the method here suggested for presenting the names of their indispensable employes and agents to the appropriate tribunal for the decision of their cases.

Respectfully yours,   Newton D. Baker

My dear Mr. President: Washington. August 29, 1918.

I have read Mr. Mott's letter of the twenty-fourth, which you were good enough to send me with your letter of the twenty-seventh, and am very sympathetic with the point of view expressed by Mr. Mott. I, of course, realize the delay which is inherent in an examination of the applications for passports by our Military Intelligence, which seems to Mr. Mott to be unnecessary in view of the previous examination of applicants through the channels of the Y.M.C.A.

I hardly see, however, how we can wisely adopt a different rule for the Y.M.C.A. than that which applies to the other organizations which are recognized by the War Department and are rendering somewhat similar service to the Army abroad. Any exceptions made for one organization would, I fear, immediately be taken by the other organizations as a discrimination which would be difficult for us to explain or justify. The experience of the Military Intelligence, on the other hand, is clear that some organizations are selecting men whom it would be unwise to send across, and only after investigation by the Military Intelligence can we exercise wise and fair discrimination.

I am asking Colonel Churchill,[1] in view of the special circumstances related in Mr. Mott's letter, if he will not expedite in every way possible passports for the Y.M.C.A. members now awaiting passage, and I am sure he will do everything possible to enable those about whom there is no question to sail at an early date.

If you feel that any further exception on behalf of the Y.M.C.A. is wise, I shall of course be very glad to follow your wishes.

Respectfully yours,   Newton D. Baker

TLS (WP, DLC).

[1] Brig. Gen. Marlborough Churchill, Assistant Chief of Staff and Director of Military Intelligence.

From Jessie Woodrow Wilson Sayre

Dearest Father,   Siaconset Mass Aug. 29, 1918

When we came back from Nantucket last night after a little supper party with the Schaufflers[1]—a brother of our Dr. Schauffler at Sea Girt,[2] do you remember him? I found your telegram and letter[3] smiling at me from the table. Maggie[4] had placed them so that they would be the very first things I would see when I opened the door. How dear of you, my darling Father! And how I love you for remembering the day when your little wee girl came into the world to love and adore you, as she has done every minute since.

Thank you so much for the lovely gift. I have many lovely plans for it, and they will all be yours.

My birthday was a beautiful one, full of sunshine and happiness. They (the cook, rather) gave me a surprise party, cake and candles and all and the children's glee was delectable.

The children are climbing all over me and I must stop.

With dearest, dearest love from us all,

                                Devotedly,   Jessie

ALS (WP, DLC).
    [1] The Rev. Henry Park Schauffler and Grace Jarvis Schauffler. He was at this time superintendent of the Brooklyn City Mission.
    [2] William Gray Schauffler, M.D., about whom see the index references in Vols. 22, 23, and 28 of this series.
    [3] They are missing.
    [4] A servant.

To Augustus Owsley Stanley

My dear Governor: The White House 30 August, 1918.

Will you pardon a suggestion about Senator James' successor? The matter of woman suffrage is critically important just now, and I am going to make bold to suggest that it would be of great advantage to the party and to the country if his successor entertained views favorable to the pending constitutional amendment.

Pardon me if I am taking too great a liberty. I am writing this because I know how serious the consequences of a rejection may be.

With warmest personal greetings,

            Cordially and sincerely yours,   Woodrow Wilson

TLS (A. O. Stanley Papers, KyU).

To Winthrop More Daniels

PERSONAL

My dear Daniels: The White House 30 August, 1918.

I believe I have already once consulted you about a suggestion similar to that embodied in the enclosed proposed proclamation,[1] but I am going to take the liberty of coming to you once more, because the financial exigencies facing many of the power companies in the country are very real and very great, and I am anxious to do anything that it is possible for me to do to assist them.

The sketch of a proclamation which I enclose with this was handed to me by the Secretary of the Treasury, whose interest of course is in maintaining as far as possible the stability of the financial situation throughout the country and who is disturbed by the fact that some eleven billions of the securities of these companies are held by banks and trust companies as well as by private persons.

I do not believe that it would be serviceable to appoint another independent body, but what I earnestly ask your advice about is this: whether in your opinion it would be wise for me to request the Interstate Commerce Commission to hear the claims of these corporations, form an independent judgment and make public recommendations with regard to their treatment by State and municipal rate-fixing bodies?

I hate to bother you about this, but the matter is of very great proportions and is very important.

Cordially and sincerely yours, Woodrow Wilson

TLS (Wilson-Daniels Corr., CtY).
[1] T MS (Wilson-Daniels Corr., CtY). This draft of a presidential proclamation called for the creation either of a National Public Utilities War Board or a National Commissioner for Public Utilities. The board, or commissioner, was empowered, upon authority of the President, to make "regulations and suggestions as to rates" to local regulatory bodies or agencies, or to the proper authorities in localities where such bodies or agencies did not exist or had insufficient powers. In the case of electric railways, where the local bodies or agencies did not exist, or had insufficient powers, or did not act with "the necessary promptness," the national board, or commissioner, was empowered "to take over ... the possession and control of such properties and fix the rates of service therefor." Finally, the board or commissioner was authorized to "exercise such further powers as may be hereafter delegated to the said (Board) (Commissioner) by the President."

To Royal Meeker

My dear Meeker: [The White House] 30 August, 1918.

I have read with sympathy your letter of yesterday, but the trouble is that I have not the legal power to regulate and control the prices and qualities of textiles and clothing in the same way that the Food Administrator regulates and controls the qualities and prices of food stuffs. The powers of the Food Administrator were specifically conferred by Congress, but no such powers have been conferred upon the Executive with regard to textiles and clothing. I wish with all my heart they had been. Just now, it seems rather futile, at the end of a hurried session, to attempt to bring this matter to action in the Congress.

Cordially and sincerely yours,   Woodrow Wilson

TLS (Letterpress Books, WP, DLC).

To John R. Mott

My dear Mott: The White House 30 August, 1918.

I took the matter of your letter of August 24th up with the Secretary of War, and he has written me that Col. Churchill, the Head of the Army Intelligence, will press the matter of the passports of the Y.M.C.A. men awaiting passage as rapidly as possible, in order to expedite the departure of those who are straining at the leash.

Cordially and faithfully yours,   Woodrow Wilson

TLS (J. R. Mott Coll., CtY-D).

To Edward Samuel Corwin

My dear Professor Corwin: [The White House] 30 August, 1918.

To tell you the truth, I do not know upon what the newspaper statements with regard to the action of certain Departments of the government with a view to getting the history of these extraordinary days we are passing through properly and promptly set forth were founded on, because I have had no part in the matter and know nothing of it.[1] I saw the same notices that you saw, and assumed that it meant merely that the military authorities in particular were seeking to have things that would not be officially recorded, studied and collated in a way which they would be sure would not be ephemeral and be lost. Personally, I do not think that this is the time to write the executive and legislative history of the war. That history will be accessible for a great many years, and more accessible in the future than it is now, in the official documents, and I have always had the feeling that an official "Remembrancer" never could do the same work that a historian could do at a later time.

With best wishes,

Cordially and sincerely yours,   Woodrow Wilson

TLS (Letterpress Books, WP, DLC).
[1] E. S. Corwin to WW, Aug. 28, 1918, ALS (WP, DLC). Corwin said that he had been very interested to learn of "the intention of the Government to begin at once the compilation of the history of our participation in the War." He was especially interested in "the legislative & administrative side of the war—that phase of it which must be written up for the student of political science: the acts of Congress, their elucidation & application thru administrative orders, Presidential proclamations, judicial decisions; the administrative machinery built up in consequence of the War; the stress & strain upon the old system, etc." Corwin asked Wilson whether he felt that he could help him to obtain "a hand" in this project.

To R. H. Windsor[1]

My dear Rev. Windsor: [The White House] 30 August, 1918.

I am writing to say with what interest and admiration I have learned of the fact that twelve of your sons are in the service of our country and the thirteenth impatiently waiting to follow them in. This is a splendid record, and I congratulate you from the bottom of my heart. The colored troops have proved themselves fine soldiers.

Cordially and sincerely yours,   Woodrow Wilson

TLS (Letterpress Books, WP, DLC).
[1] Of Rayville, La. He cannot be further identified.

From Herbert Clark Hoover, with Enclosure

Dear Mr. President: Washington 30 August 1918

You will please find enclosed herewith the executive order making the guarantee on next year's wheat, for your signature. Also a draft of a statement that I have prepared to go with the guarantee.

I would suggest that when complete they should be issued through the Committee on Public Information.

Yours faithfully,   Herbert Hoover

TLS (WP, DLC).

E N C L O S U R E [1]

MEMORANDUM

29 August 1918

In issuing today the Government's guarantee of the same price for 1919 wheat crop ⟨as⟩ that *was guaranteed* for the 1918 crop, I wish ⟨to add⟩ *it to be understood* that in the spring of 1919 I will appoint a disinterested commission who will secure for me ⟨in a broad way⟩ the facts *by that time disclosed* as to the increased cost of farm⟨ers'⟩ labor and supplies, using the three-year pre-war average prices of wheat, of labor, and *of* supply costs as a basis, and *that* from this information I shall ⟨be able to⟩ determine whether there should be an increase in price above the present level, and, if so, ⟨in a broad way⟩ what advance, ⟨should be made⟩ in order to maintain for the farmer a good return. Should it ⟨eventuate⟩ *then appear* that an increase is deserved over the present guarantee, *however,* it will be applied only to those who have by next harvest already marketed their 1918 wheat.

It is the desire and intention of all Departments of the Administration to give to the wheat-grower a fair and stimulative return in order that the present acreage in wheat ⟨should⟩ *may* be maintained.

I find a great conflict of opinion among various sections of the country as to the price that should be ⟨represented by this⟩ *named as a* minimum guarantee. It must be obvious *to all, however,* that the factors which will make for increased or decreased cost of production of next year's harvest cannot be determined until the near approach to the harvest.

In giving a guaranteed price for wheat one year in advance (the only industry guaranteed by the Government), there is involved a considerable national risk. If there ⟨is⟩ *should be* peace or increased shipping available before the middle of 1920, Europe will naturally supply itself from the large stores of much cheaper wheat now in the Southern Hemisphere; and therefore the Government is undertaking a risk which might in ⟨these⟩ *such an* event⟨s⟩ result in a national loss ⟨up to⟩ *of as much as* $500,000,000 through an unsalable surplus; or, in any event, ⟨result⟩ in maintaining a high level of price to our own people for a long period subsequent to freedom in the world's markets.

Despite this, the desirability of assuring a supply to the world of prime breadstuffs by insuring the farmer against *the* fluctuations in prices that would result from the uncertainties of ⟨this⟩ *the present* situation and from the speculation ⟨that it⟩ *these uncertainties* entail⟨s⟩, seem*s* to me to make the continuation of the guarantee for another year desirable. On the other hand, it ⟨appears to me⟩ *is clear* that before increasing this liability by large sums with the risks set forth above, ⟨or⟩ *and* before increasing the burden of the consumer, ⟨that⟩ the matter should be subjected to searching inquiry at the appropriate time⟨.⟩,—*the time when the pertinent facts will be known.*

I ⟨believe⟩ *feel confident* that with this preliminary fixed guarantee and with the assurance that justice will *in any event* be done to the grower, ⟨that⟩ he will continue the fine patriotic effort *by* which [he] has ⟨guided him⟩ *served the country* hitherto; that the

Government will have acted prudently; and *that* the consumer will be satisfied that his interests are not *unduly* sacrificed, ⟨unduly, for exhaustive consideration will be given at the proper time.⟩ *but just an exhaustive consideration given to every element of the matter at the proper time.*[2]   W.W.

TI MS (WP, DLC).
    [1] Words in the following document in angle brackets deleted by Wilson; words in italics added by him.
    [2] This statement, as revised by Wilson, was issued on September 2, 1918, and published in the *Official Bulletin*, II (Sept. 3, 1918), 7.

From William Gibbs McAdoo

Personal

Dear Governor: Washington August 30, 1918.

Will you please read the two paragraphs on the enclosed sheets from the report I am about to make to you on work done by the Railroad Administration, entitled respectively "Economies effected by reorganization of official staff," and "The salaries paid."[1] This has been a very difficult question for me to deal with because it was essential that I should retain as operating heads of the railroads in the different regions men of proven ability, who were in many cases presidents of railroad companies operating within such regions. The salaries of railroad presidents of the most important lines ranged from $50,000 to $100,000 per annum. The corporate organizations would have kept the men I have taken, and in some instances they have retained men whose services I should have been glad to have, paying higher salaries than I was willing to pay. It was imperative also that, with the great pressure upon the railroads now for adequate transportation, the best ability should be retained, and that the organized forces of the railroads themselves should not be unduly disturbed. The ferment has been bad enough at best. Therefore, I have felt obliged to fix salaries for the Regional Directors at what politicians will think as a high point, and out of which they will attempt to make political capital, but which, after all, is much less than these same men were getting under private control of the railroads and much less than many of them can now get from industrial enterprises where brains are very much in demand.

I intended to speak to you yesterday about this feature of the report, but overlooked it, and am now pointing it out to you because I want you to be informed about it.

I am sure that the course I have taken is the wise one. You will observe that in the reorganization of the official staffs of the railroads which I have effected, there is a resultant economy over private operation of $4,614,889 per annum.

Cordially yours,   W G McAdoo

TLS (WP, DLC).
   [1] T MS (WP, DLC).

Two Letters from Newton Diehl Baker

My dear Mr. President: Washington. August 30, 1918.

After a good deal of consultation with General McIntyre and others, I am disposed to recommend to you Mr. Robert Zold,[1] former Assistant Attorney General of Porto Rico, and now an assistant to the Solicitor General of the United States, as one member of the Commission to go to Porto Rico.

Mr. Wolcott H. Pitkin,[2] formerly Attorney General of Porto Rico, is thoroughly familiar with the situation there, and is recommended to me as an exceedingly intelligent and wise man. He recently made a trip to Porto Rico, and on his return I had some talks with him which led me to form a favorable judgment of his qualifications. He, however, is a Republican and held office in Porto Rico under a Republican administration. Zold, I believe, is a Democrat, but the Attorney General could undoubtedly tell you something more about his qualifications than I know.

I think in addition to either Zold or Pitkin there should be a labor representative, but Mr. Gompers has suggested one of the most radical labor men in the country, and I am afraid his activities would be provocative rather than helpful. Secretary Wilson could undoubtedly suggest a thoughtful and studious man whose sympathies with labor are great, and who would be a real counselor. In the same way, Secretary Redfield could suggest a business man of wide outlook; but I have not in the hurry of the last few days had an opportunity to confer either with Secretary Wilson or Secretary Redfield.

The matter can easily wait until my return, and if you desire I will take it up for disposition after I get back from France. There, of course, can be no reason why you should wait that long, however, if you desire to act immediately.

The purpose of the commission ought to be not merely to study labor conditions in Porto Rico, but the general industrial and agricultural conditions of the Island. Such labor difficulties as there are undoubtedly grew out of the general economic situation there.

Respectfully yours,   Newton D. Baker

TLS (WP, DLC).

[1] Robert Szold.
[2] Wolcott Homer Pitkin, Jr.

My dear Mr. President: Washington [c. Aug. 30, 1918].

Referring again to your letter of the twenty-seventh and Mr. Mott's letter of the twenty-fourth to you, I have laid the matter before General Churchill and am now convinced that not only would it be unwise to adopt Mr. Mott's suggestion that several hundred Y.M.C.A. workers be cleared by Military Intelligence without investigation, but also that everything possible is being done by Military Intelligence to relieve the situation.

It appears that the Y.M.C.A., following the suggestions of Military Intelligence is now endeavoring faithfully to use the greatest possible care in the choice of its overseas workers, but that in spite of this not a few of these persons have been found by such an investigation as Military Intelligence subsequently makes, to be unfit for service overseas either from the point of view of the Government or of the Y.M.C.A. itself. Several weeks ago, when a similar critical situation existed, Military Intelligence tried the very experiment which Mr. Mott has now suggested. The result was far from satisfactory. Subsequent reports on fully five percent of the persons thus cleared were unfavorable. Several of those who had not already sailed were held up at the Port of Embarkation, several who had sailed may have to be brought back.

This creates a situation obviously embarrassing and inimical to the Y.M.C.A., to Military Intelligence and to the best interests of the Army. I am informed that in several of the cases above mentioned, the individuals have been allowed to remain abroad because the evidence against them while certainly definite enough to have justified their being prevented from leaving this country was not considered sufficient to bring them home summarily. However, this entails the necessity of having them watched on the other side, and it is questionable whether such responsibility and additional labor should be shifted to our forces abroad, if they can possibly be spared this burden. In fact, it was largely because of complaints against the quality of a portion of the personnel of the Y.M.C.A. and similar organizations overseas that Military Intelligence found it necessary to institute the procedure of making an investigation of its own to check up that made by the organizations.

As to the present situation, about which Mr. Mott wrote, I find that all possible co-operation is being given by Military Intelligence. Officers and clerks with sympathetic appreciation of the situation are working day and night using the telegraph freely in order to clear a number sufficient to fill the twelve hundred berths that have been reserved on the ship sailing next Monday. A special committee of the Y.M.C.A. War Work Council is now in Washington, and it is understood that satisfactory arrangements have been made between this committee and the officers of Military Intelligence who are charged with the matter.

By way of explanation of the situation, several weeks ago Military Intelligence was informed by the Y.M.C.A. that the organization intended to send overseas a thousand persons a month. Arrangements were accordingly made to take care of this number. When the number was suddenly doubled, difficulty was experienced at first in meeting the increase. That the situation is being met, however, is evidenced by the fact that whereas the average clearance by Military Intelligence during the first two or three weeks in August was forty-five a day, the present average is one hundred a day. Every effort is being made that this average shall be raised in order to take care of the present accumulation and to provide for any future increase in the daily quota.

I am glad to say that the matter is simplified by the fact that Naval Intelligence is not concerned as you suggested in your letter might be the case. Military Intelligence alone is charged with these investigations.   Respectfully yours,   Newton D. Baker

TLS (WP, DLC).

From Robert Lansing

My dear Mr. President: Washington August 30, 1918.

I would like very much to have your views concerning the sending of the enclosed telegram to our Embassy at Tokio in relation to the Chinese Eastern Railway and the employment of the Stevens Mission in this connection.[1] It is a delicate matter but would prevent the road being taken over entirely by the Japanese.

I understand there is one embarrassment and that is this: That the Stevens Mission is paid by the Russian Ambassador here. I think that the cost is approximately $75,000 a month. The Ambassador, so Mr. Long informs me, states that if the interest on the Russian loan in this country is required to be paid in November he will not have funds enough to continue the payment of the Railroad Mission for more than two months.[2] In the event, therefore, of your approval of this telegram we must consider what is to be done in the matter of paying the Mission after the first of November.
                    Faithfully yours,   Robert Lansing.

President agrees after Nov 1/18 to pay Stevens Mission in some way RL. Aug. 30/18

TLS (SDR, RG 59, 861.77/471, DNA).

¹ RL to R. S. Morris, Aug. 30, 1918, T telegram (SDR, RG 59, 861.77/451, DNA). Lansing stated that the United States Government was opposed to a reported Japanese plan to change the gauge of the tracks of the Chinese Eastern Railroad to conform to those of the South Manchurian Railroad, since such a change would render the Chinese Eastern inaccessible to trains from other portions of the Trans-Siberian railroad system. The United States Government, Lansing continued, was also opposed to a suggestion that the members of the Russian Railroad Commission (about which see RL to WW, May 7, 1917, and WW to RL, May 7, 1917, both in Vol. 42) be commissioned in the United States Army. "The members of these railroad units," he said, "are the agents of Russian people and are being paid and supported by their Ambassador here from funds belonging to them, and it is felt that further complications would not arise and best results would be had, if Mr. Stevens for and in behalf of the Russian people were to have general direction of the Trans-Siberian and the Chinese Eastern Railways and their several branches." "This Government," Lansing concluded, "will be glad to have the co-operation of the Imperial Japanese Government to the end that the railways be operated by the engineers chosen by the last recognized Government of Russia and to further the efforts of these engineers to take charge, put the lines in as good working order as possible and operate them during the military occupation subject to the requirements of the military forces."

² B. Long to RL, Aug. 30, 1918, TS MS (SDR, RG 59, 861.77/471, DNA).

Sir William Wiseman to Arthur Cecil Murray

My dear Arthur,   [New York] 30 August 1918.

It has occurred to me that you might be interested to have some description of the week I spent at Magnolia with the President and Col. House. The mail is just going, but I will do my best to give you some description—though I fear it will be disjointed.

I had arranged to spend a week with Col. House particularly because Gordon Auchincloss, his son-in-law, (whom you will remember is assistant counselor of the State Department) was taking his holiday there at the same time and we had planned some golf and tennis. The morning after I arrived, however, the President and his party reached Magnolia. They had come quite unexpectedly, having only decided upon the trip the day before.

I did my best to keep my name out of the papers and the reporters were very good about it and I think only one or two papers mentioned the fact that I was there.

This was sufficient, however, for the French Embassy to ring me up on the long distance telephone and ask if there had been any special significance in the conferences between the President, House and myself. I said they had been of the utmost importance since we had proved that the President could putt at least 50 yards on his iron shots if he would only follow through. In fact it was a most interesting time for me. The President, Mrs. Wilson and Admiral Grayson, his physician and Naval Aide-de-camp occupied a beautiful colonial house over-looking the sea and about a couple of hundred yards from Col. House's bungalow, where I was staying. A company of marines kept the public at a most respectful distance and a destroyer lying off the point guarded him from ambitious U-boat commanders. The President said he was delighted to find me there and insisted on my remaining with the party. Early in the morning about eight o'clock he would motor to one of the nearby golf courses and play a round before the course was crowded. He usually played with Grayson and Mrs. Wilson went nine holes with them.

On one occasion at Myopia the Club boor came up to him at the first tee, introduced himself, and offered to play a round with the President and show him the course. With the coldest look I have ever seen the President turned to him and said, "Thank you, I have a caddy." Out of ear-shot I asked him who his friend was, "Oh just a Boston ass" was the President's reply.

As a rule the President and Mrs. Wilson came to lunch at the House's bungalow and we all went over to dine with the President in the evening. In the afternoons they generally went for a motor drive through the rarely beautiful country along the North Shore. Of course I never discussed any of the questions of the moment unless the President raised the subject, but on one or two occasions the President himself suggested that after lunch he and I and Col. House should retire and talk business. In particular we discussed the League of Nations, the economic policy of the Allies, the President's Mexican policy and the possibilities of German peace efforts. I have, as you know, cabled Reading the substance of these conversations and I will try and elaborate on them in memoranda which, however, I am afraid will not be ready for this mail.

We talked a good deal of politics in England. The President knows England much better than I supposed. Apparently, when he was at Princeton, he used to spend his summer vacations bicycling or walking through England, particularly the Lake district, and at that time had quite a wide acquaintance among University men in England and Scotland. He thinks it was a mistake for us to have a Coalition Government on the ground that the mass of the people would suspect that the Government was controlled by the more reactionary elements and the representatives of capital and privilege. He is, I am afraid, a pretty extreme radical with that curious uninformed prejudice against the so-called governing class in England. I think he would prefer the Lloyd George of Limehouse rather than of the Guildhall. He does not seem to know much of the details of continental politics and I am much impressed with the way in which he relies upon House's advice in these matters.

He does not seem to have much sympathy for Italy and thinks she entered the war as a cold blooded business transaction. Nor has he very strong feelings about Alsace Lorraine, although he says that American opinion is very determined on this point; that they will pay their debt to France by giving her back Alsace Lorraine. He has no sympathy whatever for Bulgaria or Turkey. He is convinced that there are genuine liberal elements in Austria and even in Germany who sincerely wish to follow democratic ideals, but admits that they are too small a minority to have any influence at present on the peoples, as a whole. The German people, he believes, must be made to hate war, to realize that no military machine can dominate the world today. His personal hatred of the Kaiser, whom he has never seen, is almost amusing. The elected autocrat can see no good in the hereditary tyrant. Talking of the Crown Prince he said it made him furious to think the destinies of Germany might one day be in the hands of that young ass.

I was struck by his talking one day at some length on the question of anti-British feeling in America. He ascribes it, of course, chiefly to the Irish. He does not believe in propaganda as a means of bringing the two countries closer together but thinks that the war will do much to help us understand each other better and that afterwards we shall gradually be drawn closer as we work together for the same ideals.

I find the President very interested in personalities. He was anxious to hear about our leading men, their characteristics and mode of life. He has interesting and novel ideas about the writing of history which is one of his favorite occupations. He misses, he says, the college life and the pleasant association with his fellow professors.

I must close this letter now to catch tonight's mail. It has been, as I feared, very rambling. Is there any chance of your coming back with Reading? If not, I think I shall try and get over for a short trip as soon as Reading returns.

With very best wishes and please continue to write and send me all the news you can.　　　Yours ever,　[William Wiseman]

CCL (W. Wiseman Papers, CtY).

Instructions to the Secretary of War[1]

The White House, 31 August, 1918.

In the foregoing case the sentences imposed upon Corporal Robert Tillman, Company I, Corporal John Geter, Company I, Corporal James H. Mitchell, Company I, Private First Class John H. Gould, Company I, Private Henry L. Chenault, Company I, Private Edward Porter, Jr., Company I, Private Robert Smith, Company I, Private Hezekiah C. Turner, Company I, Corporal Quiller Walker, Company K, and Private Charlie Banks, Company M, each and all of the 24th Infantry, are, in each and every case, commuted to dishonorable discharge from the service, forfeiture of all pay and allowances due or to become due and confinement at hard labor, at such place as the reviewing authority may direct, for the term of their natural lives, and as thus commuted each and every of the sentences will be carried into execution.

Woodrow Wilson

In the foregoing case the sentences imposed upon Private Babe Collier, Company I, Private Thomas McDonald, Company I, Private James Robinson, Company I, Private Joseph Smith, Company I, and Private Albert D. Wright, Company I, all of the 24th Infantry, are, in each and every case, confirmed and will be carried into execution.   Woodrow Wilson

TS MSS (WDR, RG 165, No. 114575, DNA).
  [1] Baker wrote this and the following document.

A Statement[1]

The White House, 31 August, 1918.

I have affirmed the action of the courts-martial in the so-called Washington and Tillman Cases and ordered the commutation of ten death sentences to life imprisonment; and I file this memorandum with The Adjutant General of the Army in order that the basis of my action may be a matter of record.

On the 23d of August, 1917, the so-called Houston Riot took place. A mutinous and riotous group of soldiers participated in the affair, causing in all the deaths of fifteen persons and the serious wounding of twelve others, many of whom were innocent bystanders and all of whom were peaceably disposed civilians of the city of Houston. Very searching and thorough investigations were made into the riot, its causes, and the actions of the persons who participated with the result that three groups of soldiers were tried by court-martial, the cases being known, respectively, as the Nesbit, the Washington, and the Tillman Cases. The records of these trials have been carefully examined by the Judge Advocate General and the Secretary of War, and they disclose that in each instance the Court was properly constituted, was composed of officers of experience and sobriety of judgment, and that the rights of the defendants were surrounded at every point by those safeguards which an humane administration of the law accords to those charged with grave offenses. No legal errors, prejudicing the rights of the accused, have been found; indeed, the seriousness of the cases appears to have challenged the attention of the military authorities from the outset and extraordinary precautions were taken to ensure the fairness of the trials.

The Nesbit Case was first tried. It resulted in the acquittal of five of the defendants and the conviction of the remainder with four sentenced to brief terms of imprisonment, forty-one sentenced to life imprisonment, and thirteen to death. These death sentences were reviewed by the Commanding General of the Southern Department and executed.

Later, the Washington and Tillman Cases proceeded to trial, involving altogether fifty-five persons, and resulting in death sentences imposed upon sixteen and imprisonment upon the remainder for various terms of years, except as to three in the Tillman Case, two of whom were acquitted and as to one of whom the charges were dismissed. The review which I have been called upon to make, therefore, involves death penalties imposed upon sixteen persons. Of these I have affirmed six, because the persons involved were found guilty by plain evidence of having deliberately, under circumstances of shocking brutality, murdered designated and peaceably disposed civilians. The remaining ten death sentences I have commuted to life imprisonment for the reason that, while deeply engaged in this riotous mutiny, the men involved are not shown by the record personally and directly to have caused the death of designated individuals.

The offense of which these soldiers were guilty is one of the greatest gravity. The Government relies upon its soldiers for the defense of the liberties of the people and when soldiers, forgetting their obligation, break over the restraints of discipline and become a riotous and murderous mob, the very foundations of order are shaken. When peaceably disposed and innocent civilians are the victims of this sort of riot a stern redress of their wrongs is the surest protection of society against their recurrence. I, therefore, find that the action taken by the Commanding General of the Southern Department was legal and justified by the record and direct the execution of the sentences in the six cases above referred to. I commute the remaining sentences because I believe the lesson of this lawless riot will have been adequately pointed by the action already taken and that now directed, and also because I desire the clemency here ordered to be a recognition of the splendid loyalty of the race to which these soldiers belong and an inspiration to the people of that race to further zeal and service to the country of which they are citizens and for the liberties of which so many of them are now bravely bearing arms at the very front of great fields of battle.   Woodrow Wilson

CC MS (WP, DLC).
    [1] Published in the *Official Bulletin*, II (Sept. 5, 1918), 4.

To Edward Mandell House

My dear House: The White House 31 August, 1918.

Thank you for the copies of the letters from Frank Cobb[1] and Lippmann.[2]

I am very much puzzled as to who sent Lippmann over to inquire into matters of propaganda. I have found his judgment most unsound, and therefore entirely unserviceable, in matters of that sort because he, in common with the men of The New Republic, has ideas about the war and its purposes which are highly unorthodox from my own point of view.[3]

What he says about his interviews with Sir William Tyrrell interests me very much, but if he thinks that Lord Eustace Percy is equally trustworthy, he is vastly mistaken. He is one of the most slippery and untrustworthy of the men we have had to deal with here.

In great haste, with most affectionate messages from us all,
                    Affectionately yours,   Woodrow Wilson

TLS (E. M. House Papers, CtY).
    [1] F. I. Cobb to EMH, Aug. 27, 1918, TCL (WP, DLC). Cobb suggested that, when Charles E. Hughes filed his report on the aircraft industry, Wilson should "write him a little note, and give it out for publication, thanking him for the work he had done and the public service he had rendered." This action would emphasize the fact that the Hughes report was the administration's own report and thus would blunt criticism of the administration based upon the contents of the report.
    [2] W. Lippmann to EMH, Aug. 9, 1918, CCL, and Aug. 15, 1918, TCL, both in WP, DLC.
    [3] Lippmann had been recruited for intelligence and propaganda work in Europe by Capt. Heber Blankenhorn of the Military Intelligence Branch of the army. Lippmann had consulted House about the matter and House had given his enthusiastic approval. Lippmann had arrived in France on July 22. For a discussion of Lippmann's mission to Europe and the rather complex circumstances which led to Wilson's distrust of him, including summaries of the two letters cited in n. 2 above, see Ronald Steel, *Walter Lippmann and the American Century* (Boston, 1980), pp. 141-46.

To Perl D. Decker

My dear Mr. Decker: [The White House] 31 August, 1918.

House Resolution 12776 concerns so vital and interesting a matter that I would like very much to talk with you about it, and hope

that you will make an early appointment to see me at the White
House.   Sincerely yours,   Woodrow Wilson

TLS (Letterpress Books, WP, DLC).

To Stephen Samuel Wise[1]

My dear Rabbi Wise: [The White House] 31 August, 1918.
    I have watched with deep and sincere interest the reconstructive
work which the Weitzman Commission has done in Palestine at
the instance of the British Government, and I welcome an opportunity to express the satisfaction I have felt in the progress of the
Zionist movement in the United States and in the Allied countries
since the declaration by Mr. Balfour on behalf of the British Government, of Great Britain's approval of the establishment in Palestine of a national home for the Jewish people, and his promise
that the British Government would use its best endeavors to facilitate the achievement of that object, with the understanding that
nothing would be done to prejudice the civil and religious rights
of non-Jewish people in Palestine or the rights and political status
enjoyed by Jews in other countries.
    I think that all Americans will be deeply moved by the report
that even in this time of stress the Weitzman Commission has been
able to lay the foundation of the Hebrew University at Jerusalem,
with the promise that that bears of spiritual rebirth.
                Cordially and sincerely yours,   Woodrow Wilson

TLS (Letterpress Books, WP, DLC).
    [1] This letter, with the correct spelling, "Weizmann," was printed in the *Official Bul-
letin*, II (Sept. 5, 1918), 6.

From Robert Lansing, with Enclosure

My dear Mr. President: Washington August 31, 1918.
    I have just received the enclosed telegram which appears to me
to be extremely important on account of the necessity of action
here in case the policy is adopted. I would be glad if you would tell
me your views Tuesday after Cabinet meeting.
                    Faithfully yours,   Robert Lansing

TLS (SDR, RG 59, 763.72/13369, DNA).

E N C L O S U R E

Paris. August 30, 1918.

129. Enciphered by me. Strictly confidential. For the Secretary of State and Colonel House. At the request of General Pershing, I called upon him yesterday at his headquarters to discuss an idea which he has been turning over in his mind for several days. He believes that the successful advance of the Allies on the western front will continue and while he does not consider that the Germans are yet beaten, he is satisfied that the morale of their troops is bad. Under these circumstances, he thinks that united action should be taken to bring about the end of the (*) if possible before next year. He believes that if the President were now to urge the Allies to attack simultaneously on the Italian front at Saloniki and in Mesopotamia if possible, if he were to address words of encouragement to that section of the Russian public which is pro-Ally; if an intimation from the same source were conveyed to Austria-Hungary, Bulgaria and Turkey that the time has come for them to yield and if pressure were brought to bear upon the neutrals, especially Spain, to join the Allies, the defeat of Germany which he now considers certain would be hastened. General Pershing informs me that according to his Intelligence Service, the Germans are already moving supplies to the right bank of the Rhine and that an attack by the American army is now imminent. Frazier.   Bliss.[1]

T telegram (SDR, RG 59, 763.72/13369, DNA).
[1] Robert Woods Bliss, at this time Counselor of the American embassy in Paris.

From Robert Lansing, with Enclosure

My dear Mr. President: Washington August 31, 1918.

After our conversation yesterday I prepared for your consideration the enclosed draft of a public declaration in regard to the Czecho-Slovaks.

I find there is a disposition among the newspapermen to discuss—possibly to criticize—our silence in regard to this matter. I have been fortunate enough to be able to stop it thus far but to tell the truth it is getting out of hand. I hope therefore that we can do something very shortly.

Faithfully yours,   Robert Lansing

TLS (SDR, RG 59, 763.72/11135½, DNA).

ENCLOSURE

DRAFT OF PUBLIC DECLARATION.

August 30, 1918

The Czecho-Slovaks, having taken up arms against the German and Austro-Hungarian Empires and having placed organized armies in the field, are waging war against those Empires in accordance with the rules and practice of civilized nations and under officers of their own nationality.

The Czecho-Slovaks have, in the prosecution of their independent purposes, confided to the Czecho-Slovak National Council supreme political authority.

In view of these facts the Government of the United States recognizes—

That a state of belligerency exists between the Czecho-Slovaks and the German and Austro-Hungarian Empires; and

That the Czecho-Slovak National Council is a *de facto* belligerent government slothed [clothed] with proper authority to direct the military and political affairs of the Czecho-Slovaks.

The Government of the United States further declares that it is prepared to enter formally into relations with the *de facto* government thus recognized for the purpose of prosecuting the war against their common enemies, the Empire of Germany and the Empire of Austria-Hungary.

T MS (SDR, RG 59, 763.72/11135½, DNA).

From William Gibbs McAdoo

Dear Governor: White Sulphur Springs, August 31, 1918.

From the attached clipping[1] you will see that certain Government agencies, namely, the United States Shipping Board, the Bureau of Industrial Housing and Transportation of the Department of Labor and the United States Housing Corporation, have petitioned the Public Utilities Commission of New Jersey to grant a seven cent fare to Mr. McCarter's[1] Public Service Corporation. The Government, therefore, will have to take the responsibility for this increase if it is granted.

If these independent Government agencies are to intervene in these utility questions in various places throughout the country and the Administration is forced, therefore, to take the responsibility, I think it would be much wiser to ask the Interstate Commerce

Commission to act in all such cases or to appoint an independent commission along the line of Mr. Bertron's suggestions.

Affectionately yours,   W G McAdoo

TLS (WP, DLC).
    [1] It is missing.
    [2] Thomas Nesbitt McCarter.

From Edward William Pou

My dear Mr. President: Washington, D. C. August 31, 1918.

Upon reading your letter of August 22nd to Honorable Thetus W. Sims I am reminded that very probably I misunderstood your instructions with respect to the Water Power Bill. At the time it was handed to me I did not understand it was expected that I would introduce the Bill for consideration by the House. Therefore, I simply had a thousand copies printed for distribution among the Members and Senators particularly interested. There had been so much controversy over this great subject, not entirely unmixed with a little jealousy that I really feared to introduce the Bill myself and thereby attach my name to it. Therefore, I refrained from introducing it from the very best motives, not wishing to do anything which in the smallest degree would arouse controversy or possibly a little jealousy.

However, if I had understood that you expected the Bill to be introduced by me I would certainly have carried out the instructions. After reading your letter to Mr. Sims I felt that this explanation would not be out of place. My sole desire was to help put the Bill through.

With much respect, I remain,

Sincerely your friend,   Edward W. Pou

TLS (WP, DLC).

From Paul Samuel Reinsch

Chicago August Thirty-first,
Dear Mr. President: Nineteen Hundred Nineteen [Eighteen].

On the railway journey to Chicago, which I took immediately after my conversation with you,[1] I again thought over the problems we had been talking about, and in accordance with your expressed wish that I should communicate with you on these matters, I am setting down the things that appear to me most essential, beyond the memorandum already left with you.[2]

With respect to China: the essential requirement of the situation is, that the United States should without delay take action to provide a sound basis for Chinese Finance. It is therefore of the greatest importance that a favorable reply should come from our Allies, particularly from Japan, on the proposed co-operation.

Meanwhile, there is one matter of fundamental importance, in which I hope the Government will ask the American Bankers to proceed forthwith, without waiting at all for developments in the other matter.

In July, the Chinese Government again requested the British, French and American groups, who own the Hukuang Railway concession, to provide funds in order that the railway between Hankow and Canton might be completed. This is a matter, essential like none other, to the present and future development of China.

When this trunk line is completed, the North will be closely bound to the South. Political and commercial difficulties now existing in great numbers because of the lack of this communication, will disappear. China will be in a position, more adequately to mobilize her resources for use in the War.

I have most urgently suggested to the Secretary of State, that action on this matter should be taken. It is most desirable that it should be arranged immediately, at this time. The fact that our European Allies and America are carrying out their contract with the Chinese Government will exercise a beneficent influence, scarcely second to the actual completion of a general financing arrangement. The most urgent individual need of China will be met and constructive work encouraged. The seriousness of the United States in giving actual assistance will be proven by such action.

While this matter is entirely distinct from the proposed financial co-operation and constitutes the fulfillment of a contract now held with the Chinese Government, it would clear the air and facilitate the definitive conclusion of the arrangements proposed for sound financing by International Co-operation.

With respect to Siberia, and the policy of economic assistance to Russia: the urgency of immediate action is borne in on me by every consideration.

In connection with your inquiry concerning names—I have thought of several other men, who I believe possess the qualifications for success in this important enterprise: Secretary Houston, Governor-General Harrison of the Philippine Islands, Mr. Vanderlip of the National City Bank, Mr. Jos. E. Davies, Mr. Owen Young of the General Electric Company and President Van Hise, all possess marked abilities and qualities which would fit them for this task.

I always have to recur, however, in my mind, to the unequalled qualifications of Mr. Herbert Hoover; his experience has been world-wide. He is a great engineer as well as executive, of the highest standing with our Allies, prepared as no other man to deal with the greatest problem of Russia to-day, the food situation; possessed of practical experience in Russian affairs, though now, I believe, divested of actual interests there.

He has now so organized the Food Administration with highly competent associates, that his personal presence there, appears no longer absolutely necessary. His designation for the work would at once establish the nature of our aims in the mind of the whole World.

Of the other men, perhaps Secretary Houston, Mr. Morris and Governor-General Harrison, I should consider in the second place. The other men, I believe to be likewise qualified to insure success, and at any rate to be a most admirable reserve for assisting the Commissioner when appointed, in work on this side.

I believe that these men are of the type that would achieve the fullest results from the beneficent policy of preventing unprecedented suffering and of bringing the Russian Nation back to life by the side of her Allies.

These great matters have been with me day and night; they constitute to my mind the essential foundation for guiding affairs in Asia and Russia in such a manner as to avoid disaster and to achieve the great purpose for which this War is being waged.

With highest respect, and best wishes for your continued well being, I am, Dear Mr. President,

Faithfully yours,   Paul S. Reinsch

TLS (WP, DLC).
    [1] At the White House on August 28.
    [2] It is printed as an Enclosure with WW to RL, Aug. 22, 1918.

From Gordon Auchincloss

Dear Mr. President: [Washington] August 31, 1918.

I have told Sir William Wiseman, informally, that this Government would not welcome a visit from Mr. Hughes,[1] of Australia, if he proposed to make any speeches here concerning any sort of an economic combination against Germany after the war. Sir William assures me that he believes he can arrange it so that if Mr. Hughes comes here he will give out no interviews and will make no speeches on this subject. I suggested to Sir William that Mr. Hughes might return to Australia via Canada, so that there would be no chance for him to make a speech in this country. Sir William promised to let me know whether this could be arranged.

If the matter can be satisfactorily handled in this way, do you wish me to instruct the Embassy at London to refuse to visa Mr. Hughes' passport if he requests such a visa in order to permit him to pass through this country en route to Australia?

As an additional precaution, with your approval, I will send the enclosed cable.   Faithfully yours,   [Gordon Auchincloss]

CCL (G. Auchincloss Papers, CtY).
¹ That is, William Morris Hughes, Prime Minister of Australia.

Sir William Wiseman to Lord Reading

[New York] 31 Aug. 1918. 6.10 p.m.

CXP. No. 723 Very Secret and URGENT.

The President sent me a message yesterday through the State Department as follows:

U.S.G. learns Premier Hughes of Australia contemplates visiting the United States on his way home and while here will speak on the subject of the economic policy of the Allies advocating the same policy of retaliation which he has recently expounded in England. The President wishes you to know that if this is the purpose of Premier Hughes, his visit will be most unwelcome to the U.S.G. and that if he comes here and makes public speeches on the lines indicated, the President will feel obliged to state publicly that the United States entirely disassociates itself from Hughes' policy. In order to avoid the danger of serious misunderstanding the State Department urge that Hughes shall be persuaded to abandon his tour, and if he passes through the States on his way home, he should not make any public speeches or statements.

Auchincloss told me on the telephone this morning that Lansing wished me to come to Washington at once to discuss an important matter. Afterwards he decided that it could be explained to me over the telephone, which was done in the above sense. In further conversation I learned very confidentially that the President on hearing of Hughes' intention ordered Lansing to cable London to refuse Hughes an American visa to his passport, and it was when Lansing pointed out the seriousness of this step, that the President told him to take it up with me.

May I suggest it is important that you should send a message as soon as possible, which I may communicate to the President through Mr. Lansing.

T telegram (W. Wiseman Papers, CtY).

Sir Eric Geddes[1] to Franklin Delano Roosevelt

My dear Assistant Secretary,   [London] 31st August, 1918.

When you landed in this country and I had the pleasure of your company on a visit to Queenstown, you told me that you were proposing to give attention while over here and consult with us on the subject of repeat or additional orders for naval craft in your yards, as your builders would be asking for these upon your return to the United States.

You invited me to give some thought to the question of the co-ordinated efforts of the British and American forces in waters in which the British Admiralty take particular interest. These waters may roughly be defined as the waters of the North Sea and Atlantic generally speaking north of Brest, the Mediterranean for all light craft (where the British Commander-in-Chief at Malta is entrusted by the Allies with the command of the anti-submarine war and escort work), and also all convoy and escort work organised through the British Admiralty and the escort work done by the United States naval forces based on British ports. The accompanying chart illustrates the areas to which I refer.

It is of course impossible for us to say what the United States should build, as we have no knowledge nor are we directly charged in the provision they make in their own waters, and therefore it has been necessary for us to draw up a programme which provides for what we suggest should be a fixed minimum allotment to the waters I have defined—and which for a short term I will call "British waters"—out of the total provision made by the United States. I also venture to outline certain directions in which, in the opinion of the Board of Admiralty, the United States naval authorities might usefully extend their naval shipbuilding programme.

I would first like to refer to the question of capital ships. The strength of the Allies in capital ships, apart from battle cruisers, is preponderating, and in fact a good proportion of this strength is probably excessive and at the moment not called for, nor so far as one can foresee likely to be called for in this war. We are therefore building no battleships whatsoever, and while I appreciate that I am treading upon somewhat delicate ground in referring to the matter, I venture to suggest to the United States Navy Department that as long as there is a deficiency in essential craft, it is a matter for their most serious consideration whether they are justified in continuing to build capital ships, which I understand they are still doing in accordance with the instructions of the Congress. I hope that I shall not be accused of presumption, nor of interference with

[1] At this time, First Lord of the Admiralty.

matters which do not concern me in referring to this point; but with the general shortage of skilled labour and the serious shortage of skilled ratings which I understand the United States, in common with ourselves, experience, we have not felt justified in building capital ships because of the other great demands upon our resources; and we have in addition had to sacrifice very greatly our merchant shipping output in order to meet the imperative demands of the naval war.

Coming to battle cruisers the situation is different. In no particular naval arm are the Allies so unfavourably placed as in battle cruisers. The "Goeben"[2] is a menace to which there is no entirely satisfactory reply, because battle cruisers cannot be spared to prevent a raiding exit from the Dardanelles. In the North Sea the position as regards battle cruisers between the Grand Fleet and the High Seas Fleet is by no means one of complete satisfaction. The only other battle cruisers which exist are in the Japanese Navy, and repeated efforts have been made, without effect, to obtain their co-operation in European waters. In these circumstances, and having regard to the German battle cruiser building programme, we have felt obliged to go ahead with one battle cruiser, and it is a matter of high policy, having regard to the probable duration of the war, whether we should now undertake the completion of one or more of the three which are partially built in this country.

Turning now to the craft of smaller size than battle cruisers, and dealing only with the war demands of the waters which I have called the British waters, we would suggest that you frame your destroyer programme upon a basis of allotting to those waters between now and the 31st August 1919 a minimum of 128 additional destroyers permanently in commission. Thereafter, unless the naval situation changes, it would, in the opinion of my naval advisors, be adequate if that number were maintained and not necessarily increased.

As regards minesweepers, you will be aware that the British

---

[2] The German battle cruiser *Goeben* and her consort, the light cruiser *Breslau*, had become famous in August 1914 when they escaped from a near entrapment by a much larger British naval force in the Strait of Messina and had passed through the Dardanelles to take refuge in Turkish waters. This exploit was not only embarrassing to the British but also had very serious consequences for the political and military situation in the Mediterranean and the Near East. The two vessels spent the next three and one half years in the Bosporus, bottled up by a sizable British force maintained specifically for that purpose. Then, on January 20, 1918, the German ships sallied forth from the Dardanelles to attack British patrol craft and the naval base at Moudros, on Lemnos Island, Greece. *Breslau* sank after striking several mines, but *Goeben*, despite serious damage from mines and being stuck on a sandbank in the Dardanelles for the ensuing six days, eventually made her way to safety. As it turned out, the damage to *Goeben* was too extensive to be repaired at Constantinople and, unknown to the Allies, she remained disabled for the rest of the war. See Arthur J. Marder, *From the Dreadnought to Scapa Flow: The Royal Navy in the Fisher Era, 1904-1919* (5 vols., London, 1961-70), II, 20-41; V, 12-20.

minesweeping is a very formidable task, and we actually sweep some 45,000 square miles of water every month. It is suggested that the United States might wish to undertake a proportion of this naval service, taking over definite areas to sweep, and we suggest for your consideration that you should arrange a programme of building to commission 3 minesweepers per month from the 1st January next year.

Then as regards trawlers, it is suggested that the United States might make a contribution to the trawler fleet in the areas concerned from the 1st July next year, and complete and commission at the rate of 4.5 per month for service in these waters.

As regards minelayers, as you are aware, there are two distinct classes of minelayer. There is the ordinary large minelayer of considerable size—usually a converted merchant ship—which is used on a large minefield which can be well covered by naval forces to protect it from raids by the enemy. There is also the very fast offensive minelayer used particularly at present for work close in to the German shores and in the Bight. We are at the present time using some of our destroyers for this work, but their carrying capacity is small. Similarly cruisers are fitted for this work to carry 80 mines, but having regard to the protection required by a destroyer screen it is uneconomical to use these craft for this purpose on account of their small carrying capacity. We are therefore proposing to embark upon a programme of fast minelayers for this offensive work in the North Sea, and we have two vessels of a suitable character at present under construction, and propose to go on with an improved type as soon as slips become available. We suggest, however, that the United States might desire to contribute to this offensive minelaying, and that the Navy Department might consider laying down at once two or more fast minelayers to carry 200 mines with a minimum speed of 30 knots. Should you desire it we should be glad to place at the disposal of the Navy Department any further information on the subject, together with designs if required.

A further direction in which we would invite the United States co-operation is in the construction of craft suitable for ocean escort work. As you are aware last summer, and again this summer, the sinking of merchant ships by submarines has been undertaken much further out in the Atlantic than during the intervening months. Whether this fluctuation as between inshore sinking and ocean sinking is caused entirely by the weather, or is due—in part at any rate—to the offensive measures of the Allies, we are unable to say, but the fact is undoubted that at the present time and during the last 6 months there has been a very noticeable tendency for a larger proportion of submarines, other than those of the "cruiser" type, to operate further out in the Atlantic. We think that although our methods for dealing with the submarine on passage and inshore are by no means perfect, they are proceeding on lines calculated to give the most satisfactory results as the efficiency of materiel and personnel improves, but we are not satisfied that we have got the appropriate reply to the actions of the submarine far out at sea, say between the 250 mile and 500 mile belt from the coast. Admiral Sims and his officers have been considering this matter with the British naval staff, and whatever type of craft might be considered the most desirable by our naval advisors, I suggest to you that the time has arrived when we should lay our plans to have a more suitable type of escort craft for ocean work than exists to-day in adequate numbers. We have developed a comparatively satisfactory slow ocean escort craft called the "patrol gun-boat," and if more heavily armed with say a 5.5 gun this craft may be very useful for ocean escort, but it is generally admitted that it does not combine all the qualities desired. It must be a good sea boat; its radius of turning must be small; it must have the capability of quickly attaining high speed; it must have a long radius of action; it must be mechanically simple and capable of being manned by a less experienced and less highly trained crew. A patrol gun-boat is being used with great satisfaction in the medium 10 knot through convoys to Port Said, and we have a considerable number of these under construction. Experience has shown that when all is said and done the destroyer is the most satisfactory known type of vessel for this work, but it has certain drawbacks the chief of which are the time occupied in construction and the difficulty in finding the necessary skilled personnel to man them, and I venture to suggest that the matter is one deserving the most careful consideration of the United States Navy Department as it is receiving ours.

You will of course understand that the allotments out of your total future resources, which I have outlined, are put forward as minimum allotments.

In concluding this letter I would like to reiterate that I would not presume to write in this sense had you not invited me to give the matter some consideration, and I feel sure that my action will therefore not be misunderstood.   Yours sincerely,   E. Geddes

TCL (WP, DLC).

A Labor Day Message

Labour Day, 1918. 2 September.

My Fellow Citizens: Labor Day, 1918, is not like any Labor Day that we have known. Labor Day was always deeply significant with us. Now it is supremely significant. Keenly as we were aware a year ago of the enterprise of life and death upon which the nation had embarked, we did not perceive its meaning as clearly as we do now. We knew that we were all partners and must stand and strive together, but we did not realize as we do now that we are all enlisted men, members of a single army, of many parts and many tasks but commanded by a single obligation, our faces set towards a single object. We now know that every tool in every essential industry is a weapon, and a weapon wielded for the same purpose that an army rifle is wielded,—a weapon which if we were to lay down no rifle would be of any use.

And a weapon for what? What is the war for? Why are we enlisted? Why should we be ashamed if we were not enlisted? At first it seemed hardly more than a war of defence against the military aggression of Germany. Belgium had been violated, France invaded, and Germany was afield again, as in 1870 and 1866, to work out her ambitions in Europe; and it was necessary to meet her force with force. But it is clear now that it is much more than a war to alter the balance of power in Europe. Germany, it is now plain, was striking at what free men everywhere desire and must have,—the right to determine their own fortunes, to insist upon justice, and to oblige governments to act for them and not for the private and selfish interest of a governing class. It is a war to make the nations and peoples of the world secure against every such power as the German autocracy represents. It is a war of emancipation. Not until it is won can men anywhere live free from constant fear or breathe freely while they go about their daily tasks and know that governments are their servants, not their masters.

This is, therefore, the war of all wars which labour should support and support with all its concentrated power. The world cannot be safe, men's lives cannot be secure, no man's rights can be confidently and successfully asserted against the rule and mastery of arbitrary groups and special interests, so long as governments like that which, after long premeditation, drew Austria and Germany into this war are permitted to control the destinies and the daily fortunes of men and nations, plotting while honest men work, laying the fires of which innocent men, women and children are to be the fuel.

You know the nature of this war. It is a war which industry must sustain. The army of laborers at home is as important, as essential, as the army of fighting men in the far fields of actual battle. And the laborer is not only needed as much as the soldier. It is his war. The soldier is his champion and representative. To fail to win would be to imperil everything that the laborer has striven for and held dear since freedom first had its dawn and his struggle for justice began. The soldiers at the front know this. It steels their muscles to think of it. They are crusaders. They are fighting for no selfish advantage for their own nation. They would despise anyone who fought for the selfish advantage of any nation. They are giving their lives that homes everywhere, as well as the homes they love in America, may be kept sacred and safe, and men everywhere be free as they insist upon being free. They are fighting for the ideals of their own land,—great ideals, immortal ideals, ideals which shall light the way for all men to the places where justice is done and men live with lifted heads and emancipated spirits. That is the reason they fight with solemn joy and are invincible!

Let us make this, therefore, a day of fresh comprehension not only of what we are about, and of renewed and clear-eyed resolution, but a day of consecration also, in which we devote ourselves without pause or limit to the great task of setting our own country and the whole world free to render justice to all and of making it impossible for small groups of political rulers anywhere to disturb our peace or the peace of the world or in any way to make tools and puppets of those upon whose consent and upon whose power their own authority and their own very existence depend.

We may count upon each other. The nation is of a single mind. It is taking counsel with no special class. It is serving no private or single interest. Its own mind has been cleared and fortified by these days which burn the dross away. The light of a new conviction has penetrated to every class amongst us. We realize as we never realized before that we are comrades, dependent on one another, irresistible when united, powerless when divided. And so we join hands to lead the world to a new and better day.[1]

WWT MS (WP, DLC).
[1] There is a WWsh outline of this message in WP, DLC. This message was published, e.g., in the *Official Bulletin*, II (Sept. 3, 1918), 4.

Three Letters to Robert Lansing

My dear Mr. Secretary,   The White House. 2 September, 1918.

I respectfully suggest the following as a partial modification of your wording[1] of the declaration which we must make with regard to to [the] belligerency of the Czecho-Slovaks:

The Czecho-Slovak peoples having taken up arms against the

German and Austro-Hungarian Empires and having placed organized armies in the field which are waging war against those Empires under officers of their own nationality and in accordance with the rules and practices of civilized nations; and

The Czecho-Slovaks having, in prosecution of their independent purposes in the present war, confided supreme political authority to the Czecho-Slovak National Council,

The Government of the United States recognizes that a state of belligerency exists between the Czecho-Slovaks thus organized and the German and Austro-Hungarian Empires.

It also recognizes the Czecho-Slovak National Council as a *de facto* belligerent government clothed with proper authority to direct the military and political affairs of the Czecho-Slovaks.

The Government of the United States further declares that it is prepared to enter formally into relations with the *de facto* government thus recognized for the purpose of prosecuting the war against the common enemy, the Empires of Germany and Austro-hungary.[2]

It seems to me that you have successfully stated both the actual facts and the new legal relationship which we assume.

Faithfully Yours,   W.W.

WWTLI (SDR, RG 59, 763.72/11136½, DNA).
   [1] That is, the Enclosure printed with RL to WW, Aug. 31, 1918 (second letter of that date).
   [2] This declaration was published in this revised form in the *Official Bulletin*, II (Sept. 3, 1918), 1.

My dear Mr. Secretary,   The White House. 2 September, 1918.

Such a message as this from General Pershing[1] surprises me very much. It is the first time he has undertaken to give advice, political as well as military, in this way.

I am clear that it would be out of the question for me to urge, without the (at least intimated) concurrence of the Supreme Military Council, such action in all the military theatres of the war; and it is equally clear to me that events, not any suggestions from us, will determine the action of Bulgaria and Turkey. You know the advances that have been made to us from Bulgaria and Turkey and how imprudent and unwise it would be for us to use the only channels that are open.

Baker, as you know, is now on the water, on his way to the other side, and Pershing will have an opportunity to confer with him about the whole matter. Baker['s] special commission is to have every question about the actual conduct of the war and its effective pressure to an early conclusion that can be answered now, and with the utmost possible definiteness.[2]

Faithfully Yours, W.W.

WWTLI (SDR, RG 59, 763.72/13378½, DNA).
[1] That is, the Enclosure printed with RL to WW, Aug. 31, 1918 (first letter of that date).
[2] This sentence *sic*.

My dear Mr. Secretary, The White House. 2 September, 1918.

May I not ask you to have a full conference with Mr. Baruch about this matter?[1] He is at the centre of such information. He and I were speaking of it the other day, and I found that he was familiar with the available stocks in the hands of the War Department. His information and advice ought to enable us to get a final action.

Am I not right in the impression that it was understood that the Japanese were to supply and supply at once the necessary military supplies for the Czechs?

By the way, it begins to look as if the plan of the Japanese were to do the fighting on their own plan and let the Czecho-Slovaks tag along, instead of acting themselves as a supporting force.

Faithfully Yours, W.W.

WWTLI (SDR, RG 59, 860F.24/9½, DNA).
[1] See RL to WW, Aug. 29, 1918 (second letter of that date).

To Robert Lansing, with Enclosure

My dear Mr. Secretary, The White House. 2 September, 1918.

These are the very questions Baker has gone over to settle, so far as we are concerned, and to insist that the Allies settle in a complete programme of cooperation. I have authorized him to assemble all programmes that we have had any part in formulating and discuss all the elements involved.

I think it will be sufficient to ask Barklay [Barclay] to request Lord Reading to consult with Baker immediately upon his arrival in London. Faithfully Yours, W.W.

WWTLI (SDR, RG 59, 763.72/13439, DNA).

ENCLOSURE

COMMUNICATION FROM LORD READING TO THE SECRETARY OF STATE.[1]

August 30, 1918.

The request of the United States Administration for cargo tonnage in connection with the proposed programme of transport of 80 divisions of American troops to France has been before the Allied Maritime Transport Council which has been sitting this week in London to consider the demands upon the world tonnage made by the various programme committees which include not only the food committees dealing with requirements for munitions and those raw materials which go into munitions. The American Representatives did not take part as they had no instructions from their Government.

It is plain that the furnishing of further cargo tonnage can only be effected if the three European Allies agree to sacrifice the importation of part of those commodities which had hitherto been considered essential both for military purposes and for the maintenance of the morale of the civilian population. This raises a very serious question. The Governments of the three Allied nations are prepared to ask their people to make every possible sacrifice but it must be remembered that these cannot go beyond a certain point. Reductions have already been made in order to ensure the uninterrupted shipment and maintenance of the American troops. For instance, the use of British transports now promised until the end of this year means an additional loss of 250,000 tons of cargo space per month that is of 1,500,000 tons in six months. The further grave reductions required in order to comply with the request in the telegram to General Bliss[2] must be examined with the greatest care. There is not sufficient information before us with regard to the basis of calculation of the War Department to enable the necessary consideration to be given to the possibility of France and England furnishing part of the supplies now proposed to be transported. This information will doubtless be supplied within a short period by the War Department.

Something further is, however, required. In order that the three European Governments may impose upon themselves any further sacrifice that this supreme effort for a victory in 1919 may entail, a sacrifice which we know full well that America will be ready now as in the past to share, it is vital that the Governments with whom the responsibility will rest for imposing these restrictions upon imports be able to assure that the sacrifices are imperative and are made in pursuance of a common policy followed by the four Governments. This involves joint consideration of the resources in relation to needs.

The representatives of the British, French and Italian Governments fully realize how vital and urgent it is that the question of cargo tonnage of the army supply programme should be settled at the earliest possible moment. Therefore the British and Allied Governments would earnestly request that those responsible for the allocation of American tonnage and limitation of American imports should come to London as soon as possible. We will arrange for the Ministers of Great Britain, France and Italy to meet them in London and determine the final action. It is in proof the promptest and most effective way of arriving at a decision.

The representatives of France and Italy have joined in preparing this cable and are instructing their Ambassadors at Washington to support the request contained therein in such manner as may be deemed most suitable.

T MS (SDR, RG 59, 763.72/13439, DNA).
 [1] Enclosed in C. A. de R. Barclay to RL, Aug. 31, 1918, TLS (SDR, RG 59, 76372/13439, DNA).
 [2] That is, P. C. March to T. H. Bliss, No. 74, July 23, 1918.

To Herbert Clark Hoover

My dear Hoover,   The White House. 2 Sept. 1918

The conclusions and plans stated in the enclosed[1] have my entire approval   Woodrow Wilson

ALS (Hoover Archives, CSt-H).
 [1] HCH to WW, Aug. 29, 1918, TLS (WP, DLC). Hoover stated that the Sugar Equalization Board intended to purchase large quantities of Cuban sugar at the price of five and a half cents a pound. He requested Wilson's approval to fix the retail price of sugar at nine cents a pound, which would result in an increase to the consumer of one cent a pound over the current rate. Hoover admitted that, with the price fixed at this level, some low-cost domestic sugar producers would make extortionate profits, but, he said, they would be absorbed by the excess-profits tax. On the other hand, some of the high-cost domestic producers would actually lose money, but Hoover proposed to compensate them out of the income which the Sugar Equalization Board would derive from the sale of the cheaper Cuban sugar. Hoover then pointed out that, under his proposed plan, the Sugar Equalization Board would probably accumulate a net profit of up to $25,000,000 during the next twelve months from its various operations. Although this money would ultimately either be distributed to the consumers or turned over to the Treasury, Hoover still thought that it was necessary to obtain Wilson's consent to his suggested scheme, in order to be able to meet any criticism which might arise in the future.

To Joseph Patrick Tumulty, with Enclosure

Dear Tumulty: [The White House] 2 September, 1918

I think our tip should be that it is the duty of these gentlemen to stand by their flocks, unless it is very evident that they can be dispensed with.   The President

TL (WP, DLC).

Robert Hugh Morris[1] to Joseph Patrick Tumulty

My dear Mr. Tumulty,   Stamford, Connecticut August 29, 1918

With all the multitudes of details, as well as the great moments of state, which devolve in this trying time upon our President, it is little short of criminal to lay one other, even the smallest matter, upon his mind.

I am an old Princeton man, and a minister of the Presbyterian Church. Many of the clergy of my own and of other denominations have asked me substantially this question: "What is my duty in the matter? I am within the new draft limits, am married, and have children; but I detest and abhor the very idea of being thought a slacker. Can I serve my country best by going to the front, or by staying in my parish?"

It has therefore occurred to me to ask, through you, our beloved President to give me a word which I may authoritatively pass on to my perplexed brethren, as to his judgment and wish in the matter. I realize that circumstances vary widely, but there is a sense in which many consecrated men face the self same questions in this matter. Should they refuse exemption; or are the clergy more needed in the home communities?

Busy and burdened as he is, I believe the President will give you a word for me in this matter, if you find opportunity to lay it before him.

Thanking you, and regretting to lay even a slight additional task upon you, I am, dear sir,

Very respectfully yours,   Robert Hugh Morris

TLS (WP, DLC).
[1] Pastor of the First Presbyterian Church of Stamford, Conn.; Princeton Theological Seminary, 1906; M.A., Princeton, 1905.

From Winthrop More Daniels

My dear Mr. President: Washington September 2, 1918.

Your letter of August 30th, with accompanying enclosures, were found awaiting me on my return yesterday.

Your letter propounds two different plans for the relief of certain public utilities. The first, outlined in the draft of the proposed proclamation, consists of a National Commissioner or Commission as a Public Utilities War Board; the second, contemplates that the Interstate Commerce Commission shall hear, judge and recommend to state and local rate-making bodies the proper treatment to be accorded their public utilities.

My best judgment is unequivocally adverse to the first plan. In the second my confidence is not complete. Permit me to suggest an alternative.

(1) A National Commissioner (or Commission) for Public Utilities, so far as it could only recommend rate increases to state and local rate-fixing bodies, would be impotent *de jure* and irritating *de facto*. It would nominally have power to recommend rates to bodies already vested with the right and duty to act in the premises, whose first-hand knowledge is based on longer and more intimate contact with the utilities involved than could be had by the Federal agency. Especially where state and local rate-fixing tribunals have already accorded relief by permitting rate increases,—and there are a substantial number which have so acted,—the creating of such Federal agency would inevitably create irritation. Added emphasis is given this fact by reason of the marked disquietude manifested already by certain state regulatory commissions which feel they have not been permitted to give that cooperation in transportation matters which they desired.

A still more dangerous policy suggested in the proposed proclamation is the taking over of possession and control (with rate-fixing powers) of electric railways where the

"Local regulatory bodies or agencies do not exist, or are inadequate, or do not act with the necessary promptness."

This would virtually involve the Federal Treasury's becoming responsible for their credit and finances, and would put an additional and unnecessarily heavy strain upon the National Credit.

(2) The alternative plan that the Interstate Commerce Commission shall

"Hear, form an independent judgment, and make public recommendations as to the treatment of state and local utilities by the state and the municipal rate-fixing tribunals"

would be subject to many of the infirmities inherent in an independent National Commission for Public Utilities, to wit, legal impotence and the irritation and jealousy of state tribunals. It might however happen that the Commission could act as arbiter or intermediary, in certain instances where the owners and the users of the utility property reside in different localities.

(3) My suggested alternative is that the President by proclamation press home to Governors and State and Municipal authorities the controlling fact that the burden of sustaining the credit and service of these utilities is properly a state and municipal burden which ought not to be unloaded upon the Federal Government. The steam railroads are essentially National highways. Trolleys and these utilities are in essence state highways and local enterprises. The gist of the trouble is financial. But the war has as yet hardly touched

state or municipal credit. The need may be met without issuing in competition with Federal bonds, state and municipal securities. Massachusetts has already assumed this burden by the simple but effective method of guaranteeing a moderate return upon the securities properly outstanding of the Boston Elevated and Bay State trolley systems and of putting the management into the hands of public trustees on the service-at-cost principle.

The States should, in my judgment, be exhorted to assume what is their proper burden. I believe that they would patriotically respond. State Governors might be asked to call special sessions of the legislatures, when necessary, to amend, repeal or enact laws to take care of the war needs of these utilities, leaving *post bellum* conditions to the regulatory commissions. I have ventured to draft and enclose a proclamation embodying this view.

I may add that I have conferred with my colleague, Commissioner Anderson,[1] on this matter. He thoroughly agrees in the view that it is vital that this burden of sustaining the credit of local utilities should be placed where it belongs, on the States.

Commissioner Anderson and I have also checked our own judgment by conference with Mr. Justice Brandeis who has given the matter careful consideration, and who authorizes me to say that he is in absolute concurrence with our view that the proposed burden is not one that should be assumed by the Federal Government.

With all good wishes,   Very sincerely,   W. M. Daniels

TLS (WP, DLC).
    [1] That is, George Weston Anderson.

A Statement

[Sept. 3, 1918]

No study is more important to the child than the study of the Bible and of the truths which it teaches, and there is no more effective agency for such study than the Sunday School. It certainly is one of the greatest factors in our lives in the building of character and the development of moral fibre, for its influence begins almost as soon as the child is able to talk and continues throughout life. The Sunday School lesson of today is the code of morals of tomorrow. Too much attention can not be paid the work which the Sunday School is doing.   Woodrow Wilson

TS MS (Letterpress Books, WP, DLC).

To Robert Lansing, with Enclosure

My dear Mr. Sec'y   The White House. 3 Sept., 1918

Who *is* "Captain" Lippmann and who commissioned him to assess our propaganda?   W.W.

ALI (WP, DLC).

E N C L O S U R E

Robert Woods Bliss to Robert Lansing

Paris. August 31, 1918.

131. Strictly confidential. For the Secretary of State and Colonel House. Captain Lippmann who has just returned from England informs me that while in London Sir William Urall [Tyrrell] stated to him that (despite?) President's (*) to pool all information which he could gather at the Foreign Office with some American representative at the Embassy in London he was apparently unable to find such a person amongst the staff of the Embassy. Lippmann suggests that Hoover would be an excellent man for the position of high commissioner Great Britain. He thinks it would be quite possible for Hoover to direct (readjustments?) in Europe as part of his regular functions. Lippmann has promised to give me a report on Monday for transmission to you on the shortcomings of our propaganda system in England where he has had an opportunity of studying it at close range. Frazier.   Bliss.

(*) Apparent omission.

TC Telegram (WP, DLC).

From Robert Lansing, with Enclosure

My dear Mr. President: Washington September 3, 1918.

I enclose for your consideration a letter which I have just received from Judge Gerard making application for the post of Ambassador to Great Britain.   Faithfully yours,   Robert Lansing

TLS (R. Lansing Papers, NjP).

ENCLOSURE

James Watson Gerard to Robert Lansing

My dear Mr. Secretary: New York. Sept. 1st, 1918

I hereby apply for the position left vacant by the resignation of Walter Hines Page.   Ever yours,   James W. Gerard.

ALS (R. Lansing Papers, NjP).

To Robert Lansing

Dear Mr. Sec'y   The White House. 3 Sept., 1918

It seems to me that all you need do is to acknowledge this. It is truly extraordinary!   W.W.

ALI (R. Lansing Papers, NjP).

To William Bauchop Wilson

My dear Mr. Secretary: The White House 3 September, 1918.

It isn't true, is it, that the Bureau of Industrial Housing and Transportation of your Department has joined with the United States Shipping Board in petitioning the Public Utilities Commission of New Jersey to grant a seven-cent fare to the New Jersey Public Service Corporation? Somebody has sent me a clipping from a newspaper which makes that statement,[1] and I know so much about the absolute unworthiness of that whole New Jersey Public Service crowd that I hope nothing of the sort has happened. I know you will pardon this inquiry about a matter which disturbs me.
            Cordially and sincerely yours,   Woodrow Wilson[2]

TLS (received from Mary A. Strohecker).
    [1] "War Boards Ask 7 c. Jersey Trolley Fare," unidentified newspaper clipping, WP, DLC.
    [2] Wilson made the same inquiry of the Shipping Board: WW to E. N. Hurley, Sept. 3, 1918, TLS (Letterpress Books, WP, DLC).

To Herbert Clark Hoover[1]

My dear Mr. Hoover: The White House 3 September, 1918.

As was to have been expected and indeed could hardly have been avoided, the exercise by several different agencies of the Government of the power to commandeer has resulted in some cases in conflict, not alone with one another but with the rulings of the

Priorities Committee, as to the distribution of material among the various interested departments and industries. The instances of this sort have been numerous and serious enough, I believe, to justify me in making this request: that the commandeering power should not hereafter be exercised over any of the material industries or industrial agencies of the country without first consulting the Chairman of the War Industries Board.

I think that this is one of the most important and urgent coordinations remaining to be effected. I am confident that the consultation that I request will lead to the fullest cooperation and not to embarrassment, and I hope that it will be possible by this method to effect better results than could be effected by concentrating the commandeering power in one agency.

Cordially and sincerely yours,   Woodrow Wilson

TLS (Hoover Archives, CSt-H).
  ¹ Wilson sent the following letter, on the same date, *mutatis mutandis*, to NDB, JD, E. N. Hurley, and H. A. Garfield, all TLS, Letterpress Books, WP, DLC.

To Edward William Pou

My dear Mr. Pou: The White House 3 September, 1918.

I know you so well and trust you so entirely that no such explanation as you are generous enough to make in your letter of August 31st is ever necessary, so far as I am concerned. The Water Power Bill has had so exceptional a status since the combined committee was formed that I myself had no judgment at all as to the parliamentary course that should be pursued for its introduction and, you may be sure, never gave that part of it a thought.

Cordially and sincerely yours,   Woodrow Wilson

TLS (E. W. Pou Papers, Nc-Ar).

To Raymond Blaine Fosdick

My dear Mr. Fosdick: [The White House] 3 September, 1918

May I not call your attention to a matter which has been recently engaging my thought not a little?

The War Department has recognized the Young Men's Christian Association, the Young Women's Christian Association, the National Catholic War Council, the Jewish Welfare Board, the War Camp Community Service, the American Library Association, and the Salvation Army as accepted instrumentalities through which the men in the ranks are to be assisted in many essential matters of recreation and morale.

It was evident from the first, and has become increasingly evident, that the services rendered by these agencies to our army and to our Allies are essentially one and all of a kind and must of necessity, if well rendered, be rendered in the closest cooperation. It is my judgment, therefore, that we shall secure the best results in the matter of the support of these agencies, if these seven societies will unite their forthcoming appeals for funds, in order that the spirit of the country in this matter may be expressed without distinction of race or religious opinion in support of what is in reality a common service.

This point of view is sustained by the necessity, which the war has forced upon us, of limiting our appeals for funds in such a way that two or three comprehensive campaigns shall take the place of a series of independent calls upon the generosity of the country.

Will you not, therefore, as Chairman of the Commission on Training Camp Activities, be good enough to request the societies in question to combine their approaching appeals for funds in a single campaign, preferably during the week of November 11th, so that in their solicitation of funds, as well as in their work in the field, they may act in as complete cooperation and fellowship as possible?

In inviting these organizations to give this new evidence of their patriotic cooperation, I wish it distinctly understood that their compliance with this request will not in any sense imply the surrender on the part of any of them of its distinctive character and autonomy, because I fully recognize the fact that each of them has its own traditions, principles, and relationships which it properly prizes and which, if preserved and strengthened, make possible the largest service.

At the same time, I would be obliged if you would convey to them from me a very warm expression of the Government's appreciation of the splendid service they have rendered in ministering to the troops at home and over seas in their leisure time. Through their agencies the moral and spiritual resources of the nation have been mobilized behind our forces and used in the finest way, and they are contributing directly and effectively to the winning of the war.

It has been gratifying to find such a fine spirit of cooperation among all the leaders of the organizations I have mentioned. This spirit, and the patriotism of all the members and friends of these agencies, give me confidence to believe that the united war work campaign will be crowned with abundant success.

Cordially and sincerely yours,   Woodrow Wilson

TLS (Letterpress Books, WP, DLC).

To Maurice McAuliffe[1]

My dear Sir: [The White House] 3 September, 1918.

May I not acknowledge receipt of the letter of August 31st signed by yourself, Mr. Gustafson, Mr. Hampton, Mr. Hyde, and Mr. Lowrie?[2] My announcement of the Government's present policy with regard to the price of wheat made the other day,[3] really makes an answer to your letter of August 31st unnecessary, but I wish nevertheless to acknowledge that letter and to express the hope that the policy set forth in my proclamation will seem to you and your associates a wise one. You will observe that I did not foreclose the question, but postponed its determination to a time when it will be much more possible than it is now to determine the actual elements of cost entering into the production of the next wheat harvest.

Cordially and sincerely yours, Woodrow Wilson

TLS (Letterpress Books, WP, DLC).

[1] Chairman of the executive committee of the National Wheat Growers' Association and president of the Kansas Farmers' Union.

[2] M. McAuliffe et al. to WW, Aug. 31, 1918, TLS (WP, DLC). The signers of this letter were all members of the executive committee of the National Wheat Growers' Association. They told Wilson that the wheat growers of the country could not afford to take further financial risks, and that, unless they were assured that they would not lose money on their crops in 1919, they would not be able to plant their normal acreage. They asked Wilson to let them know "very shortly" whether he intended to fix the price of wheat for 1919 and, if so, what this price would approximately be.

[3] That is, the Enclosure printed with HCH to WW, Aug. 30, 1918.

To Fred Loring Seely[1]

My dear Seely: [The White House] 3 September, 1918.

I have the most genuine sympathy with the interesting suggestion you make in your letter of August 30th,[2] but you probably do not know how perplexing and how much discussed a question you are broaching, because there is nothing not connected with the actual conduct of the war, I think, which we have debated more than the best way of recognizing services such as you refer to, and I must say that we have come to no common counsel in the matter.

At the same time, I think it would be perfectly proper and a fine thing (though you must allow me to give this opinion in the strictest confidence because it would lead to trouble elsewhere) for the Chamber of Commerce of any locality to recognize such services in any way that it deems most appropriate. Whether a copy of the seal of the United States in the form of a watch charm would be properly and legally used, is a question that I cannot answer. The gold eagle which I wear is a copy of the President's seal, which differs a little from the seal of the United States. If the lawyers of the Chamber of Commerce find that it is all right to use it, I should be very happy to send you a copy in the proper colors.

I am sincerely sorry to hear of the illness of the gentleman who, you fear, has brought it on by his labors on the Exemption Board. You do not mention his name.

Cordially and sincerely yours,   Woodrow Wilson

TLS (Letterpress Books, WP, DLC).
    [1] An old friend of Wilson's; founder and former publisher of the *Atlanta Georgian*; owner since 1917 of the Grove Park Inn in Asheville, N. C.
    [2] F. L. Seely to WW, Aug. 30, 1918, TLS (WP, DLC).

Two Letters from Edward Mandell House

Dear Governor: Magnolia, Massachusetts. September 3, 1918.

Do you not think the time has come for you to consider whether it would not be wise to try to commit the Allies to some of the things for which we are fighting?

As the Allies succeed, your influence will diminish. This is inevitable. By the time of the Conference you will be nraring [nearing] the end of your second term and this, too, will be something of a challenge to those, both at home and abroad, who have the will to oppose you. Therefore I believe that you should commit the Allies now to as much of your program as is possible. It is not probable that the person[n]el of the allied governments will be changed if things continue to go well, and you should count upon having to reckon with Lloyd George, Clemenceau, Sonninno and their kind. This would mean a hostile rather than a sympathetic membership.

While the liberals are largely with you at present, I have a feeling that you are not so strong among labor circles of either France or England as you were a few months ago. Such support, in the nature of things, is uncertain and erratic, and I do not believe will be steadfast or powerful enough to compel the reactionaries in authority to yield at the Peace Conference to American aims.

Could not a plan be thought out by which the Entente would be committed to certain things for which we stand and which are so essential, from our point of view, to the reconstruction of the world?

If the group I have mentioned come to the Congress flushed with victory, no appeal that you can make over their heads will be successful. In each country there will be men of vision and loftiness of purpose who will rally to your support, but they will be in the minority and their voices will be heard faintly by the great exultant throng intoxicated not alone by victory but by the thought of freedom from war.

If you read what Sir William Tyrrell said to Lippman[n] in the recent letters I sent you, you will be interested in his argument for forming a League of Nations now. It is not what Tyrrell says that impresses me so much, as the thought of what may be done at this time with a League of Nations and kindred things which may not be possible of accomplishment at the Peace Conference.

To agree with France, England, Italy and Japan upon the covenant for a League of Nations would not prevent its incorporation into the peace treaty. It would rather make it the more certain. The Central Powers could not object to a statement by the Allies as to a League of Nations and their conception of what it should be, and stating at the same time that they would propose its incorporation in the peace treaty.

If such a document as we have in mind should be accepted and made public, it could not have any but a good effect in the Central Powers and should shorten the war. If the convenant were published in agreement with England, France, Italy and Japan, there would be no opposition in this country worth mentioning.

If you are to take your Western trip, many things could be said in your speeches to clear the way for further action. I shall hope to be in Washington before you leave and to talk these things over in person.

With deep affection,   Devotedly yours,   E. M. House

Dear Governor: Magnolia, Massachusetts. September 3, 1918.

Lippmann was sent over by the War Department to deal with questions of propaganda in the enemy countries. You will remember that he was one of Baker's aides for a time.

I do not know how recently you have been in touch with Lippmann, but my impression is that he is not now in sympathy with the men who govern the policy of the New Republic. He went with Baker immediately after we declared war. He was always the ablest of that group and he is young enough to wean away from them and [be] broadened.   Affectionately yours,   E. M. House

Your labor day address was one of the best of its kind that you ever wrote. It will do great good.[1]

TLS (WP, DLC).
[1] EMHhw.

From George P. Hampton

Dear Mr. President: Washington, D. C. September 3, 1918

The complaint lodged with you on August 14th against the Federal Trade Commission by the Chamber of Commerce of the United States,[1] is precisely the sort of action which we anticipated certain business interests of the country would make against the Federal Trade Commission because of its conspicuous service to democracy. The Federal Trade Commission may have erred in judgment on some points but they have rendered a great service to the common people of the country. We have examined the several charges which the Chamber of Commerce makes against the Commission, and do not find any basis therefor. As you know, the agricultural interests of America had a deep rooted suspicion of the methods of the monopolistic business concerns which sought to dominate their respective fields. The attack of the Chamber of Commerce, for it cannot be otherwise designated, serves notice upon the farmers of the country that the business interests do not propose to brook any interference with their methods, however unjust and detrimental.

May we respectfully recall to your mind that the Chamber of Commerce was one of the big aggregations of business which stimulated the organization of the Advisory Commission of the Council of National Defense? The Board of Directors of the Chamber of Commerce, in their annual report of April this year, say:

"The passage of legislation by Congress, requiring that any committee member should declare his full interest in any concern with which the committee was dealing, with a view to Government purchases, brought a full realization to the Council of the necessity for complete reorganization."

Unfortunately, some business interests have made it clear that they propose, though of course we know without avail, to run the Government of the United States. The Journal of the American Bankers' Association for August this year, states editorially:

"Business after the war is to the prudent of only less concern than the present great business of winning complete victory. The world's outlook on business has changed. Everything economic is in a state of flux. Governments, by common consent, are engaging in enterprises foreign to their natures. They are 'taking over' business, we often hear. IT MAY BE NEARER THE TRUTH TO SAY THAT BUSINESS IS TAKING OVER THE GOVERNMENT."

The Federal Trade Commission has not acquiesced in such a view of the Government. It is therefore hated by the interests which rely upon privilege for existence.

On behalf of the many farm organizations for which this is the

National Headquarters, we ask that you will appoint to the two vacancies which now exist on the Commission, not men who have used their pretended loyalty as a means of enrichment during the war, nor men who believe it the function of business to take over the Government, but men of the type of Commissioners Colver and Murdock, whose aggressive fight against the grasping and illegal practices of the packers has done much to reassure farmers and city consumers alike that the people of the country are to have a square deal.

We have recently talked with many representative farmers and labor men from various sections of the country, and find they heartily approve the work of the Federal Trade Commission, and look with confidence to you, Mr. President, to appoint to the vacancies men who will aid the present commissioners carry forward to completion their great work.

Yours very truly,   Geo. P. Hampton

TLS (WP, DLC).
[1] See WW to JPT, Aug. 22, 1918, n. 1.

From the Diary of Josephus Daniels

September Tuesday 3 1918

Returned from Indianapolis. Reached cabinet meeting late.

W.W. said he was pained because W.J.B. represented Costa Rica,[1] the President[2] who had assumed the presidency after revolution. The first act of the administration, said WW, in which WJB & I were in perfect accord, was we would not encourage revolutions in Central and South America.[3] The present President, who came in by revolution, has had himself elected. Of course. He had the troops & the guns. If Mr. B. knew the forces behind him, he would not have accepted to represent him. Hardly had he usurped the place before the United Fruit Company had telegraphed from Key West seeking recognition for him. The agencies behind him are as if Wall Street proposed a plot & Mr. B would not stand for it if he knew.

Burleson said he claimed his predecessor[4] was pro-German and he had declared strongly against the Germans and ready to cooperate with us.

[1] About this matter, see WJB to WW, July 17, 1918, Vol. 48; WW to WJB, July 18, 1918; WJB to WW, July 19, 1918; and WW to WJB, July 23, 1918.
[2] That is, Gen. Federico Tinoco Granados.
[3] See the statement printed at March 12, 1913, Vol. 27.
[4] That is, Alfredo González Flores.

To Alexander Mitchell Palmer

My dear Palmer: The White House 4 September, 1918

I have no doubt that this letter is unnecessary, but several of my friends have reported to me a certain degree of uneasiness in the business world among men who want to purchase what you sell under the Alien Property Act, and therefore I am going to take the liberty of expressing the hope that you are using the power of private sale granted by my executive order of the 15th of July[1] in the most sparing manner and only where no other sort of sale is possible.

I think you have in mind as much as I have the danger and disadvantage of making any but the most sparing use of such powers, but a little reassurance between friends will do no harm.

Cordially and sincerely yours,   Woodrow Wilson

TLS (A. Mitchell Palmer Papers, DLC).
  [1] For a description of the selling arrangements announced on July 15, 1918, see "Alien Property Custodian Creates a Selling Organization To Dispose of All German-Owned Corporations," *Official Bulletin*, II (July 16, 1918), 3.

To John Wesley Wescott[1]

My dear Judge: The White House 4 September, 1918.

I am sorry to say that the government cannot in any circumstances consent to the sale of the Newport News Shipbuilding and Dry Dock Company.[2] If it passes to anybody, it must pass to the government.

I know that you will believe me when I say that this is not a hasty but a very deliberate judgment, and I am sure that nothing could come of a discussion of the matter, much as I would like to see you.

In haste,

Cordially and sincerely yours,   Woodrow Wilson

TLS (J. W. Wescott Coll., NjP).
  [1] At this time Attorney General of New Jersey.
  [2] Wilson was replying to J. W. Wescott to WW, Sept. 3, 1918, TLS, enclosing "In the Matter of the Application for Approval of a Proposition to Purchase the Newport News Shipbuilding and Drydock Company, Memorandum for the President," T MS (WP, DLC).

To George Creel

My dear Creel: The White House 4 September, 1918.

May I suggest to you a very important and immediate publicity task?

Will you not be kind enough to get from the Bureau of Labor Statistics of the Labor Department (in charge of Royal Meeker) and from the Agricultural Department, as well as from such other sources as they may direct you to, as complete a tabulation as possible of the facts with regard to increases in the cost of other articles than wheat, so that there may be systematically set forth a thorough comparison of the increase in the cost of wheat as related to other products during a particular period?

The Food Administration sent me a table of this sort,[1] and it is quite likely that they can direct you to their own sources of information.

You will see what I am after. I do not want the farmers of the country to get a wrong impression. I think they are under the impression that the price of wheat, as compared with its average price during the three year period before the war, has not increased as rapidly as the cost of things which farmers have to buy and use, whereas the fact is that the price of wheat has advanced more rapidly and to a higher point than the price of most other articles during an equal period.

If we can get these facts properly established and lucidly set forth, it will be of great service and will guide editorial comment throughout the country.

Cordially and faithfully yours,   Woodrow Wilson

TLS (G. Creel Papers, DLC).
[1] Actually, he referred to the Enclosure printed with R. Meeker to WW, Aug. 29, 1918.

From Robert Lansing, with Enclosure

My dear Mr. President: Washington September 4, 1918.

I enclose a memorandum prepared by the Division of Foreign Intelligence of the Department relative to Captain Lippmann. This is all we know about the matter. I do not know the meaning of the last paragraph.   Faithfully yours,   Robert Lansing

TLS (WP, DLC).

E N C L O S U R E

Memorandum for the Secretary: September 4, 1918.

Walter Lippmann is a Captain of Military Intelligence and is on duty in England and France in connection with propaganda in enemy countries.

A telegram from Mr. James Keeley[1] to Mr. Sisson, of the Committee on Public Information, dated August 8, stated that Walter Lippmann was in London and with other military intelligence officers desired to attend the meeting of the International Propaganda Board then about to be held.

On August 9th Mr. Keeley telegraphed to Mr. Sisson that he had arranged for Captains Lippmann and Blankenhorn to attend the conference but that Lippmann said that they would be present as observers only.

A telegram from Mr. Creel and Mr. Sisson to Mr. Keeley, dated August 13th, stated that Blankenhorn and Lippman[n] would be advisory only.

A telegram from Mr. Keeley to Mr. Sisson, dated August 20th, contained the following statement: "Possible conflict with Lippmann and his group smoothed over."[2]

T MS (WP, DLC).
[1] Former editor of the *Chicago Herald*, special representative of the C.P.I. on the inter-Allied conference on propaganda in London.
[2] About the controversy between the C.P.I. and the Military Intelligence Branch, see Steel, *Walter Lippmann*, pp. 144-47.

Three Letters from Robert Lansing

My dear Mr. President: Washington September 4, 1918.

I am to see Mr. Baruch tomorrow in regard to the matter of supplying the needs of the Czecho-Slovaks, but, while I shall proceed along the lines already suggested, I wish to offer the following as a method which seems to remove the difficulty of coordinating the different sources of supply and also to secure speedy action, which is so essential in view of the near approach of winter.

I think that in view of the fact that we have recognized the Czecho-Slovak National Council as a *de facto* government it might be possible to make them a loan sufficient to purchase the necessary supplies in this country. The entire responsibility and work of purchasing and arranging for the transportation of the supplies would by this method fall upon Professor Masaryk and his colleagues.

This course would have the advantage of giving substantial evidence of our opinion as to the probable success of the movement and our faith in the repayment of moneys loaned. But even if it was never repaid we would be no worse off than if we expend the amount on supplies and gave them to the Czecho-Slovaks.

Would you be good enough to let me have your opinion on this suggestion, and, if it meets with your approval, an authorization to lay it before Professor Masaryk either before or after discussing the plan with the Treasury as you think best?

Faithfully yours,   Robert Lansing

TLS (SDR, RG 59, 860F.24/9½A, DNA).

My dear Mr. President: Washington September 4, 1918.

In reference to your letter of August 29th, which I enclose as a reminder of its contents, I have inquired as to the situation relative to British Government prices being denied our Government in England.

I am informed by representatives of the War Trade Board that Mr. Baruch says that the matter has been satisfactorily adjusted as a result of conferences which representatives of the War Industries Board, now in London, have had with British officials; and he also suggests that the matter be allowed to rest for the present.[1]

In going over the matter I find the problem is much more complicated than appears on the face, and that the attitude which we should definitely take has not been determined. The British colonies, for example, are desirous of making large purchases in this country and it is a question to what extent we should give them the benefit of our governmental prices since, in many cases, it is almost impossible to determine whether their purchases are for military purposes or for civilian purposes. I believe it is generally agreed that the Associated Governments should give one another the benefit of governmental prices where the goods purchased are required for the conduct of military operations. This seems to be the theory, but in practice the line of demarcation between purchases for military purposes and purchases for commercial purposes is difficult to draw. This is particularly true in cases where the governments themselves are so largely purchasing for their domestic requirements and subsequently allocating their purchases among their nationals.

In view of the situation I believe it would be advisable not to rest [raise] the question at the present time.

Faithfully yours,   Robert Lansing.

TLS (SDR, RG 59, 811.24/252½, DNA).
[1] Lansing is summarizing J. F. Dulles to RL, Sept. 3, 1918, TLS (SDR, RG 59, 811.24/252½, DNA). John Foster Dulles, Princeton 1908; lawyer of New York; at this time assistant to Vance C. McCormick, chairman of the War Trade Board.

My dear Mr. President: Washington September 4, 1918.

I enclose herewith a report from Mr. Stovall (No 4079   763.72119/ 1976) to which is appended a letter dated July 30th from Doctor George D. Herron which contains his views in regard to Bulgaria.[1] I think his letter is well worth reading and considering. Will you be good enough to return it to me after you have had an opportunity to go through it, as it belongs to the files of the Department.

Faithfully yours,   Robert Lansing

TLS (R. Lansing Papers, NjP).
  [1] P. A. Stovall to RL, Aug. 6, 1918, TLS, enclosing G. D. Herron, "Ad Interim and Bulgaria," July 30, 1918, TC MS (SDR, RG 59, 763.72119/1876, DNA). Herron began this report by briefly describing the state of his negotiations with Robert de Fiori and the desperate situation which the Prussian military rulers faced. According to De Fiori, only a peace along the lines of the Bavarian proposals could save the German Empire from a sudden and violent collapse. However, the Prussian rulers, who knew that their end was certain unless they could somehow achieve victory over the Entente, would yield to nothing but military force. If they lost the war, they faced extinction of their power either at the hands of the Allies or at the hands of the "awakened and wrathful" German people. Indeed, De Fiori believed, they considered a possible defeat by the Allies more honorable and probably much more merciful than their overthrow by their own aroused and revengeful people. Thus, they would readily sacrifice the entire German nation in order to avoid the humiliation of "dismission" and death by the people whom they had kept in "docile and sordid subjection" for so long.
  After a brief comment on the continuous German propaganda activities in Switzerland, Herron discussed the recent Bulgarian "intrigue" for a separate peace and emphatically argued against a consideration of Bulgaria's overtures. A separation by the Allies of the fate of Bulgaria from that of Germany, Herron maintained, would be "both morally and politically disastrous." It would be an "essential and unforgivable betrayal" of Serbia and Rumania and would give moral sanction to a "resourceful and unrepentant enemy" to the peace of the Balkans and to that of true internationalism. Herron then launched into a vituperative attack on Bulgaria and the Bulgarian people and elaborated in great detail on the dire consequences of a separate peace with such an "unmoral nation." "Rather than discussing a separate peace," Herron concluded, "I am profoundly, yes, devoutly convinced that the high honor of America, and the lifting of our whole cause above reproach, demands a declaration of war by America against Bulgaria. Such an action will at once clear us of all doubt in the eyes of the devastated and struggling nationalities of Europe."

From the White House Staff, with Enclosure

The White House.
Memorandum for the President: September 4, 1918

Minister Morris[1] forgot to leave with the President yesterday afternoon the attached memorandum, and he asks that it be handed to him.

T MS (WP, DLC).
  [1] That is, Ira Nelson Morris, Minister to Sweden.

ENCLOSURE

Memoranda for the President:

1. Neutral sentiment, especially in Sweden where the feeling was perceptibly pro-German, has been steadily changing in favor of America and the Allies. This has been due to three causes, knowledge of which may be helpful in pointing the way to further progress. One cause is the signing recently of a commercial agreement between the Allies and Sweden to better the economic conditions in Sweden. Another cause is the excellent work done in Sweden and adjoining countries by the Committee on Public Information, headed by Mr. George Creel. This work has been characterized by intelligence and an understanding of the peoples who were to be influenced. Still another cause for the change in sentiment is the recent victories of the American and Allied armies. The neutrals swing naturally towards the victors. They are thinking mainly of their own future.

2. Any statements that may be made, especially by the President, indicating continued friendliness on the part of America towards the neutrals will be helpful, especially if they contain the suggestion that this country is anxious to aid the neutrals, once its own war necessities, and the necessities of the Allies, are satisfied. Such assurances, it is true, already have been given, but the neutrals, flooded constantly by German propaganda, would welcome a repetition of them.

3. On the way to America I heard that the Swiss Minister to the United States[1] was on his way to London to suggest that the Allies engage in a conference with representatives of the German Government to see whether some satisfactory basis for peace negotiations could not be arranged. Lord Robert Cecil advised me, while in London, that he understood that the Swiss Minister had undertaken such a mission, but remarked that he could not understand why, if it were true, the proposal were not made to the President of the United States. It is likely that this is merely one of the several efforts that have been made to lure America and the Allies, or perhaps the latter alone, into a conference.

4. The various efforts that have been made towards bringing about a conference invariably have been informal and suspicious. One of these informal proposals, made through a Liberal member of the Reichstag, was transmitted by me, with a report of the circumstances, from Stockholm to the State Department, some time ago.[2]

5. As indicating the feeling of one of the colonies of Great Britain, Sir Robert Borden, Premier of Canada, with whom I crossed the

water on my way from London to the United States, told me that
he had advised the British authorities that the Canadians could not
keep their heart in the war if they were left to understand that its
result would be the addition of more colonies to the British Empire.
His idea, which is that America should annex what were the German colonies, may be somewhat fantastic, or it may be merely
flattery, but the fact that the Canadians are very strongly in favor
of America's war aims, as they have been stated by the President,
is worthy of notice.

6. The suggestion is made that, whenever possible, the victories
of the American army be stressed in neutral countries. The influence of such victories on the neutral mind cannot be exaggerated.

T MS (WP, DLC).
[1] Hans Sulzer.
[2] I. N. Morris to RL, Feb. 26, 1918, *FR-WWS 1918*, 1, I, 139-40.

From Joseph Patrick Tumulty, with Enclosure

Dear Governor: [The White House] September 4, 1918
I agree with every word of the attached letter from Mr. Roper.
We ought not to take any part in this campaign unless this is
done.[1]   J.P.T.

How are we to get this done? Of course it ought to be done   W.W.

Dear General[2]
Secy of Navy is Ford's friend. A tip to him will suffice.
                                          Tumulty

TL (WP, DLC).
[1] About Ford's candidacy for the Senate as the administration's choice, see JPT to
WW, June 18, 1918, n. 1, Vol. 48.
[2] That is, Burleson.

E N C L O S U R E

Daniel Calhoun Roper to Joseph Patrick Tumulty

Dear Mr. Tumulty: Washington, September 3 1918.
From sources in which I have confidence I learn that Mr. Ford
can not be elected to the United States Senate from Michigan so
long as his son[1] occupies the status of an exempted man and two
sons of Mr. Newberry[2] are in the military branch of the Government.
This situation is made more acute by the fact that a large number
of voting citizens in Michigan have sons who are in the Army and
Navy by virtue of voluntary enlistment or the operation of the draft

law. Is there not some proper way in which this matter may be brought to the attention of Mr. Ford, or others interested in his success, and his son unharnessed from his exempt status and placed into a position of military or naval responsibility?[3]

Sincerely yours,   Daniel C. Roper

TLS (J. Daniels Papers, DLC).
[1] Edsel Bryant Ford, at this time secretary of the Ford Motor Co.
[2] That is, Truman Handy Newberry, former Secretary of the Navy and Republican senatorial candidate in Michigan, and his twin sons, Barnes and Phelps.
[3] Ford, in a statement issued on September 7, declared that he alone was responsible for his son's absence from the firing line in France. He had asked the army to classify his son as essential to the Ford industries. Had he been a politician, Ford said, he would have taken the "obviously easy course" of covering up his son in a uniform, with an assignment in Detroit. "When the duly authorized authority says his services are more needed in the army than here in these industries," Ford concluded, "he will be found at the front fighting, and will not be found sticking his spurs into a mahogany desk at Washington." *New York Times*, Sept. 8, 1918.

From Joseph Patrick Tumulty

Dear Governor: The White House 4 September 1918.

Referring to the Western Trip, I feel that we can withdraw from it without embarrassment of any kind. When I suggested it early in June, it seemed a necessary thing to do. With the situation on the Western Front and the increasing successes of our Troops there is no necessity for strengthening the morale of our people. I think, however, we can make a statement, outlining your reasons for not taking it, that will knock our enemies into a cocked hat and then follow it up shortly by a statement outlining the reasons why you believe a Democratic Congress necessary.

Sincerely,   Tumulty

TLS (WP, DLC).

Two Letters from David Franklin Houston

Dear Mr. President: Washington September 4, 1918.

In proceeding with the licensing of stock yards and live stock dealers, under your Proclamation of June 18, 1918,[1] new facts and conditions have developed which render it advisable to provide additional authority covering the live stock buying operations of slaughtering and meat packing concerns, rendering and serum establishments, and any other concerns buying or selling live stock in stockyards, and not specifically covered by your Proclamation of June 18, 1918.

In drafting the Proclamation of June 18th the supervision of the classes of business mentioned above was considered, but at that time it was not deemed advisable to include them, principally for the reason that the Food Administration licensed the packers as such, and it seemed that all phases of the packers' business was sufficiently under government control.

However, it now develops that it is essential to secure uniform control of all operations in the stockyards in order to accomplish the purpose of the Proclamation of June 18, 1918, and after consultation with representatives of the Food Administration, a working arrangement has been concluded between this Department and the Food Administration subject to your approval, whereby all packers' operations in the stock yards are to be regulated by this Department. It is also deemed advisable to provide more fully for the regulation of transactions in dead stock not included in the previous proclamation. In order to carry out this plan most effectively, it is desirable that an additional proclamation be issued to supplement that of June 18, 1918. Accordingly the suggested form of the supplemental proclamation has been drafted, has been approved by the Food Administration and Mr. Hoover, and is submitted herewith for your signature, if you approve it.[2]

Suitable rules and regulations pertaining to the aspects of the industry affected by this Supplemental Proclamation will be prepared promptly after its approval by you.

Faithfully yours,   D. F. Houston

[1] For the text, see the *Official Bulletin*, II (June 20, 1918), 6.
[2] Wilson signed the proclamation on September 6, 1918. It is printed in the *Official Bulletin*, II (Sept. 12, 1918), 8.

CONFIDENTIAL.

Dear Mr. President: Washington September 4, 1918.

I think perhaps you might like to have a word from me in writing to supplement what I said to you yesterday about the Federal Board of Farm Organizations. So far as I can discover, this movement was inspired by Gifford Pinchot, Charles McCarthy, and Charles W. Holman.[1] You know Pinchot. You know what an able farmer he is not. McCarthy is a wild Irishman. Holman was formerly at the University of Wisconsin in some publicity work. They had trouble with him and got rid of him. These three men were saddled on Hoover when Hoover came here. He had trouble with each of them. These three men had no difficulty in securing the cooperation of Barrett and Creasy.[2] Barrett you know. Creasy seems to be a sort of lobbyist for the National Dairy Union of which he is secretary.

These men called a convention of farmers the latter part of last winter. They had a very small attendance. They issued a memorial, of which you have a copy.[3] Some of their suggestions were good, others were bad. Their chief statement was calculated to create prejudice among the farmers and unrest. Some time ago they called another meeting for last week. They held the meeting at which perhaps 200 people were present. A number of those present were political farmers—men who are always on jobs of this sort. They selected an executive committee which contains two omissions and two additions. They omitted J. W. Shorthill[4] of York, Nebraska, and Charles W. Holman, and added R. G. Cooper of New York City,[5] and Charles A. Lyman.[6] Cooper is neither very good nor very bad. He is the President of the New York State Dairyman's League which has been very much in the limelight. Lyman is a sort of understudy for Holman. He was associated with Holman in Wisconsin and was active in the Society of Equity.[7] Some of the people I have talked with think him simply radical and erratic; others think he is not reliable.

The complete list is as follows:

W. T. Creasy, Chairman, Catawissa, Pa.

Charles S. Barrett, Union City, Ga.

R. G. Cooper, New York City.

Gifford Pinchot, Milford, Pa.

Charles McCarthy, Madison, Wis.

Charles Lyman, General Secretary, Woodward Bldg.,
Washington, D. C.

I do not think this body really represents anything in particular. Some of the more important resolutions adopted by the body you have in the file I handed you yesterday. They profess great loyalty to the Union and to the cause in which we are engaged, but some of their representations and suggestions are by no means helpful. They represent that the farmers have not been fairly treated. They attempt to give the impression that the prices of farm products have been held down while the prices of other things have not been interfered with, except perhaps to prevent undue profit. Such representations are false. They contend that a price even of $2.46 for wheat is not high enough. They ignore the action that has been taken in calling the farmers into council through the National Farmers Advisory Committee. What they wish is that they be regarded as the advisers to the Nation in agricultural matters in this crisis.

If you will glance at the latter part of Gifford Pinchot's article in the separate of the Annals of the American Academy,[8] and also at the memorial adopted at the first meeting of this body and the resolutions of the second meeting,[9] you will see that Pinchot's views run through all of them. I am reasonably sure that Pinchot in this matter is in touch with Mr. Roosevelt. Shortly after the first meeting of this body Mr. Roosevelt wrote an article in the Kansas City Star in which he rehashed the views set forth in the memorial and urged that farmers be given "fine prices," be furnished labor by the Government, and be taken into full counsel by the Government. The same thing runs through his recent speech in Springfield. It is interesting to note also that Senator Gore has recently introduced bills embodying the main suggestions of this Board.

It is somewhat difficult for me to decide what is the best method of dealing with this body. Of course, I have no earthly objection to any responsible organization of farmers. We tried to get such an organization through the National Agricultural Advisory Committee. I should welcome any better piece of machinery. I do not think this body is responsible. Its willingness to pass finally on very important matters without a reasonably full knowledge of the facts and without investigation indicates this. The question is whether to ignore the communication from the convention or to answer it. What the body wishes now is recognition from you. My present impression is that it would be better to ignore it. If you decide otherwise, it seems to me that you should, in some form, raise the question of their competency to represent the farmers of the Nation and, while expressing appreciation of their professions of loyalty and assistance, point out the danger of forming hasty judgments and of disseminating views based on inadequate consideration and calculated to cause dissatisfaction and unrest.

Faithfully yours,   D. F. Houston.

TLS (WP, DLC).

[1] Charles McCarthy of Madison, Wisc., expert on state government and legislation, organizer and director of the first state legislative reference library and bill-drafting bureau in the United States, and author of *The Wisconsin Idea* (New York, 1912); former director of investigations of the United States Commission on Industrial Relations; at this time, a member of the War Labor Policies Board, a dollar-a-year man in the Food Administration, and treasurer of the National Conference on Marketing and Farm Credits. Charles William Holman was an adviser to the Food Administration, secretary of the National Conference on Marketing and Farm Credits, and an aide to McCarthy.

[2] Charles Simon Barrett, president of the National Farmers' Union, member of the National Agricultural Advisory Committee, and member of the Price Fixing Committee for wheat; and William T. Creasy, known as "Farmer" Creasy, master of the Pennsylvania State Grange and former Democratic leader of the Pennsylvania House of Representatives.

[3] See the petition printed at February 8, 1918, n. 2, Vol. 46.

[4] John W. Shorthill, secretary of the National Council of Farmers' Cooperative Associations.

[5] Roswell D. Cooper.

[6] Charles Adelbert Lyman, secretary of the National Board of Farm Organizations.

[7] The American Society of Equity, founded in Indianapolis in 1902, was one of the earliest farmers' organizations of the twentieth century to achieve some degree of prominence. It was originally perceived as a central agency to secure equitable prices for farm products. Its basic idea was that farmers themselves would set the prices for their products and keep their crops off the market unless and until these prices could be obtained. From its inception, the Equity suffered from inept leadership and poor or-

ganization and never grew into the nationwide movement which it was intended to be. However, at various times, several of its regional branches were quite influential. After some early successes in the tobacco-growing regions of Kentucky and Tennessee, the Equity's strength became concentrated in the Midwest and the Northwest, and it gained its greatest influence in Wisconsin, Minnesota, the Dakotas, and Montana. It broadened its program to include the establishment of cooperative marketing and purchasing associations and, particularly in Wisconsin, became involved in progressive politics. Internal dissension and the establishment of rival organizations led to the waning of the Equity's power after the war, and, in the early 1920s, its remnants were absorbed by the National Farmers' Union. For a detailed discussion, see Theodore Saloutos and John D. Hicks, *Agricultural Discontent in the Middle West, 1900-1939* (Madison, Wisc., 1951), pp. 111-48.

[8] Gifford Pinchot, "Essentials to a Food Program for Next Year," *Annals of the American Academy of Political and Social Science,* LXXVIII (July 1918), 156-63.

[9] According to a brief note in the *Washington Post* of August 30, 1918, the resolutions adopted at the second conference called on Wilson to shut down all nonessential industries in order to alleviate the serious shortage of farm labor; declared that the price of wheat fixed by the government did not meet the increased cost of production; and requested the Food Administration to investigate the question of livestock waste.

From Charles Richard Crane

Dear Mr President   Chicago September 4 1918

I enclose you the information I promised in regard to Mr Robert F. Herrick.[1] His name came up one evening at Secretary Houstons and a man in whose judgment we all have confidence, Mr Roland W. Boyden, agreed to prepare me this little account of him.[2] Mr Boyden is himself a fine counsellor, an old friend of Houstons and is Hoover's legal advisor.

Mrs Crane, John[3] and I are progressing westward. This week we "stopped by" to see what kind of an idea Henry Ford has of ship-building. It is really remarkable the way he has handled this entirely new problem and it makes any talk of German efficiency look like sham. Two of the boats are already in the water. They are trim looking craft—perhaps a trifle too refined—with sharp searching looking bows. I am not quite certain that they would stand the severe christening test to which the "Quistconck" was subjected[4] but perhaps in actual service that test may never come. Please give a warm greeting to the pretty lady who invented the test from Mrs Crane, John, and me.

Always sincerely Yours   Charles R. Crane

ALS (WP, DLC).

[1] Robert Frederick Herrick, lawyer and businessman of Boston.

[2] R. W. Boyden to C. R. Crane, Aug. 28, 1918, TLS (WP, DLC).

[3] Their son, John Oliver Crane.

[4] The Wilsons had gone to Philadelphia on August 5, 1918, for the launching of S.S. *Quistconck.* It was the hottest day of the year, with temperatures reaching 105 degrees, and more than 400 people fainted during the launching ceremony. Recalling the event, Mrs. Wilson later wrote: "I swung my bottle of champagne, which was so hot that Mr. Charles M. Schwab, who stood beside me, and I received a baptism in white foam." Edith B. Wilson, *My Memoir,* p. 166; also the *New York Times,* Aug. 6, 1918, and the illustration section of this volume.

From Edward Albert Filene

My dear Mr. Wilson: Boston 4 September, 1918.

In order to save your time, I brought to the attention of Colonel House a matter which, in his reply to my letter, he suggested I take up directly with you.

As I stated in my letter to Colonel House, copy of which I enclose,[1] I want simply to state a situation which you may feel makes it wise to act in the near future in the matter of a reconstruction commission (if you have such in mind) in order to forestall the formulation of a number of separate and conflicting class programs. Evidence that such programs will be got under way presently is accumulating.

In the event that you do not care at this time to contribute any comment on this matter to the counsel of the Executive Committee of the Chamber, may I assume that in your judgment the matter would best be allowed to work itself out in this and subsequent meetings according to the best discretion of the members?

With expressions of regard, I am,

Respectfully,   Edward A Filene

TLS (WP, DLC).
[1] E. A. Filene to E. M. House, Aug. 30, 1918, TCL (WP, DLC).

From Frederick Dozier Gardner[1]

Dear Mr. President,   City of Jefferson September 4, 1918.

The Missouri Democratic State Convention was held a few days ago and your administration was endorsed from A to Z. You need have no fear about the result of the election in Missouri this fall. Fifteen Democratic Congressmen will be returned out of a total of sixteen to be elected, and a Democratic Senator.

Your administration is extremely popular out here. I have just returned from the Pacific coast where I went for a few days' rest. I found your administration very popular all through that country also.

I enclose a newspaper clipping[2] showing the endorsement the Democratic State Convention gave my administration. It is considered the strongest endorsement ever given by any State convention to any administration of Missouri. Our Republican friends held their convention the same day. As you know, they are very prone to find fault; but on this occasion they did not offer one single word of criticism of my administration.

The matter I want to bring to your attention is this: I believe the people of this country want you to accept a third term. I am well aware of the sentiment of our forefathers on this subject; but many things have changed. We are living in a new world and a new day. Personally, I can see no reason why that old theory should hold. It is almost a certainty that Colonel Roosevelt will be the Republican nominee, and I believe you should again carry Democracy's banner. I hope you will consider the matter most carefully. As one of your friends in the middle West, I want to offer you my cordial support.

Faithfully yours,   Frederick D. Gardner

TLS (WP, DLC).
[1] Governor of Missouri, a Democrat.
[2] Unidentified newspaper clipping, WP, DLC.

Royal Meeker to Joseph Patrick Tumulty

My dear Mr. Tumulty: Washington September 4, 1918.

I have read with much concern the statements in the newspapers that President Wilson is preparing to make a tour of the country in behalf of the Fourth Liberty Loan. I am sure my concern is shared by a huge majority of the American people. If any mischance should befall him, it would be an irreparable blow to our country and the Allied cause. The German spies and sympathisers in our midst realize this fact quite as clearly as any of us, and they are more desperate than ever before. They will stop at nothing in order to save the sacred Fatherland and bring about disaster to the Allies.

Of course, we all admire President Wilson for his steadfast courage which amounts to indifference for his personal safety. I would feel, however, that I had not done my duty if I did not protest against this proposed trip. I think I fully appreciate the President's desire to meet his fellow citizens face to face and to speak to them as only he can regarding the fundamental issues in the great crisis confronting us. I feel that he can speak to the people of the country almost as effectively from the safety of his office as he can from the public platform.

It makes everyone who recognizes the absolute indispensability of President Wilson to the Allied cause nervous to think of his encountering the ordinary risks of travel—the ordinary hazards from crazy fanatics and cranks. We have already lost three Presidents by assassination—two of them in times of profound peace. The hazards in ordinary times are utterly insignificant compared to the hazards of this present moment. No matter how closely the Secret Service Men may attempt to safeguard the President, he would not be safe for a single moment during this proposed journey. The loss of President Wilson at this time would be an incalculable disaster.

I beg of you for the reasons I have so inadequately set forth above to use your utmost efforts to dissuade the President from undertaking his proposed trip, not for personal safety but for the sake of the Nation and humanity. I know that you will have no easy task even to mention this subject to President Wilson, but I feel that you because of your nearness to him can perhaps exercise more influence upon him than any of his other friends and perhaps more than all of his other friends combined. I think it is your plain duty to present this subject to the President immediately in the hope that he may be induced to give up this enterprise which I regard as hazardous to the point of fool hardiness.

Sincerely yours,   Royal Meeker

TLS (WP, DLC).

From Robert Lansing

My dear Mr. President: Washington September 5, 1918.

I saw Mr. Baruch this morning in regard to the Czecho-Slovak relief and he thought it highly essential that he should be put in touch at once with Professor Masaryk. This I have arranged.

I also took the liberty of telling him of the suggestion which I had made in regard to a loan and he said that he considered it the most practical and efficient means of arranging for the supplies and expediting their transportation. Of course the matter of purchase and allocation of tonnage would still be in Mr. Baruch's hands.   Faithfully yours,   Robert Lansing

TLS (WP, DLC).

Four Letters to Robert Lansing

My dear Mr. Secretary,   The White House. 5 September, 1918.

It is my judgment that we should avoid a loan, if possible, and handle this matter directly,—possibly in the way I have just suggested over the telephone.[1]   Faithfully Yours,   W.W.

WWTLI (SDR, RG 59, 860F.24/10½, DNA).
  [1] Wilson authorized Baruch to draw upon his special war fund in the sum of $1,500,000 for supplies for the Czechs. See WW to B. M. Baruch, Sept. 17, 1918.

My dear Mr. Secretary,   The White House. 5 September, 1918.

I am glad to have seen this letter of Herron's. I agree with every word of what he says about what our attitude should be towards Bulgaria, and I think it would be well to ask Stovall to tell Herron that he might say to any Bulgarian who may approach him that we will entertain no suggestions which separate her fate from that of Germany with whom she has chosen to make common cause against mankind. I am all but persuaded by Herron's argument to advise the Congress to declare a state of war with Bulgaria. That would at least convince the Czecho-Slovaks and the Jugo-Slavs of our sincerity and would prevent the Allies from making arrangements with Bulgaria without our consent. What do you think?

Faithfully Yours,   W.W.

WWTLI (R. Lansing Papers, NjP).

CONFIDENTIAL

My dear Mr. Secretary: [The White House] 5 September, 1918.

Thank you for your memorandum about Captain Lippmann. I have a high opinion of Lippmann, but I am very jealous in the matter of propaganda. I would not think of interfering with the activities of the War Department's intelligence agents, but I want to keep the matter of publicity entirely in my own hands, and I would be very much obliged to you if you would upon every proper occasion let that be known to our diplomatic and other representatives abroad.

I am writing today to the War Department to ask about their propaganda.

Cordially and faithfully yours,   Woodrow Wilson

TLS (Letterpress Books, WP, DLC).

My dear Mr. Secretary,   The White House. 5 September, 1918.

I am content, in the circumstances you set forth,[1] that this matter should rest for the present; but I hope that we shall make sure that promises are fulfilled. Many other promises have been made which minor persons of various indirect influence have seen to it should not be redeemed.   Faithfully Yours,   W.W.

WWTLI (SDR, RG 59, 811.24/253½, DNA).
[1] See RL to WW, Sept. 4, 1918 (second letter of that date).

To Robert Lansing, with Enclosure

My dear Mr. Secretary,   The White House. 5 September, 1918.

This illustrates in the most striking way the utter disregard of General Poole and of all the Allied governments (at any rate of all who are acting for them) of the policy to which we expressly confined ourselves in our statement about our action in Siberia.

It is out of the question to send reenforcements from eastern Siberia (I presume they mean from the forces recently landed at Vladivostock) to Perm; and we have expressly notified those in charge of those forces that the Czecho-Slovaks must (so far as our aid was to be used) to [sic] be brought out eastward, not got out westward. Is there no way,—no form of expression,—by which we can get this comprehended?   Faithfully Yours,   W.W.

WWTLI (SDR, RG 59, 861.00/7381, DNA).

ENCLOSURE

Peking Dated August 30, 1918.

Urgent. The following is the substance of a mutilated telegram received from the U. S. Consul General Harris[1] by way of Uliansiuai[2] and Urga.[3] "287 August 13th. In accordance with instructions of General Poole commanding allied forces in Murman, which instructions were brought here by Captain Jones,[4] Czechs were asked to advance on and take Perm and Virdnow[5] in order to effect a junction with the Allies at Vologda at the earliest possible moment. In endeavoring to carry out this plan Czechs are meeting unexpected and strong resistance and flank attacks from organized bands of Magyars and German prisoners commanded by German and Austrian officers. (Passage undecipherable.) Taking of Perm will be delayed indefinitely and in all probability will be impossible without reenforcements from Allies in Siberia. As no reliance (?) can be placed in the Russian mobilization and as guns are not available in any case, all the burden falls on the Czechs whose losses are heavy. Please communicate with Allied forces in Siberia to hasten advance and send officers to strengthen the Czech staff. In view of the fact that recent battles have been exclusively with German and Austrian prisoners commanded by German and Austrian officers, the Allies need have no fear of fighting against Russian Bolsheviks. All ask that the Allies in East inform General Poole at Murman that unless reenforcements are forthcoming immediately it will be impossible to carry out his instructions. As above stated regarding junction at Vologda."

Remainder of telegram received undecipherable but apparently makes urgent request for information as to plans of Allies for the relief of the Czechs. Please send the above repeated to Tokyo, Harbon [Harbin], and Vladivostok for communication to American military and naval authorities.   MacMurray

T telegram (SDR, RG 59, 861.00/7381, DNA).
    [1] Ernest Lloyd Harris, Consul General at Irkutsk.
    [2] Actually, Uliassutai, now Dzhibkhalantu.
    [3] Now Ulan Bator.
    [4] Unidentified.
    [5] That is, Viatka, now Kirov.

To Benedict Crowell

My dear Mr. Secretary: [The White House] 5 September, 1918.

Returning to what I spoke of for a moment yesterday in our little war conference, may I not ask for information about a matter which I am very jealous about?

I am told that the War Department is, through its intelligence officers, in some way interesting itself in the matter of propaganda abroad, and I would be very much obliged if you would make inquiry and find how far this is true and what is being attempted, because it is my wish to keep the matter of propaganda entirely in my own hands and I had not known that any other agencies than those I had set up were attempting to interest themselves in it. I regard nothing as more delicate or more intimately associated with the policy of the administration than propaganda, and if any agency of the Army is attempting to organize propaganda of any sort or to take a hand in controlling it, I would be very much obliged if you would "call them off." You will know how to do it kindly and without intimating any criticism on my part, but only my sense of the absolute necessity of my directing that whole matter.
            Cordially and sincerely yours,   Woodrow Wilson

TLS (Letterpress Books, WP, DLC).

Two Letters to Joseph Patrick Tumulty

Dear Tumulty: [The White House] 5 September, 1918

This is of course typical of many requests which are sure to come in to me,[1] and I would like very much to have your judgment as to how we ought to handle this business.

Let me say that it is clear to me that I ought not to put such letters as are asked for on the ground of support of the administration, but rather on the ground of the support of the necessary measures, legislative and administrative, for the conduct of the war.

The President

[1] Samuel Vernon Stewart to WW, Aug. 31, 1918, TLS (WP, DLC). Stewart, Democratic Governor of Montana, requested from Wilson a statement endorsing the reelection of Senator Thomas J. Walsh. Stewart asked Wilson to emphasize that Walsh was considered "one of the able, conscientious, effective, and unswerving supporters of Woodrow Wilson and the national administration."

Dear Tumulty:　　　　　[The White House] 5 September, 1918.

I would be very much obliged if you would tell Senator Simmons that of course the impressions spoken of in the second paragraph of this letter from Mr. Fries[1] are without foundation of any kind. I am very much concerned about the whole thing but do not at present see just how to handle it.　　　The President

TL (WP, DLC).
[1] "The American Federations of Labor have laid out a plan by which they propose to organize every industry in the United States during the period of the present War. They say the Government is with them and they propose to take advantage of the Administration's attitude on this labor question." Henry Elias Fries, a prominent businessman and manufacturer of Winston-Salem, N. C., to F. M. Simmons, Aug. 28, 1918, TLS (WP, DLC). Simmons had forwarded this letter in F. M. Simmons to JPT, Sept. 3, 1918, TLS (WP, DLC).

To Willard Saulsbury

My dear Senator:　　　　　The White House 5 September, 1918.

My impulse was to answer your letter of August 29th[1] at once to the effect that of course you could use the extracts from my letters to which you refer, for I would be only too glad to have you do so if I could confine it to this one case, but there is the rub. I have a very uncomfortable recollection that I have written similar letters to men whom I believed in when I wrote the letters but whom I do not believe in now, who have in fact done everything to forfeit my confidence; and my fear and expectation is, if I gave my consent to you in this matter, that they would either ask for my consent to publish portions of past correspondence with them, or publish them without asking.

I am sure you see my difficulty and how embarrassments surround every matter of this sort, and I know you will believe that I make this reply with the utmost regret.

Faithfully yours,　Woodrow Wilson

TLS (W. Saulsbury Papers, DeU).
[1] It is missing.

To David Franklin Houston

My dear Houston: The White House 5 September, 1918

Thank you sincerely for your memorandum of yesterday about the Federal Board of Farm Organizations. I am glad to have this clear exposition of a body of persons with whom we are evidently going to be obliged to deal very frequently.

          Cordially and faithfully yours,   Woodrow Wilson

TLS (D. F. Houston Papers, NjP).

Frank Irving Cobb to Joseph Patrick Tumulty

Dear Joe: New York, September 5, 1918.

Please call the President's attention to the shocking and lawless methods taken in New York in the so-called slacker raids. If he could see what I have seen his blood would boil with indignation. I can think of nothing that will have a worse effect on public opinion and war sentiment in this city than this action of DeWoody's[1] in arresting tens of thousands of patriotic and law abiding citizens at the point of the bayonet and driving them through the streets under armed guards to remain under arrest until they prove their innocence. It is a shameful spectacle which I would not have believed could happen outside a conquered province under Prussian military control. There must be a legal and orderly way of running up slackers, but the officials in charge of this work in New York have completely lost their heads.   Frank I. Cobb.

Dear Governor:

I have suggested to the Attorney General that he send a leading representative of his office to New York at once to gather all the facts. This is the only way to convince the people of New York that the Administration is interested.   Tumulty.

T telegram and TL (WP, DLC).
  [1] Charles Frederick DeWoody, divisional superintendent of the New York division of the Department of Justice, in charge of war-intelligence service.

To Thomas Watt Gregory

          [The White House]

My dear Mr. Attorney General: 5 September, 1918.

May I not ask that you let me know at your early convenience exactly what the action of representatives of the Department of

Justice was in New York, and the circumstances of that action, in making arrests of persons charged with being slackers? The arrests have aroused so much interest and are likely to give rise to so much misunderstanding that I would be very much obliged to you if you would let me know all the facts and circumstances.

Cordially and faithfully yours,   Woodrow Wilson

TLS (Letterpress Books, WP, DLC).

To George P. Hampton

My dear Mr. Hampton: [The White House] 5 September, 1918.

I thank you for your letter of September 3rd, which I have read with interest and appreciation, and which I value for the sidelights it throws upon a very interesting situation.

Sincerely yours,   Woodrow Wilson

TLS (Letterpress Books, WP, DLC).

From Harry Augustus Garfield

Personal

Dear Mr. President: Washington, D. C. September 5, 1918.

I earnestly hope that the newspaper statement that you are to make a trip West is not true. Much as I care for your personal safety it is not that that impresses me. Should your hand be taken from the helm there is the greatest danger that reactionary forces at home will turn us back and the cause of democracy be indefinitely postponed.

It seems to me that the risk is unwarrantable. For the sake of the cause I venture to speak as I feel and believe.

Cordially and faithfully yours,   H. A. Garfield.

TLS (WP, DLC).

Three Telegrams from Sir William Wiseman to Lord Reading

CXP 730.   [New York] Sept. 5. 1918

(A) Reference my Cable No 723 of Aug. 31st.: Please cable me about this as soon as possible. The President seems to have assumed that you could arrange matters satisfactorily.

(B) It is possible that the President may be away most of October on a Liberty Loan campaign. Col. House will visit him in Washington before he leaves.

(C) Col. House asks me to remind you of your promise to discuss the Spanish situation with the War Cabinet. He thinks the time is very opportune for joint Allied and American representations to Spain, and that we might even induce her to declare war on Germany if we could assure her of full protection and satisfactory economic arrangements. He thinks in that event U.S.G. would be willing to send some troops to Spain to complete their training, if it were thought that would have a good effect. Also that U.S.G. would give war orders to Spain. He would like your views to discuss with the President.

CXP 731.   [New York] Sept. 5th. 1918.

In reply to your No. 751 of August 28th[1]:

I well understand what you mean. Some of our best friends in this country feel the same anxiety. It is obviously difficult to explain in the space of a cable, but I can touch on certain points.

The atmosphere which you detect is not part of a deliberate policy of U.S.G. If there is an apparent change of policy it is, I think, due to the friction inevitably caused in the working out of innumerable and difficult war problems between not only the heads but the minor officials of the two Governments. We all recognize, of course, that there is inherent difficulty in the attitude which the President has thought wise to adopt, namely that of an associate, not an ally. It has both advantages and disadvantages, but, combined with the great distance between Washington and Europe, and the dominating personality of the President, it means that some misunderstandings in our highest political negotiations are almost unavoidable. But the President is, after all, not anti-British—very much the contrary—and he and his Administration are striving towards the same ideals which inspire the British people.

The real danger-point, I feel, is in trade questions. We are two great independent commercial nations, both accustomed to take the lead in trade matters—the Americans in Latin America, and ourselves in European trade councils. Both nations and their representatives find it difficult to give way to each other's views and policies without apparently sacrificing their interests and principles.

It is as hard to suggest a remedy as it is to describe the complaint. My own view, as you know, has always been that we should be absolutely frank with each other; that we should be careful to avoid even the semblance of trying to appeal over the heads of the other government to any section of the people; that we should ask the American Government to adopt the same policy; and that particularly in commercial matters we should explain our policy and programme without reserve, and in our dealings avoid any suggestion of bargaining for our own trade advantage after the war.

I know this is a counsel of perfection, but I do not believe there is any other remedy or short-cut to good relations.

Finally, I think we should bear in mind that the dignity and traditions of the British Empire demand that we should be patient rather than quick to resent, sympathetic and helpful to the Administration in their many difficulties, ready to give way to American opinion on everything excepting questions of vital importance and principle. That while we should be most careful not to overdo, either by propaganda or celebrations, the outward signs of Anglo-American friendship, we should always have faith in the real tie which binds us together—that of our common traditions, ideals, and our sens[e] of what is fair.

¹ In which Reading had said, "I cannot help noticing several requests put forward recently by H.M. Government have been turned down by the U.S. Government for what, in some cases at any rate, would appear to be unconvincing reasons. I do not go into details as I am upon larger questions. I should like to know whether there are any grounds for believing this is part of a deliberate policy due either (a) to some action of ours which has antagonized the U.S. Government; or (b) to some change of policy for other reasons. If (a), I should like to know cause and of course I would do everything possible to remove it. If (b), can you ascertain reasons for the change. I am convinced there is something going awry but cannot satisfy myself as to cause." Lord Reading to W. Wiseman, Aug. 28, 1918, T telegram (W. Wiseman Papers, CtY).

CXP 732. *Very Secret and Personal.*:   [New York] Sept. 5th. 1918.

My Cable No. 731 of the 5th. was written after consultation with Col. House, who shares to some extent your present anxiety. While No. 731 represents, I believe, a true if somewhat obvious statement of the case, I must admit that our most practical difficulty is the attitude of the President himself. During his week's holiday at Magnolia, I saw a great deal of him, and, while I do not alter my own affectionate admiration for him, I realize that he is a most difficult person to deal with as head of the government. His attitude lately has tended to become more arbitrary, and aloof, and there are times when he seems to treat foreign governments hardly seriously. Col. House realises this, and any influence he has will be used to the uttermost to remedy it. Of course the rest of the Administration and officials generally take their "time" by the President and tend to treat foreign representatives in a somewhat patronizing and impatient manner. I do not think we are singled out more than any other government, excepting that we will not allow ourselves to be dictated to as some others apparently do.

I think, and Col. House agrees, that there will be some advantage and increased prestige, if you could arrange to cross the ocean fairly frequently. Coming fresh from London and Paris you would have even greater influence in Washington—particularly with the President—than if you remained there permanently; and Col. House also thinks it is of the highest importance that the British Cabinet should hear your views on American affairs fairly frequently.

T telegrams (W. Wiseman Papers, CtY).

To Joseph Patrick Tumulty, with Enclosure

Dear Tumulty: [The White House] 6 September, 1918

I do not know whether you have read this letter or not. Personally, I have no confidence at all in Mr. Wheeler,[1] the new President of the United States Chamber of Commerce, and I do not like to be seeing these gentlemen and making the impression that I am holding court with regard to the case they make against the Federal Trade Commission, and yet I do not want to put Saunders off in a way that he will not understand. What do you suggest?

The President

Mr. Tumulty doesn't see how you can get out of seeing Mr. Saunders.

TL (WP, DLC).
[1] That is, Harry Andrew Wheeler.

ENCLOSURE

From William Lawrence Saunders[1]

My dear Mr. President: New York September 5, 1918

May I not have the privilege, together with President Wheeler of the Chamber of Commerce of the United States, of a personal interview with you at your convenience to discuss the subject of the Federal Trade Commission and its relation to business?

For the first time, I have found it necessary to criticize (through the report of a committee of which I am a member) an executive body of your administration. I assure you that to do this has distressed and pained me very much.

When you were Governor of New Jersey I was asked to join and be a committee member of the Chamber of Commerce of the United States. I took the matter up with you and I recall your statement that such an organization was the right way to aid in the relations between the Government and business and that it could do much good provided it did not fall under selfish influences.

I have watched the Chamber of Commerce of the United States with an eye single to discover evidences of departure from the position about which you gave me this warning. I feel that I have been close enough to it to know that it has in no way fallen from the high plane on which it was started, and I believe to-day that it is the greatest single instrument for expression of the true public opinion of the business interests of the country.

As you know, I favored the creation of the Federal Trade Commission and gave some little aid to it in its work. Under Chairman Davies, and with his hearty co-operation, the Chamber of Commerce of the United States created a Federal Trade Committee, acting in an advisory capacity to the Commission. I have been upon that Committee from the beginning. We were welcomed by all of the members of the Commission, who gave us hearings and who called upon us for advice and co-operation.

The Commission began its work by asking business men to appear before it in various sections of the country. They established from the beginning a feeling of confidence among business men which extended up to a recent period.

When Mr. Hurley became chairman he gave evidence of his desire to make the Commission a helpful aid in conducting business properly. His work was thoroughly constructive and was much appreciated. When Mr. Harris became the chairman the same conditions existed. The Commission was careful to do nothing radical or destructive; yet it was ever watchful and strong in its determination to separate bad business from good business.

This Commission fulfilled all expectations and carried out the policy outlined by you on September sixth, 1916, when you said: "A Federal Trade Commission has been created with powers of guidance and accom[m]odation which have relieved business men of unfounded fears and set them upon the road of hopeful and confident enterprise."[2]

Senator Newlands, who did so much to aid you in the creation of this Commission, said to me in California some months afterwards: "The Federal Trade Commission will have justified its existence if it does nothing."

There has been of late a marked and lamentable change in the attitude of the Commission, which has brought about a feeling of uneasiness and a lack of confidence among business men that I regret to say threatens serious consequences.

I need hardly say that I am not directly or indirectly interested in any of the cases which have been subjects of attack by the

Commission. I am only interested in the principles involved, and I should like, together with President Wheeler, to lay the situation frankly before you.   Very truly yours,   W. L. Saunders

TLS (WP, DLC).
    [1] Distinguished engineer of New York and president of the Ingersoll-Sergeant Drill Co. A member of the Democratic National Campaign Committee in 1916, he had been active in the Democratic party in New Jersey and had been appointed by Wilson to the New Jersey Harbor Commission.
    [2] Actually, in his speech accepting the Democratic nomination on September 2, 1916. It is printed at that date in Vol. 38.

From Joseph Patrick Tumulty

Dear Governor: The White House September 6, 1918

In the matter of the proclamation which Mr. Close submitted to me this morning, I beg to make the following suggestion:

The words of a proclamation are so cold and formal that I am afraid the country will not grasp the full significance of what you really want to do. There is no doubt about the acuteness of the situation to which you wish to call the country's attention, but I think the proclamation ought to be preceded by a formal statement prepared for you by the financial authorities of the government showing how necessary it is to buttress the finances of the country by action along the lines suggested in the proclamation. For instance, if it could be shown that vast securities are held in the banks of the country that will be deeply affected if some action is not taken, the country would realize the full significance of what you are seeking to do.

Remember that what we are doing in this matter affects every man, woman and child in the country and that they ought to know why you believe this radical action necessary. I was going to suggest to you that Mr. Daniels of the Interstate Commerce Commission (who by the way, has a very facile pen) would be able to gather the facts for you and prepare a statement that would carry conviction to the country. In your letter to Mr. Daniels, you struct [struck] the keynote when you said:

"(the Secretary of the Treasury) is disturbed by the fact that some eleven billions of the securities of these companies are held by banks and trust companies as well as by private persons."

This is one of the most important questions we have had to handle since we came to Washington, and great care in the handling of it will have to be taken lest misunderstanding and misconstruction will be put upon what we are seeking to do.   Tumulty

TLS (WP, DLC).

To Joseph Patrick Tumulty, with Enclosure

Dear Tumulty: [The White House] 6 September, 1918

I quite agree with you about this. The proclamation is cold and it lacks the information which the public is entitled to. It was prepared by Mr. Daniels of the Interstate Commerce Commission and I merely changed the phraseology a little.

If Daniels would undertake a statement of the facts, nobody could make it more clearly than he. Would it be asking too much to ask you to call on him personally and see if that would be feasible?

The President

TL (WP, DLC).

ENCLOSURE[1]

PROCLAMATION
OF THE PRESIDENT OF THE UNITED STATES

WHEREAS certain of our Public Utilities,—such as Street Railways, Electric Light & Power, and Gas Companies—serve many communities, whose uninterrupted industrial activities are imperatively demanded for the successful prosecution of the Nation's War Program, many of ⟨these Public Utilities⟩ *them* directly serving Shipbuilding and Munition plants as well as other industries essential for the manufacture of materials and *for* the transportation of workers ⟨engaged in⟩ *to and from their* war work; and

WHEREAS these Public Utilities have felt, in common with other business concerns, the burden of increased expenses, occasioned by ⟨larger wages,⟩ higher cost of coal, ⟨and⟩ enhanced prices of ⟨all⟩ supplies, *and higher wages*; and

WHEREAS many of said Public Utilities are dependent upon State or local rate-fixing tribunals for authority to increase their rates and charges, and others are limited by statute⟨s⟩ or ordinance⟨s limiting⟩ *in respect of* the charges they may establish; and

WHEREAS our National Highways, the steam railroads, which ⟨now⟩ are *now* mainly under Federal control, and certain Interstate Electric Railroads, have *been authorized* by the Federal Government ⟨been authorized⟩ to increase their charges, in order to keep pace with rising costs; and

WHEREAS failure on the part of State Legislatures, State Commissions and Municipal rate-fixing bodies promptly to accord needed increases in rates and charges, where such ⟨exigency⟩ *need is shown to* exist⟨s⟩, threatens both the efficiency of *the* service and the financial solvency of some of these essential Public Utilities; and

WHEREAS several months ago, the Secretary of the Treasury directed the attention of the President to the existence of "a general apprehension regarding the adequacy, under present conditions, of the service and rates" of said Public Utility Companies,—an apprehension since reiterated by the War and Navy Departments, the Emergency Fleet Corporation, the Governors of the Federal Reserve Board, the Managing Director of the War Finance Corporation, ⟨as well as⟩ *and* by the Joint Chairmen of the War Labor Board; and

WHEREAS the burden of sustaining the solvency, credit and efficiency of service of such Public Utilities, both by granting increases in rates proportionate to increased operating costs, and, ⟨whenever necessary,⟩ by fortifying private and corporate credit by State or Municipal guaranties or loans *whenever necessary,* is a burden which properly devolves upon State and local authorities, and which ought not to be thrown upon or ⟨now be⟩ assumed by the Federal Government;

NOW THEREFORE, I, Woodrow Wilson, President of the United States of America, call upon the Governors of the several States, upon the State and Municipal rate-regulat⟨ory⟩*ing* tribunals, and upon all patrons of said Public Utilities to cooperate in making and conceding prompt and adequate response to ⟨demonstrated⟩ *the* financial needs of these Public Utilities *whenever they can be fairly demonstrated.*

To the Governors of the States, where State statutes or Municipal ordinances preclude the grant of immediate relief, I *respectfully* recommend the summoning of the legislatures in special session in order to provide promptly for just and proper rates and charges, and, *also,* where necessary, ⟨also⟩ to provide, as has already been done by the Commonwealth of Massachusetts, for the fortification of the corporate credit of menaced Public Utilities by a state guaranty. The relaxation of restrictive legislation or the temporary waiver of ordinance rights may well be limited to the duration of the war or the continuance of the present emergency.

Upon State and Municipal rate-fixing bodies I urge prompt and adequate action to the end that the service, efficiency and financial credit of these Public Utilities may not suffer.

I also appeal confidently to the great body of my fellow citizens, patrons of these Public Utilities, promptly and cheerfully to recognize the⟨ir⟩ patriotic duty of paying ⟨the⟩ increased rates ⟨obviously⟩ *wherever they have been shown to be* requisite to sustain the efficiency of service and soundness of credit of these Utilities for the adequate performance of their essential part of the Nation's War Program.

T MS (WP, DLC).
   ¹ Words in angle brackets in the following document deleted by Wilson; words in italics added by him.

To Winthrop More Daniels

My dear Daniels: The White House 6 September, 1918.

I am warmly obliged to you for your reply to my letter of August 30th concerning the difficulties now confronting the public utilities of the country. I am asking Tumulty to come over to see you about an aspect of the matter to which he has called my attention. In the meantime I have prepared the proclamation you suggest for signature. I find my judgment coinciding with yours.

I hope that your little vacation brought you refreshment.

In haste,   Faithfully yours,   Woodrow Wilson

TLS (Wilson-Daniels Corr., CtY).

To Joseph Patrick Tumulty

Dear Tumulty,   [The White House, c. Sept. 6, 1918]

This is now in shape for publication.[1]

I think it would be wise for you to send a copy to each Governor with such a note as you would know how to write.   W.W.

ALI (WP, DLC).
   ¹ Wilson enclosed a typed copy (WP, DLC) of the draft of the proclamation which he had edited. He made several new literary changes in this copy. As it turned out, the proclamation was never issued.

To William Byron Colver

My dear Colver: [The White House] 6 September, 1918.

You sent me, the other day, the bill which the Trade Commission had framed for the purpose of putting into execution the recommendations made with regard to the packers in the Commission's report on the packing industry, and I have been thinking about it a great deal.

The Railway Administration already has the legal right to take over all the cars privately owned and operated by the meat packers, and Mr. Hoover tells me that the various distributing agencies or branches owned by the packers throughout the country are already doing all that the capacity of their buildings permits, and in his judgment it would be of no real service to the public for the government to take them over and attempt to operate them.

I find Mr. Hoover in accord with the conclusions and purposes of your Commission, on the whole, with regard to the packers, but am convinced after my conference with him that no real material advantage would result from the action proposed by your bill, at any rate at this time.

I thought you were entitled to my candid opinion about this, for I know you always welcome it.

Cordially and sincerely yours, Woodrow Wilson

TLS (Letterpress Books, WP, DLC).

To Josephus Daniels

CONFIDENTIAL

My dear Daniels: The White House 6 September, 1918.

I feel so strongly that Roper is right in the enclosed[1] that I am writing to you to ask if you would think it right to give Mr. Ford the necessary tip in this matter, which is vital to his interests and vital to the interests of the country.

Cordially and faithfully yours, Woodrow Wilson

TLS (J. Daniels Papers, DLC).
[1] That is, D. C. Roper to JPT, Sept. 3, 1918, printed as an Enclosure with JPT to WW, Sept. 4, 1918.

To Harry Augustus Garfield

My dear Garfield: The White House 6 September, 1918.

Thank you for your note and your personal concern about my Western trip. As a matter of fact, I was thinking of such a trip and trying to plan it, but I have given up the idea on just the ground that you urge—that I cannot afford to be so long away from Washington. It would involve too much of the sort of danger you suggest as to what might take place in my absence.

Cordially and sincerely yours, Woodrow Wilson

TLS (H. A. Garfield Papers, DLC).

To William Julius Harris

[The White House] September 6, 1918.

No cause for concern about the price of cotton.[1] The plan is merely for an impartial inquiry to ascertain whether agreements would be serviceable in stabilizing transactions.

Woodrow Wilson.

T telegram (Letterpress Books, WP, DLC).
¹ The letter or telegram to which this was a reply is missing.

To William Gibbs McAdoo

My dear Mac: [The White House] 6 September, 1918.

The enclosed seems a very bulky paper,¹ but after all it does not, as I have found, take very long to read it, and it brings up a question of such vital importance that I am going to ask you of [if] you won't look through it and tell me what your judgment and advice would be about the suggested loan by American bankers to Mexico.

Always faithfully yours,   Woodrow Wilson

TLS (Letterpress Books, WP, DLC).
¹ The Editors have been unable to find this "very bulky paper" in any collection or repository.

To Edward Parker Davis

My dear E.P.:   [The White House] 6 September, 1918.

I did not until yesterday read your poem on The Fourth of July,¹ and I am afraid you will laugh at me when I tell you why. Because I had deliberately refrained. I had of course not forgotten it. The fact of the matter is that things have been at so anxious a stage throughout the summer, and I have been so doubtful about the outcome of the many things that I was in the midst of that, feeling instinctively that you were going to be generous enough to praise me in the poem, I felt I could not bear to read praise. It always saddens me for some reason when I am in the midst of things of doubtful success. But I have read the poem now, and read it with genuine admiration, and have derived inspiration from it. I thank you for it sincerely and affectionately.

Faithfully yours,   Woodrow Wilson

TLS (Letterpress Books, WP, DLC).
¹ E. P. Davis to WW, July 20, 1918, ALS, enclosing "Mount Vernon, July 4th, 1918," TI MS (WP, DLC).

To Robert Seymour Bridges

My dear Mr. Bridges: [The White House] 6 September, 1918.

I warmly appreciate your kind letter of August 19th which has just been put in my hands.¹ It breathes a spirit of such genuine sympathy with the greater objects of the struggle we are engaged in that I welcome it as I would a message from a friend who truly comprehends the things I am trying to express and put into action. It would indeed be worth the cost of this unspeakable war if by its means we could forever put the old statecraft aside.

I have read your poem[2] with the greatest interest and appreciation and hope that it will have just the effect you purpose for it, upon the people of India. I constantly have in my mind the waiting peoples, like the people of India, who are looking to see the dawn of a new day come after these months of strain and terror.

Cordially and sincerely yours,   Woodrow Wilson

TLS (Letterpress Books, WP, DLC).
   [1] It is missing.
   [2] It probably was "England to India," first published in *October & Other Poems* (London, 1920).

From George Carroll Todd

Dear Mr. President: Washington, D. C. September 6, 1918.

In the absence of the Attorney General, who left here Wednesday night for a few days vacation, I acknowledge your letter of the 5th instant making inquiry concerning the recent action of representatives of the Department of Justice in New York in making arrests of persons charged with being slackers.

From time to time since the enactment of the Selective Service Act representatives of this Department in cooperation with the Provost Marshal General's office have made many arrests of deserters and slackers throughout the country. The circumstances of the recent arrests in New York and vicinity, as reported in the newspapers, of course challenged the attention of the Department, and inquiries were set on foot to develop the facts. Last night Mr. John Lord O'Brian, Special Assistant to the Attorney General in charge of the enforcement of the Selective Service Law, went to New York to take charge of the investigation. The investigation will be prosecuted to a speedy conclusion and a full report made to you.

Respectfully,   G. Carroll Todd.

TLS (WP, DLC).

Two Letters from William Bauchop Wilson

My dear Mr. President: Washington September 6, 1918.

Replying to your letter of September 3d, I regret to have to state that while it is not correct to say that the Industrial Housing and Transportation Bureau of this Department has petitioned the Utilities Commission of New Jersey to grant a seven-cent fare to the

New Jersey Public Service Corporation, it has joined with the United States Shipping Board in petitioning that body to give *careful* consideration to the application of the Public Service Corporation for an increase to seven cents. Of course, the natural inference is that the petition is asking *favorable* consideration of the application. As soon as the matter was brought to my attention I directed that the petition be withdrawn, and yesterday a telegram was sent to the Public Utilities Commission of New Jersey to that effect. I have advised the Bureau that the matter of regulation of rates does not come within our jurisdiction and have had a personal talk with Mr. Eidlitz, and I feel sure there will be no recurrence of the mistake.

Faithfully yours,   W B Wilson

My dear Mr. President: Washington September 6, 1918.

The problem to which you call my attention in your letter of the 28th ultimo, which I find on my return, has for some time been receiving my anxious thought.

Undoubtedly we must work out methods of coordinating our efforts, and I gladly have acted on your suggestion to call a conference of the representatives of all the existing wage departments and adjusting agencies of the Government at my office for next Thursday to take the common counsel which as you say is essential to establish a common policy.

Faithfully yours,   W B Wilson

TLS (WP, DLC).

From Herbert Clark Hoover

Dear Mr. President: Washington 6 September 1918

In order that I may get before you as constructively as possible the problem of handling the Chicago Packers, as we view it, I have asked a number of the independent packers to come to Washington to consult with me early next week.

While the theoretical views of the Trade Commission are in my mind the ultimate desiderata, I feel there are some practical difficulties that might subject the program to a great deal of criticism.

The men I have chosen are men who have hewn their way up by sheer ability against a good deal of tyranny, and I believe their views will be of value. I am, therefore, delaying forwarding to you our recommendation until I have had the opportunity to discuss the matter with them.   Yours faithfully,   Herbert Hoover

TLS (WP, DLC).

From Samuel Lavit[1]

Honorable Sir: Bridgeport, Conn., Sept 6th 1918

At a mass meeting assembled at the Casino in Bridgeport Conn, Friday, September 6th 1918, where 6000 striking machinists were present,[2] resolutions were unanimously adopted and ordered dispatched to you.

I herewith enclose the resolutions.[3]

             Yours respectfully,   Samuel Lavit

TLS (WP, DLC).

[1] Business agent of District Lodge No. 55 of the International Association of Machinists.

[2] About this general strike of the machinists of Bridgeport, Conn., see WBW to WW, Sept. 11, 1918, and its Enclosure.

[3] Samuel Lavit *et al.*, "Resolutions Unanimously Adopted at a Meeting of 6000 Striking Machinists . . . ," TS MS (WP, DLC). The resolutions stated that the objective of the strike was to obtain a wage increase which would permit the workers to maintain a decent standard of living. To that end, the strikers demanded a classification of trades in the industries of Bridgeport which would protect workers from the arbitrary fixing of wage rates by employers. The strikers affirmed their devotion to America's war aims and to the policies of the administration and stated that they would gladly surrender everything which they had achieved in their long struggle with their employers if it would help the war effort. However, they declared, they were not prepared to make any sacrifices for the private enrichment of a few employers who were "mixing patriotism with profiteering." The resolutions then discussed at length the alleged huge wartime profits of several companies and called on the federal government to take over all essential industries.

Robert Lansing to Frank Lyon Polk

My dear Frank: [Washington] September 6, 1918.

I am in receipt of your letter of the 3d and am very glad that you have decided to remain away until the first of October. I think that you should not return as long as this rest is doing you good and I am sure that it is. While of course there is an immense amount of work in the Department we are getting along very well with it and I do not think you should feel that you are required just at this time. Of course I shall be very glad to see you back but do not want you to be anxious about the matter.

After Cabinet meeting last Tuesday I had a talk with the President about Al Smith. I told him that I intended to write him a letter of congratulation and he expressed his entire approval of my doing so. He also gave me the impression that he was very favorably inclined toward Smith and recognized that it was not a Tammany nomination but a nomination by the Democrats throughout the State. I think Gordon telephoned you that I hoped you would write him a letter. I think you should, if you have not already done so. I have written him congratulating him on his nomination and wishing him success. . . .[1]   Faithfully yours,   Robert Lansing.

CCL (R. Lansing Papers, DLC).
¹ The remainder of this letter concerned departmental and personal matters.

Lord Reading to Sir William Wiseman

[London] Sept. 6th. 1918.

No. 761 Lord Reading sends following message from PARIS this morning:

Your secret telegram of Aug. 31st.:

A.) I have not been unmindful of danger of such a situation with regard to HUGHES, but had not heard that he contemplated making such a speech or statement in passing through U. S. Let the PRESIDENT know that I shall take up matter immediately upon my return from FRANCE which will be Sunday.

B.) I am fully conscious of importance of the matter and shall do utmost to prevent any statement which might be or seemed to be not in accordance with the PRESIDENT's wishes or opinion. It is extremely difficult for BRITISH Government to appear to wish to control line which HUGHES may wish to take and any such attempt might have prejudicial effect.

C.) Understand that there is certain body of opinion which accepts eagerly a policy of retaliation. BRITISH Government has not announced such a policy. I had already communicated the PRESIDENT's views on economic question to LLOYD GEORGE and the WAR CABINET. Bear in mind that LLOYD GEORGE's position is rendered more difficult by probability of an early election although question not yet settled. Consequently attempts are being made to force his hand.

D). I feel sure HUGHES will act reasonably. I will telegraph again on my return.

T telegram (Reading Papers, FO 800/225, PRO).

To Edward Mandell House, with Enclosure

My dear House: The White House 7 September, 1918

Just a brief note to accompany the enclosed copy of the Covenant and to express my apologies for not having sent it to you sooner.

               Affectionately yours,   Woodrow Wilson

TLS (E. M. House Papers, CtY).

ENCLOSURE

COVENANT

PREAMBLE

In order to secure peace, security, and orderly government by the prescription of open and honorable relations between nations, by the firm establishment of the understandings of international law as the actual rule of conduct among governments, and by the maintenance of justice and a scrupulous respect for all treaty obligations in the dealings of all organized peoples with one another, the Powers signatory to this covenant and agreement jointly and severally adopt this constitution of the League of Nations.

ARTICLE I.

The action of the Signatory Powers under the terms of this agreement shall be effected through the instrumentality of a Body of Delegates which shall consist of the ambassadors and ministers of the contracting Powers accredited to H[olland]. and the Minister for Foreign Affairs of H. The meetings of the Body of Delegates shall be held at the seat of Government of H. and the Minister for Foreign Affairs of H. shall be the presiding officer of the Body.

Whenever the Delegates deem it necessary or advisable, they may meet temporarily at the seat of government of B[elgium]. or of S[witzerland]., in which case the Ambassador or Minister to H. of the country in which the meeting is held shall be the presiding officer *pro tempore.*

ARTICLE II.

The Body of Delegates shall regulate their own procedure and shall have power to appoint such committees as they may deem necessary to inquire into and report upon any matters which lie within the field of their action. They shall organize a Secretariat to act as their ministerial agency, and the expenses of the maintenance of the Secretariat shall be borne as they may prescribe.

In all matters covered by this Article the Body of Delegates may decide by a majority vote of the whole Body.

ARTICLE III.

The Contracting Powers unite in guaranteeing to each other political independence and territorial integrity; but it is understood between them that such territorial readjustments, if any, as may in the future become necessary by reason of changes in present racial conditions and aspirations or present social and political relationships, pursuant to the principle of self-determination, and also such territorial readjustments as may in the judgment of three-fourths of the Delegates be demanded by the welfare and manifest interest of the peoples concerned, may be effected, if agreeable to those peoples; and that territorial changes may in equity involve material compensation. The Contracting Powers accept without reservation the principle that the peace of the world is superior in importance to every question of Political jurisdiction or boundary.

H. 21[1]   ARTICLE IV.

The Contracting Powers recognize the principle that the establishment and maintenance of peace will require the reduction of national armaments to the lowest point consistent with domestic safety and the enforcement by common action of international obligations; and the Delegates are directed to formulate at once plans by which such a reduction may be brought about. The plans so formulated shall be binding when, and only when, unanimously approved by the Governments signatory to this Covenant.

The Contracting Powers further agree that munitions and implements of war shall not be manufactured by private enterprise or for private profit, and that there shall be full and frank publicity as to all national armaments and military or naval programmes.

H. 13   ARTICLE V.

The Contracting Powers agree that all disputes arising between or among them, of whatever nature, which shall not be satisfactorily settled by diplomacy shall be referred for arbitration to three arbitrators, one of the three to be selected by each of the parties to the dispute, when there are but two such parties, and the third by the two thus selected. When there are more than two parties to the dispute, one arbitrator shall be named by each of the several parties and the arbitrators thus named shall add to their number others of their own choice, the number thus added to be limited to the number which will suffice to give a deciding voice to the arbitrators thus added in case of a tie vote among the arbitrators chosen by the contending parties. In case the arbitrators chosen by the contending parties cannot agree upon an additional arbitrator or arbitrators, the additional arbitrator or arbitrators shall be chosen by the Body of Delegates.

On the appeal of a party to the dispute the decision of the arbitrators may be set aside by a vote of three-fourths of the Delegates, in case the decision of the arbitrators was unanimous, or by a vote of two-thirds of the Delegates in case the decision of the arbitrators was not unanimous, but unless thus set aside shall be finally binding and conclusive.

---

[1] This reference and the following references referred to the articles of House's draft, which is printed as an Enclosure with EMH to WW, July 16, 1918, Vol. 48.

When any decision of arbitrators shall have been thus set aside the dispute shall again be submitted to arbitrators chosen as heretofore provided, none of whom shall, however, have previously acted as arbitrators in the dispute in question, and the decision of the arbitrators rendered in this second arbitration shall be finally binding and conclusive without right of appeal.

H. 14.   ARTICLE VI.

Any Power which the Body of Delegates shall declare to have failed to submit any dispute to arbitration under the terms of Article V of this Covenant or to have refused or failed to carry out any decision of such arbitration shall thereupon lose and be deprived of all rights of commerce and intercourse with any of the Contracting Powers.

H. 15.   ARTICLE VII.

If any Power shall declare war or begin hostilities, or take any hostile step short of war, against another Power before submitting the dispute involved to arbitrators as herein provided, or shall declare war or begin hostilities, or take any hostile step short of war, in regard to any dispute which has been decided adversely to it by arbitrators chosen and empowered as herein provided, the Contracting Powers hereby bind themselves not only to cease all commerce and intercourse with that Power but also to unite in blockading and closing the frontiers of that Power to commerce or intercourse with any part of the world and to use any force that may be necessary to accomplish that object.

H. 5, 7, 8.   ARTICLE VIII.

Any war or threat of war, whether immediately affecting any of the Contracting Powers or not, is hereby declared a matter of concern to the League of Nations and to all the Powers signatory hereto, and those Powers hereby reserve the right to take any action that may be deemed wise and effectual to safeguard the peace of nations.

The Delegates shall meet in the interest of peace whenever war is rumoured or threatened, and also whenever the Delegate of any Power shall inform the Delegates that a meeting and conference in the interest of peace is advisable.

The Delegates may also meet at such other times and upon such other occasions as they shall from time to time deem best and determine.

H. 16, 17.   ARTICLE IX.

In the event of a dispute arising between one of the Contracting Powers and a Power not a party to this Covenant, the Contracting Power involved hereby binds itself to endeavour to obtain the submission of the dispute to judicial decision or to arbitration. If the other Power will not agree to submit the dispute to judicial decision or to arbitration, the Contracting Power shall bring the matter to the attention of the Body of Delegates. The Delegates shall in such case, in the name of the League of Nations, invite the Power not a party to this Covenant to become *ad hoc* a party and to submit its case to judicial decision or to arbitration, and if that Power consents it is hereby agreed that the provisions hereinbefore contained and applicable to the submission of disputes to arbitration shall be in all respects applicable to the dispute both in favor of and against such Power as if it were a party to this Covenant.

In case the Power not a party to this Covenant shall not accept the invitation of the Delegates to become *ad hoc* a party, it shall be the duty of the Delegates immediately to institute an inquiry into the circumstances and merits of the dispute involved and to recommend such joint action by the Contracting Powers as may seem best and most effectual in the circumstances disclosed.

H. 18.   ARTICLE X.

If hostilities should be begun or any hostile action taken against the Contracting Power by the Power not a party to this Covenant before a decision of the dispute by arbitrators or before investigation, report, and recommendation by the Delegates in regard to the dispute, or contrary to such recommendation, the Contracting Powers shall thereupon cease all commerce and communication with that Power and shall also unite in blockading and closing the frontiers of that Power to all commerce or intercourse with any part of the world, employing jointly any force that may be necessary to accomplish that object. The Contracting Powers shall also unite in coming to the assistance of the Contracting Power against which hostile action has been taken, combining their armed forces in its behalf.

H. 19.   ARTICLE XI.

In case of a dispute between states not parties to this Covenant, any Contracting Power may bring the matter to the attention of the Delegates, who shall thereupon tender the good offices of the League of Nations with a view to the peaceable settlement of the dispute.

If one of the states, a party to the dispute, shall offer and agree to submit its interests and cause of action wholly to the control and decision of the League of Nations, that state shall *ad hoc* be deemed a Contracting Power. If no one of the states, parties to the dispute, shall so offer and agree, the Delegates shall of their own motion take such action and make such recommendation to their governments as will prevent hostilities and result in the settlement of the dispute.

H. 22   ARTICLE XII.

Any Power not a party to this Covenant may apply to the Body
of Delegates for leave to become a party. If the Delegates shall
regard the granting thereof as likely to promote the peace, order,
and security of the world, they may act favourably on the application, and their favourable action shall operate to constitute the
Power so applying in all respects a full signatory party to this Covenant.

H. 23   ARTICLE XIII.

The Contracting Powers severally agree that the present Covenant and Convention is accepted as abrogating all treaty obligations
inter se which are inconsistent with the terms hereof, and solemnly
engage that they will not enter into any engagements inconsistent
with the terms hereof.

In case any of the Powers signatory hereto or subsequently admitted to the League of Nations shall, before becoming a party to
this Covenant, have undertaken any treaty obligations which are
inconsistent with the terms of this Covenant, it shall be the duty
of such Power to take immediate steps to procure its release from
such obligations.

T MS (E. M. House Papers, CtY).

To Robert Latham Owen

My dear Senator: [The White House] 7 September, 1918.

I have your letter of September 4th about the rates of interest[1]
and I am sincerely obliged to you for it. It is a matter in which I
am deeply interested.

          Cordially and sincerely yours,   Woodrow Wilson

TLS (Letterpress Books, WP, DLC).
  [1] R. L. Owen to WW, Sept. 4, 1918, TLS (WP, DLC). Owen called Wilson's attention
to the "propaganda" which was carried on by the *Journal of the American Bankers
Association* in favor of raising the rates of interest for the "patriotic, noble and disinterested purpose" of curtailing credits. Owen asked Wilson to throw the weight of the
administration against this propaganda and pointed out that the banks had earned an
average of over 20 per cent on their stocks during the previous year and were expected
to show similar net profits during the current year. He argued that, if the banks really
wanted to curtail credits, they could simply be stricter in granting them. Actually, Owen
maintained, interest rates should be lowered, since the present American rate of 6 per
cent was already twice as high as that of England.

To William Gibbs McAdoo

My dear Mac: [The White House] 7 September, 1918.

Here is a letter from Senator Owen which I promised him I would send you in order that you might make inquiry about the matter and correct any inequity that might be involved, if Senator Owen's information is correct.

Always faithfully yours,   Woodrow Wilson

TLS (Letterpress Books, WP, DLC).

To William Procter Gould Harding

[The White House]

My dear Governor Harding: 7 September, 1918.

I am a good deal disturbed to notice that apparently systematic propaganda is being instigated by the Journal of the American Bankers Association in favor of raising the rates of interest. I am very much concerned lest these representations should have some effect and would like your own judgment about the matter. Personally, it would seem to me that this is the very time to resist any such tendency and to go in the other direction, if possible. I should assume that any increase of rates would have a necessary reaction upon the rates of government securities.

Cordially and sincerely yours,   Woodrow Wilson

TLS (Letterpress Books, WP, DLC).

To Edward Albert Filene

My dear Mr. Filene: [The White House] 7 September, 1918.

I thank you for your letter of the fourth of September quoting your letter to Mr. House of the 30th of August. My judgment is very clear about the matter. Your instinct is right. It would be very hurtful to have a number of competitive and class schemes for reconstruction after the war, and I hope sincerely that you can convince the Executive Committee of the Chamber that it would be unwise and confusing and unpractical.

I have had in mind the formation of such a commission as you suggest, but have not satisfied myself as to the personnel of it or as to the instructions which should go to it, because I have noticed that commissions on the other side of the water have gone very far afield, and I am doubting the usefulness of their roving commissions. But I hope to address myself to the matter very soon now.

Cordially and sincerely yours, Woodrow Wilson

TLS (Letterpress Books, WP, DLC).

Two Letters from Edward Nash Hurley

Dear Mr. President: Washington September 7, 1918.

Before replying to your letter of August 29th, I wanted to refresh my mind as to whether any statement of mine might have been open to misconstruction by the British. The only statements I have made, however, were designed to show that the American merchant fleet now building would be as beneficial to the world in peace as it is intended to be in war. I have been tempted at times to argue that our ships would benefit us primarily, so that a certain discontent which unquestionably exists among many of the workers in the shipyards might be removed, but I have realized that the situation is delicate and that much harm might be done even by unwise reassurance of our own people.

Before entering the government service, I was interested in a company successfully doing business in England and came to know the British mind fairly well. It has distressed me to note constantly since the war began the very condition which you describe in your letter. I am afraid that some of the alarm they express over our shipbuilding program is simulated. You may remember that when we commandeered ships being built for British account they gave signs of deep concern. Yet at the very time they were making their arguments here, the British marine papers were rather gleefully calling attention to the fact that British owners were relieved of the high war costs in building ships, and that they would be able to replace the tonnage at half the price after the war.

In the same manner, the real shipping experts point out that our operating costs will always be higher than the British operating costs, and that this advantage quickly will restore the lead of England after the war.

Lord Reading mentioned to me before his departure for England that he would like to discuss on his return the question of pooling American and British shipping interests after the war. Of course, I shall be pleased to listen to what he has to say, but will be guarded and not commit our government in any way.

My own thought has been that they not only believe you to be entirely fair and generous, but that they know it absolutely. The

British business men are literally dominating the policy of the British government towards us. The figures they furnished us with regard to the ships they could spare were the figures their own shipping interests wanted them to put forward. These figures were quickly revised when the call came for a larger American force in France. The same thing was true with respect to coal and oil.

I agree with you that we should not give them the slightest color of provocation or excuse for what they are doing. America can afford to make sacrifices for her own ideals, but it is regrettable that interests which are identical should not have behind them an identical and single motive.

The Committee on Public Information on August 23rd requested me to make a statement on this subject for publication in Great Britain, and I take the liberty of enclosing herewith copy of same for your information.[1]

You can rest assured that I appreciate the spirit of your frank letter, and will avoid anything that might in any way lend itself to an evil interpretation of selfishness.

Yours very sincerely,   Edward N. Hurley

TLS (WP, DLC).
    [1] E. N. Hurley to the Committee on Public Information, Aug. 23, 1918, TC MS (WP, DLC). In this press release, Hurley acknowledged that the United States was building a large fleet of transports and food ships in order to carry out its military program and that, following the war, this fleet would be used in "America's enormous ocean carrying trade." However, he strongly denied that it would be used for "trade conquests" at the expense of America's present associates in the war. Any suggestion to the contrary, he asserted, was the work of enemy propagandists. Hurley summarized the uses to be made of the new American merchant marine as follows: "In building her merchant fleet America plans first of all to win the war, and after that to overcome her own neglect in providing ocean transportation for her own trade. To this end the people of the United States are preparing to develop transportation on their own trade routes, without disturbing the trade rights of other nations. And they, furthermore, hope that the American merchant marine will play a large part in bringing the neighboring democracies of the American hemisphere closer together."
    This statement was printed in the *Official Bulletin*, II (Aug. 23, 1918), 4.

Dear Mr. President: Washington September 7, 1918.

The transit situation has given all of us great concern in connection with the shipbuilding program. This problem is equal in its size and complexity to the housing problem.

After receiving your note of inquiry, I was distressed to find that our Director of Passenger Transportation and Housing[1] had, in a well-meaning, but misguided manner, joined with the Bureau of Industrial Housing and Transportation of the Labor Department in a recommendation to the Public Utilities Commission of New Jersey for "such a rate of fare upon the property of the Public Service Railway Company as will provide it with sufficient funds to pay its operating expenses and maintain its financial stability as a going concern."

Upon ascertaining the facts, I called Mr. Schwab on the 'phone at the Philadelphia offices and asked him to instruct the Director of Passenger Transportation and Housing to withdraw the recommendation immediately. Mr. Eidlits,[2] Director of the Bureau of Industrial Housing and Transportation of the Labor Department, informs me that he is following the same course.

There is no doubt that the transportation situation, as it affects the greatly augmented forces at the shipyards, is becoming serious. The problem is by no means confined to New Jersey. I haven't any doubt that some unscrupulous transit interests are trying to use this situation for their own advantage, but I have explained to the officials of the Emergency Fleet Corporation that separate dealing with the street railway companies should not be undertaken by them; that while the situation affects us vitally, the problem is of a general nature and that a solution of general nature eventually may be applied.

Only an agency devoting itself to the study of the problem will be able to separate the sheep from the goats. I have pointed out to those who are charged with maintaining transportation to and from the shipyards that they cannot possibly have sufficient information to determine the merits of cases before State commissions; that even though transportation conditions should fail completely the adjustment of the finances of the transportation companies is not within their province.

I believe the instructions I have given will prevent a recurrence of the incident and, if the New Jersey Public Service crowd have been preening themselves upon any aid given them by the recommendation, they are likely to conclude that its withdrawal leaves them worse off than they were before.

As I have indicated, we are all hopeful that there will be a national solution of the problem, which is constantly growing more acute with respect to the shipyards, but you may rest assured that there will be no further efforts by any members of our organization to seek relief in the manner that caused you to be concerned.

Faithfully yours,   Edward N. Hurley

TLS (WP, DLC).
[1] Abraham Merritt Taylor.
[2] That is, Otto Marc Eidlitz.

From Joseph Patrick Tumulty

Dear Governor: The White House September 7, 1918.

In the discussion we had a few days ago with reference to the pending "dry" legislation,[1] I tried to emphasize the fact that under the food control law you had the power to do what Congress is seeking to do in a way that will cause great irritation. Your action yesterday fixing December 1st as the day on which the prohibition of the manufacture of beer is to take place,[2] I believe, strengthens what I said. Your action and the action of the Senate a day or two ago in giving you the right to establish zones about shipyards and munitions plants[3] again shows the unnecessary character of this legislation. Your action of yesterday and the Senate's action puts you in a strong position to veto this legislation as unnecessary. Certainly the prohibitionists in view of your action could not find anything in a veto to complain about.

In your letter of May 28th to Senator Sheppard you said that you were

"very much distressed by the action of the House (and that you did not think it) wise or fair to attempt to put such compulsion on the Executive in a matter in which he has already acted almost to the limit of his authority. My own judgment is that it is wise and statesmanlike to let the situation stand as it is for the present, until at any rate I shall be apprised by the Food Administration that it is necessary in the way suggested still further to conserve the supply of food and feedstuffs. The Food Administration has not thought it necessary to go any further than we have in that matter already gone."[4]

The Springfield Republican, commenting upon the proposed legislation said:

"A Congress elected in 1916, without a mandate directly from the constituencies, is [has] virtually decided the issue by a majority vote. The establishment of national prohibition by federal statute, through the mere action of Congress, does not appeal to one as so desirable as the establishment of national prohibition by the direct action of three-fourths of the states."

The St. Louis Post-Dispatch, commenting on the proposed legislation said:

"If it were a necessary war measure everyone would accept it, but as a wanton attempt of politicians to curry favor with certain elements of voters it will be resented. The politicians of Congress seem bent on this madness. There is little hope of checking it. *But there is hope of sanity in the President.*"

The New York Evening Post, commenting on the action of the Senate and House says:

"Insincerity is stamped all over the measure. Compromise, we know, is often necessary in matters political, but this particular compromise eats up the original professed object of the whole. The scheme was put forward as one to win the war. To consent to adjourn its coming into effect for nearly a year is to admit that the bill sails under false colors. Prohibition as a war-measure is either an honest thing, honestly to be pressed as an immediate necessity, or else it is a sham and a pretence. The whole proceeding as [is] humbug."

The New York World, commenting on the legislation says: "There has been no general public demand for this measure. There has been no Administration demand for it. The provisions of the amendment were conceived by the professional Prohibition hobby [lobby] and have been carried along upon a wave of Congressional cowardice. If the bill finally becomes a law it will stand as a monument to the hypocrisy of Senators and Representatives who do not believe in it but who accepted it in the fear that the Prohibition vote may hold the balance of power in their districts and States and who are therefore convinced that political dishonesty is the best policy."

The Brooklyn Eagle characterizes it as "fake legislation," saying: "It is fake legislation because it is fastened like a parasite upon a measure otherwise excellent, and this is done over the protest of the President of the United States."

In view of all this, I wish to emphasize the dangers both of a political and commercial character that we should consider before we agree to go forward with those who favor legislation of this radical character.

I have it from inside sources that even the most ardent prohibitionists fear the reactionary effect of this legislation upon the pending constitutional amendment.[5] My principle [principal] objection to this legislation at this time, in view of the coming elections, I am frank to say, is political. I am afraid of its effects upon the voters of our party in the large centers of population throughout the country and of the resentment from all classes that is bound to follow in its path.

The average American feels that the only safe course to follow, especially in matters of legislation that seeks to regulate the morals and habits of the people, is to follow the methods set forth in the Constitution for the regulation of these matters.

The proponents of this measure, like Senator Kenyon of Iowa, agree that it is not a conservation measure, but that it is an out-and-out attempt to declare the country dry. It is mob legislation, pure and simple.

The danger of submitting quietly to any class legislation that has its basis in intolerance especially at a time like this where the emotions of people can be whipped into a fury, is obvious. Your strength in the country comes from the feeling that under no circumstances can you be "hazed" by any class. If you yield in this instance, other demands, you may be sure, will come from other sources.

The viewpoint of the gentlemen in charge of this bill is provincial. They have no idea of the readjustments that will have to come in the finances of our largest cities and municipalities through the country. I have before me an article from a leading Ohio paper, the headlines of which read as follows: "Bereft of liquor revenue, Ohio must dig up elsewhere $2,722,000. Many city treasuries to need finances. Tax rate is bound to go up, say forecasters. Dislocations arising from war conditions also to impair income and general business." The article goes on to say that the larger cities of Ohio must get more income or face the unpleasant position of occupying the bankrupt's dock in court. This comes from a State whose largest cities gave an overwhelming majority for the Democratic party in 1916.

The same financial situation confronts every large city in the east and west. Increased taxation in these cities, coming at a time when federal taxes are growing more nurdensome [burdensome] is bound to play a large part at the election, and the party in power cannot escape the responsibility.

So much in a great, broad, humanitarian way depends upon your win[n]ing the next election that I look with dread and disfavor upon anything that stands in its way. Our policy in every matter at this time should be one based upon mag[n]animity and tolerance toward every class and interest in the country.

Sincerely   Tumulty

TLS (WP, DLC).

¹ The Senate, on August 29, had adopted an amendment to H.R. 11945, a supplementary agricultural bill, which provided that, after May 1, 1919, and through the end of the period of demobilization, no foodstuffs could be used for the production of beer and wine. After June 30, 1919, and through the period of demobilization, no distilled spirits, beer, or wine could be sold for beverage purposes in the United States, except for export abroad. The date of the end of demobilization was to be determined and proclaimed by the President. The Senate passed H.R. 11945 with the prohibition rider attached on September 6 and appointed the Senate members of a Senate-House conference committee to deal with the measure. The House, on September 7, sent the Senate version of the bill to the Committee on Agriculture for a report. *Cong. Record*, 65th Cong., 2d sess., pp. 9625-51, 10070-10086, 10093.

² This decision was reached after a conference between Wilson and representatives of the Food, Fuel, and Railroad administrations and of the War Industries Board, because of shortages of fuel, grain, labor, and transportation necessary to the war effort. *Official Bulletin*, II (Sept. 7, 1918), 1. The conference presumably took place in connection with the meeting of the "War Cabinet" on September 4. The text of Wilson's proclamation ordering this curtailment, signed Sepctember 16, is printed *ibid.*, Sept. 19, 1918, p. 3.

³ Senator Frank B. Kellogg, on September 5, had introduced S.J. Res. 172, which authorized the President to establish zones around coal mines, munition factories, ship-

building facilities, and other plants producing war materials, in which the manufacture, sale, or distribution of intoxicating liquors would be prohibited. This resolution was taken verbatim from a section of the prohibition amendment to H.R. 11945, discussed in n. 1 above. Kellogg explained that he believed that it was essential for the President to have this power sooner than was likely with the slow progress of H.R. 11945 through Congress. The Senate passed the resolution that same day, the House of Representatives on September 9. Wilson signed the joint resolution on September 11. *Cong. Record,* 65th Cong., 2d sess., pp. 9976, 9979-85, 10117-18, 10696.

⁴ WW to M. Sheppard, May 28, 1918, Vol. 48.

⁵ The Eighteenth Amendment providing for the nationwide prohibition of the manufacture, sale, or transportation of intoxicating liquors for beverage purposes, had passed the House and Senate, respectively, on December 17 and 18, 1917, and was now in process of ratification.

From Breckinridge Long, with Enclosure

My dear Mr. President: Washington September 7, 1918.

At the suggestion of the Secretary over the telephone, I am enclosing you a copy of a despatch which has just been submitted to us by the Navy Department, and which is so encouragingly important as to warrant bringing it to your immediate attention.

Yours respectfully,   Breckinridge Long

TLS (WP, DLC).

E N C L O S U R E

From: Flag BROOKLYN
To: Secnav.

From the westward reliable report indicates extraordinary favorable military situation. It is reported by S. Gaida,[1] Commander Czechs troops from Central Siberia, that 90,000 Czech once [and] large force Russians under his command, total approximately 160,000. By authority of provisional government a large number of Russians are mobilizing. They are actual figures from Colonel Gaida who is now supreme Commander in Chief of Czech Forces, superseding General Dieterich. Urgently require arms and ammunition, clothing for much more force than heretofore believed possible.

Estimate that the clothing which heretofore been given should be doubled.

It is reported by Gaida that 40,000 German-Austrian prisoners under control all prisoners and Bolsheviki opposition broken down. The road is clear to point beyond Volga where formidable front already exists. Urge immediate material help.

Japanese Cavalry captured Habarosk, complete destruction of opposition prisoners. 10206.   Flag BROOKLYN

T MS (WP, DLC).
    [1] Actually, Col. or Gen. Rudolf Gajda.

From Arthur Bernard Krock[1]

Dear Mr. President:　　　Louisville, Ky. September Seventh 1918

Mr. Tumulty fully understands the situation in Kentucky, but I venture to give you the details as they appear to me. We of the Courier-Journal and The Times, it is needless to assure you, will leave no force unspent to elect Democrats to Congress from Kentucky this fall, but in my opinion your help will be needed.

Gov. Stanley has been nominated by the state committee to succeed Senator James, and this was done in the face of some sentiment for a ratifying convention or primary. This sentiment, since our newspapers represented it, can be overcome by the unwavering support we expect to give to the nominee.

The Governor appointed George Brown Martin, a worthy but little-known citizen, as ad interim Senator. It happens that he is personally acceptable to Senator Beckham, but the Governor did not consult with Senator Beckham about the matter and may thereby have lost a chance to secure ardent support in some quarters. Senator Beckham will do everything in his power for Mr. Stanley, however, and therefore this condition also can probably be overcome. There was a strong sentiment in Louisville for the appointment of a representative citizen as Senator, and the fact that the Governor did not do this seems to me to have cost the ticket some independent votes it might otherwise have gained.

A fourth condition, and the most serious, is that the Governor is personally weak with the "dry" element and with the independents. Whatever the basis, they do not give him credit for the ability and character I know him to possess. With this large element it will be difficult to win support for the Governor unless you, by whatever means you see fit, make it known that you consider his election essential to your war programme.

Without such an expression from you, I am afraid we shall have a difficult task in trying to elect Governor Stanley. Backed by you publicly, our task will be rendered much simpler.

I trust this will not seem presumptuous on my part, but as a humble worker in a great field in which you are harvest-master, I ventured to give you my opinion.

　　　　　　　　　　Very respectfully,　Arthur B Krock

TLS (WP, DLC).
    [1] Princeton 1908; at this time editorial manager of the Louisville *Courier-Journal* and the *Louisville Times*.

From Augustus Owsley Stanley

My dear Mr. President: Frankfort September 7th. 1918.

I have this day commissioned the Honorable George B. Martin, of Catlettsburg, Kentucky, to succeed the late Senator Ollie M. James. You will find in Senator Martin a jurist of ability, a genuine patriot and a man of stainless and exalted character. It affords me genuine pleasure to assure you of his earnest desire to most cordially co-operate with the President of the United States in every possible way.

I have advised Senator Martin of your attitude toward suffrage for women. While not predisposed to this reform, I have every reason to believe that his profound deference for the wisdom and sagacity of the President will induce him to waive any personal preference or preconceived opinion in this matter, and I sincerely hope that you will find in the new Kentucky Senator a tower of strength in every time of need.

Most cordially yours,   A. O. Stanley.

TLS (WP, DLC).

From Key Pittman

My dear Mr. President: [Washington] September 7, 1918.

Were I not certain of your deep interest in the General Leasing Bill now in conference between the two Houses and of the desperate situation of the legislation, I would not trespass upon your time nor place this additional burden upon you. The fact is, however, that the legislation will entirely fail unless you affirmatively aid the conference to reach an agreement that will be acceptable to the Senate and the House. No report will be adopted by congress that does not meet your pronounced approval. There are certain provisions in the House bill that a majority of the conferees on the part of the Senate will not agree to, and if agreed to by the other conferees, will result in a fight, in my opinion, upon the floor of the Senate that will prevent the adoption of the report.

You are aware, of course, that Senator Walsh and myself, have for several years been most earnestly endeavoring to formulate a bill which would be in the nature of a compromise between the extreme policies with regard to the acquisition and development of our mineral resources in public lands. The Senate bill was largely the result of such efforts and was successful to the extent that it accomplished a compromise between the opposing radicles [radicals] in the Senate. I feel that I am justified in saying that four of the five managers on behalf of the conferees of the House are in substantial accord with the managers of the conference on the part of the Senate, and would meet with the Senate conferees and agree on a bill were it not for the position taken by Mr. Scott Ferris. Mr. Ferris' attitude, as it appears to the conferees of the Senate, is inflexible and uncompromising, and he seems in no disposition to make further efforts to reach an agreement. The other managers on behalf of the House, in contradiction to their former expressions both in the Committee on Public Lands of the House and at meetings of the conferees, did at our last meeting, which was on Tuesday, announce that they intend to stand by their Chairman, Mr. Ferris. A provision of the Senate bill, which we had tentatively agreed to, was then taken up for reconsideration. It was then that the impending result became ominous, and I feel it my duty as a last resort to submit the matter to you. Permit me to say that the Senate conferees have already made great concessions, and, in my opinion, are willing to make more if the conferees on the part of the House manifest a like disposition. If they do not manifest such desire, the Senate conferees will undoubtedly do just exactly what, in my opinion, you would do if you were in their position.

I am conscious of the fact that you are vested with the power to develop and operate the coal and oil fields of the country, and that you will probably be forced to such action unless some form of leasing bill becomes a law and in the immediate future. I, for one, would deplore this necessity. Whilst I deeply sympathize with the unfortunate situation of the prospectors and producers, who have discovered and developed the great coal and oil fields of this country, that phase of the question is not the one that chiefly disturbes me. I must confess that I cannot throw off the fear that is growing upon me that the hasty and unrestricted drift into governmental paternalism and multiplying bureaus will destroy American initiative and originality and make it difficult for us to maintain the spirit of our government and our institutions. I cannot deceive myself as to the political possibilities of an united army of political employees utilizing their political influence to coerce those whom they elect and who are responsible for their employment into conceding their demands without regard to the effect upon the other citizens of our country. I trust that I will not be misunderstood. I have long favored the State ownership of all public utilities as a matter of public necessity, but beyond this I have not up to the present time felt warranted in going for the reasons that I have heretofore suggested. At the same time, in a period of war, I am firmly convinced that the government should have unlimited control over every instrumentality essential to obtaining a victory.

The oil producers are willing and anxious to increase their production, and they have the facilities to accomplish this purpose, provided the government will provide any system of rules under which they can operate and will remove the restrictions that at the present time prevent them from increasing such production. The two bills now in conference, and which have been considered during a period of five years, will provide these rules without repealing or decreasing in any way the present unlimited power of the government under other laws to control the price, the use, and the transportation of the product. There are only, as I recall, three important differences in the two bills. The first ground of dispute arises in attempting to harmonize Section 10 of the House bill and Section 12 of the Senate bill. The House bill provides in part, as follows:

"The permittee shall also be entitled to a preference right to a lease for the remainder of the land in the prospecting permit at such royalty, not less than one-eighth, *as may be fixed by the Secretary of the Interior*, for such periods and under such other conditions as are fixed for oil or gas leases in this Act."

The Senate bill provides in part, as follows:

"That said permittee shall be given a preference right to lease the remaining and unpatented lands embraced within the limits of his permit at a royalty of not less than one-eighth, and at a rate to be determined by competitive bidding, and upon the same terms and conditions as provided for other leases, or said permittee may at his election, and with like preference right, and upon like conditions, become the lessee of the entire tract embraced within said permit instead of receiving a patent for any part thereof."

The Senate conferees are opposed on principle to delegating an unlimited and unqualified discretion to any Department of the government if any definite and fixed plan can be devised. The House provision delegates such discretion. The Senate provision establishes a general method of arriving at a determination as to the fair compensation to be paid by the lessee as a royalty to the government. The Senate conferees believe that the limitations contained in the Senate provision would protect the government. They are willing, however, in my opinion, to add any other definite and reasonable limitations. I am satisfied that they will never agree to the unrestricted and unqualified authority delegated to the Secretary of the Interior in the House provision.

The second material difference is in regard to the disposition of coal lands. The Senate bill provides for either the sale or lease of coal lands, while the House bill provides simply for the leasing of coal lands, leaving the sale of coal lands to the provisions of existing laws. Under existing law coal lands are first appraised by the agents of the government and thereafter cannot be sold for less than the appraised value. Under the Senate provision coal lands are sold at competitive sale to the highest bidder, under such rules and regulations as the Secretary of the Interior may establish, with the power reserved in the Secretary to refuse any and all bids that he may consider unfair. In one case the price is fixed by an agent of the Department of the Interior, while in the other it is fixed by the Secretary of the Interior. Under existing law a geologist, who may know nothing of business or business conditions, and who may see no difference in the value of a ton of coal in Oklahoma and in Wyoming, fixes an arbitrary price, which, in many cases, has prevented the development of great coal fields. Under the Senate bill the Secretary of the Interior would be advised as to the value of coal lands by the geologist and by such other experts as necessary to the determination of the value of the coal. Senator Shafroth and other western Senators are bitterly antagonistic to the appraising system in the present law but are entirely satisfied to leave the fixing of the price to the Secretary of the Interior. I must also frankly state that Senator Shafroth and a majority of the Senate conferees consider this objection to the House bill as fundamental and involving a principle of development of the west that in their opinion is vital.

The third cause of difference is involved in the so-called remedial legislation affecting oil claims within withdrawn areas. The conferees have not yet reached the consideration of the differences in the bills touching upon this subject. The Senate bill made no attempt to deal with lands within Naval Reserves. I believe, though I have no authority for the statement, that the Senate conferees would agree to such provisions in the House bill provided that the House conferees agree with the provisions in the Senate bill affecting the lands outside of Naval Reserves. If some arrangement along this line could not be made, I still have hope that the Senate conferees would agree to a provision delegating to you the entire determination of the relief to be granted. None of the Senate conferees and none of the western Senators that I am aware of have the slightest uneasiness with regard to your ability or your desire to do absolute justice between the government and the individuals in each case. They know, however, that it would be impossible, in the circumstances, for you to give any personal attention to the matter, and that in the necessity of the case, unless other provisions were made, that you would refer the matter to the Attorney General. With all due respect to the Attorney General, and I have the highest respect for his ability and integrity, I feel personally, as do a number of other Senators, that he has become biased, if not prejudiced, in this matter through information derived from the special agents of his Department and other inexperienced but sincere legal assistants who have been chiefly moved by the belief, and sincerely no doubt, that great crimes have been committed, and by an ambitious desire to punish some one. It is very difficult for a prosecutor to sit as a judge in the case which he is prosecuting. Will you not pardon me for suggesting that possibly a solution of the matter would be the delegation of this authority to you and the execution of it through a special tribunal composed of three or five impartial, unbiased and able citizens?

I am, of course, at your service at any time that you may command me with regard to this matter as any other.

Very sincerely yours,   Key Pittman.

TLS (WP, DLC).

From Thomas Garrigue Masaryk

Mr. President: [Washington] September 7th, 1918.

Allow me to express the feeling of profound gratitude for the recognition of our Army, the National Council, and the nation.

After arriving in the United States I paid my first visit to the Gettysburg Cemetery—after a year's sad experiences in Russia I wished to collect my mind at this solemn place of America's great struggle for democracy and unity;—I read America's eternal message, cast in iron, that the government of the people, by the people, for the people, shall never perish from this Earth. At an historical moment of great significance Lincoln formulated these principles which were to rule the internal policies of the United States,—at a historical moment of world-wide significance you, Mr. President, shaped these principles for the foreign policies of this great Republic as well as those of the other nations: that the whole mankind may be liberated—that between nations, great and small, actual equality exists—that all just power of governments is derived from the consent of the governed, these, you say, are the principles in which Americans have been bred, and which are to constitute the foundation of world-democracy.

In accordance with these principles of American democracy you, and the Government of the United States, have recognized the justice of our struggle for independence and national unity; I am entitled and greatly honored to thank you, in the name of our whole nation, for this act of political generosity, justice and political wisdom. America's recognition will strengthen our armies and our whole nation in their unshakeable decision to sacrifice everything for the liberation of Europe and of mankind.

My best wishes to you, Mr. President, in your difficult and responsible work for America and the world.

Believe me,

    Most sincerely and respectfully yours,   T. G. Masaryk.

TLS (WP, DLC).

Augustus Owsley Stanley to Joseph Patrick Tumulty

My dear Mr. Tumulty: Frankfort September 7th., 1918.

Before commissioning Senator Martin, I took occasion to advise him of the President's earnest desire to have the Suffrage Amendment submitted at the present session of the Federal Congress and suggested some of the many excellent reasons given for the immediate enactment of this legislation.

I was delighted to find that the new Senator earnestly desires to co-operate in every way with the President and shares my exalted opinion of his worth and wisdom. I regret that certain over-zealous persons have attempted to commit him in the public press by suggestions as to his attitude in this matter, which I am sure is not warranted by anything that either of us may have ever said, and I fear that he may be led to regard this course as a kind of covert coercion. Such tactics are most unwise in dealing with a man of modest worth, fine self-respect, perfect courage and no further political ambition. If the new Senator should interpret such an attempt as an implied threat, it might tend to neutralize even the influence of the President of the United States supplemented by all that I may be able to do or say.

If, however, he is left to that most tactful and courteous gentleman, Woodrow Wilson, I am morally certain that he will be able to convince him of the correctness of his position, and I am the more confident since I know how genuinely anxious he is to aid the President in every way, notwithstanding the fact that under ordinary circumstances he would not be inclined to regard this reform with favor.   Most cordially yours,   A. O. Stanley.

TLS (WP, DLC).

From Benedict Crowell

My dear Mr. President: Washington. September 8, 1918.

Referring to your letter of 5th September, concerning the interest of the War Department in the matter of propaganda abroad, General March advises me that the whole question of the propaganda abroad with which Captain Lippman[n] was concerned was handled by Secretary Baker personally. The Secretary, after conferences with representatives of the Bureau of Public Information; and with the Military Intelligence Division, at which the Chief of Staff was present; and in response to the initiation of this propaganda by the Bureau of Public Information, directed the organization of the party consisting of Captain Blankenhorn, Captain Lippman, Lieutenant Merz[1] and Lieutenant Ifft.[2] These officers were to proceed to France to carry out confidential instructions which were given to them by Secretary Baker in person. Secretary Baker also wrote to General Pershing a letter in which he defined the objects of this mission and gave General Pershing necessary instructions as to his attitude toward it.

A part of the propaganda proposed consisted of getting into the territorial limits of the Central Powers certain information concerning activities of the United States in connection with the war. The Bureau of Public Information has not been able to successfully get such information into Germany and Austria hitherto. The scheme involved the preparation of certain propaganda matter which Secretary Baker proposed to visé himself or have viséd by responsible officers who would carry out his policy in the matter, so as to prevent exaggerated statements being used in the propaganda.

In accordance with the general scheme, the War Department has placed orders for a number of balloons of small dimensions, which it is proposed to start toward German territory from a base with the American Expeditionary Force when the wind is favorable, these balloons having a relatively small radius of travel so that they will be sure to get to land within the limits of the Empire of the Central Powers. The orders for these balloons have actually been placed and the carrying out of the general scheme of this propaganda would be impossible without the coordinated work of the military establishment. You will recall that in order to obtain the money for the purchase of these balloons, it was necessary to ask you for $76,000 from your war fund and this money was allotted by you for this purpose at the personal solicitation of Secretary Baker, and it was understood that Mr. Creel acted at the same time in obtaining this amount.

Captain Lippman was placed upon this committee at the suggestion of Secretary Baker himself. The committee arrived abroad and shortly after its arrival in France a cablegram was received from General Pershing announcing in general terms that the committee apparently was well selected for the purpose in hand.

In accordance with your instructions, orders have been given to the senior officer of this committee, Captain Blankenhorn, to discontinue any further activity and to report to Secretary Baker upon his arrival. A cablegram has also been sent to Secretary Baker to be delivered to him upon his arrival, announcing what your action has been in this matter and it is expected, as the entire matter was handled by Secretary Baker personally, that he will then communicate with you concerning it.

While the War Department, of course, intends to carry out exactly what you desire in this matter, it would seem that the field for propaganda of the class indicated could only be reached by the assistance of the military establishment. In propaganda work in other countries the Military Intelligence Division has never assumed any control or direction. The Military Attachés at Madrid, Berne, and other places have been told to place themselves at the disposal of the representatives of the Bureau of Public Information and to cooperate with them to any extent that they desire; but they have never attempted to initiate any such propaganda themselves.

Sincerely yours,   Benedict Crowell

TLS (WP, DLC).
¹ Charles Merz, formerly the Washington correspondent of *The New Republic*.
² George Nicholas Ifft II, Princeton 1915.

From the Diary of Colonel House

September 8, 1918.

I did not have anyone to meet McAdoo and Loulie took her dinner upstairs so we might be alone for dinner and until bedtime. Our talk was largely personal and had to do with the President, McAdoo's relations with him, and McAdoo's conduct of the Treasury and Railroads. I was amused to hear him express himself almost in my exact words, that is, he noticed signs of the President being a candidate for a third term. I confirmed this opinion. I thought there was nothing for McAdoo to do except to go on in the even tenor of his way, do his work in the efficient manner in which he has been doing it; think not at all of himself but of the public he was serving, and leave his fate in the hands of Providence. I thought it possible that the President would run, but there were many chances that he would not. I thought, too, that the President had it [in] mind stronger now than he would have later.

McAdoo tells me that the Gavin McNab letter to me, which I sent to the President,[1] advising against his speaking tour early in October, turned the scales against it, at least, McAdoo thinks the President has given it up for the moment. The President told him, too, that "I feel that I am not so strong in labor circles now as I was sometime ago." He was amused to know that this was an exact quotation from my letter to the President of September 3rd.

I explained to McAdoo the difficulty I had in advising the President. He, the President, expects me to keep absolutely abreast of both domestic and foreign situations and, in addition to that, he expects me to read his mind and know what conclusions he has come to or will come to under certain conditions. I have only received two or three letters from the President this summer. I am sure, as McAdoo says, that my influence with him is as strong as ever, perhaps stronger. There is every indication of it but I only know it from his actions and from friends to whom he happens to talk upon subjects about which I have written him. It is hardly fair to me, and less fair to him. If my advice is as valuable as he seems to think, he ought to know that it would be more valuable if he informed me oftener as to his reactions upon what I advise.

In discussing with McAdoo whether he should give up either the Railroads or the Treasury portfolio, I advised giving up the Railroads. McAdoo thought the Railroads was the easier end of his work and if he had to give up one or the other because of the hard work, it would be wise to resign from the Treasury. He thought the Railroads would give him more freedom of action and not confine him so strictly to office work.

In speaking of a possible successor as Secretary of the Treasury, he thought the President would make a serious error if he chose Houston. We agreed that Houston had a good mind but was inclined to be lazy and lacked both imagination and courage. McAdoo spoke well of Gordon and declared he was the only one in the State Department that was worth while. He liked Lansing, but considered him unable to cope with the situations that confront the State Department. He thought Baker would make a better Secretary of State and that the country would be fortunate to have him there both because of his fitness for it and because he was unfit for Secretary of War. He thought he was of the Wilson type, neither of them, in his opinion, having much executive ability. McAdoo evidently has not much opinion of his confreres in the Cabinet. He, himself, is easily the most forceful one of the lot and the most successful from the point of accomplishment, and is so recognized by the country.

McAdoo left at twelve o'clock. He walked to the station in order to observe the law regarding the use of gasolene on Sundays.

¹ G. McNab to EMH, Aug. 26, 1918, TLS (WP, DLC). McNab argued that Wilson should not be far from Washington during this critical period of the war and that his opponents would claim that a western tour to promote a Liberty Loan just before a congressional election was politically motivated.

A Statement

The White House Sept. 9, 1918

I had hoped and had even begun to plan a trip to the Western Coast and back in connection with the "campaign" for the Fourth Liberty Loan, not because I believed that the country had any need of being stimulated to subscribe to that loan by anything that I could say, but because I coveted the opportunity to discuss with my fellow-citizens the great undertaking which has made such loans necessary and in which our whole energy and purpose are enlisted. It is the third or fourth time that I have tried to persuade myself that such a trip was possible for me without serious neglect of my duties here, because I have keenly felt again and again the privation of being confined to the Capital and prevented from having the sort of direct contact with the people I am serving which would be of so much benefit and stimulation to me. To my deep regret, I find that I must again give the idea up. The questions which come to me every day, many of them questions of the utmost delicacy and involving many critical matters, convince me that it is not right for me to absent myself from Washington for more than a day or two at a time while the war continues. Questions concerning our dealings with other governments, in particular, it is impossible for me to deal with by telegraph or at a distance from the many sources of information which exist only here. I should feel myself an unconscientious public servant if I yielded to my wish in this matter and took any chance of neglecting even for a short time things that must be decided promptly and in the presence of all the facts.

Woodrow Wilson.

T MS (WP, DLC).

To Edward Nash Hurley

My dear Hurley: [The White House] 9 September, 1918.

You are certainly a brick. It is delightful to have dealings with a man who understands perfectly the spirit of everything you say, and just the right answer to give, and I thank you very warmly indeed for your two letters of September 7th about the transit situation and about the, at any rate affected, alarm of the British about the use of our shipping after the war. I am deeply interested to learn that Lord Reading purposes having a conference with you about pooling our shipping with the British after the war. That is an extraordinary proposition, and I think perhaps it would be wise to tell him that we are sure that it will not be possible for us to make special arrangements with any one nation, inasmuch as it is our fixed policy and principle to deal upon the same terms with all. But of course I leave that entirely to your discretion and to the developments of the conference.

With warmest regard,

Faithfully yours,   Woodrow Wilson

TLS (Letterpress Books, WP, DLC).

From Robert Lansing, with Enclosures

My dear Mr. President: Washington September 9, 1918.

The telegrams which you have lately received, copies of which are enclosed,[1] no doubt have greatly heartened you as they have me, particularly the one received through the Navy Department. Our confidence in the Czech forces has been justified and the fact that now a Russian military force of equal strength has joined them, combined with the gratifying reception given the Czechs by the civilian population of the localities occupied, is strong evidence to prove that the Russians are entirely satisfied to cooperate with the Czechs in Russia and that assistance to the Czechs amounts to assistance to the Russians.

At the same time, the news received has presented certain problems which, if not met and overcome by us, may seriously impair our prestige not only with those we would help—the Russians and the Czechs—but also with the Allies and Japan. It is to you that liberal opinion throughout the world is looking for a sound, constructive plan for assisting Russia. Reactionary influences in Russia and elsewhere are at work to shake off your leadership and to take advantage of any opportunity offered them to make use of Russia rather than to serve her.

You have publicly declared that you intend to stand by Russia. You have stated that our military forces sent to Russia are to render such protection and help as is possible to the Czecho-Slovaks against the armed Austrian and German prisoners who are attacking them and to steady any efforts at self-government or self-defense in which the Russians themselves may be willing to accept assistance, and that you hope and purpose eventually to send economic and other relief to the Russian people, but that this would follow and in no way embarrass the military assistance rendered to the Czecho-Slovaks. You have said you purpose not to desert the Czecho-Slovak army engaged in conflict with nationals of the Central Powers in Siberia and finally you have recognized the Czecho-Slovak Council, to which the army has sworn allegiance, as a *de facto* Government at war with the Central Powers. You have moved cautiously and deliberately and each declaration of policy has met with almost universal approval.

The problems presented by the late telegrams appear to me to fall under the following heads:

(1) The Czecho-Slovaks—a military force operating in Siberia and the Eastern part of European Russia.

(2) The civilian population of Siberia.

(3) The civilian population along the Murman Coast and in the Archangel District.

(1) In order to render protection and help to the Czecho-Slovaks it is clear we must get them military supplies, viz: clothing, shoes, arms and ammunition. This can be done with the assistance of Mr. Baruch with whom I have consulted and I understand that you are prepared to supply the necessary money from your War Fund.

(2) The relief of the civilian population in Siberia does not involve the sending of great quantities of food from this country. Clothing, shoes and certain specified commodities are required. Some months ago the United States Shipping Board chartered through the Russian Embassy certain vessels of the Russian Volunteer Fleet with the understanding that when these vessels were needed by Russia they would be returned to her. It seems to me that in good faith we are now bound to place these vessels at work carrying to the civilian population of Russia such supplies as we can spare them. Any other use of them would be making use of Russia and not serving her and would be most unjust.

(3) The rationing of the civilian population on the Murman Coast and in the Archangel District seems to me to be essential as well from a military as from a humanitarian standpoint. Certain food-stuffs have already been shipped to these points from this country by the British Government. Ambassador Francis' cables of the second and third instant from Archangel show how necessary it is that supplies be sent to that locality. The coming on of winter and the consequent closing of the ports makes it imperative that such supplies as are shipped go forward before October first. The British Government is prepared to supply the transportation and has proposed that the ultimate expense of this rationing be borne jointly by the United States, Great Britain and France. This seems to me

to be equitable and accordingly I request authority to state that this Government will contribute its share. The total expenditure has been estimated at approximately $15,000,000. However, as Ambassador Francis states, the plan is not to give away this food, except to prevent starvation, but to sell it and consequently a certain amount of the initial expenditure will be refunded. This expenditure being in the aid of and as a direct result of the sending of American troops to these points it would seem to me it might properly be met by the setting aside of $5,000,000. from your fund for the National Security and Defense and I suggest that this be done.

A number of problems of considerable difficulty are presented by (2) and (3) supra and it seems to me it would be most helpful if these problems, which involve financial questions, methods of barter and exchange, et cetera, could be studied and solutions found by one of the established War Boards of this Government working under the direction of a man who thoroughly understands your policies and who is in close personal and official contact with the heads of the various governmental agencies concerned with these problems. It has occurred to me that Mr. Vance McCormick is peculiarly fitted for such work. He has the liberal point of view and his ability to work with the heads of the various boards and departments here has been well tested. His own organization—the War Trade Board—composed as it is of representatives of the Treasury Department, the Department of Commerce, the Department of Agriculture, the Food Administration, and the Shipping Board, is almost ideally fitted to study these problems and to submit to you a report concerning them. I suggest therefore that he be requested to begin this work under your direction.

I would appreciate very much receiving instructions from you respecting the foregoing points.

I am, my dear Mr. President,

Very sincerely yours,   Robert Lansing.

TLS (WP, DLC).
[1] The telegram from Admiral Knight, printed as an Enclosure with B. Long to WW, Sept. 7, 1918, and the Enclosures printed below. D. R. Francis to RL, No. 377, Sept. 2, 1918, concerning food supplies for the Archangel-Murmansk area, not printed.

ENCLOSURE I

Tokio Sept 5, 1918

The general staff today confirmed the report that connections had been established between the Czech forces operating east of Karemska[1] and those which had been cut off in the Baikal region. This connection was effected by the capture of both Chita and

Karemska and trains are now being operated from the Irkutsk to the Onon river. The bridge over the Onon is still unrepaired. Otherwise through service could be established to Manchuli, thus releasing all the Czech forces in Siberia. The general staff still fear the activities of Austrians and Germans in the Amur region. In Central Siberia reliable reports indicate close cooperation between Czech and the Central Siberian Army.

The third Japanese division has been fully mobilized and it is expected to embark from Ujina[2] for Manchuli Saturday afternoon. It is apparently the intention of the Japanese General Staff to begin operations at Karemska eastward to clear the Amur of the Austrian and German prisoners concentrated there. In the meantime the main part of the French forces and a portion of the British contingent have left the Us[s]uri front[3] and have passed through Harbin on their way to Manchuli. The success of the expedition of the Czechs seems now assured.   Morris.

[1] That is, Karymskaya or Karymskoye.
[2] The port for Hiroshima, Japan.
[3] That is, the front along the Ussuri River.

ENCLOSURE II

Vladivostok Sept 5, 1918

Opposition which Czechs feared would prevent their reaching comrades in Irkutsk before winter has suddenly collapsed under pressure from both sides, and railway should soon be open from here to near Perm.

It is evident Czechs have been greatly assisted by Russian forces in Western Siberia which appears to be under Siberian Government and this should relieve difficult political situation in eastern Siberia. General Horvath suddenly left here night before last, is ready to confer with Czechs at Irkutsk. Military forces against Czechs and all other Allies in this district will also probably collapse within a very short time.

This makes imperative immediate assistance in transportation economic and money matters if we are alleviate any degree suffering which appears certain this winter. If it is intended to send here engines cars which were ordered for Russian railways and some of which have been stopped en route, information should be sent at once to prevent building intended for their erection being so altered by army for military purposes as to prevent or delay erection.

The addition of Allied military and associated organizations to an already overcrowded city have made the securing of any living or office accommodations so extremely difficult that I would request that I be notified as far in advance as possible of the arrival of any commission for which my assistance in securing quarters would be required.   Caldwell

ENCLOSURE III

Archangel. Sept. 3, 1918.

Situation complicated, requires adroit handling, comparatively few bourgeois here or in northern provinces where provisional government officials continued to function months after Bolshevik revolution, and would have remained in undisturbed possession if Bolshevik rule had not become inconsiderate and cruel throughout Russia. Central Soviet sent Commissaire Kedroff[1] here who arrested (?) non-Bolshevik members, city Duma taking them Moscow and committed many outrages, thus embittering the people, majority of whom had accepted anti-Bourgeois instincts. Meantime many secret organizations had been formed throughout Russia, but most, or all, suppressed by Soviet killing leaders without trial, often by German bribing or by personal jealousies. The French were prompt to encourage and financially assist every anti-Bolshevik movement. French Ambassador[2] went from Vologda to Moscow in June telling me object of his visit was to confer with French officials and nationals there; have since learned that he proposed to a non-political organization called the Center that triumvirate should be named to administer affairs after Bolshevik deposed, and demanded as two members thereof Savinkoff[3] and Chernoff,[4] the promoters to select the third, which proposition killed that movement about middle June as leaders said were distrustful of Savinkoff whom considered murderer, and that Chernoff reformed Bolshevik, unworthy of trust. They did not tell French Ambassador this, but so expressed themselves to my informant.

About July tenth when Chicherin and Radek[5] were trying to move Allied Missions to Moscow, British captain[6] visited me Vologda and stated Archangel ripe for revolution. My number 355 [350][7] narrated movements from Vologda and causes thereof until landed Archangel, see instruction of August 9th.[8] Found new government here but realize same would not have succeeded if Allied forces had not landed, neither would it survive if Allied troops taken away. Have had frequent conferences with new government which is profuse in complaints against military, claiming that orders issued by latter belittles the new government and impair its influence.

(Green) New Ministry talks irrationally about Russian laws demanding that French Colonel,[9] appointed Military Governor of Archangel city by Poole be removed, and that order issued by him with Poole's approval be rescinded. An order which was meant for protection of new government requires militia to arrest anyone accused by a citizen of Bolshevik propaganda and take accused and accusor to authorities. I told President[10] when he came to my apartment about midnight complaining of order that there was nothing objectionable therein; in fact such is law in America. The President is theorist, if not dreamer.

British who are colonizers by instinct and practice, and in control Archangel port since war began, are disposed to treat the Government contemptuously, but I remonstrate, arguing that must avoid repetition of German experience in Ukraine.

Furthermore, overthrow of this government would prolong civil dissension, strengthen Soviet Government and Bolsheviks generally, and would injure Allied cause. This Government repudiates Brest Treaty and is mobilizing army to fight Germany, consequently is our Ally and should be protected and encouraged. Do not understand that I recommend recognition now, but if as Government claims is contemplated, union with similar movement in Siberia is effected, then we could recognize. If, however, people believe that we come conquerors they will recklessly resist.

Three American battalions expected here tomorrow and their landing will not only strengthen my position, but go a long way toward reconciling Russians. I do not know what instructions these troops have, but if General Poole asks my approval I shall not object to his sending them to the interior in accordance with objects set forth in the Department's declaration of August 3rd.[11]

Have been reading American papers on Allied intervention in Russia and see that sentiment is divided; I realize enormous responsibility of the President and the Department and I am aware of conflicting appeals and influences to which you are subjected, and I highly appreciate confidence manifested in my efforts cable communication in reply as you have been advised. Observe President considering sending commission to Siberia but hope if sent will be instructed to confer with me before adopting policy. Imperative send supplies (?) here or Murman. I would appreciate it if experienced men should accompany same for distribution under my direction or with my approval.

No reply to my telegram number 364, August 13, 8 p.m. recommending authority to join British and French in guaranteeing fifteen million rouble loan of new government guaranty secured by merchandise.

Insurances [Assurances] anxiously awaited concerning vessel with

4,000 tons supplies mentioned in your unnumbered telegram July 30th.   Francis.

T telegrams (WP, DLC).
¹ Mikhail Sergeevich Kedrov, Bolshevik leader and journalist, member of the Commissariat on Military Affairs, who had been sent to Archangel in February 1918 to secure the area under Bolshevik control.
² That is, Joseph Noulens.
³ Boris Viktorovich Savinkov, Socialist Revolutionary party leader and novelist; Assistant Minister of War in the Provisional Government; planner of the terrorist assassinations of Viacheslav Konstantinovich Plehve in 1904 and of the Grand Duke Sergius Aleksandrovich in 1905.
⁴ That is, Viktor Mikhailovich Chernov.
⁵ That is, Georgii Vasil'evich Chicherin and Karl Radek.
⁶ A Capt. McGrath, sent by Gen. Poole to warn the diplomatic corps at Vologda of the impending Allied landing at Archangel and to suggest that they leave Vologda for Archangel. McGrath arrived at Vologda on July 17. See David R. Francis, *Russia from the American Embassy, April, 1916-November, 1918* (New York, 1921), pp. 250-52. The Editors have been unable to identify him further.
⁷ D. R. Francis to RL, Aug. 9, 1918, T telegram (SDR, RG 59, 861.00/2445, DNA), printed in *FR 1918, Russia, I*, 631, 633-36.
⁸ He probably refers to FLP to D. R. Francis, Aug. 3, 1918, printed in *ibid.*, p. 625. It reads as follows: "Department believes important you should remain in Russia and approves your decision to do so."
⁹ A Colonel Donop of the French military mission.
¹⁰ Nikolai Vasil'evich Chaikovskii, president of the anti-Bolshevik Supreme Administration of the Northern Region.
¹¹ That is, the press release printed at Aug. 3, 1918.

From Jean Jules Jusserand

Dear Mr. President,   Washington September 9, 1918.

My Government cables me that the method and extent of the devastations effected by the Germans in the course of their present retreat and the premeditated barbarity with which they have concealed, in the villages abandoned by them, machines and bombs with time fuses, are deeply impressing French opinion, accustomed though it has long been to germanisms of various kinds.

My Government has entrusted the competent commission with the care of collecting, as rapidly as possible, the testimony of prisoners and soldiers who have been the witnesses of those nefarious deeds. Such sworn statements will be made public, as had been done previously. But, as publicity and the condemnation of those acts by public opinion throughout the world have had no effect, and new devices are, on the contrary, put in practice by the enemy in order to cause unjustifiable pain and suffering, my Government wonders whether it might not be of use to have recourse to a solemn declaration by the Allies forecasting the punishment for all acts which are crimes in the eyes of common law, and due reparation for the same. This declaration would be couched in very general terms, no allusion being made to any particular retaliatory measures.

My Government would, I know, greatly liked [like] to be informed of the views about the matter, of one whose judgment on questions of international ethics carries such weight. I should be much obliged to you if you were so good as to enable me to inform them of your personal opinion.

I have the honor to be, dear Mr. President,

Very respectfully and sincerely yours,   Jusserand

TLS (WP, DLC).

From Josephus Daniels

My dear Mr. President: Washington. 9th of September 1918

I have your letter enclosing one from Commissioner of Internal Revenue Roper. I understand Mr. Ford is to be in Washington in a few days and I will talk with him about the matter and then inform you. I am afraid that the situation with reference to his son is the cause of the difficulty in Michigan. The exemption having already been obtained it is very difficult to see how the matter can be remedied, but I will talk with him about it.

Sincerely yours,   Josephus Daniels

TLS (WP, DLC).

From Herbert Clark Hoover

My dear Mr. President: Washington 9th September 1918

So far from the regulations of the Food Administration having accrued in large profits to the packers, I would be glad if you would read this letter which I just received from the Vice-President of Armour and Company.[1]

Faithfully yours,   Herbert Hoover

TLS (WP, DLC).

[1] Arthur Meeker to HCH, Sept. 6, 1918, TCL (Hoover Archives, CSt-H). Meeker wrote that Armour & Company was at this point not making any profit largely "due to the conditions imposed upon us by the Food Administration" and enclosed a brief financial statement which projected, for the forty-two weeks ending August 17, 1918, a net profit of $7,100,000 instead of the profit of $15,500,000 which the Food Administration had estimated that Armour & Company might earn. Meeker added that the other large packers would soon have their figures tabulated to August 1, and that they would like to arrange a meeting with Hoover "to see what can be done to compensate us for this condition."

From Edward Mandell House

Dear Governor: Magnolia, Mass. September 9, 1918.

We are breaking up here on Wednesday, September 11th, and after a few days with Mona at Chestnut Hill we will be again at 115 East 53rd Street.

If you should need me at any time quickly Gordon can reach me.
Affectionately yours,   E. M. House

P.S. Thank you for sending me the Covenant for a League of Nations which came this morning.

TLS (WP, DLC).

From George P. Hampton

Dear Mr. President: Washington, D. C. September 9, 1918

Since I wrote you on August 19th, with reference to the Water Power Bill, I have conferred with a number of farm leaders who have been in Washington as to our position, and find that they unitedly back the position on conservation of several important farm organizations, and approve my action in so writing.

We, I may say, assuredly, ask most earnestly that if by any chance the Water Power Bill with the recapture and the long term lease is passed by Congress, you will veto it. We feel it would be unjust to our soldiers and sailors to commit the Government in any way to a policy of leasing of the natural resources.

The pending Water Power Bill will in appreciable measure make life harder for every returning soldier.

We are naturally doing our utmost to prevent the enactment of this bill, but I voice the deep sense of gratitude of the farmers who realize that in you they have a clear visioned protector of the rights, not only of the soldiers, but of the army of producers here at home.
Yours very truly,   Geo. P. Hampton

TLS (WP, DLC).

From Thomas Watt Gregory

Dear Mr. President: Washington, D. C. September 9, 1918.

On returning to Washington I find your letter of the 5th instant, asking to be informed of the facts and circumstances in connection with the recent arrests by representatives of the Department of Justice in New York of persons charged with being slackers. As stated by the Acting Attorney General in acknowledging your letter, the circumstances attending these arrests as reported in the newspapers had already challenged the attention of the Department, and inquiries had been set on foot to ascertain whether any action had been taken by representatives of the Department contrary to law or to the instructions of the Attorney General.

In order to set forth intelligently the proceedings at New York, it is necessary to touch on a serious national problem. There are many deserters and slackers at large in this country. In a letter to me dated August 5th, the Secretary of War gave figures showing the number of deserters and delinquents under the first and second drafts and stated that while it was impossible to give the actual number of those who had failed to register at all—slackers, so-called—the number was large.

The Secretary of War referred to this condition "as an indictment against the honor of the Nation." To permit it to continue would weaken substantially the Nation's fighting power and do grievous injustice to the great body of the youth of the land who have so gallantly met their military obligations. Energetic measures were required. The Secretary of War naturally looked to this Department for assistance. To attempt to apprehend so great a number of offenders by running down individual cases obviously would have been futile. Some form of dragnet process, within the law of course, was absolutely essential.

Section 49 of the Rules and Regulations for the enforcement of the Selective Service Law promulgated by the President November 8, 1917, referring to slackers and delinquents, provides:

"Those who fail to return the Questionnaire, or to appear for physical examination, or to report change of status, or to report for any duty, or to perform any act at the time and place required by these regulations or by directions by Local or District Boards in pursuance thereof, are guilty of a misdemeanor under section 6 of the Selective Service Law. Under authority granted in section 6 of that law, it is hereby made the duty of all police officials of the United States and of any State, or any county, municipality, or other sub-division thereof, *to locate and to take into custody such persons and to bring them forthwith before local boards* * *." And with respect to deserters the same section provides:

"It is hereby made the duty of all such police officials to apprehend and arrest such deserters."

It was accordingly decided to adopt the plan of canvassing or rounding up in the large cities on particular days all men apparently within the draft age and arranging for a summary and immediate investigation of their status through their local draft boards. Of necessity this involved detaining, pending investigation, all such men who did not have registration or classification cards (which registrants are required by the Regulations to keep always in their personal possession), or who were not able to establish by satisfactory evidence that they were outside the draft ages. It was expected that for the most part such men would voluntarily go to the places of detention, which were usually armories, while the investigation of their status was being made. Where arrests were necessary it was never contemplated that they should be made by any but police officials of the United States or of the States and municipalities where the canvass was being conducted. The making of arrests in such cases by the military or by the members of any private organization would have been contrary to law and contrary to the express directions of the Attorney General, except in the case of deserters, where, of course, the military authorities had the power to make arrests. It *was* expected, however, that where the number detained was large this Department, in making the necessary investigations, would have the aid of the American Protective League, a private organization of established standing, which had long been participating in the enforcement of the Selective Service law by express invitation of the Provost Marshal General; and that in guarding the persons taken into custody, it would have the aid of units of the military and naval forces.

The plan was put into effect at several points before it was attempted in New York, notably at Chicago and Boston, with excellent results; and, so far as I am informed, to the satisfaction of the communities affected.

While this plan was evolved in discussions with a representative of the Provost Marshal General's office, I take full and entire responsibility for adopting it and for putting it into effect. I know that some such dragnet process is necessary unless thousands upon thousands of deserters and slackers are to remain at large; I believe the plan adopted is authorized by the regulations; I believe also, judging by the results at a number of different points, that the great body of our people will cheerfully submit to the minor inconveniences which the execution of any such plan of necessity entails, to the end that this indictment of the Nation's honor, this drain on the Nation's strength, may be removed. I shall, therefore, continue to employ the plan unless you give directions to the contrary.

Coming to the City of New York, I again accept full and entire responsibility for putting into effect there the general plan of rounding up deserters and slackers which I have described. Contrary to my express instructions, however, instructions which I have repeated over and over again, and contrary to law, certain members of the investigating force of this Department, without consultation with me or with any law officer of the Department, used soldiers and sailors and certain members of the American Protective League, I am satisfied, in making arrests. I am convinced by the inquiries which I have made that they were led into this breach of authority by excess of zeal for the public good. While this extenuates, it does not excuse their action.

Besides being unlawful, the employment of members of the military forces and of private organizations in making arrests was ill-judged, as such men are not generally fitted by training or experience to exercise the discretion required in the circumstances.

During the 3-day canvass in Manhattan and the Bronx, 11,652 persons were apprehended and temporarily held at places of detention. Of these, about 300 were inducted into the military service and at least 1,500 turned over to their local boards as delinquents. In Brooklyn, 9,750 were detained, of whom 252 have been held by order of court and at least 1,000 turned over to their local boards as delinquents. These figures do not include a large number of persons who, on being accosted, made a satisfactory showing and were not detained; nor do they include a smaller number who were taken to the police station and required to give further information before being released.

Unquestionably a considerable number of persons, who on the showing made by them should not have been detained, were detained—none, however, over-night. Such mistakes always occur in exercising the power of arrest, though in much fewer number where the power is exercised by trained police officers.

On the other hand, the investigation which I have made leads me to believe that the number of persons over or under draft age who were apprehended was inconsiderable; that there was no disorder anywhere; that no persons are known to have been assaulted or maltreated; that in general the canvass was acquiesced in with good nature.

Simultaneously with the canvass in New York, one was made in the cities of northern New Jersey, where, so far as I can learn, there was little if any criticism. The canvass in northern New Jersey was carried out in accordance with the instructions and known policy of the Department. In the city of Newark, for example, the canvass was made by groups of men composed of one regular police officer, who in every instance made the arrest, aided by members of the American Protective League and uniformed unarmed members of the State militia who assisted in the work of accosting and making inquiries. No soldiers, sailors, or members of private organizations were employed in making arrests.

There were apprehended in the five cities of northern New Jersey—Newark, Jersey City, Hoboken, Paterson and Passaic—a total of 28,875 persons. Out of this number 749 men have been ordered inducted into the army, and in addition 12,515 were delinquents whose draft records of classification were corrected by the local boards. These delinquents were persons who at one time had been given a temporary classification by reason of illness, exemption, etc., but who had failed to report for a corrected classification, or else persons who had failed to register, failed to appear for physical examination or failed to file questionnaires, etc.

I remain,   Sincerely yours,   T. W. Gregory

TLS (WP, DLC).

[1] Gregory, who said he was "besieged by inquiries and questions from the newspaper men," telephoned on September 11 to ask whether Wilson intended to make his letter public. White House Staff to WW, Sept. 11, 1918, TL (WP, DLC). "Please file the original and release the copies for immediate publication through the Committee on Public Information. Please inform the Att'y Gen'l W.W." WW to [White House Staff], c. Sept. 11, 1918 ALI (WP, DLC). Gregory's letter was printed, e.g., in the *Official Bulletin*, II (Sept. 12, 1918), 1-2.

From William Procter Gould Harding

Dear Mr. President: Washington September 9, 1918.

I have just received your letter of the 7th instant and beg to say that in my opinion discount rates are high enough, and perhaps in some cases they are too high. I do not believe that in the present circumstances any advance in rates would be effective in controlling credit transactions, but would merely react unfavorably upon Government securities. I think that we should work toward a policy of rationing credit and money along scientific lines, giving preference to the more essential industries, thus conserving to the greatest possible extent our cash and credit resources for Government use, without affecting essential production.

I have observed during the past few weeks a disposition on the part of some to create alarm because of the expansion of credit which is a necessary incident of war financing, and these critics have almost invariably suggested a sharp advance in interest rates as a remedy. I do not at all concur in these views and expressed myself plainly on the subject last Thursday in an address before the Ohio Bankers' Association at Columbus, copy of which I am sending with this letter.[1] I do not think that it would be worth your while to read it all, but I have marked a few paragraphs which may be of interest to you.

The Board is doing all in its power to discourage any further advance in rates by the banks and trust companies of the country, and I am quite sure that it would not hesitate to reduce discount rates at Federal Reserve banks if it could be assured that users of credit would be given the benefit of the reduction and that there would be no wasteful or improper use of credit for non-essential or speculative purposes.   Faithfully yours,   W P G Harding.

TLS (WP, DLC).
¹ The Enclosure was returned to Harding.

From William Byron Colver

My dear Mr. President: Washington 9 September 1918

Your letter 6 September has been duly laid before the Commission. We are somewhat in doubt as to whether or not this letter was written before you received our letter suggesting that you might wish to examine us before you closed your mind on the Packers' matter.

Naturally we hesitate to address you further on the subject and yet it does not seem to us to be possible that Mr. Hoover can have been sufficiently acquainted with the conclusions and purposes of this Commission to finally present them to you.

The Commission has made no recommendation in the nature of a war measure. It has not recommended that the Railroad Administration take over the privately owned cars. It has recommended that the Government take them over permanently using the temporary agency of the Railroad Administration.

Mr. Hoover's statement that the various distributing agencies and branches owned by the Packers throughout the country are already doing all that their buildings permit, is in a measure correct. These buildings, however, are being used to the exclusion of and to the embarrassment of other meat packers and if we could devote all those buildings and all those agencies to meat foods, employing the wholesale grocers and their storehouses for other than meat foods, we would increase very greatly the facilities for handling meat products and would also open the door to the independent meat packers who now suffer great handicap.

We are further embarrassed for the reason that the suggestions which we have made have found enthusiastic and active supporters and these men are coming to us not only from the Senate and the House but business men asking to counsel with us on a program for applying some permanent remedy to the condition of monopoly, manipulation and control which we have uncovered.

Also we have almost ready to issue, volumes of data and proof as to this situation and in view of your conclusion that "no real material advantage would result from the action proposed by your bill, at any rate at this time," we must frame some line of conduct or excuse for avoiding meetings with these men lest we find ourselves at disagreement with you.

Although the correspondence on this subject is signed by Mr. Colver, it in every instance reflects the unanimous opinion of the Commission and each letter is submitted to the Commission before it is dispatched.

By direction of the Commission.

Faithfully yours,   [W. B. Colver]

TL (WP, DLC).

From William Kent

Dear Mr. President: Washington September 9, 1918.

Concerning the water power bill: I cannot agree with the conclusion that the "net investment" amendment would work against the public interest, as it would provide that any returns in excess of reasonable bond interest and depreciation, whether used for extension of plant or for amortization of the debt, should be credited to the Government at the time of taking over the property. This is a distinct gain to the Government over "fair value not exceeding cost." I have just been talking to Secretary Lane and Senator Lenroot about this matter. Lenroot believes that the beneficial provision of "net investment" can be retained and at the same time an amendment providing for "fair value not exceeding cost" can be inserted with much less controversy than would occur if there were an attempt to throw out the "net investment" and substitute in lieu thereof "fair value not exceeding cost." Secretary Lane suggests the advisability of giving careful consideration to this matter before it comes up in the Senate.

As to Senate procedure, we all three believe that the bill should be threshed out and settled in conference, rather than have it re-referred to the Senate Committee, where the records of the conferees may come up to haunt them, and involving as it will a lot more argument on the floor of the Senate.

I believe that Senator Shields is prepared to accept the bill as you want it passed, and believe that it would be much easier for him to take his medicine as a conferee rather than to have the matter go back to the Committee. I should not intrude my suggestion except for your previous request for assistance. I feel sure that Secretary Lane and Senator Lenroot can get the wrinkles ironed out so as to be satisfactory to all concerned.

Yours truly,   William Kent

TLS (WP, DLC).

Robert Lansing to Roland Sletor Morris

Washington, September 9, 1918.

In making your observations and in framing your recommendations you will please keep in mind the aims and desires of this Government expressed in the following extracts taken from a memorandum handed to the British, French and Italian Governments at the time that activities in Siberia were decided upon by the United States Government, and of which copies were handed to the Japanese Ambassador and the Chinese Minister in Washington. The policies of the United States Government and the limitations upon its action in Siberia are set forth as follows (colon)

It is the clear and fixed judgment of the Government of the United States that military intervention in Siberia would add to the present sad confusion in Russia rather than cure it, injure Russia rather than help her and that it would be of no advantage in the prosecution of our main design to win the war against Germany. It cannot therefore take part in such intervention or sanction it in principle. Military intervention would in the judgment of the United States Government, even supposing it to be efficacious in its immediate avowed object of delivering an attack upon Germany from the East be merely a method of making use of Russia and not a method of serving her. Her people could not profit by it, if they profited by it at all, in time to save them from their present distresses and their substance would be used to maintain foreign armies and not to reconstitute their own. As we see it, military action is admissible in Russia only to help the Czecho-Slovaks consolidate their forces and get into successful co-operation with their Slavic kinsmen and to steady any efforts at self Government or self defense in which the Russians themselves may be willing to accept assistance. The only legitimate object for which American or allied troops can be employed in the mind of the United States Government, whether at Vladivostok or at Murmansk and Archangel, is to guard military stores which may subsequently be needed by Russian forces and to render such aid as may be acceptable to the Russians in the organization of their own self defense. The Government of the

United States owes it to frank council to say that it can go no further than to participate in and approve of such modest methods and experimental plans as will contribute to the objects indicated above and has no reasonable expectation of being in a position to take part in organized intervention in adequate forces from either Vladivostok or Murmansk and Archangel. It feels that it ought to add also that it will use the few troops it can spare only for the purposes herein stated and shall feel obliged to withdraw these forces if the plans in whose execution it is now intended that they should co-operate should develop into others inconsistent with the policy to which the Government of the United States feels constrained to restrict itself.

It was further announced to be the hope and purpose of this Government to take advantage of the earliest opportunity to send to Siberia a commission of Merchants, Agricultural Experts, Labor Advisors, Red Cross Representatives and Agents of the Y.M.C.A. accustomed to organizing the best methods of spreading useful information and rendering educational help of a modest sort, in order in some systematic manner to relieve the immediate economic necessities of the people there in every way for which opportunity may open. However, the execution of the plans to send such a commission will follow and will not be permitted to embarrass such military assistance as the United States in conjunction with the allied forces will render in line with the policies indicated herein-above.

You will please read very carefully the contents of this cable. It expresses the present policy of this Government in dealing with Siberian and Russian situations. In making your observations you will please keep constantly in mind the policies indicated and in making any recommendations you will please be guided by the expressed wish of this Government to conform to those policies. You may announce briefly the purpose of your visit to Vladivostock having in mind these and previous instructions of September fifth.[1]

Lansing

TS telegram (SDR, RG 59, 861.00/2719a, DNA).

[1] RL to R. S. Morris, Sept. 4, 1918, *FR 1918, Russia*, II, 366. This telegram instructed Morris to go to Vladivostok, confer with leading Russians and with Allied civil and military representatives, and to report to the State Department "how the purpose of the United States to aid the Russian people, as expressed repeatedly in public statements by this Government, may best be furthered under the conditions which you will find to exist there."

Colville Adrian de Rune Barclay to the Foreign Office

Washington. Sept. 9th. 1918.

No. 4070. Secty. of State sent for me today and said that the attitude adopted by General Poole at Archangel was causing the U.S.G. considerable concern. U. S. Ambassador to Russia had reported that General Poole had appointed a French Colonel as Military Governor of Archangel and that the latter had issued an order prescribing the arrest of anyone guilty of Bolshevist propaganda.

Secty. of State said that U.S.G.'s policy had been consistently to allow Russians to work out their own salvation, there was a local Russian Government at Archangel and he did not see that there was any necessity for a Military Governor and interference in the civil powers of the local Government was distasteful to the U.S.G.

Mr. Lansing asked me to inform you that he had taken up the matter with the President who took a serious view of it and that unless there was a change in the high handed attitude adopted by General Poole in the appointment of a Military Governor, the U.S.G. would seriously have to consider the withdrawal of the U. S. Contingent from General Poole's command.

T telegram (FO 115/2449, p. 352, PRO).

From the Diary of Colonel House

September 9, 1918.

We are busy getting ready to leave the country on Wednesday. Senator and Mrs. Hitchcock asked us to tea at Swam[p]scott. I had a long talk with him about foreign affairs. I told him what I had written the President as to the waning influence of the United States as the Allies waxed strong, and of my suggestion that we try to get an agreement with the Allies now as to our war aims. Hitchcock agreed with me as to the wisdom of this plan. He is to preside over a meeting of Czecho-Slovaks and Poles on Sunday. What he wanted particularly was to get my views regarding that situation and the fate of the Austrian Empire.

The President asked Gordon to come to the White House today. He asked him whether the State Department had sent me a copy of a cable regarding Holland's interest in a league of nations. After Gordon had assured him that I had the telegram, he asked him to telephone and find out what I thought should be done in the premises. I dictated to Gordon the following answer which he sent to the President.

"Mr. House thinks that Holland's attitude regarding a league of nations is not of sufficient importance to warrant giving them your entire program. He believes it would be well to take them in hand, and others like them, and influence them in the right direction. This can easily be done. In Mr. House's opinion, it is essential to get Great Britian [Britain] and France committed first. When this is done it will not be difficult to get the other nations."

My letter to the President today is unimportant but is a part of the record as is his letter to me enclosing his revision of my draft of the Covenant for the League of Nations. This draft, along with mine, is a part of the record. It will be seen, I think, that he has not incorporated any new ideas, but has changed the verbiage and rearranged the Articles, putting some of mine entirely out. The Preamble he has improved, some of the others I think are not as clear as mine.

Three Letters to Herbert Clark Hoover

My dear Hoover: The White House 10 September, 1918.

I wish you would "read, ponder, and inwardly digest" the enclosed letter from Daniels.[1] It has made a very great impression on me, because of the intrinsic credibility of what the Navy is afraid is taking place in the beef trade. Will you not let me have your angle and comment on the matter?

Cordially and sincerely yours,   Woodrow Wilson

[1] JD to WW, Sept. 7, 1918, CCL (J. Daniels Papers, DLC). Daniels defended the navy's specification that beef carcasses delivered to its agents had to weigh a minimum of 575 pounds against recurring demands from the packing industry that the minimum be reduced to 475 pounds. Daniels charged that the packers wished to sell, and in fact were selling, the more desirable heavy beef on the civilian market because they could get higher prices for it there than by selling it to the American armed forces and those of the Allies at the prices set by the Food Purchase Board. The packers claimed that there was not enough of the heavier beef for the army, navy, Marine Corps, and Allies, but Daniels insisted, and he cited a recent report of the Federal Trade Commission to support his argument, that there was ample heavy beef for the American and foreign armed forces, provided that civilian consumption was limited to the lighter grades of beef for the duration of the war emergency.

My dear Hoover: The White House 10 September, 1918.

I think you are mistaken in the impression you have received about the way the new draft is to be managed, or rather, exemptions from it.[1] The purpose of the new regulations, as I discussed them with General Crowder, was to take the burden of claiming exemption off of the individual and put it upon his employer or superior, and that is certainly the way in which I expect the matter to be administered.

At any time that the matter matures with regard to the men connected with the Food Administration, I should be glad to have a suggestion from you as to any action on my part that you think may be necessary, for I entirely agree with the conclusions stated in your letter of September 9th.

Cordially and sincerely yours,   Woodrow Wilson

[1] H. C. Hoover to WW, Sept. 9, 1918, TLS (WP, DLC). Hoover stated that the Food Administration at this time consisted of some 3,500 to 4,000 volunteers and 1,500 paid employees. Of the large portion of these men who would be subject to the new military draft, Hoover believed that three or four hundred were "absolutely indispensable" to carry on the work of the Food Administration. It was Hoover's understanding that, under the rules for the new draft, such men would have to apply individually for deferred classification. However, he argued, it was just these men of high character and ability who would not apply for deferment, on the ground that to do so implied a wish to escape military service. "I, myself," Hoover declared, "do not ever intend to apply for exemption from this draft." The only solution to the problem, he believed, was for him, when the appropriate moment arrived, to apply for deferred classification "for the staff in the Food Administration," and for Wilson, in turn, "to give a positive direction to this list of men to remain in this Department during the war, as being the most effective service that they can do to the nation."

My dear Hoover: The White House 10 September, 1918.

Thank you for having let me see the enclosed,[1] which I return. My fundamental trouble about all of this matter is that I do not trust the information which these men give us. I say this with hesitation and regret, but must say that the remark is justified by many circumstances and dealings of which I have knowledge.

Cordially and faithfully yours,   Woodrow Wilson

TLS (Hoover Archives, CSt-H).
[1] See HCH to WW, Sept. 9, 1918, n.1.

To Scott Ferris

My dear Mr. Ferris: [The White House] 10 September, 1918.

Replying to your letter of September 8th,[1] in which you tell me that the Toledo Blade and other papers of the Ninth Ohio District are stating that the administration desires the election of Mr. Ashley in preference to General Sherwood,[2] let me say that of course such statements are absolutely without foundation. I had not even heard anything about the contest between Mr. Ashley and General Sherwood. I cannot understand how reputable papers would engage in such misrepresentation without first according me at least the courtesy of ascertaining whether the statements they were repeating were true or not.

Cordially and sincerely yours,   Woodrow Wilson

TLS (Letterpress Books, WP, DLC).

¹ S. Ferris to WW, Sept. 8, 1918, TLS (WP, DLC).
² James Mitchell Ashley, Jr., a Republican businessman and engineer of Toledo, was opposing the Democratic incumbent, Isaac Ruth Sherwood. In the election on November 5, Sherwood defeated Ashley by a vote of 25,122 to 18,398.

To Key Pittman

My dear Senator: [The White House] 10 September, 1918.

I have your letter of September 7th and have read it with close attention and with a very sincere appreciation of its significance and of the motives of public service which lie back of it, but it is upon a matter that has too many sides and aspects to make a satisfactory answer possible in a letter. I am going to ask, therefore, if I may not have the pleasure of an interview with you about the whole matter, in order that we may go over the large field of which this particular leasing question constitutes only a part. I wonder if it would be convenient for you to come in to see me on Thursday at 4:30. You need not take the trouble of replying to this by letter. Just let my office know if that will be convenient.

Cordially and sincerely yours,   Woodrow Wilson

TLS (Letterpress Books, WP, DLC).

To William Procter Gould Harding

[The White House]
My dear Governor Harding: 10 September, 1918.

I very much appreciate your letter of yesterday and am heartily glad to have my judgment about the rates of interest confirmed by one who knows much more about the matter than I do.

I am also warmly obliged to you for letting me see the copy of your address before the convention of the Ohio State Bankers' Association at Columbus on the 5th. I have read the marked passages with interest and benefit to my own thought, and am returning the copy only because I fear you may not have any to spare.

Cordially and sincerely yours,   Woodrow Wilson

TLS (Letterpress Books, WP, DLC).

To Thomas Garrigue Masaryk

My dear Dr. Masaryk: [The White House] 10 September, 1918.

Your letter of September 7th has given me a great deal of gratification. It reassures me to know that you think that I have followed the right course in my earnest endeavor to be of as much service as possible to the Czecho-Slovak peoples, and I want you to know how much the Secretary of State and I have valued the counsel and guidance which you have given us. It will always be a matter of profound gratitude to me if it should turn out that we have been able to render a service which will redound to the permanent advantage and happiness of the great group of peoples whom you represent.

Cordially and sincerely yours,   Woodrow Wilson

TLS (Letterpress Books, WP, DLC).

From John Herbert Quick[1]

My Dear Mr. President: Washington Sept. 10th 1918

The other night I went to Keith's to see "America's Answer."[2] When the show was over I went out by the north exit. You and your party were getting into your car in the alley as I reached the stairway. I could have dropped a bomb on you and on your car with the greatest ease.

I think it is perfectly capable of demonstration that it is possible for an assas[sa]in to carry a weapon into that theatre and to murder you on almost any occasion when you go there. The thing has got on my nerves; but it has affected the minds of others in the same way.

My study of history has not furnished my mind with an instance of any man occupying a place from which his removal would have so profoundly affected world conditions. Thousands of men and women would be willing to die to get rid of you. Whole nations would be thrown into despair by such a deed. The head of Hasdrubal thrown into the camp of Hannibal seems the only case comparable in fatefulness.

And our constitution does not provide a successor in whom the world would have confidence.

Pardon me for stating this case as it appears to an outsider; and pardon an appeal in which every American would be glad to join, for greater caution.   Yours sincerely   Herbert Quick

ALS (WP, DLC).
  [1] At this time a member of the Federal Farm Loan Board.
  [2] A documentary motion picture film distributed by the Division of Films of the Committee on Public Information. It had been made in France by the Signal Corps and showed the activities of the American Expeditionary Force. It was shown during the week of August 25-31 at the Belasco (not Keith's) Theater. *Washington Post*, Aug. 25, 1918. Wilson attended the showing on August 26.

From the Diary of Josephus Daniels

1918 Tuesday 10 September

WW Any persons, except on strict military service, going abroad, I wish to know their names & mission before they are designated. Often have a sidelight and too many men go over assuming to speak for the Government & WW did not wish this

WW had letter from Gregory explaining the wholesale rounding up of slackers in New York. Senators had severely criticized the action & Gregory had justified it by calling attention to the large number and the necessity of some measure outside the usual methods. It put the fear of God in others just before new draft

To Frederick Law Olmsted, Jr.[1]

My dear Mr. Olmsted: [The White House] September 11, 1918.

Now that you are ending your second term as a member of the Commission of Fine Arts and are laying down the duties of Vice-Chairman of that body, I desire to express my personal sense of the service you have rendered to the Nation. As a member of the Commission of 1901, you were instrumental in the reinstatement of the L'Enfant Plan for the City of Washington and its logical development throughout the entire District of Columbia. The report of that commission impressed the people of the United States with the possibilities of placing Washington among the finest capital cities of the world. Also it was among the first of those impulses to civic improvement that in recent years have stirred the rapidly growing American cities to undertake an orderly arrangement of their areas.

From 1902 to the creation of the Commission of Fine Arts in 1910, you cheerfully responded to repeated calls of Congressional committees and of Executive officers for advice and assistance in the solution of questions of art affecting the District of Columbia. It was the services thus rendered unofficially by you and other public-spirited citizens that led the Congress to establish a Commission whereby it has been made possible for the Congress and the Executive Departments to obtain expert advice on questions of art and taste. The value of your services were recognized when you were asked to become one of the original members of that Commission and thus to continue to give advice made the more valuable by your familiarity with the needs of the District of Columbia and by your experience and high attainments in your profession.

For all of this service you have expected and have received no money compensation; at times the task has been attended by public misconception, so that your one satisfaction has been the consciousness of having given to your country the best that was in you to give.

You will continue to give to the Government your help in the new and perplexing task of housing workers in the industrial plants which have been created to satisfy war needs,—a task you were one of the first to recognize as essential.

Thus you are carrying on the high traditions of your family as devoted public servants in times of both peace and war.

Cordially and sincerely yours,   Woodrow Wilson

TLS (Letterpress Books, WP, DLC).
¹ Born in 1870, he had studied landscape architecture under his father and had had a distinguished career in practice on his own.

To Enoch Herbert Crowder

[The White House]
My dear General Crowder: 11 September, 1918

The Director General of Railroads, I am sure, states the hazards of the present draft as it affects the railroads with perfect accuracy in the messages which I am enclosing,¹ and I send them in order to emphasize what we were discussing the other day and to ask that you will give such advice and instructions to the local boards as will do as much as can be done to make them stiff in themselves insisting upon the exemptions which are necessary for the maintenance of the full efficiency of the railway system, for of course upon that efficiency depends the whole industrial process of the country.   Cordially and sincerely yours,   Woodrow Wilson

TLS (Letterpress Books, WP, DLC).
¹ The "messages" are missing in WP, DLC, but see WW to WGM, Sept. 13, 1918.

To John Herbert Quick

My dear Quick: [The White House] 11 September, 1918.

Your letter of yesterday makes me feel your friendship in a way that is very acceptable to my heart, and I thank you for it most warmly. You may be sure that we shall take every possible precaution, though as a matter of fact such dangers never occur to me except afterwards.

Cordially and sincerely yours,   Woodrow Wilson

TLS (Letterpress Books, WP, DLC).

To George P. Hampton

[The White House]

My dear Mr. Hampton: 11 September, 1918.

Thank you for your letter of the 9th. I am very much concerned about the present situation of the measures with regard to water power, and you may be sure have been doing some heavy thinking about them.

In haste, Sincerely yours, Woodrow Wilson

TLS (Letterpress Books, WP, DLC).

To Robert Latham Owen

My dear Senator: [The White House] 11 September, 1918.

Thank you for your letter of the 9th.[1] No subject has perplexed me or those with whom I am in daily consultation more than the question of "non essential" industries, and we have all agreed that it was practically impossible to make any confident classification of the essential and the non-essential. We have attempted to get at it, therefore, by a classification of "priorities," and some classification of the kind has been rendered absolutely necessary by the question of labor not merely (which might be susceptible of solution), but by the much more difficult and definite question of material. We have felt obliged to withhold certain materials from uses which were apparently not essential to the life of our people, and we have tried in our instructions to the Draft Boards to give some indication of the classes of employees who could best be spared from industry. But beyond this we have not attempted to go, and I share with you the view that the whole matter is difficult and dangerous. I have been trying to confine the processes to as narrow limits as possible.

Cordially and sincerely yours, Woodrow Wilson

TLS (Letterpress Books, WP, DLC).
[1] R. L. Owen to WW, Sept. 9, 1918, TLS (WP, DLC).

From Robert Lansing, with Enclosure

My dear Mr. President: Washington September 11, 1918.

In view of the fact that I am expressing views in this telegram as emanating from you I would be obliged if you would pass upon it.

In connection with the telegram I would also call your attention to the one from Ambassador Francis which arrived today and which is enclosed with my letter to you regarding instructions to Colonel Stewart.   Faithfully yours,   Robert Lansing

Approved by Prest. 9/12/18

TLS (SDR, RG 59, 861.00/2720B, DNA).

E N C L O S U R E

Amembassy LONDON.   September [blank] 1918.

The Department has received most disturbing reports concerning the high-handed methods taken by General Poole with the local Government at Archangel, whose authority he apparently ignores. The natural effect upon the Russian people will be to arouse resentment and possibly open hostility toward the Governments whose troops have been landed in Northern Russia for the purpose of aiding and not of coercing the inhabitants. The course, which General Poole is reported to have taken, is entirely at variance with the policy of this Government as set forth in the Aide Memoire handed to Lord Reading on July eighteenth and with the understanding when American troops were sent to Russian territory.

In view of this unfortunate state of affairs and the possibly serious consequences which may result in the attitude of the Russian people, not only at Archangel but elsewhere, toward the Governments whose troops are under General Poole's command you are requested to lay this matter before the British Government without delay, expressing the deep concern which the President feels as to a continuance of military interference with the local authorities at Archangel in matters of a civil nature.

You may also, in urging the British Government to instruct General Poole to be more considerate of the civil authorities, say that the President, in the event that this reported interference is not checked, will be compelled to consider the withdrawal of the American troops from the superior command of General Poole and the directing of Colonel Stewart[1] to act independently in accordance with the announced policy of this Government. The President would deplore the necessity of taking this step but he cannot permit the United States to share responsibility for the reported action of General Poole as commander of the united forces.

CONFIDENTIAL: The direct interference of General Poole with the civil authorities at Archangel has been most unfortunate and is reported to have caused great offense and humiliation to the Russians. This Government has been able thus far to retain the good will and confidence of the Russian people in general. It cannot afford to risk this friendly attitude by being a participant in an expedition whose commander apparently is indifferent to the rights and feelings of the Russian communities with which he comes in contact. I have very frankly and emphatically explained the situation to the British Chargé here who assured me he would immediately telegraph his Government.[2]

T MS (SDR, RG 59, 861.00/2720B, DNA).

[1] Col. George E. Stewart, U.S.A., who commanded the three battalions of the 339th Infantry Regiment and its auxiliaries, the 1st Battalion 310th Engineers, the 337th Field Hospital, and the 337th Ambulance Company. John W. Long, "American Intervention in Russia: The North Russian Expedition, 1918-19," *Diplomatic History*, VI (Winter 1982), 56.

[2] The above was sent as RL to American embassy, London, No. 1313, Sept. 12, 1918, 3 p.m.

From Robert Lansing, with Enclosure

My dear Mr. President: Washington September 11, 1918.

Mr. Miles, acting on my instructions, called upon the Acting Secretary of War yesterday and suggested to him that an order be sent to Colonel Stewart in command of the American troops at Archangel to consult freely with Ambassador Francis in order that he might be advised as to the policy of this Government and the possible modifications which might take place in view of new conditions.

Mr. Miles reported to me late yesterday afternoon that Mr. Crowell seemed favorably inclined to this suggestion but that on submitting it to General March the latter said he did not think it necessary to send the order as General Pershing had received by telegraph a copy of the Aide Memoire outlining our policy toward Russia (but his instructions to Colonel Stewart are certainly six weeks old.) Furthermore we have been unable to obtain from the War Department the instructions given to Colonel Stewart.[1]

I do not understand General March's attitude in this matter, but, in view of the situation which may arise if General Poole continues his high-handed methods with the Russians, I feel that it is most important that Colonel Stewart should be fully and constantly advised of the Ambassador's views. I feel this the more strongly because of the tact and judgment with which Mr. Francis has conducted himself in very trying circumstances and because I am informed that his military attaché, who would naturally be his lia[i]son officer with the military chiefs, has frequently disagreed with his policies.

I dislike to trouble you with this matter, but as it involves an important military policy as well as international affairs, I think that you alone can decide whether or not Colonel Stewart should be instructed as was suggested.

Since writing the foregoing the enclosed telegram has been deciphered. It emphasizes what I have written.

Faithfully yours,   Robert Lansing

TLS (SDR, RG 59, 861.00/2661, DNA).
[1] In fact, to this point Colonel Stewart had received no instructions at all, except to report to General Poole.

E N C L O S U R E

Archangel. Sept. 10, 1918.
Recd. 11th, 5.15 a.m.

391. Lindley[1] says confidentially has asked to be relieved if not given control over military forces which General Poole appears empowered to command; apparently friction setting [breaking] out. Poole when informed by me that supreme Government reinstated and relations between it and military be defined, today writes informally requesting nothing be decided before knowing his views as "Military dispositions in this town remain in my hands." Americans constitute decided majority of Allied forces under Poole, totalling about forty hundred; one battalion sent on railroad toward Vologda, one on Dwina[2] toward Kothelas[3] and one performing guard duty in Archangel. Americans arrived third, debarked fourth. Kidnaping occurred night of fifth.[4] Americans first assigned guard duty sixth from which community concluded Americans planned or supported coup d'état; Stewart says only orders were report to Poole. While I suspect British and probably French officers planned coup d'état American officers absolutely knew nothing about it. Your unnumbered July 30, 3 p.m. through American Consul Archangel[5] and also your circular of August 3, 4 p.m.[6] states American troops sent Archangel but gave me no instructions or authority over them. If Poole has unlimited control I fear he has learned military and colonizing instincts together with his contempt for sovereign government and his general mistrust of Russians will handicap American policy in Russia and may possibly bring about condition like that in Ukraine. I am not asking control of American troops but informing Department of conditions so that it can give instructions if so elects.

Since above written have seen Stewart who says Poole desires him to take command of railroad expedition toward Vologda; Stewart, while not shirking responsibility, dislikes leaving Archangel and I prefer he remain here as he commands three battalions and Archangel is base of operations. Tramway employees on strike because ministry kidnapped; Major Nichols[7] commanding American battalion here says was asked by military control office if had men who could run street cars and replying affirmatively was told to send such men to car barn and take out cars consequently since yesterday afternoon American soldiers have been acting as motormen and conductors but collecting no fares, public riding free and every car crowded to full capacity. I advised Nichols to request that written order be given him for such use of American Soldiers.

Please send Jenkins or Willoughby Smith or both here immediately also Flack.[8]   Francis.

T telegram (SDR, RG 59, 861.00/2661, DNA).
[1] Francis Oswald Lindley, British Commissioner in Russia.
[2] That is, the Dvina River.
[3] Kotlas, a rail junction on the northern Dvina River.
[4] Capt. Georgi Ermolaevich Chaplin, commander in chief of the anti-Bolshevik military forces in the Archangel area, had, on the night of September 5-6, led a coup against the anti-Bolshevik Supreme Administration of the Northern Region. The president of that administration, Nikolai Vasil'evich Chaikovskii, and five of his ministers had been kidnaped and deported to Solovetski Island in the White Sea. At the insistence of Lindley and David R. Francis, a British warship was sent to rescue the deposed officials, and they returned to Archangel and to power on September 8. For a brief account of this affair, together with a bibliographical note on the available source material about it, see Richard H. Ullman, *Anglo-Soviet Relations, 1917-1921: Intervention and the War* (Princeton, N. J., 1961), pp. 245-48.
[5] FLP to Felix Cole, Consul at Archangel, July 30, 1918, *FR 1918, Russia*, II, 504: "For your information the Red Cross is sending some 4,000 tons of medicines and foodstuffs to Archangel next month. This Government has also consented to send a small force of American troops to Murmansk but will not take part in any expedition into Russia from that port. Spare no effort to keep Department advised of your movements. Have cabled you fully and frequently but assume messages have been largely interrupted."
[6] The press release printed at Aug. 3, 1918.
[7] Maj. Jesse Brooks Nichols, commander of the second battalion of the 339th Infantry Regiment.
[8] Douglas Jenkins, Consul at Riga, detailed to Harbin on August 16; Felix Willoughby Smith, Consul at Tiflis; and Thomas R. Flack, clerk in the American consulate general at Moscow.

From William Bauchop Wilson, with Enclosure

My dear Mr. President: Washington September 11, 1918.

I am inclosing you herewith a letter received from the National War Labor Board relative to the refusal of certain machinists at Bridgeport, Connecticut, and the Smith & Wesson Company, at Springfield, Massachusetts, to accept the decision of the War Labor Board.

I am in entire accord with the statements contained in the Board's communication and the proposed letter to District Lodge No. 55 of the International Association of Machinists, except that I look upon the proposed penalty as being more drastic than necessary. In taking over the property of any corporation, the corporation is sooner or later compensated for the property taken, and in fact must be under our constitution. That is somewhat different from barring a workman from the opportunity of employment. The opportunity for employment is essential to secure the means of livelihood, and while other opportunity may be available outside of war industries for sometime to come, it is possible that before the war is over all of our industries will be classed as war industries.

I therefore suggest that if you issue the statement or letter the last paragraph[1] be amended so that it will read as follows:

"Therefore, I desire that you return to work and abide by the award. If you refuse, each of you will be barred from employment in any war industry in the community in which the strike occurs for a period of one year. During that time the United States Employment Service will decline to obtain employment for you in any war industry elsewhere in the United States, as well as under the War and Navy Departments, the Shipping Board, the Railroad Administration, and all other Government agencies, and the draft boards will be instructed to reject any claim of exemption based on your alleged usefulness on war production."

With this change I recommend that the letter be sent immediately and that it be given publicity.

Faithfully yours,   W B Wilson

TLS (WP, DLC).
   [1] "Therefore, I desire that you return to work and abide by the award. If you refuse, each of you will be permanently barred from employment in any war industry in the community in which the strike occurs. The United States Employment Bureau will decline to obtain employment for you in any war industry elsewhere in the United States, as well as under the War and Navy Departments, the Shipping Board, the Railroad Administration and all other government agencies, and the Draft Boards will be instructed to reject any claim of exemption based on your alleged usefulness as machinists on war production." T MS (WP, DLC).

E N C L O S U R E

William Howard Taft and Francis Patrick Walsh to William Bauchop Wilson

Dear Mr. Secretary: Washington September 10, 1918.

The simultaneous resistance of decisions of the National War Labor Board by the Bridgeport machinists and by the Smith & Wesson Company, of Springfield, Mass., presents the necessity for definite and affirmative action by the Government to the end that the authority of the War Labor Board shall be firmly established and to the end that the purposes of the President in creating this Board shall be completely realized.

Fortunately, the present situation, in which the Board's decisions and the principles approved by you and proclaimed by the President are being defied by both sides, furnishes an opportunity for affirmative action that will strike at both sides at one and the same time and permit no further misunderstanding as to the attitude of the Government toward either side in an industrial dispute.

On the one hand the Bridgeport machinists are striking because the award of the War Labor Board did not grant them the classification of trades they demanded. They got collective bargaining, the basic eight hour day, the right to organize into trade unions, equality of pay as between men and women doing the same work, and a general increase in wages for all workers receiving up to 78 cents an hour, together with a minimum wage of 42 cents an hour for all male workers over 21 years of age, and 32 cents an hour for all female workers over 18 years of age.

It should be further noted that those who refused to comply with the Bridgeport award constitute but ten per cent or less of the whole number of employees whose interests were considered and adjudged, and that small percentage are the highest paid of all who submitted to the arbitration. Their contention, therefore, with reference to the cost of living has less merit than that of the ninety per cent or more of the workers at Bridgeport who are entirely satisfied with the award and are living up to it.

On the other hand the Smith & Wesson Company has contemptuously rejected the intervention and mediation of the Board because its principles and rules of decision approved in the proclamation of the President, imposed upon the management the necessity of dealing with its employees collectively.

The War Department is prepared to uphold the War Labor Board in the Smith & Wesson case by taking over the plant, and a commandeering order is signed and awaiting delivery.

It is the opinion of the War Department and of the chairmen and secretary of the War Labor Board[1] that drastic action also should be taken with regard to the Bridgeport strike, and the attached letter has been prepared,[2] with the approval of the War Department, with the suggestion that the President address it to the Bridgeport locals.

It is the purpose of the War Department upon the same day that this letter is issued for publication to issue a statement announcing the commandeering of the Smith & Wesson plant, together with a statement of the reasons for the action.

The necessity for speedy action is imperative if the Government is to turn this unusual opportunity to good account.

> Wm H Taft }
> Frank P. Walsh } Chairmen
>
> For the War Department.
> Benedict Crowell
> Acting Secretary of War.

TLS (WP, DLC).
[1] That is, Taft, Walsh, and William Jett Lauck.
[2] T MS (WP, DLC). With W. B. Wilson's substitute final paragraph included, it is printed as WW to the members of District Lodge No. 55, Sept. 13, 1918.

From Robert Russa Moton

My dear Mr. President:

Tuskegee Institute, Ala.
September 11, 1918

I notice in today's paper that Liberia has been granted a loan of Five Millions of Dollars, as requested by the Committee which waited on you last April.

This act will serve not only to help a struggling people, but it will tremendously strengthen the morale of the American Negroes: and I do not mean to intimate that the morale of the Negroes is at all weak at this time, for your address on mob law, as well as the commuting of the sentences of the ten Houston rioters, with the accompanying expression, has sent a thrill of joy which reacts in loyalty and patriotism on the millions of my people.

I am taking this opportunity now to thank you for your efforts in our behalf, and I know that I speak the sentiments of all of the colored people of this country and of Liberia, when I tell you how grateful we are to you for what you have done in this instance.

> Very truly yours,   R. R. Moton

TLS (WP, DLC).

From Herbert Clark Hoover

Dear Mr. President: Washington 11 September 1918.

In response to your request, I beg to set out my observations on the recommendations of the Federal Trade Commission, with regard to the five large packing firms.[1]

[1] W. B. Colver et al. to WW, July 3, 1918, Vol. 48.

I scarcely need to repeat the views that I expressed to you nearly a year ago, that there is here a growing and dangerous domination of the handling of the Nation's foodstuffs.

I do not feel that appreciation of this domination of necessity implies wrong doing on the part of the proprietors, but is the natural outgrowth of various factors which need correction. In an objective understanding of this situation, it is necessary to review the underlying economics of its growth.

At one time our food animals were wholly slaughtered and distributed locally. The ingenious turning to account of the byproducts from slaughtering when dealt with on a large scale gave the foundation for consolidation of slaughtering in the larger centers. From this grew the necessity for special cars for livestock transport and the large stockyards at terminals. The creation of these facilities were largely stimulated and to a considerable extent owned by the packers. Added to this was the application of refrigeration processes for the preservation of meat, which at once extended the period of preservation and the radius of distribution from the slaughter centers, enabled larger slaughtering nearer the great Western producing area, and further contributed to the centralization of the industry. This enlarged scope, particularly the refrigeration operations require not only the expensive primary equipment, but a network of refrigerator cars, icing stations and cold storage at distribution points. This special car service in products is of the nature of the Pullman Service; it must traverse railroad lines independent of ownership, and moreover, it is seasonal and varies regionally in different seasons. For each railway to have foreseen and to have provided sufficient of this highly specialized equipment is asking the impossible, and, in any event, no particular railway could be expected to provide sufficient of these cars to answer the shifting of seasonal and regional demands outside its own lines.

Thus, the provision of a large part of the stock yards and car services has naturally fallen in considerable degree to the larger and more wealthy packers who have used their advantages as in effect a special and largely exclusive railway privilege with which to build up their own business.

From the stage of establishment of a multiplicity of marketing facilities, such as cold storage, warehouses, branch offices, etc., grew direct dealings with retail dealers and finally resulted in a large elimination of the wholesale traders.

Through this practical railway privilege, the numerous branch establishments, the elimination of wholesale intermediaries, and with large banking alliances, this group have found themselves in position, not only to dominate the distribution of interstate animal products, but to successfully invade many other lines of food and other commodity preparation and distribution. Their excellence of organization, the standing of their brands, and control of facilities now threaten even further inroads against independent manufacturers and wholesalers of other food products. They now vend scores of different articles, and this constantly increasing list now approaches a dominating proportion of the interstate business in several different food lines.

It is a matter of great contention as to whether these five firms compete amongst themselves, and the records of our courts and public bodies are monuments to this contention. Entirely aside from any question of conspiracy to eliminate competition amongst themselves and against outsiders, it appears to me that these five firms, closely paralleling each other's business as they do, with their wide knowledge of business conditions in every section, must at least follow coincident lines of action and must naturally refrain from persistent, sharp, competitive action towards each other. They certainly avoid such competition to considerable extent. Their hold on the meat and many other trades has become so large through the vast equipment of slaughter houses, cars and distributing branches, and banking alliances which each of the five controls, that it is practically inconceivable that any new firms can rise to their class, and in any event even sharp competition between the few can only tend to reduce the number of five and not increase it. Of equal public importance is the fact that their strategic advantage in marketing equipment, capital and organization must tend to further increase the area of their invasion into trades outside of animal products. Furthermore, as these few firms are the final reservior [reservoir] for all sale of animals, when the few yards where they buy become erratically over supplied with more animals than their absolute requirements, it remains in their hands to fluctuate prices by mere refusal to buy—and not necessarily by any conspiracy. In other words, the narrow number of buyers undoubtedly produces an unstable market which reacts to discourage production. It can be contended, I believe, that these concerns have developed great economic efficiency, that their costs of manufacture and profits are made from the wastes of forty years ago.

The problem we have to consider, however, is the ultimate social result of this expanding domination, and whether it can be replaced by a system of better social character, and of equal economic efficiency for the present and of greater promise for the future. It is certain, to my mind, that these businesses have been economically efficient in their period of competitive upgrowth, but, as time goes on, this efficiency cannot fail to diminish and, like all monopolies, begin to defend itself by repression rather than by efficiency. The worst social result of this whole growth in domination of trades is the undermining of the initiative and the equal opportunity of our people and the tyranny which necessarily follows in the commercial world.

The Federal Trade Commission's recommendations fall into three parts:

(A) That the Railroad Administration take over all animal and refrigeration car services.

(B) That they take over the stockyard terminals.

(C) That the Federal Government itself take over the packer's branch houses, cold storage warehouses, etc., with view, I assume, to the establishing of equal opportunity of entrance into distribution among all manufacturers and traders.

As to the first part of this recommendation on car service, I am in full agreement and may recall to you that soon after its installation, we recommended that the Railway Administration should take over and operate all private car lines in food products. This has, to some degree, been accomplished through their car service division.

These arrangements are purely under war powers, and if the reforms proposed are to be of any value, they must be placed upon a permanent basis and not merely for the war. There can be no doubt that the car services, in order to obtain the results desired and the greatest national economy, must be greatly expanded and must be operated from a national point of view, rather than from that of each individual railway. Moreover, they are highly technical services beyond the ordinary range of railway management and need to embrace all cooled cars as well as meat cars. Whether this service on a national scale should be conducted by the Government or by private enterprise, under control as a public utility, seems to me to require further thought and, in any event, to depend upon the ultimate disposal of the railway question.

As to the stock yards, I am in agreement that they should be entirely disassociated from the control of the packers. A distinction must be drawn between the stock yards as a physical market place and the buying and selling conducted therein. In the first sense, the complaints largely center around the exclusion not of buyers and sellers, but of the prevention of competitors from establishing packing plants either upon land of the yards, or of obtaining track and other connections therewith. The solution of this problem in permanent form will also depend upon the ultimate solution of the Railway problem. If the Government should acquire the railways, it would appear to me that it should, as a part of the system, acquire the yards. If the Government returns the railways to their owners, it would appear to me that these ends could be accomplished by appropriate regulation under the Interstate Commerce Commission, and this should be done ad interim. As to the wrong practices between buyers and sellers, these would not be corrected by the Government owning or controlling the physical yards; they are, in fact, now under war regulation by the Department of Agriculture.

As to the recommendation that the Federal Government should at once take over the packers' branch houses, cold storage and warehouse facilities, I find much difficulty. I do not assume that the Trade Commission contemplates the Government entering upon the purchase and sale of meat and groceries at these establishments. Nor does it appear to me that the individual separate and scattered branch houses of the packers furnish any proper physical basis for free terminal wholesale markets. In discussion with the independent packers, I find no belief that the packers' branch houses would serve as a basis of universal market service, and I find much differences of opinion as to public markets as a solution. Any of the great packers' equipment in this particular would in any event require a great deal of extension to effect such objectives, and we are in no position to find the material and labor during the war.

We do need an absolute assurance to the food trades of such terminal facilities as will allow any manufacturer or dealer in any food product equal opportunity to handle and store his goods pending their final distribution. The usefulness of either public, wholesale, or retail markets in the promotion of these ends is a matter of great division of opinion. The most predominant feeling in the independent trades is that if sites can be made advilable [available], adjacent to railway facilities, the trades themselves would solve the matter. In any event, the whole public market question is peculiar to each city and town, and my own inquiries find little belief that the present branch houses of the packers would serve this purpose. Furthermore, my own instinct, in any event, is against Federal Ownership of such facilities, and our own inquiries rather indicate that if transportation questions, together with factors mentioned later on, are put right, this problem will solve itself. Altogether, I do not consider that the prime objective of maintaining the initiative of our citizens and of our local communities is to be secured by this vast expansion of federal activities.

There are certain matters relating to the development and control of the packing industry which are not referred to in the report of the Trade Commission, which appear to me of first importance. One effect of the great centralization of this industry has been the stultification or decline in slaughter near many large cities and towns. I believe this has been initially due to the inability to recover byproducts to such advantage as under the centralization, a disability that does not now generally exist, for most of these products now have an outlet. It has also been partially due to the cheaper animals from the cheaper lands of the West—and this disparity in costs of animal production has greatly diminished with settlement of the country. It is also partially due to at least the fear that the great packers would direct their power of underselling against such enterprises. If proper abattoirs could be extended near the larger towns, possibly with municipal help and the operations therein protected from illegitimate competition, I believe they would not only succeed, but would greatly stimulate the local production of meat animals. One effect would be a great stabilization of prices by a wider based market than that now so largely dependent upon a small group of buyers.

Another phase of the question lies around the fact that I feel the solutions propounded by the Trade Commission will not entirely solve the problem of the invasion of many other lines of food handling besides animal products. This portion of their business is more largely supported by their larger credits and their elimination of the wholesale grocer, rather than upon railway privilege. As to whether such goods can be vended more economically direct than through the wholesaler is a matter of much contention. It seems to me, however, that this whole phase of absorption of other food industries requires consideration. It appears to me at least worth thought as to whether these aggregations should not be confined to more narrow and limited activities, say those involved in the slaughter of animals, the preparation and marketing of the products therefrom alone. Such a course might solve the branch house problem, and it is not an unknown legislative control, as witness our banks, railways, and insurance companies.

One other cause also chokes the free marketing of food in the United States, which will not be reached by the ultimate action on the above lines, and that is the present insufficient standardization of our food products, and this would contribute to strengthen the independent manufacturer.

In summation, I believe that the ultimate solution of this problem is to be obtained by assuring equal opportunity in transportation, equal opportunity in the location of manufacturing sites and of terminal sites, and the limitation of the activities of these businesses. In this situation, I believe that the fifty minor meat packing establishments and the hundreds of other food preservers could successfully expand their interstate activities and that local slaughter would increase with economic gain to the community, and all through continued competition constantly improve our manufacturing and distribution processes to the advantage of both producer and consumer. The detailed methods, except in the manifest case of car and stock yard control, require much more thought.

The activity of the Food Administration is necessarily founded on securing the largest service and the least disruption and danger to distribution during this period of national strain. To take such a radical step as to seize the packers branch houses for the war, would effect no permanent values and would surely disrupt distribution at this time. The packers are today performing their economic duties of preserving and distributing the meat supplies to our own population and the Allies, as distinguished from the social results of their organization, and the only outstanding question from a purely win-the-war point of view is whether the packers are today imposing upon their competitors and whether their remuneration is exorbitant. These are matters which can be remedied during the war by regulation and taxation.

I would, in any event, separate the whole problem into a question as to what should be done as a war emergency and what should be done as a permanent solution of the whole question. I do not feel that the Government should undertake the solution of the problem by the temporary authority conferred under the war powers of the Railway and Food Administrations, which must terminate with peace, but rather that it should be laid before Congress for searching consideration, exhaustive debate and development of public opinion, just as has been necessary in the development of the public interest in our banks, insurance companies and railways.

Yours faithfully,   Herbert Hoover

TLS (WP, DLC).

From William Julius Harris

Atlanta, Ga., Sept. 11, 1918.

My majority overwhelming and it continues to increase.[1] Suggest you send Clark Howell strong telegraphic message congratulating him and through him other newspapers and the people who so loyally backed your administration.   William J. Harris.

T telegram (WP, DLC).
[1] Harris carried 114 of the 152 counties in Georgia in the primary election held on September 10. The other thirty-eight counties were divided among Senator Hardwick, Representative William S. Howard, and Emmet R. Shaw, a former state senator. About Georgia's county-unit system, see W. J. Harris to WW, July 27, 1918, n. 1.

To Robert Lansing

My dear Mr. Secretary: The White House 12 September, 1918.

Thank you for letting me see the enclosed.[1] Will you not be kind enough to have copies of it sent to Mr. Baruch, Mr. Vance Mc-Cormick, and Mr. Hurley? At my little war board meeting yesterday I arranged with those three gentlemen that they were to actively cooperate to see that the necessary supplies get off to Russia at the earliest possible time, and information like this will of course be very necessary to them.

Cordially and sincerely yours,   Woodrow Wilson

TLS (SDR, RG 59, 861.48/651, DNA).

[1] Henry St. George Tucker and Rudolf Bolling Teusler, M.D., to H. P. Davison, Sept. 6, 1918, TC telegram (SDR, RG 59, 861.48/651, DNA). They reported on a recent meeting in Vladivostok with Gen. Rudolf Gajda, commander of the Czech forces in western Siberia. Gajda claimed to control "practically all Siberia." However, there was a dire shortage of equipment. Supplies of all kinds, especially those for winter, were urgently needed for at least 160,000 Czechs and 200,000 of their Russian allies. Teusler requested that thirty-one medical specialists and sixty trained nurses be sent to Siberia, as well as X-ray and other specialized equipment.

Tucker (1874-1959), Protestant Episcopal Bishop of the Diocese of Kyoto, Japan, was at this time serving as a member of the American Red Cross Commission with the Allied forces in Siberia. Teusler, medical missionary, founder and director of St. Luke's Hospital in Tokyo, and a first cousin of Edith Bolling Wilson, was also serving on the Red Cross Commission in Siberia.

To Augustus Owsley Stanley

The White House
My dear Governor Stanley: 12 September, 1918.

Thank you warmly for your letter of September 7th. It was gracious of you to have in mind my solicitude about the attitude of your appointee to the Senate on the subject of woman suffrage, and I shall look forward with real interest to meeting Senator Martin and discussing the matter with him.

I warmly appreciate your kind letter.

Cordially and sincerely yours,   Woodrow Wilson

TLS (A. O. Stanley Papers, KyU).

From Peyton Conway March, with Enclosure

My dear Mr. President: Washington. September 12, 1918

I have just received a letter from General Bliss, with certain enclosures,[1] all of which refer to the problem at Archangel, which I am sending you, thinking perhaps you would be interested in reading General Bliss' account of the attitude of the military representatives of the Supreme War Council towards this matter. General Bliss is always interesting and he always talks good sense.

Very sincerely yours,   P. C. March

TLS (WDR, RG 120, Records of the American Section of the Supreme War Council, 1917-1919, File No. 366-5, DNA).
[1] The Editors have not found these enclosures.

ENCLOSURE

Tasker Howard Bliss to Peyton Conway March

No. 18.

My dear March: Versailles. September 3, 1918.

I suppose that the Secretary of War has started by this time. I am just informed that the Washington courier leaves here to-day and I therefore write to you hastily about two or three things in order to keep you advised as to the situation here at Versailles.

1. From the various papers that have drifted in here, presumably originating in the French General Staff in Paris, I have foreseen that sooner or later the question of sending reinforcements to the expeditions in Russia would come up. I supposed that it would come up from the French, but as a matter of fact it has come from the British who, nevertheless, seem to take less interest in the matter than the French do. Two or three days ago the British Representative received from the British War Cabinet in London the copy of a telegram sent by Admiral Kemp,[1] the British Admiral commanding the naval force at Murmansk and Archangel. I inclose a copy of it. The War Cabinet asked to have early consideration given to it by the Military Representatives. When I received the copy from the British Representative it contained a note from the British Chief of Staff in London saying that as the Military Representatives here had prepared the organization of the expedition to Murmansk and Archangel he wanted their opinion as to the matter of reinforcements. In conversation I expressed quite plainly my opinion as to the accuracy of this statement, whereupon that copy of the telegram was withdrawn and a new one submitted without the remark which I had criticized.

If you will consider this telegram in connection with the instructions sent to General Poole by the British Government,[2] to govern his campaign, you will see that the situation presented to us is somewhat extraordinary. The Military Representatives had rec-

[1] That is, Rear Adm. Thomas Webster Kemp.
[2] See T. H. Bliss to NDB and P. C. March, Aug. 18, 1918.

ommended that a force be sent to General Poole, merely in order to enable him to hold the ports of Murmansk and Archangel during the winter, which force was identical with that which General Poole himself had requested. This was approved by the Supreme War Council. The British War Cabinet then drew up the instructions for the campaign and sent them to General Poole without the Military Representatives knowing anything about it until a copy was finally sent here. However, the instructions of the British War Cabinet were, so far as I can see, quite in accord with the original intention. General Poole was told that he could have no further reinforcements this year. With that as a basis he was told to do certain things, provided he could do them. In case he could not do them he was to confine himself to the object of defending the ports during the winter months. From Admiral Kemp's telegram it would appear that the conditions have arisen which would require him to obey the instructions limiting him for the winter to the defense of the Arctic ports. General Poole makes his reports to the British Government. We do not know what they are. We have heard nothing from him except that the War Cabinet says that he concurs in the recommendation[s] of Admiral Kemp. These recommendations of Admiral Kemp mean nothing. He says that 5,000 reinforcements should be sent to the Murmansk column, without giving the slightest analysis of the situation or showing why he asks for 5,000 rather than 50,000 men. In regard to the Archangel column he simply says that sufficient reinforcements should be sent. It is absurd to suppose that General Poole would have made such a demand, without stating the number and composition of the reinforcements that he wants and what he needs them for.

I have no reason to suppose that the United States would engage in this venture any further than it has done. In previous letters I have stated very plainly my conviction that the Allies think that having made a beginning in Russia and having put the foot in the crack of the door the whole body must follow. I have told my colleagues that I did not believe the United States would send any more troops there and that I individually would not approve it. I determined, if possible, to head off the question from going to Washington, and I do not think that it will go there. When we discussed the matter yesterday, I commented on the situation, as it was put up to us, and send you an abstract of my remarks taken from the minutes of yesterday's meeting. The substance of those remarks was embodied in a telegram sent last night to the British War Cabinet. They made the plan of campaign and if they want to change it, they must do it themselves and then obtain the approval of the Supreme War Council. I do not believe that the British will send more troops there, nor will the French, and unless you have changed your mind very decidedly in Washington, I am sure that the United States will not do so. If this is the case, it will require General Poole to do that which he was originally supposed by the Military Representatives to do.

2. I think that with the British and French, more particularly the latter, the idea of pushing the movement from Murmansk and Archangel grows out of their belief that nothing of material value will result from the movement in Siberia from Vladivostok. In regard to the situation in Siberia we are quite in the dark. A number of papers from the French General Staff indicate their belief that the Allied forces in Siberia will have to be increased. How this is going to be obtained, I do not know. There is no available source of reinforcements except the Japanese. If the question should come up, I shall take no action on it without definite instructions. The only information that I have from Washington as to why some 7,000 Americans were to be sent into Siberia via Vladivostok is that they, together with certain other Allied forces, were to help the Czecho-Slovaks there. But no one knows what the Czecho-Slovaks will do or want to do if they can once unite. It is one thing to help the Czecho-Slovaks to keep from being wiped out by the Bolsheviks and then march them to Vladivostok and help them to get out of the country. But suppose that it should develop that the Czecho-Slovaks do not now want to get out of Russia, and that they propose to set up a Government of their own there? or, that they want to fight their way through Russia to reach the Germans on the Eastern front? I certainly do not suppose that we are going to help the Czecho-Slovaks if they want to set up a government of their own; nor do I suppose that we want to face the possibility of having a force of 7,000 Americans wiped out in an attempt to reach Germany's Eastern front against the will of the Russians. In any event I do not see how we can do anything more in Russia, even if we wanted to do so. As I have said before, if our Allies have any axes to grind in Russia, let them go and do it. I think that the war has got to be ended on this Western Front and I fully agree with you and Pershing that every effort of ours should be concentrated here.

I think that it is easy to see what is at the bottom of the minds of our Allies in all of these distant expeditions. They are haunted by a fear that *something* may happen that will bring the war to an end before the Allies will be in a position to impose what terms they please on Germany and undo all that the latter has done during the war in various parts of the world. The thing to stiffen up our Allies and convince them beyond peradventure of a doubt that the war will end the way we want it, is to continue piling our troops into France as rapidly as they can come.

3. In further reference to what I said just above, I ask your attention to the letter, written in my own hand, which I sent by the last courier to the Secretary of War.[3] It was about the Conference that was had that day between Marshal Foch and the Military Representatives. In that interview he laid great stress on "manpower." He said that of course he wanted all the artillery that he could get and all the tanks and aeroplanes; but he reiterated that what he most wanted was "man-power." He meant by that that if we could not send all of our divisions completely equipped with the auxiliary services and materiel, to send them with their rifles and small arms ammunition. And I think that he is right. I do not think that there is any doubt that the British and French will both have to consolidate quite a number of divisions in order to maintain the remaining ones at reasonable strength. This consolidation will be due to infantry losses and not losses in artillery materiel. A good deal of artillery materiel will become available for our troops which might otherwise be short of it. And I have discovered that a good deal of materiel becomes available when an emergency approaches, the very existence of which materiel was denied before the emergency came. All of the Armies here have necessarily a certain reserve of materiel. It is difficult to learn what it is because they do not like the idea of giving any of it up. But if our troops are here requiring some of this equipment and if all are convinced that the time will have come next year to bring the war to a conclusion on this front, they will see that no better use of this reserve materiel, or some of it, can be made than to let our troops have it.

4. Another burning question of reinforcements is the sending of additional American troops to Italy. Ambassador Page from Rome stopped to see me some days ago on his way to London. He, like everyone else that goes to Italy, has become saturated with the Italian idea. He insisted that we should send 500,000 men to Italy. I told him that I had nothing whatever to do with that question. I told him to go and talk to General Pershing and Marshal Foch. He did not seem to think that it would do much good to talk to Marshal Foch. He said that the Italians disliked the French very much and that the French reciprocated the feeling. He did not believe that he would get much encouragement at the Marshal's Headquarters. I told him frankly that I did not think he would get much encouragement at General Pershing's Headquarters.

A few days later, General Diaz appeared on the same mission and for the purpose of interviewing both General Pershing and Marshal Foch. Marshal Foch is pressing General Diaz to make an offensive in Italy before the winter sets in in the mountains. I think

---

[3] It is missing in all collections known to the Editors.

that General Diaz is using that request as a club to force the consent
of the French to have Americans go to his aid. I know that Marshal
Foch's views are radically opposed to this. When he had his conference with the Military Representatives last week, General di
Robilant broached this subject and the Marshal replied that he
would not send troops from the front in France to Italy unless it
should be necessary to resist what might otherwise be a successful
enemy drive. There are three reasons which, it seems to me, un-
derlie the insistance of the Italians in getting a large force of Americans in that country. These are

a) Fear. They are mortally afraid of the Germans. Day after
day they send to me reports from the Italian Secret Service which
make the positive assertion that such and such a number of
German divisions have been moved from this front to reinforce
the Austrians in Italy. Thus far there has been no verification
whatever of these statements. If the Germans can stabilize themselves in France in sufficient time before the season closes, it is
very possible that they might send divisions to Italy in order to
take advantage of this very fear which the Italians have of them.
Of course the Germans will not want to have the winter set in
with the knowledge on the part of their people that they have
failed on all fronts. If they can possibly get even a partial success
anywhere before winter, it is most likely that they will try it. But
thus far there is no sign of their attempting any movements to
Italy. They are kept too busy on this front.

b) Money. I have seen numerous references in the principal
political papers of Italy to the great sums of money which they
say France is making out of the presence of the American troops.
Of course their Government does not allege this as a reason for
their desire to have our troops, but the fact remains that great
pressure to get our people there is put upon that government by
men who are thinking mainly of the money return. I have seen
violent attacks made on the Italian Government for its alleged
failure in diplomacy in allowing all the American troops to come
to France.

c) Political. As you know, the Secret Treaty signed (I think)
on April 26, 1915, between Russia, Great Britain and France, on
the one hand, and Italy on the other, promised Italy large territorial rewards (among them, on the East coast of the Adriatic)
provided Italy would enter the war within 30 days after the signature of the Treaty. Moreover, there was an unknown concession to Italy on the part of the other Allies which may cause great
trouble after the war. This concession was that if the Allies at
the end of the war, should be aggrandized by the acquisition of

German colonial possessions she (Italy) would be entitled to corresponding compensation elsewhere. This can only mean compensation in Europe or North Africa. The Treaty was signed and Italy entered the war exactly 30 days afterwards. There is a general undercurrent of belief here that the Allies will not give Italy even that which they specifically promised. Italy knows this. Therefore she would like to have the decisive blow struck from Italy rather than from France, with her army as a predominating factor. That is the third reason why Italy wants large American reinforcements.

5. Lord Reading is here, having arrived late on Saturday night. He is at the British Embassy here and Lord Darby[4] telephoned me yesterday to come to lunch. I could not do that so Lord Reading then asked me to come to see him at half past five, which I did. I had a two hour's talk with him. It would do you good to hear the cordial way in which he expresses himself about the United States and the tremendous efforts which are being made there. He talked to me about the shipping problem, having seen the shipping people in London just before he came over here. I think that he believes, as all of us do, that if there be a well-grounded hope that we can end the war next year, the shipping will be forthcoming. But he says the question can be settled only by getting together the shipping men of the United States and those of the Allies, in London. He asked me to make arrangements for an interview with General Pershing so that he could arrange for a two or three day's visit to the American troops. It will be a fine thing for him to see them before he returns to the United States. I got General Pershing on the 'phone and it was arranged for an interview with him and Lord Reading this morning to fix the details.

I have written very hastily in order to not miss the courier. Along with this I send some miscellaneous documents which may be of interest. I do not know how much of it you may get from other sources but even if they duplicate previous information they may not come amiss.

With best regards, I am

Cordially yours,   Tasker H. Bliss.

TLS (WDR, RG 120, Records of the American Section of the Supreme War Council, 1917-1919, File No. 366-5, DNA).
4 That is, Edward George Villiers Stanley, 17th Earl of Derby.

From George Creel

My dear Mr. President: Washington, D. C. September 12, 1918.

I have just talked with Mr. Baruch about the withdrawal of his appointment of Lindbergh, of Minnesota.[1] While the Torry papers of Minnesota credited me with the appointment, I knew nothing of it until this morning. However, I feel strongly that the appointment, having been announced, should be stood by. Lindbergh and all of his followers are your loyal supporters, and this is their one crime as far as the Minnesota reactionaries are concerned. I have followed this situation very closely and very dispassionately, and I can conceive of nothing more harmful to the Nation's interest than that we should be put in the position of backing down under the threat of a lot of Republican politicians, willing at all times to put their party above their country.

Please forgive this liberty, but the matter is one in which I feel very deeply.   Respectfully,   George Creel

TLS (WP, DLC).
[1] Baruch had offered Charles A. Lindbergh an appointment to membership on the War Industries Board on August 23. Lindbergh accepted on August 26 and was sworn into office in early September. However, publicity about the appointment stirred up furor, especially in Minnesota, on the ground of Lindbergh's alleged disloyalty to the American cause in the war. At Baruch's request, Lindbergh sent him a letter of resignation on September 10. See Bruce L. Larson, *Lindbergh of Minnesota: A Political Biography* (New York, 1973), pp. 250-54, and G. Creel to WW, Sept. 18, 1918.

Walter Hines Page to Robert Lansing

London. Sept. 12, 1918.

Urgent. 1834. Confidential. Lieutenant Charles Merz, assistant to Captain Walter Lippmann, suggests the following, with regards to the inter-Allied Labor Conference which meets in London next week September 17th to 19th, the first conference of the kind attended by representatives of American labor: "Now is the moment for the President to address a message to the inter-Allied Labor Conference, not only reaffirming that this is a working mans war but winning more securely than ever to his standard, the great force in the Allied labor movement which will not long remain latent. Definite declarations are necessary. Such declarations in their most effective form would include: First, a repetition of the President's own statement that this war must end in no selfish economic leagues; second, that it is the firm intention of America to help create a league of nations; third, that the creation of this league removes the last excuse for those strategic protections which nations seek in new colonies or economic advantages; fourth, that

America is ready to accept her share in the world responsibility for the fair treatment of native peoples and backward races; fifth, that future peace in the world demands a scientific allocation of exportable food stuffs and raw materials after the war and new world legislation against sweating and the exploitation of women and children; sixth, that it is the conviction of the American Government that the reestablishment of a Tsarist regime in Russia can end only by playing into the hands of the reactionary German Government upon which any Tsarist regime in Russia must lean." I submit the above without comment for your consideration.   Page.

T telegram (WP, DLC).

A Memorandum

The White House. September 12, 1918.

Since the transmission to the President of the letter of Secretary Wilson and other documents in the case of the Bridgeport strike, I have written to the strikers requesting their immediate return to work under penalty of suspension of their local from the international. Today they replied by telegram that they would continue to strike, and by telephone officers of the local said the men would return to work only upon request of President Wilson.

Wm. H Johnston[1]

TS MS (WP, DLC).
[1] That is, William Hugh Johnston.

Sir Eric Drummond to Sir William Wiseman

[London] Sept. 12th. 1918.

No. CXP 770. Your telegram No. 716 of August 27th. We are grateful for your description of views held by President Wilson as to declaration of war by United States on Turkey and Bulgaria. Theory that presence of American missionaries in Turkish territory has up to now prevented massacres and atrocities is quite untenable. Armenian massacres which were witnessed by Americans have probably surpassed for savagery anything in war. No doubt missionaries dislike idea of a war between Turkey and United States as this would imperil security of their important properties and institutions which they possess on Turkish soil. Morgenthau and Elkus' influence and advice would also I believe be against declaration of hostilities. However this may be it would seem we must abandon idea of declaration of war on Turkey by United States.

Your views on Bulgaria are more encouraging. On the whole we have come to conclusion that if President Wilson consents to threaten Bulgaria with a declaration of war within a limited time, say six weeks, from when threat was first made considerable political advantages might accrue whether United States had declared war on Turkey or not. Conditions which we should like to see attached to threat have been set out in my previous telegrams. As I have already explained at present Bulgarian Government are much strengthened by being able to announce they are still friends with United States. Every agent reports one thing they are afraid of is a declaration of war by United States. At present they tell their country that not only have they secured great territorial expansion at cost of Serbia and Greece but that they are on good terms with Allied Powers of the greatest importance as regards after war reconstruction and finance. They no doubt add that the United States must take a favourable view of their territorial ambitions as otherwise she would not have adhered to her present attitude. All this would be changed by threat I have suggested and we trust therefore that President may be persuaded to make it.

T telegram (W. Wiseman Papers, CtY).

A Translation of a Letter from Jean Jules Jusserand to Stéphen Jean Marie Pichon

[Washington] 12 September 1918.

No. 424. The American labor organization which comes nearest to the Russian extremists is the one called the Industrial Workers of the World, or I.W.W., according to the mode, so often abused, of designation by initials. It will soon be necessary to have special dictionaries in order to recognize them. Undermine, destroy, overthrow, kill if necessary—one will see afterward—seems to be the fundamental principle which inspires this organization composed in large part of people who are American in name only or who are not even that.

The President, who regards himself as well informed on these problems, spoke to me of them not long ago. He said that the danger of conflagrations and revolutions menaces all organized states if the necessary precautions are not taken in time to assure the maintenance of order and the triumph of law, which represent the sober will of the nation and not the destructive passions of some demagogues. "I hope," he says to me, "that, as for us, we will have done what is necessary in time." And he alluded there to the demoralizing role of the I.W.W. and to the steps already taken to cut it short. . . .

TCL (Papiers Jusserand, Vol. 17, pp. 303-304, FFM-Ar).

To the Members of District Lodge No. 55 and Other Striking Workers

Gentlemen: [The White House] 13 September, 1918.

I am in receipt of your resolutions of September 6th announcing that you have begun a strike against your employers in Bridgeport, Conn. You are members of the Bridgeport branches of the International Union of Machinists. As such, and with the approval of the National officers of your Union, you signed an agreement to submit the questions as to the terms of your employment to the National War Labor Board and to abide the award which in accordance with the rules of procedure approved by me might be made.

The members of the Board were not able to reach a unanimous conclusion on all the issues presented, and as provided in its constitution, the questions upon which they did not agree were carried before an arbitrator, the unanimous choice of the members of the Board.

The arbitrator thus chosen has made an award which more than ninety per cent of the workers affected accept. You who constitute less than ten per cent refuse to abide the award although you are the best paid of the whole body of workers affected, and are, therefore, least entitled to press a further increase of wages because of the high cost of living. But, whatever the merits of the issue, it is closed by the award. Your strike against it is a breach of faith calculated to reflect on the sincerity of National organized labor in proclaiming its acceptance of the principles and machinery of the National War Labor Board.

If such disregard of the solemn adjudication of a tribunal to which both parties submitted their claims be temporized with, agreements become mere scraps of paper. If errors creep into awards, the proper remedy is submission to the award with an application for rehearing to the tribunal. But to strike against the award is disloyalty and dishonor.

The Smith & Wesson Company, of Springfield, Mass., engaged in government work, has refused to accept the mediation of the

National War Labor Board and has flaunted [flouted] its rules of decision approved by Presidential proclamation. With my consent the War Department has taken over the plant and business of the Company[1] to secure continuity in production and to prevent industrial disturbance.

It is of the highest importance to secure compliance with reasonable rules and procedure for the settlement of industrial disputes. Having exercised a drastic remedy with recalcitrant employers, it is my duty to use means equally well adapted to the end with lawless and faithless employes.

Therefore, I desire that you return to work and abide by the award. If you refuse, each of you will be barred from employment in any war industry in the community in which the strike occurs for a period of one year. During that time the United States Employment Service will decline to obtain employment for you in any war industry elsewhere in the United States, as well as under the War and Navy Departments, the Shipping Board, the Railroad Administration, and all other Government agencies, and the draft boards will be instructed to reject any claim of exemption based on your alleged usefulness on war production.

Sincerely yours,   Woodrow Wilson

TLS (Letterpress Books, WP, DLC).
    [1] On September 13. See Conner, *The National War Labor Board*, p. 133.

To Robert Lansing

My dear Mr. Secretary: The White House 13 September, 1918.

Frankly, I think that Mr. Root is past his period of active usefulness and I do not want to reappoint him to the Permanent Court at the Hague.[1] Have you someone else in mind whom international lawyers would accept as a suitable successor?

Cordially and faithfully yours,

TL (WP, DLC).
    [1] Wilson was responding to RL to WW, Sept. 11, 1918, TLS (WP, DLC). The international bureau of the Permanent Court of Arbitration had called attention to the fact that Root's term of six years had expired on December 15, 1916.

From Joseph Patrick Tumulty

Dear Governor: The White House. 13 September 1918.

I have read your letter to the Secretary of State, declining to reappoint Mr. Elihu Root.

I am afraid of the impression your refusal to reappoint him will make. Our enemies will look upon it as an attempt to belittle and humiliate him. If you are going to make any change, I suggest that you hold back until at least after the election.[1]

Sincerely,   J P Tumulty

TLS (WP, DLC).
[1] Wilson's letter was not sent.

To Joseph Patrick Tumulty

Dear Tumulty: [The White House] 13 September, 1918

Won't you say to Mr. Saunders that I will be very glad to see him.[1] Just say nothing about Mr. Wheeler. Please suggest Tuesday of next week at 4.30, immediately after Cabinet.

The President

TL (WP, DLC).
[1] See WW to JPT, Sept. 6, 1918.

To Robert Russa Moton

My dear Major Moton: [The White House] 13 September, 1918.

Thank you sincerely for your letter of September 11th. It has given me real gratification. You rightly interpret my desire, which is to help in every way that is possible and legitimate, and I am always glad when thoughtful men agree that I am doing the right thing.   Cordially and sincerely yours,   Woodrow Wilson

TLS (Letterpress Books, WP, DLC).

To William Gibbs McAdoo

My dear Mac: The White House 13 September, 1918.

I cannot exempt any more classes by executive order, because the exemptions already made have worked unhappily, but I hope and believe that the expectations of General Crowder with regard to the successful working of the machinery provided will serve the purpose which I think he is as willing to serve as I am, the safeguarding of the railways against a too great depletion of their working forces. I feel confident that when you read the regulations and such statements as this that General Crowder has put forth,[1] you will agree that every facility has been afforded for doing the thing in as businesslike and effective a manner as circumstances make possible.   Always affectionately yours,   Woodrow Wilson

TLS (W. G. McAdoo Papers, DLC).

¹ E. H. Crowder to WW, Sept. 12, 1918, TLS (W. G. McAdoo Papers, DLC). Crowder stated that everything was being done to insure that workers truly necessary to the continued functioning of organizations and industries essential to the war effort would be given deferred status under the draft. He outlined briefly the steps being taken to this end. He especially called attention to a statement which he had issued on September 9 and which was printed in the *Official Bulletin*, II (Sept. 11, 1918), 1-2, 6. In this statement, Crowder urged both public and private employers to furnish to the draft boards the information about essential employees which would enable the boards to make correct decisions in such cases.

Two Letters to Benedict Crowell

My dear Mr. Secretary: [The White House] 13 September, 1918.

The case referred to in the enclosed letter from the Secretary of State¹ is one about which one cannot form a confident judgment, but I am clear that the Secretary of State is entirely right about the serious aspects the case may assume, if this man is forced to undergo trial by court martial. Will you not be kind enough to give instructions that the course suggested by the Secretary of State be followed; namely, that the man be allowed to return to camp, and upon his return immediately receive his discharge without judicial processes of any sort?²

As you know, no cases are giving us more embarrassment or uneasiness than those of aliens drafted into the service who are subjects of countries with which we have specific treaty engagements such as we have with Spain, and in the present circumstances treaty engagements take on a peculiar sacredness.

Cordially and sincerely yours,   Woodrow Wilson

¹ RL to WW, Sept. 12, 1918, TLS (WP, DLC). Lansing called Wilson's attention to the case of Private Telesforo Samperio, a Spanish subject mistakenly drafted into the United States Army. His release had been requested and granted under a provision of a treaty between the United States and Spain which exempted Spanish subjects from compulsory military service. However, before the discharge was delivered to Samperio, he had deserted, in the belief that he was about to be sent to France. The War Department demanded that he return to camp to face a court martial for desertion. The Spanish Ambassador, who knew of Samperio's whereabouts, argued that he could not be tried in a court martial since he was illegally in camp in the first place and hence had no obligation to remain there. Lansing recommended that the tangled situation be resolved by granting Samperio a discharge without court martial, provided that he immediately return to the camp from which he had deserted.

² Crowell agreed to the proposed solution. B. Crowell to WW, Sept. 16, 1918, TLS (WP, DLC).

My dear Mr. Secretary: [The White House] 13 September, 1918.

I have little enough sympathy with the conscientious objector, but I am sure we all want to avoid unnecessary harshness and injustice of any sort, and I would be very much obliged if you would read the letter of Mr. Hochbaum and its enclosure,[1] with a view to remedying any injustice that may have been done.

Cordially and sincerely yours,   Woodrow Wilson

TLS (Letterpress Books, WP, DLC).
[1] A White House memorandum dated Sept. 13, 1918, T MS, (WP, DLC) reveals that this letter was Hays L. Hochbaum to WW, Sept. 8, 1918, which complained of the treatment of his brother, who had "enrolled" in the army as a conscientious objector.

To William Graves Sharp

The White House

My dear Mr. Ambassador: 13 September, 1918.

The bearer of this letter, Dr. Stockton Axson, is my brother-in-law. It would not do, therefore for me to say that he is a particularly fine fellow. But I am at least at liberty to say that he is the Secretary of the American Red Cross and is anxious to serve the purposes of that organization in any way possible not only, but is also anxious to serve you in any way that you may suggest, in the exercise of his duties.

Cordially and sincerely yours,   Woodrow Wilson[1]

TLS (WC, NjP).
[1] Wilson wrote the same letter, *mutatis mutandis*: to J. J. Pershing, Sept. 13, 1918, TLS (Letterpress Books, WP, DLC).

From Robert Lansing, with Enclosure

My dear Mr. President: Washington September 13, 1918.

I do not know whether this telegram received by the War Department from General Graves has been called to your attention. I am, therefore, sending it to you.

Faithfully yours,   Robert Lansing.

TLS (SDR, RG 59, 861.00/2760½A, DNA).

E N C L O S U R E

Received at the War Department, Sept. 12-18. 9:51 AM
Vladivostok.

The Adjutant General, Washington. Number 20 September 11th. Secret.

Paragraph Number 1. Captain Hasurak[1] Czech forces arrived here today with the message from General Guida[2] for Admiral Knight

and myself in substance as follows: The railroad is clear from Vladivostok to Samara; *most of* German and Austrian prisoners in
Siberia are now confined in prisons under *guard* of Russians organized and operating with Czechs; the Czech situation west of
Urals is such as to demand immediate assistance from the allies
and if the assistance is not furnished soon there is danger that the
Czechs will suffer military reverse and that the Russians will feel
that the allies do not intend to give material aid to Czechs and will
no longer affiliate with them in rehabilitating Russia. My investigation of all available sources which include Captain Hasurak, General Dietrichs and Doctor Girza[3] lead to the conclusion that Czechs
need moral and material aid. As the situation in *Siberia is* such
that there is no longer any *need* for anything more than a small
allied military force it is easy for the enemy to make the Russians
believe that the allies have no intention of doing anything in Russia
if the allies do not send all available allied troops to aid the Czechs.
The American flag is best for moral effect but Japan is the only
nation in a position to give *much* material assistance at this time.
The Czechs undoubtedly need clothing, blankets, arms and ammunition especially field artillery. The Russian troops forming will
need careful examination and I believe from available information
if allied troops go to eastern Russia as many *scouting* troops can
be organized as can be equipped. There is no need for more than
one thousand American troops at Vladivostok. The farther *we go*
the better the effect will be. As decision in the matter involves
questions other than military the situation as *mentioned* by General
Guida's representative is submitted to the department notwithstanding my instructions. If it be decided to send troops west of
the Urals to aid the Czechs, and it seems that from military standpoint alone this should be done, I request 9th Cavalry, all field
artillery and engineers be sent here from Philippine Islands.

Graves

T telegram (SDR, RG 59, 861.00/2760½A, DNA).
    [1] K. Husarek. In William S. Graves, *America's Siberian Adventure, 1918-1920* (New
York, 1931), p. 67, "Captain Hasurak" is described as "General Gaida's Adjutant." Col.
"K. Husarek" is pictured in Rudolf Gajda, *Moje Paměti: Československá Anabase* (Prague,
1920), facing p. 24.
    [2] That is, Rudolf Gajda.
    [3] That is, Vaclav Girsa.

From Robert Lansing, with Enclosure

My dear Mr. President: Washington September 13, 1918.

I am enclosing to you a memorandum on Irish conditions prepared by Professor Charles McCarthy, of Madison, Wisconsin, who

has just returned from Ireland. He is a man of exceptional ability and last spring refused to act as Counsel for the Chinese Government because he preferred to serve with Mr. Hoover and also with Mr. Frankfurter in England.

I think you will find this memorandum of unusual interest because he offers suggestions of a constructive nature in dealing with the problem of Ireland. He visited the Governor-General[1] and also came in contact with the Sinn Fein leaders there. He seems to be a man of extraordinary ability and he offers to serve the Government in any capacity where he will be most useful. I am sure you will agree that his suggestions are more or less practical and certainly valuable.   Faithfully yours,   Robert Lansing.

TLS (SDR, RG 59, 841D.00/15A, DNA).
  [1] He presumably meant the Lord Lieutenant, or Viceroy, of Ireland, Field Marshal John Denton Pinkstone French, Viscount French of Ypres and High Lake. There was no Governor-General of Ireland at this time.

E N C L O S U R E

Washington, D. C. September 12, 1918

MEMORANDUM ON IRISH CONDITIONS

(1) The Irish Sinn Fein movement is very likely to control the whole English Government in the near future. The Liberal majority has always been very slight. The Sinn Feiners are now electing members to Parliament, to stay away from Parliament. The result will be that the old combine of Nationalists, Liberals, and Labor members which has ruled England will be on the point of dissolution. If the Sinn Fein movement goes much further, the Labor Party will be more uneasy than it is, for it cannot hope to carry out its policies unless it has greater power than it now has. This is the reason why the Trade Union Congress went by acclamation for Irish Home Rule. The Sinn Fein leaders will try to thrust Ireland onto the Peace Table by using Labor as a fulcrum. Therefore, what is now going on in Ireland is of the utmost importance to America.

(2) All news about what is going on in Ireland is harshly censored. The result is that something may slip through which may arouse the American public, especially the Irish-Americans, and intrude this question into American politics.

(3) Our sailors and soldiers and the Irish population are in constant clashes. There is an angry feeling in our Navy towards the Irish. Certain individuals have fanned this flame, and the controversy is growing more and more bitter as more and more Irish soldiers from America come to Europe and try to find their way into Ireland.

CONSTRUCTIVE SUGGESTIONS

(1) As the Irish will not recruit under the English Flag, and as there are 150,000 British soldiers in Ireland, it is of great importance to us, whether we have to bring over 300,000 soldiers or can take 300,000 soldiers (British and new Irish recruits) who are now in Ireland. I am much inclined to think the British would welcome some way out of the difficulty. With a little tactful negotiation they would be willing to grant the American Army the right to recruit in Ireland. I am quite sure the Sinn Fein element would approve. I found no pro-German spirit in Ireland, and I am quite sure we would get 100,000 soldiers from Ireland in this manner.

(2) At the present time there are a very few women to aid the American Army in France; we have asked for 5,000 W.A.A.C.'s;[1] we have practically no V.A.D.'s or Auxiliary Hospital Workers. All parties agree that you could get 10,000 Irish women to organize into a corps to aid the American Army.

(3) Some sort of a commission should be set up, with well known American Irishmen on it, to deal with American-Irish relations in the ports of Ireland. It may be that Mr Fosdick will work this out.

(4) If three American convalescent hospitals could be established in Ireland, it would lead to friendly relations. The warmhearted Irish would take a special delight in caring for the wounded soldiers. At the present time, where boys are recovering in Paris and London, they are hedged about by vicious conditions. Boys of Irish parentage could be sent to Ireland. It would have a great effect upon the morale of Ireland, and would be a connecting link between Ireland and America.

(5) A special body of Irish women could be set up in Ireland to invite American soldiers over on leave from France, particularly officers, who would be *persona grata* to the Irish. For instance, Father Duffy,[2] who was cited for bravery the other day and given a medal, should be invited to Ireland on leave. All of that would help out with the Irish situation.

It is respectfully submitted that the above constructive ideas be considered at once. There is a possibility that in the middle of October terrible conditions may occur, if the British insist upon dragging out the Irish who refuse to fight under the British Flag. Some little spark will escape and set up a great conflagration. As Sir Horace Plunkett says, "They will shoot the wrong Bishop." I saw one instance of this kind when I was in Ireland; a Mrs O'Connor had been arrested for having in her house some birdshot; the next day the papers carried a paragraph that her son, Lieutenant Joseph O'Connor, had been killed in France in doing a desperately gallant deed. Such things as this, together with the suppression of Gaelic meetings, dances, hurling, football games, and of all assemblies, have been goading the people to the point of desperation.

C McCarthy

TS MS (SDR, RG 59, 841D.oo/15A, DNA).
[1] He presumably referred to the British Women's Army Auxiliary Corps. There was no counterpart of it in the American army. However, the United States Navy enrolled 11,000 female "yeomen" and 269 females in the Marine Corps.
[2] The Rev. Francis Patrick Duffy, a well-publicized chaplain with the 165th Infantry Regiment (formerly the 69th Regiment of the New York National Guard) of the A.E.F. He had recently received the Distinguished Service Cross for heroism under fire while caring for wounded and dying soldiers in the village of Villers-sur-Fere from July 28 to 31. He later published an account of his wartime experiences: *Father Duffy's Story: A Tale of Humor and Heroism, of Life and Death with the Fighting Sixty-Ninth* (New York, 1919). See also the *New York Times*, Sept. 6 and 8, 1918.

From Bainbridge Colby

My dear Mr. President: Washington September 13, 1918.

Your ringing letter of today addressed to the striking machinists in Bridgeport is a great step forward.

I have heard men say of late, in commenting on the recurrent threat of strikes, and the continual breakdown of accommodations with labor, which have been conscientiously sought by the employer in a spirit of justice and conciliation, that we needed a new theorem in coping with labor disaffection. In other words, that ingenuity was exhausted and mere concession futile, and that a solution could not be hoped for until the mind of the nation worked out some new formula.

I believe you have supplied it. Your letter is brave and has the note of true leadership.

Faithfully yours,   Bainbridge Colby

TLS (WP, DLC).

From Raymond Poincaré

[Paris] September 13, 1918.

I cannot await the conclusion of the operations in which the American Army is now engaged to congratulate you, Mr. President, on a victory, the first objectives of which have been already so brilliantly attained. General Pershing's magnificent divisions, assisted by their brothers in arms, the French troops, have now, in a spirit of splendid enthusiasm, liberated towns and villages of Lorraine which have groaned for the last four years under the yoke of the enemy. I express to the people of the United States the heartfelt thanks of France. Permit me to add the expression of my profound personal emotion. I have represented for a quarter of a century in the French Chambers the regions liberated this day. I know better than anyone else how patriotic their inhabitants are, how attached they are to justice and liberty, and how faithful are their hearts. The great sister republic may rest assured of their undying gratitude.   Raymond Poincaré.

T MS (WP, DLC).

From Edward Mandell House, with Enclosure

Dear Governor,   New York. September 13, 1918.

Instead of stopping in Chestnut Hill I came directly through and shall be here from now.

The enclosed letter and cable[1] I think you will find well worth reading   Affectionately yours,   E. M. House

TLS (WP, DLC).
  [1] [Sir Walter Beaupré Townley? to the Foreign Office?], Aug. 3, 1918, TC telegram (WP, DLC). The significant portion of this telegram reads as follows: "Editor of the Leipziger Neueste Nachrichten has arrived in Holland in connection with the New Peace Movement. Editor frankly admitted his mission and says that Germany must have peace this year. Editor says that shortly Holland will be asked to secretly but officially act as intermediary for peace proposals." House commented in the margin as follows: "I got this from Sir Wm. The Dutch will bear watching on this subject, for they may be acting for Germany. E.M.H."

E N C L O S U R E

Lord Robert Cecil to Sir William Wiseman

This, I think, will interest you. E.M.H.

My dear Wiseman: London. Monday, 19 August 1918.

Many thanks for your letter of July 18 about the League of Nations.[1]

I think I look at the problem like this. Here we are suffering from the greatest catastrophe that has perhaps ever occurred, and the worst part of it is that it seems to herald an era of destruction. No one can yet estimate the moral injury that has been wrought. But personally I believe it to be very great, and of infinitely greater importance than the material waste, prodigious as that has been. This will, I hope, grow clearer as the excitement of war subsides, and will create a very powerful reaction against war.

It is that feeling we must harness, if any good is to be done. It will not last long, so we have not much time. Its tendency will be against all force. And to be utilised we must aim at converting it into international public opinion. That is why the main thing I look for is to get nations into the habit of co-operation rather than competition.

Our economic need should help, since the various Inter-Allied organisations which we are creating for the War must last into and over the so-called period of reconstruction. Into these organisations we should be ready to admit all nations as and when they are really to be trusted as peaceful members of the International Society.

But all this will fail as a unifying force unless we add something more. It is a delusion to suppose that the pursuit of material wealth tends to peace. What is wanted is a great ideal, and that must be found in the old Hebrew—and let us add, Christian—conception of the reign of Peace. I believe that a great formless sentiment of this kind exists. If it does not, we can do nothing. If it does, we must give it an organ for its expression. That must be found in a League of Nations which shall operate directly by discussion, and indirectly by taking charge of some of the national problems left to us by the war, such as the care of backward nations, the government of such special districts as Palestine, and perhaps some of the great social problems which can scarcely be treated except internationally.

Since beginning this letter, I have seen your telegram giving an account of the President's views.[2] We shall of course comply with his wishes as to the publication of the Phillimore Report.

I am not sure, however, whether he realises the immense difficulties there will be in the way of establishing a League of Nations. All the European bureaucracies will be against the idea, including probably the bureaucracy of this country. Nor must it be forgotten that the heresies of Militarism have unfortunately extended beyond the limits of Germany, and all the militarists will be against the idea. Finally there will be many people who will fear that the Germans may use the League for their own purposes: lulling us and others to sleep, and then falling on us when we have been disarmed. All these people are working already, more or less secretly, against the idea. I wished to publish some thing, therefore, in order to create and focus public opinion, and make it vigorous.

It is, however, very good to hear that the President is ready to discuss the matter, and I hope that Reading, when he returns to Washington, will be able to take it up with him in detail.

If I venture to insist upon the strength of the bureaucracies in Europe, it is because no one who has not actually seen them at work can form any idea of their resisting power. They are very able and honourable, but past masters in the arts of obstruction and resistance.   Yours very sincerely,   Robert Cecil.

TCL (WP, DLC).
  ¹ That is, W. Wiseman to R. Cecil, July 18, 1918.
  ² That is, W. Wiseman to Lord Reading, Aug. 16, 1918.

From Herbert Clark Hoover

Dear Mr. President: Washington 13 September 1918

You will please find attached hereto a Proclamation for signature with regard to the Brewing Industry.¹

At a conference yesterday morning with Messrs. McCormick, Garfield and Baruch, it was decided to recommend to you the present form. The effect of this is to limit the making of beer to the use of malt alone from the first of October to the first of December, and at the latter date a complete cessation of the use of foodstuffs including malt. I would like to mention that on December 1st, there will be a good deal of beer in the vats all over the country and we shall have, no doubt, a great deal of pressure from these industries to allow them to use some fuel to revive these beers so that they can be marketed, and they will represent an alternative that there will be enormous losses for them to suffer by the throwing into the sewers of material which otherwise would otherwise have food values.   Faithfully yours,   Herbert Hoover.

TLS (WP, DLC).
  ¹ Hoover summarizes it below. Wilson signed the proclamation on September 16. It is printed in 40 *Statutes at Large* 1848.

Two Telegrams from Colville Adrian de Rune Barclay to Arthur James Balfour

Washington. r. September 13th 1918.
Personal and very secret.

Doctor Masaryk very frequently hears in State Department that English exert some influence on press and that their eagerness to intervene in Russia and Siberia is so great that it suggests some doubts as to what may be real plans of Great Britain.

He has impression that even President is under spell of some such propaganda and that it is very important to remove it.

Probably a speech by you proclaiming anew our complete disinterestedness and that our only aim is that Russia shall not fall under domination of Germany together with a large immixture of high principles which find so much favour in this country, especially in highest quarters, would best meet situation.

Dr. Masaryk told Mr. Hohler¹ the above in strictest secrecy and only because he is so desirous of removing any obstacle to complete harmony of co-operation. He is disposed to fear some source of propaganda perhaps catholic or Irish.

[1] That is, Thomas Beaumont Hohler, since February 2, 1917, Counselor of the British embassy in Washington.

Washington. r. September 13th 1918.

Personal and most secret.

My telegram personal of to-day.

First two paragraphs were dictated by Doctor Masaryk who is of course most apprehensive of it becoming known that he had repeated substance of President's conversation with him[1] as this would destroy President's confidence in him which at present is very high. I cannot too strongly urge need of extreme secrecy.

T telegrams (A. J. Balfour Papers, Add. MSS 49748, British Library).
[1] On September 11.

INDEX

NOTE ON THE INDEX

THE alphabetically arranged analytical table of contents at the front of the volume eliminates duplication, in both contents and index, of references to certain documents, such as letters. Letters are listed in the contents alphabetically by name, and chronologically within each name by page. The subject matter of all letters is, of course, indexed. The Editorial Notes and Wilson's writings are listed in the contents chronologically by page. In addition, the subject matter of both categories is indexed. The index covers all references to books and articles mentioned in text or notes. Footnotes are indexed. Page references to footnotes which place a comma between the page number and "n" cite both text and footnote, thus: "418,n1." On the other hand, absence of the comma indicates reference to the footnote only, thus: "59n1"—the page number denoting where the footnote appears.

The index supplies the fullest known form of names and, for the Wilson and Axson families, relationships as far down as cousins. Persons referred to by nicknames or shortened forms of names can be identified by reference to entries for these forms of the names.

All entries consisting of page numbers only and which refer to concepts, issues and opinions (such as democracy, the tariff, and money trust, leadership, and labor problems), are references to Wilson's speeches and writings. Page references that follow the symbol Δ in such entries refer to the opinions and comments of others who are identified.

Two cumulative contents-index volumes are now in print: Volume 13, which covers Volumes 1-12, and Volume 26, which covers Volumes 14-25. Volume 39, covering Volumes 27-38, is in production.

INDEX